THEOLOGY
OF THE
NEW TESTAMENT

VOLUME 2

LEONHARD GOPPELT

THEOLOGY
OF THE
NEW TESTAMENT

VOLUME 2

The Variety and Unity of the Apostolic Witness to Christ

translated by
John E. Alsup

edited by
Jürgen Roloff

WILLIAM B. EERDMANS PUBLISHING COMPANY
Grand Rapids, Michigan

Copyright © 1982 by Wm. B. Eerdmans Publishing Co.
255 Jefferson Ave., S.E., Grand Rapids, Mich. 49503

Translated from the German edition *Theologie des Neuen Testaments*
© Vandenhoeck & Ruprecht, Göttingen 1976

Library of Congress Cataloging in Publication Data

Goppelt, Leonhard, 1911-1973.
Theology of the New Testament.

Translation of Theologie des Neuen Testaments.
Bibliography: v. 1, *passim;* v. 2, *passim*.
Includes indexes.
1. Bible. N.T.–Theology. I. Roloff, Jürgen.
II. Title.
BS2397.G6313   1981   230   80-28946
ISBN 0-8028-2384-X (v. 1)
ISBN 0-8028-2385-8 (v. 2)

71038

Contents

EDITOR'S (REVISED) FOREWORD

With the publication of this second volume, Leonhard Goppelt's understanding of New Testament theology is now available in as complete a form as possible under the circumstances. Comprehensiveness could be achieved at least in regard to the work's overall outline; it corresponds essentially to the author's intentions. Nothing would suggest that Goppelt had planned additional major sections and chapters. Wherever certain New Testament writings and groups of writings remained outside his purview it was surely because Goppelt did not yet consider it possible to offer a representative picture and evaluation in such cases. Here he was of the opinion that it would be premature in light of the status of research. This is particularly true for the Gospel of Mark; redaction-historical studies in recent years were unable to convince Goppelt that there was much point at the moment in trying to reconstruct for a Theology of the New Testament the theological profile of the oldest evangelist. He found such studies too diverse in matters of methodology and substance. This caution in making judgments, so characteristic of the author, also prevented him from devoting a separate chapter to the deutero-Pauline epistles. It is important to note here that Goppelt counted the Epistle to the Ephesians—contrary to his earlier opinion—along with the Pastoral Epistles among the deutero-Pauline writings while maintaining to the end the Pauline authorship of the Epistle to the Colossians (cf. §28,1)

To be sure, it will become apparent to the reader that in spite of the comprehensive character of the overall scope unfortunate gaps could not be remedied within certain chapters. The representations, e.g., of the Pauline teaching on justification (§39) and ecclesiology (§40) existed as much in the form of a preliminary draft as the concluding chapter on Johannine theology (§49). The two sections on Pauline ethics and eschatology, which according to Goppelt's outline were planned for the third major section, remained on the whole undeveloped. In this case, however, the gap is of no major consequence since both themes are discussed with relative completeness within the fourth major section. Hence, the Pauline ethic is held up as a basis for comparison to the ethic of the epistles of I Peter and James in §§43 and 45; similarly, the sections on the eschatology of the post-Pauline writings (§§44,8; 48,3; 49,6) contain elaborations on Pauline eschatology. For more information see the Subject Index.

The undeniable gaps in this second volume are more than compensated for by the fact that areas of the New Testament receive comprehensive treatment in it that in other New Testament theologies available until now have had little more than marginal attention. It could not have been otherwise than that the keen interest always shown by Goppelt in the writings of the post-apostolic generation, e.g., the historical composition of Luke, the epistles of Peter and James, and the Revelation of John, should also manifest itself in his overall representation of New Testament theology. He wanted to show that these writings interpreted the apostolic kerygma in the context of new historical situations without relinquishing its decisive features in the process. He saw in them normative models for the task of interpreting the message of salvation that is given anew to the church in every generation.

The diverse state of the materials available necessitated a higher degree of editorial involvement in the second volume than in the first. Consequently I would like to recount for the reader the kind and goal of my redactional work. The second and third major sections were available as manuscripts completed for the most part by Goppelt himself. Here it was necessary only to look through the material for purposes of polishing and to fill minor gaps with sections from the author's articles and addresses on related themes. In contrast, only one lecture manuscript and the typed form of a tape-recorded lecture that was given during the summer semester of 1973 were available for the fourth major section. Here it was sometimes necessary to shape, polish, and document in order to supply the volume with requisite formal unity. In all such matters my singular concern was to enable Leonhard Goppelt himself to address the issues as clearly as possible.

Accepting the editorial responsibilities of this project was not merely the gesture of gratitude that might be expected of a student for his teacher. I did so rather in the conviction that Goppelt's voice needs to be heard precisely in the contemporary theological context. It is a voice that encourages us not to content ourselves resignedly with the confusing plurality of theological positions past or present, but to search for the apostolic witness to Christ behind them. That witness alone is the norm of Christian faith and life that is to be developed reflectively in the context of present-day realities.

In the five years since it was first published Goppelt's *Theology* has come a long way. Having appeared in several editions, it has had an influence on the German-language theological scene that its author with his characteristic modesty would not in the least have dared to expect. It has become an indispensable theological textbook for students; moreover, it has furnished the theological discussion with new impulses. Most of all, it has achieved fundamental significance for the attempt to reclaim a biblical theology that comprehends the Old and New Testaments. I am delighted that my colleague and friend, John Alsup, has accomplished the difficult task of translating this book into English so that it can now enjoy an even greater circulation.

Erlangen, November 6, 1981   Jürgen Roloff

TRANSLATOR'S FOREWORD

With the publication of the second volume the English reader now has the completed *Theology of the New Testament* by Leonhard Goppelt. Familiarity with the introductory apparatus of Vol. 1 is to some degree presupposed in Vol. 2; for convenience, however, the list of abbreviations has been repeated. As the Editor's (Revised) Foreword makes amply clear, there are certain areas in this second volume that Professor Goppelt would have extended in scope and perfected in detail had he lived to complete it with the thoroughness and care that were typical of his style. Yet this does not in the least detract from the valuable contribution that Vol. 2 makes to the present discussion of New Testament theology in church and academic settings. The way it groups the writings of the New Testament by affinity of direction and substantive content provides the student with a valuable overview for further reflection. The footnote references to additional publications of Professor Goppelt and other representative voices furnish the reader with helpful guidance for follow-up study. In this regard, appended to this volume and contributing to its usefulness are a comprehensive list of publications by Leonhard Goppelt and a general literature supplement.

In my introduction to the first volume I tried to give the English reader some insight into the place of Leonhard Goppelt in contemporary New Testament theology, e.g., his relationship to other representatives of *Heilsgeschichte* (cf. also Vol. 2, pp. 56-62, 267ff., etc.). It remains to direct the reader's attention to a modest selection of passages in Vol. 2 that—especially in light of his sudden and unexpected death—present in the author's own words Leonhard Goppelt the man as he spoke personally about Christian faith and hope and the life of the church. One such passage is quoted here to give expression to Goppelt's own experience of resurrection hope; additional passages are referred to simply by page number.

> Hence, for Paul coming to salvation stood or fell with the reality that those who believed would be raised just like Jesus himself in their in-person totality to an abiding existence before God. For him, the justification of those who believed had to come to its goal in the redemption of the body and of all creatures (Rom. 8:18-30). A new existence as person, however, also meant a new communication

with others, a new fellowship, and thereby a new situation for life—a "new world." The whole New Testament, including the Gospel of John, advocated this view. Even today, bound together with faith is the hope that the I-Thou relationship with God endures and will be consummated beyond death, and that the new human being that Jesus had claimed and mediated in secret will step forth in the way patterned by the Easter event (p. 196; cf. also pp. 33f., 114ff., 126ff., and 209).

I hereby express my appreciation and indebtedness to the Austin Presbyterian Theological Seminary for a generous sabbatical leave to complete this translation project, to Frau Dora Goppelt for many kindnesses in providing hospitality and a place to work in her home during the completion of Vol. 2, and to family and friends in Munich and Austin for unwavering support. Providing valuable help were my assistant, Ms. Catherine Robinson, and with regard to the comprehensive list of Goppelt publications Herr Walter Kotschenreuther of the University of Erlangen. The manuscript was typed with care and skill by Mrs. Dorothy Andrews. Finally, I express my gratitude to the editor of the *Theology*, Prof. Dr. Jürgen Roloff of the University of Erlangen, for his support in all phases of my work; an extended conversation during a visit in Erlangen led to some minor revisions in text and footnotes of the original.

Tutzing, W. Germany   John E. Alsup
November 6, 1981

ABBREVIATIONS

Included here is only frequently cited literature. Additional abbreviations for Jewish, Hellenistic, and early Christian literature can be found in the list of abbreviations in Kittel's *Theological Dictionary of the New Testament.* Abbreviations for the rabbinic literature receive more exact clarification in H. Strack, *Introduction to the Talmud and Midrash* (1931). Regarding the circumstances in which the Jewish and early Christian literature arose compare the information in the reference works: O. Eissfeldt, *The Old Testament: An Introduction* (1965); B. Altaner, *Patrology* (1960/61).

1. The Books of the Bible

They are designated according to the ecumenical standard of abbreviation.

2. Extracanonical Jewish Literature

Arist.	The Letter of Aristeas (ca. 90 B.C.)
Asc. Isa.	Ascension of Isaiah (Christian/Jewish A.D. 2nd cent.)
As. Mos.	Assumption of Moses (ca. 4 B.C.)
Bar.	The apocryphal book of Baruch (LXX)
Gr. Bar.	Greek Apocalypse of Baruch (ca. A.D. 200)
Syr. Bar.	Syrian Apocalypse of Baruch (ca. A.D. 100)
CD	Damascus Rule (Fragments of a Zadokite Work; Qumran document, 2nd/1st cent. B.C.)
I Enoch	I Enoch (Apocalypse; 2nd/1st cent. B.C.)
II Enoch	II Enoch (Apocalypse; 2nd/1st cent. B.C.)
IV Ezra	IV Ezra (Apocalypse; ca. A.D. 95)
Jos. As.	Joseph and Aseneth (Hellenistic/Jewish missionary document from Egypt, end of 1st cent. B.C.)
Josephus *Ant., Ap., War, Life*	Flavius Josephus (Jewish historian, A.D. 37-97), *Antiquitates, Contra Apionem, Bellum Judaicum, Vita*

Jub.	Book of Jubilees ("Little Genesis") (2nd/1st cent. B.C.)
LXX	Septuagint
1, 2, 3 Macc.	1, 2, 3 Books of Maccabees (LXX)
4 Macc.	4th Book of Maccabees (Philosophical tractate, Hellenistic/Jewish, ca. 50 B.C.-A.D. 50)
Mart. Isa.	Martyrdom of Isaiah (= 1st part of the Ascension of Isaiah, Jewish, 1st cent. B.C.)
Philo	Philo of Alexandria (Jewish philosopher of religion, 20 B.C. to A.D. 50): abbreviations for his writings from the *TDNT*.
Ps. Sol.	Psalms of Solomon (1st cent. B.C.)
1(4)Q	out of Cave 1 (4) at Qumran
1QH	Hodayot: Psalms of Thanksgiving (Qumran)
1QM	Milhamah: War Scroll (Qumran)
1QpHab	Pesher Habakkuk: Habakkuk Commentary (Qumran)
1QS	Serek Hayaḥad: Community Rule/Manual of Discipline (Qumran)
1QSa	Fragment: Rule for the entire community of Israel in the end time (Qumran)
1QSb	Fragment: Words of blessing (Qumran)
4Qtest	Testimonia (Qumran)
4Qflor	Florilegia (Qumran)
4Qpatr	Blessings of the Patriarchs (Qumran)
11QMelch	Fragments of eschatological Midrashim from Qumran (Cave 11)
Sib.	Sibylline Oracles (Jewish/Christian)
Sir.	Jesus Ben-Sirach or Ecclesiasticus (LXX)
Test. XII Test. Ash., Ben., Dan, Gad, Jos., Iss., Jud., Levi, Naph., Reub., Sim., Zeb.	Testaments of the 12 Patriarchs (Jewish with Christian revision, 2nd/1st cent. B.C.)
Tob.	Tobit (LXX)
Vit. Ad.	Life of Adam and Eve (Christian/Jewish document, originally ca. A.D. 50?)
Wis. Sol.	Wisdom of Solomon (LXX)

3. Extracanonical Early Christian Literature

Act	Apocryphal Acts of the Apostles: Andrew-, John-, Paul-, Peter-, Acts of Thomas (cf. Hennecke II).
Barn.	Epistle of Barnabas (ca. A.D. 130)
I, II Clem.	I, II Epistles of Clement (ca. A.D. 96/ca. A.D. 140)
Clem. Al. *Strom.*	Clement of Alexandria (ca. A.D. 200); *Stromateis*

Did.	*Didache* (Teaching of the Twelve Apostles, ca. A.D. 100)
Eus. *EH*	Eusebius of Caesarea (A.D. 263-339), *Ecclesiastical History*
Herm. *M.*, *Sim.*, *Vis.*	Shepherd of Hermas (Apocalypse, ca. A.D. 140), *Mandata, Similitudines, Visiones*
Ign. Eph., Magn., Trall., Rom., Phld., Sm., Pol.	Ignatius of Antioch (Martyr, ca. A.D. 110), Epistles to Ephesus, Magnesia, Tralles, Rome, Philadelphia, Smyrna, and Polycarp
Iren. *Haer.*	Irenaeus of Lyon (Martyr, A.D. 202), *Adversus haereses*
Jer. *Vir.*	Jerome (A.D. 340/50-420), *De viris illustribus*
Just. *Ap.*, *Dial.*	Justin (Martyr, ca. A.D. 165), *Apology, Dialogue with Trypho the Jew*
Mart. Pol.	Martyrdom of Polycarp (ca. A.D. 150?)
Od. Sol.	Odes of Solomon (Christian/Gnostic hymns, ca. A.D. 120)
Orig. *C. Cels.*	Origen (A.D. 185-254), *Contra Celsum*
Pol.	Epistle of Polycarp from Smyrna (Martyr, A.D. 155/168?)
Pol. Phil.	Epistle of Polycarp to the Philippians
Tert. *Bapt.*, *Marc.*, *Praescr. haer.*, *De pud.*, *De spec.*	Tertullian (A.D. 160-220), *De baptismo, Adversus Marcionem, De praescriptione haereticorum, De pudicitia, De spectaculis*
Gospel Thom.	Gospel of Thomas (Coptic/Gnostic collection of logia, ca. A.D. 140)

4. Journals, Collections, Reference Works, Commentary Series

ANF	The Ante-Nicene Fathers
BHH	*Biblisch-historisches Handwörterbuch*
BDF	Blass-Debrunner-Funk, *A Greek Grammar of the New Testament* (1961)
BZ	*Biblische Zeitschrift*
CSEL	*Corpus Scriptorum Ecclesiasticorum Latinorum*, ed. Wiener Akademie der Wissenschaften
DB	*Deutsche Bibel*, Martin Luther
EKL	*Evangelisches Kirchenlexikon*
ELKZ	*Evangelisch-lutherische Kirchenzeitung*
ETL	*Ephemerides theologicae lovanienses*
EvK	*Evangelische Kommentare*
EvTheol	*Evangelische Theologie*
HNT	Handbuch zum Neuen Testament, ed. Hans Lietzmann
HTK	Herders Theologischer Kommentar zum NT
JBL	*Journal of Biblical Literature*
ICC	The International Critical Commentary

Int	*Interpretation*
JThSt	*Journal of Theological Studies*
KEK	Meyers Kommentar zum NT
KuD	*Kerygma und Dogma*
LCL	Loeb Classical Library
LThK	*Lexikon für Theologie und Kirche*
NovTest	*Novum Testamentum* (Journal)
NTD	Das Neue Testament Deutsch
NTS	*New Testament Studies*
PW	Pauly-Wissowa, *Real-Encyklopädie der klassischen Alter-tumswissenschaft*
RAC	*Reallexikon für Antike und Christentum*
RB	*Revue Biblique*
RE	*Realencyklopädie für protestantische Theologie und Kirche* (3rd ed.)
RGG	*Die Religion in Geschichte und Gegenwart*
RQ	*Revue de Qumran*
SAB	*Sitzungsberichte der Preussischen bzw. Berliner Akademie der Wissenschaften, phil.-hist. Klasse*
SAH	*Sitzungsberichte der Heidelberger Akademie der Wissenschaften, phil.-hist. Klasse*
SBS	Stuttgarter Bibelstudien
SSAW	*Sitzungsberichte der sächsischen Akademie der Wissenschaften*
StEv	*Studia Evangelica*
StTh	*Studia Theologica*
TDNT	*Theological Dictionary of the New Testament*
ThBl	*Theologische Blätter*
ThEx	*Theologische Existenz heute*
ThLZ	*Theologische Literaturzeitung*
ThR	*Theologische Rundschau*
ThHK	Theologischer Handkommentar zum NT
ThZ	*Theologische Zeitschrift*
VF	*Verkündigung und Forschung*
Vig Chr	*Vigiliae Christianae*
WA	Martin Luther, *Werke*, Weimarer Ausgabe
ZAW	*Zeitschrift für die alttestamentliche Wissenschaft*
ZKG	*Zeitschrift für Kirchengeschichte*
ZKTh	*Zeitschrift für katholische Theologie*
ZNW	*Zeitschrift für die neutestamentliche Wissenschaft und die Kunde der älteren Kirche*
ZRGG	*Zeitschrift für Religions- und Geistesgeschichte*
ZThK	*Zeitschrift für Theologie und Kirche*
Zahn-K	Kommentare zum NT, ed. T. Zahn
ZEE	*Zeitschrift für evangelische Ethik*
ZBK	Züricher Bibelkommentar (formerly: Prophezei)

5. Frequently Cited References

Barrett: C. K. Barrett, *The New Testament Background: Selected Documents* (1957, 1971⁵).

Beginnings: F. J. Foakes Jackson and K. Lake, *The Beginnings of Christianity* I: *The Acts of the Apostles* I–V (1920-33).

Billerbeck I–VI: H. L. Strack und P. Billerbeck, *Kommentar zum Neuen Testament aus Talmud und Midrasch* I–IV (1922-1928), V-VI (1956/1961).

Bornkamm, *Aufsätze* I–IV: G. Bornkamm, *Gesammelte Aufsätze* I–IV, (1952-1971) (Eng. trans. of parts of vols. I and II: *Early Christian Experience* [1970]).

Bousset, *Judentum*: W. Bousset, *Die Religion des Judentums im späthellenistischen Zeitalter*, ed. H. Gressmann (1926³; 1966⁴) (HNT, 21).

————, *Kyrios*: W. Bousset, *Kyrios Christos* (1970).

Braun, *Qumran* I, II: H. Braun, *Qumran und das Neue Testament* I–II (1966).

————, *Radikalismus* I, II: H. Braun, *Spätjüdisch-häretischer und frühchristlicher Radikalismus. Jesus von Nazareth und die essenische Qumransekte* I–II (1957; 1969²).

Bultmann, *Glauben* I–IV: R. Bultmann, *Glauben und Verstehen. Gesammelte Aufsätze* I–IV (1933-1965). (I, 1966⁶; IV, 1967²). Vol. 2: *Essays Philosophical and Theological* (1955). Vol. 1: *Faith and Understanding* (1969).

————, *Theology*: R. Bultmann, *Theology of the New Testament* (I, 1951; II, 1955)

————, *Tradition*: R. Bultmann, *The History of the Synoptic Tradition* (1968); *Ergänzungsheft* (1971⁴), compiled by G. Theissen and P. Vielhauer.

Charles: R. H. Charles, ed., *The Apocrypha and Pseudepigrapha of the Old Testament in English* (2 vols., 1913; repr. 1963).

Conzelmann, *Theology*: H. Conzelmann, *An Outline of New Testament Theology* (1969).

Cullmann, *Christology*: O. Cullmann, *The Christology of the New Testament* (1959).

Dibelius, *Tradition*: M. Dibelius, *From Tradition to Gospel* (1965).

Goppelt, *Apostolic Times*: L. Goppelt, *Apostolic and Post-Apostolic Times* (1977).

————, *Christologie*: L. Goppelt, *Christologie und Ethik. Aufsätze zum Neuen Testament* (1968).

————, *Typos*: L. Goppelt, *Typos. Die typologische Deutung des Alten Testaments im Neuen* (1939; repr. 1969 with appendix: "Apokalyptik und Typologie bei Paulus").

Hahn, *Titles*: F. Hahn, *The Titles of Jesus in Christology: Their History in Early Christianity* (1969).

Hennecke, I, II: E. Hennecke and W. Schneemelcher, *New Testament Apocrypha* I–II (1963/1965).

Hennecke²: E. Hennecke, ed., *Neutestamentliche Apokryphen . . . in deutscher Übersetzung* (1924²).

Historische Jesus: H. Ristow and K. Matthiae, eds., *Der historische Jesus und der kerygmatische Christus. Beiträge zum Christusverständnis in Forschung und Verkündigung* (1961; 1962²).

Holtzmann, *Theologie* I, II: H. J. Holtzmann, *Lehrbuch der neutestamentlichen Theologie* I–II, 2nd edition by A. Jülicher and W. Bauer (1911).

Jeremias, *Eucharistic Words*: J. Jeremias, *The Eucharistic Words of Jesus* (1966³).

—————, *Parables*: J. Jeremias, *Rediscovering the Parables* (1966).

—————, *Theology*: J. Jeremias, *New Testament Theology* I: *The Proclamation of Jesus* (1971).

Käsemann, *Exegetische Versuche* I, II: E. Käsemann, *Exegetische Versuche und Besinnungen* I–II (1960/64) (cf. *Essays on New Testament Themes* [Studies in Biblical Theology 41, 1964]; *New Testament Questions of Today* (1969).

Koester-Robinson, *Trajectories*: H. Koester and J. M. Robinson, *Trajectories through Early Christianity* (1971).

Kramer, *Christ*: W. Kramer, *Christ, Lord, Son of God* (Studies in Biblical Theology 50, 1966).

Kraus, *Psalmen* I, II: H.-J. Kraus, *Psalmen* I–II (1961; 1966³) (Biblischer Kommentar. Altes Testament, Bd. XV).

Kümmel, *Introduction*: W. G. Kümmel, *Introduction to the New Testament* (rev. ed. 1975).

—————, *Investigation*: W. G. Kümmel, *The New Testament: The History of the Investigation of Its Problems* (1972).

—————, *Theology*: W. G. Kümmel, *The Theology of the New Testament according to Its Major Witnesses: Jesus—Paul—John* (1973).

Leipoldt, *Umwelt*, I–III: J. Leipoldt and W. Grundmann, eds., *Umwelt des Urchristentums* I–III (1967).

von Rad, *Theology* I, II: G. von Rad, *Old Testament Theology* I–II (1962/1965).

Roloff, *Kerygma*: J. Roloff, *Das Kerygma und der irdische Jesus. Historische Motive in den Jesuserzählungen der Evangelien* (1970).

Schlatter, *Erläuterungen* I–III: A. Schlatter, *Erläuterungen zum Neuen Testament* I–III (1928⁴; repr. 1961/65).

—————, *Theologie* I, II: A. Schlatter, I: *Die Geschichte des Christus* (1923²); II: *Die Theologie der Apostel* (1922²).

—————, *Mt.* (etc.): A. Schlatter, *Kommentare* (on the NT books named) (1929/ 37; repr. 1960/65).

Schreiner, *Gestalt*: J. Schreiner, ed., *Gestalt und Anspruch des Neuen Testaments* (1969).

Schürer, *Geschichte* I–III: E. Schürer, *Geschichte des Jüdischen Volkes im Zeitalter Jesu Christi* I–III (1901-1909³⁻⁴). Rev. Eng. tr.: *The History of the Jewish People in the Age of Jesus Christ (175 B.C.—A.D. 135)* I, 1973; II, 1979).

Schweitzer, *Quest*: A. Schweitzer, *The Quest of the Historical Jesus* (1910).

Schweizer, *Lordship*: E. Schweizer, *Lordship and Discipleship* (Studies in Biblical Theology 28, 1960) (trans. of 1st Ger. ed.).

Taylor, *Mark*: V. Taylor, *The Gospel According to St. Mark* (1959).

Volz, *Eschatologie*: P. Volz, *Die Eschatologie der jüdischen Gemeinde im neutestamentlichen Zeitalter* (1934²).

Part Two

THE PRIMITIVE
CHRISTIAN COMMUNITY
(THE CHURCH WITHIN ISRAEL)

§24. The Sources and Their Evaluation

Goppelt, *Apostolic Times*, pp. 1-7 (review of research and older literature); pp. 25-81
(the primitive community); F. V. Filson, *A New Testament History* (1964), pp. 153-174;
H. Conzelmann, *History of Primitive Christianity* (1973), pp. 21-67; for further Lit. cf.
below, n. 2.

1. THE SOURCES

Jewish sources are almost entirely silent on the matter of the groups into
which Jesus' disciples formed themselves within the Jewish theocracy of Palestine after Jesus' exit. They are equally silent about Jesus himself.[1] These
sources are historically valuable, nonetheless, as they provide exact information
about the environment of the earliest Christian community. Regarding that community itself, however, one must rely entirely on Christian sources. The earliest
literary documents of Christianity, the Pauline epistles, came from the period
between A.D. 50 and 62 and were written to the communities between Asia
Minor and Rome. The distance in time and geography, therefore, between them
and the beginnings of Christianity in Palestine is considerable. Information about
the twenty "dark" years between the conclusion of Jesus' life and the period of

---

[1]Josephus, the Jewish historian of the epoch, provided only one brief reference about the end of
James (*Ant*. 20.9.1); the reference in *Ant*. 18.3.3 is an interpolation. Lit.: H. L. Strack, *Jesus, die
Häretiker und die Christen nach den ältesten jüdischen Angaben* (1910); H.-J. Schoeps, *Aus früh-
christlicher Zeit* (1950), pp. 239-254; Billerbeck IV, 1241 (s.v. *Jünger*).

1

the Pauline epistles can be ascertained only by reasoned deductions based on the following sources:

a) The Pauline epistles make reference on occasion to the early period when they report matters in retrospect. Such is the case in Gal. 1f. They quote particular didactic traditions that can be traced back as far as the primitive Christian community and its Aramaic-language roots (I Cor. 11:23; 15:1-3). By means of form-critical standards it is possible, moreover, to detect in those epistles a considerable number of formulaic expressions that have been passed on from the pre-Pauline period (§26,2).

b) Some forty to fifty years after the beginnings of Christianity, around the year A.D. 80, Luke wrote the book of Acts. He wrote it as a description of the spread of the gospel from Jerusalem to Rome and intended thereby to present the foundational emergence of the church. In this extensive report about the primitive Christian community one encounters important traditions provided one utilizes the appropriate critical means.[2] One basic criterion would be, of course, that comparison be made to the actual statements of Paul himself.

c) It was in the Palestinian church that the traditions about Jesus' earthly ministry were conceived in their basic form. These traditions were then written down in the synoptic Gospels after the lengthy period of history-of-tradition development between A.D. 65 and 85. Their formulations were always shaped with the circumstances of the community in mind. For this reason the circumstances of the community are reflected in the synoptic tradition: it arose, was passed on, and finally redacted in connection with them. The degree to which pointers to the early stages ot tne Palestinian church are to be found in the synoptic tradition is, of course, very uncertain and a controversial matter. Coming to terms in a scientifically responsible way with such pointers as they surface with the aid of form-critical analysis depends on their critical comparison with the historical situation reflected in the Pauline corpus and the book of Acts (on the discussion, cf. §2).

d) The above-mentioned sources are supplemented only slightly by the Palestinian traditions found in the book of Revelation, in the Didache, and in isolated references of the church fathers.

In view of the sources available, the picture of the primitive Christian community and its witness appears to be based on very fortuitous pieces of information. Upon closer examination, however, such information proves not to be so fortuitous, but rather it emerges consistently in connection with a focused line of questioning belonging to the sources that contain them.

---

[2]Reports on the history of research: E. Grässer, "Die Apostelgeschichte in der Forschung der Gegenwart," *ThR* NF 26 (1960), 93-167; I. H. Marshall, "Recent Study of the Acts of the Apostles," *Expository Times* 80 (1968/69), 292-96; Marshall, *Luke: Historian and Theologian* (1970); the commentaries by H. Conzelmann (HNT 5 [1972²]) and E. Haenchen (Westminster, 1971) look at Acts too one-sidedly as kerygma for the community of its time; in contrast, G. Stählin (NTD 5 [1970⁴]), C.S.C. Williams (Harper/Black, 1964²), and K. Lake-H. J. Cadbury (*Beginnings* I-V) inquire primarily into that which was reported about the community.

2. THE LINE OF QUESTIONING OF THE SOURCES AND OF THEIR PRESENTATION

The three New Testament sources mentioned above did not have as their goal the retelling of what was believed and taught by certain individual members of the primitive Christian community. They intended rather to relate what was normative and valid proclamation. In order to pass this on, Paul appropriated formulaic traditions of the primitive Christian community and sought out a consensus for it from the apostles and representatives of the community in Jerusalem during the Apostolic Council (Gal. 2:2, 8f.; I Cor. 15:1-5, 11). Historically speaking, of course, he always selected and interpreted the traditions according to his own theological point of view. According to Luke, whatever was taught first by "the apostles" in Jerusalem and then subsequently by Paul between Jerusalem and Rome (Lk. 1:1-4; Acts 1:21f., 42; 28:23-31) and whatever else documented itself in keeping with this line of the church's expanding shape was to be constitutive in the church for all time. Seen historically, he described the words and actions of "the apostles" and of Paul historically, often by reproducing small segments of tradition in a freely interpretive manner. Lastly, standing behind those pointers derived from the synoptic tradition is the other principle shared by both Paul and Luke: normative finally is that which is to be addressed to the community situation from the life and ministry of Jesus. Historically, it must, therefore, be questioned in particular whether or not this interpretive shaping of the Jesus-tradition actually corresponded to the intention of Jesus.

These basic perspectives of the New Testament sources are, in spite of the necessary critical questioning, fundamentally accurate in substance, and therefore historical reasons are not the only ones for taking those perspectives into consideration here. On the one hand we must ask: Which theological perspectives were in fact represented in the preaching of the primitive church in Palestine, especially in the primitive Christian community of Jerusalem? At the same time, however, we ask: What was considered normative according to the criteria, mentioned above, coming from our New Testament sources? Both questions can be answered only in limited fashion because of the dearth of information; this state of affairs will be quite different later for the Hellenistic church of Paul's ministry. This history-of-tradition question will accompany our study throughout and take up the matter of the mutual relationship of the data from these three sources and their distinct orientations.

In terms of content, the theological reflection manifest in the statements of the first community will begin with two themes determined by the historical situation: (1) the self-understanding of the community and its own practices of worship in the context of the Jewish national community; (2) the interpretation of Jesus' activity against the backdrop of the religious traditions of Israel. These themes are related to each other: in discipleship people constantly sought to interpret their situation afresh from the perspective of their Master, and in doing so they learned new aspects about his activity.

Up to this point (§§5-22) we have concerned ourselves with what happened to people from Jesus' activity to the time of the event of Pentecost. Now we want to turn our attention to a description—even if only in very brief form—of the self-understanding of the first Christian community. From there we will be able to pursue the christological reflection the community developed for its situation.[3]

§25. Following Jesus in Discipleship as the Church

On 1 and 5a: A. von Harnack, *The Mission and Expansion of Christianity in the First Three Centuries* I–II (1904-05; repr. 1972); J. Jeremias, *Jesus' Promise to the Nations* (1958); F. Hahn, *Mission in the New Testament* (1965); D. Georgi, *Die Gegner des Paulus im 2. Korintherbrief. Studien zur religiösen Propaganda in der Spätantike* (1964); H. Kasting, *Die Anfänge der urchristlichen Mission* (1969); M. Hengel, "Die Ursprünge der christlichen Mission," *NTS* 18 (1971/72), 15-38. **On 2**: O. Cullmann, *Baptism in the New Testament* (1950); J. Jeremias, *Infant Baptism in the First Four Centuries* (1960); G. Braumann, *Vorpaulinische christliche Taufverkündigung bei Paulus* (1962); O. Kuss, "Zur vorpaulinischen Tauflehre im Neuen Testament," in Kuss, *Auslegung und Verkündigung* I (1963), 98-120; G. Delling, *Die Taufe im Neuen Testament* (1963); G. Kretschmar, "Die Geschichte des Taufgottesdienstes in der alten Kirche," in *Leiturgia* V (1964/65), 1-160; G. R. Beasley-Murray, *Baptism in the New Testament* (1962); F. Lentzen-Deis, *Die Taufe Jesu nach den Synoptikern* (1970); K. Aland, *Taufe und Kindertaufe* (1971). **On 3**: K. Holl, *Der Kirchenbegriff des Paulus in seinem Verhältnis zu dem der Urgemeinde* (*SAB*, 1921), in Holl, *Gesammelte Aufsätze* II (1928), 44-67; O. Linton, *Das Problem der Urkirche in der neueren Forschung* (1932; older Lit.!); N. A. Dahl, *Das Volk Gottes* (1941; repr. 1963); A. Oepke, *Das neue Gottesvolk* (1950); E. Schweizer, *Church Order in the New Testament* (Studies in Biblical Theology 32 [1961]); R. Schnackenburg, *The Church in the New Testament* (1965); W. G. Kümmel, *Kirchenbegriff und Geschichtsbewusstsein in der Urgemeinde und bei Jesus* (1943; 1968[2]). **On 4a**: cf. §21 Lit. and Goppelt, *Apostolic Times*, pp. 45ff., 202ff.; G. Delling, *Worship in the New Testament* (1962); G. Dix, *The Shape of the Liturgy* (1945; 1959[7]); O. Cullmann, *Early Christian Worship* (1953); F. Hahn, *The Worship of the Early Church* (1973). **On 4c**: M. Simon, *St. Stephen and the Hellenists of Acts* (1958); J. Bihler, *Die Stephanusgeschichte im Zusammenhang der Apostelgeschichte* (1963). **On 5d**: I. H. Marshall, "Palestinian and Hellenistic Christianity: Some Critical Comments," *NTS* 19 (1972/73), 271-287.

1. THE MISSIONARY WITNESS

a) Jesus and the movement he started. Jesus did not dedicate himself to religious contemplation, but to ministry among people. He did not seek out the company of a few like-minded persons, but concerned himself with Israel as a whole and consequently focused his attention finally on Jerusalem. Following his direction, therefore, after his exit his disciples set out on a path that was entirely different from that of the Essene movement, a movement comparable to

---

[3]For a reconstruction of the historical setting, cf. Goppelt, *Apostolic Times*, pp. 25-60.

it in so many respects. The disciples did not renounce further association with society and think of themselves as enthusiast apocalypticists waiting for the imminent appearance of the Son of man. The majority of the disciples, who had their roots primarily in Galilee, moved their residence to Jerusalem. This is not only the view of the book of Acts (1:4; 8:1); it was in Jerusalem that Paul too sought out the leading voices among the disciples after his conversion between A.D. 35 and 40 (Gal. 1:18). The disciples wanted to reach all Israel in Jerusalem. Here the people themselves came from the Diaspora to be assembled during pilgrim festivals. In Jerusalem the disciples awaited the salvation that was dawning (Isa. 2:1-4; 60; Mt. 8:11f. par.; Rev. 21). To be sure, however, the witness was proclaimed from the very beginning outside of Jerusalem as well, all over Judea and Galilee (Acts 9:31; Gal. 1:22) and in the Diaspora. At the time of his conversion, Paul met disciples of Jesus in far-off Damascus (II Cor. 11:32f.; Acts 9:1f.).

Behind this movement stood the sending out of witnesses that took place in the Easter appearances and that was reinforced by the Spirit. The commission was carried out by the "apostles," according to the book of Acts,[1] and by such people as Stephen and Philip (Acts 6:8; 8), who were later described as evangelists (21:8). Most comprehensively, however, the work was carried out by unnamed members of the community, those Hellenists who had fled from Jerusalem (8:4; 11:19ff.). These schematized and isolated pieces of information correspond to a large extent to the historical events. To begin with, the mission was carried out by the apostles commissioned in the Easter appearances, the number of which according to Paul, however, exceeded the twelve disciples (cf. I Cor. 15:7; Rom. 16.7).[2] Traveling missionaries also were soon involved. They were commissioned by the Spirit or by the community and in Palestine were even referred to as apostles (Acts 14:4, 14; II Cor. 11:13), although in the Pauline realm the designation evangelist was developed for them later (Eph. 4:11; II Tim. 4:5). The only explanation for the rapid spread of the mission is that every disciple became a missionary witness in his or her own setting.

Missionary activity did not generally take place in Jerusalem in the way it is redactionally portrayed in the book of Acts (2:6, 41; 4:4, 33; 5:12-16, 28), i.e., in large public assemblies, but by conversations in small groups and on a person-to-person basis as people met each other in the routine of daily life. The pairing of missionaries who would go from house to house as described in the commissioning discourses of the synoptic tradition (Mk. 6:7-11 par. Lk.; Lk. 10:3-12 [Q]; Mt. 10:5-16) never was the practice according to all that we are able to ascertain from both Paul and the book of Acts. This was not carried out either in the early period in Palestine or thereafter. I Cor. 9:4f. reflects a quite different picture of the journeys of the apostles. According to Did. 11–13 it was only later in Syria that these directives were followed to the letter.

---

[1]Regarding the discussion of the origin of the apostolic office, cf. J. Roloff, *Apostolat —Verkündigung —Kirche* (1965), pp. 9-37.

[2]Ibid., pp. 57-64.

b) The oldest missionary kerygma. The sermons of Peter found in Acts 2–5 were formulated by Luke. This can be seen in the style, the use of the LXX, and other indices.[3] He did not draft them as independent compositions, however, in the way that was expected of an ancient historian seeking to characterize the situation he was writing about. Instead, he made use of traditions in the interest of giving witness here as well to the event that established the church. His use of tradition for this witness was directed at addressing the reader. This also meant that the sermons contained not a few elements foreign to his theology. The design of the sermons, however, offers an astonishing congruence with the earliest kerygma in I Cor. 15:3-5 and turns out to be, therefore, historical at its base.[4] From this it is quite apparent that at the heart of the missionary proclamation stood the Easter witness: "this Jesus . . . you killed"— "but God raised him up" (Acts 2:22ff.; 3:13ff.; 4:11; 5:30f.); "this has happened according to scripture" (2:25-31; 3:18; 4:11); "of that we all are witnesses" (2:32-36; 3:15b, 16; 5:32). On the basis of this witness all Israel was summoned to turn back to its God who now in fulfillment of prophecy and in an ultimate way was addressing his people (2:38f.; 3:19; 4:12; 5:31b). Undoubtedly, this summons to repentance was originally more forceful than the book of Acts indicates and was underscored by the reference to the imminently near consummation through the coming of Jesus the Messiah (cf. Acts 3:19f. and §25,5). The expectation of an imminent end of the world was, nevertheless, also announced by others in the disciples' environment; unique to them, in contrast, was the Easter witness. In that which occurred at Easter and Pentecost the event of the end time had begun for them. In but a brief span, they maintained, that final hour would strike through the gathering of the community of salvation and the all-transforming coming of "their Lord."

The goal toward which the missionary witness pressed as it stood in this eschatological frame of reference was from the beginning, however, baptism. In baptism the requisite and invited repentance as well as entry into the community of salvation was accomplished (Acts 2:38).

2. BAPTISM

a) Its origin. From the earliest beginnings, following Jesus in discipleship was accompanied by baptism as a rite of acceptance and initiation. This information from the book of Acts (2:38, 41; 8:12f., 36, 38; 9:18, etc.) is substantiated by Paul in his epistles. He presupposed that by the time of his own conversion baptism was already generally practiced (I Cor. 12:13) and that all those in the community at Rome—of which he had no firsthand knowledge— had been baptized (Rom. 6:3).

b) Its meaning. According to Acts 2:38 the baptism that was offered by Christian missionaries was described as follows: "Repent, and be baptized every

---

[3] U. Wilckens, *Die Missionsreden der Apostelgeschichte* (1974³).
[4] Goppelt, *Apostolic Times*, pp. 36ff.

one of you in the name of Jesus Christ for the forgiveness of your sins; and you shall receive the gift of the Holy Spirit." As the expression "Jesus Christ" indicates, this description represented a later, probably Lukan formulation, but it contained older tradition. We must determine to what extent the three elements articulated here were connected to baptism in the initial period.

1) The baptism of the disciples was undoubtedly similar to that of John the Baptist, a baptism of repentance for the forgiveness of sins, i.e., a bath that cleansed from former things. It communicated forgiveness and, correspondingly, repentance. (From the beginning it was probably accomplished in part as a baptismal bath, in part through the pouring of the water.)[5]

2) In all probability, this act was connected from its inception to one's calling upon the name of Jesus. Just as one called upon the name of Jesus on the occasion of healings (Acts 3:6), so too fundamentally at baptism; for the disciples repentance and forgiveness were mediated by Jesus. The name was called upon over the act of baptism and not over the water or over the person being baptized. This invocation was uttered by the one baptizing and not, as has been deduced on the basis of Acts 22:16,[6] by the one being baptized as his or her prayer. It was the role of the baptized one rather to confirm the invocation by a baptismal confession (e.g., Rom. 10:9; cf. Acts 8:37). Calling upon the "name" was certainly shaped by the Hebrew expression *l*ᵉ*shem*, which in cultic ceremonies articulated the causal and concluding relationship.[7] Translating this background into Greek, one had to use two expressions. One baptized "in the name of Jesus" (*en [epi] tō onomati Iesou*, Acts 10:48; 2:38). By saying this one expressed that the exalted One was accomplishing through baptism that which baptism promised, namely, forgiveness and repentance. Used more commonly was the formula baptized *eis to onoma*, "into the name."[8] This expressed that baptism connected a person to the exalted One. Both belong together: baptism accomplishes repentance and forgiveness because the exalted One places the person being baptized into relationship with himself.

3) The Spirit was promised to the one who was baptized in this way. R. Bultmann[9] conjectured that this third element, perhaps even the second, was added later in the Hellenistic Church. This conjecture is unfounded. To be sure, the book of Acts reports that on occasion baptism and the bestowal of the Spirit took place separately (8:12; 10.44, 47f.; 11:15f.; 19:2-6). But this was consistently the result of extraordinary circumstances. These reports presupposed,

---

[5]*baptizein (baptisma)*, actually "to immerse," was used in the LXX for *ṭabal (ṭᵉbilah)*; in Judaism it was a technical term for the religious baths of immersion through which purification was achieved (A. Oepke, *TDNT* I, 535). Regarding its formal accomplishment, cf. Acts 8:36; Did. 7:1-3; and L. Goppelt, *TDNT* VIII, 332.

[6]Thus, e.g., G. Stählin, *Die Apostelgeschichte* (1970⁴), p. 285; yet, in contrast, G. Delling (Lit., §25,2), pp. 32-36.

[7]H. Bietenhard, *TDNT* V, 274-76.

[8]Acts 8:16; I Cor. 1:13, 15; cf. Rom. 6:3; Gal. 3:27: *eis Christon*; I Cor. 10:2: *eis ton Mousēn*; Mt. 28:19 developed the expression for the first time trinitarily; it was developed further in Did. 7:1; Just. *Ap.* 1:61; cf. G. Kretschmar (Lit., §25,2), pp. 32-36.

[9]*Theology* I, §6,3.

therefore, that baptism and the bestowal of the Spirit ordinarily were bound together. Of course, the coming of the Spirit was never bound exclusively to baptism, but that coming was promised to and widely experienced by those baptized, and that from the earliest period on. Such was in keeping with the substantive context that whoever was brought into relationship with the exalted One was also delivered over to the work of the Spirit.[10]

The three elements mentioned in Acts 2:38 were not merely a theological interpretation of the baptismal event, but were basic to the substantive context. From this starting point was developed the further explanation of the effects of baptism as, e.g., second birth, or the expansion of the invocation of Jesus' name to the trinitarian formula in Mt. 28:19. The truly decisive question, however, is: By what means were the disciples authorized to baptize in this way?

c) Its foundation. Jesus himself did not baptize anyone,[11] but he brought about repentance and forgiveness through his personal involvement with people, especially through his summons to discipleship (§12). Alongside this experience of the disciples, was there room substantively for a ritual mediation like the one attempted by John the Baptist—basically to no avail? It is not sufficient to explain the baptismal activity of the disciples by making reference to the history-of-religion principle of correlation, and saying, "the Church took this practice over from John the Baptist."[12] To be sure, the baptism of the primitive church was related to the baptism of John and like it stood within the stream of Jewish rites of cleansing (§4,3). But through what means would one have been motivated substantively to reach back and appropriate John's baptism? In the early church two motifs were mentioned. These are in need, however, of fundamental historical and substantive correction.

1) According to Mt. 28:19f. and the inauthentic ending of Mark (Mk. 16:15f.) a "command to baptize" was given to the disciples in the Easter appearances. These directives were formulated redactionally in accord with the practice of baptism at the time of their composition. Seen from a history-of-tradition point of view, a common, three-part schema formed the base for the words of commission in Mt. 28:18b-20b; Lk. 24:46-49; Mk. 16:15-18. This schema expressed Jesus' reception of authority through his exaltation, his commissioning, and the promise of his presence. The commissioning most certainly goes back to the Easter appearances (cf. I Cor. 15:7f.). Of some question, however, is whether or not a directive to baptize was connected to it. If it were, it would explain satisfactorily why baptism was generally practiced from the beginning. But it cannot be demonstrated on history-of-tradition grounds. Theologically, in any case, no higher premium accrues to this directive in principle than to the command to repetition in the institution of the Eucharist (§20,6). Clearly the disciples were authorized through the commissioning, the apostolate, to minister "in the

---

[10]Cf. E. Schweizer, *TDNT* VI, 413; Goppelt, *Apostolic Times*, pp. 68-71.

[11]A historicizing of the remark in Jn. 3:22 that reflected a situation of the community is prohibited by Jn. 4:2.

[12]Conzelmann, *Theology*, p. 47.

name of Jesus," and therefore also to call upon him in baptism. Furthermore, the promise on the night of Jesus' betrayal assured them that Jesus' personal involvement would extend itself through a symbolic act.

2) Jesus himself was called into his new existence through the baptism of John. Could not this have been understood as the instituting of the post-Easter call to discipleship? That Jesus' baptism was seen in this light is not expressed in the New Testament; it is found for the first time in Ignatius and there in a strange way.[13] Jesus allowed himself to be baptized by John (Mk. 1:9ff.) and made it known through his conduct as well that he acknowledged the baptism of John as the sign of eschatological repentance given by God (Mk. 11:30 par.). In the synoptic tradition, the pericope about Jesus' baptism (Mk. 1:9ff. par.) intended primarily to make only a christological statement (cf. Jn. 1:31); even its redactional reworking made no use anywhere of Christian baptism. Yet it could not have escaped either the various redactors of this pericope or the readers that what would be communicated at baptism into Jesus' name happened here when Jesus entered into John's baptism of repentance. In the one instance as in the other sonship and Spirit were communicated.[14] If one looks at this substantive context as given,[15] then baptism just like the Eucharist was not a rite that came about or was instituted more or less fortuitously. Rather, it grew just like the Eucharist out of Jesus' actual entry into fellowship with sinners who were called to repentance.

These two resulting theological bases for baptism—the authorization for a symbolic act in the name of Jesus and its "institution" through Jesus' own behavior—were rooted in Jesus even if it is unclear how widely they were shared in the explicit consciousness of the primitive church. Baptism is not, therefore, simply a matter of lapsing back into ancient ritualism. Even Jesus did not make simply a general call to repentance, but he brought about its accomplishment by his offer of vital discipleship. In the post-Easter setting, the universal symbolic act of baptism replaced in substance the call to discipleship that was restricted to a few prior to Easter.

Baptism joined the baptized person not only to the exalted One, but also to other baptized persons or disciples who at Pentecost had received the Spirit without baptism; it also distinguished such a person from the remainder of the Jewish national community.

3. THE *EKKLĒSIA*

Unlike those who returned home once they had been baptized by John the Baptist, the baptized Christians became a distinct group within the religious

---

[13]Ign. Eph. 18:2: "He was born and baptized that by his suffering he might purify the water" (LCL, *Apostolic Fathers*, I, 193); Clem. Al. *Paedagogos* I.6.25f.; *Eclogae propheticae* 7.1; Tert. *Bapt.* 4.8.9; Pseudo-Cyprian *De pascha computus* 22; the baptismal pericope, however, was, in contrast to the account of eucharistic institution, never appropriated into the ancient church's liturgy as a word of institution (Kretschmar, op. cit. [n. 8], pp. 89ff.).

[14]The Christian experience of baptism certainly contributed to the shaping of the pericope.

[15]Thus also Kretschmar, op. cit. (n. 8), pp. 16f.

community of the Jewish people. "They devoted themselves to the apostles' teaching and fellowship, to the breaking of bread and the prayers" (Acts 2:42). The elements mentioned here were characteristically structural elements both of the common life of this group and of their own service of worship.

How did this group understand itself? When reading the book of Acts one has the impression that subsequent to Pentecost the group was led by the twelve and lived autonomously as church. It would seem that it carried out its mission within its Jewish milieu, doing so in the initial period unchallenged for the most part and with considerable success. Commenting on this picture in 1904, E. von Dobschütz stated that it had been the firm conclusion of historical research for some one hundred years that the primitive community was not a church among the Jews and had not wished to be this either. It had been rather—in his view—a "school" of Jews that "saw in their Master the Messiah," and that sought to win fellow Jews over to its confessional direction by means of as quiet a propaganda as possible.[16] This view of things emphasized quite accurately a sociological fact that the book of Acts presupposed without emphasis; in sociological perspective, the group of Jesus' disciples lived within the religious community of the Jewish people. It was referred to by its Jewish milieu as a *hairesis* (Acts 24:5, 14; 28:22), just like the Pharisees (Acts 15:5; 26:5) or the Essenes (Josephus *War* 2.8.7). *Hairesis* (Heb. *min*) was a designation for a religious-political group within Jewish society. The meaning "heresy" was attached to the word only toward the end of the 1st century. The criterion for membership in Judaism was the fundamental acceptance of the Mosaic Law. On the matter of what was to be expected regarding the end time and on many other issues differences of opinion were common. By all indications, Jesus' disciples—in contrast to Jesus himself—held to the Law, even to the levitical regulations for purity. Peter gave assurances of such according to Acts 10:14. The remark in Gal. 2:12 about the incident in Antioch confirmed this portrayal of Acts. Jesus' disciples also continued to participate in temple worship services (Acts 2:46; 3:1) or attended the synagogue (Mt. 10:17). They lived in closer contact with the religious community of the Jews than did the Essenes. The closest sociological analogy to the Christian community was the community of the Pharisees.

But how did they understand themselves? Their self-understanding found expression in the ways that they referred to themselves. In both Paul and the book of Acts the community at Jerusalem was referred to with special emphasis as "the saints" (*hoi hagioi*). Most probably, this designation came from within their own ranks (Rom. 15:25f., 31; I Cor. 16:1; II Cor. 8:4; 9:1, 12; Acts 9:13, 32, 41; 26:10). The same can be said when the synoptic apocalypse spoke about "the elect" (Mk. 13:20, 22, 27 par. Mt.), and certainly when the word to Peter (Mt. 16:18) referred to *ekklēsia*, the people of God or of Jesus. The Jewish Christians in Palestine referred to themselves as "the poor," the Ebionites, however, for the first time toward the end of the 1st century. On these matters the history of research is generally in agreement; controversial nevertheless is what precisely was intended by these self-designations.

The understanding of Bultmann was given exact formulation after the dis-

---

[16]*The Apostolic Age* (1910), pp. 20f.

covery of the Dead Sea Scrolls when he said in the preface to his *Theology*:
"The most significant analogy [namely, to the community at Qumran] may well
be that just like the Qumran sect the primitive Christian community understood
itself as the true Israel of the end time."[17] The group at Qumran did, in fact,
also refer to itself exclusively as the saints, the elect, the *ekklēsia* (Heb. *qahal*).
They wanted to be the true Israel that would soon inherit Israel's promises. In
essence, the Pharisees also made this claim when they called themselves "the
saints."

Did those who followed Jesus in discipleship also understand themselves to
be the "true Israel" that prior to the final hour separated itself from the bankrupt
mass of the "national church" of Israel in order to inherit Israel's salvation?
Removed from the context of their proclamation, almost all of these self-
designations could be understood in such a way. Only one cannot be so construed.
According to Mt. 16:18,[18] the disciples no longer referred to themselves like the
others as the *ekklēsia* of God, but as the *ekklēsia* of Jesus: "You are Peter, and
on this rock I will build my *ekklēsia*. . . !" *Ekklēsia* translated *qahal* in the
LXX. The *qᵉhal Yahweh* (LXX =*ekklēsia kyriou*) was the people called forth
by God.[19] When the Christian community referred to itself as the *ekklēsia* of
Jesus against this backdrop it was saying that it was the people of Jesus, the
messianic Ruler; it belonged to God through him. The community was the end-
time community of salvation. For it stood the words in the following clause:
"the gates of hell"—which close behind every human being (Isa. 38:10)—"shall
not prevail. . . ." It was to be built up as a spiritual temple—the Essenes also
likened themselves to this image—upon Peter, the rock. Peter was the rock
because he confessed Jesus as the Christ and was entrusted by Jesus with the
office of the key, because he was an apostle. The saying about Peter expressed
what was ascribed to all the apostles in Eph. 2:20 and Rev. 21:14. The apostles
were, therefore, the foundation because the church according to I Cor. 3:11 was
built upon Jesus. That is to say, the apostles transmitted the primitive witness to
Jesus. They were the foundation of the church, but did not constitute the basis
for a succession of officeholders. This saying, which was inscribed on the ceiling
of the dome of St. Peter's in Rome, contradicts—when correctly understood—
the claim of the papacy. It calls Peter the rock upon which the *ekklēsia* was
founded, and not the succession of Roman bishops.

From all this it is clear that the *ekklēsia* of Jesus did not understand itself to
be the true Israel like the Essenes and the Pharisees did, but as the eschatological
Israel that already had been taken into the end-time *basileia* of the Messiah and
thereby of God. To put it in terms of a phrase developed later, it was not the
true Israel within the false one, but the new Israel. It called forth the whole

---

[17]*Theologie* (1958³; not in Eng. trans. of 1951), p. VII.

[18]Thorough analyses of this word which was formulated in the early Palestinian church can be
found in O. Cullmann, *Peter—Disciple, Apostle, Martyr* (1962²), and A. Vögtle, "Messiasbe-
kenntnis und Petrusverheissung. Zur Komposition Mt. 16,13-23 par.," in A. Vögtle, *Das Evangelium und die Evangelien* (1971), pp. 137-170.

[19]K. L. Schmidt, *TDNT* III, 530.

people of the promise to Abraham and of the covenant at Sinai over into the dimension of the new across the barrier created by Jesus' rejection and resurrection. For this reason there was no need for the disciples of Jesus to migrate out of Israel like the Essenes or later out of Hellenistic society, but rather they could live together with them in the distance of the "now" but "not yet."

4. THE NEW SERVICE OF WORSHIP ALONGSIDE THE OLD

a) The breaking of bread. Within the context of a summary report based on tradition in Acts 2:46 the following remark was made: "And day by day, attending the temple together and breaking bread in their homes, they partook of food with glad and generous hearts." They did not visit the temple just to engage in missionary activity, but to participate in the temple's service of worship (Acts 3:1). The mealtimes referred to alongside attendance at the temple, therefore, were themselves occasions of worship. They were the new special service of worship for the Christian community.

These mealtimes were designated "the breaking of bread." In Judaism, the breaking of bread was an act at the beginning of every meal (§20,4). In the Christian community, it became the term for its special mealtime worship service. Later in Acts 20:7, Luke called *the* worship celebration "the breaking of bread"; in I Cor. 11:20, Paul called it the Lord's Supper. Differences existed in the shape taken by the celebration as described by Luke and Paul. Yet, in both descriptions the celebration was constituted by that sacramental eating and drinking which was expressed in the liturgical formula of I Cor. 11:23ff., the so-called account of institution. Was this also valid for "the breaking of bread" of the primitive church in Jerusalem? In the views of H. Lietzmann[20] and R. Bultmann,[21] the meal celebration of the primitive community represented a type of meal distinct from the Lord's Supper of the Hellenistic community. The former was celebrated (Acts 2:46) "with gladness" (concerning the end-time salvation) as an eschatological meal of joy; the latter proclaimed (in the interpretation of Paul, I Cor. 11:26) the death of the Lord. A meal of joy without connection to the accounts of institution was presupposed by the meal prayers in Did. 9f. And so Lietzmann assumed that the Palestinian type of meal lived on in those prayers. As he saw it, the first community did not appropriate the (supposed) institution on the night of betrayal, but continued the table fellowship from the days of Jesus' earthly ministry. That first community—reasoned Lietzmann—was conscious of the unseen presence of the resurrected One in its midst, just as the disciples on the road to Emmaus had experienced him perhaps in a visionary way. Regarding this hypothesis, it has become clear in the meantime that the meal prayers of Did. 9f. referred from the very beginning to the meal *(Sättigungsmahl)* that was linked to the sacramental eating and drinking. The accounts of institution, moreover, have shown themselves to be at their core his-

---

[20]*Mass and Lord's Supper* (1979), pp. 193-99.
[21]*Theology* I, §§6,4; 8,3.

torical (§20,1). The promise expressed by those accounts corresponded to the way in which the exalted One in fact continued to minister after Pentecost. He was present among the community in a divine way. The Palestinian tradition (Mt. 18:20; 28:20; Rev. 3:20) emphasized this more drastically than either Paul or John. He was present by ministering among his own through his Spirit or to them through his name. Thus the members of the community linked an eating and drinking in accord with the accounts of institution with their daily common meals. Like everything else that was given to them by the Easter event, this eating and drinking was unique in their environment.

b) The so-called community of goods. The common mealtimes not only were suggested by the meaningful table fellowship of Jesus' earthly ministry, but also were conditioned by the social setting. Many of the disciples had given up their means of livelihood in Galilee and had moved to Jerusalem. There it was difficult for them to support themselves. Everyone received the necessities of life through the voluntary giving of the few who owned property; such giving also meant the loss of personal economic resources such as houses and fields. The summary reports of Acts 2:44f.; 4:32, 34f. convey the impression of a community of goods. According to the individual accounts of Acts 4:36f.; 5:1-11, however, they did not introduce a compulsory collective economy as in Qumran,[22] but the members contributed to the community through voluntary offerings. These offerings included making available the necessities of life and far exceeded the considerable amounts of money offered for the care of the poor in the synagogal community. This extraordinary giving was conditioned by the unusual social situation of the primitive community. Consequently, it did not repeat itself hereafter in early Christianity. Luke did not report it so that it might serve as an example to be followed, but so that it might serve as a demonstration of what the church is. It was a demonstration of the faith that was established by Jesus, the faith that was free to provide for one's neighbor the things needful for living. It was free because it had given up the worry of calculating (Mt. 6:25).

c) The gospel and the law—conflict and compromise. It is evident that the community lived on the basis of the kerygma in accord with Jesus' Sermon on the Mount; yet, simultaneously, it still observed the Mosaic Law, which was also the civil law. It lived according to the regulation, "these you ought to have done, without neglecting the others" (Mt. 23:23). It lived—as strange as it may sound—a kind of two-kingdoms ethic. Before long it became apparent that here too it was difficult to maintain the tension between the two. The tension led to conflict and therefore also to a compromise that relativized the tension.

The conflict came about when Stephen, one of the "Hellenists" (Acts 6:5), emphasized in the context of missionary dialogue the priority of that which was

---

[22]Josephus *War* 2.8.3f.; *Ant*. 18.1.5; 1QS 1:11-13; 5:2f.; 6:18-23; *CD* 16; regarding care of the poor by the synagogue, cf. Billerbeck II, 643ff.; Lit. in H. Bolkestein, *Wohltätigkeit und Armenpflege im vorchristlichen Altertum* (1939); M. Hengel, *Property and Riches in the Early Church* (1974), esp. pp. 31-34.

new. It is probable that his Jewish partners in conversation wished to avoid the radical call to repentance by pointing to God's gracious presence in the temple. In any case, Stephen referred to Jesus' saying about the end of the temple, a saying the Palestinian disciples had transmitted but had not realized (Acts 6:14; cf. §24,1). This said in essence that God's salvation was finally not to come from the temple. As far as we can tell from the limited traditions, Stephen did not, moreover, appropriate the statements of Jesus that were critical of the Law. The Hellenists of Jerusalem, whom he represented, apparently were not yet advocating freedom from the Law; this was not critical in Jerusalem.

This critical statement directed at the temple was enough by itself to get Stephen thrown out of the Jewish national community. His execution according to Jewish custom unleashed further attacks on the Christians. All disciples who were in agreement with his views had to flee Jerusalem if they did not want to fall victim to a similar fate. They belonged basically to the group of Hellenists, i.e., to the Greek-speaking portion of the community that had emerged from among those Diaspora Jews who had returned to Jerusalem. (The account in Acts 7:54–8:3 should be understood in this way.) For these disciples, the return to the Diaspora was not difficult, particularly when Jesus' saying about the end of the temple was allowed to stand and to cancel the notion of salvation's fulfillment in Zion.

The events surrounding Stephen and the Hellenists show just how much the rest of the Christian community in Jerusalem maintained the Law. It did not consider breaking the sabbath or the ordinances of purification in the way recorded in the synoptic tradition about Jesus (§9,2). Pericopes like Mk. 2:21-28; 3:1-6 were not formulated in order to justify the conduct of the community. They were written to clarify the singular path tread by Jews alone.[23] This much is clear: after the departure of the Hellenists, the longer it stayed the more the Christian community that remained in Jerusalem held to the Law. Because of this, it lost sight of the priority of the call to that which was new, as well as Jesus' critique of that which belonged to former things. The later Palestinian church was in danger of becoming in its structure that which it was not in the beginning, namely, a Jewish *hairesis* honoring Jesus as Messiah and living according to a radicalized Law. This danger was averted for the Palestinian church as a whole first of all by the enlarged vision that was prompted by the flight of the Hellenists.

5. THE ALTERED MISSIONARY SITUATION AND THE BEGINNINGS OF GENTILE CHRISTIANITY FREE FROM THE LAW

a) The centripetal mission in Jerusalem. Astonishingly the apostles remained in Jerusalem during the first years after Jesus' exit and did not set out

---

[23]R. Bultmann (*Theology* I, §8,2) thought that the community in Jerusalem knew an early period of freedom in which it was different, but this is a postulate that cannot be verified at all by historical references.

on missionary travels. It was in Jerusalem that Paul sought them out, according to Gal. 1:18f. The book of Acts depicts a similar picture (cf. 8:1). This conduct was based on a substantive connection: they expected that Israel would turn to its Messiah very soon and that the nations would then follow; i.e., they hoped for a development corresponding to the tradition of the pilgrimage of the nations to Zion (Isa. 2:2-4). It was in this sense that they had understood the saying of Jesus, "many will come from east and west and sit at table with Abraham, Isaac, and Jacob . . ." (Mt. 8:10f. par.).

b) The rise of missionary travels. After but a few years it became evident, however, that the message of the apostles would not be heeded either by the population as a whole or by Israel's leaders. The apostles and disciples in Palestine would not accept this at first. The legendary account of Hegesippus says that James, the brother of the Lord, prayed daily in the temple throughout the decades for the conversion of Israel,[24] until in A.D. 62 he was brought to trial by the high priest and thereby the community's contact with the temple was severed. While the community in Jerusalem continued to concern itself with Israel, the Hellenists who had been driven away from Jerusalem began a spontaneous mission as they traveled about. So it was that only about three years after Jesus' exit, alongside the centripetal mission in Jerusalem there emerged a centrifugal mission of traveling missionaries (Acts 8:4f.; 11:19f.).

c) The mother church of Gentile Christianity. Through the spontaneous work of traveling missionaries there arose after a brief time a community made up primarily of Gentile Christians. It was located in Antioch on the Orontes in Syria, a major Hellenistic city with a population at that time of approximately 300,000 inhabitants. This Christian community as a whole no longer lived according to the Mosaic Law (cf. Gal. 2:11f.). It became the mother church of Gentile Christianity. It came into being not because of a theological program or an ecclesiastical strategy, but through the dynamics of the gospel. As the "Hellenists" preached in the synagogues, uncircumcised Hellenistic people who had contact with the synagogues here as in other places became believers. They were baptized without circumcision and thereby without being placed in subjection to the Law.

Luke mentioned this epoch-making turn of events only briefly in Acts 11:20f. He attempted to explain it as a development whose roots were to be traced fundamentally to Jerusalem. He did this by describing in detail the baptism of the uncircumcised Cornelius by Peter and its discussion in Jerusalem before mentioning the incident in Antioch (Acts 10:1–11:18). He let Peter justify the baptism of the uncircumcised before the community of Jerusalem with the words: "If then God gave the same gift to them as he gave to us when we believed in the Lord Jesus Christ, who was I that I could withstand God?" (Acts 11:17). This sentence describes correctly the empirical reality; this was and is the way the church comes into being. The Hellenistic, Gentile Christianity that came

---

[24]Eus. *EH* 2.23.11-19.

about like this could survive and acquire its own shape as church, however, only by means of theological clarification. And there were many more issues to be clarified theologically than were addressed in the Cornelius story. What was needed was an advancement of the very foundation of preaching and the church within Israel to the emerging image of the church made up of Jews and Gentiles and to a proclamation and theology that would gather and support them.

d) *The preparation for the transition to Hellenistic Christianity.* It was very important for the extended development that emanated from Antioch that the transition from the Aramaic to the Greek linguistic realm had already taken place during the initial years in Jerusalem. This meant that from the earliest period the tradition of the primitive community was bilingual. This also accomplished a first step out of the thoughts and imagery of Palestinian Judaism into those of Hellenism. Of course—as has become clear through contemporary research— the exchange between Judaism and Hellenism had been underway for a long time even in Palestine.[25] Nevertheless, the step from the one to the other realm was for Christianity anything but unproblematical. Even in Jerusalem there arose considerable tension between that segment of the primitive community which came from Palestine and that which came from the Jewish Diaspora. Luke himself, who very much suppressed and simplified the controversies of the early period, reported the conflict between these two groups, the "Hebrews" and the "Hellenists" (Acts 6:1-6). It is to be determined whether this difference can be observed as early as among the few didactic traditions that came from the early Palestinian church. We want to keep this question in mind as we turn now to inquire about the central matter that supported the emergence and life of the community and made the fundamental preparation for further development. This means the inquiry into the Christology that was expressed by the community's preaching, confessing, and praying.

§26. The Beginnings of Christology

Presentations as a Whole: Bousset, *Kyrios*; Cullmann, *Christology*; Schweizer, *Lordship*; Hahn, *Titles*; Kramer, *Christ*; P. Vielhauer, "Ein Weg zur neutestamentlichen Christologie? Prüfung der Thesen Ferdinand Hahns," *EvTheol* 25 (1965), 24-72; K. Wengst, *Christologische Formeln und Lieder des Urchristentums* (1974²). **On Methodology**: H. R. Balz, *Methodische Probleme der neutestamentlichen Christologie* (1967); F. Hahn, "Methodenprobleme einer Christologie des Neuen Testaments," *VF* 15 (1970), 3-41. **On 2 and 6**: E. Haenchen, "Die frühe Christologie," *ZThK* 63 (1966), 145-159; W. Thüsing, "Erhöhungsvorstellung und Parusieerwartung in der ältesten nachösterlichen Christologie," *BZ* NF 11 (1967), 95-108; J. Ernst, *Anfänge der Christologie* (1972); M. Hengel, "Christologie und neutestamentliche Chronologie," in *Neues Testament und Geschichte, Festschrift für O. Cullmann* (1972), pp. 43-67. **On 3**: A. von Harnack, *Die Bezeichnung Jesu als "Knecht Gottes" und ihre Geschichte in der alten Kirche* (*SAB*, 1926), pp. 212-238; J. Jeremias, *pais theou*, *TDNT* V, 700-05. **On 5**: K. G. Kuhn, *maranatha*, *TDNT* IV, 466-472; S. Schulz, "Maranatha und Kyrios Jesus,"

---

[25]M. Hengel, *Judaism and Hellenism* (1974).

ZNW 53 (1962), 125-144; B. Sandvik, *Das Kommen des Herrn beim Abendmahl im Neuen Testament* (1970).

1. THE RELATIONSHIP TO THE PREACHING OF JESUS

a) The difference. According to the structural outline upon which Peter's sermons in Acts 2–5 were based, the earliest missionary kerygma stated: you killed Jesus; God raised him from the dead; therefore, repent! (§25,1b). Jesus, on the other hand, preached: Repent, for the Kingdom of God is at hand! The difference is clear: Jesus called people to repentance in view of the imminent coming of the kingdom; the disciples did the same but in view of Jesus' resurrection that had taken place.

In his lecture "What is Christianity?" (1900), A. von Harnack expressed this difference in terms of a memorable formula: the gospel of Jesus was turned into the gospel about Jesus Christ.[1] As Bultmann put it: "the proclaimer became the proclaimed. . . ."[2]

b) How is this shift to be understood? For Harnack, liberal theology, and the history-of-religion school that followed the latter theologically, this transformation was the decisive break that constituted the forfeiture of the simple gospel of Jesus. Said Harnack: "The Gospel, as Jesus proclaimed it, has to do with the Father only and not with the Son."[3] The Easter kerygma and the Christology that was developed from it were to be eliminated. Bultmann, on the other hand, explained the difference in terms of the formula "implicit-explicit," i.e., "Jesus' call to decision implies a christology . . . (namely) the implications of the positive answer to his demand for the decision, the obedient response which acknowledges God's revelation in Jesus."[4] Similar is the judgment of H. Conzelmann. Prior to Easter it was a matter of "indirect" Christology; after Easter, "direct Christology." For him, the historical Jesus considered himself to be the spokesman of God's message, but not its mediator. For this reason "the unity of the pre- and post-Easter Jesus" became "clear only in the proclamation of faith."[5]

It has become clear above that the earthly Jesus had already been the "mediator." He did not simply announce the coming of the kingdom, but made possible repentance and forgiveness and thereby a share in the kingdom (§6,3). Yet he brought this about only preliminarily, since he himself was bound by time and space, and was moving toward the completion of his service in death and resurrection. Consequently, Jesus' proclamation was a veiled and preliminary offering of salvation while that of the apostles after Easter was the offering of salvation open and final. In this sense, Jesus represented a Christology as a

---

[1] A. von Harnack, *What is Christianity?* (1957), pp. 142ff. and 178ff.
[2] *Theology* I, 33.
[3] Op. cit. (n. 1), p. 144.
[4] *Theology* I, 43.
[5] "Jesus von Nazareth und der Glaube an den Auferstandenen," in *Historische Jesus*, p. 198.

veiled witness to himself; the apostles developed this Christology as an open confession and from there as teaching that gave clarity to this confession.

2. THE STARTING POINT OF CHRISTOLOGY

As soon as we ask where the Christology that the primitive church of Palestine developed for its situation was to be found, we encounter some difficult methodological and substantive problems.

a) Regarding methodology. In the traditions that have come down to us from the primitive church we find titles and formulas, but no connected discussions. Studies of Christology take as their starting point, therefore, in part titles and in part formulas.[6] The recent work by F. Hahn focused on titles, while that of W. Kramer focused on formulas (*Christ* [Ger. 1963]). How does one come to understand what the titles and brief formulas meant? In the opinion of the history-of-religion school—here we look to the classical expressions of W. Bousset—the disciples responded to the enduring impression that the religious personality of Jesus had made upon them with the faith of Easter. They talked about him, moreover, in the terms of their time by taking over and applying to Jesus the mythical schemata that were current, e.g., the Son of man expectation of Jewish apocalypticism.[7] In the meantime, careful investigation of the content of this expectation has shown that precisely this Son of man title was used in a fundamentally different way in the synoptic Gospels than in Jewish apocalypticism (§18). The same can be said about other titles. That which can be derived from history-of-religion analysis about a title's meaning in the milieu of the church cannot be assumed without differentiation to be true for Christian usage. The usage of the environment and that of the church must be confronted with each other so that out of the comparison the Christian meaning of the title and statement as a whole may become clear. It is essential that the study of Christian formulas be carried out within the context of the actual life of the community, i.e., in terms of its *Sitz im Leben* and that which truly motivated its behavior. What caused people to apply to Jesus specific titles and to make specific formulaic statements about him? While Bousset pointed here to the impression made by Jesus' personality, Bultmann considered the christological titles to be the existential response to his call to decision (*Theology* I, §7,2). E. Schweizer, who gave special attention to this question in his book *Lordship and Discipleship*, regarded the setting of discipleship established by Jesus as the starting point.

In terms of methodology both here and elsewhere what we come to understand about Christology will be the product of overlapping explorations into the content

---

[6]A. Seeberg, *Der Katechismus der Urchristenheit* (1903; repr. 1965), came upon this formulaic tradition while searching for the preliminary stages of the Apostles' Creed in the New Testament. Concerning further research of this tradition, cf. the report of K. Wengst (Lit., §26), pp. 13-25.

[7]On the basis of historicism's principle of correlation, Bousset, *Kyrios*, pp. 45f., formulated: "along with the title (Son of man), however, the primitive community—and here we stand in the presence of a fact of most decisive importance—also appropriated the total contents of the representations which are connected with it."

of the titles and formulas, their history-of-religion background, and the actual motivation behind their usage in the community.

b) The substantive issue. When reconstructing the Christology of the primitive community a question arises. The question is characteristic of the overall problem one faces in studying Christology and is one that is raised from within the sources themselves: What is the relationship between the Christology found in the traditions from the Pauline epistles and the book of Acts and that found in the early strata of the synoptic Gospels? The interpreters associated with the history-of-religion school assumed that the primitive community lived by the Christology of the synoptic sayings concerning the Son of man and looked for that One to appear in the near future at the *parousia*. How did this compare to the Christology expressed in the epistles of Paul and the book of Acts through the titles and formulas that on the basis of the Easter kerygma directed one's attention to the exalted One? Did this Christology rest on a narrow selection of traditions? Did it flourish in segments of the community or in whole communities distinct from those claiming the Son of man concept? Is the relationship to be explained only in terms of subsequent or parallel historical developments? Should their substance be understood along mutually complementary lines?

c) The approach to the task. In resolving this problem we should avoid an initial isolation of the distinct traditions from each other. We should attempt to characterize their relationship to each other. We shall take as the starting point the information about the Christology of the primitive community that we find in the Pauline epistles and the book of Acts and then make constant comparison with corresponding elements found in the synoptic tradition. In a second stage of inquiry it will be necessary to reverse the process, starting with the synoptic tradition. From both sides then we shall attempt to characterize the christological structure in overview.

d) The christological titles. In both the Pauline and Lukan traditions—the differences that existed between them notwithstanding—we find four basic christological titles that were used in the primitive community, though leading from case to case in quite different directions. The title "Servant of God" linked the course of Jesus' ministry to the contemporary life of the community. "Christ" and "Son of God" referred to the activity of the exalted One. The invocation: "Come! O Lord!" looked at his imminent coming and toward the consummation. The first and last of these four flourished primarily in prayer formulas, the second and third in kerygmatic and confessional formulas. We shall take a look now at each of the somewhat meager traditions in order to gain as much understanding as possible about the roots and the structure of the earliest Christology.

3. THE SERVANT OF GOD

a) The origin of the designation. In the account of Acts 3:1–4:31, which contained considerable material from earlier sources, Jesus was referred to four times as the "(holy) servant of God" (3:13, 26; 4:27, 30). Elsewhere in the New

Testament he was called this only one other time, i.e., in the proof-from-prophecy reference in Mt. 12:18-21 (= Isa. 42:1-4). In this reference the Hebrew text was followed in vv. 18-20c and the LXX in v. 21. This would indicate that the reference already had undergone a considerable history-of-tradition development. In the extracanonical Christian literature up to ca. A.D. 160 this designation for Jesus is found only some seventeen times, and always in the liturgical context of prayers.[8] Thus, for instance, it was used doxologically in I Clem. 59:4 and in Mart. Pol. 14:1f., but otherwise always in the phrase "through Jesus (Christ), Thy (beloved) Servant." Such was also the usage in the Agape-feast prayers of Did. 9:2f.; 10:2f., in the large prayer for the church in I Clem. 59:2f., and in the prayers of Mart. Pol. 14:3; 20:2. In Acts 3f. the designation was also brought together with the phrase in a prayer at 4:30, but at 3:13, 26 and 4:27 in the kerygma. Where did this designation come from? The usage in Acts and in Mt. 12 shows that we are dealing here not merely with an expression of prayer that was constructed in correspondence to Jewish statements about servants of God like David.[9] "Servant of God" was actually a title for Jesus. The title was certainly not conferred on him as such in the Hellenistic church since, for it, in relationship to God Jesus was the Son and not the Servant. The usage in Mt. 12, which proceeded initially from the Hebrew text, and that in Did. 9f., also suggest an origin in the Palestinian church. The Lukan account also contained other traditional material from this church. It is likely that Luke appropriated this expression, which he doesn't use elsewhere, from this traditional material. Speaking decisively in favor of this origin is the content that is to be derived on the basis of the formulaic phrases.

b) *The content expressed.* An image of the servant was reflected in the four statements of Acts that was noticeably comparable to that of the proof-from-prophecy reference of Mt. 12:18-21 and later liturgical tradition. Two motifs were well defined: (1) Jesus was the "Servant of God" because God performed healings through him (Acts 3:13; 4:30; Mt. 12:15-21), in fact, accomplished the very salvation that the community encountered (Did. 9:2f.; 10:2f.; I Clem. 59:2f.). (2) Jesus was the servant—and this was original to his being so designated—as that One who was rejected by the powerful but now since Easter had been "glorified" by God through the dawn of salvation accomplished "in his name." That is to say, he was the servant as the One who was identified, exalted, and established as the promised Messiah (3:13; cf. 3:26; 4:26f.).

Was this content anticipated in some prior history of the designation? (1) The essential motifs of this image corresponded strikingly to those Old Testament references that were referred to by the texts; these were the sending of the messianic prophet that Second Isaiah promised under the servant-name in 42:1-4 (Mt. 12:18-20a) and the servant's announced exaltation from unimaginable hu-

---

[8]Hahn, *Titles*, p. 376 n. 172 (= pp. 400f.).

[9]Contra E. Haenchen, *Acts*, and H. Conzelmann, *Apostelgeschichte*, regarding Acts 3:13, Luke himself surely understood *pais*—just like the rest of the liturgical tradition—not as "son" but as "servant."

miliation in Isa. 52:13f. (= Acts 3:13). The designation could therefore have been applied originally to Jesus in the way understood by these references. (2) It was not developed, however, purely on the basis of meditation upon the scriptures. It was much more the product of the stimulus found in the widely known titular use of "Servant of God." In several places David too was called the "servant of God" (Acts 4:25; Did. 9:2). "Servant of God" was frequently an honorific title in the Old Testament/Jewish realm for the bearer of God's mandate in relationship to his people, e.g., also with regard to the prophets (cf. Rev. 11:18; 22:9). The title seemed appropriate for Jesus, therefore, when he was understood to be the end-time prophet just like some felt regarding the Teacher of Righteousness at Qumran. To see Jesus in this light was suggested by his earthly ministry. Jesus himself had made the typological comparison between himself and the Old Testament prophets (§17,2) and this comparison was extended at once in the Palestinian church. Behind the Moses typology of Acts 7:22b, 25, 37-52a, 53 stood traditions that reached back to Jewish Christianity in Palestine.[10]

Much is to be said, therefore, for localizing the "Servant of God" title for Jesus in the primitive community. By doing so it was saying in general that he was the promised end-time prophet; specifically, however, it saw his image in Isa. 42:1-4 and 52:13f.[11] The Servant of God, working in a way concealed from everyday sight, ushered in God's salvation among people; he was the abased One who was exalted. None of the references to Jesus as the "Servant of God," however, contained a pointer to an atonement and corresponding liturgical formulas such as "for Jesus' sake." Isa. 53, therefore, was not envisaged here.[12]

The conceptual background out of which the designation grew was broader than the designation's use and broader also than that which it expressed. The voice from heaven at Jesus' baptism (Mk. 1:11 par.) and his transfiguration (Mk. 9:7 par.) that marked out the course of his life in a programmatic way, did appropriate the vocational call of the servant of God in Second Isaiah (Isa. 42:1),[13] but the direct address was taken from the vocational call of the messianic king in Ps. 2:7, "You are my son." It is improbable that the word *pais* originally was used here, and on the basis of a double meaning was understood later as "son."[14] The degree to which, from a history-of-tradition perspective, the reverse interpretation of Ps. 2:1f. goes back to the servant in Acts 4:27 is uncertain.

At least the use of the designation "Servant of God" indicated to the primitive community that a line of thought from its preaching and its prayers led to a

---

[10]Cf. Hahn, *Titles*, pp. 372-74.

[11]Thus also Cullmann, *Christology*, pp. 69ff.; J. Jeremias, *TDNT* V, 704 (cf. Ger. 701f. for ref.); Schweizer, *Discipleship*, pp. 49ff. In contrast, Bultmann, *Theology* I, §7,5, and Conzelmann, *Theology*, p. 85, restricted the meaning to the general honorific title, and Hahn, *Titles*, pp. 372f., to the end-time prophet like Moses (Deut. 18:18).

[12]Neither was Isa. 53 of influence elsewhere in early Christian theology; J. Jeremias failed to note this in *TDNT* V, 704-712; cf. above, §18,8b.

[13]The connection becomes especially clear when one compares the rendering of Isa. 42:1 according to the Masoretic text in Mt. 12:18.

[14]Contra Jeremias, op. cit. (n. 11), 701f.

comprehensive conceptual reservoir with whose help the course of Jesus' life was interpreted as the course of the "prophet" or the "righteous One." Whether it originated with Jesus himself or with his witnesses, its roots were attested from the oldest strata of the synoptic tradition on.

The absence of such a suggestive reference to Isa. 53 indicates that for the primitive community Jesus' death was initially connected to the history of Israel in the sense of the missionary kerygma (cf. Acts 3:13-15), the passion narrative, and the announcements of coming suffering; it was not developed in its special saving significance for the community. It was enough to take the *hyper*-formula from the tradition of the Last Supper and to incorporate it into the kerygma (I Cor. 15:3-5; Rom. 4:25). For this reason we find this traditional context first of all in Paul (§35,3). Salvation was expected in such a way that God's activity to save "through his servant Jesus" was now being carried out in its entirety by the exalted One. Hence, his exaltation was confessed as his authority to minister historically as "the Christ" or as "the Son of God in power."

4. THE RESURRECTION AS THE EXALTATION TO MESSIANIC RULER

a) The documentary support. Three references in the New Testament pointed out that Jesus had become the messianic ruler through the resurrection. Acts 2:36, "God has made him both Lord and Christ, this Jesus whom you crucified." According to Acts 13:33, Jesus fulfilled Ps. 2:7 through the resurrection: "Thou art my Son, today I have begotten thee." In Ps. 2:7 the messianic king was referred to as "God's son." Hence, the content was the same as that expressed in Acts 2:36. The third and most important reference is also the most reliable from a history-of-tradition perspective; the formula of Rom. 1:3, 4a, whose subject originally was Jesus, stated:

> [Jesus], who was descended from David according to the flesh and designated Son of God in power according to the Spirit of holiness by his resurrection from the dead.

According to these three references Jesus became the Christ or the Son of God or the Lord through the resurrection.

b) What kind of Christology is this? This Christology has been labeled repeatedly "adoptionistic." Such is supposed to mean according to Bultmann[15] that this earliest Christology did not consider the earthly ministry of Jesus to be messianic; for it Jesus first became the Messiah through the resurrection. This disclaimer regarding the earthly ministry that was characteristic of the adoptionist Christology of subsequent Jewish Christianity, however, was not yet contained in these formulas. What Jesus was before the resurrection was at least left open by them. According to the formula of Rom. 1:3f., he was indeed characterized before his exaltation as descended from David, i.e., in fact as the One destined

---

[15]*Theology* I, §4,1.

to become the Messiah. One could certainly conclude that if he became the Son of God in power through exaltation, then he was that earlier in weakness. Decisive is that the formulas spoke of the conveyance of a function and not of an ontological title. The function of the resurrected One was, to be sure, quite different from that of the earthly Jesus. Hence these statements ought to be classified as exaltation Christology because they sought to express the function of the exalted One. This was accomplished through the aid of three designations: Christ, Son (of God), and Lord.

c) The statement. The exalted One was at work as "the Christ." Within the Jewish context, "the anointed One" was the expected Davidic King of salvation or in a more general sense the end-time Bringer of salvation (§17,4). Inasmuch as designations like Lord (Acts 2:36), Son of God in power (Rom. 1:3f.), and Son (Acts 13:33 following Ps. 2:7) stand alongside the predicate "Christ" as corresponding interpretive clarifications, the Christ was certainly thought of as the ruler over his people (cf. Mt. 16:18); he was the One who would establish his dominion in history. The manner and context of his dominion, however, could only be derived from the historical appearance of Jesus. Through his exercise of dominion, the dominion of God, the *basileia* that Jesus had proclaimed, was established (§6).

While the terms "Christ" and "Son of God" were developed from their Old Testament/Jewish prior-history, there was no such point of contact for the designation "Lord." This designation was found in the form of a title in the one christological formula of the Aramaic-speaking primitive community that has been preserved verbatim, namely, in the call *maranatha*.

5. MARANATHA!

a) Tradition and meaning. In I Cor. 16:22 and Did. 10:6 the call *maranatha* was found in portions of the liturgy of the Lord's Supper. The Hellenistic church had taken over this formula from Aramaic usage. The expression represented two words. How to relate and translate them is a matter of philological uncertainty. According to Palestinian Aramaic they should probably be divided: *maran 'atha'* (our Lord has come) or *maran 'atha'* (our Lord, come!). The latter option could also read: *marana' tha'*.[16] The context of Did. 10:6 required the use of the imperative. Such was also the rendering of the oldest Greek translation (Rev. 22:20): "Amen. Come, Lord Jesus!" This call in both Rev. 22:20 and Did. 10:6 did not refer to a present coming at the Eucharist,[17] but to the eschatological coming at the *parousia*. From its inception the call was probably located in the liturgy of the meal of celebration;[18] perhaps the use of the address was helped

---

[16]K. G. Kuhn, *TDNT* IV, 466-472; regarding the discussion, cf. H. Conzelmann, *A Commentary on the First Epistle to the Corinthians* (Hermeneia), at I Cor. 16:22.

[17]Contra B. Sandvik (Lit., §26,5), pp. 13-36.

[18]Contra K. Wengst (Lit., §26), pp. 49-54.

along by the eschatological saying in the account of institution of the Supper (Mk. 14:25; cf. I Cor. 11:26b).

  b) **The emergence of the address.** 1) The address was in no way prepared by the Old Testament/Jewish expectation of the Messiah. This expectation did not include a calling upon the Messiah nor his designation as Lord. Moreover, in other contexts the address *mari'* (my Lord) and the designation *mare'* (Lord) in Aramaic linguistic usage were not applied to deities. Rather it was an address of respect; it had special application to higher officials in matters of judicial administration.[19] An isolated religious usage can be found in the Genesis Apocryphon of Qumran. Here the Aramaic *mari'* (my Lord) was also used as a form of address in prayer. In the synagogue, on the other hand, the Old Testament name of God was reproduced customarily by using the Hebrew term *'adonai* (Lord). In a way to be distinguished from the linguistic usage of these surroundings the ministry of Jesus offered the substantive and linguistic presuppositions for the formation of the call.

  2) Substantively, the request for the eschatological coming of Jesus came about because he himself had announced a twofold coming: the coming of the kingdom of God and the coming of the Son of man. The disciples prayed for the coming of the kingdom in the Lord's Prayer (Mt. 6:10 par.). This request always retained for them the meaning that it might come through Jesus. After his exaltation the request underwent consolidation in a personal direction with the coming of the Son of man (cf. Lk. 12:8). Yet the designation "Son of man" was not taken over into prayer, confession, or proclamation. It was not suited linguistically for this, but only for the enigmatic witness of Jesus to himself.[20] It was replaced by the address "our Lord."

  3) Regarding the history of the term, this address suggested itself because Jesus' charitable intervention had already been sought during his earthly ministry as people probably addressed him not only as *rabbi* but also as *mari'* (lord). The term was mentioned in Q, however, only at Mt. 8:8 par., where the centurion from Capernaum said, "Lord, I am not worthy to have you come under my roof; but only say the word . . . ," and in Mark only at 7:28 (par. Mt.) in the words of the Syrophoenician woman. Directed at Jesus the address of respect *mari'* and the address *rabbi* were combined with the concept of his *exousia*.

  Whereas the earthly Jesus was addressed only occasionally as "lord," it probably became customary very early in the Palestinian community to draw on former usage and to refer to him as "the Lord." One probably first spoke about the "brothers of the Lord" in the setting where they had a role to play (Gal. 1:19; I Cor. 9:5); reference to the "words of the Lord" (I Cor. 7:10, etc.) probably also arose in this setting.

  It was out of this address and reference to the earthly Jesus with their basic

---

[19]Cf. S. Schulz (Lit., §26,5), 136f.; M. Hengel's objections (Lit., §26,2 and 6; p. 56, n. 43) do not alter this overall picture.

[20]The address "Thou son of man" as it was used in relationship to the prophet Ezekiel makes sense with God as the speaker but not on the lips of a human being.

understanding about his *exousia* that one was able to call the exalted One "a Lord" in order to designate "the Christ" as ruler. The reference took on a different tone when one sought his eschatological coming with the address "our Lord" and summarized in this call the request for the coming of the *basileia* promised by Jesus and thereby the entire expectation of salvation.

c) *The content of the address.* This call referred of course to "our Lord" who would bring the *parousia*, but it was intended to be heard by the exalted One. In this way the call ascribed to the exalted One a function that was without analogy in the conceptual world of Judaism. Here only God and never the Messiah was addressed. Thus in an unreflected manner the call took on the character of a prayer. The concept that was instinctively applied in this way to the exalted One was clarified and filled out very early with the aid of Ps. 110:1: "The Lord said to my lord: 'Sit at my right hand. . . .' " Originally this was a prophetic word spoken to the king by a cult prophet. According to Acts 7:55 and Mk. 14:61f. this passage was already linked to the exaltation of Jesus to messianic-ruler within the Palestinian church. Accordingly his relationship to God was clarified through the metaphorical expression "at my right hand." That is, he shared in the *basileia* of God; it was established by him.

By using Ps. 110:1 the pericope in Mk. 12:35-37 par. expressed in contrast to Jewish messialogy that Jesus was the Christ as "Lord" at the right hand of God, not merely as *ben-dawid* (§17,3). This understanding is more clearly apparent in the Greek text of the Psalm than in the Hebrew. Consequently the pericope could have been formulated in the Greek-speaking Jewish-Christianity of Palestine.

Just like the formula in Acts 2:36, the pericope did not turn "Lord" into a title, but thereby only described the place and function of the exalted One. "The Lord" as reference to the earthly Jesus and "our Lord" in liturgical acclamation took on titular character.

These formulas that were transmitted by Paul established a bridge to the synoptic sayings about the coming of the Son of man. From this connection it is possible to clarify further the key problem of the primitive church's Christology.

6. REGARDING THE STRUCTURE OF EARLY CHRISTOLOGICAL STATEMENTS

a) *Research on the Christology of the early layers of the synoptic tradition.* W. Bousset thought that the Christology of the primitive community of Palestine was to be found in the synoptic Son of man sayings.[21] H. Koester[22] chose as his starting point a renewal of the history-of-religion school's line of questioning and ascertained recently four history-of-religion types of Christology in the synoptic tradition. They are: (1) The earliest community was an enthusiast-apocalyptic sect. It did not base its life on the Easter kerygma, but on

---

[21]*Kyrios*, pp. 35-42, also Conzelmann, *Theology*, pp. 136f.

[22]Koester-Robinson, *Trajectories*, pp. 205-231.

"prophetic utterances and apocalyptic traditions . . . and in the cultic anticipation of that future" . . . and expected Jesus as the "Son of man" and as "the Lord."[23] (2) Additional Christologies also began with the early collecting and shaping of synoptic material, but only became fully developed at the time of their integration into Hellenistic Christianity. Here a *"theios anēr"* Christology emerged that was based on collections of miracle stories about Jesus. For this view Jesus became the prototype of wandering miracle worker-missionaries like the ones Paul opposed in II Corinthians.[24] (3) Among collections of sayings Jesus had already been understood in the Palestinian-Syrian setting as the envoy of wisdom. With the aid of corresponding proverbial sayings Jesus himself was soon heralded as *the* wisdom by a Sophia-Christology. It was in opposition to such groupings of wisdom teachers that I Cor. 1–4 was written.[25] (4) Of the pre-Pauline synoptic tradition only the passion narrative was oriented toward the Easter kerygma; yet it was the passion narrative then that gave the canonical Gospels their shape, causing the other tendencies to be suppressed.[26] Here Jesus was referred to as "the Christ" and confessed as the One who through his suffering accomplished reconciliation, who "died and was raised."[27] Corresponding to this confession was the self-understanding of the disciples as *ekklēsia*.[28]

Even though the particulars of this imaginative reconstruction cannot be demonstrated either historically or exegetically, it does note correctly that in the earliest period there certainly was no unified Christology. Characteristic for the thought of Koester is that he—like Bousset and Bultmann—divides the statements of the New Testament into types that were based on abstractions of religious phenomena. Among them were the two christological developments whose relationship to each other is the subject of inquiry at this point in our study: the synoptic Son of man expectation and the exaltation to the Christ according to Pauline-Lukan tradition. As Koester sees it, they were the two extreme wings of a widespread side-by-side relationship of different Christologies and were represented by two mutually contradictory groups within the church. But can they not be related to each other in a different way?

b) A dialogical relationship among various christological traditions. Regarding the derivation of the *maranatha* formula it became clear that the address "our Lord" and the title "Son of man" were not used side by side in the Christology of the community. The Son of man sayings were addressed to the community as Jesus' witness to himself, as his claim and promise; the community appropriated the sayings about the coming of the Son of man (e.g., Luke 12:8) by praying for the coming of its Lord. To be sure, the Son of man sayings were not merely collections of sayings of the earthly Jesus. As noted above (§18,2), they were reworked and multiplied. The very fact that they were reworked

---

[23]Ibid., pp. 214f.
[24]Ibid., pp. 216-19.
[25]Ibid., pp. 219-223.
[26]Ibid., p. 228.
[27]Ibid., pp. 224-231.
[28]Ibid., pp. 228f.

shows, however, that they were not the spontaneously produced sayings of prophets, but represented the Jesus tradition in ongoing development. So it was that the Christology of the first community was developed in accord with its unique situation simultaneously along two tracks. Proceeding from the Easter kerygma, on the one hand, the Jesus tradition was reworked christologically and, on the other, a kerygma and confession Christology was developed. In the early period, as both traditions were taking shape, they were regularly related to each other in dialogical fashion. The Jesus tradition was shaped on the basis of the community's christological understanding; for that understanding the former remained the criterion and source, even where that Jesus tradition was advanced through kerygmatic reinterpretation in new situations.

Even the two titles "Christ" and "Son of God," which expressed the function of the exalted One in the primitive community, were used in the synoptic tradition in dialogical correspondence and not as synonyms.

The title "Christ" appeared only in the oldest layer of the synoptic tradition in two unique settings, namely, the confessional response of the disciple: "You are the Christ" (Mk. 8:29 par.) and the question of the representatives of Judaism at the trial of Jesus (Mk. 14:61 par.). Such moments of confessing and questioning were the practice generally, however, in the primitive community. In these synoptic passages we do not have the primitive community's act of confessing represented and anticipated; rather through them the community was confronted with the question: In what sense was the earthly Jesus the Christ in its situation? The confession of the community did not articulate who Jesus had been, but who the exalted One was for it.

The title "Son of God" also appeared in the earliest synoptic layer only at certain points; it was found in profiled individual settings that did not reproduce the community situation but addressed it. That Jesus was the Son of God was spoken to him by a heavenly voice at his baptism and transfiguration (Mk. 1:11 par.; 9:7 par.). No disciple acclaimed him thus; it was expressed only by an outsider, by the one who directed his execution (Mk. 15:39 par.). These passages were formulated among other things with the aid of the community's confession of the exalted One and its Old Testament background; they did not anticipate the confession, but wished to summon it forth and define it with respect to content. It was first during redactional work, like Mt. 14:33f., that the situation of the community was mirrored.

Growing out of the context of statements about Jesus' exit was the designation "Servant of God." It was stated in the Jesus tradition only as a reflection upon the course of Jesus' life (Mt. 12:18) and was supposed—as we saw—to bring together an extensive complex of this tradition with a particular emphasis relating to the situation of the community.

So we may conclude: the Jesus tradition was not formulated as a competing Christology alongside the growth of the Easter kerygma; rather it wished from the very beginning to represent the origin of salvation history. The course of Jesus' life, his words and actions, were reported as claim and promise, and the community in relationship to the exalted One was supposed to reply to them in view of its situation. Conversely, replying included, nonetheless, in a dialogical circle the possibility of understanding and representing that which had taken place formerly.

c) Theological principles. The dialogical connection between the shape of the Jesus tradition and the reflective development of the Easter kerygma was the principle of preaching and teaching in the primitive community; here active theological engagement was worked out.

In contrast to all those which came after it, the primitive community did not have the Jesus tradition and the primitive kerygma passed on to it; in the context of its life both received their basic shape. Even if some sayings and parables were already passed on as tradition during Jesus' earthly ministry, the act of collecting sayings for transmission and of shaping narratives about him was a post-Easter phenomenon. Just like the molding of the Easter kerygma, this collecting and shaping was in large measure made possible and enhanced by the flow of religious traditions and the language of Palestinian Judaism. Yet it is difficult to overestimate the unique value of this theological achievement of discriminating vision and perceptive expression. As in Judaism, its core was the determination to understand the present—the ministry of Jesus and the emergence of the church—in the light of scripture. Our conclusions above demonstrated that to an astonishing degree the primitive community did not simply appropriate already existing traditions but struck essentially new directions both in conceptual language and the interpretation of scripture. This active theological engagement focused predominantly on the shaping of the Jesus tradition was not carried out simply as the collective achievement of "the community" but was done by "apostles . . . prophets . . . teachers" (I Cor. 12:28). Primarily it was the work of "the apostles" in Jerusalem, who according to Gal. 1:18f. were recognized in the whole church as the constitutive witnesses. Their work was not done, however, along the lines of chroniclers but along those of missionary and catechetical teachers. In this respect their work developed in regular conversation with the community (Acts 2:42; Rom. 1:11f.). The decisive stimulus for the direction of their thought had come to them from Jesus himself (§18,6-9). The Jesus tradition was transmitted within the communities as a central content of instruction and was, therefore, also that which was initially reshaped in terms of their respective understandings. But until the redaction of Matthew and Luke the Jesus tradition was understood as an account of the events of former times to which the community of the present was to respond from the perspective of the Easter kerygma for its own situation. Though each pericope and each collection of pericopes had an independence the tradition grew as a whole, transmitted complex; this can be seen by the stylistic agreement even of the special source material.

Hence the most ancient Christology was developed primarily in dialogue between the Jesus tradition and the kerygmatic confession of the community and not, as H. Koester supposed, as parallel and successive theological constructions that interpreted the Jesus tradition kerygmatically. Undoubtedly this dialogue was already being carried out in an astonishing variety of ways within the primitive church of Palestine. The members of that community had been familiar with various Jewish traditions and thus introduced into the community the great religious variation of Judaism. In addition, the position taken on questions that had recently come upon them, especially those that were a consequence of missionary outreach and conduct in relationship to the Law and the temple, led to further examples of differentiation. The tension between "Hebrews" and "Hellenists" was far from the only one (Acts 6:1). Claiming the backing of the Palestinian church was not only Paul, but also the Judaizers in Galatia (Gal. 2:6-9) and the "spiritualizers" in Corinth (I Cor. 1:12). The distinct points of view of Peter and James, the brother of the Lord, made themselves felt as far as Antioch and beyond (Gal. 2:11-13). Most of all, however, it was not only the synoptic Jesus tradition that emanated from the Palestinian church, but also the first rudiments of the Johannine tradition. It is critical to recognize that this theological variety should not—in contrast to the commonly accepted notion from F. C. Baur to the present—be likened to the model of Jewish factions (*haireseis*), special groups like the Pharisees and the Essenes, and even less to that of Hellenistic philosophical schools. The formation of such groups and schools would contradict the essence of the community. In the latter, service was basic; it was service that brought the various gifts into use.

This was Paul's point in I Cor. 11:18f.; 12:4-6 where the community in Corinth had adapted itself to the formation of the schools and groups of its environment (I Cor. 1:12). This perspective was already an extension of the Jesus tradition (cf. Lk. 11:39-47; Mk. 10:41-45).

The discrete christological conceptions then are not to be traced in accord with those models back to various communities and community groups. Rather they are to be examined as to whether they cannot be understood in a mutually supplementary way as the variety of proclamation in the same community. By doing this one does not reduce in a harmonizing way that which was distinguishable; rather profile is gained in accord with the historical situation. At the same time the question about the limitation of variety arises. This limitation becomes relativized through the Jewish-Hellenistic concept of school positions. A way of looking at the structure of the primitive church in Palestine is achieved through this line of questioning that corresponds to the sources since, according to the epistles of Paul, this church was a community of service well acquainted with tension. As such it was precisely not to become a coexistence of separate groups.

The image of the primitive church in Palestine, therefore, came about to a large degree only through the extended developments of its history in the Hellenistic church. Whether or not the basic structure of its Christology—the dialogical correspondence between the Jesus tradition and the kerygmatic confession of the community—persisted in the Hellenistic community is to be determined under the question of "Paul and the synoptic Jesus tradition" (§28,4). It will be necessary, moreover, to clarify more precisely then the question of interpretive aids employed during the reflective development of early Christian theology. This is to be done in an analysis of the broad spectrum of material that was available to Paul (§29).

Part Three

PAUL AND
HELLENISTIC CHRISTIANITY

INTRODUCTION

§27. The Problem of Hellenistic Christianity

W. Heitmüller, "Zum Problem Paulus und Jesus," *ZNW* 13 (1912), 320-337 (repr. in *Das Paulusbild in der neueren deutschen Forschung*, ed. K. H. Rengstorf [1964], pp. 124-143); R. H. Fuller, *The Foundations of New Testament Christology* (1965); H. R. Balz, *Methodische Probleme der neutestamentlichen Theologie* (1967), esp. pp. 129-137; J. N. Sevenster, *Do You Know Greek?* (1968); M. Hengel, "Christologie und neutestamentliche Chronologie," in *Neues Testament und Geschichte, Festschrift für O. Cullmann*, ed. H. Baltensweiler and B. Reicke (1972), pp. 43-67; I. H. Marshall, "Palestinian and Hellenistic Christianity: Some Critical Comments," *NTS* 19 (1972/73), 271-287; Bultmann, *Theology* I (1951), §§9-15; Hahn, *Titles* (1969), esp. pp. 12ff.; Conzelmann, *Theology*, pp. 29-32.

1. ON THE DISCUSSION

a) In 1912, W. Heitmüller advanced the thesis: "Paul was separated from Jesus not only by the primitive community, but also by one other link in the chain. The order ran like this: Jesus—primitive community—Hellenistic Christianity—Paul."[1] For Heitmüller this meant that Paul stood at a far greater distance from Jesus and Palestinian Christianity than had been assumed heretofore. According to this view, Paul became acquainted with Christianity not in Jerusalem but in the Hellenistic communities of Damascus and Antioch. His contact

---

[1]Op. cit. (Lit., §27), 330.

with Jerusalem was restricted to a fourteen-day visit with Peter and James three years after his conversion (Gal. 1:18). Otherwise his starting point was Hellenistic Christianity. The traditions to which he made reference in I Cor. 11:23ff. and 15:3ff. did not come from Jerusalem but from Antioch. The structure of Hellenistic Christianity in fact was fundamentally different from that of Palestinian Christianity.

W. Bousset attempted to reconstruct the image of the Hellenistic Christianity on which Paul is supposed to have depended.[2] His reconstruction was designed to evoke the impression that Palestinian and Hellenistic Christianity were two separate religions. While Christians in Jerusalem expected Jesus as the coming Son of man, those in Antioch venerated him as the heavenly Lord. While the meal of celebration in Jerusalem was a meal of joy, in Antioch it was celebrated as one of mystery.

b) R. Bultmann aligned himself expressly with this view of the historical phenomena and was the first to construct a corresponding overall image of Hellenistic Christianity within the framework of a New Testament theology.[3] His reconstruction of the kerygma of Hellenistic communities was based on that which was presupposed as a commonly accepted understanding in the Christian literature from the Pauline epistles to the Apostolic Fathers. Actually, this reconstruction was not only hypothetical; it was also abstract: the kerygma was never represented in this form. This reconstruction did not do justice to the structure of Hellenistic Christianity.

2. THE STRUCTURE OF HELLENISTIC CHRISTIANITY

Around the year A.D. 40 a community emerged in Antioch that distanced itself from the Law and was made up of Jews and Gentiles. It was the mother church of "Gentile Christianity" in the Hellenistic world (Acts 11:20-26; Gal. 2:3ff., 11ff.). Hardly ten years subsequent to this emergence the Emperor Claudius banned the Jews from Rome in A.D. 49 because they "constantly made disturbances at the instigation of Chrestus (*impulsore Chresto*)."[4] The disturbances in the synagogues arose as Jewish Christians, who had come to Rome among the many travelers of the time, represented in the synagogues a Christianity bearing the Antiochean stamp. The Epistle to the Romans presupposed the same community situation for Rome as did the book of Acts for Antioch. What had taken place in Antioch soon was carried forth to or repeated itself in many Hellenistic cities. What were the theological problems that accompanied this movement from Jerusalem to Antioch?

a) The history-of-religion school focused on what it believed to be the transition from one cultural context to another. This view introduced an important

---

[2]*Kyrios*, esp. pp. 119-152.

[3]*Faith and Understanding*, pp. 220ff.; *Theology* I, §§9-15.

[4]Suetonius *Vita Claudii* 25 (*Lives* V.25.4=LCL II, 52f.). Regarding dating, cf. Goppelt, *Apostolic Times*, p. 62 n. 4.

aspect into the scholarly discussion that had always traced all differences back to the debate about the Law between Paul, Peter, and James. It was in fact true that both the gospel and the existence of the church had to be transposed from the linguistic and conceptual world of Palestinian Judaism into that of Hellenism. Today we recognize, however, that the borders between the two was more fluid than the history-of-religion school assumed. Palestinian-Jewish and Hellenistic culture overlapped considerably in those very circles where Christianity had gained a footing. Elements of the Hellenistic world view had made significant inroads even into Palestinian Judaism despite attempts to resist.[5] Most important, however, was the fact that a Greek-speaking community coming out of the Jewish Diaspora was already growing up in Jerusalem almost simultaneously with the Aramaic-speaking one. This meant basically that from the very beginning Christian traditions were formulated in two languages (§25,5d). Outside of Palestine, however, the first communities sprang up and took shape in all the important centers of the network of Diaspora Judaism; in most of these the Jewish Christians made their influence felt. The difference in this respect, therefore, can be described only in degree; in Jerusalem the gospel and the church stood primarily in the sphere of Palestinian-Jewish thought, while in Antioch they stood primarily in Hellenistic thought. It is with this qualification that the various expressions of proclamation, church life, and theology that emerged in these contexts need to be heard. By paying attention to such within the vital statements of the Christian writers a spectrum comes to light that stretches from an Aramaic Jewish Christianity through a Hellenistic one to a Hellenistic Gentile Christianity. This spectrum, however, did not represent itself throughout sociologically in a chronological and geographical distribution among communities and groups of communities, but in the form of currents of thought flowing mostly side by side.[6] As can be seen in the divisions in Jerusalem (Acts 6:1) and in Corinth (I Cor. 1:11f.), they were frequently active at the same location. Moreover, they almost never existed as "pure" types. Seen in this perspective, the differentiation of these types can, nonetheless, serve the end of the historical derivation and characterization of early Christian statements. In doing so, one must take care not to neglect the other aspects of their structural analysis.

Substantively, the occurrences that were involved in the initial transition of the gospel from one cultural context to another are of special importance to those of us today who are working toward a theologically responsible analysis of and posture toward corresponding occurrences in Asia and Africa. It is es-

---

[5] M. Hengel, *Judaism* (1974).

[6] This has been emphasized correctly by I. H. Marshall (Lit., §27), 272f. and 286, and M. Hengel (Lit., §27), pp. 43-67. The latter pointed out above all that the development stretching from Jesus' exit to the Christology represented by Paul took place at most in fifteen years, perhaps in an even shorter span of time. One can see, of course, from the acute hellenization of Christianity against which Paul struggled in I Corinthians, just how quickly a total estrangement could become established; nevertheless, one cannot generalize even this development. In any case, Hahn, *Titles*, esp. pp. 12-14, still divided the development of the christological predicates much too schematically over the four streams of thought alluded to.

pecially noteworthy that when the gospel first crossed the border it was not simply poured into already existing vessels. The new content also created new vessels; it created its own conceptual language and life forms. New faith formulas and ethical constellations arose in the new circumstances of proclamation. At the same time, however, fundamental traditions from the primitive church of Palestine were taken over and adhered to. Hellenistic communities sought not only to win over Hellenistic people, but also to maintain fellowship with the communities in Palestine. Both in teaching and in the shape of their life they understood themselves to be responsible for each other. Close personal contact was a high priority toward this end. Palestinian and Hellenistic Christianity did not live at the distance from each other that the broadly distinct origin of their conceptual languages might otherwise suggest.

b) The step from Jerusalem to Antioch, however, involved more than a mere transition of the gospel from one cultural context to another, like that which has been repeated so often down to the present. It involved the fundamental departure once and for all from the realm of the old covenant people. Based on their understanding of the God of the Old Testament, the Jewish Christians in Palestine had come to the confession that Jesus was the promised One. They summoned Israel to the promise of its God. They lived together with Israel in the realm of the Law. But who was Jesus for the uncircumcised Gentile Christians in Antioch? If he was not to remain the promised One of the Old Testament for them he would have to become a Hellenistic redeemer god like Serapis and Isis. Should they, therefore, also adopt the Old Testament as canonical scripture? But they— in contrast to the Jewish Christians—did not observe the Law, that portion of scripture decisive for the Jews, and that precisely for the sake of their faith. It suggested itself that they should dispense with the canonical scripture of the Jewish Christians altogether. In the Gnostic movement, against whose precursors Paul struggled in I Corinthians and Colossians, Jesus was extricated from the God of the Old Testament and misunderstood as the Hellenistic redeemer. This was the case even though its advocates felt just as free to adopt Old Testament/Jewish traditions as Hellenistic ones. If the Gentile Christians were not to end up as a syncretistic religious fellowship the life and ministry of Jesus would have to be combined for them with the Old Testament theologically to form a new unity. The same had to transpire, moreover, with other indices for the Jewish Christians of Jerusalem if they were not to end up as a Jewish sect. This task of combining Jesus with the Old Testament theologically and by doing so shaping the gospel for one church out of Jews and Gentiles was the decisive ecclesiastical-theological problem of that hour.[7]

To fulfill this unique task a human being who had not been a disciple of Jesus was called to be an apostle quite unexpectedly; this was the Diaspora Jew, Paul of Tarsus. He was not the theological mind behind a school of universalistic

---

[7]For the most part this has not been recognized in research because it has been assumed that the manifestation of Jesus was interpreted strictly with the aid of Old Testament/Jewish and Hellenistic traditions, but was not understood seriously as the fulfillment of scripture (cf. §30).

Christianity (F. C. Baur).[8] Nor was he the great but rarely understood theologian of popular Gentile Christianity (A. von Harnack),[9] nor the theologian of influence who through critical appropriation clarified myth-laden Hellenistic Christianity (R. Bultmann).[10] Rather Paul was the one who through fundamental theological solutions in the context of missionary and pastoral activity articulated the gospel for the church of Jews and Gentiles. Understood in this way he was the one he wanted to be, namely, the apostle of Jesus Christ to Gentile peoples (Rom. 1:1,5).

At the end of his career in the East he wrote down the gospel for the community in the capital of the world. He was not the missionary founder of that community. What he had to say about the gospel was shaped precisely by his understanding of the church throughout the world; it was the gospel that justified Jews and Gentiles by faith "apart from law" and yet in accord with "the law and the prophets," i.e., scripture (Rom. 1:16f.; 3:21). As this kind of apostle he received fundamental recognition in the church between Antioch and Rome. As early as in the First Epistle of Clement (ca. A.D. 96 in Rome) and for Ignatius of Antioch (ca. A.D. 110) his letters constituted a normative witness to Christ; this was possible only because in the intervening period they had been regarded as such. Decisive historically was not his theological influence—it was in fact astonishingly limited[11]—but the fundamental recognition of his gospel as a binding direction of interpretation.

3. CONSEQUENCES FOR THE REPRESENTATION OF NEW TESTAMENT THEOLOGY

What consequences should be drawn from this structure of Hellenistic Christianity for the representation of New Testament theology? Trying to represent the kerygma of the Hellenistic church in cross-section, like Bultmann did, leads to nonhistorical abstractions. Historical realities were always traditions and the specific word of proclamation and shape of life together with their theological reflection that grew out of those traditions. Historically discernible and especially

---

[8]"The Pauline didactic term was the most important moment in the history of the development of primitive Christianity. . . . if Christianity was that which was in accord with its true essence primarily in distinction from Judaism by virtue of the special consciousness of its principle distinct from that of Judaism, so too it was first elevated to this independent, absolute meaning through the Apostle Paul. . . ." (F. C. Baur, *Vorlesungen über neutestamentliche Theologie*, ed. F. F. Baur [1864; repr. 1963], p. 128).

[9]". . . the doctrinal formation in the Gentile Church is not connected with the whole phenomenon of the Pauline theology, but only with certain leading thoughts which were only in part peculiar to the Apostle. His most peculiar thoughts acted on the development of Ecclesiastical doctrine only by way of occasional stimulus" (A. von Harnack, *History of Dogma* I [1961], 92).

[10]"The historical position of Paul may be stated as follows: Standing within the frame of Hellenistic Christianity he raised the theological motifs that were at work in the proclamation of the Hellenistic Church to the clarity of theological thinking; he called to attention the problems latent in the Hellenistic proclamation and brought them to a decision; and thus . . . he became the founder of Christian theology" (Bultmann, *Theology* I, 187).

[11]K. H. Schelkle, *Paulus, Lehrer der Väter* (1959²).

relevant, however, in terms of historical effect and theological expression were the preaching and theology of Paul. They can only be reiterated in accord with their own origin and intention when, at the same time, the traditions with which Paul was in conversation and the situation with which he was in debate are viewed together. When both are represented, a historically defensible picture emerges both of the preaching situation in the early Hellenistic church and of the Pauline gospel that gave interpretive direction for all ages of the church.

Chapter I

THE PRESUPPOSITIONS OF PAULINE THEOLOGY

§28. The Course of Paul's Life and Christian Traditions

On the History of Research: A. Schweitzer, *Paul and His Interpreters* (1951); R. Bultmann, "Zur Geschichte der Paulusforschung," *ThR* 1 (1929), 26-59; 6 (1934), 229-246; 8 (1936), 1-22; A. M. Denis, "S. Paul dans la littérature récente," *ETL* 26 (1950), 383-408; G. Delling, "Zum neueren Paulusverständnis," *NovTest* 4 (1960), 95-121; B. Rigaux, *The Letters of St. Paul* (1968 [Lit.!]). **Presentations as a Whole of Paul's Life and Work**: W. Bousset, *Der Apostel Paulus* (1906); W. Wrede, *Paul* (1962); A. Deissmann, *Paul, a Study in Social and Religious History* (1926); P. Feine, *Der Apostel Paulus. Das Ringen um das geschichtliche Verständnis des Paulus* (1927); K. Pieper, *Paulus, seine missionarische Persönlichkeit und Wirksamkeit* (1929); A. D. Nock, *St. Paul* (1938); W. von Loewenich, *Paul, His Life and Work* (1960); J. Knox, *Chapters in a Life of Paul* (1950); G. Ricciotti, *Der Apostel Paulus* (1950; comprehensive overview of historical background and of older research!); M. Dibelius-W. G. Kümmel, *Paul* (1953); E. Fascher, "Paulus," in PW Suppl. VIII (1956), 431-466; J. Perez de Urbel, *S. Paul, Sa vie et son temps* (1956); G. Bornkamm, "Paulus," *RGG*[3] V, 166-190; G. Bornkamm, *Paul* (1971); O. Kuss, *Paulus. Die Rolle des Apostels in der theologischen Entwicklung der Urkirche* (1971). **Representations of Pauline Theology**: E. Lohmeyer, *Grundlagen paulinischer Theologie* (1929); A. Schweitzer, *The Mysticism of Paul the Apostle* (1931); H.-J. Schoeps, *Paul, the Theology of the Apostle in the Light of Jewish Religious History* (1961); D.E.H. Whiteley, *The Theology of St. Paul* (1964); R. C. Tannehill, *Dying and Rising with Christ. A Study in Pauline Theology* (1967); E. Käsemann, *Perspectives on Paul* (1971); H. N. Ridderbos, *Paul: An Outline of His Theology* (1975); G. Eichholz, *Die Theologie des Paulus im Umriss* (1972). **On 1**: W. G. Kümmel, *Römer 7 und die Bekehrung des Paulus* (1929; repr. in Kümmel, *Römer 7 und das Bild des Menschen im Neuen Testament* [1974]); H. Windisch, *Paulus und das Judentum* (1935); W. L. Knox, *St. Paul and the Church of the Gentiles* (1939); E. Pfaff, *Die Bekehrung des H. Paulus in der Exegese des 20. Jahrhunderts* (1942; older Lit.!); P.-H. Menoud, "Révélation et Tradition. L'influence de la conversion de Paul sur sa théologie," *Verbum Caro* 7 (1953), 2-10; J. Munck, *Paul and the Salvation of Mankind* (1959); H. G. Wood, "The Conversion of St. Paul: Its Nature, Antecedents and Consequences," *NTS* 1 (1954/55), 276-282; U. Wilckens, "Die Bekehrung des Paulus als religionsgeschichtliches Problem," *ZThK* 56 (1959), 273-293 (= Wilckens, *Rechtfertigung als Freiheit. Paulusstudien* [1974], pp. 11-32). **On 2-4**: O. Michel, *Paulus und seine Bibel* (1929); H. Windisch, *Paulus und Christus. Ein biblisch-religionsgeschichtlicher Vergleich* (1934); E. Jüngel, *Paulus und Jesus* (1964; 1972⁴); J. Blank, *Paulus und Jesus. Eine theologische Grundlegung* (1968).

1. PRELIMINARY OBSERVATION: THE SOURCES[1]

It is generally recognized that the majority of those thirteen letters transmitted in the New Testament under Paul's name constitute the authentic sources for knowledge about him. These are Romans, I and II Corinthians, Galatians, Philippians, Philemon, and I Thessalonians. To these may be added, in spite of certain peculiarities, Colossians and II Thessalonians; in these two cases, however, one must pay special attention to the internal consistency of Pauline statements. Ephesians, which is related to Colossians, distinguished itself in language and style of presentation so radically from these other letters that its statements can only be considered at a distance in the task of representing Pauline theology. Finally, in light of conceptual language and theological content, the Pastoral Epistles are clearly to be counted among the writings of the later Pauline school; they will receive subsequent treatment of their own. The speeches of Paul in the book of Acts are quite clearly not directly from him but from Luke and his traditions.[2] It will be necessary to make regular and critical comparison of the biographical data in the book of Acts with Paul's own statements in his letters.[3] The apocryphal literature on Paul did not preserve any reliable traditions.

When one observes differences of terminology and content within the Pauline corpus one asks such questions as: To what degree do they go back to a reworking of extraneous tradition? Should one reckon with growth and development within Pauline theology?[4] Did the apostle's fellow workers join in on the composition of his letters?

2. HIS LIFE AND PILGRIMAGE

We cannot make a detailed study of Paul's biography here;[5] we shall concentrate on that which is important for the understanding of his theology.

    a) Three aspects of the apostle's pilgrimage[6] became important for his theology:

---

[1]The following evaluation of the sources agrees in essence with the judgment of W. G. Kümmel, *Introduction*, pp. 250-387.

[2]M. Dibelius, "Die Reden der Apostelgeschichte und die antike Geschichtsschreibung," in M. Dibelius, *Aufsätze zur Apostelgeschichte* (1953²). pp. 120-162.

[3]Cf., recently, C. Burchard, *Der dreizehnte Zeuge* (1970).

[4]Regarding the discussion, cf. C. Buck and G. Taylor, *Saint Paul. A Study of the Development of his Thought* (1969); W. G. Kümmel, "Das Problem der Entwicklung in der Theologie des Paulus," *NTS* 18 (1972), 457f.

[5]Cf. G. Bornkamm, *Paul* (1971), pp. 3-106.

[6]The questions about Paul's pre-Christian past were last examined by Blank, loc. cit. (Lit., §28), pp. 238-249, and Burchard (loc. cit. [n. 3]).

1) Paul was probably born during the first few years of the 1st century in the Hellenistic city of Tarsus in Cilicia; he was a "Hebrew of Hebrews," i.e., born into a family loyal to the traditions of the fathers (Phil. 3:5f.; Acts 21:39; 22:3). He was, therefore, a Diaspora Jew and was familiar from his youth with the Hellenistic world as far as was possible for a Jew true to the Law.

2) His loyalty to Judaism was deepened through his scribal study in Jerusalem (Acts 26:5). Though Paul stated in Gal. 1:22 that he was not known personally by the Christian communities of Judea, this in no way necessitates the conclusion that, in his pre-Christian days, Paul never resided in Jerusalem at all.[7] It may be, of course, that some of the references of the book of Acts on his activity as persecutor are to be discounted.[8] Prior to his conversion, therefore, Paul was a student of rabbinic Judaism, following the direction of the Pharisees. This latter aspect he himself emphasized in Gal. 1:14; the former speaks for itself most admirably in the intensive and creative valuation of scripture in his letters.

3) What he expressed in Gal. 1:13f. about his pre-Christian orientation toward the Jesus movement was consistent with this course of his development: he was devoted to the Law and persecuted the community of the crucified Christ! For him the Damascus Road experience was not the crowning moment of a spiritual pilgrimage but the unexpected, painful break with that which had gone before (Phil. 3:6). He could only view that break as a personal revelation of the resurrected One; it happened to him apart from his initiative and he regarded it as fundamentally comparable to the Easter experiences of the first apostles (I Cor. 15:8; 9:1; Gal. 1:15f.; cf. Acts 9:1-9; 22:3-11; 26:9-18). For him it represented his summons to faith and, at the same time, to the apostolic office. On the basis of his own development he had understood devotion to the Law and faith in the crucified One as the Messiah to be mutually exclusive options. Here lies the starting point of his Christian existence and of his theology.

b) As an apostle Paul passed through the following phases: 1) Lasting from ca. A.D. 32/34 until ca. A.D. 40 was the time of his preparation with limited ministry in Arabia (region of the Nabateans) and Cilicia (Gal. 1:15-24; II Cor. 11:32f.; Acts 9:19-30). During this period three years after his conversion there took place a noteworthy encounter with the representatives of the primitive community of Jerusalem (Gal. 1:18f.). 2) What his own task would be became clear to him when he was brought to Antioch and into the mother community of Gentile Christianity (Acts 11:25-30). 3) From here began the so-called first missionary journey and with it a far-reaching missionary and pastoral activity. Through this activity, historically speaking, the church was founded in the cultural center of the then-known world, the Greek world of Asia Minor and Greece. The high points of this activity were the Apostolic Council in Jerusalem (Gal. 2:1-10; Acts 15:1-35) and the journey with the collection for the saints in Jerusalem that ended with his arrest (Rom. 15:25-32; Acts 21:15-36). This

[7]Thus R. Bultmann, *Theology* I, 187; H. Conzelmann, *History of Primitive Christianity* (1973), pp. 60f.; nevertheless, contra is Hengel, op. cit. (Lit., §27), p. 49.

[8]Burchard, op. cit. (n. 3), pp. 40-50.

phase, during which the apostle became the one he was, lasted the brief decade from A.D. 46-56. 4) The final phase spent in prison in Caesarea and Rome lasted from ca. A.D. 56 until ca. A.D. 62/63. It culminated with his death as a martyr in Rome (I Clem. 5:4-7; II Tim. 4:16). He may have been freed for a time in this last phase and may have visited the communities in the East (Eus. *EH* 2.22.2ff. according to II Tim. 4:13).

3. THE COMMUNICATION OF THE GOSPEL TO PAUL

a) The starting point and the problem. On the basis of his pilgrimage, whence did Paul come to know the gospel, the preaching of which was the focus of his life for three decades?

In Gal. 1 and I Cor. 15, Paul answered in a way that, on the surface, sounds contradictory; the tension between them makes clear the fundamental problem before us. Gal. 1:11f. reads, "For I would have you know, brethren, . . . the gospel. . . . For I did not receive it from man [as tradition], nor was I taught it, but it came through a revelation of Jesus Christ." And we find in I Cor. 15:1, 3, "Now I would remind you, brethren, in what terms I preached to you the gospel. . . . For I delivered to you [as tradition] as of first importance what I also received [as tradition], that Christ died for our sins in accordance with the scriptures, that he was buried. . . ." Hence, in Gal. 1 the gospel was the revelation that the crucified One was the representative of God, and in I Cor. 15 it was a tradition that gave witness by faith to the events of salvation history (§36,4).

How are these two qualifications of the gospel related to each other? The reply of exegetes is a reflection of various theological and ecclesiastical points of view. According to R. Bultmann, Gal. 1 was a genuine, and I Cor. 15 an inconsistent statement of the apostle.[9] The gospel was in essence pneumatic-kerygmatic tradition and could not, as Bultmann saw it, be captured in didactic formulas; it could only be passed on in the proclamation that in turn gave birth to further proclamation. In contrast to this view of kerygmatic theology, the Roman Catholic New Testament scholar H. Schlier and the Anglican patristic scholar J.N.D. Kelly placed the accent on I Cor. 15. They emphasized that the gospel was the appropriation of a fixed tradition for a particular situation.[10]

Was Paul then inconsistent? Did he allow himself to be overly influenced by the situation when he made the two statements? It is clear that in Gal. 1 he emphasized the immediacy of revelation from above over against a Judaism seeking to legitimize itself in a historical framework, and that in I Cor. 15 he emphasized the historical tradition over against a spiritualistic outlook void of history. He could give emphasis to both equally because for him they belonged together. They had been combined in his own experience: on the way to Damascus he was given access to the exaltation of the crucified One to God and

---

[9]*Theology* II §54,2f.

[10]H. Schlier, *Die Zeit der Kirche* (1956), pp. 216f.; J.N.D. Kelly, *Early Christian Creeds* (1952²), pp. 11f.

thereby the significance of Jesus' appearance in history; yet this was only possible because he was already familiar with that appearance in history as such through Christian tradition. He was familiar not only with the direct assertion that a crucified human being was the Messiah, but also with the Easter kerygma and certainly some of the Jesus tradition, e.g., the matrix of missionary preaching (§25,1). But one thing is fundamentally clear from this perspective of his own experience: in essence the gospel was/is always both historical tradition and pneumatic kerygma. To the extent that it was information about Jesus' life, ministry, and person—also therefore about historical events—it could only be passed on as formulated, historical tradition. This tradition only became gospel, the good news of salvation coming from God, when it was encountered as kerygmatic address. Indeed, Paul himself not only restated the tradition in I Cor. 15, but in the course of the chapter he interpreted it kerygmatically. Along the same line, the traditional, christological expression of the gospel in Rom. 1:2-4 was immediately interpreted soteriologically in the thematic statements of the epistle (1:16f.); in this sense it was enlarged upon kerygmatically, moreover, through to the end of the letter.[11]

The content of Pauline theology therefore grew out of both the tradition of the Easter kerygma and the Damascus Road experience. The immediate revelation had opened up for him the way of understanding to the tradition. What happened to him fundamentally, however, did not differ in the least from the experience of anyone touched by the pneumatic kerygma. For this reason in both Rom. 1 and I Cor. 15 Paul made the kerygmatic enlargement of the transmitted Easter kerygma the principle of his theology, and not the Damascus Road experience.

b) *The traditions behind the Pauline gospel.* Express references and form-critical analyses bring to light three different types of traditions in the epistles:

1) Clearly of fundamental significance were the didactic and confessional formulas[12] that interpreted Jesus' death and resurrection christologically and soteriologically. They can be traced in part back to the church of Palestine (I Cor. 15:3-5; Rom. 1:3f.; 4:25; perhaps also 3:25f., etc.), and in part back to the Hellenistic church (I Cor. 12:3; Rom. 10:9, etc.). The latter were extended in I Thess. 1:9f.; I Cor. 8:6 through theological confessions and in Phil. 2:6-11; Col. 1:15-20 by hymnic development.

2) In addition to these Paul appropriated parenetic material from ecclesiastical tradition. The parenesis in Rom. 12f., e.g., was related at several points to that found in I Pet. 2:11–3:22. These points of contact are attributable not to literary dependence—as is generally recognized today[13]—but to a common oral tradition. This explains the sometimes verbatim agreements between Rom. 12:17 and I Pet. 3:9, and Rom. 13:1-7 and I Pet. 2:13-17.

---

[11]P. Stuhlmacher, "Theologische Probleme des Römerbriefpräskripts," *EvTheol* 27 (1967), 374-389.

[12]Kramer, *Christ*, esp. pp. 19-128.

[13]E. Käsemann, *Commentary on Romans* (1980), at Rom. 12:1.

3) Only four times did Paul refer in his letters to "words of the Lord," i.e., for him *logia* of the earthly Jesus. He gave these words a special prominence; while he offered all his pneumatic opinions and instructions for discussion in the Spirit who was at work in the community (I Cor. 14:37), the words of the Lord were the very criteria of the Spirit (I Cor. 7:10). Yet these words did not form their own complex of tradition; they took their place rather within the parenetic (I Cor. 7:10; 9:14), liturgical (I Cor. 11:23ff.), and apocalyptic traditions (I Thess. 4:15). Especially in the parenetic tradition one can observe beyond direct quotation the tacit appropriation of additional Jesus *logia* through history-of-tradition analysis. Such was the case, e.g., in Rom. 12:14, 17; 13:7, 10; 14:14; I Cor. 4:12; 6:1ff., 7.

Nowhere did Paul directly address or make verbatim appropriation of that Jesus tradition which was written down in the synoptic Gospels during the two decades subsequent to the death of the apostle. In order to understand this peculiar fact it is necessary to explain comprehensively the relationship between Paul and Jesus.

4. PAUL AND JESUS

a) Did Paul know Jesus personally? According to the biographical references in the book of Acts, while studying in Jerusalem to be a rabbi Paul could have seen Jesus die (Acts 22:2ff.; 26:4). On this matter he expressed himself only once; in II Cor. 5:16 he declared to opponents who called his apostleship into question and who set themselves apart from him by laying claim to the earthly Jesus, "even though we once regarded Christ from a human point of view, we regard him thus no longer." The expression "from a human point of view" (*kata sarka*) belongs grammatically and substantively both to the verb and the object.[14] The statement meant that for Paul, therefore, the strictly human knowledge of the strictly human Jesus was over. It would be irrelevant for him, e.g., what kind of impression Pilate or Caiaphas had had of Jesus. Whether or not Paul himself had once had an occasion to meet Jesus in this external human way cannot be determined by this statement; it can be taken as a conditional sentence according to fact or contrary to fact. The perfect tense of the verb gives the edge to the former perhaps, but finally the question must remain unanswered.[15] Much more important, nonetheless, is a further question.

b) What was the significance of Jesus' earthly ministry for Paul the Christian and for his theology? R. Bultmann interpreted the substance of the expression "from a human point of view" in II Cor. 5:16 as applying solely to "Christ." Based on this interpretation he advanced the thesis that in Paul's view the earthly Jesus was no longer of consequence for faith. This thesis was accurate as long as Bultmann directed it toward the historical Jesus of his teachers' liberal the-

---

[14]Blank, op. cit. (Lit., §28), pp. 304-326 (here a detailed debate with the various attempts at interpretation).

[15]Thus also ibid., pp. 313-325.

ology; that Jesus was of course the product of a strictly historical knowledge, a knowledge "from a human point of view."[16] But its general application is by no means justified.

At first glance it does appear that the thesis is consistent with the fact that Paul did not appropriate anything from Jesus directly. It is certainly correct to maintain in light of the available data:

> All that is important for him in the story of Jesus is the fact that Jesus was born a Jew and lived under the law (Gal. 4:4) and that he had been crucified (Gal. 3:1; I Cor. 2:2; Phil. 2:5ff., etc.).
>
> Jesus' death-and-resurrection, then, is for Paul the decisive thing about the person of Jesus and his life experience . . . it is the sole thing of importance for him—implicitly included are the incarnation and the earthly life of Jesus as bare facts. That is, Paul is interested only in the *fact* that Jesus became man and lived on earth. *How* he was born or lived interests him only to the extent of knowing that Jesus was a definite, concrete man, a Jew. . . . But beyond that, Jesus' manner of life, his ministry . . . play no role at all; neither does Jesus' message.[17]

This assessment puts the question in bold relief: Was Paul really interested only in the "that"—that the One sent by God was crucified and that God, however, exalted him—or was he not also interested in the "how"? It would be helpful at this point to make a comparison between the preaching of Jesus and the theology of Paul in terms of content.

c) The theology of Paul and the preaching of Jesus. A review of the scholarly discussion will help us to gain access to the issue facing us today. In 1905, W. Wrede came forward as spokesman for the history-of-religion school with the provocative thesis that Paul was the second founder of Christianity. He "turned Christianity into the religion of redemption. . . . Of that which is to Paul all and everything, how much does Jesus know? Nothing whatever."[18] According to Paul people were to believe in the acts of redemption, according to Jesus they were to surrender themselves to God. W. Heitmüller explained the distinction historically by means of the thesis already mentioned above that between Jesus and Paul stood not only the primitive community but also Hellenistic Christianity (cf. §27,1). In the reconstruction of W. Bousset then the latter was regarded as a different religion.

R. Bultmann appropriated this historical/history-of-religion perspective,[19] but came to the quite different theological evaluation that Paul was in substantive

---

[16]*Theology* I, §22,3 ("in the flesh," pp. 236-39). In the final analysis Bultmann contradicted his own philological analysis of II Cor. 5:16 with this interpretation.

[17]*Theology* I, 188, 293f.

[18]*Paul* (1962), p. 163; cf. also pp. 147f. In the same period bitter criticism of Paul was expressed by P. de Lagarde, *Deutsche Schriften* (1886); F. Nietzsche, *Antichrist* (1888); and H. S. Chamberlain, *Foundations of the Nineteenth Century* (1899; Eng. 1910); after 1933 A. Rosenberg, *Der Mythos des 20. Jahrhunderts*, propagandized their theses (cf. M. Dibelius, *Paulus* [1964³], pp. 6f.). Representative for a philosophical critique of Paul from a neo-Marxist point of view is E. Bloch, *Atheism in Christianity* (1972), pp. 131, 173-77.

[19]*Theology* I, §16.

agreement with Jesus in his teaching about the Law and justification.[20] This agreement, however, was to be explained not through a historical/history-of-tradition connection, but through the same rational starting point; both Jesus and Paul considered the human situation to be determined by God's eschatological intervention.[21]

For A. Schlatter[22] and J. Schniewind,[23] on the other hand, the fundamental, substantive agreement between Paul and Jesus was based on the reworking of the Jesus tradition under the conviction that the exalted One and the crucified One were one and the same person. Schniewind summarized his observations in a hermeneutical program. "One cannot read one word of the gospels unless one reads in light of Paul." And: "We cannot understand one word of Paul unless it is understood in light of the gospels."[24] Neither Schlatter nor Schniewind, however, was able to show how this reworking actually took place. So we come in the final analysis to the conclusion that Schlatter, Schniewind, and Bultmann represented the three options to be taken most seriously today on the issue of Paul and Jesus. Bultmann's view, however, has the advantage that it offered a clear hermeneutical key.[25]

This much can be said: it would seem that regarding essential statements Paul was in substantive agreement with Jesus; there is, however, no outward indication that Paul relied on the Jesus tradition. The problem, therefore, can be summed up in the hermeneutical question: Could Paul, in spite of outward silence, have known and appropriated the Jesus tradition?

5. THE JESUS TRADITION AND PAUL'S HERMENEUTICAL METHOD

a) Could Paul have known the Jesus tradition even though he did not mention it? When one examines the rest of the early Christian literature outside the Gospels with an analogous inquiry one finds that it quoted the Gospel tradition as little as Paul did, even though that literature was familiar with it. Luke, e.g., did not point back to the accounts of his Gospel in any of the missionary sermons of the book of Acts; the only saying of Jesus quoted in the book of Acts (20:35) was an *agraphon*! The author of I John was just as reluctant to direct attention back to the Fourth Gospel. Even II Clement, a homily written around the middle of the 2nd century, made hardly any use of the Gospel tradition though its author was undoubtedly familiar with it. Paul too, therefore,

---

[20]*Faith and Understanding*, pp. 223-35.

[21]*History and Eschatology* (1957), pp. 44ff. (cf. Ger. for specific reference: *Geschichte und Eschatologie* [1964²], p. 53).

[22]*Theology* II, 389-397; cf. the presentation in E. Güttgemanns, *Der leidende Apostel und sein Herr* (1966), pp. 373-383.

[23]*Nachgelassene Reden und Aufsätze* (1952), pp. 16-37.

[24]Ibid., pp. 22, 29.

[25]Thus Güttgemanns, op. cit. (n. 22), pp. 372-412 after an extensive review of the status of research (pp. 329-372). Under a different dimension the review of research can be found in Blank, op. cit. (n. 14), pp. 61-132.

could have known the Jesus tradition that was written down later in the synoptic Gospels although he did not quote it. This becomes even more probable when one considers the reason why he did not quote it.

b) *One attempt: Paul's individual rejection.* The reason for not quoting the Jesus tradition has been sought recently by a segment of scholarship in the individual, substantive rejection by Paul of certain early stages of the synoptic tradition. In II Cor. 10–13, Paul rejected Jewish peripatetic missionaries who characterized Jesus as a miracle-working hero, a *theios anēr*; they developed thus—it is maintained—a pre-form of the synoptic miracle stories, which Mark nevertheless corrected from the perspective of the passion kerygma.[26] In the same vein it is supposed that the wisdom teaching polemicized in I Cor. 1:18–3:23 represented a sayings tradition standing close to Q. For this reason—it is argued—Paul himself appropriated some Jesus sayings in I Corinthians, but rejected this collection of wisdom sayings.[27] Consequently, Paul rejected in his day the developmental tendencies of the synoptic tradition, for the most part on substantive grounds, because it portrayed Jesus as a miracle-working hero or as a teacher of wisdom. Even if these hypotheses contained modest elements of truth, they could not explain the actual problem of why Paul, along with the whole early Christian epistolary literature, did not make use of the Gospel tradition.

c) *The hermeneutical reason.* The general silence of the epistolary literature receives substantive explanation when one observes that the ministry of the earthly Jesus was tied strictly to its particular eschatological situation and in any case lost its substantive center—namely, its person—when it came to an end historically. As such it could not be appropriated into the situation of the community that, regardless of various interpretive directions, took as its starting point the Easter event.

This was forcefully evident for those portions of Jesus' earthly ministry that were appropriated more directly and more often than others, namely, for words of instruction. They were passed on throughout the parenetic tradition in a different form than in the synoptic tradition. The expressions of the commandment to love one's enemy, e.g., in Rom. 12:17a; I Thess. 5:15a; and I Pet. 3:9, maintained a high level of mutual agreement, but represented a typically different shape from the words in Lk. 6:27a and Mt. 5:44a. In the Gospels the commandment was the striking expression of Jesus' eschatological summons to repentance. In the parenetic tradition it was addressed to people who already stood in eschatological repentance. As an orientation aid for the living out of eschatological existence in history it was linked with the proverbial expressions of historical experience; but this was done in such a way that it would remain a criterion of choice for that existence. It was not to become "letter," a letter-perfect prescribed moral ideal, or a new Law. Even Jesus' prohibition of divorce was introduced in I Cor. 7:10 as a final standard for decision, but it did not

---

[26]H. Koester, in Koester-Robinson, *Trajectories*, pp. 189f., with reference to D. Georgi.

[27]H. W. Kuhn, "Der irdische Jesus bei Paulus als traditionsgeschichtliches und theologisches Problem," *ZThK* 67 (1970), 295-320 with reference to those mentioned in n. 26 et al.

become Law. In I Cor. 7:15, Paul opened the way for separation in marriages between partners of different religions wherever the non-Christian partner insisted on it. The word of instruction was incorporated into the framework of the kerygma that called to salvation. By way of contrast, in the Gospels it was an eschatological summons to repentance; or to put it another way: it was the pre-Easter form of the kerygma itself!

Even the instructions of the earthly Jesus could not be appropriated by Paul into his proclamation directly. They had to be transposed into a not only historically but also salvation-historically different situation! The Gospels, however, wished primarily to portray the past ministry of Jesus; blending in the situation of the community was done for the most part only suggestively during their redaction. A transformation comparable to that of Paul happened only in the case of the Gospel of John; yet here it was done in such a way that—distinct from Paul—the tradition persevered as text. In John 6:1-15, e.g., the miraculous feeding was narrated first, and then in the bread-of-life discourse of John 6:26-58 its meaning for the post-Easter situation was developed.

Our inquiry about the posture of Paul toward the Jesus tradition can therefore receive adequate resolution only by a study of the degree to which Pauline statements issued forth from such a transformation of the Jesus tradition. Examining this in detail will show itself to be a fruitful hermeneutical principle for the interpretation of Pauline theology. On the other hand, it will also indicate that the Jesus tradition reworked in this manner stood behind Pauline theology to an extent rarely recognized until now.[28]

The successful formulation of this line of questioning depends on a recognition of the interpretive aids that Paul called upon during this transformation and under which the Easter kerygma and the particular situation of the community were advanced.

§29. The Christ Event and the Interpretive Aids of the Religious Environment

On 1: U. Wilckens, "The Understanding of Revelation Within the History of Primitive Christianity," in *Revelation As History*, ed. W. Pannenberg (1968), pp. 55-121; R. Bultmann, "Ist die Apokalyptik die Mutter der christlichen Theologie?" in *Apophoreta. Festschrift für E. Haenchen* (1964), pp. 64-69; E. Käsemann, "On the Subject of Primitive Christian Apocalyptic," in *New Testament Questions of Today* (1969), pp. 108-137; H. H. Rowley, *The Relevance of Apocalyptic* (1964); P. Stuhlmacher, *Gerechtigkeit Gottes bei Paulus* (1965; 1966²); H. D. Betz, "Zum Problem des religionsgeschichtlichen Verständnisses der Apokalyptik," *ZThK* 63 (1966), 391-409; J. M. Schmidt, *Die jüdische Apokalyptik. Die Geschichte ihrer Erforschung von den Anfängen bis zu den Textfunden von Qumran* (1969 [Lit.!]); J. Becker, "Erwägungen zur apokalyptischen Tradition in der paulinischen Theologie," *EvTheol* 30 (1970), 593-609; K. Koch,

---

[28]D. L. Dungan, *The Sayings of Jesus in the Churches of Paul* (1971), strove to show a broad influence of the Jesus tradition upon Paul, but he failed to develop the precise line-of-questioning. Much the same can be said for B. Fjärstedt, *Synoptic Traditions in I Corinthians* (1974).

The Rediscovery of Apocalyptic (1972); W. Schmithals, *The Apocalyptic Movement* (1975). **On 2**: R. Reitzenstein, *Hellenistic Mystery Religions* (1978); C. Colpe, *Die Religionsgeschichtliche Schule. Darstellung und Kritik ihres Bildes vom gnostischen Erlösermythos* (1961); C. Colpe, "Gnosis," *RGG* II³, 1648-1652; G. Wagner, *Pauline Baptism and the pagan mysteries: the problem of the Pauline Doctrine of Baptism in Romans VI.1-11 in light of its religio-historical "parallels"* (1967); H. D. Betz, *Der Apostel Paulus und die sokratische Tradition. Eine exegetische Untersuchung zu seiner "Apologie" 2 Korinther 10–13* (1972).

Scholarly research has produced a long chain of studies that have investigated the connections between the theology of Paul and a great number of religious traditions in his non-Christian environment. Everything has been examined, from Pharisaic-rabbinic Judaism, apocalypticism, and the beliefs of the Essenes of Palestine found in Hellenistic Judaism of various types to the expressions of Hellenistic syncretism, the *kyrios* cults, the mystery religions, gnosticism, and popular philosophy.[1] Among these, two areas commanded special attention: Old Testament/Jewish apocalypticism and Hellenistic syncretism.

1. OLD TESTAMENT/JEWISH APOCALYPTICISM

a) The discussion. Following A. Schweitzer's lead,[2] H.-J. Schoeps,[3] E. Käsemann,[4] and U. Wilckens,[5] each in his own way, represented the point of view that apocalypticism was the "mother" of Pauline theology. For Schoeps apocalypticism as a history-of-religion category meant the dominant Jewish eschatology of the New Testament period. The Jewish apocalypses and the writings of the rabbis were basically in agreement with each other as representatives of this eschatology. For Wilckens, though, apocalypticism meant a theological system that emerged as the product of Old Testament theology; it was a way of looking at all of history from hindsight like that offered by the classical apocalypses (Daniel, I Enoch, IV Ezra, and the Syrian Apocalypse of Baruch). For Käsemann, finally, apocalypticism was a systematic designation for a futuristic, cosmic eschatology shaped by the expectation of the imminent *parousia*. Further distinctions among the three approaches can be seen as well regarding the manner in which Paul made use of apocalypticism as an interpretive aid.[6]

b) What is apocalypticism? To orient ourselves on this question we may make the following general comments:

1) The prismatic word apocalypticism referred basically to the special theological view of history and the cosmos that, in spite of considerable variations,

---

[1]H.-J. Schoeps, *Paul* (1961), pp. 13-50, provided a good overview of scholarly research.
[2]*The Mysticism of Paul the Apostle* (1931).
[3]Loc. cit. (n. 1).
[4]*New Testament Questions of Today* (1969), pp. 108-137.
[5]Op. cit. (Lit., §29); the same perspective was most recently represented in the "polemical work" of K. Koch, *The Rediscovery of Apocalyptic* (1972).
[6]Presentation and position taken by L. Goppelt, "Apokalyptik und Typologie bei Paulus," in *Christologie*, pp. 237-244.

surfaced in each of the following Old Testament/Jewish documents: Isa. 24–27, Daniel, I and II Enoch, IV Ezra, and the Syrian Apocalypse of Baruch. This view, expressed in classical form in Dan. 7,[7] brought together a universal history of the end time and an imminent climax to the cosmos out of which would follow a new world. Only the community of the elect that had persevered during the history of the end time would be delivered out of this radical climax. This history of the end time was understood to proceed as a fixed succession of times and periods whose (entirely fictitious) prophecy made possible the calculating of the hour in which the world found itself. Equipped with such secret knowledge the pious were bolstered in their faithful obedience to the Law and their endurance of persecutions for its sake. Standing above the events in time that were approaching their climax was a supraterrestrial world in which the events transpiring below were predetermined and guarded. This world above corresponded by and large to the coming new world, the coming aeon.[8]

2) The conceptual world of apocalypticism and its terminology were known to Paul in part directly as Jewish tradition (beyond what he found in the Old Testament—however, not literarily) and in part through the medium of early Christian tradition that had reshaped it into a Christian apocalypticism (§44,1).

3) In addition to the historical and cosmic conceptual framework of Old Testament/Jewish and early Christian apocalypticism through which he perceived the life of Jesus, the emergence of the church, and thereby even his own pilgrimage, Paul also appropriated its corresponding terminology.

4) The criterion he used in this appropriation was the kerygma about Christ. That meant that for its sake essential elements had to be eliminated from this conceptual framework. Such elements as the cosmological graphics and the dividing of the course of history into periods were eliminated; most especially, Paul never spoke about the "coming aeon"[9] because for him the *eschaton* was not to be identified with a coming new world. The *eschaton* was no longer linked to time and space. Rather it had already appeared with Christ and was yet to come with him.

5) Consequently, new dimensions were introduced into the apocalyptic conceptual framework and its terminology altered its content. The term "resurrection," e.g., now took its content from Easter, and the coming Judge of the world meant not only Jesus, but also this Judge was now going to act quite differently from the expectations of Jewish apocalypticism. Paul appropriated these alterations in part from an already developed early Christian apocalypticism.

c) The significance of apocalypticism for Paul. We may characterize in general then the use made of Old Testament/Jewish apocalypticism as an interpretive aid as follows: it provided Paul a historical and cosmic framework as well as terminology with which to express the eschatological situation. But it was not able to articulate the decisive matter, namely, the way in which the *eschaton* that

---

[7] Cf. I Enoch 89:59ff.; Syr. Bar. 36–40; IV Ezra 11f.

[8] I Enoch 91:16; Sib. 5:420; Syr. Bar. 32:6.

[9] Otherwise in the New Testament only at Eph. 2:7; Mk. 10:30 par. Lk. 18:30.

had already dawned was present through the death and resurrection of Christ. This could not be because it was only familiar with an *eschaton* as the climax of history and not like Paul with an *eschaton* within history. Paul appears to have gone elsewhere for interpretive aids to express the new presence of the Divine in history. The scope of Judaism, which for Paul represented the Old Testament tradition in the present, was for him by no means restricted to apocalypticism; in fact, he was more profoundly influenced by Pharisaism: it was life under the Law. As he himself stated emphatically (Phil. 3:5), he had been the product of Pharisaism.[10]

2. HELLENISTIC SYNCRETISM

a) The course of research. We shall consider a few prominent examples of works coming out of the first wave of history-of-religion analyses of Pauline concepts against the backdrop of Greek thought. R. Reitzenstein,[11] renowned for his work in the language and thought of the ancient world, regarded Paul's statements about the renewal of the human being as reflecting the mystery of rebirth in the mystery religions and in the tractates of the Corpus Hermeticum. W. Bousset[12] went further in that he traced the reverence accorded the exalted One as Lord to the *kyrios* cult. R. Bultmann[13] ascertained the Christology of a preexistent redeemer from a pre-Christian gnosticism whose chief figure descended from the light world and then led the redeemed as his body back to that realm. During the last decade progressive studies in the history of religion have clearly shown that for the most part concrete historical proof is wanting that these conceptual possibilities were ever directly adapted by primitive Christianity in the way one had assumed. Earlier studies had been based on abstractions from the phenomenology of religion. C. Colpe[14] demonstrated that Bultmann's view of gnosticism was not supported by the sources, and particularly that the Gnostic redeemer myth that he had postulated could not be found in the pre-Christian period. G. Wagner[15] pointed out that the interpretation of baptism as the sharing of death toward the sharing of life could not be derived directly from the mystery religions.

b) The significance of Hellenistic syncretism for Paul. Today we recognize

---

[10]Cf. Acts 23:6; 26:5. Pursuing the continuing effects of Pharisaic and rabbinic forms of thought on Paul were J. Bonsirven, *Exégèse rabbinique et exégèse Paulinienne* (1939); W. D. Davies, *Paul and Rabbinic Judaism. Some Rabbinic Elements in Pauline Theology* (1955²); D. Daube, *The New Testament and Rabbinic Judaism* (1956); H. Müller, *Die Auslegung alttestamentlichen Geschichtsstoffes bei Paulus* (Diss. Halle, 1960 [typewritten]), pp. 64-179.

[11]*Hellenistic Mystery Religions* (1978) (excerpt of Reitzenstein in Ger. in K. H. Rengstorf, *Das Paulusbild in der neueren deutschen Forschung* [1964], pp. 246-303); cf. Bultmann, *Theology* I, §13,3.

[12]*Kyrios*, pp. 138-148.

[13]*Theology* I, §12,3; cf. also §15.

[14]*Die Religionsgeschichtliche Schule* I (1961); C. Colpe, "Gnosis," *RGG* II³, 1648-1652.

[15]*Pauline Baptism and the pagan mysteries: the problem of the Pauline Doctrine of Baptism in Romans VI.1-11 in light of its religio-historical "parallels"* (1967).

that the points of contact between Pauline theology and the traditions of the Hellenistic church that preceded it with the religious environment of Hellenism were much more differentiated than assumed by the generation that pioneered their study. The schemata of myths were not simply taken over. Rather, faith made use of already existing terms and concepts on a selective basis in order to develop the aspects of its content for a new situation of proclamation. Thus these concepts of the Hellenistic world were made available to Paul in a variety of ways; they came to him through direct contacts with Hellenistic people, through Hellenistic Judaism, and through Hellenistic Christianity.

The ways in which the Jewish and Hellenistic religious environment was responsible, each in its own right, for contributing positive stimuli and conceptual and linguistic aids to the theology of Paul and to the ecclesiastical traditions that he developed will become clear from theme to theme in the subsequent analysis. Paul's indebtedness to both of these areas was of a quite different type than to that of a third interpretive aid: the Old Testament.

3. THE OLD TESTAMENT

While Paul deliberately maintained a critical distance toward Judaism and Hellenism he expressed himself with emphasis in connection with that document which he referred to at first as "the Old Testament" (II Cor. 3:14). In I Cor. 10:1-11 he placed over against a Hellenistic misunderstanding of baptism and the Eucharist the God of the Old Testament; the God whom Israel knew in the wilderness wanderings was the same One encountered inescapably in the sacraments and yet he was not at human disposal. In a corresponding way Paul laid claim to the Old Testament witness to Abraham's justification in debate with a Judaizing (Gal. 3:6-18) and with a Jewish (Rom. 4:1-25) misunderstanding of the way of salvation. It would appear that for Paul the Old Testament was the decisive interpretive aid of the Christ event.

The historical investigation of scripture in the 19th century had already come to the fundamentally correct recognition that the exegetical method of the apostle corresponded formally to that of the Judaism of his time.[16] A broad stream of research from the past 150 years,[17] however, drew the conclusion that Paul, just like the rabbis and Philo, did not derive his theology from scripture, but subsequently acquired its foundation from it. In contrast to the way Paul himself portrayed it, the relationship of his theology to Judaism and Hellenism on the one hand, and to the Old Testament on the other, would be precisely the reverse. As this stream of research would have it, Pauline theology derived its shape with the help of Jewish and Hellenistic traditions and then later drew upon the Old Testament, i.e., was transported into this connection. The references of the apostle to the Old Testament, therefore, would be substantively irrelevant for his

---

[16]Goppelt, *Typos*, pp. 8-10.
[17]It was represented by F. C. Baur, A. von Harnack, and R. Bultmann; cf. in this regard Vol. I, §23,II-III.

theology. Since the middle of the 19th century, in contrast, another direction of the historical investigation of scripture[18] sought to become acquainted with the substantive principles—relevant then and now—for understanding the Old Testament used by Paul in connection with contemporary forms of interpretation. The question of the relationship between Paul and Jesus excepted, this issue represents *the* key problem for understanding Pauline theology. We now turn our attention to this issue.

§30. The Christ Event and the Old Testament according to Paul

On 1-3. N. J. Hommes, *Het Testimonialboek. Studien over OT citaten in het NT* (1935); W. D. Davies, *Paul and Rabbinic Judaism* (1948); C. H. Dodd, *According to the Scriptures. The Substructure of New Testament Theology* (1952); E. E. Ellis, *Paul's Use of the Old Testament* (1957); P. Vielhauer, "Paulus und das Alte Testament," in *Studien zur Geschichte und Theologie der Reformation, Festschrift für Ernst Bizer* (1969), pp. 33-62. **On 4:** L. Goppelt, *Typos* (1939; repr. 1963; Eng. trans. 1982); idem, "Apokalyptik und Typologie bei Paulus," in *Christologie und Ethik* (1968), pp. 234-267; R. Bultmann, "Ursprung und Sinn der Typologie als hermeneutischer Methode," *ThLZ* 75 (1950), 205-212; J. Daniélou, *Sacramentum futuri. Études sur les origines de la typologie biblique* (1950); S. Amsler, *L'Ancien Testament dans l'église. Essai d'herméneutique chrétienne* (1960); W. G. Kümmel, "Schriftauslegung," *RGG* V³, 1517-1520; J. Schniewind-G. Friedrich, *epangellō*, etc., *TDNT* II, 576-586; L. Goppelt, *typos*, *TDNT* VIII, 246-259 (Lit.!). **On 5:** O. Cullmann, *Christ and Time* (1950); O. Cullmann, *Salvation in History* (1967); U. Luz, *Das Geschichtsverständnis des Paulus* (1968); G. Klein, "Römer 4 und die Idee der Heilsgeschichte," in *Rekonstruktion und Interpretation* (1969), pp. 145-169; U. Wilckens, "Die Rechtfertigung Abrahams nach Römer 4," in U. Wilckens, *Rechtfertigung als Freiheit. Paulusstudien* (1974), pp. 33-49; U. Wilckens, "Zu Römer 3,21-4,25. Antwort an G. Klein," ibid., pp. 50-76; O. Michel, *oikonomia*, *TDNT* V, 151-53.

1. THE FUNDAMENTAL RECOGNITION OF THE OLD TESTAMENT CANON

a) Appropriation. Normally Paul called the Old Testament "scripture" (*hē graphē*), and he often used the formula for quoting, "it is written" (*gegraptai*). According to Jewish linguistic usage, this meant that Paul was referring to the Old Testament as canon.[1] The scope of the canon was not limited until some fifty years after Paul by the Sanhedrin of Jamnia, but the validity of the major documents had stood firm for a long time.[2] Like the rest of the New Testament writers (Jude 14ff. excepted), Paul did not quote as scripture anything beyond

[18]Thus J.C.K. von Hofmann, J. T. Beck, A. Schlatter, J. Schniewind; cf. in this regard Vol. I, §23,V and Goppelt, *Typos*, pp. 11-18.
[1]The rabbis and Philo characterized the Old Testament books with the expressions "the holy scriptures," "the scriptures," as binding documents of revelation. Occasionally the expression "the scripture" was also used among the rabbis (G. Schrenk, *TDNT* I, 751-55).
[2]O. Eissfeldt, *The Old Testament. An Introduction* (1965), pp. 568-570.

the twenty-two books listed by Josephus (*Ap*. I.40), which were also the standard at Qumran.[3] Those books, referred to apparently since the 16th century as the apocrypha and transmitted as cursive writings of the LXX in extension of the Hebrew canon, were not judged to be canonical even by Philo.

b) The new perspective. Yet Paul did not simply appropriate the Old Testament as a formal authority. Perhaps we may find even the shift of terminology an indication of his new understanding. While the Old Testament in Jewish linguistic usage normally was designated as "the holy scriptures" and on occasion as "the scriptures" or "the scripture," for Paul, on the other hand, "the scripture" was the dominant designation; he meant by this the book as a whole.[4] Except for Rom. 1:2 he did not call it "holy" nor did he ever single out the inspiration of particular statements; later the Pastoral Epistles (II Tim. 3:16) and II Peter (1:20f.) emphasized this once again as in Judaism. Paul knew, in any case, that scripture as such can also be "the written code" (*gramma*) that "kills" (II Cor. 3:4-11). For him the inner structure of scripture had undergone a complete change from that which it had in Judaism. After the composition of Deuteronomy, the book that constituted the foundation stone of the Old Testament canon, obedience to the Law and prophetically interpreted historical experience represented the poles of scripture linked with each other.[5] According to Paul, however, Christ and no longer the Torah constituted the foundation of existence for the believer (Rom. 10:5). For this reason the Old Testament was no longer primarily Torah for him, but the history of promise (Rom. 4:13-15; Gal. 3:17f.). The Torah, to be sure, was also "holy" (Rom. 7:12), but scripture was primarily that authoritative witness generated by God himself about his address and acts toward Israel during the course of its history; that witness pointed to the end time that now was dawning (I Cor. 10:11). This structure of the Old Testament and its meaning were unveiled, of course, to the one who had turned in faith to Christ (II Cor. 3:12-18). Perhaps it was also for this reason that Paul designated the Old Testament singularly as "the scripture" because "the scriptures" appeared to him to be a unity from this new vantage point. In any case, for him the Old Testament was in no way the inherited authority upon which he documented his theology with apologetic interest. He viewed it from a new perspective.

c) The new authority base. But precisely from this new perspective Paul affirmed the Old Testament because its God had encountered him as his God in a new way. His summons to faith was not the transition from the Jewish to the Christian religion, but a new revelation of the God of scripture who had always been his God. Paul represented this change by drawing on the Old Testament account of the call to Jeremiah: "But when he who had set me apart before I

---

[3]The quotations in I Cor. 2:9 and 15:45b (Eph. 4:8; 5:14) cannot be identified specifically; they probably represent free restatement of Old Testament texts and were not derived from apocryphal sources (Ellis, op. cit. [Lit., §30], pp. 34-37).

[4]Not strictly the individual scriptural passage as do the synoptic Gospels, Acts, and the Gospel of John! This was shown by Schrenk, op. cit. (n. 1), 752ff., especially by the personification of scripture in Gal. 3:8, 22.

[5]J. Maier, *Geschichte der jüdischen Religion* (1972), pp. 20-30.

was born, and had called me through his grace, was pleased to reveal his Son to me . . ." (Gal. 1:15f.). For him the gospel was not the message of salvation of an until-then unknown God, as it was for Marcion, but the promised, final proclamation (cf. Rom. 10:15) announced in Isa. 52:7: "Your God reigns." Even the content of the gospel was, as Paul already understood it along with the primitive kerygma (I Cor. 15:3-5), "in accordance with the scriptures." In Rom. 1:2, Paul (speaking traditionally) expressly adopted as his own this understanding of the entire church in relationship to the community unknown to him in Rome: ". . . the gospel of God which he promised beforehand through his prophets in the holy scriptures." But how can Paul have found the gospel of Jesus Christ announced in the Old Testament?

2. THE FORMAL HERMENEUTIC

By giving attention to the apostle's customary style in dealing with scripture we discover certain characteristic traits of his understanding.

a) A statistical breakdown of quotations[6] shows that the references to scripture have been determined with an eye toward content in connection with the theme he happened to be covering and not by the need for formal reliance on an authority. Far and away the largest number of quotations are found in the Epistle to the Romans; there are fifty-two of them, twenty-eight in chapters 9–11 where the concern was his existential program and not scribal apologetics. The First Epistle to the Corinthians, which is of almost the same length, contains only sixteen quotations, II Corinthians only nine, while the much briefer Epistle to the Galatians has ten quotations. In the remaining letters of Paul there are indirect references, to be sure, but no express quotations are to be found.

b) The quotation formulas[7] used by Paul were the customary Jewish expressions "it is written" (Rom. 1:17; 2:24; 3:4, 10; 4:17; 8:36, etc.—29 times), "scripture says" (Rom. 4:3; 9:17; 10:11; 11:2; Gal. 4:30; cf. I Tim. 5:18), "David says" (Rom. 4:6; 11:9), "Isaiah says" (Rom. 10:16, 20; 15:12), "Moses says" (Rom. 10:19), "the Law says" (Rom. 3:19; I Cor. 14:34), "God says" (II Cor. 6:16; cf. Rom. 9:15; II Cor. 6:2; Rom. 11:4), or "he says," whereby God (or scripture) was the antecedent to be supplied (Rom. 15:10; Gal. 3:16). One cannot conclude from these quotation formulas—in spite of Rom. 10:20f.— that Paul wanted to accentuate the difference between God's revelation and the human authors. The great variability of his quotation formulas indicates that he did not take his point of departure from a theory of inspiration—in contrast to Philo[8]—but formally speaking maintained a posture of great flexibility over against scripture; it also indicates that for him the decisive thing was the content of the particular Old Testament statements.

c) Corresponding perspectives are to be derived from the form of the quo-

---

[6]A reliable overview is to be found in the lists of Ellis, op. cit. (n. 3), pp. 150-188.
[7]Cf. regarding the following, ibid., pp. 22-25, 48f.
[8]*Spec. Leg.* IV:49.

tations. Here he followed the LXX just as Philo did. Paul did so even when it departed from the Hebrew text (e.g., Rom. 4:3, 7f.). But more than a third of his quotations distanced themselves from every verifiable text.[9] This was not only the result of faulty memory—in contrast to Philo and the Essenes, Paul wrote while he was travelling—but also of intuitive selection and interpretation. For this reason one also finds a clustering of combined quotations that allowed texts to flow into one another; this trait represented virtually a unique Pauline feature.[10] A comparison with the Old Testament quotations in other New Testament documents produces but occasional agreement in the sequential ordering of quotations, which was not based, however, on specific wording.[11] One may conclude from this that, in contrast to the sect at Qumran, early Christianity did not work with messianic promise/fulfillment texts (florilegia), but at best in various instances used similar quotations and quotation groups as tradition.[12]

d) It was characteristic of the practice and method of interpretation that they were much less unified in Paul than among the rabbis or in Philo. Paul could at one point interject Old Testament statements without quoting the sources (e.g., Rom. 12:20), or he could quote them as supporting evidence without interpretation (Rom. 1:17); then again he could follow the practice of taking words and incidents of the Old Testament and making a broad exegetical development of them (Rom. 4 and I Cor. 10:1-11).

With respect to these developments he could also, on occasion, appropriate methodologically two of the seven rules drawn up for rabbinic exegesis by the school of Hillel,[13] namely, the conclusion from the few to the many (*a minore ad maius*, Rom. 5:15, 17) and the conclusion based on the principle of analogy (Rom. 4:3-8). On the other hand, he was once able to establish an allegorical interpretation as Philo did (I Cor. 9:9f.). Similarly, Paul combined rabbinic and Hellenistic-Jewish interpretive traditions; in I Cor. 10:4 he could state with the Palestinian midrash that the rock from which water came forth in the desert accompanied Israel and then relate the rock in the same way to the preexistent Christ as Hellenistic Judaism linked it to Sophia or the Logos.

In sum, it can only be established that he was obligated more to the Palestinian-rabbinic interpretive method and traditions than to those of the Hellenistic-Jewish. It is decisive, however, that in contrast to the rabbis and to Philo he did not follow a particular rule and tradition of interpretation but operated eclectically. This practice would have had to have appeared even to the thinking of his contemporaries as unsound if behind it there had not stood defensible, substantive hermeneutical principles.

---

[9]Rom. 2:24; 3:10-12, 14, 15-17; 9:9, 17, 25, 26, 27f., 33; 10:6-8, etc.; cf. Ellis, op. cit. (n. 3), pp. 150-52.

[10]Rom. 9:32f.; 11:26f., 34f.; I Cor. 15:45, 54f.; II Cor. 6:16-18. From these. the series of quotations in Rom. 9:12f., 25-29; 10:5-8, (11-13), 19f.; 11:8-10; 15:9-12 are to be differentiated.

[11]E.g., we find the same quotation link in I Pet. 2:6-8 as in Rom. 9:32f.; for a complete overview, cf. Ellis, op. cit. (n. 3), p. 187.

[12]Discussion in Vielhauer, op. cit. (Lit., §30), p. 39.

[13]Ellis, op. cit. (n. 3), p. 41.

3. THE HERMENEUTICAL STARTING POINT AND ITS PROBLEMATIC

a) Paul himself saw that he could not prove his interpretation of scripture to any Jew. ". . . to this day, when they read the old covenant, that same veil remains unlifted, because only through Christ is it taken away . . . but when a man turns to the Lord the veil is removed." These statements from II Cor. 3:14 and 16 indicate that the actual meaning of the Old Testament was to be understood only from the perspective of faith in Christ.

b) How should one evaluate this position? 1) P. Vielhauer[14] was an exponent of the school of research represented by R. Bultmann[15] when he wrote that Paul's interpretation of the Old Testament cannot be accepted by those who follow the historical interpretation of scripture. Not only is this obviously so, he maintained, but more than this such interpreters do not observe the exegetical standards of Paul's contemporaries. (Among the latter the particular groups did in fact relate the Old Testament variously to their understanding of the situation seen through the optic of tradition, but in doing so did eliminate caprice by means of exegetical rules and obligation to interpretive tradition.)

In the case of Paul, said Vielhauer, an examination shows "that Paul, consistent with what he implied in II Cor. 3:14, always knew the 'substantive meaning' beforehand and did not derive it from the Old Testament; rather he placed into the text what he then later took from it interpretively."[16] The one hermeneutical principle found by Vielhauer was the certainty that the God of the Old Testament was identical to the One of the Christians; he was, namely, the God who justified the ungodly. We too—concluded Vielhauer—are able to take this principle alone as the connection between the Old and New Testaments.[17] This certainty, however, was only to be derived from the Christ event; the Old Testament, on the other hand, contributed nothing to the understanding of the Christ event.[18]

2) The opposite point of view was represented by G. von Rad. In his eyes, the Old and New Testaments interpret each other reciprocally now as before! For von Rad the Old Testament is to be interpreted finally in relationship to Jesus Christ. This is in accord with its own intention. And the reverse is true also: the New Testament is to be grasped finally as the fulfillment of the Old Testament.[19]

In order to be fair to Paul, therefore, one must examine whether he developed his position in defensible hermeneutical principles.

---

[14]Op. cit. (n. 12), p. 51.
[15]*Theology* I, §11,3b.c.
[16]Op. cit. (n. 12), pp. 51f.
[17]Ibid., p. 61.
[18]Ibid., p. 56.
[19]*Theology* II, 244-48.

4. HERMENEUTICAL PRINCIPLES

The hermeneutical starting point developed by Paul in II Cor. 3 did not remain a pneumatic postulate. It was applied according to clear hermeneutical principles for which Paul developed in part his own terminology.

a) Promise. In contrast to an interpreter like Philo, Paul did not transport into the Old Testament a philosophical-religious system with the aid of allegorical interpretation as eternal truth. For him the Old Testament did not contain the gospel, but promise (*epangelia*) and Law (*nomos*). This structural shaping of the Old Testament had been derived from faith's recognition that Christ was both the yes to all God's promises (II Cor. 1:20) and the end of the Law (Rom. 10:4). Paul summarized this view of the Old Testament in the paradoxical key statement with which he began the development of the gospel of justification by grace: "But now the righteousness of God has been manifested apart from law although the law and the prophets bear witness to it" (Rom. 3:21). "The law and the prophets" was a designation for "the scripture."[20] Scripture itself pointed, therefore, to salvation's path for the justification by faith that suspended the Law and turned the covenant with Moses into "the old covenant." To the degree to which it announced the salvation experienced through Christ it was *epangelia*.

Only a short time before the New Testament period the word *epangelia* had sometimes been used in the realm of Greek-speaking Judaism for the promises (*Zusagen*) of the Old Testament. Septuagint usage conformed to that of customary Greek, i.e., announcement, making a promise (*das Versprechen*). It was Paul who first vested the word with pregnant theological meaning.[21] "The promises" (*Verheissungen*) or "the promise"—plural and singular were substituted synonymously—represented the promise of eschatological salvation that was made to Abraham before all others (Gal. 3:16, 18; Rom. 4:13). In Rom. 4 and Gal. 3 Paul developed the thought that this promise surpassed circumcision and the Law and was valid independent of both so that it was fulfilled in those who believed in correspondence to Abraham (Rom. 4:23f.). Much like Rom. 4:21-23, Rom. 9:8f. underscored that the promise was given only to the elect of God and not merely to the physical descendants of Abraham. When he spoke of promises or promise without express connection to Abraham it is probable that Paul was also thinking of the other salvation promises of the Old Testament (Rom. 9:4; 15:8; II Cor. 1:20; 7:1). Hence he turned "promise" into a collective term for salvation promises that—with respect to their content—superseded the meaning they had as individual Old Testament references. What was specified as the content of the promise were life (Gal. 3:21; Rom. 4:17), righteousness (Gal. 3:21), the spirit (Gal. 3:14; cf. Eph. 1:13), sonship (Rom. 9:8f.; Gal. 4:22ff.), in brief, eschatological salvation. The promise had the character of a *diathēkē*, of a binding testamentary enactment (Gal. 3:17; cf. Eph. 2:12).

---

[20]The three constituent parts of scripture were named comprehensively in Lk. 24:44 just as already in the Prologue to Sir. (ca. 130 B.C.): "In the law of Moses and the prophets and the psalms."

[21]J. Schniewind/G. Friedrich, *TDNT* II, 579-584.

Thus the line of the Old Testament leading to Christ was not understood as prophecy but as promise. Essential here is not that the realization of prediction could be demonstrated apologetically, but that God had verified his promise, that he had proven his loyalty to his promise (Rom. 15:8). The Christ event was characterized correspondingly as the "yes" of God (II Cor. 1:20; cf. Rom. 15:8) or as the "guarantee" of the promise (Rom. 4:16), and not as by Matthew as "fulfillment."[22] In this way the signpost "promise" was erected for the entire history of Israel as reported in the Old Testament; moreover, that history itself became promise.

b) Typos. In Rom. 4 the report about Abraham's justification was first treated exegetically (vv. 1-8); then it was argued in contrast to both the Jewish and the historical view of the Old Testament that this declaration of righteousness stood independent of circumcision and the Law (vv. 9-12, 13-17). Finally in vv. 18-25 the arch was drawn between the justification of Abraham and that of the Christians; both were not tied to each other through the continuity of history. Such continuity existed through circumcision and the Law and along with them was abolished here. Abraham was linked to the Christians by the similarity of the summons to faith that issued forth there from the promise (vv. 18-22) and here from its realization (vv. 23-25). "But the words, 'it [faith] was reckoned to him,' were written not for his sake alone, but for ours also. It will be reckoned to us who believe in him that raised from the dead Jesus our Lord" (Rom. 4:23f.). In the passage that sounds much the same (1 Cor. 10:11), Paul used the technical term with which he expressed the relationship intended here between the Old and the New Testament event. "All these things that happened [the events of the wilderness wanderings] to them were symbolic (*typikōs*), and were recorded for our benefit as a warning. For upon us the fulfillment of the ages has come" (NEB). The events of the wilderness wanderings were, as was stated above, promissory images of the time of salvation (*typoi*). In Rom. 5:14 Paul called Adam *typos tou mellontos*, a type of the one who was to come. Adam was the antithetical announcement beforehand of the second Adam, Christ.

The Greek word *typos* was rich in meaning and designated at its root the raised image like the face of a printing font or of a stamp that leaves an impression. Paul turned this word into a technical term[23] as a means for interpreting Old Testament history that had been current in Old Testament tradition since Second Isaiah. Occurrences of the past history of election were understood as an announcement of the eschatological intervention of God. The first exodus became an announcement of the second, more glorious one (Isa. 43:18f.); David became a pointer to the Monarch of salvation (II Sam. 7:12; Isa. 11:1), and Moses a pointer to the end-time Prophet (Deut. 18:18).[24] Jesus was the first one who had linked this estimate of election-history for end-time expectation not with the eschatological future but with his own time (§6,3). Paul followed his

---

[22]Cf. G. Delling, *TDNT* VI, 294ff.; regarding *plērōma* in Gal. 4:4; Eph. 1:10 cf. ibid., 305.
[23]L. Goppelt, *TDNT* VIII, 251-56.
[24]von Rad, *Theology* II, 244-48.

lead in this way of looking at things. The typological understanding of the Old Testament was not an exegetical method but a distinctly defined angle of vision that was applied meditatively. Looking back from the Christ event Paul observed in persons, institutions, or events of the Old Testament advance signals of God's activity in the end time. These types were not something like historical analogies. They were God's connections to the human being that were witnessed to by the Old Testament and that announced—positively or antithetically—a corresponding but at the same time eschatologically elevated, final connection. The announcement character rested on God's loyalty to his promise. For this reason typology was, to a considerable extent, independent of the historicity of the Old Testament representation of history. Abraham's relationship to God, e.g., expressed in Gen. 15:6 was a prophetic account that was also quite valid apart from the historical religiosity of Abraham.

How did Paul derive Old Testament types? Prompted by the typological interpretive tradition already underway in the Old Testament, his eye moved back and forth from the Christ event to Old Testament history in order to interpret the one in relationship to the other. In this way arose the Adam-Christ typology of Rom. 5:12-21 (cf. I Cor. 15:21, 44-49) that spanned the breadth of human history, and the Abraham typology of Rom. 4:1-25; Gal. 3:6-18 that illuminated the history of election. So it was also possible specifically in I Cor. 10:1-11 to avoid a misunderstanding of the sacraments by the wilderness wandering typology and to provide elucidation of their ethical implications. It is therefore quite unfounded to maintain that New Testament insights were brought into the Old Testament simply out of apologetic interest.

Quantitatively, among the many references of the apostle to the Old Testament the typologies actually made up but a small number,[25] but along with the reference to "promise" they were characteristic of his overall use of scripture and established for him the standard. Paul saw all scripture as a unity within a frame of reference set off by either of the two key words "promise" and "typos"; for him this unity was the "Old Testament" (II Cor. 3:14).

5. SCRIPTURE INTERPRETATION AS INTERPRETIVE VEHICLE

From this vantage point we must now inquire into the theological significance of the Old Testament as interpretive vehicle. What was the result of this estimate of the Old Testament for the understanding of the Christ event?

[25]Other typologies in Paul's writings cannot be separated sharply because he did not develop this interpretive approach strictly in the form of developed comparisons, but carried it over into allusions to Old Testament texts (e.g., I Cor. 5:7) or into designations like "Israel of God" (Gal. 6:16) or "circumcision" (Phil. 3:3; Col. 2:11). The development of thought about the relationship between Ishmael and Isaac (cf. Gen. 21:2, 9) in Gal. 4:21-31 was a typology that to a considerable degree crossed over to allegory. The reference to the covenant of Law and its office in II Cor. 3:4-18 can be understood as antithetical typology. When Paul referred to the community (I Cor. 3:10-17; II Cor. 6:16; cf. Eph. 2:20ff.) or even to individual Christians (I Cor. 6:19) as the true temple of God, this was a graphic form of expression whose typological background was no longer in view. In contrast, Rom. 3:25 was a genuine and, for Paul, important typology; Good Friday was the eschatological Day of Atonement (§35,4a). Cf., regarding the whole, Goppelt, *Typos*; Ellis, op. cit. (n. 3), pp. 126-134.

a) The correspondence between promise and fulfillment and the typological relationship between the Old Testament and New Testament event as well as the general applicability of Old Testament sayings to the Christian situation that existed in this realm all expressed the selfsameness of God's activity. This self-sameness guarded against a misunderstanding of the Christ event from the side of Hellenistic as well as Judaizing concepts of God (cf. I Cor. 10:1-11; Gal. 3:1-5). It kept the eschatological message of salvation from being separated from the horizon of creation and history and from becoming a suspended utopia. The God who made himself known through Jesus remained the Creator and the Lord of history with the result, e.g., that coming on the heels of the proclamation of love in Rom. 12:9-21 could follow words of obligation toward political authority in Rom. 13:1-7. The character of his revelation as address through people stood in effective connection with the particular historical situation. Such revelation was made powerfully vivid through the Old Testament, understood in a fundamentally historical perspective, so that, e.g., the revelation of the cross could not so easily be supplanted by a self-supporting system of speculative wisdom (I Cor. 1:19, 31; 2:16; 3:19f.).[26] By means of the selfsameness of God's activity the Christ event was ultimately verified internally for faith. According to the Abraham typology, e.g., justification by faith alone was not an arbitrary incident but the basic point of reference from God's activity of election (Rom. 4:23f.). In the same sense the role of the Law became internally perceptible.

b) The typological supersession of the relationship to God in the Old Testament, and the character of the Christ event as fulfillment of the promise made, however, a conclusive announcement. Here was the *eschaton* in the form of the *kainē diathēkē*, the new covenant (I Cor. 11:25; II Cor. 3:6), the final, holy relationship to God through which everything becomes holy! It rested upon the Spirit and not upon the letter; God's will was no longer encountered as code but it took hold of people from within; it was no longer written on "tablets of stone" but "on the heart" (II Cor. 3:3). The *eschaton* had become a present reality even if the course of history marched on. Following out of the connectedness of the Christ event to the Old Testament was that which could not be derived from apocalypticism, namely, that the *eschaton* was present for faith (II Cor. 5:17). To be sure, it was not present as demonstrable change in the world available for viewing, but nevertheless there as the universal, physical becoming new that followed from creation (Rom. 8:18-30). Paul could therefore distinguish the present from what had gone before by means of the great "now" (*nyn*). "Behold, now is the acceptable time; behold, now is the day of salvation" (II Cor. 6:2). This "now" was not merely a chronological point in time or a period of time. Rather it was the time since the resurrection of Jesus that was always present whenever the good news of him was preached and received. This kerygmatic, time-related meaning was perhaps already intended by the *nyn* of Rom. 3:21, although there it was used only in the adversative sense, "but now." In any case,

---

[26]Bultmann, *Theology* I, §11,3b, noted correctly that through the adherence to the Old Testament since early Christianity the fundamental recognition was communicated that "man becomes aware of God and of his own nature not by free-soaring thought but by historical encounter" (p. 117).

it was the force of Rom. 3:26 (*en tō nyn kairō*, "at the present time"; similarly 11:5; II Cor. 8:14); Rom. 5:9, 11; 6:19; 8:1; 11:30; 13:11; (16:26); II Cor. 5:16; Gal. 2:20; 4:9, 29.[27]

6. CHRIST AND HISTORY

With respect to the question of how Paul understood the connection between the Christ event and the passage of world events the gamut of opinion in Pauline research is divided. In point of fact, the various positions can be illustrated schematically by comparing their interpretation of Rom. 4. One can ask critically: How do they seek to do justice to the way in which Paul in Rom. 4 linked the Christ event with the history that began with Abraham?

a) O. Cullmann characterized the ministry of Christ as "the center of time" in his books *Christ and Time* (Eng. 1950) and *Salvation in History* (Eng. 1967). Christ was represented here as the point of intersection where all the lines of God's manifestations in history converged in order then again universally to radiate forth from him. For Paul, however, the typological images of Rom. 4 and 5:12-21 were not like the mosaic tiles of a universal plan of salvation; they cannot be fit together in this way. Paul shaped the terms *epangelia* and *typos* but he did not develop a term for "plan of salvation" or "process for salvation." The word *oikonomia*, meaning basically "house administration," first took on the rudiments of meaning for "divine decree, plan of salvation, or economy of salvation" in Eph. 1:10 and 3:2, 9;[28] this usage reflected the theology of the 2nd century (Ign. Eph. 18:2; 20:1). Irenaeus then was the first one to turn it into a major theme for the process of salvation history in which—similar to Cullmann's position—Christ stood as "the center of time."[29] The apocalyptic term *mystērion* (secret), however, meant for Paul the secret counsel of God regarding the end time but not a plan for history.[30]

b) It is even less in correspondence to the thinking of Paul when U. Wilckens[31] claimed to find in him the desire to turn the Christ event into an apocalyptic universal history. For Wilckens, Paul looked at the resurrection of Jesus, the gathering of the community of faith, and the *parousia* as one, singular apocalyptic event of the end time. He found this portrayed in I Cor. 15:20-28. In Rom. 4, however, Wilckens thought Paul understood the event of the end time

---

[27]G. Stählin, *TDNT* IV, 1112-1123, has made substantive comments about the character of this *nyn*. In contrast, P. Tachau, *"Einst" und "Jetzt" im Neuen Testament* (1972), merely pursued the origin of this schema.

[28]Discussion in E. Lohse, *Colossians* (Hermeneia) regarding Col. 1:25, and O. Michel, *TDNT* V, 151-53.

[29]Cf., in this regard, J. Reumann, "*Oikonomia*-Terms in Paul in Comparison with Lucan Heilsgeschichte," *NTS* 13 (1967), 147-167.

[30]Rom. 11:25; I Cor. 2:1, 7; 13:2; 14:2; 15:51; Col. 1:26f.; 2:2; 4:3; cf. E. Lohse, *Colossians* (Hermeneia), at Col. 1:26.

[31]"Die Rechtfertigung Abrahams nach Römer 4," in *Rechtfertigung als Freiheit. Paulusstudien* (1974), pp. 33-49.

to grow in continuity out of the history-of-election traditions because Christ was the end of the Law as its replacement.

c) In contrast, R. Bultmann[32] understood Christ to be encountered only in the kerygma; he was seen here as the eschatological summons for decision issued to history that furnished the individual with a new self-understanding in the midst of history. The apocalyptic framework merely indicated through the nearness of the end the eschatological character of the message. The same was being expressed through the cloaking of Christology in the Gnostic redeemer myth in which Christ descended out of the dualistically other, upper world, came into this world, and then returned to the other. Because Bultmann understood Christ as the summons to decision he was able to grasp in what preceded him in the Old Testament only a history "of failure." No matter how important the Old Testament was for Bultmann as a pointer to the historical character of revelation he could only see here the rejection of God's summons. Along this line G. Klein[33] interpreted Rom. 4 in debate with U. Wilckens. For Klein, Abraham had been brought together with Christ here merely "under the timeless aspect of the example"; Abraham had been separated from him "under the historical aspect of the chronological distance" that "made the history of Israel profane and paganized" and freed "the one who believed from the power of history."

d) When Paul brought the Christ event together with the Old Testament, however, he had in mind neither a salvation-historical nor a universal-historical master plan, nor merely a call to decision expressed in mythical terms. In my opinion his point was rather the correspondence between the events of promise and fulfillment. Both were for him, however, not only address but also the commitments given in covenant relationships. They were certainly not linked to each other through historical continuity but through the arch of promise. The realization of the promise had not come about coincidentally; it corresponded rather to the "design" and the "election" of God that became effective in history as "calling" (Rom. 8:28-30; 11:28f.). Paul was therefore familiar with "salvation history" not in the sense of a historical process but clearly in that of covenantal commitments in history that furnished the heading for historical occurrences. These covenantal commitments were bound together, to be sure, only by the arch of promise, but they were encountered as "calling" according to the "divine decree" of God in a particular "now." Paul was familiar with salvation history as the history of election, promise, and calling.[34]

In I Cor. 15:20-28 and Rom. 8:18-30 Paul stated in apocalyptic terminology

---

[32] "History and Eschatology in the New Testament," NTS 1 (1954), 5-16(16); Bultmann, "Prophecy and Fulfillment," in Essays on Old Testament Hermeneutics (ed. C. Westermann [1963]), pp. 50-75 (esp. pp. 72ff.); also in Bultmann, Essays Philosophical and Theological (1955), pp. 182-208 (esp. pp. 205ff.); with particular reference to Rom. 4: Bultmann, "Ursprung und Sinn der Typologie als hermeneutischer Methode," ThLZ 75 (1950), 210 (also in Exegetica, pp. 369-380).

[33] Op. cit. (Lit., §30,5); cf. also further discussion between H. Conzelmann and G. von Rad in EvTheol 24 (1964), 57-73, 113-125, 388-394.

[34] More detailed development of this conception in Goppelt, "Paul and Heilsgeschichte. Conclusions from Romans 4 and I Corinthians 10:1-13," Int 21 (1967), 315-326 (slightly revised Ger. form in Christologie, pp. 220-233).

that the fulfillment in the "already" of faith would be culminated by a (future) visual fulfillment. These apocalyptic statements formed not the basis for but rather the consequence drawn from the starting point of the history of promise.

It was of considerable significance for the entire theological discussion of the 20th century that G. von Rad succeeded in such fundamentally convincing fashion in demonstrating Paul's theological-typological view of promise in contemporary historical-critical study of the Old Testament. Bultmann's minimalist thesis of the bare identity of God in both Testaments, however, was turned by H. Braun into the codeword "God"[35] with certain consequences. When today the question of God more than ever has become the test question for all theology, the theme Christ and the Old Testament according to Paul is not only a key question of Pauline interpretation but of all theology.

Paul opened up in this way the decisive theological-ecclesiastical question of that hour (§27,2b): How could Jesus and the Old Testament be combined for Jewish and Gentile Christians into a new unity? It is therefore no coincidence that we are confronted here with a new perspective on the structure of the Old Testament as well as its relationship to Christ. It corresponds to the starting points provided by Jesus' preaching and the course of his life and must therefore stand as an effective guidepost for the church even if this new perspective has been explicitly adopted only rarely in theology.

Paul could also speak about the gospel without direct reliance upon the Old Testament. There are no direct quotations, e.g., in First and Second Thessalonians, Philippians, Colossians, and Philemon. But when the gospel was supposed to be articulated centrally and clearly for Jewish and Gentile Christians, it had to be portrayed with the aid of scripture as the message of the fulfilled promise and of the suspension of the Law; such was the case for the Epistle to the Romans.

§31. The Arrangement of Pauline Theology

Literature: compare that of §28.

In what order should we arrange the theology that was expressed in the epistles of Paul but was nowhere—not even in the Epistle to the Romans—summarized systematically? Paul followed neither the path of the objectifying theology that issues forth in teachings and the data of salvation nor that of the speculative-apologetic theology that turns subjective experiences and insights into its bases and criteria. His theology was a dialogue toward faith (cf. Rom. 1:16f.). It sought to put into words the promising address of God that had gone forth through Christ; it sought to evoke the human response of trusting acceptance toward God. Paul's statements, therefore, did not constitute a close-knit theoretical framework into which all reality could be ordered and contained.

---

[35]"Vom Verstehen des Neuen Testaments," in *Gesammelte Studien zum Neuen Testament und seiner Umwelt* (1962), pp. 297f.

a) R. Bultmann tried to do justice to this insight by portraying Pauline theology from the vantage point of the human being who was being addressed. He wrote, "Every assertion about God is simultaneously an assertion about man and vice versa. For this reason and in this sense Paul's theology is, at the same time, anthropology." Marking the way for the recognition of its structure was for Bultmann also the insight that ". . . every assertion about Christ is also an assertion about man and vice versa; and Paul's christology is simultaneously soteriology. Therefore, Paul's theology can best be treated as his doctrine of man."[1] For this reason, Bultmann wrote about Pauline theology in the form of a kerygmatic anthropology. But although Bultmann—thanks to this orientation— was able to state some essential matters, nevertheless he was able to offer predominantly only the one side: the reflection of God's revelation in human existence. He offered too little about this revelation itself.

b) In contrast, W. G. Kümmel[2] and H. Ridderbos[3] began with the salvation-historical realm in which Paul did his thinking, i.e., in Rom. 4. For Paul himself this realm was, however—and such is also acknowledged by both—not the normative rational starting point. Paul came to the latter by way of an interpretation of the public ministry of Jesus in the light of scripture.

c) In light of the foregoing it appears to me consistent with the nature of things to develop Pauline theology from the reception of the tradition about Christ. This is also suggested through the arrangement of the book of Romans. Paul first characterized the gospel as the promised message about Jesus Christ (Rom. 1:2-4), pointed at the same time to its communication through his preaching (Rom. 1:1, 5-15; 15:14-33), and then extended it soteriologically (Rom. 1:16f. as the theme of the letter). Soteriology, however, achieved shape in history as a community of faith[4] and as new ethical conduct (cf. Rom. 12f.), and anticipated the consummation for all eyes to see (cf. Rom. 8:18-30). We shall now develop Pauline theology following this arrangement.

---

[1]*Theology* I, 191.
[2]*Theology*, pp. 141-150.
[3]*Paul* (1975), pp. 44-57.
[4]This was not developed explicitly in the Epistle to the Romans; yet cf. I Cor. 12:4-31.

Chapter II

JESUS CHRIST (CHRISTOLOGY)

§ 32: The Line of Questioning

O. Michel, "Der Christus des Paulus," *ZNW* 32 (1933), 6-31; O. Cullmann, *The Earliest Christian Confessions* (1949); N. A. Dahl, "Formgeschichtliche Beobachtungen zur Christusverkündigung in der Gemeindepredigt," in *Neutestamentliche Studien für R. Bultmann zu seinem 70. Geburtstag* (1954), pp. 3-9; 993-96; Cullmann, *Christology*, pp. 166-181; I. Herrmann, *Kyrios und Pneuma. Studien zur Christologie der paulinischen Hauptbriefe* (1961); H. Lietzmann, "Die Anfänge des Glaubensbekenntnisses," *Kleine Schriften* III (1962), 163-181; Schweizer, *Lordship*; Hahn, *Titles*, pp. 189-193; A. Vögtle, "Der Menschensohn," in *Studiorum Paulinorum Congressus Internationalis Catholicus 1961* I (1963), 199-218; W. Thüsing, *Per Christum in Deum* (1965); H. R. Balz, *Methodische Probleme der neutestamentlichen Christologie* (1967); E. Güttgemanns, "Christos in 1 Kor. 15,3b—Titel oder Eigenname?", *EvTheol* 28 (1968), 533-554; J. Jeremias, "Nochmals: Artikelloses *Christos* in I Kor. 15,3," *ZNW* 60 (1969), 214-19; F. Hahn, "Methodenprobleme einer Christologie des Neuen Testaments," *VF* 15 (1970), 3-41; C. Burger, *Jesus als Davidssohn* (1970); W. Grundmann, *chriō*, *TDNT* IX, 551-560.

1. THE HISTORY-OF-TRADITION STRUCTURE OF PAUL'S CHRISTOLOGICAL STATEMENTS

The Christology advanced by Paul was expressed in titles, formulas, and brief statements. Nowhere in his letters did he develop his Christology thematically. It was, to be sure, the starting point and criterion of his critical exchanges and written reflections but not their theme.

As we shall see in the following analysis, titles and formulas were taken over in general from ecclesiastical tradition. In fact, it was the Christology of the Hellenistic church that was being expressed in the layer of this tradition available to Paul. This Christology was clearly distinguishable from that of the Palestinian church. The latter appeared directly in Paul's writings through formulas that were appropriated, yet in the case of Rom. 1:3f., e.g., were altered through context or revision.

In contrast, the traditions of the Hellenistic church taken up by Paul did not simply repeat their Christology. They represented a selection for which Paul was responsible and that corresponded to certain streams of tradition. Already in the Pauline period traditions stood alongside them that made their appearance—in further development—in I Peter, in later layers of the synoptic tradition, in the book of Hebrews, and in the Johannine writings.

The Christology developed by Paul without making it a separate theme was therefore distinct because it rested on a critical selection of tradition that, in some respects, would not have come about without his work. Its distinction depended, moreover, on his interpretation with its differentiated and developed application.

One observes even apart from the necessary history-of-tradition differentiation that basic elements of the Christology of the Hellenistic church, distinguishable both generally and typically from those of the primitive church of Palestine, were reflected in the traditions appropriated by Paul.

2. ALTERATIONS IN COMPARISON TO THE PRIMITIVE CHURCH OF PALESTINE

a) Titles. If one views Paul here as representative, christological titles were used in the Hellenistic church in a fundamentally different manner than in the Palestinian church.

The dominant title of the synoptic tradition, i.e., "Son of man," was probably known to Paul; in I Cor. 15:28 he interpreted Christ in light of Ps. 8, which spoke of the Son of man, although he did not include this term in his quotation. It could be that he was prompted to interpret Christ as the second Adam (§35,6c) through this designation. In the rest of the New Testament epistolary literature as well and correspondingly in the community language of the Hellenistic church the designation "Son of man" was not in use because it was not at all comprehensible to Hellenistic peoples. It had its place in the Gospel tradition (§18) and appeared outside this context only isolatedly in the portrayal of apocalyptic visions (Acts 7:55f.; Rev. 1:13).

Also to be found neither in Paul nor in the other New Testament epistles was the designation "son of David" (Mk. 12:35-37 par.; cf. §17,3), used only with reserve even in the Palestinian church. The tradition about the Davidic lineage of Jesus was the only one retained by Paul (Rom. 1:3f.) and thereafter (II Tim. 2:8; Rev. 5:5; 22:16).

Of the four christological titles from the language of the Palestinian community the unusual term "servant of God" was not used anywhere by Paul. The dominant title "the Christ" had become a name, but "Son of God" and "Lord" took on new conceptual associations and became the decisive vehicles of christological address.

b) Content. How the substantive structure of these statements was altered shows up, e.g., in the context of the Palestinian formula in Rom. 1:3f. Paul placed the prepositional phrase "concerning his Son" before the formula and thereby turned the birth from the lineage of David into the incarnation of the preexistent Son. He added at the end: "Jesus Christ our Lord." The One who was exalted to "Son of God in power" was now called "Jesus Christ" and designated "our Lord."

Did these alterations signify a linguistic accommodation to the changed environment and a substantive expansion for a new realm of inquiry or the replacement of one interpretation of Jesus' life and ministry by another? According to H. Braun this alteration was in fact a substantive break with previous interpretation so that Christology would be a variable quantity and only anthropology would remain the constant factor of the New Testament.[1] In light of this key question a thorough examination of the new titles and statements becomes imperative.

3. THE NAME "JESUS CHRIST"

a) "Christ" as name. No other proper noun even approached the frequency of usage by Paul of "Christos"; it occurred in his writings nearly four hundred times. He was aware that "Christos" in its root meaning was a Jewish honorific designation and therefore he combined the word with the verb *chriō* as, e.g., in II Cor. 1:21. But for him as for the entire Hellenistic church it was no longer a Jewish or a primitive Christian title but a personal name.

That "Christos" was used by Paul ordinarily as a personal name was not dependent upon the presence of the definite article. The word occurred for the most part without the article, but it is found sometimes with the article as well. In Greek as in Hebrew, however, the word also stood as a title without the article[2] and, on the other hand, personal names were also linked with the article in both languages (cf. Mk. 15:43ff.; Lk. 23:35). Paul used "Christos" syntactically in such a way, however, that in all instances it can and should be translated as a name.[3]

This does not mean that a title that was foreign to the Hellenistic church simply had been hardened into a surname. It had become an epithet with the capacity to speak. The name Jesus was common, the epithet "Christos" was unique. The latter retained a type of titular emphasis and therefore was never combined directly with the title "Kyrios"; from time to time the name Jesus was placed between them: "our Lord Jesus Christ." Hellenistic Christians heard this

---

[1] "The Meaning of New Testament Christology," in *God and Christ: Existence and Province* (ed. R. W. Funk [1968]), pp. 95ff., 115, 118f.

[2] Jn. 4:25: "I know that Messiah [*Messias*] is coming (he who is called Christ [*ho legomenos Christos*])"; to what extent the word without the definite article was found in pre-Christian–Jewish linguistic usage has been discussed primarily in the debate about the Aramaic source for I Cor. 15:3-5 (cf. W. Grundmann, *TDNT* IX, 541 n. 319).

[3] Individual supporting references in W. Grundmann, *TDNT* IX, 541-43.

threefold sound nearly like that of "Imperator Caesar Augustus." In accord with this special name the non-Christian members of their environment called them "Christians" (Acts 11:26; I Pet. 4:16).

b) The use of the names. Because the names were capable of saying something they were purposely recast in corresponding statements. "Jesus" became for the most part the earthly One, only occasionally the resurrected One and the coming One (I Thess. 1:10; II Cor. 4:5). "Christ" alone was connected by Paul, and even earlier in the appropriated formulaic tradition,[4] most often with the One who died and was raised. The twofold name "Jesus Christ" reflecting a preference referred to the exalted One and the One who would appear at the *parousia* (e.g., Rom. 1:4, 6; 6:3; I Cor. 1:8). The combinations "our Lord Jesus Christ" (Rom. 15:30; I Cor. 1:2; II Cor. 1:3; Gal. 6:14, 18) or "Jesus Christ, our Lord" (Rom. 5:21; 6:23; 7:25; 8:39; I Cor. 1:9; 15:31) served the end of celebrative emphasis, as, e.g., at the beginning or end of the epistles.

While the title "Christ" became a name capable of speaking so meaningfully and thus was used predominantly, the designations "Son of God" and "Lord" took on new dimensions. Within a new horizon of understanding the one referred to Jesus' relationship in a heavenly direction and the other to that in an earthly one.

§33. The Son of God

On 1-3: Cullmann, *Christology*, pp. 270-305; Hahn, *Titles*, pp. 279-333; M. Hengel, *The Son of God: The Origin of Christology and the History of Jewish-Hellenistic Religion* (1976); E. Schweizer, *huios*, TDNT VIII, 363-392. On 4: E. Schweizer, "Zur Herkunft der Präexistenzvorstellung bei Paulus," in Schweizer, *Neotestamentica* (1963), pp. 105-09. On 5: E. Lohmeyer, *Kyrios Jesus. Eine Untersuchung zu Phil 2,5-11* (*SAH*, 1927/28, 4. Abh., 1928; repr. 1961); D. Georgi, "Der vorpaulinische Hymnus Phil 2,6-11," in *Zeit und Geschichte. Dankesgabe an R. Bultmann zum 80. Geburtstag* (1964), pp. 263-293; E. Käsemann, "A Critical Analysis of Philippians 2:5-11," in *God and Christ: Existence and Province* (ed. R. W. Funk [1968]), pp. 45-88; G. Strecker, "Redaktion und Tradition im Christushymnus Phil 2,6-11," *ZNW* 55 (1964), 63-78; G. Schille, *Frühchristliche Hymnen* (1965); J. Jeremias, "Zur Gedankenführung in den paulinischen Briefen," in Jeremias, *Abba* (1966), pp. 269-276; R. Deichgräber, *Gotteshymnus und Christushymnus in der frühen Christenheit. Untersuchungen zu Form, Sprache und Stil der frühchristlichen Hymnen* (1967); R. P. Martin, *Carmen Christi. Philippians ii. 5-11 in Recent Interpretation and in the Setting of Early Christian Worship* (1967); K. Wengst, *Christologische Formeln und Lieder des Urchristentums* (1967; 1973[2]); C.-H. Hunzinger, "Zur Struktur der Christus-Hymnen in Phil 2 und 1. Petr 3," in *Der Ruf Jesu und die Antwort der Gemeinde, Festschrift für J. Jeremias* (ed. E. Lohse [1970]), pp. 142-156; M. Rese, "Formeln und Lieder im Neuen Testament. Einige notwendige Anmerkungen," *VF* 15 (1970), 75-95; J. T. Sanders, *The New Testament Christological Hymns: Their Historical and Religious Background* (1971). On 6: C. Maurer, "Die Begründung der Herrschaft Christi über die Mächte nach Kolosser 1,15-20," *Wort und Dienst* NF (1955), 79-93; J. M. Robinson, "A Formal Analysis of Colossians 1,15-20," *JBL* 76 (1957), 270-287; E. Käsemann, "A Primitive Christian Baptismal Liturgy," in Käsemann, *Essays on New*

---

[4]Cf. Kramer, *Christ*, pp. 38ff.

Testament Themes (1964), pp. 149-168; H. J. Gabathuler, *Jesus Christus. Haupt der Kirche—Haupt der Welt. Der Christushymnus Kolosser 1,15-20 in der theologischen Forschung der letzten 130 Jahre* (1965; Lit.!); N. Kehl, *Der Christushymnus im Kolosserbrief. Eine motivgeschichtliche Untersuchung zu Kol 1,12-20* (1967); E. Lohse, *Colossians* (Hermeneia, 1971), pp. 41-61; T. Ahrens, *Die ökumenische Diskussion kosmischer Christologie seit 1961* (Diss. Hamburg, 1969); R. Schnackenburg, "Die Aufnahme des Christushymnus durch den Verfasser des Kolosserbriefes," in *Evangelisch-katholischer Kommentar. Vorarbeiten* I (1969), 33-50; E. Schweizer, "Kolosser 1,15-20," ibid., pp. 7-31.

1. THE HELLENISTIC SCOPE OF UNDERSTANDING

a) Hellenistic concepts of the Son of God. Hellenistic peoples linked other concepts with the designation "Son of God" than Jewish ones. In Old Testament/Jewish tradition the designation called up thoughts about covenant relationships of various kinds to God. It was used in this sense during the growth of the synoptic tradition and within the confession of the Palestinian church as it was also applied to Jesus (§18,9). For Hellenistic thought, however, the designation pointed largely no longer to membership within a family of deities but rather to the manifestation of the divine; consequently, it was applied to people. It was thus possible for the divine to manifest itself in the successful political wisdom and the ability to act of a ruler like Augustus and in the practical philosophical guidance and the miraculous power of an itinerant philosopher like Apollonius of Tyana. Through such people, as also through heroes, the divine manifested itself for the healing of the world; they represented in the phenomenology of religion the *theios anēr* type, the divine man. In the ancient world these types bore—with qualifications, of course—the title "sons of God."[1] An entirely different manifestation of the divine was represented by the Gnostic revealer of the Hermetic Tractates dating from the period about A.D. 100. The revealer called upon the souls of light, who had become preoccupied with the world, to remember their divine origin in order that he might lead them back to the world above but not in order to improve this world. Simon Magus, who called himself "that power of God which is called Great" (Acts 8:10), possibly a precursor of gnosticism, was, according to later accounts,[2] supposed to have said about himself, "I am God (or a son of God, or a divine Spirit)."[3]

b) The transference theory. According to Bultmann, Hellenistic Christians ascribed to Jesus "divinity" and "divine nature" on the basis of their rational presuppositions by passing on the designation "Son of God." Hence, "by virtue of which [this ascription] he is differentiated from the human sphere" and "filled with divine 'power.' "[4]

In Bultmann's opinion, the major types of Hellenistic concepts for "Son of God" can each be found in the New Testament in transference to Jesus. (1) In

[1]P. Wülfing von Martitz, *TDNT* VIII, 340; thus, e.g., Augustus (ibid., 337), but hardly one of the philosophers, and basically not Apollonius of Tyana either (ibid., 339).

[2]Origen *C. Cels.* 7. 9 (cf. H. Chadwick, p. 402).

[3]Additional material: Wülfing von Martitz, op. cit. (n. 1), 339.

[4]*Theology* I, 128f.

the synoptic tradition, above all in Mark, Jesus was represented as the Son of God in the sense of a *theios anēr* "who reveals his divine power and authority through his miracles."[5] (2) Found in the pre-Pauline christological hymn of Phil. 2:6-11 and in similar texts was a concept of the Son similar to that found in the myths of the Near Eastern son-deities Osiris, Adonis, and Attis, who were honored above all in the mystery cults. Here the son-deity suffered the fate of a human death and emerged from it as the deliverer and *kyrios* of those who honored him. (3) Taking a place alongside these soteriological types was a cosmological. The divine son of the Gnostic redeemer myth was the agent of emanation in primeval time; during the course of things the divine sank progressively deeper into the material world and became entrapped in it. By means of a subsequent descent of the son the souls of light imprisoned in the cosmos were set free and led back into the higher world. As Bultmann conceded, this myth was not explicitly portrayed in any pre-Pauline text, but Hellenistic Christianity derived the concept from it that the Son was preexistent, that he was the "image of God," the agent of creation, and that through his descent and ascent he became the redeemer who drew the redeemed as his body after him.

This analysis of Bultmann has been advanced and corrected in the meantime by H. Koester,[6] whose approach is quite similar methodologically. Here the *theios anēr* Christology has been extended broadly, but the derivation from the Gnostic redeemer myth through that of the Jewish Sophia and of the mystery religion types has been replaced by that of the Easter kerygma. This is an indication that the history-of-religion analyses out of which Bultmann developed these three types from the phenomenology of religion have been revised now to a considerable extent by historical research. The redeemer myth from which Bultmann derived the most important statements of Hellenistic Christology in Paul cannot be shown to have existed in a pre-Christian form.[7] While knowledge of this fact has had considerable impact, awareness must yet increase that making a standard of the *theios anēr* by this school of research also needs to be critically reviewed and in terms of history-of-religion comparison to be differentiated and made more precise.[8] Moreover, neither the "divine men" nor the dying and rising deities of the mystery religions were in essence "sons of God," even though they were on occasion, but far from always, designated as such.[9]

---

[5]Ibid., 130.

[6]Koester-Robinson, *Trajectories*, pp. 270ff.

[7]Thus C. Colpe, *Die Religionsgeschichtliche Schule* I (1961); regarding Gnostic research, cf. Goppelt, *Apostolic Times*, pp. 92-102; R. M. Wilson, *Gnosis and the New Testament* (1971); U. Bianchi, *The Origins of Gnosticism* (1967).

[8]The material was collected without the necessary critical stratification by L. Bieler, *Theios Anēr. Das Bild des "göttlichen Menschen" in Spätantike und Frühchristentum* I (1935); II (1936 [repr. 1967]). It was set forth in the line of Bultmann most recently by D. Georgi, *Die Gegner des Paulus im 2. Korintherbrief* (1964), and appropriated in this sense by H. Koester. In critique, cf. Wülfing von Martitz, op. cit. (n. 1), 339 n. 27; M. Hengel, *The Son of God* (1976), pp. 31f.

[9]A good overview of the myths about the dying and rising of the gods is found in G. Wagner, *Pauline Baptism and the pagan mysteries* (1967).

c) Fundamental historical and substantive objections to the transference theory. In addition to individual corrections based on history-of-religion research the clarification of early Hellenistic Christology by recourse to the transference theory must face two fundamental objections.

1) The types of son-of-God concepts referred to here from Hellenistic backgrounds and, moreover, the types of Christology emerging by transference from them were based on abstractions from the phenomenology of religion. These abstractions differentiated too little among the data available from the history of religion. A historical analysis of Hellenistic Christology will show that what took place was not simply the transference of mythical schemata to Jesus, but rather the collective influence of various factors and motifs upon the shaping of these christological concepts. The theory of transference developed on the premises of the history-of-religion school when critiqued methodologically turns out to be an oversimplification.

2) What the theory of transference reconstructed also falls short of the key substantive starting point. Hellenistic Christians did not think about divine sonship any longer in terms of Hellenistic concepts about deity but in terms of the God of the Old Testament. They had turned away from the former and come to the latter; that was the central content of their conversion (1 Thess. 1:9). The designation "Son of God" expressed for them precisely not "divine being," "divine origin," etc. The word "divine" that recurs in the discussion so often was never applied to Jesus by Paul. In fact, it occurred only twice in the whole New Testament, and that without a christological connection (Acts 17:29; II Pet. 1:3f.). Even for Hellenistic Christians the title "Son of God" placed Jesus in a special relationship to the God of the Old Testament. He was not the depth of the cosmos but the personal One standing in relationship to all that existed in the world. The theory of transference thus overlooked the key substantive question for the emergence of Hellenistic Christology: How could Jesus, who had died but a few years earlier, be placed in connection with the God of the Old Testament in the way expressed by the title "Son of God" in the tradition appropriated by Paul from the Hellenistic church?

2. THE DESIGNATION "SON OF GOD": OVERVIEW OF USAGE

a) Word usage. Even the usage of the word is instructive. The title "Son of God" and the absolute use of "the Son" are found in Paul's writings only once each (II Cor. 1:19; cf. Eph. 4:13; and I Cor. 15:28); otherwise, "Son" was used regularly with the possessive pronoun "his Son" because God was the subject of the remarks. The expression was used, therefore, not generally as a traditional title, but in accord with its specific content in order to express Jesus' relationship to God. Son (of God) "in Pauline usage indicates the very close relationship between the one who brought salvation and God himself."[10]

---

[10]Kramer, *Christ*, p. 185.

b) Occurrence. In all, Paul employed the designation fifteen times. He used it relatively less frequently than the authors of the Epistle to the Hebrews and the Gospel of John. In terms of the history of tradition, six of Paul's usages certainly belonged to formulas and expressions that had been passed on to him (Rom. 1:4; 8:3, 32; Gal. 2:20; 4:4f.; I Thess. 1:10). Nine of them were the apostle's own formulations (Rom. 1:3, 9; 5:10; 8:29; I Cor. 1:9; 15:28; II Cor. 1:19; Gal. 1:16; 4:6).[11]

With the exception of the exaltation formula coming from the Palestinian church in Rom. 1:3b, 4, the traditional statements were represented by a commissioning formula (Rom. 8:3), two consecration formulas (Rom. 8:32; Gal. 2:20), and a *parousia* formula (I Thess. 1:9b, 10). The Pauline formulations were not restricted to specific areas of comment.

When one observes the content of the statements as a whole a considerable amount of development becomes evident between the confession of the Palestinian church in Rom. 1:3f. and Paul.

3. THE INCEPTION OF THE SON'S ACTIVITY

a) According to the most ancient confession of the Palestinian church Jesus was "designated Son of God in power" through the resurrection or exaltation (Rom. 1:3f.; §26,4). What was he before this? Was he the Son of God in weakness? The confession intended to express the summons to an activity and not the nature of his being.

b) The statement of the Palestinian Christology of exaltation regarding his activity as Son was developed on the one hand with an eye toward his historical prominence, and on the other toward his relationship to the cosmos.

1) According to a very early layer of the synoptic tradition Jesus was called at the baptism of John to serve as "the beloved (= only) Son" (Mk. 1:10f.; §4,3). Thus his earthly ministry was carried out under this heading.

In the birth and early years narratives of Matthew and Luke the question was raised about the historical origin of his life. The reply there was that Jesus' life in terms of its roots was uniquely determined by God's Spirit. Hence, according to Lk. 1:35 he was to be called "Son of God" from his birth. This was the case, moreover, not because his birth out of the Spirit corresponded to mythological conception through a deity (cf. §3,2).

Both of these perspectives are missing from the writings of Paul, even though the first one certainly and probably the second as well were already represented in traditions of the Palestinian church during Paul's lifetime. They simply belonged to the frame of reference of the Gospel tradition.

2) Paul appropriated, in contrast, what was concluded on the basis of the exaltation Christology in the confession of the Hellenistic church: Jesus was the incarnation of the preexistent Son! How could one designate a person in this

---

[11]Made probable by ibid., p. 183.

manner hardly fifteen years after his end? How did the preexistence Christology emerge?

4. THE EMERGENCE OF THE PREEXISTENCE AFFIRMATION

a) The substantive motif. If Christology came about merely by the transference of mythical schemata to Jesus—as the history-of-religion school assumed—then it is difficult to understand why a preexistence of the Son of man was not already expressed in the synoptic tradition. For, according to Jewish apocalyptic, the Son of man was hidden from time eternal at the throne of the Most High.[12] Moreover, it would have been possible in Mt. 11:25f. and similar locations to assimilate the interpretation of Jesus as the representative of wisdom and the concept of the preexistence of wisdom (Prov. 8:22ff.; Sir. 24:3ff.). The preexistence Christology, however, was first developed in the hour when it was imperative for the sake of the kerygma and of faith. That was when the gospel encountered Hellenistic people. Palestinian-Jewish people experienced the world as history and therefore they understood Jesus as the One who brought history to its eschatological completion. For Hellenistic people, however, the world was the cosmos, the world edifice ruled by principalities and powers. All those statements about Jesus that were to have meaning for the existence of these Hellenistic people had thus to be connected to the cosmos as well. The emergence of the preexistence affirmation can be understood substantively on the basis of this motivation. A recognition of faith was developed that linked Jesus' coming in accord with his essence to the cosmos.

b) The linguistic vehicles. In order to bring this recognition of faith to expression various linguistic and conceptual vehicles were available in Hellenistic Judaism. Here personified wisdom had been connected with the cosmos. Close points of contact show that Hellenistic Christianity made use of this concept.[13] Gal. 4:4 spoke of the sending of the Son like Wis. Sol. 9:10 spoke of that of wisdom: "Send her forth out of the holy heavens, and from the throne of thy glory bid her come!" (= Charles, I, 550). Just as in Gal. 4:6 there followed in Wis. Sol. 9:17 a parallel statement about the sending of the Spirit. Only in these two places did Paul use the verb *exapostellō* for "send," the verb that was also used in the wisdom literature. This coming into the world led, however, strictly to a dwelling of wisdom in the midst of Israel in the shape of the Torah (Sir. 24:11) or to the inspiring of prophetic people. "And from generation to generation passing into holy souls She maketh them friends of God and prophets" (Wis. Sol. 7:27 = Charles, I, 547). Its coming did not lead, however, to an incarnation.

In Paul and the wisdom literature an agency of creation was affirmed con-

---

[12]I Enoch 39:6; 40:5; 48:3, 6; 62:7; IV Ezra 13:20, 52.

[13]Supporting references in E. Schweizer, *Neotestamentica*, pp. 106-111 and *TDNT* VIII, 375f.; cf. R. G. Hamerton-Kelly, *Preexistence, Wisdom and the Son of Man. A Study of the Idea of Preexistence in the New Testament* (1972).

cerning the preexistence that preceded the coming into the world. Thus it was stated concerning Christ in I Cor. 8:6, etc. and concerning wisdom in Prov. 3:19; 8:22-31; Wis. Sol. 9:1f., 9; Sir. 24:3; Philo, *Det. Pot. Ins.* 54 and passim.

With the aid of these linguistic vehicles the following observations about preexistence were drawn together in keeping with the above-mentioned substantive motif.

5. THE SENDING AND INCARNATION OF THE PREEXISTENT SON

a) Formulas. In Gal. 4:4f. and Rom. 8:3 we find the statement: "God sent his Son." This statement had the character of a formula since it recurred independent of Paul in Jn. 3:(16), 17; I Jn. 4:9. The synoptic tradition had spoken of Jesus' coming in the *ēlthon*-sayings (Mk. 2:17 par.; Lk. 19:10) and in doing so had meant only his commissioning by God. This coming now had to be characterized in cosmic coordinates as a "coming" from the beyond that stands over against everything known as world. And its goal could not be merely a historical commission but only the incarnation. "God sent forth his Son, born of woman, born under the law" (Gal. 4:4). He was born as a human being and, like all others, was subject to the Law. Yet he distinguished himself from all others. He was sent "in the likeness of sinful flesh" (Rom. 8:3f.). That he became "flesh" (Jn. 1:14) was something that Paul too could say, but not "sinful flesh." He belonged to the flesh (Rom. 9:5; cf. II Cor. 5:16), but he did not allow himself to be determined by it. He did not follow "the mind of the flesh," sin (Rom. 8:5-7). This distinction from ordinary human existence was suggested here by means of the distancing "likeness." It was clarified further in Phil. 2:6-11.

b) Hymns. The Christ-hymn in Phil. 2:6-11 did not portray the coming of Christ as God's sending but as the divestment of the preexistent One. The presence of a large number of expressions not typical for Paul suggests that he appropriated the entire hymn or at least its essential elements from tradition and altered its shape only in minor ways.

In v. 5 the hymn was introduced by the preface: "Have this mind among yourselves, which is yours in Christ Jesus." Four double lines in *parallelismus membrorum* constituted the first of the two strophes.[14]

> I   (6)   who, though he was in the form of God,
>   did not count equality with God a thing to be grasped,
>   (7)   but emptied himself,
>   taking the form of a servant,
>   being born in the likeness of men.
>   And being found in human form
>   (8)[15]   he humbled himself
>   and became obedient unto death (even death on a cross).

---

[14]Thus Deichgräber, op. cit. (Lit., §33,5), p. 122.
[15]Versification of Greek text (Alsup).

II   (9)   Therefore God has highly exalted him
           and bestowed on him the name which is above every name,
    (10)   that at the name of Jesus every knee should bow,
           in heaven and on earth and under the earth,
    (11)   and every tongue confess that Jesus Christ is Lord,
           to the glory of God the Father.

This hymn took as its point of departure the Old Testament/Jewish concept of humiliation and exaltation of the righteous One, just as did the exaltation Christology of the Palestinian church and a primary line of synoptic interpretation of Jesus' passion (§21,2c).[16] The identifying mark of the humiliated righteous One was the obedience that in certain circumstances would bear final witness in his martyrdom. This development was set in cosmic dimensions here, resulting in two declarations.

(1) According to v. 7 the preexistent Son came in "the likeness of men" and was "found in human form," i.e., Jesus was truly human. Yet, in contrast to all others, he was "obedient." Whereas he was seen in the synoptic tradition as the righteous One par excellence, here he was the obedient One. This absolute obedience was not a moral quality but the realization of the Father's sending (Gal. 2:20). He was not, therefore, "pure human being"—as has often been explained following Bultmann[17]—so that this Christology would exclude a portrayal of Jesus along the lines of our Gospels.[18]

(2) This unique and yet unlimited human existence was not humiliation on the basis of historical developments—as was the case for the synoptic Gospels—but was already such from the beginning. "He humbled himself" (v. 8a), "he emptied himself" and became a human being (v. 7a). The subject of these statements was the preexistent Son even if the title as such does not appear here. The preexistent One exchanged the *morphē* of God for that of man. *Morphē* did not mean here the outward form alone, but also the mode of existence, the position. What was given him he did not use in the manner of flesh to his advantage but placed it at the disposal of God's sending. He "emptied" himself, i.e., divested himself of God's mode of existence, and he "humbled himself," i.e., took on "the servant's" mode of existence (v. 7b). He became a "servant" not like the Old Testament righteous One as the instrument of God; he became such because he made himself subject to the forces that held sway in the cosmos.

The hymn left unanswered the question that interests us, namely, how this subject of the preexistent One who emptied himself was related to the subject of the obedient One.

With reference to Jesus these statements about the kenosis of the Son like those about the sending of the Father made it clear that Jesus was not a human being who distinguished himself through religious-moral achievements. He came

---

[16]Thus, correctly, also Schweizer, *Lordship*, pp. 61-63.

[17]*Theology* I, §§4 and 12.

[18]Thus Conzelmann, *Theology*, p. 80 (". . . because the actions of the Incarnate One have no role in it").

rather from the beyond that stood over against all human existence. He became "poor" for our sakes (II Cor. 8:9). On the other hand, he was also not a half-god, but with respect to his existence he was fully human; yet he was the One who lived in accord with his destiny, the obedient One (cf. Mk. 10:45).

As the second strophe developed, this origin of Jesus was confirmed by his exaltation. That this affirmation about his origin in preexistence had existential and not speculative character becomes quite evident through the statements about preexistence itself.

6. THE PREEXISTENT ONE AS THE AGENT OF CREATION

a) *Formulas.* In I Cor. 8:6 a two-part confessional formula can be distinguished from the context.

> One God, the Father,
>   from whom are all things, and for whom we exist,
> And one Lord Jesus Christ,
>   through whom are all things and through whom we exist.[19]

When Hellenistic Christians asked within the frame of reference of their cosmology about the relationship of Jesus to God and the world they were told that God did not represent or reside in the superior part of the cosmos but stood in relationship to it as the Creator (Rom. 4:17; 11:36; II Cor. 4:6). For Hellenistic people that notion was a foreign concept coming from the Old Testament.[20] That Jesus did not belong to the side of that which was created but to that of the Creator had already become clear when in God's place the earthly One announced the new commandment and in his place received sinners. For Old Testament thought, however, God was not the Highest Being but Will in purposeful action. For this reason, in the realm of the preexistence concept to belong to him could only be expressed as taking part in his creative activity, i.e., as agency in creation. The structure of this concept becomes transparent in the affirmations about the end-time lordship of God through the exalted One (§34,2c). Creation through the preexistent One corresponded to the new creation through him: "through whom we exist" (v. 6b; cf. II Cor. 5:17; Gal. 6:15).

b) *Hymns.* These statements were shaped and enlarged upon at the time a pre-Gnostic movement in the community of Colossae was instating Christ in the

---

[19]Regarding the structure of this formula, cf. §34,2b.

[20]Instructive is the differentiation between *dēmiourgos* and *ktistēs* in Philo *Som.* I:76: "And above all, as the sun when it rises makes visible objects which had been hidden, so God when he gave birth to all things, not only brought them into sight, but also made *(epoiēsen)* things which before were not, not just handling material as an artificer *(dēmiourgos)*, but being Himself its creator *(ktistēs)*" (= LCL, *Philo*, V, 337). *Dēmiourgos*, the customary Greek designation for the Creator of the of the world, was in everyday speech the craftsman who fashioned the material furnished him; *ktistēs*, however, was, e.g., the ruler through whose command a city would be built. The LXX used the latter and not the former to reproduce the Old Testament statements about God as Creator; his will articulated in speech summoned everything into existence and gave it shape (W. Foerster, *TDNT* III, 1023-28).

cosmos as an intermediate being beneath the world powers. Countering this move, the Christ hymn in Col. 1:15-20 confessed:

I. 15 He is the image of the invisible God,
        the first-born of all creation;
    16 for in him all things were created,
        in heaven and on earth,
        visible and invisible,
        whether thrones or dominions or principalities or authorities—
        all things were created through him and for him.
    17 He is before all things,
        and in him all things hold together.
    18 He is the head of the body, the church;[21]

II.   he is the beginning,
        the first-born from the dead,
        that in everything he might be pre-eminent.
    19 For in him all the fulness of God was pleased to dwell,
    20 and through him to reconcile to himself all things,
        whether on earth or in heaven,
        making peace by the blood of his cross.

Being the agent of creation meant accordingly not merely participation in an event at the beginning but an enduring relationship to the cosmos. He was the "first-born of all creation" (v. 15b) not because he was the first one to be created and as such would introduce the succession of that which was created, but because he "is before all things" (v. 17). He was "before all things," i.e., set above all things, and "in him all things hold together." For Greek thought that meant that he guaranteed the harmonious order; for biblical thought it meant that he upheld everything by giving shape and direction (Sir. 43:26; Heb. 1:3).

7. THE ENDURING SIGNIFICANCE OF THE AFFIRMATIONS ABOUT PREEXISTENCE

The history-of-tradition structure and the kerygmatic tendency of the preexistence concept provide the basis for recognizing what remains as theologically significant today in a changed situation for preaching.

Not only for us but also for the New Testament statements themselves the chronological prior-time and the spatial upper region are secondary vehicles of expression. Even for Paul they were intended more or less as visual aids since for him God stood above time and space and was not the resident of the top floor in the cosmos. Jesus had not been fit here into the ancient view of the

---

[21]*tēs ekklēsias* is considered by most scholars to be an interpretive vehicle that did not belong to the original hymn (in contrast, Kehl, op. cit. [Lit., §33,6], pp 41, 43, 93). Concerning the problem, cf. W. Pöhlmann, "Die hymnischen All-Prädikationen in Kol. 1,15-20," *ZNW* 64 (1973), 53-74 (55).

world but had been related to the understanding of the world held by Hellenistic people.

When the cosomological terminology is allowed to recede, quite in keeping with the intention of the New Testament, the preexistence affirmations gave expression to the concept of *extra nos*. That is to say, what had happened in Jesus came upon all that existed in the world from the absolute One standing in relationship to it. This was also emphasized by the position of existential interpretation,[22] but the preexistence affirmations intended to express still more. They intended to open up a new dimension of Jesus in comparison to the Palestinian tradition. They spoke of his relationship to the Creator and to creation. What was encountered in Jesus was not a divine principle in a pagan, purely secular world, but the Creator as the Redeemer. The God who opened up a new opportunity for life in Jesus was the same One to whom we have been related all along as Creator and Lord of the world, though of course in hiddenness.

And that means at the same time that God did not become encompassed altogether in the human being Jesus and in his ministry. In Jesus—as was formulated conclusively in Jn. 1:14—the Logos, the God who was revealing himself eschatologically, and not God himself, became a human being.

8. THE ESSENCE OF SONSHIP

For the Palestinian church Jesus was the Son because he stood in a unique covenant with God and was determined by the Spirit. For preexistence Christology he was the Son because his activity was one with God's on an essential level and therefore reflected the essence of God.

a) In II Cor. 4:6 Paul confessed that when he came to faith he had seen the glory *(doxa)* of God in the face of Christ. Whoever turned away from faith failed to see "the light of the gospel of the glory of Christ, who is the likeness *(eikōn)* of God" (II Cor. 4:4). According to II Cor. 4, "the likeness *(eikōn)* of God" was Christ as the crucified and exalted One; according to Col. 1:13 it was the "beloved Son" from preexistence on.

In Gen. 1:27 the original Adam had been characterized as the likeness of God, and Paul was able in I Cor. 11:7 to relate this reference to adamite man. In christological statements, however, he followed the application of this reference to the wisdom that was called the "image of his goodness" and the "effulgence *(apaugasma)* from everlasting light" in Wis. Sol. 7:26 (= Charles, I, 547). With the aid of this concept Paul expressed what he had come to recognize by faith in Christ, namely, the essence of God in his turning to the world. *"Eikōn"* was not merely the pattern but the shape of a reality itself (cf. Rom. 1:23).[23] Heb. 1:3 expressed it this way: the Son was "the effulgence of God's splendour and the stamp of God's very being" (NEB). According to Jn. 1:1-18 he was the Logos of God himself; whoever saw him, saw the Father (Jn. 14:9).

[22]Bultmann, *Theology* I, §33,6b; in contrast, Conzelmann, *Theology*, p. 80.
[23]H. Kleinknecht, *TDNT* II, 389.

b) Paul called Christ the "likeness of God" but not "God." The reference in Rom. 9:5, which has often been interpreted in this latter sense, was a doxology to God, not to Christ.[24] Christ was placed in relationship to God by Paul in a graduated arrangement: "all are yours; and you are Christ's; and Christ is God's" (I Cor. 3:22f.; cf. 11:3). Consequently he was able to expect of the consummation: "When all things are subjected to him, then the Son himself will also be subjected to him who put all things under him, that God may be everything to every one" (I Cor. 15:[23f.], 28). The end was not to be—as expressed by similar Hellenistic formulas[25]—the identity of God with the totality of the universe, but his exclusive dominion of salvation in which that dominion of the Son presently distinguishable from it would be encompassed.

c) In keeping with this way of relating things the activity of the two toward each other was described as a personal unity: God sent his Son and gave him over; the Son, however, was obedient, humbled himself (Phil. 2:6ff.), and gave himself over (Gal. 2:20). Only in this way did he become what he was for the community of faith. Preexistence Christology did not negate what the exaltation Christology of the Palestinian church had determined. According to Rom. 1:3f. the preexistent "Son" became "Son of God in power" only after the course of his earthly life and his exaltation. The exalted One was the Son in a different sense than the preexistent One; he had been "highly exalted" (Phil. 2:9), he had become the *kyrios* (Phil. 2:10f.).

§34. The *Kyrios*

Bousset, *Kyrios*, pp. 119-152; W. Foerster, *Kyrios, TDNT* III, 1081-1094; Cullmann, *Christology*, pp. 195-237; S. Schulz, "Maranatha und Kyrios Jesus," *ZNW* 53 (1962), 125-144; Hahn, *Titles*, pp. 68-128; Kramer, *Christ*, pp. 65-107; P. Vielhauer, *Aufsätze zum Neuen Testament* (1965), pp. 147-175; J. A. Fitzmyer, "The Semitic Background of the New Testament Kyrios-Title," in Fitzmyer, *A Wandering Aramean: Collected Aramaic Essays* (SBL Monograph Series 25, 1979), pp. 115-142 (cf. also his "New Testament *Kyrios* and *Maranatha* and Their Aramaic Background," in Fitzmyer, *To Advance the Gospel. New Testament Essays* [1981], pp. 218-235).

In the epistles of Paul the noun *kyrios* (Lord) was used almost exclusively as a designation for Christ, but occasionally, in connection with the LXX, as a designation for God. In light of formulaic expressions it can be seen that Paul appropriated here the primary designation for Christ of the Hellenistic church.

1. THE *KYRIOS*-CONFESSION OF THE HELLENISTIC CHURCH

a) The formula "Jesus is Lord" can be found three times in Paul's writings (Rom. 10:9; I Cor. 12:3; Phil. 2:11). It must have represented the basic confession of the Hellenistic church because the pre-Pauline hymn of Phil. 2:6-11 even

---

[24] E. Käsemann, *Romans*, at Rom. 9:5 (cf. pp. 257-260 for a presentation of the discussion!).
[25] Cf. E. Norden, *Agnostos Theos* (1971⁵), p. 241.

culminated with it in v. 11. Baptismal candidates made this confession at their baptism since Rom. 10:9 sounds like a baptismal promise: "because, if you confess with your lips that Jesus is Lord . . . you will be saved." At the same time it had its place in the worship service of the community. With the hymn of Phil. 2:10f. the community expressed the confession for the present on behalf of the entire creation until it would be voiced universally at the consummation. It also stood as the criterion by which spirits were distinguished (I Cor. 12:3).

Uttering this formula was designated expressly as the act of confessing *(homologein)* in Rom. 10:9a and in Phil. 2:11. According to Rom. 10:9 the faith that came to expression in this confession was the one that relied on the crucified One as its Lord because God had raised him from the dead and thereby exalted him to be the eschatological Ruler over the cosmos. In Phil. 2:9-11 the confession assumed the place of the acclamation in the Eastern coronation ceremony (§33,5). In the ancient world[1] an acclamation was the spontaneous cheer of the crowd in public assembly that expressed the recognition appropriate to the situation. This recognition had validity as a binding legal action and as such was duly recorded.[2] The confession would assume this character when all creatures recognize their Creator at the consummation. In the community of faith, however, the *kyrios*-confession was hardly expressed in this form—at least its binding character was never that of a collective legal action but rather that of immediate, personal faith. It is therefore inappropriate to designate the confession an acclamation of the community.[3]

b) It was for the sake of this confession then that Christians were referred to as those who "call upon him" (Rom. 10:12f. with reference to v. 9). With this confession Jesus was recognized by the name *kyrios* (Phil. 2:9-11); the one confessing him placed himself under his care and direction, i.e., "called upon him." The same thing happened in all those acts of worship in which "the Lord" was named in order that he might accomplish what he promised. In his name baptism purified (I Cor. 6:11), and "assembled in the name of our Lord Jesus" the community of faith was then in his "power" to withhold fellowship from the one living in incest (I Cor. 5:4, NEB). The "breaking of bread" of the primitive church became in the Hellenistic church "the Lord's Supper" *(kyriakon deipnon)* that was linked to the Lord in a variety of ways (I Cor. 11:20, 26; 10:21). Accordingly the Christians referred to themselves as "those who call on the name of the Lord" (cf. I Cor. 1:2; Acts 2:21; 9:14; 22:16).

c) Whereas both the formulas above functioned primarily in the context of the community's own life, the expression "one Lord, Jesus Christ" *(heis kyrios Iēsous Christos,* I Cor. 8:6) had its place in the community's missionary-apologetic confession.

d) One can certainly question whether or not the closing greeting of the

---

[1]E. Peterson, *Heis Theos* (1926), pp. 133f., 141-45.

[2]An acclamation, e.g., was the cry of the crowd in the theater of Ephesus: "Great is Artemis of the Ephesians!" (Acts 19:28).

[3]Contra Kramer, *Christ*, p. 65.

Pauline epistles, "the grace *(charis)* of the Lord Jesus be with you" (or "with your spirit" or "with you all") in contrast to the introductory greeting can be traced to a liturgical formula of the community. In I Cor. 16:23 the closing greeting linked up with liturgical pieces in vv. 20b and 22 and, independent of Paul, cropped up again in Rev. 22:21. Even if this reference to *charis* just as in the introductory formula should come from Paul, the expression "our Lord Jesus (Christ)" could very well be the traditional language of the community; it is also found in the opening part of the eucharistic *paradosis* (I Cor. 11:23). The same is true perhaps for the expression "and Father of our Lord Jesus Christ" (I Cor. 1:3; 11:31; Rom. 15:6) and the thanksgiving "through our Lord Jesus Christ" (or "through Jesus Christ our Lord," I Cor. 15:5-7; Rom. 7:25; Col. 3:17), less so for the characterization of the saving benefits through this expression (Rom. 5:1, 11, 21; I Thess. 5:9; cf. Rom. 15:30).

With all these formulas and expressions it was quite natural that the distinction between pre-Pauline tradition or the language of the community and Paul's own formulations would not be a hard and fast one. After all, such tradition and language to a large extent here as elsewhere were not developed without the apostle's influence.[4] With regard to the predicate as such that was quite clearly in use before and independent of Paul we must ask: How did it arise?

2. THE ORIGIN AND CONTENT OF THE HELLENISTIC *KYRIOS*-CONCEPT

In Paul's epistles the designation *kyrios* was connected to three *kyrios*-concepts outside the Hellenistic church. These then offer themselves in terms of the history of tradition as the three possible starting points for its emergence. Since W. Bousset's incisive study *Kyrios Christos* (1913) there has been considerable scholarly debate over which of these three concepts provided the primary or even the exclusive matrix for the *kyrios*-predicate of the Hellenistic church. One sought to clarify which one left its stamp with respect to content.

a) Found among the liturgical formulas in I Cor. 16:22 there appeared the expression *maranatha* of the Palestinian church (§26,5). The Hellenistic church appropriated the Aramaic form of this key summary of one's expectation regarding salvation just as it did regarding the word *'abba'*. Yet the confession that stood at the heart of its own *kyrios*-affirmations, "Jesus is Lord," distinguished itself markedly in form and content from this expression of the Palestinian church. The latter spoke of "our Lord" while the Hellenistic church referred to "the Lord" in an absolute sense. The one anticipated salvation as the consummation to history, the other understood salvation to be present with "the Lord." In view of these differences one must ask if it could have happened that the second formula grew out of the first on the basis of an altered preaching context. Since Bousset many have assumed that the *kyrios*-confession grew exclusively

---

[4]There is a thorough discussion of this formulaic tradition in ibid., pp. 65-107.

out of Hellenistic roots.[5] Yet bridges from the one to the other can also be found. The primitive church prayed to "its Lord" that he should come. In doing so it did not think only about the coming One but also about the exalted One since its prayer certainly had to have had an addressee and had to be heard. This tradition could have formed a starting point for confessing the exalted One as the Lord at a time when the community of faith in the Hellenistic world sought to answer how he related in the present to the cosmos. Just as much involved in the process, however, of shaping this confession were the *kyrios*-concepts of the Hellenistic environment. These then had a considerable effect on the confession's form and content.

b) Paul himself referred to the Hellenistic *kyrios*-concept when in I Cor. 8:6 (§33,6a) he introduced the confessional formula with the remark, ". . . as indeed there are many 'gods' and many 'lords.' . . ." Paul recognized that *ho kyrios* was a religious technical term, something that was never the case for the Aramaic *mare'* (in contrast to the Heb. *'adonai*).

For the ancient Near East of the 1st century B.C. *ho kyrios* became a standard designation for the salvation deities that were looked upon by their devotees exclusively as their patrons and commanders. The Egyptian deities Isis and Serapis, and Artemis of Ephesus, were very often addressed in this sense as lord.[6] Typical for the kind of piety were votive inscriptions like, "I thank the Lord Serapis that he delivered me when I was in danger upon the sea."[7] The devotee looked upon this deity as his personal lord-protector and guide; to this deity he directed his prayer requests and intercessions as well as his acclamations. He worshipped this one cultically at the sacred sites of pilgrimage, e.g., at the artemisium in Ephesus, at the serapeum in Alexandria, as well as in the worship communities that sprang up around such deities in Hellenistic cities. Such cultic groups frequently took on mystery-religion form too, but this was not necessarily

---

[5]W. Bousset created a basic awareness that the absolute use of "the Lord" was the specific Christ-predicate of the Hellenistic but not of the Palestinian community (*Kyrios*, pp. 121-138). "It is, in fact, the *Hellenistic* community in which this development so important for the history of religions took place, through which, out of the future Messiah Jesus, the present cult-hero as Kyrios of his community came into being" (p. 136). ". . . this peculiar doubling of the object of veneration in worship is conceivable only in an environment in which Old Testament monotheism no longer ruled unconditionally and with absolute security" (p. 147). In this way Bousset grasped pointedly the new situation of the Hellenistic church and its problematic. It was not at all necessary in addition for him to have the *maranatha*, as it were, first emerge as effect of the *kyrios*-cult in the linguistically mixed region of Syria (p. 129). The philological presuppositions of the predicate were clarified further most recently by Schulz (op. cit. [Lit., §34]). A purely phenomenological way of looking at things prevented him, however, from considering the substantive connections so that he concluded concerning the predicate: "A still narrower passageway did not exist that led from this apocalyptic-enthusiast Maranatha-theology . . . to the kyriology in which the present God became manifest . . . !" (143).

[6]W. Foerster, *TDNT* III, 1049-58; Schulz, op. cit. (n. 5), 127. It first became customary in the course of the 1st century after Christ under influence from Egypt to refer to rulers in the sense of this divine predicate as *kyrioi* as well. The first supporting reference from the Greek realm for this usage of the absolute *ho kyrios* applied to the Roman emperor was surely Acts 25:26. A description of Jesus' confrontation with this concept was first given in the post-Pauline passages (e.g., Rev. 19:16).

[7]*TDNT* III, 1051 (Gr.).

connected with the *kyrios*-concept. It should be remembered that the *kyrios* was not the Lord of history or of the cosmos; the *heimarmenē* or the *fatum* and not the *kyrios* ruled over what took place in the world and cosmos as a whole. The *kyrios* was merely able "to temper the storms of fate"[8] for his devotees because his was a relative power over nature and history. The following acclamation, which reminds one of I Cor. 8:6, was intended in this sense:

heis Zeus Serapis   [We have one Zeus, namely Serapis,
megalē Isis hē kyria   and great (i.e., divine) for us is Isis, the Lord.]

When one compares this formula to I Cor. 8:6 two things become clear. (1) This missionary confession was not simply designed apologetically to counter Hellenistic *heis-theos* formulas[9] but was also formulated in reliance upon their shape. (2) Similarly the designation of the exalted One as the *kyrios* was developed in apologetic reliance upon this *kyrios* concept. Nevertheless, in content the *heis* (one) and the *ho kyrios* (the Lord) in the Christ-confession went far beyond what was meant by these others. *Heis* in I Cor. 8:6 was not merely "the one" for us but the only one absolutely. In terms of substance it had a meaning like that of the fundamental confession of the Old Testament/Jewish community—Dt. 6:4—which stated (in the LXX form):

kyrios ho theos hēmōn   [The Lord, our God, is the one Lord (i.e., the only Lord).]
kyrios heis estin

In the same sense that God, according to I Cor. 8:6, was exclusively the One, so too the exalted One was the only Lord. The Christians did not go the direction of the *kyrios*-cults and grant that others call on another *kyrios*.

Thus the exalted One was presented to Hellenistic people through analogy with the *kyrioi* as the Lord who protected them against the powers of the cosmos and gave direction to their lives if they placed themselves under his care and called upon him in prayer. He was this not because he himself was one of the cosmic powers (Col. 2:8ff.), but because he established the eschatological *basileia*. The theology rejected by the Epistle to the Colossians had misunderstood this. The Lord not only replaced the salvation deities but also the *heimarmenē*! This became clear to Christians not alone on the basis of the concept of the Christ passed on to them, but also directly by way of the *kyrios*-designation. The notion that he replaced both was suggested by the *maranatha*-expression, and was—as we shall see—communicated by way of a third association.

c) In the *kyrios*-formulas appropriated by Paul in Phil. 2:9-11 as in I Cor. 12:3, and in his own formulations as well, the LXX affirmations about the *kyrios*, i.e., Yahweh, already were being applied to the exalted One as the *kyrios*.

The path for such an application had been prepared philologically. In the context of Greek-speaking Judaism the Old Testament name for God, Yahweh, had already been translated with the name *kyrios*, the Near Eastern designation

---

[8]Apuleius *Metamorphoses* 11.25.2 (regarding Isis: "Thou art she that puttest away all storms and dangers from men's life by stretching forth Thy right hand . . ." [LCL, *The Golden Ass*, p. 583]).
[9]Cf. n. 1.

for the Deity. Used in the LXX was the Tetragrammaton (YHWH)—as became clear in recent study—but when read aloud *ho kyrios* (the Lord) was pronounced.[10]

From the beginning, whenever quotations from the LXX were employed in the New Testament, the Greek form was retained consistently in writing. Since the exalted One was also characterized as the *kyrios* in the Hellenistic church, the application to him of Old Testament affirmations about the *kyrios*, i.e., Yahweh, suggested itself linguistically and was able, moreover, to influence the shape of this predicate.

Yet this application process did not take place at important junctures without selection. It was accomplished with a surprisingly high degree of concern for content. Preferred for application to the exalted One were affirmations about Yahweh's eschatological activity. This can be seen by turning to two key formulas that Paul already found in use as tradition.

The formula "to call upon the name of the Lord" made use of Joel 3:5, as Rom. 10:13 expressly pointed out. In Joel 3:5 eschatological deliverance on the Day of Yahweh was promised to the one who called upon his name. This promise now reached fulfillment by calling upon the exalted One.

Still more important was the other example. The second strophe of the Christ-hymn (cf. §33,5) appropriated several expressions from Second Isa. 45:23 (shown below in italics):

> (9) Therefore God has highly exalted him
>   and bestowed on him the name which is above every name,
> (10) that at the name of Jesus *every knee should bow*,
>   in heaven and on earth and under the earth,
> (11) *and every tongue confess* that Jesus Christ is Lord,
>   to the glory of God the Father.

This strophe had been formulated in conformity with the coronation ceremony of the ancient Orient; such was also appropriated in I Tim. 3:16; Heb. 1:3-13; Rev. 5:6-14 (hardly, however, in Mt. 28:19f.). The coronation would begin, as v. 9 would have it, with the presentation of the new ruler and the proclamation of his name. The name by which the new position was assigned was called here *kyrios*. It was linked to the human name "Jesus" that represented the basis and presupposition for the exaltation. For this reason, the cosmic proskynesis (obeisance) in v. 10 was carried out with respect to the naming of the name. This proskynesis and the acclamation, following in v. 11, belonged together. In this way the *kyrios* was to be recognized with legally binding character in the consummation by the entire creation. This had not yet happened, however, because of the powers of the cosmos. In the hymn here as in Rev. 5:13 it had been announced in the kerygmatic indicative what would happen finally in history at the end, and what nevertheless had already been established at the exaltation of the obedient One. Beforehand then the community of faith confessed by means of this hymn and in a representative way for creation that Jesus was the *kyrios*.

---

[10]Schulz, op. cit. (n. 5), 128-134.

This content of the designation was qualified here by a deliberate link to Isa. 45:23 (LXX). The link was not actually restricted to this one verse but had the whole passage in mind from which the verse was taken. What the whole passage had to say was directly in conformity with the link's intention. This key passage (Isa. 45:18-25) in the theology of Second Isaiah expressed the fundamental question for every theology concerning itself with history. Its question was: How can God be called the Lord of history? It answered by saying that there was a distinction between God's being Lord in the present and his becoming Lord in the *eschaton*. At the beginning of the passage there was a confession made in spite of what appeared on the surface that as the Creator Yahweh was already the Lord of history. "For thus says the Lord, who created the heavens (he is God!), who formed the earth and made it (he established it . . .)" (v. 18, LXX). Only when the time of salvation came would he require that those from among the nations fleeing the catastrophe recognize him as their God. "Turn to me and be saved, all the ends of the earth! . . . 'To me every knee shall bow, every tongue shall swear.' Only in the Lord, it shall be said of me, are righteousness and strength . . ." (vv. 22ff.). When the Christ-hymn appropriated these expressions in spontaneous association it wished to say that this end-time, universal recognition of the Creator offering himself to his world anew was taking place in the confession, "Jesus is Lord."

Inasmuch as the *kyrios*-confession was shaped like this by the Old Testament concept of God, two consequences existed for the *kyrios*-Christology. (1) The exalted One was not a divine being alongside God so that the suspicion of polytheism might arise. Rather he was the One through whom God's end-time activity was taking place. He was incorporated into the singularity of God. (2) Understood as the *kyrios* in this sense the exalted One had a profiled relationship to the cosmos that was quite different from the Hellenistic *kyrioi*. He was not the *Cosmokratōr*—that was applied to "the powers" in Eph. 6:12 and in the ancient church to "Satan."[11] Rather he was established as the eschatological Lord of the cosmos that was created by him.

On the matter of how his being Lord in relationship to the cosmos was realized, there are a variety of statements in the New Testament. According to the hymns of Phil. 2:9-11; Col. 2:10, 15; Eph. 1:20-23, as well as I Pet. 3:22 and Rev. 5:11-14, the exalted One was already Lord of all powers. In contrast, I Cor. 15:25-28 (Rev. 6-19; Heb. 2:5-9; 10:13) said that he was yet doing battle with them and would finally put them down only at the end of history and establish his dominion. How is the tension to be understood? E. Käsemann maintained that in the hymns a pre-Pauline, enthusiast perfectionism expressed itself like that which Paul rejected in I Cor. 4:8 in order to counter it with his

---

[11] W. Michaelis, *TDNT* III, 913f. Characteristically the exalted One was never called "Lord of the world" in the entire New Testament. This frequent rabbinic address to God that meant his sovereignty in the affairs of this world was applied to the exalted One for the first time in Barn. 5:5: it de-eschatologized his lordship. The designation of God as the *Pantokratōr* that later was also applied to the exalted One had, in contrast, a stronger eschatological character (ibid., 913f. [W. Foerster], 1085).

own conception in I Cor. 15:25-28.[12] In point of fact, however, the hymnic "already now" was an expression of the doxological indicative. The community confessed what had been established by God through Jesus' exaltation (Phil. 2:9), but it did not fail to recognize that this still had to be established conclusively in history. This was expressed not only by I Cor. 15:25-28, but also by the parenetic imperative of Col. 2:20 and even by Eph. 6:12. These imperatives served no more the function of subsequent correction to the hymns than did Rev. 6–19 to Rev. 5:11-14.

On the question of the lordship of Christ in relationship to the cosmos in the mind of Paul—a matter that has been argued endlessly in the last generation— it can be said: Jesus had been established as eschatological Lord of the cosmos through his exaltation in order to become just that through the confessing of the community and the overcoming of the enemies of God.[13] The establishment of Jesus as Lord in relationship to the cosmos was not to be accomplished in history conclusively by proclamation in conjunction with propaganda and power, as in the case of the dominion of the new emperor; it was to happen rather by the preaching that allowed faith to be born as "new creation." Its reverse side was judgment, and its goal was the consummation itself. Neither Paul nor any other New Testament writer knew of a coming of Christ's dominion apart from preaching and believing that would mean salvation and not judgment for human beings. Christ's being Lord in relationship to the world maintained a strict kerygmatic character because it maintained an eschatological and soteriological character.[14]

As regards the history-of-religion emergence of the *kyrios*-Christology it can be said: the determinative motif was the kerygmatic inquiry of Hellenistic man in his relationship to the cosmos. Added to this, an apologetic understanding of the Hellenistic *kyrios*-concept was brought together with the Old Testament expectation, communicated by the LXX, of God's eschatological turning as the *kyrios* to his creation; the process of bringing such together was stimulated by the primitive church's words about Jesus as the Lord. By means of the Old Testament expectation mentioned above, the exalted One's being Lord retained the character of the dominion of God that Jesus sought and ushered in, and that the cry *maranatha* expected from him. In this sense the *kyrios*-Christology of the Hellenistic church preserved substantive continuity as it extended the concepts about Jesus as Lord from the Palestinian church.

3. THE FUNCTION OF THE *KYRIOS* FOR THE COMMUNITY

On the basis of what we have found regarding the content of the *kyrios*-concept we ask now about its functions for the community of faith.

[12]*New Testament Questions of Today*, p. 206; cf. "A Critical Analysis of Philippians 2:5-11," in *God and Christ: Existence and Province* (ed. R. W. Funk [1968]), pp. 78-82. Regarding the discussion, cf. Kramer, *Christ*, pp. 65-84.

[13]Regarding the discussion, cf. Goppelt, "Die Herrschaft Christi und die Welt," in *Christologie*, pp. 121-26.

[14]This was emphasized correctly by E. Schweizer, "Jesus Christus, Herr über Kirche und Welt," in *Libertas Christiana, Festschrift für F. Delekat* (ed. E. Wolf and W. Mathias [1957]), pp. 175-187.

a) According to Phil. 2:8, Jesus was the Lord because "he became obedient unto death, even death on a cross." In the *kyrios* the redeeming work of Jesus was present. For Paul, as for the rest of the New Testament, Jesus was not seen primarily as the *Pantokratōr* (the almighty), but as the defender who interceded at God's right hand on behalf of those belonging to him (Rom. 8:34; 5:1). For the Epistle to the Hebrews (8:1–10:18) he was seen as the high priest who presented his atoning blood before God. For the book of Revelation (5:6, 9f.) he was seen as the Lamb with the mortal wounds who purchased with his blood people of every nation for God on behalf of his *basileia*. Accordingly, his dominion in history was realized pointedly through the *koinōnia* that produced the Lord's Supper at "the Table of the Lord" and through "the cup of the Lord" (I Cor. 10:16f., 21).

b) Yet the exalted One was never seen in the same light as the Hellenistic *kyrioi* merely as the patron and guide of his followers. He was always looked upon as the One who had been established as Lord of the cosmos in such a way that he was changing it eschatologically toward the new world (I Cor. 15:25f.; cf. Heb. 1:4-14; Rev. 5:10b, 13f.). This process of change was a historical one that nevertheless would reach its conclusion not by a historical development but when that which had been accomplished by cross and resurrection finally had been established in an unequivocally observable way.

Hence, even in the Hellenistic church the position of Christ that was expressed in titles and the Christ event—especially the course of his life—were inseparably united.

§35. The Course of Christ's Life as Saving Revelation: The Cross

On 1: E. Stauffer, *New Testament Theology* (1955), pp. 116ff.; Bultmann, *Theology* I, §33,5f.; J. T. Sanders, *The New Testament Christological Hymns* (1971). On 2: J. Behm, *haima*, TDNT I, 172-76; F. Grandchamp, "La doctrine du sang du Christ dans les épîtres de Saint Paul," *Revue de théologie et de philosophie* 11 (1961), 262-271. On 3: Kramer, *Christ*, pp. 26-32; W. Popkes, *Christus Traditus. Eine Untersuchung zum Begriff der Dahingabe im NT* (1967); K. Wengst, *Christologische Formeln und Lieder des Urchristentums* (1973²), §§3-6. On 4: J. Hermann/F. Büchsel, *hilastērion*, TDNT III, 318-323; Goppelt, *Typos*, pp. 178f.; W. G. Kümmel, *"Paresis* und *endeixis,"* in Kümmel, *Heilsgeschehen und Geschichte* (1965), pp. 260-270; D. Zeller, "Sühne und Langmut. Zur Traditionsgeschichte von Röm 3,24-26," *Theologie und Philosophie* 43 (1968), 51-75; W. Schrage, "Röm 3,21-26 und die Bedeutung des Todes Jesu Christi bei Paulus," in *Das Kreuz Jesu (Forum* 12, ed. P. Rieger [1969]), pp. 65-88; E. Käsemann, "Zum Verständnis von Römer 3,24-26," in *Exegetische Versuche* I, 96-100; Käsemann, *Romans*, at this place (Lit.!); Käsemann, "The Saving Significance of the Death of Jesus in Paul," in Käsemann, *Perspectives on Paul* (1971), pp. 32-59; P. Stuhlmacher, "Zur neuen Exegese von Röm 3,24-26," in *Jesus und Paulus, Festschrift für W. G. Kümmel* (1975), pp. 315-333. On 5: O. Schmitz, *Die Christus-Gemeinschaft des Paulus im Lichte seines Genitivgebrauchs* (1924); H. Lietzmann, *HNT*, Excursus on Rom. 6:3; O. Kuss, *Der Römerbrief* (1957/59; 1963²), pp. 319-381; W. Michaelis, *sympaschō*, etc., TDNT V, 925-935; E. Larsson, *Christus als Vorbild* (1962); G. Wagner, *Pauline Baptism*

(1967); R. C. Tannehill, *Dying and Rising with Christ* (1967); W. Grundmann, *synmeta, TDNT* VII, 786-794 (766 Lit.!); E. Schweizer, "Die 'Mystik' des Sterbens und Auferstehens mit Christus bei Paulus," *EvTheol* 26 (1966), 239-257 (= Schweizer, *Beiträge zur Theologie des Neuen Testaments* [1970], pp. 183-203); E. Güttgemanns, *Der leidende Apostel und sein Herr* (1966); E. Lohse, *Colossians* (Hermeneia, 1971), at Col. 1:24 and 2:12; E. Käsemann, *Romans*, pp. 160ff. **On 6:** A. Deissmann, *Die neutestamentliche Formel "in Christo Jesu" untersucht* (1892); A. Oepke, *en, TDNT* II, 541-43; F. Neugebauer, *In Christus* (1961); M. Bouttier, *En Christ* (1962); W. Thüsing, *Per Christum in Deum* (1965; 1969²).

1. CHRIST'S LIFE AS A WHOLE

The content of the honorific titles regarding Christ's position ensued from the course of his life, and vice versa. The primitive kerygma, I Cor. 15:3-5, referred to his life only in terms of death and resurrection, while the Christ-hymn, Phil. 2:6-11, extended it from cosmic preexistence to eschatological dominion over the universe. Yet even this hymn did not describe a uniform succession of events like the second article of the Apostles' Creed or the *ordo salutis* of early Protestant dogmatics. The hymn, like the kerygma, concerned itself rather with the proclamation of two moments: Christ's self-abasement that brought him to death on the cross and the response of his being exalted by God. One observes corresponding perspectives among other Pauline statements about the course of Christ's life.[1] Consequently, the steps along the path of his life were never recounted by Paul or other New Testament writers in as "complete" a fashion as in the second article of the Apostles' Creed. The representation in I Pet. 3:18-22 came the closest to this article of the creed. But even in I Peter the series concluded with the dominion of the exalted One and not with the *parousia*. The New Testament statements closed by proclaiming a soteriological offering of Christ and not—as in the case of the Apostles' Creed—by describing his person through the course of his life. Within the context of the 2nd century the omission of a portion would have meant an alteration of the overall picture, whereas in the lst century one could still proclaim the whole by referring to some fundamental moments from the course of his life.

When one compares the Pauline statements about Christ's life with those of other New Testament writers—especially with those of Hebrews and the Gospel of John—the following distinctions become evident.

a) The subject of Christ's life for Paul was primarily God. Paul understood the second half of Christ's life—resurrection or exaltation—exclusively in terms

---

[1]Rom. 1:3f.; 8:3; Gal. 4:4; I Cor. 15:20-28; Col. 1:15-20 (Eph. 2:14-16; I Tim. 3:16); cf. Heb. 1:3; Jn. 1:1-14.

of God's activity. God raised him from the dead,[2] God exalted him.[3] In contrast, for Hebrews Christ himself brought his offering before God as high priest (Heb. 9:11f., 24; 10:12f.). According to the Gospel of John, ". . . I lay down my life that I may take it again" (Jn. 10:17) or he proceeded to the Father (Jn. 13:33; 14:3). But even regarding the first half of Christ's life Paul preferred to speak in terms of God's activity on behalf of the world. God sent his Son (Rom. 8:3; Gal. 4:4); he gave him up (to death, Rom. 3:25; 4:25; 8:32; II Cor. 5:21). In conjunction with this Paul could also, of course, make Christ the subject. He humbled himself (Phil. 2:6-8); he gave himself over (Gal. 2:20; Rom. 5:6-8; II Cor. 8:9).

In the final analysis Paul looked upon the course of Christ's life quite one-sidedly as God's eschatological intervention in the world. In this Paul is basically to be distinguished from all other New Testament writers.

b) The critical point about this intervention, i.e., about the course of Christ's life, was for Paul the cross. For him Christ stood in the midst of history not as the Word become flesh (Jn. 1:14), not as the high priest who declared his solidarity with us (Heb. 4:14-16; 5:5-10), and not as the eschatological martyr-prophet (Acts 3:13; 4:27). For Paul Christ was the crucified One. "For I decided to know nothing among you except Jesus Christ and him crucified" (I Cor. 2:2).

R. Bultmann laid decisive emphasis upon this aspect. In his view, for Paul the whole course of Christ's life was summed up in the cross; all other statements really did no more than to express that the cross was the activity of God.[4] The cross, however, only became effective through the kerygma. In Bultmann's view the cross became the saving event when the word of the cross as God's address caused a human being to give up his previous self-understanding and to allow himself to be crucified with Christ.[5]

By means of these two theses the two problems present here were addressed uncompromisingly, and yet this solution was too one-sided.

1) What was the saving significance that accrued to the individual steps of the course of Christ's life? Seen homiletically, what was the special message of Christian festivals? E. Stauffer said that every stage of Christ's life brought as a consequence a change to the world's existence for the glory of God, for the triumph over the powers opposing God, and for the salvation of man.[6] It is clear that this concept of advancing apocalyptic world change interpreted Paul far less

---

[2]Rom. 4:24f.; 6:4, 9; 7:4; 8:11. "Jesus . . . rose again" (only I Thess. 4:14) still meant for Paul—entirely in the sense of the Old Testament—the same as "he was raised" (hence he could also say about Christians in I Thess. 4:16: *anastēsontai*, "they will rise"). Cf. also Rom. 14:9: "lived again" *(ezēsen)*.

[3]Phil. 2:9-11; Rom. 1:3f. Both times "exalted" or "designated" did not stand for an act after the resurrection, but in its stead! It is different in Eph. 1:20: ". . . he raised him from the dead and made him sit at his right hand" (cf. Col. 3:1; Rom. 8:34). Regarding the substantive issue, cf. more remotely Vol. 1, §22,3.

[4]*Theology* I, §33,1f.

[5]Ibid. I, §33,6a.

[6]Op. cit. (Lit., §35), pp. 116-142.

accurately than Bultmann's concept, which stood in direct opposition to it. To some degree the latter had an affinity with the model of the Gnostic redeemer who brought the individual call to decision.[7]

For Paul the cross was the crucial moment of the Christ event, but it was this only because it was the dying of the obedient One (Phil. 2:8f.), the One sent from God, and because the crucified One was raised/exalted (I Cor. 15:17-22). Through these statements about the course of Christ's life that preceded the cross and that followed it Paul showed that the significance of the cross as God's saving work was not merely symbolic. Its significance was actually constituted through both sides,[8] although this was a matter of what happened in secret.

2) How did the course of Christ's life become effective in the world? Certainly not directly as apocalyptic world change, but also not only as preaching! Christ had already become the *kyrios* in relationship to the cosmos through the course of his life, as became clear above, but he was that only in such a way that his dominion established itself through proclamation and its reverse side, judgment.

> What had already been established between God and the world by means of the course of Christ's life and what was yet to occur through preaching should not be played off one against the other. The substance of preaching is reduced when preaching is regarded more as a public announcement of what has already been established; Karl Barth tended to go this direction. But preaching is also overloaded when the decisive action of God is not grasped as always preceding it; what takes place does so within and only through that decisive action of God. These limits became especially clear when ca. 1970 both the "word" and "kerygma" theologies and the homiletical concepts they shaped became less prominent.

Now that a critical overview has emerged it remains to be understood more precisely in just what sense the cross was the crucial moment for the course of Christ's life. That which stood on the one side, his coming in the flesh, and that which stood on the other, his exaltation to Lord, came up in previous portions of our study with regard to honorific titles (§§33 and 34). How Paul understood the cross can be deciphered by considering terminology and the appropriation and development of formulaic tradition.

2. THE CROSS: TERMINOLOGY

Just like the primitive kerygma before him (I Cor. 15:3ff.), Paul spoke often about the "dying" of Christ.[9] Parallel to *thanatos* (death, Rom. 5:10) Paul placed

---

[7]Stauffer called upon Rom. 4:25 for support of his apportioning of the effects of salvation: "Christ was delivered up for our trespasses, and was raised up for our justification" (ibid., p. 136). This apportionment, however, was strictly a rhetorical stylization since in Rom. 3:25 justification followed from his dying as here from his resurrection. Only both together as inseparable saving-act of God meant salvation. One should not play off a theology of the cross against a theology of the resurrection and vice versa!

[8]Regarding the discussion, cf. more remotely E. Käsemann, *Perspectives on Paul* (1971), pp. 54-59; B. Klappert, *Die Auferweckung des Gekreuzigten. Der Ansatz der Christologie Karl Barths im Zusammenhang der Christologie der Gegenwart* (1971), pp. 348-397.

[9]Thus with the verb *apothnēskein* (Rom. 5:6, 8; 6:10; 8:34; 14:9 and passim) and with the substantives *thanatos* (Rom. 5:10; 6:3, 4f.; I Cor. 11:26) and *nekrōsis* (II Cor. 4:10).

the term *haima* (blood) of Christ in Rom. 5:9. This term was used here as elsewhere in the New Testament (cf. Heb. 9:14-19) as an image for the dying of Jesus. The image that stood behind it was developed as an abbreviation from the word about the cup in the tradition of the Eucharist. It can be found in Mk. 14:24 par. Mt.: ". . . my blood of the covenant, which is poured out. . . ." Its Hellenistic formulation in I Cor. 11:25 substituted: ". . . the new covenant sealed by my blood . . ." (NEB), i.e., sealed by my dying.[10] Paul, however, introduced a term that remained his own, *ho stauros* (the cross).

Of course, the passion narrative recounted that Jesus had to carry his cross *(stauros)* as a condemned man to the place of execution (Mk. 15:21 par.), that he was "crucified" and in ridicule was challenged to come down from the cross (Mk. 15:30 par., 32 par.). Missionary polemic made the Jews responsible for this crucifixion (Acts 2:36; 4:10; Rev. 11:8). The term *stauros* as such took on theological significance only in the discipleship saying about taking up one's cross that used it as an image (Mk. 8:34 par.; Mt. 10:38 par.). The same was true in the remark about those people who were "standing by the cross of Jesus" (Jn. 19:25), and the one about "the cross" of "shame" that Jesus took upon himself (Heb. 12:2). For Paul, however, "the cross" became a theological code word for the dying of Christ in its theological significance; the aorist passive participle "having been crucified" became a theological designation for Christ.[11] This linguistic usage suggested itself when Paul added the phrase to the hymn of Phil. 2:8, "even death on a cross"; yet the cross here, as in Col. 2:14, remained an instrument of execution. In contrast, it became a theological technical term in I Cor. 1:17f.; Gal. 5:11; 6:12, 14; Phil. 3:18; Col. 1:20; cf. Eph. 2:16. This word, which we use confidently today in connection with its theological heritage, was a word that repelled the contemporaries of Paul just the way the word "gallows" repels us today. For this reason, no other early Christian author appropriated this Pauline linguistic usage.[12]

Just what Paul intended by using this shocking theological word-picture becomes clear when considering the context of usage, which was always polemical. With his words about the "cross" Paul was attacking a Jewish or a wisdom-oriented mitigating of the offense of Jesus' dying! The Judaizers in Galatia wanted a righteousness based on the Law, a moral Jesus, and a moral human being because they wanted to avoid the cross; the cross was the sign of human failure and of human condemnation by God; it was the sign that provoked the contradiction of people who tried living by the Law (Gal. 6:12; cf. 5:11). According to Phil. 3:18f., the Libertarians were those whose "god [was] the belly" and who were "enemies of the cross," because at the cross was manifested the termination of self-exalting desire. Most of all, Paul opposed the wisdom teachers of Corinth who in pseudo-spiritual *securitas* had stood for the principle "all

---

[10]Also I Cor. 10:16; 11:27; Rom. 3:25; 5:9; Col. 1:20; cf. Eph. 1:7; 2:13.

[11]I Cor. 1:23; 2:2; II Cor. 13:4 (cf. I Cor. 2:8; Heb. 6:6); Gal. 3:1; 6:14 (cf. 5:24).

[12]Also in the writings of Ignatius the cross did not have the Pauline meaning (Eph. 9:1; 18:1; Trall. 11:2; Rom. 5:3; Phld. 8:2; Sm. 1:1); cf. J. Schneider, *TDNT* VII, 579f., 583.

things are lawful for me," for " 'all of us possess knowledge' " (I Cor. 6:12; 8:1). He did so by rebutting them in the first two chapters of the First Epistle to the Corinthians with the great statements of his *theologia crucis*. "Christ sent me . . . to preach the gospel, and not with eloquent wisdom, lest the cross of Christ be emptied of its power." "But we preach Christ crucified, a stumbling block to Jews and folly to Gentiles" (I Cor. 1:17, 23; cf. 1:18; 2:2). Paul pointed in this polemical way to the cross because—as he stated in Phil. 3:4-11—he himself had experienced that the attempt to shape one's existence according to wisdom, i.e., according to empiricism and its standard, led one finally to inhumanity. For the person who by means of the cross allowed himself to be released from the fascination with having one's own way and with the fashioning of the world and to be led to the God of the resurrection, for this one the cross as "the power of God and the wisdom of God" would become effective as the foundation and illumination of his existence (I Cor. 1:24f.).

Paul not only taught but also lived this theology of the cross. He understood his life right down to flesh and bone to be marked by the cross. ". . . always carrying in the body the death of Jesus" (II Cor. 4:10; cf. 6:4-10). His prayer for the healing of a chronic illness was heard not with bodily results but through the promise: "My grace is sufficient for you, for my power is made perfect in weakness" (II Cor. 12:9).

Hence the dying of Jesus was understood as "the cross," i.e., as the signpost that marked the collapse of the human desire to establish one's own being in one's own power. It was the signpost by which, in light of the collapse, a place for God as God was created, namely, for the One "who . . . calls into existence the things that do not exist" (Rom. 4:17).

Paul undoubtedly came to this understanding of Jesus' dying by the resolution of the offense that he himself as one bound to the Law had taken at the crucified One. This was only possible, however, because he already found in Christian tradition a fundamental interpretation that had come from Jesus himself.

3. THE *HYPER*-FORMULA

The primitive kerygma that was cited as tradition in I Cor. 15:3-5 already contained the formulaic statement: "Christ died for our sins in accordance with the scriptures." This "for/on behalf of" (normally Gr. *hyper* with the genitive = "for the benefit of")[13] occurred frequently in Paul's writings as fixed expression. For this reason, one refers to the expressions as *hyper*-formulas. For the time being we shall leave open the question whether or not in each detail and location we have a genuine formula before us that had its own *Sitz im Leben* or whether it is a matter of a fixed expression that could have been interjected into various contexts.

---

[13]Occasionally *peri* with the genitive case ("for") or *dia* with the accusative ("on account of") also appear. Only in the two "for"-passages of the synoptic tradition was *anti* ("for," "in one's stead") used.

A history-of-tradition study of the "on behalf of"-statements points up two formulaic traditions.

a) The dying formula. The statement of the primitive kerygma noted above appropriated, as we saw earlier (§18,8), by means of formulaic simplification the intention of Jesus' vivid words about the significance of his death. The expression occurred again in Rom. 5:8 with the same characteristic words (Christ as subject—*apethanen*—*hyper*): "Christ died for us." In Rom. 5:6, Paul made the interpretive addition: "while we were yet . . . ungodly." The expression has been worked into the context at Rom. 14:15 and I Cor. 8:11 (in the latter stands *di' hon*). In Gal. 2:21 it was used without *hyper* and in I Thess. 5:10 and II Cor. 5:14f. with a circumscription of the subject (cf. I Cor. 1:13). Outside the immediate context of Pauline tradition it appeared in I Pet. 3:18: "For Christ also died for *(peri)* sins once for all"; in I Pet. 2:21 "[he] suffered" was used instead of "[he] died." This *epathen* (he suffered [unto death]) was also to be found frequently elsewhere, e.g., Ign. Sm. 2:1; 7:1; II Clem. 1:2; Barn. 5:5; Mart. Pol. 17:2.

Even in all those passages where the removal of sins was not mentioned expressly on the order of I Cor. 15:3 and I Pet. 3:18, "dying for" meant the vicarious atoning death. This was the weight that Paul placed on the expression, e.g., in Rom. 5:1-11.

b) The "he was given over" formula. We also find the statement that characterized Jesus' dying as his having been given over *(paradidonai)* expressed in the framework of a traditional formula. Such was the case in Rom. 4:25: "who was put [Gr.: given over] to death for our trespasses and raised for our justification."

The point of departure for this tradition may well lie in the announcement of coming suffering of Mk. 9:31 par., which probably can be traced back to Jesus. It said, "The Son of man will be delivered [*paradidotai*; namely, by God] into the hands of men" (§18,6). To begin with, this *logion* designated Jesus' dying only as the realization of God's end-time plan of salvation; it did not, however, ascribe to that death as such any saving significance. This did not happen until the catechetical formula of instruction (Rom. 4:25) developed from the announcement of coming suffering. It appears that in the process Isa. 53:12 was of some influence; at the end of the LXX version it said: "and on account of their sins[14] he was given over." Christ's dying was designated as vicarious atonement. The same formulaic expression appeared in Rom. 8:32: "He . . . gave him up for us all." In other passages Christ was the subject: "who gave himself for our sins" (Gal. 1:4; 2:20). In Gal. 2:20 the motif of love and in Eph. 5:2, 25 that of sacrifice were added.

We must now ask in conclusion: In what form did dying and the "he was given over" formulas circulate? Without a doubt, I Cor. 15:3-5 and Rom. 4:25 were independent pieces of tradition. Were these pieces put together from brief

---

[14]*dia tas hamartias*; when in Rom. 4:25 *dia ta paraptōmata* was used it corresponded to Pauline linguistic usage. (This portion of Isa. 53:12 is not included in the RSV. Alsup).

formulas according to a building-block system?[15] In all probability the brief formulas in Rom. 5:8 and 8:32 were merely fixed expressions; they had to become independent statements by being restated within a context. Only in this sense would they qualify as formulas.

4. THE DEVELOPMENT OF THE *HYPER*-FORMULA

The interpretation of Jesus' death as vicarious atonement was developed with the word about the cup and that about the ransom (Mk. 14:24; 10:45) as an outgrowth of Jesus' earthly ministry (§18,8). This interpretation was preserved in formulaic fashion for community catechesis within the *hyper*-formulas, but these in turn were explicated theologically. When Paul accomplished this he did so with the aid of various concepts that in part were already available to him from Christian tradition. At first glance these concepts appear to have been graphic illustrations, but actually they were expressions of substantive contexts to which the dying of Jesus was connected. Especially important was the conceptual realm of cultic atonement.

a) Old Testament rites of atonement. According to the Old Testament God provided cultic atonement because he wished to forgive but also wished to remain faithful to the order he established (§18,8). A link with Old Testament rites of atonement existed more or less clearly in the following statements about Jesus' dying.

1) In I Cor. 5:6-8, Paul appropriated the tradition of a Passover homily and explained: "For Christ, our paschal lamb, has been sacrificed." Just as the dying of the Passover lambs, which was valid as atonement in rabbinic interpretation, accomplished the first redemption, so the dying of Jesus accomplished the final one. The latter brought ultimate freedom from the former way of life.[16]

2) According to I Cor. 11:25, the word about the cup within the eucharistic liturgy of the Pauline church ran: "This cup is the new covenant sealed by my blood" (NEB). This formulation reminded one of the statement in Ex. 24:8 where the Sinai covenant was sealed by sprinkling the people with the "blood of the covenant." Actually it probably rested on a concept of Hellenistic-Jewish Christianity that was prompted by Old Testament/Jewish traditions about covenant renewals[17] without being identical to them. According to Rom. 3:25b, the trespasses committed under the old covenant—and that meant all the trespasses of the old man—which God in deliberate forbearance *(anoché)* until now really

---

[15]Thus Wengst, op. cit. (Lit., §35,3), §0.

[16]A balanced view of the discussion is found in W. Huber, *Passa und Ostern* (1969), pp. 108f.

[17]Ex. 34:6f.: "The Lord, the Lord, a God merciful and gracious, slow to anger, and abounding in steadfast love and faithfulness, keeping steadfast love for thousands, forgiving iniquity and transgression and sin, but who will by no means clear the guilty, visiting the iniquity of the fathers upon the children and the children's children, to the third and the fourth generation." Finally, this was appropriated by the Damascus Rule (CD) 2:4f.: "Patience and much forgiveness are with Him towards those who turn from transgression" (G. Vermes, *The Dead Sea Scrolls in English*, p. 98), i.e., for those who had entered into the new (= renewed) covenant.

did not punish, but "passed over" *(paresis)*, these trespasses were atoned through the dying of Jesus in such a way that God demonstrated his fidelity to himself. Something comparable was expressed even more clearly in Heb. 9:15, 22. Based on this atonement through Jesus' dying, i.e., "sealed by his blood," the new covenant, a new relationship to God, could legitimately replace that which came before. The atonement, however, through which this took place was designated in Rom. 3:25a through reference to a further conceptual tradition that was also connected in Heb. 9 to the one just discussed.

3) The key expression about *hilastērion* in Rom. 3:25a stated: "whom God put forward [namely, the crucified Christ] as an expiation by his blood *(hilastērion en tō autou haimati)*. . . . This was to show God's righteousness."

What was intended by *hilastērion*? In Greek the word referred to that which atoned, the means of atoning (cf. IV Macc. 17:22). If one began here with this general meaning, as frequently has been done,[18] the result was a very weak statement: Jesus' public death was a means of atoning and therefore "to show God's righteousness." Why an act of atonement as such should be a demonstration of the righteousness, the covenant loyalty of God, no one was able, however, to explain. To the readers of the Epistle to the Romans, who were familiar with the LXX, this very uncommon word in Greek was known in connection with its central usage. The LXX translated the Hebrew word *kapporet*[19] with *hilastērion*. This *kapporet* was the cover-seat of the Ark of the Covenant in the Holy of Holies in the temple. It was that which marked the gracious presence of God among his people. According to Lev. 16:14f., this seat (or, in the second temple, its place) was sprinkled with the blood of the atoning sacrifice on the occasion of the great day of reconciliation (actually, "on the day of atonement" *[hēmera exhilasmou]*; Lev. 23:27; cf. 16:30; 25:9) by the high priest. God, who was present on this spot, accepted the atonement he had made possible here. In New Testament times the Day of Atonement was still the great day of remission for every Jew; through this act of atonement all the sins of the previous year of which one had repented were cancelled.[20] Our passage recalled the rite of atonement almost unavoidably when it referred to the crucified Christ as the "*hilastērion* by his blood."[21]

This image was nevertheless unwieldly. Present in the crucified One simultaneously were "the mercy seat" that represented the presence of the God who provided and in turn accepted the atonement, and the atoning blood, the atoning death. That was intended to affirm that God was present in the crucified One and that he accepted his dying as atonement. This concept corresponded to the structure of Pauline theology. It was characteristic of Paul's thought that Jesus' dying was understood primarily as the activity of God. "God was in Christ

---

[18]Thus, most recently, E. Käsemann, *Romans*, at Rom. 3:25; Wengst, op. cit. (n. 15), p. 83; Schrage, op. cit. (Lit., §35,4), p. 81.

[19]Some twenty times in the LXX (e.g., Ex. 25:16ff.; Lev. 16:2, 13ff.).

[20]Billerbeck III, 165-185.

[21]Thus, after others, A. Schlatter, *Gottes Gerechtigkeit*, at Rom. 3:25; F. Büchsel, *TDNT* III, 320f.; H.-J. Schoeps, *Paul*, pp. 146ff.

reconciling the world to himself" (II Cor. 5:19). This statement and the image above were quite harmonious even if "to reconcile" did not signify "to atone" (§39,3). The imagery of which Paul availed himself was of course rarely without its drawbacks.

In Rom. 3:25, moreover, it was not just a matter of imagery; Paul was not merely illustrating. For him the act of atonement of Lev. 16 was nothing less than it was for its accomplishment during the time of Moses (I Cor. 10:6, 11); it was the promissory prefiguration of the hour of fulfillment, *typos*. If Jesus' dying was the typological correspondence to the act of atonement of Lev. 16, then Good Friday was the eschatological day of reconciliation that once and for all brought atonement for all "transgressions" (Rom. 4:25; cf. 3:25b). And it brought freedom from the bondage to sin as a power (Rom. 6:10). Since this act of atonement was carried out in accord with the institution of the old covenant in Lev. 16 it was the demonstration of God's fidelity to his covenant. In other words, it was the demonstration of his righteousness. Good Friday as the eschatological day of reconciliation was the demonstration of the righteousness of God.

The connection to Lev. 16 that was drawn implicitly in Rom. 3:25 by means of terminology was filled out explicitly in Heb. 8–10 (9:7, 11-14, 24-28; 10:3). There Christ was seen as the high priest who offered to God his own blood, while in Rom. 3 he was the mercy seat where God accepted his blood. Apparently the writer of Hebrews and Paul, each in his own way, made use of the same early Christian tradition that intepreted typologically the dying of Jesus with the aid of Lev. 16 (cf. §47,4c). Numerous pointers clearly suggest that Paul reworked traditional elements in Rom. 3:25.[22]

It is decisive to remember that this meditative use of the Old Testament did not merely draw out the *hyper*-formula in the framework of a rational construction. Rather it placed the formula within the reality of the relationship between God and man as revealed and set by the Old Testament, and as it was traced back to a reconstitution through Jesus. Until then human life stood universally under the provisional preservation and retribution that the covenant at Sinai secured explicitly for Israel. This reality was not annulled by the word of the cross; it was not dismissed as some incorrect theory. Through atonement it was recognized and suspended. Only in this way could the empirical reality that was fixed by the covenant of the Law be suspended credibly by the eschatological covenant. The latter covenant rested alone upon the new demonstration of God's grace and alone upon the voluntary responsibility of people that was called forth by this grace. Thus the Old Testament concept of atoning sacrifice could help make the *hyper*-formula understandable and internally verifiable as long as the

---

[22]In v. 22 no other term for the righteousness of God appeared than that found otherwise in Paul (§39). But the double-sided connection of the granting of righteousness with the universal former-time of patience (v. 25b) and with the present-time of righteousness (v. 26a)—the reverse side of which was wrath (1:18)—was not specifically Pauline; it was suggested through the tradition of the day-of-atonement typology and of the covenant renewal (cf. n. 17); moreover, the sentence was linguistically overloaded: *dia pisteōs* stood between *hilastērion* and *en tō autou haimati*.

arrangement was seen as set forth by God and not as a theory of ancient religiosity. The arrangement was founded in a reality and at the same time pointed promisingly beyond itself as *typos*.

This line of development was continued in a second group of Pauline statements that took up the justice of God in order to explain the atoning significance of the cross.

b) The Justice of God. The doctrine of satisfaction of Anselm of Canterbury, which has continued to influence Western theology up to the present, explained the atoning significance of Jesus' dying in terms of Germanic legal thought, i.e., in terms of a presupposition that was historically and substantively foreign to it. In contrast to this doctrine Paul took the Old Testament view of God's justice as his starting point when in Gal. 3:10 he quoted the conclusion of the curse ceremony in Dt. 27:15-26: "Cursed be every one who does not abide by all things written in the book of the law, and do them." This curse formula was appropriated not only with respect to the obligation to keep the Dodecalogue at Shechem (Dt. 27:[11], 15-26), but also cultically at the covenant-renewal festival at Qumran (1QS 2:4-19). In light of this Old Testament tradition active in Judaism Paul understood that people who lived by the Law's order of retribution—according to Rom. 2:6 that meant everyone—had come under this curse. And then he looked upon the crucified One and added in Gal. 3:13: "Christ redeemed us from the curse of the law, having become a curse for us—for it is written, 'Cursed be every one who hangs on a tree' " (cf. Dt. 21:23). Christ became a curse, though not as one who was accursed. He bore the curse of the Law, though not as though he bore the sum of the punishments people deserved. II Cor. 5:21 explained more precisely: "For our sake he made him to be sin who knew no sin, so that in him we might become the righteousness of God." He did not become a sinner, but One who was marked by sin. Sin separates one from God and delivers one over to dying. Christ suffered this separation and being delivered over in his dying representatively and atoningly. The group of statements that came from the concept of Old Testament justice emphasized more the representative aspect, while those that came from the rites of atonement emphasized more the atonement. Both were nevertheless always bound together.

Because this representative bearing of the curse was at the same time atonement it "redeemed us," as it says in Gal. 3:13. It bought freedom from the curse of the Law and—according to Gal. 4:5—at the same time from its claim by having placed us in the relationship of sonship to God. In place of "redeem" *(exagorazein)* in I Cor. 6:20 and 7:23 we find "bought" *(agorazein)*. The intent was to make clear that the existing link could only be replaced by another one. This traditional expression from early Christianity (cf. Rev. 5:9; 14:3f.) did not intend to interpret Jesus' dying as the price of purchase like, e.g., what was paid when freedom from slavery was purchased.[23] It had in mind even less the powers that receive such a purchase price. It only wanted to say that his dying had made

---

[23] F. Büchsel, *TDNT* I, 124-28.

legally free because it was atonement for everyone. In Rom. 8:3f., moreover, the freedom achieved was given foundation: "For God . . . sending his own Son in the likeness of sinful flesh and for sin [i.e., as a sin offering], condemned sin in the flesh, in order that the just requirement of the law might be fulfilled in us." Joining here the "for" was a "together with"; that is to say, "sin in the flesh" was condemned with respect to us just as much as with respect to Christ.

Paul did not restrict himself to a theological development of the *hyper*-formula of community confession; he also extended it into *syn*- and *en*-formulas. These formulas expressed something in common with Christ that followed from the "for/on behalf of." Following the vivid *hyper* in Rom. 3:21–5:21 came a similarly profiled *syn* in Rom. 6:1-10 (6:4, 6, 8).

5. BEING WITH CHRIST (*SYN CHRISTŌ*) AND BAPTISM

a) Overview. The *syn*-expressions linked to Christ were made up partly of compound verbs[24] and partly of simple verbs, the preposition *syn* (= with), and the dative of association. They are found among four distinct groups of statements within the writings of Paul.

1) There were *syn*-statements for Paul that meant a being-with, such as being together with Christians.

A group of statements can be found in the New Testament that have the same meaning but were not formed by using *syn* with the dative of association but by using *meta* (= with) and the genitive case. Fellowship with Jesus, especially table fellowship with him (Mk. 2:16 par.; Lk. 15:1f.), was thus emphasized in the synoptic tradition,[25] and a corresponding fellowship in the consummation was promised.[26] This line of thought was appropriated in the book of Revelation; to those who persevered were promised the victory and the consummation "with" the "Lamb."[27]

For Paul the "with"-statements of this type take their emphasis in the reply to the question about death. Christians who have died will be "with Christ," i.e., in his company, be it at the *parousia* (I Thess. 4:15-17) or independent of the *parousia* following their death (Phil. 1:23; cf. II Cor. 5:8). For the present and the future this being-with was established on our behalf through Jesus' dying. "[He] died for us so that whether we wake or sleep we might live with him" (I Thess. 5:10).

2) The future, eschatological being with Christ brought forth the notions of "inheriting with" and "being glorified with" that corresponded to a "suffering together with him" in the present (Rom. 8:17; cf. Col. 3:4; I Pet. 4:13: 5:1). Believers were "conform[ed] with him" *(symmorphos)* and participated in this

---

[24]Paul used fourteen such composites (W. Grundmann, *TDNT* VII, 786f.).

[25]Mk. 3:14 par.; 14:67 par.; cf. Lk. 15:31.

[26]Inserted into the eschatological saying Mk. 14:25 in the par. Mt. 26:29 was a "with you" in keeping with the intent. Cf. Mt. 8:11; Lk. 22:29f.; 23:43.

[27]Rev. 17:14; 3:4, 20f.; 14:1; 20:4, 6.

way in the likeness of God (Rom. 8:29; Phil. 3:20f.).[28] Whoever was with Christ was given his likeness! This was already the meaning of the discipleship of his followers (Lk. 10:16) and that of the table fellowship with the tax collectors (Mk. 2:17). We can see here a bridge to two other conceptual groups whose distinctions, however, should not be overlooked.

3) Only Paul and the deutero-Pauline epistles spoke of a "with Christ" that did not mean a being together with him or a resultant being shaped to his likeness. This third group of sayings referred to a spiritual participation in his dying and rising. This dying-with toward living-with came about through baptism as a result of Jesus' dying and rising; this was expressed in Rom. 6:4, 6; Col. 2:12; probably also in Gal. 2:19. According to II Cor. 5:14 (cf. 4:14) it was established directly through Christ's cross and resurrection, though here a "with" was not expressed. The "with" that was communicated through baptism was appropriated in Col. 2:(13), 20; 3:1, (3, 4; cf. Eph. 2:4ff.).

4) Also original with Paul was the conviction that Jesus' dying and rising manifested themselves, moreover, in Paul's own being and ministry as apostle (Phil. 3:10f.; II Cor. 1:4-7; 4:7-15; 6:3-10; Gal. 6:17; cf. Col. 1:24). A "with" is to be found among these statements only occasionally (II Cor. 4:14), while the fellowship with the destiny of Christ was otherwise expressed by means of genitive connections like the "suffering of Christ" or the "life of Christ."

How did the statements about dying-with toward living-with, so characteristic for Paul, come about?

b) On the discussion. In the discussion about the origin and intention of the statements about dying-with toward living-with one finds a reflection of the particular interpretations of Pauline theology as a whole.

1) The psychological interpretation of Paul traced the statements back to the "mystical experience of Christ" and to a contemplation "most strongly inspired . . . by the Christ-cult."[29] The cross "has become, instead of a historical conception, altogether a spiritual, mystically realized and living reality."[30] The mysticism of death described the mystical-secretive dying of Christ in the symbolic act of baptism; the mysticism of suffering described the confirmation of this death repeated in experience.[31]

2) This way of interpreting by psychological reconstructions gave way in the history of research to history-of-religion analysis. The understanding of the history-of-religion school was summarized as follows by H. Lietzmann.[32] The dying-with toward living-with came out of the mystery religions. The concept was passed on to Paul by the Hellenistic church; the latter understood the rite of initiation of baptism in terms analogous to the consecrations of the mystery

---

[28]The expectation of "ruling together with" (Rev. 5:10; 20:4, 6; 22:5) was referred to in I Cor. 4:8, but—perhaps coincidentally—not appropriated positively by Paul.

[29]A. Deissmann, *Paul* (1957 [= 1927²]), p. 191.

[30]Ibid., pp. 202f.

[31]Cf. supporting references in the review of research in Güttgemanns, op. cit. (Lit., §35,5), pp. 16-20.

[32]H. Lietzmann, *Römerbrief*, at Rom. 6:3 (excursus, pp. 65-68).

religions. The Isis consecration was practiced "like to a voluntary death and a difficult recovery to health." The deity cared (for the consecrated ones) "to make them as it were new-born and to reduce them to the path of health" (Apuleius *Metamorphoses* 11.21 and 23 = LCL, pp. 575 and 581). This all became possible through supernatural powers, which the rite laid hold of, and through contemplative vision. "I approached near unto hell, even to the gates of Proserpine, and after that I was ravished throughout all the elements, I returned to my proper place: about midnight I saw the sun brightly shine, I saw likewise the gods celestial and the gods infernal, before whom I presented myself and worshipped them." Analogous to this, baptism was understood as consecration into the mystery religions. "The submersion in water transferred (sacramentally efficacious) death to the body, the emerging from the water (also sacramentally) transferred the resurrection of Christ to the body." By this means, eternal life was guaranteed to the baptized one under all circumstances. Paul, however, provided this concept of the Hellenistic church with an ethical dimension. He shifted the idea of rising with Christ in the direction of a new ethical conduct and of the future. This history-of-religion derivation of Paul's statements was taken over by R. Bultmann[33] and combined with a kerygmatic interpretation.

3) Bultmann drew his conclusions out of this derivation regarding the relationship of the *syn-* to the *hyper*-statements and at the same time regarding the interpretation of Jesus' dying altogether. Interpreting theologically he reasoned that the *hyper*-statements (Rom. 3–5) explained Jesus' dying with the help of Old Testament/Jewish concepts about the cult and justice; the *syn*-statements (Rom. 6), on the other hand, by using the categories of the Hellenistic mystery religions. Both ways of interpreting mutually excluded each other as images and concepts. Interpreted existentially the cross could only be understood as the question, "whether a man is willing to give up his old understanding of himself and henceforth to understand himself only from the grace of God. . . ,"[34] i.e., in the sense of Rom. 6:11.[35] What this means, however, is that both the cross and human existence are restricted to the narrows of self-understanding. Man, however, lives historically, even in all those relationships into which Paul placed the cross. Man lives, as Paul saw it (Rom. 3–5), under the laws of the existing world order and in the expectation of a different future; and he lives, as Paul thought in Rom. 6, in a "body of sin" and "of death" (Rom. 6:6; 7:24). The interpretation of the cross as dying-with toward living-with was directed quite deliberately at this anthropological frame of reference. This will become clear upon a differentiated analysis of the concept's origin and intention.

c) The effect of the cross as dying-with toward living-with. On the issue of this concept's origin the history of research has moved beyond psychological reconstructing as well as the transference scheme of historicism. As I see it, the

---

[33]*Theology* I, §§13,1; 34,3.
[34]Ibid. I, §33,3f. (quotation, p. 301).
[35]H. Conzelmann did not go beyond this in *Theology*, pp. 205-08.

three factors out of which Pauline theology grew generally also combined their influence to bring about this concept.

1) Here as elsewhere Paul's environment—here his Hellenistic environment—provided the linguistic vehicles and the conceptual aids. The notion of dying-with toward living-with as concept called to mind the mystery religions.

The mystery religions regarded as fundamental the dying and coming-to-life of deities; the initiations into the mysteries made it possible to die to the former ways and to be born again to a new life. Nowhere, however, was this transaction designated in the texts available to us as a dying-with toward a living-with. This was the conclusion of the thorough history-of-religion study of the available sources by G. Wagner.[36] Consequently it is no longer possible to hold the transference theory that Bultmann was still able to accept in his time.[37] On the other hand, one should not altogether reject every genetic connection, as Wagner did. The way people thought in the mystery religions supplied as one factor among several an impetus for these Pauline statements.[38]

Since the conceptual world of the mystery religions did not cover the range of Paul's syn-statements, it was supposed that the conceptual model operative here was the notion of the corporate person.[39] In this concept Adam, e.g., left his mark on all his descendants. Paul, however, did not appropriate this concept into his syn- but rather his en-statements (I Cor. 15:22). Influencing the shape of the syn-statements alongside the reflective impetus provided by the mystery religions was also an inner-Christian tradition. To it we now turn.

2) The concept of dying-with toward living-with corresponded in substance to that of discipleship, which was a constitutive part of the Jesus tradition (§19,2). It corresponded because discipleship meant not only to be together with Jesus, but also to become directed by the course of his life. It produced a total break with the former existence; not only the separation from occupation and family, but also that from one's customary manner of life. This separation was also represented graphically as dying: "If any man would come after me, let him deny himself and take up his cross . . ."—like the condemned person who was led to the place of execution (Mk. 8:34 par.; Mt. 10:38 par.). To follow Jesus in discipleship meant to know oneself no longer, to see oneself as condemned to death, and after Easter that signified to see oneself condemned like him.

Is it thinkable that this substantive parallel helped shape the Pauline concept? After Easter it was no longer possible "to follow," "to follow behind someone" in the literal sense in relationship to Jesus. Consequently it is by no means astonishing that this term from the synoptic Gospels was never employed in the Pauline epistles. If one takes into account that the Jesus tradition was often transformed into the kerygma of the community, it can be assumed with con-

---

[36]Op. cit. (Lit., §35,5).

[37]Theology I, §33,3d.

[38]Similarly, Larsson, op. cit. (Lit., §35,5), pp. 48-80.

[39]Thus W. Grundmann, TDNT VII, 789-792.

siderable probability that Paul substituted the concept of discipleship among other options by talking about dying-with toward living-with Christ.[40]

3) Finally, it needs to be clarified why only Paul and the writings in early Christian literature linked directly with him spoke about a dying-with toward living-with Christ. The similar statements in Ignatius (Sm. 4:2; Pol. 6:1) have a different intent! This very observation makes it improbable that Paul took this concept over from the Hellenistic community. In contrast, it can be explained in terms of a specific principle of his theology; he understood the course of Christ's life in a strictly theocentric manner as the intervention of God. Thus, in II Cor. 5:14f. he developed the following theological deduction: ". . . one has died for all; therefore all have died. And he died for all, that those who live might live no longer for themselves but for him who for their sake died and was raised." This effect was made possible not only through baptism; it already came into force on the basis of the cross. Already through the dying of Christ all have been marked by the cross before they know it! Why? In the dying of Jesus the condemnation of God upon adamitic man was carried out (Rom. 8:3). Hence in God's eyes all adamitic people stand under a death sentence carried out representatively for them. According to God's judgment and therefore in his eyes they are all dead in order that—based on representation—they may live to the One who died and was raised for them. Because Paul viewed Jesus' dying and rising in strict theocentric terms, as God's action for humanity, he also understood it as the action of God upon humanity that marked everyone.

d) Baptism as dying with Christ. 1) The difficult formulation of Rom. 6:5 spoke about a "growing together" of Christians in the context of this sign. "For if we have [become] grown together [through baptism] with the likeness of his death, we shall also be so with that of his resurrection" (Gr.).[41] The *homoiōma* (likeness) of the death of Jesus was in fact that dying of every adamitic man according to II Cor. 5:14, i.e., it was Jesus' dying as universal event. Prior to baptism Jesus' dying meant a judgment of God that stood over all people (Rom. 8:3) and was proclaimed as such along the lines of II Cor. 5:14: "they all died." In baptism this proclamation became the very experience of the individual. The individual human being was drawn into this judgment in a unique, historically concrete act in such a way that "he died with him."

2) The genetic derivation of the dying-with toward living-with motif also helps to clarify in what sense all baptized people died with him in order to live with him, as Rom. 6:3ff. put it. We observe in Rom. 6:3-10 that Paul talked about what happened to one in baptism first of all in the indicative mood as something that had occurred; this was something that for the imperatival sentences thereafter (Rom. 6:11-13) was supposedly waiting yet to be recognized as having happened. In proximity to v. 4, "We were buried therefore with him by baptism into death," stood v. 11, "So you also must consider yourselves dead

---

[40]Pondering this also were Larsson, op. cit. (n. 38), pp. 25f. and Schweizer, *Lordship*, p. 91 (expanded in Ger. revision, pp. 140-43).

[41]Cf. the thorough discussion in J. Schneider, *TDNT* V, 191-95.

to sin and alive to God, . . !" The indicative and imperative were related to one another not simply as theory and practice. They intended to say rather that the dying-with toward living-with was not to be found on an empirical level. It was neither an experience of conversion nor a supraphysical transformation. Rather the indicative proclaimed the death sentence that had come upon adamitic man, that was carried out representatively upon Christ, and to which baptism, therefore, subjected itself. The imperative stated the challenge to let this sentence become valid for oneself: "consider yourselves dead. . . !" "to consider your-self" *(logizesthai)* meant to see yourself with God's eyes, to let become valid for oneself what had happened from God's side, i.e., to believe! The statement in the indicative, "our old self was crucified with [through baptism]" (Rom. 6:6), bore the same intent fundamentally, therefore, as the indicative statement in II Cor. 5:18f. that God reconciled the world, humanity, unto himself through Jesus' dying before it learned of it through missionary preaching. In both cases there was a witness to what had taken place from God's side. Seen historically, baptism was an equivocal human action in the same way as the cross. What had taken place in, with, and under this action from God's side could only be proclaimed and confessed out of faith. The imperative, however, summoned us to allow this action to become effective for us and upon us through faith.

3) That this proclamation was valid generally for all baptized people was confirmed by the way in which the living-with was brought together with the dying-with Christ. Paul never said that in baptism you have died with and been raised with Christ. Rather the living-with Christ was a deduction out of the dying-with Christ in these ways.

3.1 It was an eschatological future dimension to be hoped for. "If we have died with Christ, we believe that we shall also live with him" (Rom. 6:8; cf. 6:5).

3.2 It was a present dimension for faith. "So you also must consider yourselves dead to sin and alive to God . . ." (Rom. 6:11).

3.3 It was therefore a calling to be obedient in faith, to show forth love. "We were buried therefore with him into death, so that . . . we too might walk in newness of life" (Rom. 6:4). This "newness of life" was not a natural nor an ethical condition, but just like righteousness it was the new reality that determined who a person was and that God had brought about in Jesus' rising from the dead. In Rom. 8:1-4 Paul called this reality the Holy Spirit.

4) In Rom. 6:6-10, 12f. Paul discussed what the new manner of life looked like in practical terms within our human existence. The "I" that lived with Christ and shall live with him was the "I" of faith. In contrast to this "I" was the "I" of adamitic man, according to Rom. 6:6f. To be sure, the "I" of adamitic man had been judged through the cross of Christ and had been buried in baptism; yet it had never become a past tense as long as we live in the flesh; we must consider it crucified with Christ again and again. The new life always realized itself, as Gal. 5:16-24 stated further, strictly as the battle of the Spirit, who supported the "I" and took it into service, against the flesh. The new "I" could only exist

when its life was sustained through the word of proclamation and through the Spirit present in the word. In this way it was also possible for the new "I" to take into service the parts of the old man, his mouth and hands. "Do not yield your members to sin as instruments of wickedness, but yield yourselves to God as those who have been brought from death to life, and your members to God as instruments of righteousness" (Rom. 6:12f.).

5) There was fundamental agreement between Rom. 6 and Col. 2:12 when the latter stated in hymnic style: ". . . buried with him in baptism, in which you were also raised with him through faith. . . ." The conditional clause of Col. 3:1, "If then you have been raised with Christ . . . ," was also not meant in a perfectionistic sense but as an imperative along the lines of Rom. 6:11. Col. 2:13, however, added the assurance to the baptismal event parallel to 2:12 in the language of the synoptics: "And you, who were dead in trespasses [not: through the cross were crucified with him!] . . . God made alive together with him, having forgiven us all our trespasses. . . ." Only the "with" in this statement went beyond what was said in Luke 15:24. The hymnic statement in Eph. 2:4-6, on the other hand, which began like Col. 2:13, anticipated the consummation while speaking doxologically in a way that went far beyond Rom. 8:30: ". . . [God] made us alive together with Christ . . . and raised us up with him . . . in Christ Jesus."

e) The dying and rising of Christ at work in the history of the apostle. In II Cor. 4:11, Paul emphasized about himself "we are always being given up [by God] to death for Jesus' sake, so that the life of Jesus may be manifested in our mortal flesh." The latter would not only transpire at the consummation (4:14), but also right then in the present in all the experiences of God's power, the power that made deliverance and renewal possible (4:8f., 12, 16; 6:3-10). This existence of the apostle did not come as the result of imitation or mystical contemplation. Rather he understood this existence as the dying and rising of Christ at work and becoming evident in his life.[42] This was made possible, however, by Christ having taken the apostle into his service. Being delivered over to death (II Cor. 4:11), e.g., happened for the apostle, just as it did for Christ himself (Rom. 4:25), because they both trod the path of obedience. This was stated about the apostle in II Cor. 4:1-6 (the introduction to 4:7-18), and about Christ in Phil. 2:8.

According to Rom. 6:1-13, no one would become obedient, in fact, in any other way than through this dying-with toward living-with Christ! Where the history of the apostle was marked in secret by Christ's dying and rising it was the consequence of his own spiritual dying-with toward living-with him. Paul's having died with Christ was documented in his having suffered with him! Yet

---

[42]This explanation was developed by Güttgemanns, op. cit. (n. 31), pp. 195-98 in connection with E. Käsemann (*ZNW* 41 [1942], 53f.): "Since the sufferings of the apostle only became understandable as christological epiphany, terms like that of 'analogy,' 'imitation,' 'discipleship,' and 'continuation' had to be carefully avoided in making interpretation" (ibid., p. 195).

this substantive context was articulated nowhere in Paul's writings. The suffering of Christians was interpreted, however, both as participation in the suffering of Christ (4:13) and as the killing of the flesh (4:1, 6) in the First Epistle of Peter.

In any case, Paul understood the *syn*-concept not as a partnership-connection, but as something that came to one from without, established and generated from God through Jesus' dying and rising. Hence this *syn* led frequently to the much more plentiful uses of the preposition *en*. And *en Christō* in Rom. 6:11 followed the *syn Christō* in 6:2-10, just as it did in II Cor. 5:17 after 5:14f.

6. "IN CHRIST"

a) Occurrence. This expression is to be found in Paul's writings with much greater frequency than the *syn*. It occurred ca. 164 times. It too was original with him; it is found elsewhere in the New Testament only in the deutero-Pauline epistles and in the First Epistle of Peter. The *en*-expressions of the Johannine writings had a different shape and intention; in shape they had interchangeable forms: "we are in Christ"— "Christ is in us." In terms of content they expressed the mutual relationship between the exalted One and the disciples. The Pauline *en Christō*-formula, however, pointed to something that was at work quite one-sidedly from Christ.

b) Variable intention. The intention of this expression in many passages was quite naturally varied. *En Christō* corresponded to the numerous other Pauline *en*-expressions. Man existed *en sarki* (in the flesh), *en nomō* (under the Law), *en pneumati* (in the Spirit), *en kyriō* (in the Lord). The *en* in these expressions could be causal, instrumental, or modal in meaning. It never had, however, the meaning of location, mainly because Christ was always event and person in relationship. The expression *en Christō* could mean that one's direction was determined by Christ or also that one simply belonged to him. In the latter sense it frequently stood for the adjective "Christian," which was not yet current. But even for the refined use of the term the precise basic meaning was also important.

c) Basic meaning. The precise intent was that of the causal and instrumental: "in Christ" was the person who was determined by him. But how was Christ understood in this concept? One did not have the exalted One primarily in mind as one did in the *en kyriō* concept. A. Oepke derived the precise intent of the expression quite correctly from I Cor. 15:22: "For as in Adam all die, so also in Christ shall all be made alive."[43] "In Adam" was the person who was determined by Adam's fall; "in Christ" was accordingly the person who was determined by Christ's act of obedience, i.e., by his dying and rising.[44] His dying and rising, however, were of course present in a determining way in the exalted

---

[43] *TDNT* II, 541-43.
[44] Similarly also Neugebauer, op. cit. (Lit., §35,6); *en Christō* pointed back to the event in cross and resurrection and sought to grasp in that event the consummation at the end already in the present (ibid., pp. 34-44, 147-49).

One who was at work through the Spirit.[45] He laid hold of the individual through proclamation, pointedly through baptism. Thus, "in Christ" were those who through baptism had been taken into his body, the community of faith, and through this action were exposed to the activity of the Spirit through the word. They as individuals were thus also shaped by him as person. This experience that happened to them was appropriated by faith, but it always preceded faith as its foundation so that "the ones 'in Christ' " were not simply identical with the ones having faith. The significance of Jesus' dying awaited full expression in soteriological and ecclesiological terms as well.

So it was that Jesus' dying in the strength of its manifold significance reached out to people in various ways. It directed its attention toward the individual and yet did not seek out only religious individuals, like the mystery religions did, who would gather together in cultic association. It was intent upon a transformation of all humanity: "And he died for all, that those who live might live no longer for themselves . . ." (II Cor. 5:14-17).

---

[45]This side was emphasized by J. Gnilka, *Philipperbrief*, at Phil. 2:5 against Neugebauer. But even he, of course, did not return to the position of Deissmann (op. cit. [Lit., §35,6]), who also appropriated the work of Bousset (*Kyrios*, pp. 153-181); according to this position *en Christō* circumscribed "the sojourn in a pneuma-element comparable to air."

Chapter III

THE CONTINUED MINISTRY OF JESUS

§36. The Event of Proclamation (the Gospel)

R. Asting, *Die Verkündigung des Wortes im Urchristentum* (1939); D. Lührmann, *Das Offenbarungsverständnis bei Paulus und in den paulinischen Gemeinden* (1965). **On 3:** E. Klostermann, HNT, at Mk. 1:1; J. Schniewind, *Euangelion* I/II (1927/31); G. Friedrich, *euangelizomai*, etc., *TDNT* II, 707-737; G. Kittel, *legō*, *TDNT* IV, 114-19; P. Stuhlmacher, *Das paulinische Evangelium. 1. Vorgeschichte* (1968), O. Michel, "Evangelium," *RAC* VI, 1107-1160; E. Käsemann, *Romans*, at 1:1. **On 4:** W. Michaelis, *mimeomai*, *TDNT* IV, 666-673; H. D. Betz, *Nachfolge und Nachahmung Jesu Christi im NT* (1967), pp. 137-169; Goppelt, *typos*, *TDNT* VIII, 249f.; H. Conzelmann, *1 Corinthians: A Commentary on the First Epistle to the Corinthians* (Hermeneia, 1975), at 11:1 (Lit.!).

1. INTRODUCTION: THE PROBLEMATIC

a) Analogies. Jesus was not to Paul God's witness in history as the prophets were to the Old Testament or the martyrs and the rabbis were to Judaism. For Paul Jesus was the personal event of salvation. In Jesus' dying and rising God intervened in history eschatologically. The Old Testament/Jewish analogies for the continuation of Jesus' ministry, in Paul's eyes, were therefore the Exodus — especially the Passover (I Cor. 5:7; cf. 10:5) — or, antithetically, Adam's fall (Rom. 5:12-21; I Cor. 15:20, 22, 44-49). As was true for those events in the Old Testament, the public activity of Jesus was realized through proclamation, confession, and cult. The closest analogy in the Hellenistic world was not Socrates but Julius Caesar to whom was acribed an apotheosis through ideological-political propaganda and cultic celebration. For Caesar the result was that he maintained influence throughout the centuries as the ideal *cosmokratōr*. We shall now consider the structure of Jesus' continued ministry more precisely against this backdrop.

b) The structure of Jesus' continued ministry. The continued ministry of Jesus took place, as it were, on two different levels.

1) Jesus was mediated to subsequent generations, as it were, from above in a threefold manner, in "trinitarian" fashion if you will.

Jesus was present as the *kyrios* who interceded for his people with God (Rom. 8:34) and who was establishing his eschatological dominion over the world by gathering his own in the *ekklēsia* and putting down the powers opposing God (I Cor. 15:23-28).

He was also present because God had established a new world condition through him, decisively through his cross and his resurrection; God set up the new covenant through him (I Cor. 11:25; II Cor. 3:6); he reconciled the world, humanity, to himself (II Cor. 5:18f.).

The eschatological engagement of both God and the *kyrios* was encountered in the present whenever people were taken hold of through the Spirit of God (II Cor. 3:6). The new "above" brought about the emergence of a new humanity through three substantively identical occurrences (I Cor. 12:4-6):

and there are varieties of gifts, but the same Spirit;
and there are varieties of service, but the same Lord;
and there are varieties of working, but it is the same God. . . .

Gift, service, and working were three sides of the same event. The three who accomplished them were in their activity one God. This activity was eschatological because it accomplished the new, ultimate relationship to God that transcended the range of historical relationships. But it was at the same time essentially historical because it intercepted man not observably as apocalyptic event but secretly within this-worldly occurrences that let him become eschatologically new through faith I Cor. 2:6-11; II Cor. 5:7).

2) The mediation from above transpired in history through—to use the words of II Cor. 5:18f.— "the message of reconciliation" and through "the ministry of reconciliation," the "office" that the message bore. In its structure, the message was tradition that was passed on as kerygma, i.e., as a human word going forth out of tradition, a word that was an address from above. The kerygma took on consistency in the sacraments. It was portrayed through the witness of a manner of life (§36,5).

The problematic behind this starting point emerged out of the intersecting of the pneumatic-eschatological line "from above" and the historical line "from below."

c) The problematic. The thought processes of the modern world since the Enlightenment have been able to understand in Jesus only the appearance of a historical personage, but not an intervention of God in history and a continued ministry of the exalted One through the work of the church. How then can the figure of Jesus so remote in time be at work in the present? The Tübingen school of F. C. Baur replied that it happened through the power of the idea embodied in Jesus that was progressively unfolding itself. The school of A. Ritschl saw its realization through the psychological effect of Jesus' religious personality.

R. Bultmann and his school saw it happening in a human recounting that took on the form of the address that offered a new self-understanding from *extra nos*. Bultmann wrote, ". . . the salvation-occurrence is nowhere present except in the proclaiming, accosting, demanding, and promising word of preaching."[1] But did this summons to decision of the proclamation of the Christ event in fact show itself to be at work? In 1968, the crisis began for the word- and kerygma-theologies with this question of critical empiricism. Why did that kerygma not accomplish the change that took place through the preaching of Paul—as his letters indicate—on a worldwide scale? With this statement of the issue in mind we shall now examine the decisive factors of the process of communication addressed by Paul; we begin with proclamation.

2. THE TERMINOLOGY OF PROCLAMATION: STATISTICAL BREAKDOWN

How did Paul refer to the word by which he represented the Christ event as missionary and pastor?

We shall see more clearly what was characteristic for Paul if we compare his terminology to that of the book of Acts, to the way the latter described the work of Paul and the other missionaries. Acts designated this word event with the following verbs in roughly comparable frequency: *euangelizomai* (to preach the gospel—Acts 13:32; 14:15, 21; 15:35; 16:10), *didaskō* (to teach—Acts 18:11; 20:20; 21:28; 28:31), *martyreō* (to give witness—Acts 13:22; 14:3; 23:11), *kēryssō* (to proclaim—Acts 19:13; 20:25; 28:31), and *parakaleō* (to admonish, to exhort—Acts 11:23; 20:2). This was the customary linguistic usage of the church of the time in its entire breadth.

For Paul, however, *euangelizomai* was far and away the most frequently used verb (in ca. 20 passages); occurring with even greater frequency (ca. 57 times) was the substantive *euangelion* (gospel, gospel proclamation), a word that is to be found in Acts only twice and in the rest of the New Testament only ca. 15 times. Coming next in importance was *kēryssō* (to proclaim—15 times), while the substantive *kerygma* (proclamation) played a role neither for him (it appeared only four times) nor for the rest of the New Testament (four times). In contrast to the book of Acts there was in Paul a noticeable retreat of usage for *didaskō* (to teach—seven times) and *martyreō* (to give witness; nowhere of pregnant significance); the latter was characteristic for Acts and with another meaning in combination with *martyria* (witness) also for John's Gospel. It is noteworthy that *parakaleō* (to admonish, to exhort, to comfort) occurred very frequently (44 times; the substantive cognate, *paraklēsis*, occurred in 22 passages [of that number 12 times in the Second Epistle to the Corinthians]). This term was supplemented through use of *noutheteō* (to admonish; six times, but only once in the rest of the New Testament).

---

[1] *Theology* I, 302.

On the basis of this statistical breakdown we can see that Paul understood himself as a herald whose task it was to represent good news, and as a "paraclete" who was to address people personally and to give them exhortation. He qualified this kind of speaking, above all through references back to his missionary work, as "the word of God," or "the word of the Lord," or simply "the word" (cf. §36,4c). Quite deliberately he adopted this early Christian missionary terminology for himself and, analogous to the expression already in use elsewhere "the word of truth" (II Cor. 6:7; Col. 1:5; Eph. 1:13), he coined the expressions "the word of the cross" (I Cor. 1:18) and "the word of reconciliation" (II Cor. 5:19).

The theological intention behind this terminology can be deciphered primarily in connection with the key term "gospel."

3. "GOSPEL" AS A RELIGIOUS TERM PRIOR TO PAUL

For Hellenistic people as well as for Jews and for Christians most of all, the verb *euangelizesthai* and the substantive *euangelion* had become religious terms long before Paul used them.

a) The Hellenistic world. In the everyday linguistic usage of Hellenistic people *euangelion* meant the good news that everyone welcomed because it brought with it an increase in the quality of life; most importantly it served, however, as a sacral technical term in the cult of the emperor and in the theological rationale of the empire. Important news about the emperor and his edicts, which because of the dearth of other means of communication was proclaimed orally and preserved in inscriptions, was referred to as *euangelion* (joyous news); it was called this because it mediated peace and prosperity for the entire society. This word usage came to be known above all through the inscription from Priene on the Meander in A.D. 9, published in 1906. It can be reconstructed and translated as follows: "But the birthday of the god was for the world the beginning of tidings of joy on his account."[2] It has been frequently maintained in the history of research that this was the linguistic resource of Pauline usage[3] because one simply could not find a terminological usage of the substantive in the Old Testament/Jewish realm.

b) The Old Testament. The prior history of the Old Testament and Judaism took its starting point from the verb *euangelizesthai*. In Deutero- and Trito-Isaiah it designated the proclamation of the end-time news of salvation through which salvation would dawn (Isa. 40:9; 52:7; 60:6; 61:1; Ps. 95[96]:3). In Isa. 52:7, the herald of joy *(euangelizomenos)* was announced who would make known good news for Zion: "Your God is [has become] king" (NEB). This proclamation spelled the release from foreign domination through the ultimate reign of God.

---

[2]Cf. A. Deissmann, *Light From the Ancient East* (1910), p. 371.
[3]Thus ibid., pp. 371f.; E. Klostermann, *Markus*, at Mk. 1:1; E. Hennecke/W. Schneemelcher/ R. M. Wilson, *New Testament Apocrypha* I (1963), 71-75.

Euangelizesthai meant to proclaim Yahweh's eschatological ascent to the throne of dominion and to realize it through that proclamation.

c) *Jesus.* In all probability Jesus himself appropriated this Old Testament usage and introduced it into Christian vocabulary through the saying in Mt. 11:5. He characterized his preaching and teaching by drawing on Isa. 61:1 in the sentence: "the poor have good news preached to them" *(ptōchoi euangelizontai).* The verb was given direction through dependence on the prophecy. Its content was the joyous news about the establishment of the end-time kingly reign of God; it was to come about in secret through Jesus' ministry (§6,3b). The prophecy of Deutero-Isaiah remained alive in Judaism. In 1QH 18:14 the herald of joy was probably identified with the Teacher of Righteousness, in 11QMelch with Melchizedek.[4]

d) *Jewish-Christianity.* After Easter the message about Jesus as the Christ who was establishing the reign of God was developed from his message about the coming reign. In the book of Revelation, which appropriated Palestinian traditions, the Jewish theological expression *euangelion euangelizein* (Heb. *biśśar bᵉśorah)* was used at 14:6; it stood for the "liberating message of salvation," and above all for the "prophetic message of salvation and destruction"[5] (cf. Rev. 10:7). It is thus possible that the message about Jesus, the Christ, was already characterized with this terminology in Palestinian Jewish-Christianity. A pointer in this direction could be that didactic traditions from the Palestinian church were referred to as "the gospel" by Paul in I Cor. 15:1f. and Rom. 1:1 though he normally employed "gospel" as a *nomen actionis* for his preaching. Apparently he appropriated a linguistic usage along with the formulas that preceded his own.

Thus the use of this central term grew within the Hellenistic church in a kind of continuity, starting with the Old Testament/Jewish tradition that depended on Deutero-Isaiah, and was passed on through Jesus and the Palestinian church.[6] For this reason its usage was influenced by the tradition's concept of God. But gospel was a term that also got the attention of Hellenistic people.

4. "GOSPEL" IN PAUL

Paul appropriated this resplendent term in order to designate the shape and content of his commission to labor among people. He could speak about "his gospel"[7] because the one gospel was laid upon him with a charge and not because

---

[4]Stuhlmacher, op. cit. (Lit., §36,3), pp. 144ff.

[5]Ibid., p. 152.

[6]Advocating this path are Schniewind, op. cit. (Lit., §36,3); G. Friedrich, *TDNT* II, 728f.; and with further observations, Stuhlmacher, op. cit. (n. 4), pp. 153, 204f., 289; and Michel, op. cit. (Lit., §36,3).

[7]More reliable than the debated expression "my gospel" (Rom. 2:16; 16:25) was "our gospel" (II Cor. 4:3; I Thess. 1:5; II Thess. 2:14) and especially "the gospel which was preached by me" (Gal. 1:11; cf. Gal. 1:8; 2:2; I Cor. 15:1) or the gospel "that I had been entrusted with" (Gal. 2:7; cf. I Thess. 2:4).

he represented his peculiar conception of the gospel. He was "called to be an apostle, set apart for the gospel of God" (Rom. 1:1). "Gospel" meant for Paul both the act of proclaiming and the content of proclamation. Rom. 1:1f., e.g., can be restated in keeping with its intent as, ". . . set apart for the [preaching of the] gospel of God, the gospel that he [as content] . . . promised in former times."[8] In I Cor. 9:14, the two meanings stood side by side in the same sentence: "In the same way, the Lord commanded that those who proclaim the gospel [as content] should get their living by the gospel [as act of preaching]."[9] Thus, "the gospel" was both a *nomen actionis* and yet a specific content.

Regarding content, it was qualified through the use of two genitives. It was "the gospel of God,"[10] the message that God caused to be preached, even that which he himself uttered (*genitive of author*). As was said more frequently, it was "the gospel of Christ,"[11] i.e., the gospel about Christ, "about his Son" (Rom. 1:3). Jesus Christ was the central content of the gospel. Most certainly he was not this as a thing but as the One who was at work in and through the proclamation of the apostle.[12] But the expression thought of him primarily as this active content.[13] He was himself present in the gospel; to be ashamed of the gospel and of God or Christ was the same thing (Rom. 1:16; Phil. 1:27; I Thess. 2:12; Col. 1:25). In a way characteristic for him, Paul filled out this twofold, formal qualification of a word generally used elsewhere absolutely[14] and turned it into an instructive key term within the church. It was characterized in his thought by three aspects.

a) Not only the content of the gospel, but also his preaching was an eschatological event; his preaching was the fulfillment of a promise. The content of his gospel corresponded to prophecy (Rom. 1:2; I Cor. 15:3f.) and the prophetic word about the eschatological herald of joy was fulfilled in his proclamation (Rom. 10:15 = Isa. 52:7). Hence Paul understood his work as a cosmic event prior to the end of the world, i.e., in an apocalyptic framework (Rom. 15:14-33). Aside from certain sayings of Jesus (Mt. 11:5), the proclamation of the gospel was characterized nowhere else in early Christianity so strictly as eschatological event as by Paul (not I Pet. 1:12 nor even Lk. 4:17ff.; 24:44).

b) The content of the gospel was not restricted to a certain language but it was distinguished in a theologically precise manner over against "another gospel."

Surprisingly, Paul did not call the kingdom of God the content of the gospel

---

[8]Cf. I Cor. 1:17; 9:16; Gal. 1:16.

[9]Similarly I Cor. 9:18; further as a technical term for the carrying out of proclamation: II Cor. 8:18; Phil. 4:3.

[10]Rom. 1:1; 15:16; II Cor. 11:7; I Thess. 2:2, 8, 9; cf. I Pet. 4:17.

[11]Rom. 15:19; I Cor. 9:12, (18); II Cor. 2:12; (4:4); 9:13; 10:14; Gal. 1:7; Phil. 1:27; I Thess. 3:2; also "of his Son" (Rom. 1:9); "of our Lord Jesus" (II Thess. 1:8).

[12]Rom. 15:18; II Cor. 5:20; 13:3.

[13]It was in this sense an objective genitive and not a subjective one (differing is G. Friedrich, *TDNT* II, 730f.).

[14]Even the verb *euangelizomai* was used in an absolute sense by Paul—Gal. 1:23 ("the faith") excepted—while Luke, who used it just as often, linked it for the most part with objects.

as the synoptic tradition, congruous with the Old Testament, had done.[15] In keeping with its fulfillment character he described the content christologically. This can be seen especially in two passages: I Cor. 15:3-5 with its Easter kerygma of the Jewish-Christian church and Rom. 1:3f. with an enclosed formula of the Palestinian Christology of exaltation. In Rom. 10:8f. he made use of the confession of the Hellenistic church for the message that he later on referred to as the gospel. Corresponding to these christological descriptive actions were the soteriological ones in Rom. 1:16f.; through the gospel God's righteousness was at work. The gospel could thus be summarized in various formulas; starting with each it would then be developed in a different direction and manner.

Yet Paul certainly did not believe that every proclamation that referred to Jesus was gospel! It was in fact the historical goal of most of the Pauline epistles to clarify the gospel so that its acute misrepresentation might be prevented.[16] In Galatians Paul interpreted the gospel as the message of justification by grace alone and by faith alone in order to fight against its Judaizing misrepresentation. It was interpreted as *theologia crucis* in the First Epistle to the Corinthians because it had been misunderstood syncretistically as an enthusiast doctrine of wisdom. Both II Corinthians and Colossians also showed opposition to syncretistic distortions that had a Judaizing impact, just as did I Corinthians.

These distortions were provoked, to put it pointedly, by the gospel itself. The distortions were attempts to make the gospel, in keeping with its intention, relevant for Jewish and Hellenistic people and to present it as the solution to their problems. In addition there emerged, unintentionally, a "conformity" (Rom. 12:2) to the thought-forms of the addressees. Heresy arose, quite tragically, right where the gospel was advancing into a world of altered circumstances. For this reason heresy could not be overcome through repetition of what was said earlier but only through a more adequate application of the gospel to new questions. It was hardly coincidental that the Pauline gospel took shape positively in the midst of these very controversies.

The perspectives Paul rejected were not merely those theological schemes that differed from his own. He was fully prepared to approve the validity of other theologies, like that of a Peter or a James, next to his own (Gal. 2:6-10; I Cor. 3:5-15; 15:11). But then he did draw an absolute limit from time to time and totally rejected specific outgrowths of the gospel. He called them "turning to another gospel—not that there is another gospel" (Gal. 1:6f.; II Cor. 11:4); those proclamations had forfeited the identity of Jesus and of the Spirit (II Cor. 11:4) and perverted Christian existence (Gal. 3:1-3; 5:4; I Cor. 15:17-19; II Cor. 13:5, etc.).

---

[15] "the gospel of the *basileia*" (Mt. 4:23; 9:35; 24:14; cf. Mk. 1:14f.); "preach the good news of the kingdom of God" (Lk. 4:43; 8:1; 16:16; Acts 8:12).

[16] Regarding the historical course of these debates, cf. Goppelt, *Apostolic Times*, pp. 71-77, 92-102; regarding the substantive issue, cf. L. Goppelt, "The Plurality of New Testament Theologies and the Unity of the Gospel as an Ecumenical Problem," *The Gospel and Unity* (ed. V. Vajta [1971]), pp. 106-130 (ibid., pp. 117f.: response to H. Koester, "Häretiker im Urchristentum als theologisches Problem," in *Zeit und Geschichte, Festschrift für R. Bultmann* [1964], pp. 61-76).

What criterion determined where this limit was to be drawn? Paul took his stand on two principles: (1) To be taken as gospel was only that message which came from the primitive witness of the apostles (Gal. 1:11f.; 2:1f.; I Cor. 15:1-11). But, of course, Paul's opponents also laid a counterclaim to the apostles of Jerusalem! (2) That which represented the gospel's proper development and that which was distortion could not be derived from the transmitted formula as such; it could only be determined on the basis of one's explication of genuine tradition. The guideline and criterion for this explication was the exclusive role of mediation exercised by Christ with regard to salvation. God's ultimate and gracious turning toward the world was represented by him alone. In Gal. 2:21, Paul countered the Judaizers in Galatia who wanted to incorporate Jesus into the system of a humanly produced righteousness: ". . . for if justification were through the law, then Christ died to no purpose." And he countered the enthusiast teachers of wisdom in Corinth (I Cor. 1:18-25; 2:1f.) with his preaching of the cross: "For I decided to know nothing among you except Jesus Christ and him crucified" (2:2). And in II Cor. 4:7-18; 11:23-33; 12:7-10 he rejected the view of a synergistic alteration of the world through divine demonstrations of power; these were propagated by pseudo-apostles in Corinth and were countered by Paul with the mark of the cross upon his apostolic ministry.

How were those listening to this debate able to recognize the truth? They could not cling to the "objective" authority of a formula or of a person; Paul considered them capable of thoughtful listening within their bond to Christ and deciding for themselves (Gal. 3:1-5; II Cor. 10:3-6). Viewed in this way, the discernment of spirits in I Cor. 12:10 was a charisma because it was recognized by faith. Thus what emerged as the result of debates in the community was not an accumulation of dogma but a new confessional formula that took a stand on the new questions in the recognition of faith. The new confession of the Hellenistic church—"Jesus is *kyrios*!"—also served the discerning of spirits, according to I Cor. 12:3. And at the time when the First Epistle of John was written one went beyond Paul in opposition to Docetism and confessed: "Jesus Christ has come in the flesh" (I Jn. 4:2).

No witness of the New Testament, however, established the limits of the message of Christ as the one gospel theologically more precisely over against the distortions that arose under Jewish and Hellenistic influences than did Paul; no one developed that message as gospel in so profiled a manner for people's lives as he.

c) Linked to this substantive profiling of the gospel was its qualification as word of God. That which brought forth the community of faith was called by Paul "gospel" (I Cor. 15:1f.) and "the word of the Lord" (I Thess. 1:8) or "the word of God" (I Thess. 2:13). These two expressions were already employed in the LXX as technical terms to reproduce the Hebrew expression *d^ebar Yahweh* (word of Yahweh); subsumed in the understanding of the Old Testament under this expression were then the particular directives of the God of the covenant that were represented by the prophets. For Paul, however, these two terms designated the word about Christ, i.e., the gospel. This linguistic usage had already emerged in the church before Paul; it also occurred in early Christian traditions independent of him.[17] Paul himself used it comparatively seldom.[18]

1) Even this designation of the message about Christ assumed a face of its own in Paul. For him it did not refer primarily to a formal authority or a symbol of power but to the trustworthiness of a statement. This was developed in connection with the Old Testament word of God. According to Rom. 3:1f. and 9:4, this word was initially directed at Israel. It did not communicate general truths but gave expression to an election in relationship to a concrete partner within his historical situation (Rom. 9:11; 11:5; 7:28; cf. *proorizō* [Rom. 8:29f.]), to a calling (Rom. 9:12; 11:29; cf. 8:30), and to a promise (Rom. 9:4, 8, 9; cf. 15:8).[19] With an eye toward this "word of God" Paul advanced the thesis that represented the theme of Rom. 9–11 and the foundation of his theology as well as of his faith: "But it is not as though the word of God had failed" (Rom. 9:6). The calling of Israel, held together by promise and established upon election, would not become a deception even if Israel as a whole refused to accept the gospel. God would remain faithful to the calling through which he bound himself to people. His word was not the call to decision at a given point in time, as understood by Bultmann. It was not information made public about God's accomplishments at a given point in time, as understood by Barth; for the latter it was through this public disclosure that the Spirit was given *ubi et quando visum est deo*. Rather God's word was his bond, which was based on a promising call in relationship to concrete, historical partners. That word established a continuity of the bond between God and man in history and, seen in this way, it established salvation history. Dependent upon the interpretation of Rom. 9–11 was the interpretation of "the word" and thereby proclamation and the existence of the church.[20] In Rom. 9–11, Paul came to the assurance that God's word to Israel was accomplishing exactly what it had said it would. In fact, God would do still more in the end than he had said he would; he would give all Israel a share in the promised salvation (Rom. 11:25). God would not withdraw his "calling" (Rom. 11:29)!

Paul did not ask, therefore, why the gospel did not prove to be at work in relationship to Israel although it was the word of God. Rather he asked: Why has God not brought to faith the people that he called for salvation through his word of promise? Was he not faithful to his word?

2) At this point Paul presupposed, as it were, that which was the second aspect: God "was able to do what he had promised" (Rom. 4:21); through his

---

[17]Jas. 1:18, 21ff.; Heb. 4:12; 13:7; Rev. 1:2, 9; 6:9 and passim; cf. G. Kittel, *TDNT* IV, 115.

[18]"the word of God": I Thess. 2:13; I Cor. 14:36; II Cor. 2:17; 4:2; Col. 1:25; "the word" (used absolutely): I Thess. 1:6; Gal. 6:6; Phil. 1:14; Col. 4:3; "the word of the Lord": I Thess. 1:8; II Thess. 3:1; "a word of the Lord" used sometimes as a designation for individual sayings of the earthly Jesus: I Thess. 4:15; for this also "give charge . . . the Lord," and such (I Cor. 7:10; 9:14).

[19]In contrast, "to reveal" *(apokalyptō, phaneroō)* was not bound to "the word" (§28,3a).

[20]This has now also been set forth correctly by E. Käsemann, *Romans*, pp. 253-263; Discussion and Lit. to Rom. 9–11; cf. above at §38,3.

word he even "gives life to the dead and calls into existence the things that do not exist" (Rom. 4:17). Even this innate power of the word, however, was characterized by Paul in a way that corresponded to the essence of the word as gospel. In proclamation the innate power of the word was hidden beneath its apparent contradiction. The word about Christ as word about the cross was "weakness" and "folly" to the natural man; for faith alone did it become "the power of God" and "the wisdom of God" (I Cor. 1:18-25).

Functioning in this form, the word was to force the issue on the negative side with regard to the crisis of salvation; it would become "to one a fragrance from death to death, to the other a fragrance from life to life" (II Cor. 2:15f.; I Cor. 1:18). It would call forth a crisis as separation between people because it would produce the separation in each; it would repel in everyone "glorying in oneself," the desire to secure one's being autocratically, and would offer an existence that came from God (I Cor. 1:31; II Cor. 10:17).

The word took this form on the positive side in order to bring deliverance on the basis of faith. In II Cor. 5:20, its specific structure stood out when the apostle said with regard to his preaching, ". . . God making his appeal through us. We beseech you on behalf of Christ, be reconciled to God." The word was the personal confrontation of God. God desired to win a person over as a partner; whoever believed, agreed to be brought into partnership. But everyone who thus agreed also confessed that he had not done so on his own but that he had been won over. The word was "received . . . with joy inspired by the Holy Spirit" (I Thess. 1:6)[21] because the listener had been laid hold of by it. The gospel came in the form of human speech but at the same time "you received the word . . . with joy inspired by the Holy Spirit" (I Thess. 1:5), i.e., as "the word of God" (I Thess. 2:13).

Paul did not link the word with *exousia* (the authority to say what shall be done) as the synoptic tradition did, but with *dynamis eis sōtērian* (the power to deliver). Like Christ himself (I Cor. 1:24) this was the power of God that intervened to shape history in the direction of salvation (Rom. 1:16; I Cor. 1:18). That meant, however, that this power was the one, seen eschatologically, that brought about the resurrection and the *basileia* (I Cor. 4:20; 6:14; 15:43; Phil. 3:10). The dialectic with regard to this power that can only accomplish its ends in the form of "weakness" was represented in the apostle's own person; we hold the treasure of the gospel "in earthen vessels," he said, "to show that the transcendent power belongs to God and not to us" (II Cor. 4:7; cf. 12:9). So formed, Paul showed himself to be an apostle through "truthful speech, and the power of God" (II Cor. 6:7); it was the word of truth because it measured up to reality.

Thus Paul, like no other author of the New Testament, characterized the message about Jesus as a strictly eschatological event in history, as a theologically profiled witness to Christ for people within the context of their lives, and as

---

[21]*dechomai* ("to receive") as technical term in I Thess. 1:6; 2:13; cf. Acts 8:14; 11:1; 17:11; Jas. 1:21.

God's active involvement through people under the cross, an involvement that changed human lives. The gospel was not only something that was uttered; in that gospel the active involvement of God that took place in Jesus' dying and rising was at work in the present and received people as partners. Because it established an in-person relationship in history, it was inextricably connected with the witness of human behavior.

5. PROCLAMATION THROUGH ACTS

Time and again Paul linked the word of his preaching with the acts practiced at baptism and the Lord's Supper. Both these acts, which were called "sacraments" in post-New Testament times, were taken together for the first time as the means of God's saving activity in I Cor. 10:1-5. To them we now turn within the context of the community of faith.

Our attention is drawn here to another embodiment of the word. Paul did not present the gospel through his preaching alone, but through the shape of his life as well (II Cor. 6:4-10); moreover, to a degree he expected the same from the congregations. He was inclined to express this by using two catchwords; they appeared together in I Thess. 1:6f.; II Thess. 3:9; and Phil. 3:17.

a) Mimēsis. Paul could refer to himself as the father of a community of faith because he had become its parent through the gospel; he could challenge it: "be imitators of me" (I Cor. 4:16; Phil. 3:17). In I Cor. 11:1, the content and character of this imitation were clear: "Be imitators of me, as I am of Christ." Paul was an imitator of Christ not because he appropriated the conduct of the earthly Jesus as an example, but because he permitted himself to be shaped by Christ's work of salvation (Phil. 2:4ff.). People thus imitated Paul when they permitted themselves to be directed by that which shaped his life. In I Thess. 1:6 Paul could state as an unintended conclusion: "And you became imitators of us and of the Lord, for you received the word in much affliction, with joy inspired by the Holy Spirit." The Christians in Thessalonica became of themselves imitators because they let themselves be directed by the same word as the other two who were named. One did not become an imitator here by selecting a behavior pattern or by taking on the obligation of following an example, but by permitting oneself to be directed by that which shaped and expressed itself in the life of the other.

b) Typos. This understanding of imitation was confirmed by the second key term, *typos*. The community of faith that imitated Paul, according to I Thess. 1:6, itself became a *typos* (influencing example) for others (I Thess. 1:7); they were this no differently than Paul himself (Phil. 3:17; II Thess. 3:9). The context of II Thess. 3:9 explained how this came about by mentioning, alongside the example influencing others, the tradition to which one was obligated (3:6) and instruction (3:10ff.).[22] Accordingly, the *typos* portrayed what the word—here

---

[22] In the same way, I Cor. 11:1 was more closely qualified through 10:31ff. (perhaps also through 11:2), and 4:16 through 4:14f.

the word of parenesis—was saying. The more a life was shaped by the word the more it became an example influencing others. This example was not at work only through human authority or through the *eros* of the one accepting it, but subliminally through the word that expressed itself in the *typos* and the faith that perceived it.

Hence proclamation through behavior was not something added to the word; it emerged spontaneously wherever the word was authentically present. Like all proclamation, that of behavior was connected to the Spirit and to faith.

§37. The Work of the Spirit

R. Bultmann, "Zur Geschichte der Paulus-Forschung," *ThR* NF 1 (1929), 29-59; A. M. Hunter, *Paul and His Predecessors* (1961), pp. 90-97; E. Käsemann, "Geist und Geistesgaben im NT," *RGG* II³, 1272-79; E. Schweizer, *pneuma, TDNT* VI, 415-437 (434 Lit.!); I. Hermann, *Kyrios und Pneuma. Studien zur Christologie der paulinischen Hauptbriefe* (1961); H. Conzelmann, *charisma, TDNT* IX, 402-06.

The Spirit appeared in Paul's thought to be the content, bearer, and gift of the gospel in a more immediate way than God and Christ. Apart from Luke (especially in Acts 1–12), no other New Testament writer referred more persistently to the *pneuma*, the Spirit, than Paul. In a group of passages (Rom. 1:9; 8:16; I Cor. 2:11; 5:3f.; 7:34; II Cor. 2:13; 7:1; Phil. 4:23; I Thess. 5:23; Philem. 25) it meant the human spirit; in the vast majority of passages, however, it meant the Spirit of God. Especially whenever its connection with God was at stake, the Spirit was designated with this Old Testament expression as "the Spirit of God" (12 times).[1] In contrast, there was a decline in usage (13 times) of the customary early Christian designation "Holy Spirit" (cf. Rom. 1:4) that predominated in the synoptic tradition and in Luke's redaction. The terms "Spirit of Christ" (Rom. 8:9; Phil. 1:19) or "Spirit of his Son" (Gal. 4:6) or "Spirit of the Lord" (II Cor. 3:17), all referring to the exalted One, appeared as new expressions and remained—I Pet. 1:11 (cf. Acts 16:7) excepted—within the New Testament Paul's own. For the overwhelming majority of passages, however, Paul used the absolute *to pneuma* (the Spirit; ca. 45 times). What reality was Paul calling Spirit with these expressions?

1. REGARDING HISTORY-OF-RELIGION ANALYSIS

a) The history-of-religion analysis of the *pneuma*-concept grew out of the "purely historical" branch of New Testament research in a rational process that sheds informative light on its structure.[2]

---

[1] In the Hebrew Old Testament, in the LXX, and in the Jewish apocrypha and pseudepigrapha the Spirit from above was called "God's ('his,' 'thy') Spirit," also "Spirit of Yahweh," or "of the Lord," or absolutely "the Spirit," but only sporadically "the Holy Spirit"; in contrast, the latter expression was the standard designation in the rabbinic literature. In the LXX and in Hellenistic Judaism (Philo) the expression "divine Spirit" was also used (cf. F. Baumgärtel, *TDNT* VI, 362f.; E. Sjöberg, *TDNT* VI, 381).

[2] Supporting references for the following are to be found in the important review of research by Bultmann, op. cit. (Lit., §37), 29-41.

In this branch of research the trinitarian *pneuma*-understanding of the church was abandoned and the references of Paul to the Spirit were interpreted in terms of the philosophy of the day without thinking much about it. F. C. Baur raised the following considerations. In Paul, the Spirit stood in contrast to the flesh, i.e., it was the eternal, the absolute in contrast to the temporal. Anthropologically that meant: Spirit was something other than understanding; understanding always perceived only with regard to something else, while Spirit was the knowledge of oneself. This, however, was not only the knowledge of one's own individuality, but the knowledge of the absolute Spirit, the absolute self-awareness that Paul called faith, since Christ was the manifestation of the absolute Spirit. The hermeneutical root of these perspectives is clear: Baur translated the categories of Pauline theology into those of the philosophy of Hegel. Among other supports along the way he was bolstered here and there by the Greek thought expressed in I Cor. 2:11. Operating on the same principle, representatives of liberal theology at the end of the 19th century identified Spirit in Paul in a psychologizing manner with that which that era understood under the notion of spirit. For them then that meant rationality, mental attitude, the capacity for introspection that stood in contrast to material existence and nature.

Against this naive translation game, which is reviving again today, the history-of-religion school came up with the historical effect of estrangement. Just as A. Schweitzer opposed the Kantian kingdom of God of liberal theology with the apocalyptic kingdom of God of the 1st century, so H. Gunkel opposed the 19th-century concept of the spirit with that of the Hellenistic world. Gunkel showed in his epoch-making monograph *Die Wirkungen des heiligen Geistes nach der populären Anschauung der apostolischen Zeit und der Lehre des Apostels Paulus* (1888) that for Hellenistic Christians as well as for their contemporaries *pneuma* in I Cor. 14 referred to a supernatural, miraculous power. In Gunkel's view, this power filled man like an influence and announced its presence in strange psychic phenomena, e.g., glossolalia and miraculous deeds. Paul corrected these popular notions, said Gunkel, and taught that one should not look upon these unusual phenomena as the work of this miraculous, divine power but rather the new manner of life as a whole.

b) After this confrontation it was no longer possible to interpret Paul's statements, nor those of other early Christian writers before him, about the Spirit independent of the concepts of the Spirit in the Jewish and Hellenistic environment. The decisive problems and the contours of possible solutions are generally agreed upon today in New Testament research; they are presented with a variety of emphases.[3]

1) Among Jewish Christians the Spirit was primarily thought of as the power of the future world, among Hellenistic Christians as the power of the world

---

[3]Representative are the articles mentioned above (Lit., §37) by E. Käsemann and E. Schweizer, and in part also the book by A. M. Hunter. R. Bultmann (*Theology* I, §§14,1; 38,3) made his judgment along the lines of the history of religion in a less differentiated manner and, pertaining to substance, too much in the sense of existential interpretation.

above. For the former the Spirit was regarded more as the prelude to the consummation, for the latter more as salvation in the present. The former considered the Spirit more as a force at work, the latter tended more in the direction of substance. Both understood the Spirit, nevertheless, theologically as the eschatological gift of God mediated through the exalted Christ.

2) With regard to its work in man the Spirit was seen by Jewish and Hellenistic Christians alike sometimes animistically as a personal power that laid hold of people like a demon, sometimes dynamistically as a personal force that filled people like an influence (cf. I Cor. 12:13; I Thess. 5:19). This personal or impersonal force sometimes appeared to seize people for a short period so that under the Spirit's influence they came forward, sometimes it was attributed to each baptized person at his or her baptism.

3) What special insight did Paul add to this concept of the Spirit? It is generally conceded that Paul was responsible for the view that the work of the Spirit was to be seen in the context of Christian existence as a whole—and that as life lived by faith, and not primarily in ecstatic and miraculous phenomena. For Paul the Spirit was "the Spirit of faith" (II Cor. 4:13). Yet on the one hand he did not limit it to the ethical side, and on the other hand he did not exclude the ecstatic side. He himself experienced visions (II Cor. 12:6-9), worked "miracles" by the gift of the Spirit (Rom. 15:18), and spoke in tongues (I Cor. 14:6). For Paul, the link to the life lived by faith was the result of the decisive insight that the Spirit was not only the gift of the exalted One—as was generally perceived in early Christianity according to Acts 2:32f.—but in an immediate sense it was the way he was at work in the present. Paul interpreted the Spirit in a strictly christological sense and therefore also included the bodily side: "The Lord is the Spirit!" and "the body is . . . for the Lord!" (II Cor. 3:17; I Cor. 6:13). Hence the work of the Spirit was neither a prelude of that which was to come nor already participation in the heavenly world. Rather it was the sign of that which was yet to come and, yet, already the pledge of the resurrection because the resurrection of Jesus was at work in it (Rom. 8:23; II Cor. 1:22; 5:5). How did Paul understand the Spirit within this conceptual frame of reference with regard to theological particulars?

2. THE EXPERIENCE OF THE SPIRIT IN PAUL

From the very beginning of the Christian community the Spirit was not a theological theory, but something that had happened to people empirically and that they had sought to interpret. According to Paul, the Spirit was experienced primarily in two ways.

a) The most genuine utterance of the Spirit in the assembly of believers was not ecstatic speech, glossolalia—opinion to the contrary in Corinth notwithstanding—but prophecy, since the intention and the criterion of the worship service was that God should become manifest for people. If an outsider should come into the service of worship glossolalia would strike him necessarily as "madness." Prophetic speech, however, would be relevant; it would uncover his existence *sub specie Dei* so that he could make the confession: "God is really among you." At such a moment the character of the assembly as worship service had become manifest (I Cor. 14:23-25).

b) The individual believer experienced the Spirit primarily in prayer when he could call upon God in the words of the Lord's Prayer: "Abba, Father!" (Rom. 8:15; Gal. 4:6). This immediacy of devotion to God did not come forth from innate human capacity but from the Spirit. The Spirit brought to light an awareness in the depth dimension out of which prayer sprang forth that man has been accepted through the love of God. When the Spirit reached out, the love of God reached out: "because God's love has been poured into our hearts through the Holy Spirit which has been given to us" (Rom. 5:5).

So Paul understood two fundamental expressions of the life of early Christianity—the new way of speaking with authority and the new way of praying—and thereby the new openness of people toward God and one's neighbor as the work of the Spirit. The Spirit made known its presence as the consciousness-generating power that created openness for the God of Jesus Christ. How did Paul come by this interpretation?

3. THE INTERPRETATION OF THE EXPERIENCE OF THE SPIRIT

a) The experience of the Spirit as fulfillment event. In II Cor. 3:3, (6) Paul brought together the prophecy of the new covenant (Jer. 31:31-34), under which God would "write" his will "upon their hearts," and that of the renewal of the heart through the Spirit (Ezek. 36:26). The image of the one who was circumcised according to the Spirit and not according to the letter in Rom. 2:29 was also drawn out of this reference in Ezekiel. So for Paul the Spirit was the word accomplishing the work that came from God, the word that changed man on the day of salvation and bound him to the gracious will of God. According to II Cor. 3:3a, however, this word proceeded from Christ; the community of faith was a "letter from Christ," the letter written by him through the ministry of Paul. The gospel encountered people as the life-changing word of the day of salvation, i.e., as the Spirit, while the Law as statute requiring achievement became the killing letter. The presence of the Spirit brought "righteousness, peace, joy," the fundamental elements of God's end-time reign (Rom. 14:17).

b) The Spirit as the presence of Christ. In the Spirit promised for the day of salvation not only was God now at work in the present but also Christ. "The Spirit of God" is in you, "the Spirit of Christ" is in you, "Christ" is in you; these words were written side by side in Rom. 8:9-11 as synonyms. The Spirit was the "Spirit of the Son" (Gal. 4:6) and the "Spirit of the Lord" (II Cor. 3:18) not simply because it was his gift (Acts 2:33) but because this One offered himself in the Spirit; Christ himself became "a life-giving spirit" (I Cor. 15:45). ". . . the Lord is the Spirit" (II Cor. 3:17)! This statement, which was an exegesis of an Old Testament passage, did not wish to equate the exalted One with the Spirit[4] but to interpret the work of the Spirit christologically; the exalted One was at work through the Spirit and therefore was at work as the Spirit within man. If it were not so intended, then the confession "Jesus is Lord" could not be, conversely, the criterion of the Spirit (I Cor. 12:3). Among the many spirits that buffeted man (I Cor. 2:12; 12:10; II Cor. 11:4), among the many forces that pressed upon him and shaped human consciousness, the Spirit of God identified itself by causing people to become dependent on the crucified Jesus as their Lord. Because Christ himself was turning to people in the Spirit, their turning to him made known, on the other hand, that the Spirit of God truly was at work in them. In the same way the Spirit of God and only the Spirit of God led people to the knowledge of God (I Cor. 2:10-16).

c) *The body as "the temple of the Spirit."* Just as Paul linked the Spirit to the historical life and ministry of Jesus, he also linked it to the physical conduct of Christians. The Christians with whom Paul debated in the First Epistle to the Corinthians understood themselves to be *"pneumatikoi,"* spiritual specialists. This catchword was appropriated in this epistle fourteen times (in the remaining Pauline epistles it appeared only nine times!). While these specialists in matters spiritual downgraded bodily existence over against the *pneuma* in the sense of Hellenistic dualism, Paul did not look upon the body as the Spirit's "prison," but as its "temple" (I Cor. 6:19).[5] In it and together with it the worship of God was taking place (Rom. 12:1), for the body made historical activity and in-person communication possible. The body of Christians was "the member of Christ," the organ through which the exalted One was acting in history (I Cor. 6:15). The spiritual specialists in Corinth, on the other hand, looked upon the body as unimportant; in their opinion, "All things are lawful for me" in the realm of the body, even traffic with prostitutes (I Cor. 6:12-17). The "spiritual food" [Gr.] of the Lord's Supper (I Cor. 10:3f.) relieved them of obligation to physical obedience, while for Paul that meal led precisely to such obedience (I Cor. 10:1-13). For them a future, bodily resurrection was an absurd notion (I Cor. 15:12), for Paul that resurrection would bring the "redemption of our body" [Gr.] and of the entire creation (Rom. 8:22f.). A reinstatement of the "mortal body" (cf. Rom. 8:11) would be no redemption whatsoever; the resurrection would produce a "spiritual body" that would participate in "glory" (I Cor. 15:42-44). Like the gift in the Eucharist this body would be "spiritual" *(pneumatikos)*; it would be this not because it would consist of a heavenly substance but because it would be created through God's work of salvation.[6] This was seen analogous to Israel's "spiritual" food during the wilderness wanderings (I Cor. 10:3f.). Accordingly, this future resurrection for Christians, in

---

[4]Regarding the interpretive history and problematic, cf. Hermann, op. cit. (Lit., §37), pp. 17ff., 57f.

[5]The same image was used in I Cor. 3:16 for the community. Regarding the history-of-religion background, cf. H. Conzelmann, *I Corinthians*, at I Cor. 6:19. According to Philo (*Som.* I:139, 149) the soul was the house of God; the body, however, was the prison of the soul.

[6]Regarding the discussion, cf. L. Goppelt, *TDNT* VI, 146f.; and E. Schweizer, *TDNT* VI, 436f.

the same way as for Christ (Rom. 1:3f.), was assured in the present through the Spirit at work in the "mortal body."[7] It brought this assurance not as a supernatural strength, but because even now it took the mortal body into service for the Lord.

Through such taking one into service the *charismata* came into being (charisms, gifts of grace, deeds of grace). Paul introduced this term[8] in order to designate the *pneumatika* (works of the Spirit, I Cor. 12:1; 14:1; Rom. 1:11) as works of *charis*, of God's gracious turning to people through Christ (Rom. 12:6; I Cor. 1:4; Rom. 5:15f.). They were *charisma pneumatikon* (a spiritual gift of grace, Rom. 1:11). Qualifying as *charismata*, therefore, were not merely the ecstatic phenomena of the Spirit but all acts of service that were rendered to the Lord in the community of faith in order to live out the life that came from faith (I Cor. 12:5, 7-11).

d) "The spirit of faith." As becomes clear again in relationship to the *charismata*, the working of the Spirit was experiential but it was recognizable neither unequivocally nor compellingly as the manifestation of God through Christ; its point of reference was faith.

Wherever Paul was able to point to the works of the Spirit as well as to those of Christ he used only the indicative and imperative. According to Rom. 8:2-11, the gospel assured baptized members in the indicative: "For the law of the Spirit of life . . . has set me free from the law of sin and death" (Rom. 8:2); and in Rom. 8:12f. it challenged in the imperative, therefore, to live according to the Spirit, to be obedient to the work of the Spirit. Gal. 5:25 expressed the same tension in the sentence: "If we live by the Spirit, let us also walk by the Spirit." Whoever had been claimed by Christ and taken into the community of faith so as to live within it under the word was *en pneumati* (in the Spirit), given over to the working of the Spirit (Rom. 8:9; I Cor. 12:13; II Cor. 6:6). Nevertheless, this one must be summoned repeatedly to allow this to happen, i.e., to live this life by faith.

The Spirit was "the Spirit of faith" (II Cor. 4:13); whoever had received the "earnest money" of the Spirit walked by faith (II Cor. 5:5, 7). Spirit and faith stood in an interchangeable relationship to each other. The summons to faith was the challenge to follow the working of the Spirit. And, conversely, the Spirit was received through "hearing [the preaching] with faith" (Gal. 3:2; 5:5). Thus faith was the vessel that received the Spirit and at the same time was created, formed, and maintained by it; this is true even if Paul never spoke directly about the creation of faith by the Spirit.

Christians "received" the Spirit (Rom. 8:15 and passim) and "had" it (I Cor.

---

[7]According to some, the body that died in baptism, according to others—surely correct—the body that is subject to dying (cf. E. Käsemann, *Romans*, at Rom. 8:11).

[8]It is not found prior to Paul and was used by him only in Romans and II Corinthians; after him it was used only in the Pastoral Epistles and in I Pet. 4:10; cf. H. Conzelmann, *TDNT* IX, 402ff. (Lit.!).

7:40 and passim) in the same sense that they accepted and had the gracious turning of the faithful God through Christ; yet they received and had the "Spirit" as creative address in the midst of their lives as persons.

e) The essence of the Spirit. In light of the foregoing we can attempt the following definition. The Spirit was the awareness-generating power of the word of God about Jesus the Lord, the power that created the life lived by faith. As Spirit of the day of salvation it led people into freedom over against all nomism (II Cor. 3:6, 17; Rom. 7:6), as also over against enthusiast dualism (cf. I Cor. 6:12; Col. 2:16-23) and over against one's own flesh.

But is not the Spirit more than word-related power (Rom. 15:13, 19; I Cor. 2:4)? Is it not a person? Paul was not yet referring to it as person when he personified it like other abstractions such as wisdom, law, sin, and death, and when he spoke about the "teaching" or "thinking" of the Spirit. He came closer to this concept of person when he referred to Spirit alternately with Christ (Rom. 8:9-11; cf. II Cor. 3:17) or with God (I Cor. 3:16; cf. 14:25; II Cor. 6:16) as acting subject, or made them parallel to one another in triadic formulas (I Cor. 12:4-6; II Cor. 13:13; elsewhere in the New Testament, cf. Eph. 2:18; I Pet. 1:2; Mt. 28:19; Rev. 1:4f.).[9] In all this, however, the Spirit was not taken as an autonomous subject, as a "person"—a term foreign to the Greek and Hebrew languages; to the contrary it was emphasized that it was the word-related power through which God himself or Christ himself was at work in the present. Paul did not wish to explain the inner structure of the Godhead, like the doctrine of the trinity did later, but to characterize the soteriological experience that dawned in people's lives as the stepping-forth-out-of-himself of the one God. For this reason, that which stood in relationship to the Spirit on the human side could only be faith!

§38. Faith

A. Schlatter, *Der Glaube im NT* (1927⁴; 1963⁵); E. Wissmann, *Das Verhältnis von Pistis und Christusfrömmigkeit bei Paulus* (1926); R. Bultmann, *pisteuō, TDNT* VI, 217-222; F. Neugebauer, *In Christus* (1961); H. Ljungmann, *Pistis* (1964); H. Binder, *Der Glaube bei Paulus* (1968). **On 3b**: L. Goppelt, *Jesus, Paul, and Judaism* (1964), pp. 151-167; Goppelt, "Israel und die Kirche, heute und bei Paulus," in *Christologie*, pp. 165-189; J. Gnilka, *Die Verstockung Israels. Jes 6,9-10 in der Theologie der Synoptiker* (1961); C. Müller, *Gottes Gerechtigkeit und Gottes Volk* (1964).

1. THE DEVELOPMENT OF THE CONCEPT OF FAITH IN PRIMITIVE CHRISTIANITY

a) Even a glance at the breakdown of vocabulary shows what significance was ascribed to the substantive *pistis* (faith) by Paul; of the 224 references in

---

[9] "The fellowship of the Holy Spirit" was the Spirit's gift of participation in itself (subjective genitive; thus also E. Schweizer, *TDNT* VI, 434), alongside the "grace of the Lord Jesus Christ" and the "love of God."

the New Testament 108 are found in Paul, 13 in the Pastoral Epistles, 24 in Hebrews 11, 11 in James 2, one in the First Epistle of John, and none in the Gospel of John. The verb *pisteuō* (to believe), on the other hand, was used by Paul only 46 times; it is found 6 times in the Pastoral Epistles and 198 times in the rest of the New Testament; of this last figure 106 references are in the Gospel of John and the First Epistle of John. How did Paul come to regard faith with the significance that is apparent in this statistical breakdown?

b) From a schematic point of view, the pre-Pauline development of the term passed through three phases. (1) In his public proclamation Jesus required repentance, but then effected repentance in the form of discipleship or faith by involving himself with individuals. The new, vital act of believing was the inner-historical goal of Jesus' earthly ministry (§15,3); such believing stood alongside the act of following in discipleship that—though not stated—depended on it. (2) After Easter, the primitive church of Palestine through its missionary kerygma summoned once again to repentance; but this time it was realized decisively through the acceptance of the Easter kerygma, i.e., through the faith that expressed itself along the lines of Rom. 1:3f. (3) In the Hellenistic world, however, the missionary kerygma aimed comprehensively at the "turning toward" or the "turning back" to the "living God" (I Thess. 1:8f.; Heb. 6:4-6). This turning toward God was directly identifiable with the faith whose core was the acceptance of the Easter kerygma (1 Cor. 15:11). Whereas faith was the heart of repentance for Jesus and for the primitive church in Palestine, it had become here the whole of it.[1] Paul was able to refer directly to the goal of his missionary work as "the obedience of faith" (Rom. 1:5), even though *epistrephō* (to turn back, to turn oneself toward) remained the technical missionary term (I Thess. 1:9f.; cf. II Cor. 3:16; Gal. 4:9; and passim in Acts). In any case, he then addressed baptized people in the interest of faith but almost never in the interest of "repentance."[2]

Thus the emergence of faith in the Hellenistic church was founded upon two factors: for one thing upon the key role that Jesus himself had ascribed to it, and for another upon the mission to the Gentiles. Through the first it became

---

[1]This emphasizing of faith had already been anticipated in Jewish missionary activity. According to Philo, Abraham was "the first person spoken of as believing God [cf. Gen. 15:6], since he first grasped a firm and unswerving conception of the truth that there is one Cause above all, and that it provides for the world and all that there is therein" (*Virt.* 216 [= LCL, *Philo*, VIII, 295]; cf. *Op. Mund.* 170-72). This faith, however, was not the beginning but the end of Abraham's turning to God; he came to this faith not through acceptance of the word, but on the basis of viewing the world. In order to know that which existed he lifted his eyes for so long over heaven and the stars until he had achieved a clear concept of God's being and providence (cf. *Virt.* 211-15). His faith meant both—and with this point a further element of Jewish theology of mission was appropriated—the renunciation of the deification of the world and—this was original with Philo—the renunciation of the temporal in favor of the eternal. With the latter aspect he appropriated Platonic thought and with the characterization of this posture as "faith" he appropriated later motifs of later Stoicism. Yet for him faith was not fidelity to oneself as it was in Stoicism, but—and in this he remained close to the Old Testament—trust in the God who had become for him, of course, pure being. Cf. Schlatter, op. cit. (Lit., §38), pp. 60-63, 69ff.; R. Bultmann, *TDNT* VI, 201f.

[2]*Metanoia*, only II Cor. 7:9f.; *metanoeō*, II Cor. 12:21.

the heart of the behavior prompted by Jesus; through the second it became the whole that comprehended this behavior. For Paul, however, there was a third factor with which he took these two a step further.

c) Paul emphasized faith in order to distinguish Jesus' path toward salvation from that of the Law.[3] He set faith over against "works." The two terms faith and works signaled for him two separate contexts for life that were expressed through a series of expressions. One series was: sin, law, works, flesh, wrath, death; the other, corresponding antithetically to the first, was: righteousness, Christ, faith, Spirit, grace, life. In this way the substantive "faith" emerged as a key theological term. It, along with the verb "to believe," appeared cluster-fashion in Rom. 3:20–5:2 and in Gal. 3, on both occasions as the correlate of justification. Twenty-seven of the 35 faith-passages in the entire Epistle to the Romans and 18 of the 21 faith-passages in the Epistle to the Galatians addressed the issue of justification. In contrast, neither the substantive "faith" nor the verb "to believe" appeared in Rom. 5:3–9:30, ch. 6:8 excepted! How was the relationship to God or Christ expressed in this section? This question has hardly been addressed in research to the present and needs careful examination. In I Corinthians the substantive and the verb appeared 7 times each, but "knowledge" of God 10 times and the verb "to know" 12 times. Thus faith received a special accent in Paul through the interpretation of the gospel as justification.

Paul therefore not only laid hold of the development of the missionary kerygma in his references to faith,[4] but also designated through it the new existence that the gospel brought to life over against Jewish and Hellenistic religious understanding and practice. This development of the term faith was reflected in Pauline statements about its content.

2. THE CONTENT AND ESSENCE OF FAITH

As Paul appropriated the early Christian development of the term faith he availed himself of its Old Testament/Jewish prior history. He made that clear by the very way he reached back to the Old Testament at key junctures. In contrast to someone like Philo, Paul did not evidence contact here with Greek-Hellenistic usage. While in the view of classical Greek the divine was grasped rationally but not "believed," in the Hellenistic world it was stated on occasion that one "believed" in the existence of gods in spite of skepticism. In Stoicism, *pistis*, which at its root in Greek meant trust, conviction, that which was reliable, became a technical term for loyalty to oneself.[5] In order to grasp more precisely what Paul understood by faith we take as our starting point here his statements about its content.

a) Paul often used the substantive and the verb in an absolute sense. Wherever

---

[3]In order to free one from that which had gone before, the Jewish theology of mission had already made reference to faith as well; cf. n. 1.

[4]Rom. 1:5, 8, 12; (16:26); Gal. 1:23; I Thess. 1:8ff. and passim.

[5]R. Bultmann, *TDNT* VI, 179-182.

he qualified them more closely, he used with the verb a reference to God in the dative case or as the object of the preposition *epi* with the dative, just as the LXX had done. We see this in Gal. 3:6; Rom. 4:3: "Abraham believed God . . ." (dative according to Gen. 15:6); Rom. 9:33; 10:11: "he who believes in him . . ." (*epi* with the dative according to Isa. 28:16). Wherever Christ, on the other hand, was referred to as the content, he used with the verb the preposition *eis*. This we see in Rom. 10:14; Gal. 2:16; Phil. 1:29[6] (Col. 2:5 also with *pistis*). The substantive was often connected with the objective genitive and is always to be translated "faith in," namely, in "Jesus Christ" (Rom. 3:22; Gal. 2:16; 3:22), "Jesus" (Rom. 3:26), "Christ" (Phil. 3:9), the "Son of God" (Gal. 2:20). Only two prepositional expressions were used of God and of Christ, namely, *pistis pros* of God in I Thess. 1:8, and of Christ in Philem. 5, as also *epi* with the accusative case (seldom in the LXX) of God in Rom. 4:5, 24, of Christ, however, only in Acts (9:42 and passim). These formulations had in mind one's turning to God; I Thess. 1:8 expressly looked back to the missionary setting, but even in Rom. 4:5, 24 Paul had in mind the moment of conversion to what was new. The same can be said of *eis Christon* in Gal. 2:16 ("we have believed in Christ Jesus") and in Rom. 10:14 ("But how are they to call upon him in whom they have not believed?")—both used the inceptive aorist. Turning to God took place first as turning to Christ because God offered himself in him through the gospel. This turning to God led to the result that one's existence was dependent upon God. This was reflected by the expressions in the dative case.

Thus the content of faith was Christ himself or God himself; however, not in the sense of Highest Being but in their self-offering through the gospel. The gospel itself appeared nowhere as the content of faith.[7] The events of salvation, which were referred to frequently with a description of faith's content through a *hoti*-clause (that . . .), were not meant as facts that should become the objects of faith. Rather these events were to specify God or Christ more closely. The that-clauses of Rom. 10:9: "if you . . . believe in your heart that God raised him from the dead," or of I Thess. 4:14: ". . . believe that Jesus died and rose again," had the same function as the participles or the relative clauses that described God or specified him more closely (Rom. 4:24: belief "in him that raised from the dead Jesus our Lord" or Rom. 4:5: in "him who justifies the ungodly"). Hence the descriptions of faith's content provided clear contours in connection with which we can now continue our inquiry.

b) How is the content of faith therefore to be specified more exactly?

1) Paul developed a fundamental explication of faith in Rom. 4:16-25 while comparing the faith of Christians typologically to that of Abraham. Abraham believed God on the basis of his promise although humanly speaking there was nothing to hope for. "Abraham, for he is the father of us all, . . . in the presence

---

[6]This expression recurred frequently in the New Testament, especially in the Gospel of John (ibid., 210 n. 266).

[7]"Faith of the gospel" (Phil. 1:27) was "the faith that the gospel sustained" (J. Gnilka, *Philipperbrief*, at Phil. 1:27).

of the God in whom he believed, who gives life to the dead and calls into existence the things that do not exist" (4:16f.). The faith of Christians corresponded to this on the level of fulfillment. "But the words . . . were written not for his sake alone, but for ours also . . . who believe in him that raised from the dead Jesus our Lord" (4:23f.). This was the actual content of faith; Christians believed, in light of the cross and on the basis of the gospel, in God as the One who raised Jesus and thereby brought life to light for all. Finally, therefore, faith had one content: God himself; but who God was, conversely, became visible only to the eyes of faith.

To believe did not mean to accept God hypothetically as the depth of being or as the power of history; this was the direction of Philo's thought about faith.[8] For Paul to believe meant to receive the promise of God. Abraham believed, i.e., he trusted the One who addressed him that he would sustain his pledge in creative fashion. ". . . he gave glory to God, fully convinced that God was able to do what he had promised" (Rom. 4:20f.). So the one who "believed" now was the one who accepted the message of Jesus' dying and rising as the ultimate pledge of the Creator and let this One who was confronting by his address be his God. He let him be the One who ". . . justifies the ungodly" (Rom. 4:5) and who "will bring them [those who died as Christians] to life with Jesus" (I Thess. 4:14, NEB). So faith was, at its core, trust in God on the basis of his promise.

2) This trust in God encompassed "faith in Jesus Christ" since the address that established faith went out through the resurrection of the crucified One; that resurrection proclaimed the gospel. The familiar formula "faith in Jesus Christ" summarized briefly then what the confessional formula said in Rom. 10:9: "because, if you confess with your lips that Jesus is Lord and believe in your heart that God raised him from the dead. . . ." Accordingly, the person who believed in Jesus Christ was that one who accepted his dying and rising as God's revelation of salvation or him as the *kyrios* in order to live by that faith (cf. Rom. 1:17).

Out of the combination of the two statements in Rom. 10:9 there followed consequences, on the other hand, for the question of "faith and fellowship with Christ" as well. The accepting of the exalted One as Lord was not realized as a mystical partnership or *unio* but always as the faith that received the word of the cross and resurrection as the pledge of God.

Why did the sections in Rom. 6:1–8:17, which directed one into the realization of the life "in Christ," "in the righteousness of God," and "in the Spirit" (Rom. 6:11, 18; 8:9), have nothing to say—6:8 excepted—about faith? These sections proclaimed in the indicative mood the new field of relationships to which Christians had been related through baptism; they challenged in the (kerygmatic) imperative mood to allow oneself to be determined by that field of relationships. The participation of man therefore was expressed in the imperative,

---

[8]Cf. n. 1.

but Paul never formulated the imperative of the verb: "believe!"[9] The imperative addressed to the baptized members stated rather: "So you also must consider yourselves dead to sin and alive to God in Christ Jesus!" (Rom. 6:11). "Consider yourselves" meant to see oneself through God's eyes, i.e., to believe. The imperative was realized through faith, much like the missionary imperative, "repent!"[10] The same was true of the summons in Rom. 6:19: ". . . yield them [your bodies] to the service of righteousness" (NEB), and in Rom. 8:12f.: "So then, brethren, we are debtors" to live according to the Spirit, and most especially of the challenge in II Cor. 5:20: "be reconciled to God!" Thus it was not only the surrendering of Christ on our behalf that was accepted and lived "by" and "through" faith, as Rom. 3:21-26 would have it, but also the dimension of being "with Christ" and "in Christ." Paul summarized both compactly in the style of a personal confession in Gal. 2:14-21; he was delivered into the right relationship to God through faith as his turning to Christ (vv. 15f.). Out of this relationship arose the new life-situation; Paul was crucified with Christ and now Christ lived in him as the subject who determined who he was; yet Paul lived his life as he experienced it "by faith in the Son of God," who had demonstrated love for him as he sacrificed himself for him (vv. 19f.).

Just as faith, therefore, could not be replaced by a mystic relationship with Christ but endured as that which mediated the relationship to Christ, so too, conversely, the bond to Christ or to God could not be replaced through the act of believing as such. H. Braun notwithstanding,[11] it was precisely not the consequence of this understanding of faith—a consequence Paul had not yet drawn—that faith as "the renunciation of boasting" and the "knowledge of the paradoxical manifestation of God's grace" could do without the "metaphysical data of Christology," i.e., that faith alone was already salvation as a new life-relationship. Faith rather brought salvation alone through the binding of man to his Creator. To stand in faith (II Cor. 1:24) corresponded to standing "in the Lord" (I Thess. 3:8), "in the gospel" (I Cor. 15:1), and "in grace" (Rom. 5:2).

3) This becomes clear, furthermore, through the manner in which Paul joined faith with salvation. The conditional clauses in Rom. 10:9 (". . . if you confess with your lips . . . and believe in your heart . . . , you will be saved") could evoke the impression that they were indirect imperatives that made faith the condition for salvation. The context of vv. 5-13, however, was determined by the antithesis of vv. 5-8; faith was not placed in contrast to the "doing" that was made the condition for "life" by the "righteousness of the Law," but "the word of faith" was given that function. And "the word of faith" was the gospel that

---

[9]In the New Testament it is found in the missionary formula of Acts 16:31: "Believe in the Lord Jesus. . . ." This extended further a formula of the synoptic healing-narratives that stood in the imperative redactionally at Mk. 5:36 par. Lk. 8:50: "Do not fear, only believe!"; cf. also Mk. 1:15: "believe in the gospel!"

[10]In Rom. 6:8 *syzēsomen* ("we shall live together with") was not a logical but an eschatological future; therefore, "we believe"—about the same as "we hope."

[11]"The Meaning of New Testament Christology," in *God and Christ: Existence and Province* (ed. R. W. Funk [1968]), p. 90.

drew near to man establishing faith (vv. 6ff.). The conditional clauses linked in a causal sense in v. 9 explained how this "near" word accomplished salvation. The "confessing" and the "believing" were presuppositions of the "salvation," but were not conditions to be achieved by man. The entire sentence was not a requirement but, like v. 11, a pledge, probably a baptismal promise that accomplished as gospel what it stated.

The section in Rom. 10:5-13 explained what the short formulas "righteousness" and "life," "out of" or "through faith" implied.[12] The one who believed was righteous not because he fulfilled the condition but because faith itself signified that one let oneself be placed in the right relationship to God. Righteousness, the right relationship of man to God that God himself established, was the other side of faith, of the entering into or abiding in this relationship. This abiding was so little a matter of the acknowledgment of man's own position that Rom. 4:5 emphasized expressly: faith was not acknowledged like a work, but was "reckoned as righteousness." That is to say, it was only accepted by grace as an always-deficient response to God's pledge. And yet faith was not simply the echo of the word!

3. THE EMERGENCE OF FAITH

a) The problem that the statements about the emergence of faith raised becomes clear when one observes that Paul, while never using the imperative to challenge people to believe, nevertheless characterized the goal of his ministry as "the obedience of faith" (Rom. 1:5).

In the scholarly discussion R. Bultmann laid the emphasis one-sidedly upon the latter side and characterized faith as the decision to be obedient.[13] In contrast to this F. Neugebauer thought that faith was primarily the decision of God,[14] and E. Jüngel, referring to him, wrote "that faith is not the doing of man, but an event that happens to man," since faith "comes" to man, according to Gal. 3:25.[15] The pointed word of Gal. 3:23, 25 elucidated, however, not the emergence of faith but the replacement of the Law's order of salvation by faith's. The problem of the emergence of faith, however, is the question how Paul was able to characterize faith both as the work of God and as the responsible behavior of man.

---

[12] "Righteous through faith": Rom. 1:17; 4:16; 5:1; 9:30, 32; 14:23; Gal. 2:16; 3:8, 12, 22, 24; (5:5); "through faith": Rom. 3:22, 25, 31; Gal. 2:16; Phil. 3:9; for this also the instrumental dative: Rom. 3:28; "live through faith": Rom. 1:17; Gal. 3:11, (9); "through faith": Col. 2:12 (cf. Eph. 2:8; 3:17); similarly Gal. 3:14, 26.

[13] *Theology* I, §35; also Conzelmann, *Theology*, p. 172, and E. Käsemann, *Romans*, p. 109 ("act and decision of the individual person").

[14] Op. cit. (Lit., §38), pp. 165ff.

[15] " 'Theologische Wissenschaft und Glaube' im Blick auf die Armut Jesu," *Ev Theol* 24 (1964), 430; Schweizer concurred (ibid., 417) with the remark: "I come to faith only because faith comes over me"—as a power that comes over the world. With considerable one-sidedness Binder (op. cit. [Lit., §38], pp. 56ff., 64ff.) characterized faith as a transsubjective divine reality-in-action (*Geschehenswirklichkeit*).

b) Nowhere else in his writings did Paul express himself more thoroughly and with greater personal involvement regarding the emergence of faith than in Rom. 9–11.[16] Here he reflected on the unbelief of Israel because it not only worried him humanly speaking but also conflicted with the foundation of his certainty of salvation because he saw the summons to faith and the election to salvation as inseparably united.

Paul heard in Rom. 9–11 three replies to his question: "Why did Israel not believe?"

1) Rom. 9:6-29: "So it depends not upon man's will or exertion, but upon God's mercy" (9:16). Whoever believed owed this to God's grace alone. Thus the believer had to see in all unbelief hardness of heart and be afraid (Rom. 9:18, 22-24).

2) But unbelief in Rom. 9:30–10:21 was understood in insoluble antinomy to this: it was both disobedience and the fault of man. "But they have not all obeyed the gospel; for Isaiah says, 'Lord, who has believed what he has heard from us?' " (10:16). Hence the faithfulness of God's election that continued to invite those who had refused appeared all the greater (10:21).

3) After Paul had confessed both of these, the prophetic announcement was finally given him in Rom. 11: ". . . a hardening has come upon part of Israel, until the full number of the Gentiles come in, and so all Israel will be saved" (11:25f.). In other words, not every individual but indeed Israel as a whole will come to faith in the God who had sought them out through Christ and in this way will be led to salvation. Paul expected this through a miraculous turn of events immediately before the imminent *parousia* (Rom. 13:11) after the nations of the world as a whole had turned to their Creator.

This prophecy was not fulfilled in the way Paul had imagined it. The great turning of events in both the nations of the world and in Israel did not happen just as the imminent *parousia* did not. In the book of Revelation the opposite of what Rom. 15:19-24 had in mind came about from the apocalyptic turning of the nations to Christ (Rev. 11:7-10); yet John also saw in the consummation a flock too great to be counted (Rev. 7:9f.). The narrowed perspective, however, by no means displaced the theological content of the universal expectation of Rom. 11 since its foundation in Rom. 11:26-32 corresponded at its heart to the gospel.[17] Old Testament prophecies had already announced repeatedly since the fall that a saving turn of events was coming for Israel (vv. 26f.); this corresponded to the faithfulness with which God sustained his calling (vv. 28f.). Above all, however, the expectation corresponded to the manner in which God

---

[16]Regarding the discussion about the understanding of Rom. 9–11, cf. L. Goppelt, *Jesus, Paul, and Judaism*, pp. 151-167; L. Goppelt, *Christologie und Ethik*, pp. 177ff.

[17]The special election for the sake of the fathers did not make the Jewish people into the other wing of the church, but certainly into a continuation of Old Testament Israel; the Jews continue to live on the level of the promise of the Law. They are nevertheless distinct from Old Testament Israel because they have not entered into the level of fulfillment; even more, because they stand in opposition to it. They maintain against Christ their covenant with God already replaced through Christ (II Cor. 3:12-18).

through Christ accomplished salvation. "For God has consigned all men to disobedience, that he may have mercy upon all" (11:30ff.). God's judgment would finally be replaced by his love; passing through his wrath, in the end it would be his love that would be grasped. This certainty was given through the cross, according to Rom. 5:5-8; of course, the counter image stood in the book of Revelation (11:8). Through these considerations about the realization and the foundation of the prophecy of Rom. 11:25 its special meaning becomes clear:

3.1 God's summons and the election that stood behind it always preceded faith. Its life depended on the love of God that spoke forth in that summons and election which was greater than God's wrath and therefore was greater than all human failure (Rom. 8:29f.; Phil. 3:12).

3.2 The love that God demonstrated in the sending of Jesus for the entire human race that had resisted him (Rom. 5:6-11) applied to Israel too; but God's electing love was directed toward Israel especially "for the sake of the fathers" (i.e., for the sake of the promise given to Abraham). This special election remained intact even though the promise given to Abraham was fulfilled exclusively through Jesus Christ and thereby in his community of faith (Gal. 3; Rom. 4). It remained intact on the basis of God's faithfulness that bound him to human beings, here to this people (Rom. 9:4f.; 11:16), without giving anyone the right to demand anything (Rom. 9) and in spite of all human failure (Rom. 10); this was so because the promise was dependent from the very beginning on the *creatio ex nihilo* (Rom. 4:7).

3.3 What was said about the election of Israel through the promise to the fathers was now valid all the more for the election through baptism. In Rom. 8:30 Paul said about the baptized: "And those whom he predestined he also called; and those whom he called he also justified; and those whom he justified he also glorified." When through such apparently coincidental circumstances and finally through baptism a human being was called to faith, then faith was not an idea that dawned on him and that could vanish again at any time; rather God's election had made its appearance historically within that person. For this reason, faith may be certain that it shall finish the course (Phil. 3:12). Because this certainty was thrown into question through the failure of Israel, Paul pointed out finally in Rom. 9–11 that even the word of election given to Israel would finish its course (Rom. 9:6; 11:25f.). So, what was said in Rom. 9–11 about Israel's relationship to faith was true, when applied in keeping with its intent, of all baptized people; this was true even if they did not find their way to faith for a time, as Israel had not.

3.4 Is it possible, moreover, to verify the expectation for "the full number of the Gentiles" (Rom. 11:25) by making use of the Pauline gospel? If Christ died "for all," should not then all "come in" to the fellowship with their Creator as well? The universal statements in Rom. 5:18f. and 11:32 (cf. I Cor. 15:22) were not meant to be taken in the sense of a "retrieval" of all; this concept is an erroneous postulate. The election found in Paul, however, was a final risk of faith that was based on the tradition that sprang forth from Jesus' statement about himself (Mk. 14:24), that he died "for the whole." From this came not only the universal mission, but also the expectation that "every knee" shall bow voluntarily to the exalted One (Phil. 2:10). The gospel did not aim at a mystery religion society but at a new creation![18]

c) In this way, one can speak about the summons to faith that God shall see through to its completion because faith was established by God, although it was at the same time the responsible behavior of man.

Paul could characterize his own path to faith only dialectically. He could not say that he had made up his mind to believe, but also not that God had forced him to believe. Rather he had to confess on the one hand that a new beginning had been created within him: "The God who said, 'Let light shine out of darkness,' . . . has shone in our hearts to give the light of the knowledge of the glory of God in the face of Christ" (II Cor. 4:6). The word that allowed faith to emerge was just as creative as that which let light shine forth at creation. The "I" that believed was a new "I" (II Cor. 5:17). Faith did not emerge by man's changing his self-understanding on his own initiative or by coming to the insight that a new "I" had now confronted the old "I." The new "I" regarded the old "I" as "crucified with him" (Rom. 6:6, 11). Thus, later New Testament writings called the rise of faith rebirth (Jn. 3:3, 5; I Pet. 1:3) or the seeing-again of one born blind (Jn. 9).

Still, all this remained on the one side: faith was also the response of the entire man. Described as human behavior, it was at its core a becoming certain, trust in God's pledge (Rom. 4:16-25), a statement of feeling; furthermore, it was obedience (Rom. 1:5; 6:16ff.; 10:16f.), a new orientation of the will, and finally knowledge (I Cor. 8:2f.), a new way of thinking. The whole man turned to the reality of God and conducted himself accordingly.

Just as faith freed the will in Rom. 1-8, so it freed knowledge in I Cor. 1f. (I Cor. 1:21, 24; 2:9-16). The new orientation toward God, through which it was possible to know his reality, Paul called, nevertheless, loving and, for the most part, not believing. "If any one imagines that he knows something [to be correct], he does not yet know as he ought to know. But if one loves God, one is known [= elected] by him" (I Cor. 8:2f.). "Yet among the mature we do impart wisdom," i.e., " 'What no eye has seen, nor ear heard, . . . what God has prepared for those who love him' " (I Cor. 2:6, 9). Paul appropriated hereby the Old Testament/Jewish context for the term according to which one only knew God, i.e. (in the Old Testament), recognized (e.g., Isa. 43:10) who loved him—as a member of his people—(cf. Dt. 30:6) because he himself was known by God (e.g., Amos 3:2; Jer. 1:5) and was loved (e.g., Dt. 7:6ff.; Hos. 11:1-4), i.e., elected.[19] Nevertheless, Paul spoke quite sparingly, only in this conceptual frame of reference really, about a love to God (Rom. 8:28; I Cor. 2:9; 8:1, 3) and emphasized much more God's (or Christ's) love to us in that he was there

---

[18]Cf. E. Käsemann, *Romans*, p. 156.
[19]R. Bultmann, *TDNT* I, 696-703.

for us (Rom. 5:5, 8; cf. 15:30; 8:35, 37, 39; 9:13, 25; II Cor. 5:14; 9:7; 13:11, 13; Gal. 2:20).

So faith brought knowledge with it. It not only comprehended God's revelation of salvation; it also saw in its light the structure of pre-Christian existence, anthropologically and in terms of the theology of history. Not only the revelation of salvation of Rom. 3:21-28 was received by faith and thereby realized; the existence beneath the wrath of Rom. 1:18-23 and 7:7-25 was also seen for the first time in retrospect from the vantage point of faith and experienced as the reality of the old man. We shall develop this in the next major section.

4. FAITH IN THE CONTEXT OF PARENESIS

Alongside the decisive function of faith represented thus far as the human receptor created by the revelation of salvation in order to receive it, faith appeared sometimes also in the context of parenesis as conduct in relationship to the environment. Christians related to their environment as people who were sustained by faith in God. Paul referred to them on occasion not only by the formulaic expression "the believing ones" (I Thess. 1:7; 2:10, 13; cf. Eph. 1:19; Acts 2:44; 4:32, etc.), as was already customary before him; he also expressed faith together with hope and love as the armor with which Christians could survive in the world (I Thess. 5:8), and emphasized this triad, which likely was already community tradition before him, in I Thess. 1:3; I Cor. 13:(7), 13; Rom. 5:3ff. as well.[20]

---

[20]Preliminary stages of this triad in Paul are: faith and love (I Thess. 3:6; I Cor. 16:13f.; Philem. 5; Gal. 5:6, 22 [in a catalogue of virtues]; cf. II Cor. 8:7; faith and hope (Gal. 5:5). It is found further in I Tim. 6:11; II Tim. 3:10; Eph. 1:3ff., 15-18; Col. 1:4f.; Heb. 10:22-24; Barn. 1:6. Preliminary stages are also found in the Old Testament/Jewish realm (IV Macc. 17:2, 4: faith, hope, patience), but none is a direct counterpart. The Gnostic parallels are late (Lietzmann, *Der Erste Korintherbrief*, excursus to I Cor. 13:13, pp. 66-68).

Chapter IV

THE SAVING EFFECT OF THE CHRIST EVENT: THE GOSPEL AS THE REVELATION OF GOD'S RIGHTEOUSNESS

§39. Justification and Reconciliation

H. Cremer, *Die paulinische Rechtfertigungslehre im Zusammenhange ihrer geschicht-lichen Voraussetzungen* (1900²); G. Quell/G. Schrenk, *dikē, dikaios*, etc., *TDNT* II, 174-225; H.-D. Wendland, *Die Mitte der paulinischen Botschaft. Die Rechtfertigungs-lehre des Paulus im Zusammenhange seiner Theologie* (1935); P. Bläser, *Das Gesetz bei Paulus* (1941); A. Oepke, "Dikaiosynē theou bei Paulus," in *ThLZ* 78 (1953), 257-263; C. Haufe, *Die sittliche Rechtfertigungslehre des Paulus* (1957); A. Schlatter, *Gottes Gerechtigkeit. Ein Kommentar zum Römerbrief* (1959³); E. Käsemann, " 'The Righ-teousness of God' in Paul," in Käsemann, *NT Questions*, pp. 168-182; E. Jüngel, *Paulus und Jesus. Eine Untersuchung zur Präzisierung der Frage nach dem Ursprung der Christologie* (1962); R. Bultmann, "*Dikaiosynē theou*," in *Exegetica*, pp. 470-75; C. Müller, *Gottes Gerechtigkeit und Gottes Volk* (1964); K. Kertelge, "*Rechtfertigung*" *bei Paulus. Studien zur Struktur und zum Bedeutungsgehalt des paulinischen Rechtfer-tigungsbegriffs* (1967); L. Goppelt, "Der Missionar des Gesetzes," in Goppelt, *Chris-tologie*, pp. 137-146; J. Blank, "Warum sagt Paulus: 'Aus Werken des Gesetzes wird niemand gerecht?' ", in *Evangelisch-Katholischer Kommentar zum NT. Vorarbeiten* 1 (1969), 79-96; G. Klein, "Gottes Gerechtigkeit als Thema der neuesten Paulusfor-schung," *VF* 12 (1967), 1-11 (= Klein, *Rekonstruktion und Interpretation* [1969], pp. 225-236); U. Wilckens, "Was heisst bei Paulus: 'Aus Werken des Gesetzes wird kein Mensch gerecht?' ", in *Evangelisch-Katholischer Kommentar zum NT. Vorarbeiten* I (1969), 51-78; J. A. Ziesler, *The Meaning of Righteousness in Paul. A Linguistic and Theological Enquiry* (1972); E. Käsemann, *Romans*, pp. 21-32; E. Lohse, "Die Ge-rechtigkeit Gottes in der paulinischen Theologie," in Lohse, *Die Einheit des NT* (1973), pp. 209-227; H. Conzelmann, "Die Rechtfertigungslehre des Paulus. Theologie oder Anthropologie?", in Conzelmann, *Theologie als Schriftauslegung* (1974), pp. 191-206. **On the Jewish Background**: F. Nötscher, *Zur theologischen Terminologie der Qumran-Texte* (1956); S. Schulz, "Zur Rechtfertigung aus Gnaden in Qumran und bei Paulus," *ZThK* 56 (1959), 155-185; J. Becker, *Das Heil Gottes. Heils- und Sündenbegriffe in den*

Qumrantexten und im Neuen Testament (1964). **On 3**: F. Büchsel, *allassō*, . . . *katallassō, TDNT* I, 251-59; J. Hermann/F. Büchsel, *hilastērion, TDNT* III, 318-323; E. Käsemann, "Erwägungen zum Stichwort 'Versöhnungslehre im Neuen Testament,' " in *Zeit und Geschichte, Festschrift für R. Bultmann* (1964), pp. 47-60; G. Fitzer, "Der Ort der Versöhnung nach Paulus," *ThZ* 22 (1966), 161-183; L. Goppelt, "Versöhnung durch Christus," in *Christologie*, pp. 147-164; H. Ridderbos, *Paul* (1975), pp. 182-204.

1. REGARDING TERMINOLOGY

Paul described the effect of God's revelation of salvation with a number of different terms. In I Cor. 1:30, he said that Christ had become for us "righteousness *(dikaiosynē)* and sanctification *(hagiasmos)* and redemption *(apolytrōsis)*." What later ecclesiastical usage came to associate with these various terms was not, for the most part, what Paul meant. For him justification and sanctification were by no means two events following each other in succession. The terms *dikaioun* (to justify) and *hagiazein* (to sanctify) intended simply to describe the same event from two different sides. That was also true especially for *dikaioun* (to justify) and *katallassein, katallagē* (to reconcile, reconciliation), terms that Paul used in a parallel sense in II Cor. 3:9 and 5:18. Such was also the case for *zōē* (life) and *sōtēria* (salvation/deliverance); in Rom. 10:9f. *sōzein* (to deliver) was used thus as a parallel to *dikaiosynē* (righteousness).

2. THE DIFFERENT ASPECTS OF SALVATION'S EFFECT

The observation is of course decisive that all these terms met in a threefold perspective.

a) The indicative. Seen from the verbal structure of the Greek language, these terms were used aoristically in order to express what had already been accomplished in the present through the summons to faith. "And those whom he called he also justified; and those whom he justified he also glorified" (Rom. 8:30; cf. Phil. 3:9; Rom. 5:1, 9f.).

In a way distinct from the other terms mentioned above, reconciliation could be expressed, moreover, as already having occurred for the whole world as a direct consequence of the cross prior to the summons and faith. "All this is from God, who through Christ reconciled us to himself and gave us the ministry of reconciliation" (II Cor. 5:18f.). For their part, the other terms expressed what had happened to people as the result of the cross or of baptism through the summons to faith.

b) The imperative. These terms also served to describe a task that was set before faith (Rom. 6:13, 16, 19; I Thess. 4:3; 5:23). This imperative took the form of the call to the obedience of faith.

c) Hope. Since righteousness as well as sanctification was always given strictly as gift and task, they always remained in the course of this world the object of hope as well. "For through the Spirit, by faith, we wait for the hope of righteousness" (Gal. 5:5). The tension between the "already" and the "not yet" could be seen most clearly through the description of what happened to people in salvation. On the one hand, the "already" was expressed: "now is the day of salvation" (II Cor. 6:2; cf. I Cor. 1:18; II Cor. 2:15); on the other, it was said as in Rom. 8:24, "For we have been saved, though only in hope" (NEB).

Hence salvation *(sōtēria)* appeared as that end toward which expectation looked in the final judgment as a risk in faith based on justification in the present (Rom. 5:9f.; 13:11).

3. JUSTIFICATION AND RECONCILIATION AS SPECIFIC PAULINE TERMS

Two of the terms in this field of expression gained special prominence for Paul: "to justify" and "to reconcile." Although the number of passages was relatively small—only Romans and Galatians spoke with emphasis about justification, and the technical terms *katallassein/katallagē* actually appeared in three passages only (Rom. 5:10f.; 11:15; II Cor. 5:18-20)—nevertheless these terms had considerable theological weight for Paul.

It is noteworthy that he linked justification and reconciliation together both in Rom. 5 and in II Cor. 5. In Rom. 5, he moved from justification (5:1a) to reconciliation (5:1b, 10) and in II Cor. 5, the reverse, from reconciliation (5:18-20) to justification (5:21). Both terms apparently described the same event, the becoming "saved" of the relationship between God and man. This can be seen also in the way that Paul used them as parallels to each other in a series of statements. Thus the statement about reconciliation in Rom. 5:10 corresponded in form and content to that about justification in Rom. 5:9. Serving the gospel could be called the ministry of reconciliation *(diakonia tēs katallagēs)* or the ministry of justification *(diakonia tēs dikaiosynēs*, II Cor. 3:9; 5:18). The two terms represented two conceptual contexts that described in human images that which happened to a person in salvation as the relationship between God and man. And this occurred in connection with distinct settings that were already shaped by the Old Testament.

a) Justification *(dikaiōsis* or *dikaioun)* interpreted the relationship to God in terms of the legal character of the Old Testament covenant of God (cf. Rom. 3:2-6); its starting point was the demonstration "of the righteousness of God," which removed "the condemnation" of the "unrighteous one" and made him into the "righteous one."

With the help of justification Paul was able to express that in Christ the God of the Old Testament acting in faithfulness to his pledge bound himself to man in a perfectly legal way and made him his covenant partner. The message of justification encompassed the core of God's relationship to man; and it set that human being in the midst of the mass of humanity as a responsible individual related back to God.

When Paul designated the effect of the cross in Rom. 3:25f. as the demonstration of the righteousness of God and in Rom. 1:17 the gospel thematically as the revelation of the righteousness of God, he was appropriating the most central theological term of the Old Testament. God encountered people in the Old Testament as the God of the covenant. He was the One who established the relationship upon which all Israel was to depend for life. This is why it was so critical that God should remain faithful to this relationship and act accordingly. This demonstration of his covenant faithfulness was his righteousness.

For the Old Testament, righteousness therefore was not a measuring stick as it has become for Western thought, but a relationship! For man everything depended on his finding satisfaction in this relationship established by God, in being "righteous." Thus, for people of the Old Testament righteousness was the highest value in life.[1]

The concept of "justification" comprehended the depth of the relationship to God when it characterized the corruption of man, his fallenness to sin and to death, as the condemnation of God (Rom. 5:18f.; 8:1f.); it also comprehended that depth, on the other hand, when it expected all that meant salvation to come from God's righteousness, i.e., from God's loyalty to his pledge (Rom. 3:2; 9:6), from the demonstration of his promissory and covenantal faithfulness (Rom. 3:3-6; 9:4f.). For Paul, the righteousness of God was precisely not, in a general way, his faithfulness to his creation. This has been misunderstood frequently in recent times.[2] Rather God's righteousness was his faithfulness to the pledge witnessed to in the Old Testament; precisely this faithfulness as such was universal because the promise given to Abraham encompassed "all peoples" (Rom. 4:16f.). God's pledge was for Paul the starting point for believing and thinking. "But it is not as though the word of God had failed" (Rom. 9:6). Christ, moreover, was the "yes" of God to all his promises (II Cor. 1:20), the demonstration of God's righteousness in person (I Cor. 1:30).

b) Reconciliation *(katallagē)* interpreted the relationship to God in terms of the Old Testament covenant of God as electing love (cf. Rom. 9:11, 13; Col. 3:12). It took as its starting point the demonstration of "the love of God," which turned the "enemy of God" into one who had "peace with God."

One should note that the parallel term here was "peace" *(eirēnē)* and not something like "expiation" *(apolytrōsis,* Rom. 5:1; Col. 1:20; cf. Eph. 2:14). Paul used the infinitive "to reconcile" *(katallassein)* for the relationship between

---

[1] von Rad, *Theology* I, 370-383.

[2] E. Käsemann, " 'The Righteousness of God' in Paul," in *New Testament Questions of Today*, pp. 168-182; Stuhlmacher, op. cit. (Lit., §36), pp. 89f.

God and man with the same philological meaning it had in I Cor. 7:11 for the restoration of the separated marriage partner (cf. *diallassein*, Mt. 5:24). The concept of a settlement between two partners through an accomplished atonement was not contained in this word at all;[3] and yet it took on a special character through the way in which the reconciliation took place here. In every passage, the subject who was responsible for the reconciliation was God!

In the Hellenistic world,[4] the verbs *katallassein* and *diallassein* were used synonymously with various connotations; among them also "to reconcile," but almost never applied to the relationship between God and man. In contrast, though not in the Old Testament, nevertheless in Judaism there were some modest beginnings. The LXX used the words rarely; a development took place, however, in a late writing, II Maccabees. There the statement was used with a certain formulaic shape that God would give up his wrath if people petitioned him or if they repented, and that he would reconcile himself to them, i.e., become gracious toward them once again (II Macc. 1:5; cf. 7:33; 8:29; also 5:20). To apply the word in this way to God was apparently current practice for the Greek-speaking Judaism from which Paul came; this formula, after all, did find usage in Josephus (*Ant.* 6.143 = LCL, V, 239).

That people in the primitive church before Paul already spoke about reconciliation through Christ is improbable. In all the Christian literature of the 1st century this word is found only in Paul. It corresponded to his way of seeing Christ's work of salvation strictly as the work of God. The God of the New Testament was the strictly in-person God of the Old Testament. He gave his word to people so that a partnership was established that could be compared to a marriage between two people (Rom. 3:2-5). Only because Paul saw God as person in this way could he speak about reconciliation between God and man.

Whereas justification said that God in Christ sought the responsible individual, reconciliation said that he sought the heart of man; "God's love has been poured into our hearts . . ." (Rom. 5:5). Yet reconciliation too said precisely that he did not seek merely peace of soul for the individual or peace for a cloister, but peace for the world. If justification exposed the depth of the event between God and man as a legally binding status, reconciliation encompassed its cosmic breadth. As for the former the word about the eschatological reconciliation (Rom. 3:25f.) constituted the central starting point, so for the latter the word—formulated no less theocentrically—about the eschatological peace agreement (II Cor. 5:19): "God was in Christ reconciling the world to himself." It was not coincidental that Paul nowhere said that God had justified the world since justification meant the establishment of a right relationship through the creation of faith. In contrast he could say that God had turned with a universal demonstration of his love in the dying of Jesus to the humanity that stood hostile against him long before it knew anything about it.

---

[3]L. Goppelt, "Versöhnung durch Christus," in *Christologie*, pp. 147f.
[4]Ibid., p. 149; F. Büchsel, *TDNT* I, 254.

4. JUSTIFICATION IN PAULINE THEOLOGY AS A WHOLE

a) Regarding the history of the problem. Here we must content ourselves with some brief references.

1) The Reformers understood justification to be the center of Pauline theology and, in addition, the center of the New Testament.

2) The history-of-religion school, in contrast, devalued justification to an anti-Jewish polemic teaching and posited as the ostensible center of Pauline theology the so-called Christ-mysticism.[5]

3) R. Bultmann attributed once again to justification a central place in terms of his word/kerygma theology. Sections 28-30 of his *New Testament Theology* constituted the center of his presentation of Paul and, perhaps not coincidentally, of his whole book. Bultmann understood justification in a strictly forensic sense; God's righteousness (objective genitive) was the righteousness given as gift by God and announced to man.[6]

4) H. Conzelmann made emphatic appropriation of this and took sides with Luther (and Bultmann)[7] against A. Schlatter[8] who had interpreted the genitive in *dikaiosynē theou* (Rom. 1:17; 3:4) as a subjective genitive and thus God's righteousness as the righteousness "possessed by God."

5) With this defense, however, Conzelmann also opposed the line of interpretation in New Testament research forged by E. Käsemann and P. Stuhlmacher. Both of them do not wish to understand God's righteousness forensically but—in company with Schlatter—as a power that took man into service, and then and from that perspective as a gift.

So it is that justification once again has assumed a focal position in New Testament theology as otherwise could be said only of the question about the historical Jesus. Its position as the center of Pauline theology is uncontested. In order to understand this position one must grasp the starting point of the Pauline statements about justification.

b) The starting point of the statements about justification. Paul interpreted Jesus' life and ministry, especially his cross, in terms of the center of God's revelation in the Old Testament; he understood it as the demonstration of God's righteousness or as the justification of sinners (Rom. 4:6f.). The activity of God that let Jesus die the death of the sinner in an atoning and representative way came to us as the "demonstration of the righteousness" of God. This demonstration "justified," i.e., made us righteous. It did not convey a quality but placed one in an in-person relationship. It turned the believing one into a covenant partner of God.

Justification meant that God placed man in a right relationship to himself. He apportioned to him a place at his table. To take one's place in order to live meant

---

[5]Regarding the first aspect, cf. W. Wrede, *Paul* (1908), pp. 74ff.; regarding the latter aspect, cf. A. Schweitzer, *The Mysticism of Paul the Apostle* (1931), esp. pp. 205-226.

[6]*Theology* I, §30,3.

[7]*Theology*, pp. 213-220.

[8]*Gottes Gerechtigkeit* (1935), pp. 36-39.

to believe. God created for himself the believing one as partner. Hence justification was certainly always forensic to begin with (Rom. 1:23–4:25). But according to Rom. 6:17-23, one only had justification when one served justification, i.e., lived in terms of this relationship! Whoever took up the place apportioned him by God—believed—that one was justified. To believe meant to agree with God from the position of Jesus.

Justification put man in the place of final solitude before God. It was something that happened to faith. No one could believe for another. But the believing one did not remain alone. Justification linked God and man together in a new way. Rom. 12–13 placed the one who believed into wide-ranging social relationships; through justification this one became a member of the body of Christ (Rom. 12:4-8), participated in the relationship to neighbor within the community of faith (Rom. 12:9-21), and was incorporated into the walks of life of this world (Rom. 13:1-7).

Chapter V

THE EMERGENCE OF THE GOSPEL AS VISIBLE FORM IN THE CHURCH

§40. The Church

H. Schlier, *Christus und die Kirche im Epheserbrief* (1930); O. Linton, *Das Problem der Urkirche in der neueren Forschung* (1932; repr. 1957); E. Käsemann, *Leib und Leib Christi* (1933); A. Wikenhauser, *Die Kirche als der mystische Leib Christi nach dem Apostel Paulus* (1940²); N. A. Dahl, *Das Volk Gottes* (1941; 1963²); E. Percy, *Der Leib Christi* (1942); Bultmann, *Theology* I, §§13,2; 34,2; A. Oepke, "Leib Christi oder Volk Gottes bei Paulus?", *ThLZ* 79 (1954), 363-68; H. Schlier, "Corpus Christi," *RAC* III, 437-453; J. Reuss, "Die Kirche als 'Leib Christi' und die Herkunft dieser Vorstellung bei dem Apostel Paulus," *BZ* NF 2 (1958), 103-127; R. Schnackenburg, *The Church in the New Testament* (1965); E. Schweizer, "Die Kirche als Leib Christi in den paulinischen Homologumena," in Schweizer, *Neotestamentica* (1963), pp. 272-292; Schweizer, *sōma*, *TDNT* VII, 1049-1094; J. Roloff, *Apostolat—Verkündigung—Kirche* (1965); Conzelmann, *Theology*, pp. 254-265; E. Käsemann, "The Theological Problem presented by the Motif of the Body of Christ," in *Perspectives on Paul* (1971), pp. 102-121; L. Goppelt, "Kirchentrennung und Kirchengemeinschaft nach dem NT," *Ökumenische Rundschau* 19 (1970), 1-11; H. Schürmann, "Die geistlichen Gnadengaben in den paulinischen Gemeinden," in Schürmann, *Ursprung und Gestalt. Erörterungen und Besinnungen zum NT* (1970), pp. 236-267; J. Hainz, *Ekklesia. Strukturen paulinischer Gemeinde-Theologie und Gemeinde-Ordnung* (1972); J. S. Vos, *Traditionsgeschichtliche Untersuchungen zur paulinischen Pneumatologie* (1973).

1. THE STARTING POINT

What the church meant for Paul can be deciphered quite effectively by reading the First Epistle to the Corinthians. It was an epistle about the church! Paul wrote in I Cor. 1:2 to the *ekklēsia* of God that was at Corinth.

But how would this group, which Paul addressed with this lofty designation, be portrayed if seen through the eyes of an outsider? According to I Cor. 1:26ff., belonging to their number were "not many . . . wise according to worldly standards, not many . . . powerful, not many . . . of noble birth"; they were not of the intellectual and economic upper class. And in I Cor. 6:9ff., Paul used strong words when considering the former existence of the community members, who had been "immoral, idolaters, adulterers, thieves, greedy, drunkards," etc. To be sure, this was a traditional catalogue of vices; nevertheless, they were the kind of people who could be reminded about their former existence with such references. But now, of course, it was true of them: "But you were washed . . ." (I Cor. 6:11).

Was that other side, that which was debased and had shaped their former life, really behind them now? This question is quite in order when one looks at 1:11 where Paul mentioned the arguments, factions, and the differences between various theological positions and interest groups (cf. also I Cor. 3:12). Paul was worried not only about the dearth of quality in the Christian life of the Corinthians, but even more about that which they claimed with regard to its content. There were people in Corinth who lived by the conviction, " 'All things are lawful for me,' " for " 'all of us possess knowledge' " (I Cor. 6:12; 8:1). The community of faith there understood all that for which Paul reproached them, even fornication, as the pneumatic demonstration of Christian freedom.

How could Paul regard this group of people, which by outward appearances composed such a questionable picture, as the community of God? As answer all those explanations come to mind that have been tried throughout the course of church history. Was the community of God for Paul the invisible flock of believing souls? Or did he mean a core-community that was distinguishable from the mass of merely baptized people? Or was the church for Paul only present in the form of functions? There are probably moments of truth in all of these explanations.

How Paul understood things can be seen in I Cor. 1:2. In the prescript of the letter he developed the designation *ekklēsia tou theou* (community of God) by means of the clarifying phrase, "those sanctified in Christ Jesus," "called to be saints." As we saw earlier (§39,1), Paul used "to sanctify" in a way parallel to "to justify" (e.g., I Cor. 6:11). The Palestinian church had already referred to itself as "the saints" (*hoi hagioi*; §25,3).

A person's belonging to the community of God was therefore evident and effective in the same way as his justification and sanctification. That a flock of people was the community *(ekklēsia)* of God was a matter—just like our justification—of believing the pledge and grace of God, if the signs of his effective grace were discernible. Thus *ekklēsia tou theou* was not an objectifiable sociological designation for Paul, but a kerygmatic specification of something's essence.

According to Paul, the designation *ekklēsia* was applicable to three different possibilities. (1) In I Cor. 10:32 it meant the people of God in its entirety. (2) In I Cor. 1:2 it meant the particular local community. (3) In I Cor. 11:18 it meant the worshipping assembly of the community. The word did have the same basic meaning in all three usages: the eschatological people of God that came into existence as the Christian church, as total community, and as worshipping assembly.

2. THE IDENTIFYING MARKS OF THE CHURCH

What indications cause faith to see in a host of people the community of God?

Paul called the saints *klētoi* as well (the called ones, I Cor. 1:2), i.e., those people who were grasped by the word and summoned to faith. But how was it possible to recognize that "called ones" were in Corinth?

Paul was not thinking here of cases of conversion that one could exhibit, but of baptism (I Cor. 6:11). The indicatival aorists *apelousasthe* (you were washed), *hōgiasthēte* (you were sanctified), and *edikaiōthēte* (you were justified) proclaimed what had happened in baptism so that it might happen always afresh in faith. Baptism as well was not simply an observable credential that one belonged to the community, but a concealed sign always confessed anew. The one who was called showed that he belonged to Christ by confessing. Those who were baptized were also always those who called upon the name of the Lord (I Cor. 1:2; Rom. 10:13f.). Furthermore, people could be found in Corinth who said "Jesus is Lord" (I Cor. 12:3). According to Rom. 10:9, this corresponded to faith in one's heart; according to I Cor. 12:3, it corresponded to the working of the Spirit. But even the confession of one's mouth was, on the other hand, no proof but a sign for both.

In I Cor. 10:1-13 Paul compared the community to Israel during the wilderness wanderings. As Israel came forth from the deliverance at the Red Sea, so the community came forth from baptism. What manna and water from the stone had been for Israel back then in the wilderness wanderings, the Lord's Supper was now for the new people of God as provision for the journey. The Lord's Supper (I Cor. 10:17) was the most immediate portrayal of the community of the Lord in time.

Let us summarize: The community of God was for Paul the flock that was comprehended by the electing summons of God in missionary proclamation and by baptism. It was therefore the flock *en Christō* by which and through which the word was preached and the Lord's Supper was celebrated. It was the flock that responded to the gospel, confessing, praying, and serving by faith, and that thus traveled the road through the cross to the resurrection.

3. THE CHURCH AS THE ESCHATOLOGICAL PEOPLE OF GOD

In addition to *ekklēsia* Paul applied a series of further designations to the people of God that came out of the Old Testament/Jewish realm. He called it the temple of God (I Cor. 3:10ff.; cf. Rom. 15:20; Col. 2:7; Eph. 2:20), the planted field of God (I Cor. 3:5-9; Col. 2:7), the flock of God (I Cor. 9:7), [God's] administration/*oikonomia* (I Cor. 9:17 [Gr.]), the Israel of God (Gal. 6:16), the offspring of Abraham (Rom. 4:13, 16, 18; Gal. 3:16).

The situation of the community corresponded typologically to the situation of Israel in its wilderness wanderings (I Cor. 10:1-13). That signified two things.

a) It signified a salvation-historical correspondence. What was spoken to Israel in the Old Testament as the people of God was now to be connected typologically with the church. It alone was the community that could understand itself as the heir of the Old Testament promises.

b) It also signified an eschatological difference. The church was no longer like Israel a people among other peoples; it was not the "third gender" *(tertium genus)* alongside Jews and Gentiles. Rather the church stood in relationship to all peoples as the eschatological people of God, as the new creation. Even if the people of any nation belonged almost entirely to the church, nation and church, ecclesiastical and political activity, could no longer coincide as they had in Israel. Gal. 3:28 emphasized this eschatological character of the church: "There is neither Jew nor Greek, there is neither slave nor free, there is neither male nor female; for you are all one in Christ Jesus."

Yet this was not to be misunderstood in a perfectionistic sense as in Corinth. The difference had been removed only for faith and for the activity that came from faith. Christians were thus to remain in the stations to which they were called (I Cor. 7:17-24). Most of all, the community was to know that, for as long as it still lived in the flesh, in history, it was always subject to wrestling with doubts (I Cor. 10:6, 12).

4. THE CHURCH AS THE BODY OF CHRIST (SŌMA CHRISTOU)

In order to express that which was eschatologically new about the church Paul used a designation that did not come from the Old Testament. For him the church was the *sōma Christou* (body of Christ).

Paul did not regard the "body" the way the Greeks did, as formed matter, but as an organism of acting members. In Rom. 6:13, the word "members" was used as a synonym to the word "body" (Rom. 6:12). On the basis of this conception Paul not only compared the community to a body (I Cor. 12:12-26), the image known to the ancient world,[1] but also went on to say: "Now you are the body of Christ and individually members of it" (I Cor. 12:27). Disciples were members of Christ (I Cor. 6:15), his mouth and his helping hands, and thus in their entirety his body, for Christ was at work historically through them (I Cor. 12:4-6). Because he was present as the One at work in this way through all of them, and not through a community-for-action with whose cause they should join forces, they were bound to each other. The starting point for this concept was not to be found in the Gnostic myth of the "primal man"[2]—frequent suppositions in the history of research to the contrary notwithstanding—but in the Pauline understanding of the Lord's Supper. That can be seen in I Cor. 10:17

---

[1] Cf. the well-known fable of M. Agrippa (Livy *Roman History* 2.32) as well as the material in E. Schweizer, *TDNT* VII, 1036-1041.

[2] Thus H. Schlier, op. cit. (Lit., §40); E. Käsemann, *Leib und Leib Christi* (1933); yet contra, E. Percy, *Der Leib Christi in den paulinischen Homologumena und Antilegomena* (1942); E. Schweizer, "Die Kirche als Leib Christi in den paulinischen Homologumena," in *Neotestamentica* (1963), pp. 272-292.

(cf. §41,2). Because Christ was currently at work among the members of the community in the Lord's Supper through the offering of his body, his person, he made them his *sōma*, i.e., his "total person," the organism of functioning members, the community of his body.

§41. The Lord's Supper

Cf. also Lit. to §21 and §25,4a; H. von Soden, *Sakrament und Ethik bei Paulus* (1931; repr. in *Das Paulusbild in der neueren deutschen Forschung* [ed. K. H. Rengstorf (1964)]); K. Stürmer, "Das Abendmahl bei Paulus," *EvTheol* 7 (1947/48), 50-59; G. Bornkamm, "On the Understanding of Worship," in Bornkamm, *Early Christian Experience* (1969), pp. 161-179; E. Käsemann, "The Pauline Doctrine of the Lord's Supper," in Käsemann, *Essays on New Testament Themes*, pp. 108-135; P. Neuenzeit, *Das Herrenmahl. Studien zur paulinischen Eucharistieauffassung* (1960); Goppelt, *Apostolic Times*, pp. 202ff.; G. Delling, "Das Abendmahlsgeschehen nach Paulus," in Delling, *Studien zum NT und zum hellenistischen Judentum* (1970), pp. 318-335; J. Roloff, "Heil als Gemeinschaft," in *Gottesdienst und Öffentlichkeit* (ed. P. Cornehl/H.-E. Bahr [1970]), pp. 88-117; L. Goppelt, "Der eucharistische Gottesdienst nach dem Neuen Testament," in *Erbe und Auftrag, Benediktinische Monatsschrift* 49 (1973), 435-447.

1. THE LORD'S SUPPER CELEBRATION OF THE PAULINE COMMUNITIES

a) How the institution of Jesus (§20,6) was appropriated liturgically and interpreted theologically in the Hellenistic community can be drawn from the oldest interpretive tradition contained in the New Testament. In I Cor. 10:15, Paul directed the community's attention to an interpretation of the Eucharist with which it was apparently already familiar. He quoted it in I Cor. 10:16 in order that he might thereafter draw consequences from it for the community's situation (I Cor. 10:17-22). That we have a transmitted formula in I Cor. 10:16 is also suggested by the presence of non-Pauline terminology and the skilled formulation in *parallelismus membrorum*.

The cup of blessing which we bless,
is it not a participation in the blood of Christ?
The bread which we break,
is it not a participation in the body of Christ?

The interrogatory form, as well as the switching of the series bread and wine, was presented that way because Paul wanted the statement of v. 17 to be the conclusion of the formula. The formula depended—and that is an indication of its age—on Jewish table-custom and separated in clarifying fashion the eucharistic liturgy from that custom in the two parallel relative clauses.[1] Here it was no longer the Jews that blessed but "we!" Here it was no longer that one "blessed" over the bread and cup, i.e., pronounced the laudation, but for them!

---

[1] Supporting references for the following are found in L. Goppelt, *TDNT* VI, 156ff.; Goppelt, *Apostolic Times*, pp. 217-221.

In Jewish table-custom, "the cup of blessing" was the cup filled with wine over which the table-prayer of thanksgiving, the "blessing," was spoken at the end of each meal that had included wine. Here in the Eucharist one no longer gave thanks for the meal through the cup, but rather the cup itself was "blessed." To bless *(eulogein)* meant here "to give thanks with praise." For this reason, Paul replaced it in the account of institution (I Cor. 11:24), in comparison to Mk. 14:22, with the word *eucharistein* (to give thanks), which was more readily understood by his Greek readers.

What exactly was said in thanks for the cup is not reported anywhere in the New Testament. But we can derive what it was with considerable probability from the substantive context. The cup was "blessed" by giving thanks with praise for the gift that the Lord in accord with the cup's institution offered through it. In I Cor. 11:24, Paul emphasized the institution of these gifts, while in I Cor. 10:14-21 he specified that the Lord himself offered them.[2] Even on the basis of the parallelism one must conclude that the phrase "the bread which we break" intended to speak in a corresponding sense. "To break bread" had here a special meaning that is familiar in connection with Luke 24:35 and appeared on occasion in Jewish linguistic usage too. The formula summarized here four stages of Jewish table-custom. The bread was taken into the hand, the benediction was prayed, the bread was broken, and the pieces were distributed. The pronouncement of laudation, which in the Eucharist was no longer spoken over the bread but for this gift, corresponded to the content that we concluded for the blessing of the cup.

b) What did this prayer of thanksgiving mean? We can derive an answer from the effect that was ascribed in the New Testament even to the thanksgiving for everyday meals. "Nothing is to be rejected when it is taken with thanksgiving, since it is hallowed by God's own word and by prayer" (I Tim. 4:4f., NEB; cf. Rom. 14:23; I Cor. 10:25f., 30). Thus the elements of the Eucharist were "hallowed" through the giving of thanks. They were removed from the profane realm and received back from the hand of the Lord as the mediator of that which was given through them according to the word of institution. The cup that was blessed was "participation in the blood of Christ." It was this not in an objective sense but in the accomplishment of the meal *(in usu)*. This confessing and proclaiming thanksgiving for the elements was the apostolic form of the "consecration." In early Christianity the thanksgiving for the elements was so important that the celebration received the name "Eucharist" from it.

---

[2]In fact, the oldest liturgical formulary that has come down to us, the church order of Hippolytus (31:7ff.), offered here a prayer of thanksgiving for redemption through Christ that then flowed into the account of institution. To this thanksgiving were added three other elements that were found repeatedly in the liturgy of the Eucharist: (1) an anamnesis, (2) an offertory prayer, and (3) an epiclesis. ". . . (1) being mindful of his death and resurrection, (2) do offer unto thee this bread and this cup, giving thanks unto thee for that thou hast deemed us worthy to stand before thee and minister as thy priest. (3) And we beseech thee that thou wouldst send thy Holy Spirit upon the oblation of thy holy Church . . ." (H. Bettenson, *Documents of the Christian Church* [1963²], p. 107).These three elements were not, however, already represented in I Cor. 10 as Lietzmann had assumed *(Mass and Lord's Supper*, pp. 146f.; and in *ZNW* 22 [1923], 265ff.).

Following the thanksgiving came the distribution that was linked with a bestowal formula. Its original content may have corresponded to the words that, according to the account of institution, accompanied the distribution of bread and wine. According to I Cor. 11:24f., they went as follows in the Pauline congregations: "This is my body which is for you!—This cup is the new covenant in my blood!"[3] Within the context of the worship-service celebration for which people gathered in a small area around the table, the bestowal formula grew directly out of the "giving of thanks." Its pluralistic form indicated an important aspect of the meal's significance. The meal mediated not only fellowship with the Lord but also fellowship among the celebrants.

2. PAUL'S INTERPRETATION OF THE LORD'S SUPPER

a) Following up here on previous understanding, Paul applied ecclesiologically the statement of the interpretive tradition about the soteriological effect of the meal. He elevated *koinōnia* to a key term for the entire section, I Cor. 10:14-22. In English the word is usually translated "fellowship," but for Paul it did not mean an association that arose through subjective inclination but a bond that had been established. In vv. 17 and 21 he could use *metechein* (to participate) for this. Just as, according to the tradition, the elements mediated participation in the blood and body of Christ, i.e., participation in Christ as determined by his dying, independent of the attitude of the recipient, so too, as Paul concluded in v. 17, those elements established a bond among the concelebrants. "Because [if] there is one bread [that we eat], we who are many are one body." That intended to say that participation in the body of Christ as the gift of the Eucharist turned the celebrants into the body of Christ, i.e., into the community of faith! (§40,4).

b) Whenever one denied that Christ united the celebrants with each other through his offering of himself in order to be at work through them in society, the meal was received to one's destruction (I Cor. 11:27-34). This happened in Corinth since people celebrated there in order to satisfy individualistic religious needs (I Cor. 11:17-22). Without reservation, therefore, people thought that it was possible to participate both in the "table of the Lord" and in the "table of demons" (I Cor. 10:21). The "table of demons" was the meal that was dedicated—even if mostly only in a formal sense—not to God but to the gods of people. Christians were also attracted to such a meal because it served primarily social ends and not cultic ones.

This misuse of the Lord's Supper was the product of a deep misunderstanding of its content. In Corinth, people interpreted the formulas known to them in terms of the piety of the mystery religions, i.e., in terms of a deity other than

---

[3]Generally it can be observed that as the accounts of institution were transmitted the introduction of the words about the bread and cup was shaped increasingly in the direction of a formula of bestowal. Thus in Mt. 26:26f. the challenge "take" was shaped more pointedly than in Mk. 14:22f. and I Cor. 11:24f.: "Take, eat . . . !" "Drink . . . all of you!"

the Father of Jesus. Apparently they referred to the gifts of the Lord's Supper as "spiritual food" and "spiritual drink" (I Cor. 10:3, Gr.). They intended thereby to say that the sacrament mediated a heavenly *pneuma*-substance that emancipated one from bodily existence and elevated the true reality of man. They took this in such a way that they could live by the motto, "all things are lawful for me" (I Cor. 6:12; 10:23) because we "possess knowledge" (I Cor. 8:1).

c) This reinterpretation of the sacraments was countered by Paul in I Cor. 10:1-11. He did so by referring to the God of the Old Testament as he had made himself known to Israel in the wilderness period. Food and drink in the wilderness period, as well as in the Lord's Supper, were for Paul "spiritual" because in both places they were the gifts and mediators of God's work of salvation.[4] In the meal God was at work just as inescapably as he was in the provision in the desert, but people were no more able to take possession of him in the meal than they were in the desert provision. The gracious turning of God for the purpose of fellowship that mediated wholeness of life obligated one here as there to comply with his will; otherwise his turning accomplished judgment. In I Cor. 12:13, Paul could refer to the typological correspondence in fact not only as "spiritual," but also as the Spirit itself: "and all were made to drink of one Spirit." The Spirit, however, was not for Paul a heavenly substance but the Lord (II Cor. 3:17). Not that Paul thought about the identity of person here, but certainly about the manner of being at work. The coming of the Spirit was identical to the present giving of himself of the exalted One. Thus Paul developed Jesus' instituting of the Supper in trinitarian fashion as he related it to the God of the Old Testament. He proclaimed the meal as the most immediate moment of the continued ministry of the historical Jesus; moreover, he proclaimed the meal as the visualization of the promise that was fulfilled through him and that also opened the way for the future. Seen in this way, this meal can be understood in the context of faith today as it was in New Testament times and the worship-service celebration can become the center of responsible Christian conduct in history.

---

[4]Cf. L. Goppelt, *TDNT* VI, 146ff. and E. Schweizer, *TDNT* VI, 436f.

Part IV

THE THEOLOGY OF THE POST-PAULINE WRITINGS

INTRODUCTION

§42. The Apostolic Period Draws to a Close

M. Werner, *The Formation of Christian Dogma* (1957); E. Grässer, *Das Problem der Parusieverzögerung in den synoptischen Evangelien und in der Apostelgeschichte* (1957); Goppelt, *Apostolic Times*, pp. 1-7 (Lit.!). **On 3:** E. Käsemann, ed., *Das Neue Testament als Kanon. Dokumentation und kritische Analyse zur gegenwärtigen Diskussion* (1970).

1. THE SITUATION AT ITS CLOSE

The designation "apostolic period" employed in the title was used as a technical term as early as in the first—for us—extant written history of the church; Eusebius used the term *hoi apostolikoi chronoi*.[1] According to a concept already current in the 2nd century, the beginning period of the church was not simply the first chapter of the church's history, but it was a unique and, for all time, normative epoch. In what sense we shall make use of this concept and are able to speak of a "closing of the apostolic period" should become clear in the course of this section.

The first question to be asked is: Did this concept have a historical content? Without doubt the apostle was the leading figure among the representatives of a dawning Christianity, not the prophet or the pneumatic teacher. That much is certainly to be inferred from Gal. 1:1 and I Cor. 15:11. The apostle held this position because the gospel, according to its primitive form as represented in

---

[1]Eus. *EH* 3.31.6 (=LCL, I, 272).

I Cor. 15:3-5, was the testimony to the historical course of Jesus' life and to his resurrection. The apostle was the authorized, authentic witness. But already in I Cor. 15:1-8 the authentic testimony was not bound to the person of the apostles; it had become tradition.

This observation leads further to the question concerning the chronological range of the apostolic period. Did it extend only for as long as the apostles represented the testimony personally? Or did it continue for as long as genuinely apostolic tradition was represented orally? Let us inquire how the writings of the post-Pauline period view this question!

a) In the well-known foreword to his gospel (Lk. 1:1-4), Luke made clear that he looked back to the lifetime of the apostles, but that he had, nevertheless, direct and genuine apostolic tradition at his disposal. As he stated, it was his desire to report what those had passed on who were from the beginning eye-witnesses and servants of the word (§48,lc). According to the Lukan definition in Acts 1:21, those were in fact the apostles. Their lifetime lay for him evidently in the past. It was very important to him that their circle be limited; for this reason he reserved the designation "apostle" for the twelve. This group had already declined in importance by the second part of the book of Acts, while Paul, who for Luke was not an apostle, came to the fore as the representative of the post-apostolic period.

b) The supplemental chapter that was published along with John's Gospel ca. A.D. 90-100 sounded quite different. In Jn. 21:24, the so-called Beloved Disciple was named as the historical eyewitness and as the author of the Gospel. Here the claim was made, therefore, that more than a generation beyond Paul an apostolic witness was alive.

c) This concept, however, was not confirmed by the Gospel of John itself. Prior to the supplemental chapter the Beloved Disciple was not a historical figure but the type of the true disciple and in this sense the guarantor of the Gospel. Here claim was made, above all, that this Gospel reproduced the witness of the one who had really understood Jesus (Jn. 13:25f.; 19:35; 20:8). In addition, one may also have intended to refer to a personal witness who was the guarantor of this tradition.[2]

d) Thus, with regard to our question we take note of a varying self-under-standing already in the post-Pauline period itself. If we go on beyond the New Testament documents to the Apostolic Fathers whose earliest document was written at a time contemporaneous with the Gospel of John, we note that they look back throughout to the time of the apostles (e.g., I Clem. 5:3ff.; 42:1; II Clem. 14:2; Ign. Eph. 13:1f.; Pol. 6:3; Herm. *Vis*. 3:5; *Sim*. 9:17). Even that consciousness of having immediate and genuine Jesus tradition at one's disposal

---

[2]Similarly and most recently cf. O. Cullmann, *The Johannine Circle* (1976), pp. 76ff.; regarding the problem cf. the literature below at §49,1!

no longer appeared as it did in Luke 1:1-4. That does not exclude the possibility that in practice the Jesus tradition continued to be quoted freely from memory.[3]

e) The result of this was that for those who themselves were involved the lower limit of the apostolic period was fluid. Decisive in the matter was that the post-Pauline New Testament literature documented a period of transition between two poles. On the one side stood the period of the first witnesses that was represented literarily by Paul alone, and on the other, the situation of the evolving early catholic church that was represented by the Apostolic Fathers, like the First Epistle of Clement and Ignatius. What had validity as "apostolic" in the range in between has to be determined according to historical-theological criteria.

"Apostolic" had reference, generally speaking, to whatever was an immediate and genuine witness to Christ. What was valid as "apostolic" was, from the earliest beginnings, never a given; it always had to be decided upon. Paul wrote the majority of his epistles to fight for this outcome for himself. The concept extending from the 2nd century down through the centuries that the apostolic period was a time of the ideal unity and purity of the church is a positivistic image of the ideal.

2. THE THEOLOGICAL AND HISTORICAL PROBLEMATIC OF THE CLOSING APOSTOLIC PERIOD

By what criteria, however, should we evaluate theologically the literary statements of this period of transition? This question too involves the overall historical and theological evaluations that have come out looking quite varied in the course of the history of research.

a) One became aware of the theological problematic during the debates over the limits of the canon in the early church and then anew in the Reformation. The latter observed that the church dogma of the Catholicism of the Middle Ages contradicted the Pauline gospel. The histories of the church written in the Reformation inquired into the beginnings of this difference and came to the conclusion in the Magdeburger Centurien that since the opening of the 2nd century a falling away from the apostolic truth had been occurring! In contrast to this, Roman Catholic research throughout was inclined to regard the path from Paul to the constitution of the Catholic Church at the end of the 2nd century as a positively progressive, consistent evolution. This perspective has been emphasized, e.g., by the Catholic exegete R. Schnackenburg.[4] More recent Protestant research has been inclined, in contrast, to judge this development as depravation: and for R. Bultmann this depravation did not begin with the 2nd century but already with Luke!

b) Intersecting this theological way of looking at things is the historical. Since the beginning of the historical study of scripture one of its main themes was

---

[3]Neither Conzelmann, *Theology*, p. 294, nor H. Koester, *Synoptische Überlieferung bei den Apostolischen Vätern* (1957), did justice to this complex state of things.

[4]*New Testament Theology Today* (1963), p. 18.

considered to be that of making clear the path from Paul to the constituting of the Catholic Church as historical development. This path ought not to be judged either as theological apostasy or as theological evolution, but was supposed to be explained as historical development. Motivated by this intention then the bold accounts of the early history of Christianity were written, for the most part, within the "purely historical" direction of research (cf. Vol. I, §23, II, 2-3). Each of these accounts meant an overall evaluation of the New Testament's compositional whole that located a place for every document and every statement. The great milestones were the accounts of F. C. Baur, A. Ritschl, those of the history-of-religion school, and those of the school of R. Bultmann that followed it.[5]

3. AN ATTEMPT AT DETERMINING THE POST-PAULINE PERIOD

a) The historical situation at its close. We shall use the term "post-Pauline period" because it is historically more precise than the term "post-apostolic period." The post-Pauline period began with three decisive historical events that took place chronologically between the years A.D. 63 and 70. These events fundamentally altered the historical situation of the church. We refer to the martyrdom of the original apostles, the destruction of Jerusalem, and the Neronian persecution.

1) Between A.D. 60 and 64 the three most prominent representatives of early Christianity ended up as martyrs: Paul, Peter, and the Lord's brother James. These apostles were referred to, e.g., in Gal. 2:9 as the decisive representatives of the then-known world at the Apostolic Council. The ministry of Paul, which by means of his epistles had mediated decisive impulses to the entire region of the church between Asia Minor and Rome, came to an end. The influence of James and Peter had also come to an end. Paul had encountered that influence not only in Syrian Antioch, but also in Galatia and Corinth.

Along with these figures of worldwide influence there disappeared the organic context of the Christian movement. Regional figures came to the fore so that church development from then on assumed in the particular regions a distinctive, individual appearance. The ecclesiastical situation developed differently in the Palestinian-Syrian realm than in that of western Asia Minor, and there differently than in Greece and Italy. One looked at the mission of the church no longer, as Paul had (cf. Rom. 15:19ff.), as an apocalyptic event of the whole that, like the sun, illuminated the whole world from East to West. Rather, one looked at mission now as a historical event of the particular location that verified itself in many particular encounters of everyday life.

2) The destruction of Jerusalem and of the temple in the year A.D. 70 signified the most profound turning point in the history of the Jewish people that spanned millennia. The catastrophe had a twofold effect on the church. The Jewish-Christian church in Palestine was forced to survive at the poverty level. Because of this it lost all influence upon the Hellenistic Gentile church from

---

[5]Cf. the representation and critique of these accounts in L. Goppelt, *Jesus, Paul, and Judaism*, pp. 15-19 (see Ger. pp. 3-11 for this point); cf. also Goppelt, *Apostolic Times*, pp. 108ff.

Antioch to Rome. Only those particular representatives of the Palestinian church who immigrated to Syria and Asia still managed to work there with some influence; but even their influence died out with this generation. The polarity between Palestinian Jewish-Christianity and Hellenistic Christianity that had been so characteristic of and so significant for the Pauline period became a thing of the past.

Not only Jewish-Christianity but also Judaism itself declined in influence for the church. The Judaism that reconstituted itself after the catastrophe closed itself off toward outsiders, especially in opposition to the church. Of course that did not exclude the possibility, in fact even promoted it, that traditions of Hellenistic- but also of Palestinian-Judaism poured into Christianity through literary channels; as the years wore on this occurred increasingly. In the progress of the 2nd century, Christianity drew mainly upon those Jewish traditions that were rejected by the rabbinic Judaism that was establishing itself: apocalypticism, as well as the literature of Hellenistic Judaism and of the Jewish baptismal movement.

3) Just as the relationship of the church to Jewish-Christianity and Judaism was altered drastically during the few years after A.D. 70, its relationship to the Hellenistic world of the Roman Empire was likewise altered. This change was signaled and triggered by a third event in these years: the so-called Neronian persecution of A.D. 64.

For the general public during the Pauline period the Christians represented a Jewish sect and enjoyed the protection of the *religio licita*, as did the synagogues. Neither in the Corinthian correspondence nor in the Epistle to the Romans were conflicts with the Hellenistic environment mentioned. All other conflicts were of a local nature. Even the measures taken by Nero were at first an arbitrary act of local significance; it did of course presuppose an already altered situation. He placed the Christians under suspicion of having set Rome on fire in order to free himself of such. He could do that only because the Christians at that time already were considered outsiders by the population in this capital city of the world and in the provinces. This suspicion created by the events in the capital reached out into public consciousness throughout the empire and was greeted everywhere with considerable readiness. From that moment on the Christians were recognized as a separate religion and were strapped correspondingly with a label of discrimination.

Thus, between the years of A.D. 63 and 70 three historical events altered the historical situation of Christianity in the whole world in a quite decisive manner. Going hand in hand with equally profound influence were the alterations in the inner structure of Christian faith.

b) **Structural changes to the posture of faith.** The self-understanding of Christian existence underwent change since the A.D. 60s primarily through two factors.

1) In the discipline of the history of missions one talks about the problem of the "second generation."[6] In every community of faith founded by pioneer missionaries the transition from the first to the second generation creates certain

typical problems and structural changes. The second generation seeks to institutionalize that which the first generation had shaped in dynamic participation. The disappearance of vital substance is compensated for through ritualism and legalism. This is in part an unavoidable experience since a repentance movement as such cannot be sustained forever.

In the second Christian generation these typical problems cropped up too. The forms of ecclesiastical life that were so animated in the initial period anchored themselves firmly. That was true both for the constitution and the shape of the worship service and of piety. The tendency also became noticeable that people began once again to conform to the very way of life practiced in the environment from which they had found freedom during the period of conversion. The question of conformity became a critical issue in the communities of faith. These general problems of the second generation became all the more critical through a specifically primitive Christian dimension.

2) The other important factor was the delay of the *parousia*. As the Gospel of Matthew was being circulated in the communities ca. A.D. 80, everyone understood it allegorically when in the parable of the evil servant it said: "that wicked servant says to himself, 'My master is delayed,' and begins to beat his fellow servants, and eats and drinks with the drunken" (Mt. 24:48). After all, this statement described the situation perfectly; the delay of the *parousia*, and not something like the disappointment surrounding the imminent expectation, caused people to fall back into a life formed by this world. How is this thesis to be explained?

The "consistent eschatology" developed by A. Schweitzer and the history-of-religion school produced the concept that the primitive Christianity of the first generation was motivated by an enthusiastic imminent expectation whose disappointment then in the second generation led to a profound crisis and a total alteration of Christian self-understanding. M. Werner, in his book *The Formation of Christian Dogma* (1957; a shortened form of his *Die Entstehung des christlichen Dogmas* [1941]), derived the entire shift of Christianity in the direction of the Catholic Church from the disappointment of the imminent *parousia*. In the Bultmann school as well these concepts of consistent eschatology were close at hand. For example, the monograph of E. Grässer, *Das Problem der Parusieverzögerung in den synoptischen Evangelien und in der Apostelgeschichte* (1957), saw in the disappearance of the imminent expectation the most important motif for the formation of the synoptic Gospels. H. Conzelmann[7] distanced himself, with good reason, from this perspective. It is not only not to be supported within the literature of the post-Pauline period, but can actually be flatly disproved on the basis of those sources! The failure of the *parousia* to take place was regarded as a problem within the literature of the post-Pauline period only quite sporadically. The question of the community concerning the *parousia* was addressed only rarely and quite on the fringe of concern; such was the case, e.g., in Jas.

---

[6]W. Freytag, "Das Problem der zweiten Generation in der jungen Kirche," in W. Freytag, *Reden und Aufsatze* I (1961), pp. 245-257.

[7]*Theology*, pp. 307-317.

5:8f.; Heb. 10:36-39; I Clem. 23; II Clem. 11; II Pet. 3. One observes also that the announcement of the imminent end by no means disappeared in this literature; it was in fact repeated again and again more or less with emphasis well into the 2nd century. It did not stop with I Cor. 7:29ff. and Rom. 13:11; they were followed rather by I Pet. 4:7, Jas. 5:8f.; Heb. 10:36-39; Rev. 22:20; Did. 10:6; I Clem. 23:5; II Clem. 12:1, 6; Barn. 4:3; Herm. *Vis*. 3.8.9; *Sim*. 9.12.3; 10.4.4. In only two of the major writings of each epoch was the reference to the imminent end absent: in the historical composition of Luke and in the Gospel of John.

Thus the problem of the second generation was not the disappointment of the imminent expectation, but the practical delay of the *parousia*, i.e., the extension of time. This was the problem because the Christians understood themselves as called into eschatological existence through total repentance. Put another way: the commandments of the Sermon on the Mount had freed them from the conventional form of life and turned them into strangers in society (I Pet. 1:1). But they were also obligated not—like the community at Qumran—to emigrate out of society, but on the contrary to remain in their marriages, in their families, in their occupations, and within political life. They stood on the one hand within the eschatological existence regarding which was valid: "There is neither Jew nor Greek, there is neither slave nor free, there is neither male nor female" (Gal. 3:26ff.; cf. Col. 3:11); they were also given instruction on the other hand: "Every one should remain in the state in which he was called [to faith]" (I Cor. 7:20). What resulted was a sharp tension between the calling into the new existence of eschatological freedom and the abiding link to the structures of historical life. To maintain the tension permanently was the actual problem caused by the unfulfilled *parousia*. This problem was addressed repeatedly in the post-Pauline literature because everywhere in the communities of faith the tendency arose to conform oneself again to the routine forms of life in the environment. Classic examples of this problematic are the Epistle to the Hebrews (Heb. 12:12f.) and the Shepherd of Hermas.

3) The lengthening of time created a problem also for the maintenance of the tradition of proclamation from which the church lived; this was the problem of the preservation of the Jesus tradition and the kerygma tradition. One began to reflect about how these traditions could be maintained without counterfeit. Out of interest in this issue and others Luke wrote his historical composition (Lk. 1:1-4). In the composing of the remaining Gospel literature it may also have stood in the background. The maintenance of the *paratheke*, the entrusted apostolic teaching, was the chief theme of the Pastoral Epistles. As solution to this question one finally opted in the early catholic church for the New Testament canon, the *regula fidei*, and the succession of the bishops.

Hence historical presuppositions and ecclesiastical-theological lines of questioning become visible that the post-Pauline period took as its starting point. The manner in which these questions were stated and then resolved is the decisive and substantively appropriate theological criterion by which we can group the theological statements preserved for us from this epoch and ascertain its limits as a whole.

4. THEOLOGICAL GROUPINGS AND LITERARY FORMS OF THE POST-PAULINE PERIOD

a) Consideration of the line of questioning shown here itself makes clear the lower limit of this epoch. This line of questioning occupied the attention of the church during the second and third generations, i.e., until ca. A.D. 120. After this, new lines of questioning were taken up among the apologists, the early catholic fathers, and the large Gnostic schools. One also notices that there was a standard way of working on the line of questioning in this period up to A.D. 120. It was responded to, formally speaking, primarily in three literary ways: (1) In the editing of the Gospel tradition, (2) in letter writing that followed the formal example of Paul (the letter became a Christian literary genre; most of the letters of this epoch were more on the order of tractates, epistles rather than letters), and (3) in apocalypses.

b) The limit of the canon was being fixed throughout this literature so similar in genre since the closing of the 2nd century and ultimately since the 4th. This literature has come down to us, in part among the post-Pauline writings of the New Testament and in part among the writings of the Apostolic Fathers. The limit of the canon was fluid up into the 4th century in the very realm of these writings. On the one hand, the canonicity of the Epistle of James, the Second Epistle of Peter, and the Epistle to the Hebrews was challenged in the Western church; and in the East that of the book of Revelation. On the other hand, for a long time several writings of the Apostolic Fathers were read in the service of worship and passed on in editions of the New Testament. This was the case in Syria for the Epistle of Barnabas, frequently in the East for the First and Second Epistles of Clement, and in the West for the Shepherd of Hermas, often also for the Didache and the Apocalypse of Peter. Was it substantively justified that the Easter celebration letter of Athanasius in the year A.D. 367 should set the limit of the canon at that point where it has remained right to this very day?

The limit was not fixed by a chronological date. Most of the writings of the Apostolic Fathers were written, to be sure, after the later writings of the New Testament; but by no means all of them were. Can the limit then be determined according to other criteria? In the 4th century one inquired about apostolic authorship. This criterion no longer exists for us for historical-critical reasons as well as theological ones. We can only apply the criterion we have just acquired as we ask: How were the key ecclesiastical-theological problems of the epoch overcome?

When one compares the substantive replies that were given from I Peter to II Peter to II Clement with regard to the questions raised by the ecclesiastical situation, a noteworthy difference can be delineated. The Epistle to the Hebrews, e.g., countered a relaxed standard in the community of faith with nothing other than a renewed proclamation of the eschatological message of salvation; Hebrews placed full confidence in the power of the word. The Shepherd of Hermas, however, sought to meet the problem by establishing a pedagogical-legal system of penance. This system was *in nuce* the penance system of the Catholic Church that emerged near the end of the 2nd century. Based on this observation we may conclude that the Shepherd of Hermas was early catholic; the Epistle to the Hebrews, in contrast, was "apostolic." "Apostolic," therefore, referred to that which agreed with the theological guideline extending from Jesus to Paul and still reproduced this tradition of proclamation directly out of oral tradition. The same corresponding differences can be observed between Luke and I Clement, John and Ignatius. It is thus true that the limit between "apostolic" and "early catholic" solutions extended approximately to the point where the 4th century set the limit of the canon, even if it did so frequently for secondary reasons.

Thus the literature that was accepted by the early catholic church continually developed for the problems of its day two solutions that were similar but distinct: the "apostolic" and the "early catholic."

c) Alongside this, a third solution was offered in the Eastern ecclesiastical regions: the Gnostic. Over against this-worldliness it proclaimed an apparently consistent other-worldliness. In a practical way it eliminated the tension between eschatological and historical existence in favor of a pneumatic supernatural state. It combined this partly with asceticism, partly with libertinism. Corresponding to this anthropology was Docetism in Christology. It also solved the problem of tradition in this one-sidedly pneumatic way; it supplanted the bishops and presbyters of early catholicism with the free pneumatic teacher and prophet, and the *regula fidei* with the pneumatic secret-tradition. The perspectives of this Gnostic movement of that epoch we know only on the basis of what was said against them in disputation. Almost nothing has survived of the Gnostic writings. The extensive finds from the library at Nag Hammadi come from a later period. In the earlier epoch the Gnostic movement was represented by the opponents against whom the Pastoral Epistles, the book of Revelation, the First Epistle of John, Ignatius, the Epistle of Jude, and the Second Epistle of Peter were written. Sociologically, gnosticism in this period still appeared, as in its primitive forms in Corinth or in Colossae (documented in the epistles to these places), as a movement within the community, and not as later when it took the form of a closed school or group.

d) Alongside the apostolic, early catholic, and Gnostic streams there was in this period, finally, a Jewish-Christianity that was localized in Palestine and Egypt and distanced itself more and more from Hellenistic Christianity. We have received only a few documents from this Ebionite Jewish-Christianity.[8]

In the following sections we shall portray more precisely the theological kerygma of the particular New Testament writings of this epoch. The comparable

---

[8]Cf., regarding the whole, Goppelt, *Apostolic Times*, pp. 135-151.

writings of the Apostolic Fathers will only be drawn upon briefly as pertains to background. We shall proceed in such a way as to begin with an analysis in the first chapter of the two decisive position statements on the situation of the Christian in society: the First Epistle of Peter and the book of Revelation. Thus the sociological dimension of the church's situation and its theological evaluation will become clear. In this way we shall achieve a graphic frame of reference for the inner-ecclesiastical and inner-theological developments that we will then wish to portray in further chapters arranged according to church regions.

Chapter I

CHRISTIANS IN SOCIETY

§43. The Responsibility of Christians in Society according to the First Epistle of Peter

E. G. Selwyn, *The First Epistle of St. Peter* (1952); K. H. Schelkle, *Die Petrusbriefe und der Judasbrief* (HTK, 1961; Eng. in prep.); J.N.D. Kelly, *The Epistles of Peter and of Jude* (1969). **On 1**: Goppelt, *Apostolic Times*, pp. 109-114; J. H. Elliott, *The Elect and the Holy* (1966). **On 2 and 3**: W. Schrage, *Die konkreten Einzelgebote in der paulinischen Paränese* (1961); H.-U. Minke, *Die Schöpfung in der frühchristlichen Verkündigung nach dem 1. Clemensbrief und der Areopagrede* (Diss. Hamburg [1966], pp. 27-66); L. Goppelt, "Die Herrschaft Christi und die Welt," in Goppelt, *Christologie*, pp. 102-136; P. Stuhlmacher, "Christliche Verantwortung bei Paulus und seinen Schülern," *EvTheol* 28 (1968), 165-186 (esp. 173-183); H.-D. Wendland, *Ethik des Neuen Testaments* (1970), pp. 69-88, 101-04; K. Philipps, *Kirche in der Gesellschaft nach dem 1. Petrusbrief* (1971); L. Goppelt, "Prinzipien neutestamentlicher Sozialethik nach dem 1. Petrusbrief," in *Neues Testament und Geschichte*, Festschrift für O. Cullmann (ed. H. Baltensweiler and B. Reicke [1972]), pp. 285-296; Goppelt, "Prinzipien neutestamentlicher und systematischer Sozialethik heute," in *Die Verantwortung der Kirche in der Gesellschaft* (ed. J. Baur, L. Goppelt, G. Kretschmar [1973]), pp. 7-30. **On 3c** *(Haustafeln)*: K. Weidinger, *Die Haustafeln* (1928); M. Dibelius, "Excursuses" on Col. 4:1 and Eph. 5:14 (HNT), pp. 48ff., 91f.; D. Schroeder, *Die Haustafeln* (Diss. Hamburg [1959]); G. Delling, *hypotassō*, *TDNT* VIII, 39-48; E. Kamlah, "*Hypotassesthai* in den neutestamentlichen 'Haustafeln,' " in *Verborum Veritas*, Festschrift für G. Stählin (ed. O. Böcher and K. Haacker [1970]), pp. 237-243; L. Goppelt, "Jesus und die 'Haustafel'-Tradition," in *Orientierung an Jesus*, Festschrift für J. Schmid (ed. P. Hoffmann [1973]), pp. 93-106; J. E. Crouch, *The Origin and Intention of the Colossian Haustafel* (1972). **On 4**: W. Nauck, "Freude im Leiden," *ZNW* 46 (1955), 68-80; Schweizer, *Lordship*, esp. pp. 22-31; E. Lohse, *Märtyrer und Gottesknecht* (1963²); Lohse, "Paränese und Kerygma im 1. Petrusbrief," in Lohse, *Die Einheit des Neuen Testaments* (1973), pp. 307-328; H. Millauer, *Die Leidenstheologie des 1. Petrusbriefes* (Diss. München [1975], pub. as *Leiden als Gnade* [Europäische Hochschulschriften XXIII Theol./56. 1976]). **On 5**: A. Schulz, *Nachfolgen und Nachahmen* (1962); R. Bultmann, "Bekenntnis- und Liedfragmente im ersten Petrusbrief," in Bultmann, *Exegetica* (1967), pp. 285-297;

R. Deichgräber, *Gotteshymnus und Christushymnus in der frühen Christenheit* (1967), pp. 77f., 140ff.; K. Wengst, *Christologische Formeln und Lieder des Urchristentums* (1973²), pp. 83-85, 161-64.

1. PRELIMINARY CONSIDERATION: COMPOSITIONAL CIRCUMSTANCES

a) The letter was addressed to Christians in Asia Minor from Rome. The regions mentioned in the address of 1:1 were the Roman provinces of Asia Minor, while the place of composition, referred to in 5:13 with the code word "Babylon," was probably Rome. The letter says in 5:12 that it had been written by Peter through Silvanus. It is certainly thinkable that it really was composed by the Silas who, according to Acts 15:22, came from Jerusalem and accompanied Paul on his second missionary journey (Acts 15:40; II Cor. 1:19).

b) The time of composition, however, has to be ascertained independently on the basis of the circumstances that the letter presupposed. Christianity had already spread throughout all of Asia Minor. That is thinkable at the earliest possible date some twenty years after the beginning of Paul's missionary activity, i.e., from A.D. 65 on. The situation of the Christians throughout the entire then-known world was marked by social discrimination. It actually was discrimination, to be sure, but not persecution as customarily assumed. Regarding the circumstances of the Christians in society the following can be derived from the letter itself.

1) The Christians were not tracked down in some systematic way by civil authorities and brought to court. The malice toward them came from their environment, from their social world.

2) This happened in keeping with the nature of their predicament. The hostilities consisted of malicious accusations (2:12; 3:15f.), which from case to case, nevertheless, could very well have led to an appearance in court for the Christians. One could have had to "suffer" for the reason alone of having belonged to the Christian religion. "But let none of you suffer as a murderer, or a thief, or a wrongdoer, or a mischief-maker; yet if one suffers as a Christian (*hōs Christianos*), let him not be ashamed . . ." (4:15f.).

3) Why were the Christians discriminated against by society in this way? The answer to this question reveals not merely historically coincidental perspectives, but those of a fundamental nature. I Pet. 4:3f. stated: "Let the time that is past suffice for doing what the Gentiles like to do. . . . They are surprised that you do not now join them in the same wild profligacy, and they abuse you." This motivation recreates in polemic fashion but fundamentally in an accurate way the mental attitude of Hellenistic people.

Philostratus remarked regarding the Jews (*Vita Apollonii* 5.33): "[They] cannot share with the rest of mankind in the pleasures of the table nor join in their libations or prayers or sacrifices; [they] are separated from ourselves by a greater gulf than divides us from Susa or Bactra or the more distant Indies" (= LCL,

I, 541). This distancing of themselves of Jews was tolerated basically by the Gentiles, to be sure, because they had the status of an ethnic entity. It belonged to the order of the world, according to Celsus (*C. Cels*. 5.34), that every people should preserve its inherited religion and custom and should tolerate those of another; it was not in order for one to lay claim to absolutism the way the Jews did (*C. Cels*. 5.41). Apparently, in the eyes of the Hellenistic environment, the Christians also had offended against these basic categories of Hellenistic metaphysics. They acted contrary to the principle of living together in peace and harmony (*eirēnē* and *harmonia*) that according to popular philosophy had been shown to man by nature.[1] Hence contradiction and suspicion had to surface in everyday life since here not the members of a foreign people, the Jews, distanced themselves personally as Christians from the ways of living in their environment, but one's very fellow citizens, neighbors, and relatives. And it was these very people who let it be known that they, like already the Jews, laid claim to this offensive notion of religious absolutism. Christianity had to have appeared more or less as that which Celsus repeatedly labelled as *stasis*, rebellion against the divine harmony (*C. Cels*. 5.33ff., 41; 8.14) in which all people were to live together tolerantly in a fundamental syncretism. Hence Christianity looked like a "new and mischievous superstition" (Suetonius *Nero* 16=LCL, II, 111).This conflict put its stamp not coincidentally but out of substantive necessity upon the social situation of the Christians until finally after ca. 300 years the Hellenistic world view was replaced by a Christian one; this conflict made its appearance for the first time in the First Epistle of Peter.

4) When was this stage reached in the historical development? The epistles of Paul and the accounts of the book of Acts about the Pauline period presupposed an entirely different situation. Mention of conflicts with the environment and with Roman authorities referred throughout to those of local and personal but not to those of fundamental character. In the Pauline period the Christians appeared to their environment, just like the "God-fearers," as an appendage to the synagogue community, the religion of the Jews toward which one was fundamentally tolerant. For I Peter, however, the Christians were known to the public under a new designation of their own, *Christianoi* (4:16). According to Acts 11:26, this designation was developed in all places where Christianity distinguished itself, even for outsiders from Judaism, as a religion of its own.

This stage was first reached, as far as the public life of the empire was concerned, as noted above when the Neronian persecution broke out. In the year A.D. 110 Tacitus reported in retrospect (*Annals* 15.44 = LCL, IV, 283-85): "Therefore to scotch the rumour [that the fire had taken place by order], Nero substituted as culprits . . . a class of men, loathed for their vices, whom the crowd styled Christians. . . . First, then, the confessed members of the sect were arrested; next, on their disclosures, vast numbers were convicted, not so

---

[1]Minke, op. cit. (Lit., §43), pp. 24ff.

much on the count of arson as for hatred of the human race" (cf. §2,4). Non-conformity was understood as *odium generis humani*.

When one reads reports like these one thinks with good reason about I Pet. 2:12 and 4:15. The mental attitude over against the Christians—that was the starting point for Nero's action, according to Tacitus—had spread in the mean-time over the whole then-known world (cf. 5:9). This context was fundamentally the lot of the Christians since the Neronian persecution. It continued in this form until toward the end of the reign of Domitian when it became more acute through the cult of the caesar. This turn for the worse is not yet observable in the First Epistle of Peter; it was reflected, however, in the book of Revelation. According to I Pet. 5:13, Rome was Babylon, the capital of the world that was the enemy of God and his people. According to Rev. 17:5 Rome was this for the Christians since the Neronian persecutions; for the Jews Rome was this since the destruction of Jerusalem, according to IV Ezra, although even before this people connected the statements of the book of Daniel about Babylon naturally with Rome. But it was only from Domitian on that Rome represented the Antichrist (Rev. 13; cf. §44,5).

On the basis of the above we may conclude regarding the time of composition: the circumstances presupposed by the letter suggest that it was written between the years A.D. 64 and 90. All indicators favor the beginning rather than the end of this period since for the recipients of this letter the conflict with society was still quite new and unprecedented. "Beloved, do not be surprised at the fiery ordeal which comes upon you to prove you, as though something strange were happening to you" (I Pet. 4:12).[2]

c) The letter has frequently been misunderstood because its main theme was not recognized. Even one of the most recent commentaries on I Peter to appear in German stated as its theme, "the affliction that had already begun and would in the future increase."[3] Of course, the issue of Christian suffering wove its way through the letter like Ariadne's thread. But this issue was not its theme; it was rather the occasion for composition and a consequence of its theme. In 1:1–2:11, readers were addressed not as the persecuted but as the "[chosen] exiles of the Dispersion" or as "aliens and exiles." The letter addressed them then in terms of their situation in society. Consequently, its theme was the question that is discussed today throughout ecumenical Christianity: Christian responsibility in society.

---

[2]This statement frequently provided the occasion for literary-critical considerations since R. Perdelwitz (*Die Mysterienreligionen und das Problem des 1. Petrusbriefes* [1911]) expressed the conjecture that 1:3–4:11 was a baptismal address that later because of persecution was enlarged through the words of comfort and exhortation in 4:12–5:14 and was then put into circulation with the address in 1:1f. as a letter. Cf. on this W. G. Kümmel, *Introduction*, pp. 346ff. This perspective, however, is indefensible because the section beginning at 4:12 in no way presupposed a different situation from that of the preceding one. That only after 4:12 anything was said about the current experience of suffering is already refuted by 1:6. Correct is only that the letter developed traditional material in progressive stages.

[3]K. H. Schelkle, *Der Erste Petrusbrief*, p. 3 (Eng. in prep.).

2. THE ESSENCE OF BEING A CHRISTIAN IN SOCIETY

a) The situation of diaspora. When one compares the way Paul addressed his readers with the address here in I Pet. 1:1f. it becomes apparent at once that the author was speaking here in another dimension. The address "to the [chosen] exiles of the Dispersion" spoke, as it were, to the horizontal dimension of Christian existence, while the addresses of the Pauline epistles (e.g., I Cor. 1:2: "to the church of God . . . [to those] called to be saints" brought to mind the vertical dimension of Christian existence.

The address of I Peter raised to a conscious level the social dimension of the community of faith and clarified it by use of a model known to the readers. Up to this point the Jews had characterized themselves as Diaspora living as they were outside their homeland of Palestine between Persia and Spain in the Hellenistic cities of the Roman Empire. The Christians lived among their neighbors in a way comparable to the—until then—Jewish Diaspora. These Christians understood themselves accordingly as a particular shared community spanning the entire then-known world, the new people of God (I Pet. 2:9) and not as a movement with a special world view like the Stoic popular philosophy, e.g., or as a cultic association like the mystery religions. Thus the Christians from the time of I Peter to the close of the first three centuries referred to themselves as Diaspora. In the 4th century at the time of Constantine this designation disappeared quite necessarily.

b) The eschatological exodus community. The way the Christians became strangers among their fellow-citizens became clear by use of a second model that stood behind the exposition of ideas as background though it was not expressly stated. The expressions used to relate the essence of being a Christian in 1:3–2:10 continuously called to mind the way that the special community in Qumran spoke about itself. In their self-understanding, therefore, the Christians were comparable to a degree to this Jewish Exodus community that lived in the desert of Qumran. Like this group, they praised God because he had granted them an entirely new beginning to their existence and thereby a whole new life. In 1:3 it said, "Praise be to the God . . . who in his great mercy gave us new birth into a living hope by the resurrection of Jesus Christ from the dead!" (NEB). In the psalms of thanksgiving from Qumran the one praying confessed in similar fashion regarding his acceptance into the sect: "I thank Thee, O Lord, for Thou hast redeemed my soul from the Pit . . . and I know there is hope for him whom Thou hast shaped from dust for the everlasting Council" (1QH 3:19-21 = Vermes, *The Dead Sea Scrolls in English*, p. 158).

Thus the terminology and substantive content were quite similar; both spoke of a new beginning that could only be compared to a new creation and bore the significance of the Exodus. The baptized members were summoned to the Exodus; I Pet. 1:13 said, "Therefore gird up your minds!" They would live from now on as strangers (1:1, 17) and thus until the consummation in suffering (1:6), since they were "elect" (1:1), "saints" (1:16), "God's people" (2:9). Correspondingly, with almost the same terms it was said of the Essenes in the Damascus Rule (CD) 4:1-6: "[Those] are the converts of Israel who departed from the land of Judah . . . and the elect of Israel . . . who shall stand at the end of days . . . and the number of their trials, and the years of their sojourn, . . . (They were the first men) of holiness whom God forgave" (Vermes, *Scrolls*, p. 100).

According to these and many other similarities one can assume that the First Epistle of Peter appropriated an early Christian tradition of Essene origin in order to designate the Christians as a group of people who were transferred to an entirely new existence and in this way were estranged from society precisely as eschatological Exodus community.

c) Exodus as faith, not as emigration. Quite apart from this correspondence, however, the formulaic expressions have a fundamentally different meaning in the two contexts.

1) The new existence was of a different kind for each. For the Essenes the new being registered itself in the new way life was lived in keeping with firm rules. This perspective has repeatedly found proponents among Christians since the Epistle of James and its theology of empiricism (§45,3). The indicative of I Pet. 1:3 ("[he] gave us new birth into a living hope" [NEB]) cannot be misunderstood as a description of an empirical state because the imperative followed it immediately in 1:13 ("set your hope fully!"). This dialectic corresponded to the existence lived by faith.

2) This difference in the structure of the new being, moreover, was the consequence of its distinctive root. In Qumran, this root consisted in a radicalized form of the Law whose realization could be checked upon and was made possible by the strength received as a gift of grace.[4] In I Peter, to the contrary, everything sprung forth from the gospel of the redemption that happened in secret through cross and resurrection and would come forth in full view in the near future (I Pet. 1:3ff., 18f.; 4:7).

3) In Qumran, therefore, the subjective point of departure was a conversion experience strengthened each year at the covenant renewal celebration (1QS 1:16–3:20), while for I Peter it was the summons to faith accomplished by baptism.

At the conclusion to the first section (2:9) and at the conclusion to the whole letter (5:10) "summons" stood for that which was called "new birth" in 1:3; new birth and summons to faith corresponded to each other here. With these two terms, in fact, the starting point of Christian existence was expressed.

4) Thus the status of being a stranger became an image for the eschatological existence into which the Christians had been placed through faith. Whoever obeyed the commandments of the Sermon on the Mount and the call to discipleship would become estranged from the everyday life of society and would break out of the familiar form of life into a new human existence. This transition

---

[4]Qumran certainly was familiar with *sola gratia*. But grace actually served there the realization of the radicalized Law; cf. J. Becker, *Das Heil Gottes* (1964), esp. pp. 276ff.

and not the emigration out of society practiced by the Essenes was the Exodus offered to Christians.

3. RESPONSIBLE CONDUCT IN THE INSTITUTIONS OF SOCIETY[5]

a) Motivation (2:11f.). What was said about the conduct of Christians in the institutions of society began in 2:11f. with two sentences that gave the reasons why Christians were not allowed to emigrate out of the institutions of society, even though they were forced into the role of strangers. The first sentence was extraordinarily sobering: "Beloved, I beseech you as aliens and exiles to abstain from the passions of the flesh." For those who were called, to be estranged from society always meant in the first instance, therefore, to be estranged from one's own old human existence. Exodus began here!

But because this old human existence never became a thing of the past until bodily death (4:2), Christians always had to experience the Exodus out of the old existence anew through the faith that overcame their own old human existence but could not succeed in relegating it to a thing of the past. It would be sheer hypocrisy should they want to emigrate out of society as though the old dimension now lay behind them. Far beyond this they had received, as 2:12 added, a positive commission of their own within the institutions: "Maintain good conduct among the Gentiles, so that in case they speak against you as wrongdoers, they may see your good deeds and glorify God on the day of visitation." Christians were supposed to bear witness to the gospel that sought to save all people through Christian conduct in the institutions of society. While the Qumran community in the process of emigration armed itself as a community of action for the holy war against the unrighteous ones, the Christians were supposed to sojourn among people, as their Lord had done, and also thorugh their conduct in politics, economics, and marriage let it be known that God desired to lead all into a whole human existence. Socio-ethical responsibility motivated by the love of God stood here within the brackets of the missionary commission.

b) The principle: good conduct in relationship to every creature for the sake of the Lord. Good conduct (*agathopoiein*) was required of Christians in the institutions of society and not something on the general order of "love" (2:13-15, 20; 3:6, 17). But what was this good conduct supposed to look like?

The section 2:13–3:7 answered this question by appropriating in 2:18–3:7 the household code tradition that was already employed in Col. 3:18–4:1 and Eph. 5:22–6:9. Combined with this in 2:13-17 was the same kind of tradition over political conduct that had already been used by Paul in Rom. 13:1-7. The principle of this the New Testament's own social ethic was taken up by I Peter. In

---

[5]That which today in sociological terminology is designated mostly as "institution" or in a somewhat different sense as the "structure of society," was called in the Reformation "worldly stations" and, in more recent Lutheran social ethics from P. Althaus to H. Thielicke "orders of creation or preservation." The distinctions among these designations have signaled, of course, a change in the ways of looking at things.

2:13 this principle is referred to by catchwords in the introductory sentence, "Be subject for the Lord's sake to every human institution!"[6]

c) The content of good conduct: responsible abiding in the institutions (the household codes). Precisely as strangers Christians were obligated to involve themselves in the existing institutions.

1) This statement was implied by the key word of the household code tradition; this key word introduced the individual instructions to the one social partner: *hypotagēte* (order yourselves under, 2:13, 18; 3:1; cf. Rom. 13:1; Col. 3:18; Eph. 5:24). This key word of New Testament social ethics quickly alienates readers today and appears to them as an expression of a bygone social order. For readers today marriage is not a matter of the wife's subordination beneath the husband (Eph. 5:24) but of partnership. This reservation, however, misses the point of the statement. We hear the word automatically in terms of the prefix "sub" (under). In the New Testament, however, the accent did not fall on the prefix but on the root *taxis* (order) or *tassesthai* (to order itself or oneself).

At its core the directive did not address itself in opposition to rebellion but to the flight of emigration. It wanted to say primarily: enlist yourselves in the given institution! In relationship to this, the prefix "sub" (under) that corresponded to the social order of the time did not bear any theological emphasis. The intrinsic sense of the directive therefore endures even where institutions are thought of in terms of partnership as well.[7]

The later period of the ancient world was familiar with a very profiled notion of *taxis* wherever Stoic thought had been influential. This notion was then appropriated into Christianity at a very early date. Thus in I Clem. 20, the order of human social existence in nation, family, and church was to be seen in the cosmos as the principle of organization.[8] This concept was able to be developed further into a natural law. In comparison, the concept in Rom. 13:1f., where the term *taxis* appeared in clusters, was not one of an order that could be deciphered from nature or in the cosmos but one of a relationship among people established proportionately by God in history. In the one passage where the New Testament used the substantive *taxis* in a parenetic context (I Cor. 14:40), Paul brought this term together with that of peace, i.e., with that of the *shalom* that God, according to Old Testament/primitive Christian concepts, willed and accomplished. *Shalom*

---

[6]In both its parts were bound together, as it were, both foundational elements that were appropriated each for itself by two important recent contributions to Protestant social ethics. The appeal to subordinate oneself "to every human institution" (namely, that God has set over) calls to mind the ethic of orders represented from P. Althaus to H. Thielicke, while the expression "for the Lord's sake" calls to mind the "christocratic" ethic that was placed over against the ethic of orders from K. Barth to E. Wolf.

[7]The philological findings also correspond to this meaning of the term developed from the substantive context; cf. G. Delling, *TDNT* VIII, 43-45. The word could therefore encompass in parenesis a whole succession of meanings from subordination under authority to attentive personal engagement. Distinguishable from the view of Delling who circumscribed *hypotassesthai* in the household codes with the expression "acquiescence in a divinely willed order," I would prefer to talk about an enlisting of oneself. Also, one really ought not speak about an order established by God since this designation is missing here as well as elsewhere in the New Testament.

[8]Ibid., 46.

was the right relationship of all people to each other, the relationship that meant prosperity and life for all.[9] As can also be concluded from Rom. 13:4, the social orders served this prosperity as well. But the peace of God did not come through these orders *per se* but through the establishment of the eschatological dominion (Rom. 8:6; 14:17).

The challenge to subordinate oneself did not come, in I Peter any more than in Paul, from a mental image of a historically necessary or even an ideal, cosmologically grounded order of society, but from the concept that the Christian bore an obligation to the particular historical forms of life and lived responsibly in them.

2) This perspective finds confirmation through the history-of-tradition origin of the household code schema.

The manner in which the household codes issued socio-ethical directives, the way they guided one into marriage, the occupational relationship, and the political order, called to mind the Stoic ethics of human relationships. Epictetus, e.g., taught his students that whoever had become wise and had found the correct foundational orientation or attitude should also work to fulfill the *scheseis*, those relationships to other people into which one had been placed by fate or choice. The relationships would reveal themselves to this student by virtue of the "names" he bore. "[I must be one to] maintain my relations, both natural and acquired, as a religious man [in relationship to the gods], as a son [in relationship to parents], a brother, a father, a citizen" (Epictetus *Dissertationes* 3.2.4 = LCL, II, 23; cf. also 4.6.26). The obligations (*ta kathēkonta*) attendant to these relationships, the *scheseis*, or, as one could also say, the obligations ascertained from the role in each individual case, were not specified by Epictetus. He did not do so because appropriate and correct conduct was only that which corresponded to the nature of one acting and the particular relationship to the other person. The wise could and must find for themselves, therefore, the particular obligation. The wise were only reminded of them by means of a question that would invite reflection. "Consider who you are. To begin with a Man. . . . In addition to this you are a citizen of the world, and part of it. . . . What, then, is the profession of a citizen? . . . Next bear in mind that you are a Son. What is the profession of this character?" (*Dissertationes* 2.10.1ff. = LCL, I, 275f.).

To an extent, this socio-ethical principle certainly corresponded to the schema of the household codes. In both contexts rules to be applied casuistically were not dictated but rather one was directed into a social relationship that was then to be filled out in spontaneous responsibility. For this reason, K. Weidinger[10] in his day, in connection with the thought of M. Dibelius,[11] put forward the frequently accepted hypothesis that Christians had simply taken over the popularized schema of Stoic duty codes mediated to them through Hellenistic Judaism. This took place, thought Weidinger, at the time they began to settle into society as

---

[9]Cf. W. Foerster, *TDNT* II, 412, and G. Delling, *TDNT* VIII, 30 n. 22.

[10]Op. cit. (Lit., §43,3c).

[11]*Kolosserbrief* (HNT), at Col. 4:1 and Eph. 5:14.

a consequence of the delayed *parousia*. They merely Christianized the schema, continued Weidinger, through the motivating reference to the *kyrios* (e.g., Eph. 4:17; 5:17, 22; Col. 1:18, 20; I Pet. 2:13). In contrast to this view, D. Schroeder[12] showed that the household codes did not simply Christianize the Stoic schema with respect to appearances, but did so to the very core. They were distinct from the Stoic duty codes particularly in two ways. They were distinct in style. The duty codes of the Stoa spoke in the style of Stoic diatribe; the household codes, in contrast, spoke in the style of the apodictic justice of God. They were thoroughly stylized to fit a specific schema, e.g., Eph. 6:1: address ("Children"), imperative ("obey your parents"), rationale ("for this is right"). When instead of the imperative in I Pet. 2:18; 3:1, 7 one encounters a participle, this represents an alternate rabbinic form of expression.

Behind this stylistic distinction stood one of profound substance. For the Stoa, the specified social relationships were possibilities through whose full exploration the person considered wise by Stoic standards came to self-realization. In the household codes, on the other hand, the fulfillment of these social relationships was the commandment of God. It was a consequence of this that noticeably fewer social relationships were addressed here than in the Stoic duty codes; only the rudimentary forms of historical existence were addressed: marriage, family, occupation, and the political order. To these one actually can be obligated in an apodictic way. Mentioned, therefore, were not the relationships of choice, like friendship, but only the structures or institutions of society.

3) The Stoic ethic of relationships could be appropriated in this altered form only because an inner-Christian tradition provided the substantive starting point for it. Early Christianity did not concern itself with the institutions of society only after the delay of the *parousia* became an issue. Rather, already Jesus had obligated people in a new way regarding marriage and paying taxes to Caesar (§10,3), alongside his summons to the eschatological existence of discipleship. In doing so he developed precisely the principle of the ethic of relationships. In response to the question of paying taxes to Caesar, e.g., he pushed aside the objections of the Jews that came from the Law and the election of Israel so that he might make reference to the historical situation stamped there upon the coin (Mk. 12:16f.). Following the same principle Jesus replied to the question about one's neighbor by telling the parable of the Good Samaritan (Lk. 10:29-37).[13]

New Testament social ethics, defined in the sense given by the tradition, began with the directive that those called to faith ought to enlist themselves in the social orders in which they found themselves and to conduct themselves in accord with their "rules for playing the game" (cf. I Cor. 7:17, 20, 24). This socio-ethical principle was extraordinarily flexible because it started with the historically existing structures of society and not with a rigid concept of natural justice nor a postulated ideal order.

---

[12]Op. cit. (Lit., §43,3c).

[13]Regarding Mk. 12:13-17 and the tradition developing from it, cf. L. Goppelt, "Die Freiheit zur Kaisersteuer," in *Christologie*, pp. 208-219.

4) But did not this principle lead of necessity to unlimited conformity as it caused Christians to align themselves passively with the various social structures and rules for playing the game and to accept, e.g., even slavery?[14] In I Peter we observe the opposite. And this was the most important difference in the shaping of the household code tradition in relationship to Paul. The socio-ethical parenesis of I Peter focused on conflict, while Rom. 13:1-7, along with the household codes of Colossians and Ephesians, did not appear to be familiar with such conflict and therewith the evil connected with these institutions. The household codes of Colossians and Ephesians, moreover, addressed themselves to different social situations; they presupposed the situation between Christians within a Christian household. In contrast, I Pet. 2 had in mind the individual Christian within the institutions of a non-Christian society. This tension was addressed expressly regarding slaves and wives, but in 2:13-17 was also to be felt regarding one's duty in relationship to Caesar.

Thus, in the First Epistle of Peter the early Christian starting point was developed further with substantive consistency. It guided, like Paul did, into the existing institutions, but it also obligated one strongly toward responsible, critical conduct within them; Paul more or less presupposed this conduct in silence. "Good conduct" meant for I Peter not only enlisting oneself in the existing institutions, but also conducting oneself responsibly and critically within them.

d) Critical responsibility and its criteria. What the obligation to conduct oneself critically in institutional life meant was developed in terms of the extreme example of slavery. It was said to them: "Servants, be submissive to your masters. . . . For one is approved if, mindful of God (*dia syneidēsin theou*), he endures pain while suffering unjustly" (2:18f.). The Christian slave therefore should not run away from his master, but should, however, when the master required something unjustly, follow his conscience, refuse to obey, and bear the suffering inflicted by the master's reactions. How this example was handled clarified to an extent how Christians could take a position responsibly and critically within institutions and their standards. We note the following criteria and starting points.

1) The conscience. I Pet. 2:19 referred to a formal capacity for making judgments: the conscience bound to God (*hē syneidēsis tou theou*).[15] I Peter talked about conscience here in a way similar to Paul, for whom conscience was an evaluatory capacity that responded to human behavior by making judgments (I Cor. 4:4; Rom. 2:15; II Cor. 4:2; 5:11; cf. also Jn. 3:19-22). This aspect of

---

[14]Thus, most recently, S. Schulz, *Gott ist kein Sklavenhalter* (1972), esp. pp. 193-219; yet contra, H. Gülzow, *Christentum und Sklaverei in den ersten drei Jahrhunderten* (1969); G. Klein, "Christusglaube und Weltverantwortung als Interpretationsproblem neutestamentlicher Theologie," *VF* 18 (1973), 47-54.

[15]C. Maurer, *TDNT* VII, 914ff.; J. Stelzenberger, *Syneidesis im Neuen Testament* (1961), pp. 45-49. Stelzenberger argued against the translation "conscience" and proposed instead "consciousness of God" since it was not a matter here of the autonomous decision-making of the personality according to the standards that are accepted by it for itself; yet in my opinion this is unfounded because it is oriented on too narrow a philosophical definition of conscience.

Paul's view was in keeping with customary Hellenistic-Jewish understanding.[16] But he also developed beyond this a concept of conscience that thanked the Hellenistic world for its origins only in modest beginnings. According to this concept of Paul, the conscience not only judged in response to what had taken place, but also made a decision as to what ought to happen. It was "a judgment that established itself in the consciousness of man and prescribed his behavior to him";[17] it was the reflecting and judging "I" of faith that sought to determine in various situations what the will of God was (Rom. 12:2; cf. I Cor. 8:10; Rom. 14:1).

2) For the exercise of this judging, however, the conscience, the reflecting "I" of faith, was equipped with substantive standards of measure. As such standards I Peter, like the rest of the New Testament, did not mention in a general way social motifs or goal-oriented concepts such as love, peace, righteousness, or freedom. When the letter talked about the conscience bound to God it was specifying rather a standard of measure with content; after all, for it God was not a code word without content.

How God was understood for social ethics can be observed in the introductory motivational statements of 2:13. They point to the *ktisis* (the created thing) and thereby to the Creator, and further to the exalted One, through whom God was now establishing his end-time dominion.

What is to be ascertained from the reference to the Lord, which also dominated the Pauline household codes (Col. 1:18, 20; cf. Eph. 5:17, 22), for social ethics, for conduct in the structures of history?[18] The exalted One had the face of the Jesus to whom the Gospel tradition gave witness. Through him God was establishing his end-time dominion rich in salvation. He represented the goal of all history, the kingdom of God that would be realized in full view only on the other side of history in the world of the resurrection. This goal itself cannot be a direct standard of measure, e.g., for conduct in marriage (cf. Mk. 12:25). Just as futile would be the attempt to shape political life directly according to principles of the kingdom of God since the kingdom of God took on shape through service. Service was the central expression of the eschatological demonstration of love that laid no claim to right and might (Mk. 10:43ff.). According to I Pet. 4:10, this service was the principle of life for the community of faith in which the kingdom of God in fact was to take on shape proleptically. Political life, however, was based on the application of right and might, according to Rom. 13:1-5. Thus political life could not be shaped directly in analogy to the dominion of Christ. It was the case, however, that the dominion of Christ as the eschatological goal of all history even now established the frame of reference and the final point of orientation for the use of right and might. This standard

---

[16]This concept of conscience as *elenchos*, the convincing judgment about what has taken place, was developed by Hellenistic Judaism; it advanced thereby the popular-Hellenistic concept of an evil conscience.

[17]A. Schlatter, *Paulus, der Bote Jesu* (1970⁴), p. 260.

[18]Cf., hereto, L. Goppelt, "Prinzipien neutestamentlicher Sozialethik," op. cit. (Lit., §43), p. 25.

of measure was expressed magnificently in I Pet. 3:7: the eschatological goal obligated partners to encounter each other in institutional life as people destined to be "joint heirs of the grace of life" and as people who should become just that through the conduct of Christians.

It was not possible, however, to decipher from this last criterion just how, e.g., marriage and political engagement should be shaped in terms of particulars. Rather this was to be deciphered from the other criterion, the character of these realms of living as *ktisis*. It was a matter here of God's relationship to his creation. It was Jesus who already had referred to creation and not to the kingdom of God for the constitution of a marriage (Mt. 19:4-8; Eph. 5:22-33 did not contradict this; cf. §10,3a). It was noted, of course, that the original will of the Creator could only be realized after the "hardness of heart" that currently distorted creation had been overcome. The will of God as Creator could not be grasped directly in terms of the present state of the creation and history. The existing structures and institutions of society were, to be sure, established by God's sovereignty over history (Isa. 10:5ff.: Dan. 2:21; Rom. 13:1f.), but they were not as such already an expression of the will that desired to sustain creation in forbearance toward the consummation (Gen. 9:21f.; Rom. 3:26). For Israel, this will was expressed in the Mosaic Law (cf. Gal. 3:22f.); to some degree it corresponded in this respect to the orders of justice among the nations (Rom. 1:32; 2:14f.; 13:3f.). Christians were supposed to seek this will of God for preservation behind the structures of society as they looked back from the perspective of the eschatological dominion of God that appeared in Jesus; this angle of vision penetrated the existing historical situation that, especially with the help of the Old Testament, could be analyzed in terms of the theology of history. New Testament parenesis presupposed that this analysis would be accomplished in pneumatic intuition by the conscience bound to God. For this conscience God was revealed through preaching that had substance and was discriminating. According to a socio-ethical parenesis of this kind, the "good conduct" of Christians in institutional life was possible for I Peter and the rest of the New Testament. This was so precisely because their actual existence transcended the society that lived under the constraints of "law," "death," and "sin"; for this reason they always understood or even broke through to God's will for preservation in terms of the original and ultimate destiny of man.

e) The historical effects. I Peter was in agreement with the rest of the New Testament that the conduct of Christians in the institutions of society produced considerable effects. The effects were seen on two sides.

1) Paul reckoned with the possibility of positive change. According to the Epistle to Philemon, Paul had determined to send the runaway slave Onesimus, who had become a Christian, back to his master. At the same time he challenged this master, Philemon, to accept Onesimus into his house from then on not only as a slave but also as a beloved brother (Philem. 16). As this happened the institution of slavery was, as it were, undermined in this particular instance. As the household codes presupposed, an extended family formed by Christian faith

emerged without the structures of society as such having been altered. But as individual institutions in which Christians participated were thus altered for good in the process, so this represented an occasion that had to have an altering effect on the institution as such in the future.

2) The other side of the change was conflict. I Peter took special note of this. Conflict arose because Christians living in institutions were always conducting themselves on the basis of other motives, and according to other criteria, and therefore always differently than their non-Christian partners expected. In order to cope with the conflict and to master it, I Peter pointed toward only one path: "But if when you do right and suffer for it you take it patiently, you have God's approval" (2:20). Only when willingness—said I Peter—constituted the basis for such suffering and was repeatedly practiced would the responsible conduct of Christians in society become the witness to Christ that it was finally supposed to be. It became thereby also the witness to the new existence of the *eschaton* because it did not ignore the conditions for living in history but made itself appropriately subject to them. The directive to women married to non-Christian husbands, e.g., was to be understood in this sense; they were to accept and to change this difficult situation by appropriate marital conduct so "that some, though they do not obey the word, may be won without a word by the behavior of their wives" (3:1).

Because responsible, critical conduct in the structures of society was only possible through the willingness to suffer in every situation, I Peter attempted to give foundation to the willingness to suffer for the sake of good conduct; it did so from section to section of the letter in increasing proportion.

4. THE THEOLOGY OF SUFFERING

I Peter's theology of suffering had in mind quite pointedly the suffering whose model in the Old Testament was Daniel and not Job. As two groups of difficult sayings explained, this suffering was both the judgment and grace of God. Such an interpretation of suffering came to the letter by way of a stream of tradition whose source was the theology of martyrdom in Judaism and Jesus' beatitude about those who were persecuted for righteousness' sake (§18,7).

a) Suffering as judgment. 1) Since the Maccabean revolt many Jews like Daniel were in conflict with the religious state ideologies of the Hellenistic empires because they remained loyal to the Law of the God of Israel. Their loyalty led to martyrdom.[19] This commitment was interpreted in Jewish theology with considerable attention (e.g., II Macc. 6:18–7:42) in order then in turn to endorse this path in a corresponding parenesis (II Macc. 6:12-17). This path was not understood here in essence to be a social act and in this sense an example for one's own fellow citizens; nor was it understood in essence to be a moral force and a demonstrative warning for the opposition, although such ideas were not totally absent either. Martyrdom was seen rather *sub specie Dei* within the

---

[19]E. Lohse, *Märtyrer und Gottesknecht*, pp. 66-77.

field of influence of the Creator and Lord of history. Compulsory surrender of life and dying meant for the Jew therefore to be cut off from life with the Creator, hence judgment. According to Jewish understanding, however, as judgment martyrdom was an atonement for the martyr's own shortcomings and, moreover, representative atonement for the debts of the people. In IV Macc. 6:28f., the martyrs died with the plea: "Let our punishment be a satisfaction in their behalf. Make my blood their purification and take my soul to ransom their souls" (Charles, II, 674).

2) Appropriating such traditions of the Jewish theology of martyrdom, the affliction that came upon the Christians from their environment throughout the then-known world from Rome to Asia Minor and Syria in innumerable incidents of ordeal was understood by I Peter first of all as judgment. In 4:17 it was said with an Old Testament image that the community of faith should know: "For the time has come for judgment to begin with the household of God." The end-time judgment, under which all evil in this world was to come so that this world would be purified of evil, would not pass by the "household of God," the temple, but would begin there. The temple was thereby an image for the community of faith among which God was now graciously present.

3) Even the Christians and precisely they need the judgment. They certainly have been called to freedom from evil, but they still remain in its grip. As the perplexing sentence in I Pet. 4:1f. said, through suffering the natural side of human existence would be dispatched. "Since therefore Christ suffered in the flesh, arm yourselves with the same thought, . . . so as to live for the rest of the time in the flesh no longer by human passions but by the will of God."

b) Suffering as grace. As participation in union with the crucified and resurrected Lord, suffering for the sake of good conduct was paradoxically not only judgment but also grace. To impress this upon the reader was a central concern of the writer. In view of the extreme example of the Christian slave in relationship to a "perverse" (NEB) master the guiding principle was formulated: "For one is approved if, mindful of God, he endures pain while suffering unjustly" (2:19).

The bitter counterblows that strike the one bound to God in his conscience may be seen as indications of the love of the One from whom and to whom all is, because these blows—as this assurance went on to say—were an expression of calling (2:21). Whoever trod this doubt-filled path would not come to naught, but would fulfill his destiny and reach his goal since he had traveled the path of discipleship. Discipleship—and not imitation of Christ or Christ-mysticism— was the meaning of the sentence that summarized the assurance and was packed with substance (2:20f.): "But if when you do right and suffer for it you take it patiently, you have God's approval. For to this you have been called, because Christ also suffered for you, leaving you an example, that you should follow in his steps." Whoever had been drawn into Jesus' path by the obedience of faith became one who followed in discipleship. At this point the letter's theology of suffering went on to its Christology.

5. CHRISTOLOGY

a) The Christ formulas. On three occasions when the writer had reached key junctures in his thoughts about the existence of Christians in society he used confessional-type statements in hymnic form about the life and ministry of Christ. These christological formulas are to be found each time in the center of the first three chapters: 1:18-21; 2:21-25; and 3:18-22.

> The last account of the history-of-tradition origin of these christological formulas and their investigation was given by K. H. Schelkle.[20] He followed to a considerable degree the hypothesis of R. Bultmann[21] according to which the author of I Peter took over, similar to Paul in Phil. 2:6-11, existing hymnic and confessional fragments from the community tradition. The chief support for this view was not found merely in the metrical form but in the content of the formulas. They went, supposedly, far beyond what the context called for. This hypothesis, however, stood on weak footing. On the one hand, it cannot be shown conclusively that the content of the passages in question went far beyond what the context called for. On the other hand, an analysis of the passages demonstrates that, in contrast to how it was in Phil. 2:6-11 and Col. 1:15-20, it could by no means have been a matter here of the author having taken over completed pieces of tradition (Bultmann himself spoke about fragments for this very reason). More realistic therefore is the supposition that the author of the letter here as in other places did of course make use of traditions available to him, but that he reworked them independently. This is confirmed, moreover, by the way he linked together Christology and parenesis.

b) The connection between Christ formulas and parenesis. This issue can be clarified by reference to the second christological section of the letter in a way that exceeds this example. The confession of 2:21-25 provided the foundation, as shown above (§43,4b), for the challenge to maintain good conduct even while suffering. To this the line of connection was drawn between the suffering of Christians and the suffering of Christ. But how does such happen?

The Catholic exegete A. Schulz advocated the position[22] that in the whole New Testament "discipleship" was used synonymously with "imitation of Christ" only in this passage; Schulz drew the conclusion that the New Testament basis for the Catholic ideal of the *imitatio Christi* was very narrow. This concept, however, is not even to be found, in the sense Schulz intended, in I Pet. 2:21! Rather, the suffering of Christ was connected here with Christians in a twofold way:

> For to this you have been called,
> because Christ also suffered for you,
> leaving you an example,
> that you should follow in his steps.

Two connections have obviously been drawn here. (1) Christ's suffering unto death was a suffering for Christians, and (2) it was a suffering whose footprints they were supposed to follow. The second expression was a favorite image in

---

[20]*Die Petrusbriefe*, pp. 110ff.
[21]Op. cit. (Lit., §43,5).
[22]*Nachfolgen und Nachahmen* (1962), pp. 289-292.

the Hellenistic world for the imitation of an example.[23] In what way the two connections belonged together can be ascertained from the following context that appropriated both sides. In vv. 24 and 25 the *hyper* (for) was explained; here the disciples were introduced into a way of conduct through Christ's suffering for them, conduct that had as a consequence suffering for the sake of righteousness. Through his suffering for them he accepted them into this path of his. From this then followed for vv. 22f. that his suffering became the determinative prototype that they should follow in their own suffering. Accordingly, the *syn* (with) was given foundation through the *hyper* (for) for I Peter just as for Paul (§35,5).

c) *The Christological themes of the formulas.* The three confessional-type formulas, 1:18-21; 2:21-25; and 3:18-22, in each case furnished the parenesis with a christological foundation. The first one (1:18-21) made the point that Jesus' dying was the eschatological ransom or redemption that had established the Exodus, i.e., eschatological existence. The second formula (2:21-25) referred to the suffering of the righteous One for us as prototype; Jesus' suffering unto death as the suffering of the righteous One for us led to "good conduct" in order to become the prototype of our suffering for the sake of righteousness. The third formula (3:18-22) explained that the path of Jesus marked by suffering unto death was a path of blessing; the same was true for his disciples as they followed in suffering. Out of suffering of this kind came forth far-reaching blessing. The theme addressed in 3:18-22 prompted, in fact, the most detailed representation of the path of Christ in the entire New Testament.

d) *The path of Christ according to I Pet. 3:18-22* 1) In no other passage of the New Testament were so many elements mentioned of what later became the second article of faith than here: he "suffered" or "died" (v. 18), "he went . . . to the spirits in prison" (v. 19), "through the resurrection" (v. 21) "gone into heaven and is at the right hand" (v. 22). This christological formula was in fact a preliminary stage of the second article.

2) An extraordinarily far-reaching saving effect was ascribed to this path as a whole, and not, as it were, to its individual stages. It was valid for "us" (*hēmin*, v. 18), i.e., for the community of faith, but it extended far beyond this as well (vv. 19f.), since it included also that portion of pre-Christian humanity most without hope, the generation of the flood abiding in the world of the dead. Concluding then, vv. 21f. stated that this saving effect was now being offered quite universally to all through baptism.

e) *The proclamation of salvation to the deceased (I Pet. 3:19f. and 4:6).* The reference of I Pet. 3:19f., "in which he went and preached to the spirits in prison, who formerly did not obey, when God's patience waited in the days of Noah," is the only one in the New Testament that spoke about Jesus' preaching in hades. It provided the starting point for the obscure saying of the second article of faith: "he descended into hell."

The spirits in prison were not fallen angels, as has been assumed frequently

---

[23]A. Stumpff, *TDNT* III, 402ff.

in recent exegesis, but were the souls of the generation of the flood. If this is correct,[24] then our passage contained a remarkable soteriological statement. In rabbinic tradition the generation of the flood was regarded as being lost completely and forever.[25] Our passage said, however, that Christ had now offered salvation to this the most hopeless portion of humanity as well! The saving work of Jesus' dying even reached all the way to those people who in this life had never come to a conscious encounter with Christ, and even to those who were the most without hope among them. I Pet. 4:6 stated in general correspondence: "the gospel was preached even to the dead."

Is this not a fanciful speculation that is cancelled out along with the ancient view of the world? It is characteristic that these two passages did not make graphic portrayal of a cosmic-spatial concept or a mythical proclamation. The accent lay alone upon the proclamation before the lost. I Peter only introduced this element into the concept, common to the New Testament, that Jesus had passed through the world of the dead.

> In the 2nd century, this concept of a descent into hell was developed in two ways. For one thing, the statement about the battle in hell was developed. Christ conquered the powers of the underworld. For another thing, the concept of the preaching in hades was extended in such a way that it corresponded exactly to the growth of soteriology. The early Catholic Fathers taught that Christ preached to the righteous ones of the past, especially to the patriarchs. In opposition, Marcion explained that Christ preached to all the sinners in the underworld, but precisely not to the righteous ones of the Old Testament.

In I Peter, the statement about preaching in hades, which was already tradition for the author, intended to appropriate the existential question: What significance does Christ have for those who have not come to a conscious encounter with him in this life? Its reply was that we could leave them to the grace of the One who died for the unrighteous ones and was raised; we could leave them to the grace from which the community of faith lived.

If one looks back from this vantage point to the overall theme of the letter it provides an impressive overview. The letter replied to the wave of discrimination from the side of society with an unbroken preparedness for universal missionary witness through proclamation and through conduct: The First Epistle of Peter was the New Testament document that most vigorously united the witness of the word with the witness of Christian presence in society.

§44. Christians in the Post-Christian Society of the End Time according to the Book of Revelation

J. Behm, *Gott und die Geschichte. Das Geschichtsbild der Offenbarung* (1925); C. Clemen, "Die Stellung der Offenbarung Johannes im ältesten Urchristentum," *ZNW*

---

[24]Regarding the discussion, cf. Schelkle, op. cit. (n. 20), pp. 106f. (Lit.!).

[25]"The generation of the Flood has no share in the world to come nor shall they stand in the judgment" (Mishnah Sanhedrin 10:3 = H. Danby, *The Mishnah* [1933], p. 397).

26 (1927), 173-186; H.-D. Wendland, *Geschichtsanschauung und Geschichtsbewusstsein im NT* (1938); H. Bietenhard, *Das tausendjährige Reich* (1944); L. Goppelt, "Johannes-Apokalypse," *EKL* II, 365-69 (Lit.!); O. A. Piper, "The Apocalypse of John and the Liturgy of the Ancient Church," *Church History* 20 (1951), 255-266; J. Schniewind, "Weltgeschichte und Weltvollendung," in Schniewind, *Nachgelassene Reden und Aufsätze* (1952), pp. 38-47; A. T. Nikolainen, "Über die theologische Eigenart der Offenbarung Johannes," *ThLZ* 93 (1968), 161-170; A. Satake, *Die Gemeindeordnung in der Johannesapokalypse* (1966); M. Rissi, *Was ist und was geschehen soll danach. Die Zeit- und Geschichtsauffassung der Offenbarung des Johannes* (1966); cf. Rissi, *Time and History; a study on the Revelation* (1966); P. Prigent, "L'Apocalypse et Liturgie," *Cahiers Theologiques* 52 (1964), 7-81; R. Halver, *Der Mythos im letzten Buch der Bibel. Eine Untersuchung zur Bildersprache der Johannes-Apokalypse* (1964); T. Holtz, *Die Christologie der Apokalypse des Johannes* (1962); L. Goppelt, "Heilsoffenbarung und Geschichte nach der Offenbarung des Johannes," *ThLZ* 77 (1952), 513-522; W. Thüsing, "Die theologische Mitte der Weltgerichtsvisionen in der Johannesapokalypse," *Trierer Theologische Zeitschrift* 77 (1968), 1-16; G. Delling, "Zum gottesdienstlichen Stil der Johannesapokalypse," in Delling, *Studien zum NT und zum hellenistischen Judentum* (1970), pp. 425-450; K.-P. Jörns, *Das hymnische Evangelium. Untersuchungen zu Aufbau, Funktion und Herkunft der hymnischen Stücke in der Johannesoffenbarung* (1971). **Important Commentaries:** W. Bousset (1906), KEK (historical background interpretation); W. Hadorn (1928), ThHK (historical-theological interpretation); E. Lohmeyer (1953²), HNT (supra-historical interpretation); E. Lohse (1966), NTD (historical background interpretation); H. Kraft (1974), HNT (end-time interpretation).

The problem of church and society stands under a different heading for the book of Revelation than it did for I Peter. Both were familiar with conflict, for both it appeared inevitable. Yet while the conflict was the result of the discrimination prompted by an active, missionary responsibility for the world in I Peter, in Revelation it was the result of the anti-Christian activity of a post-Christian world.

1. PRELIMINARY CONSIDERATION: COMPOSITIONAL CIRCUMSTANCES, CONTENT, AND INTERPRETIVE PROBLEMATIC

A special difficulty in interpreting the book of Revelation is that its theological statements were encoded in a language of apocalyptic imagery. Before we shall be able to interpret those statements it is indispensable that we consider the compositional circumstances, the content, and the procedures for interpreting this document.

a) Regarding composition. This book is the most outstanding document produced by primitive Christian prophecy. It offered prophecy, however, that was transmitted literarily in accord with its essence and not directly through oral delivery (1:19). This form of transmission as well as its corresponding language calls to mind Old Testament/Jewish apocalypticism. Yet the very particulars regarding the compositional circumstances of apocalypticism necessitate their differentiation. The author of the book of Revelation, e.g., did not conceal himself behind a pseudonym from the past the way the writers of Jewish apocalypticism did. Rather, along with mentioning his name he addressed himself directly to the community of faith in a letter-type opening (1:4-8).

The name alone was enough for the author to identify himself to the addressed communities, the seven leading communities of faith in the Roman province of Asia (2:1, 8, 12, 18; 3:1, 7, 14). Hence this author John could possibly be identical to the disciple of the Lord bearing this name who came from Palestine. This John had personally met the presbyters of Asia, Papias of Hierapolis and Polycarp of Smyrna, around the end of the 1st century in Ephesus (Eus. *EH* 3.39.3f.; 5.20.4). We cannot say, of course, whether or not this John was the same person as John the son of Zebedee, the pillar apostle of Gal. 2:9, as has been claimed since Justin Martyr and Irenaeus.

The author wrote while on the little rocky isles of Patmos, probably as an exile (1:9). That provides a reference to the time of composition; the exiling of Christians was first practiced around the late part of the reign of Domitian. This and other indications suggest that the prophecies came about near the end of Domitian's reign (A.D. 81-96), as Irenaeus had assumed (*Haer.* 5.30.3). The occasion for writing may have been the claim of Domitian on divine majesty that increased more and more toward the final years of his reign and the measures he took against all those who resisted this claim.[1]

b) Regarding content. To characterize the content one should begin with the statement of theme in 1:19: "Now write what you see, [namely] what is and what is to take place hereafter." Accordingly, the revelation that John received from the exalted Son of man encompassed two parts: (1) prophecy for the present ("what is") in the letters to the seven communities (chs. 2–3), and (2) the revelation regarding the future ("what is to take place hereafter," chs. 4–22).[2]

This revelation for the future was introduced by a vision of the One upon the throne and of the lamb (chs. 4f.); to the exalted Christ has been committed the

---

1. Further, Goppelt, *Apostolic Times*, pp. 109-114.
2. In particular the following schematic breakdown emerges:

<table>
<tr><td>Introduction</td><td>1:1-20</td></tr>
<tr><td>A. Revelation for the Present</td><td></td></tr>
<tr><td> 1. Cycle: Letters to the Seven Churches</td><td>2:1–3:22</td></tr>
<tr><td>B. Revelation for the Future</td><td>4:1–22:5</td></tr>
<tr><td> 2. Cycle: Introduction of the Future Picture</td><td>4:1–5:14</td></tr>
<tr><td>   and the Seven Seals (7:1-17: the community)</td><td>6:1–8:1</td></tr>
<tr><td> 3. Cycle: the Seven Trumpets (10:1–11:14: the community)</td><td>8:2–11:14</td></tr>
<tr><td> 4. Cycle: the dragon and the lamb</td><td>12:1–14:20</td></tr>
<tr><td>   (the forces of the world and the community of God)</td><td></td></tr>
<tr><td>   (12:1-18: the mother with child, and the dragon;</td><td></td></tr>
<tr><td>   13:1-18: the two beasts;</td><td></td></tr>
<tr><td>   14:1-20: the consummation through Christ)</td><td></td></tr>
<tr><td> 5. Cycle: the Seven Bowls</td><td>15:1–16:21</td></tr>
<tr><td> 6. Cycle: the Fall of Babylon</td><td>17:1–19:10</td></tr>
<tr><td> 7. Cycle: the *parousia* of Christ and the Consummation</td><td>19·11–22:5</td></tr>
</table>

    (19:11-21: the *parousia* and the judgment over the Antichrist; 20:1-10: Satan falls from power and the perfection of the community on earth; 20:11-15: the judgment of the world; 21:1-8: the new creation; 21:9–22:5: the new Jerusalem)

Conclusion   22:6-21

carrying out of God's plan for history. Then followed a chain of vision-cycles (seven seals: 6:1–8:1; seven trumpets: 8:2–11:19; seven bowls: 15:1–16:21) whereby—like the stages of a rocket launch—each time the next cycle came forth out of the last vision of the previous cycle (8:1; 11:15; 15:5; 16:1). A further principle of division was that between the sixth and seventh seal (7:1-17) and between the sixth and seventh trumpet (10:1–11:14) pauses occurred. In each, attention was turned from world events to the destiny of the community of God. Thus two partners stand over against each other in the final hour: the world and the community of God.

The vision-cycle in chs. 12–14 assumed a special position. In it these two partners of the last hour were placed over against each other, as it were, in photographic enlargement. It constituted, so to speak, a little apocalypse within the larger one. The next to the last cycle, the fall of Babylon (17:1–19:10), described the end of world history in the rebellion of humanity against its Creator. Then followed the concluding series of images, 19:11–22:5, that portrayed the end of world events.

c) *Regarding the problematic of interpretation.* The method of interpretation is quite decisively dependent upon how one judges the relationship of the book of Revelation to classical apocalyptic prophecy.

Let us take as an example of the latter the four-kingdom vision of Dan. 7:2-27. It began with the typical I-report about a vision (Dan. 7:2-14): Daniel saw four fantastic beasts, one after the other, coming up out of the sea that had been agitated by four winds. The first was like a lion, the second a bear, the third a leopard, the fourth a prehistoric monster. Then the image changed: in a heavenly throne room "the Ancient of Days" carried out the judgment of the world, the power was taken from the beasts and given to the Son of man descending from heaven. These images were then interpreted in Dan. 7:15-27 by an *angelus interpres*. The seer was informed that the four beasts were the last kingdoms, i.e., figured from the vantage point of Daniel, the kingdoms of the Babylonians, the Medes, the Persians, and Alexander including the Seleucids. Among the latter, one was singled out especially, the one that blasphemed the Most High and afflicted his people. Intended was the Seleucid, Antiochus IV Epiphanes, who had wanted to subject the Jewish people by force to Hellenistic syncretism. By this focusing of the prophecy it is not hard to determine that it was written at the time of this confrontation ca. 165 B.C. and not, as indicated, during the Exile ca. 550 B.C. Through the prophecy the reader of that day who was loyal to the Law was to be strengthened in perseverance until the imminent change of all relationships. To this person was said: the course of history has been fixed from the beginning, the end is near!

When one compares the book of Revelation with this classical model of apocalyptic prophecy, moments of correspondence are unmistakable. In both there was a frequent use of traditional linguistic imagery that did not describe directly viewed images—the "images" of Revelation were not actually portrayable—but prophecies clothed in the language of symbol. In both there was an expansion of evil toward the end, and finally the end would come as cosmic catastrophe and world judgment. The way of dividing into periods characteristic of the apocalyptic prophecy also appeared to be reproduced by the vision cycles of Revelation. Based on the assumed analogy to apocalypticism the following modes of interpretation have emerged.

1) According to an uncritical understanding Dan. 7 prophesied the entire course of world history from the vantage point of the author. Analogous to this is how the book of Revelation has been understood in the church-historical or world-historical interpretation. Interpreters saw in Revelation predicted history from the days of the seer—thus from the time of Domitian—to the end of the world. The focus of the prophecy, the Antichrist in Rev. 13 as well as the "little horn" in Dan. 7:8, was then identified with some figure contemporaneous with the interpreter. Thus, both beasts in Rev. 13 were interpreted during the Reformation and also in the late Middle Ages as representing empire and papacy.

2) The scholarly commentaries[3] generally follow the interpretation linking Revelation to the world of its time. Like Dan. 7, Revelation was written in point of fact for its period of composition. It did not intend to prophesy the course of world history but to analyze in apocalyptic language the situation current in its world up to the end, which was expected in the near future. In this view the Antichrist of Rev. 13 would be Domitian.

3) In the 17th century, Pietism developed the interpretation of history's end as a further variant. It took as its starting point the assumption that the prophecy beginning in Rev. 4:1 was a matter of the yet future end to history both for the author and for the present-day interpreter.

All three modes of interpreting Revelation fail to recognize that the structural arrangement and the content of the book differ fundamentally from apocalyptic prophecies.

1) The starting point of the prophesied event was not the vantage point of the seer but that of the exaltation of Christ. The prophecy went forth from chs. 4f. where the lamb bearing mortal wounds stood before God's throne and was given the book with the seven seals. That is to say: the carrying out of God's plan for history was given over to the exalted Christ. Revelation intended therefore to represent the consummation of the earthly drama that began with the exaltation of the crucified One. This conclusion based on Rev. 4 and 5 is confirmed by the little apocalypse in Rev. 12–14 since the event from which it took its starting point was the birth of the world's Savior and his translation to heaven.

2) As in the case of the starting point, so too the goal is qualitatively different. The alteration of the earthly drama that began with the exaltation of Christ would be completed at the *parousia*. Both the little apocalypse in 14:14ff. and the main one in 19:11ff. closed with the *parousia*. Accordingly, Revelation portrayed the drama that began with Christ's exaltation and was directed toward the consummation by him through his *parousia*.

---

[3]Op. cit. (Lit., §44).

3) For this reason, even the drama that was depicted itself had a different character than in apocalypticism. In the latter, a particular portion of the earthly drama was portrayed that came to a close through the intervening *eschaton*. Revelation, on the other hand, described an earthly drama that was determined by the reign of God that had already dawned in secret and that would be consummated by the intervening reign of God in full view. Hence, according to the passage that is decisive for the understanding of the book (5:9), the sealed book was given to the lamb because it had already established the *basileia*. Therefore, this reign was now to triumph in history so that at the end could be proclaimed: "Alleluia! The Lord our God, sovereign over all, has entered on his reign!" (19:6, NEB). The structure of Revelation has been fundamentally misunderstood when one explains that for Paul and the Gospel of John the *eschaton* was already present (II Cor. 5:17; Jn. 5:24), but for Revelation it was still in the future. Rather the *eschaton* was also and precisely for Revelation both present and future. Because the already and the not yet were both true for it, Revelation fulfilled an important criterion for apostolicity.

4) Because Revelation, therefore, did not merely portray the course of history but history's encounter with the *eschaton*, its type of portrayal was also fundamentally different from those of the Jewish apocalypses. This can be illustrated in terms of the following example. The image of the beasts in Rev. 13:1 united in itself the aspects of the beasts in Dan. 7. In Rev. 13 therefore, in contrast to Dan. 7, a succession of worldly kingdoms was no longer portrayed, but the essential character of the worldly kingdom *per se*. The reader was not supposed to determine which ruler was intended out of a succession of rulers and figure out his own point of reference. Rather he was supposed to grasp the essential character of the anti-Christian ruler so that he would not worship him like the other members of society. In Rev. 17:8ff., in fact, a pointer was given to the readers that in principle this Antichrist figure was already to be found in history. But the figure of the beast as such was an image of essential character, born of the spirit of prophecy, even if the occasion for its composition was the appearance of Domitian, and even if the readers could recognize in him a certain in-principle realization of that image. The image was not simply a cipher beneath which Domitian was hiding, but a figure of essential character. The four apocalyptic horsemen (6:1-8) —to suggest still a second example—also represented not singular events following one upon the other, but essential moments of history's climax: world conquest, war, hunger, and pestilence. The prophecy did not list a succession of events, but depicted essential moments of history's climax.

Thus Revelation distinguished itself fundamentally through the four points above from Old Testament/Jewish apocalypses. It is also not to be interpreted, therefore, in analogy to them. The interpretation that looks purely at the world of that time is just as much off the mark as the church-historical or world-historical positions. Revelation did not portray simply a course of history, in an interpretive way, either the history of that time or the history of the world; rather it proclaimed, from the perspective of Jesus' exaltation, the essential character of the historical drama, the essential character that resulted from the encounter with the dawning *eschaton*. It proclaimed this in order to make the recognition of faith and the decision of faith possible for the community. This type of portrayal characterized the synoptic apocalypse in Mk. 13 par. as well. We are dealing therefore with a specific stream of tradition for primitive Christian apocalypticism!

2. GOD AND HISTORY

Revelation responded to the fundamental theme of all theology: God and history—and that always means as well: God and the absurdity of history. It developed this theme of Old Testament prophecy in terms of the new historical situation that had come to pass through the life and ministry of Jesus and the emergence of his community. For that matter, one could also label the thematic concern here "Christ and history" or "the final-hour revelation of salvation and history."

If we are to attend to its essential theological statements we shall have to follow its own structure and begin with the general theme "God and history." We shall then consider the life and ministry of Christ as well as that of the church and their effect on history.

The prophecy began in ch. 4 with the vision of the One upon the throne. Before a single word about the course of history had been uttered, attention was directed toward the One from whom and to whom all things were. Two doxologies proclaimed in this image the two basic starting points typical for the theology of history.

a) The first doxology expressed what had already been said in symbolic language[4] through the image of the One upon the throne. Sovereign above all that happened in the world was not, as ancient man assumed, *heimarmenē* (fate), but the One upon the throne. He was the Almighty who determined everything that happened—past, present, and future. "Holy, holy, holy, is the Lord God Almighty, who was and is and is to come!" (4:8).

Did it represent a change within the New Testament concept of God when Revelation introduced God not as the Father but in the Old Testament sense as the Almighty (*Pantokratōr*)?[5] The predicate was certainly prompted by the special theme of Revelation. As in no other book of the New Testament, Revelation saw in the earthly drama dark evil forces at work and people who not only rebelled against their Creator but also rejected his gospel. And yet it did not lapse into dualism; God was the *Pantokratōr*, i.e., he alone was Lord over all that happened. He also fixed the time frame and the extent of operation for the forces of evil that raised themselves against him; indeed, he turned them into agents of his wrath. Thus, in Rev. 13:5 and 7 it was said four times about the

---

[4]Sitting upon the throne is a typical image for the function of ruling or of judging; cf. O. Schmitz, *TDNT* III, 162ff.

[5]*Pantokratōr* is a typical predicate for God; cf. W. Michaelis, *TDNT* III, 914f.

anti-Christian world-ruler, "and it was allowed" that he rule over the nations and that he wage war against the saints. This divine passive construction meant that God had allowed this to be. And in Rev. 17:17 it was clarified expressly that no one other than God himself had put into the hearts of the ten kings, who were in league with the Antichrist to do battle against Christ, to put their royal power at the disposal of the beast. This One was the God of Rom. 9:17f. who once hardened Pharaoh's heart so that he would rescind his order and not permit Israel to leave. Only by including this final dark possibility of a hardening effect of wrath does God really become present in history.

Because God was and remained the Lord over all that happened could he show the seer "what must take place after this" (4:1). This *dei* (it must) did not have in mind simply God's plan for history, as it did in apocalypticism, but, as it was in the announcements of coming suffering (§18,7), God's resolution to save.

b) The earthly drama, however, was not merely a monologue of the *deus semper ubique actuosus*, but also a dialogue, since man participated with shared responsibility in this drama. This was expressed by the second doxology in the vision of the One upon the throne. "Worthy art thou, our Lord and God, to receive glory and honor and power, for thou didst create all things" (4:11). Historical life did not exist of its own doing but owed its existence to the Creator. It was man's destiny to appropriate this into his self- and world-understanding in a reflective way and to acknowledge its truth in relationship to God. In 14:7 came the challenge in this respect, "Fear God and give him glory, for the hour of his judgment has come. . . !" Man was destined and called to respond to the Creator as the voice of his creation. Revelation further developed this perspective impressively as it related everything in the earthly drama to the relationship between God and man. The cosmos collapsed over the humanity that refused to give the honor to its Creator, but for the new humanity that had turned to God a new world was created (21:1ff.).

This was underscored with urgency in Rev. 20:11ff. through the image of the judgment of the world: "Then I saw a great white throne and him who sat upon it; from his presence earth and sky fled away, and no place was found for them. And I saw the dead. . . ." The whole creation sank here before its Creator into the nonexistence from which he had called it. Then the real partners of the earthly drama stood over against each other in great solitude—man, and God as his Judge. In this reciprocal relationship the course of the whole had been decided, and in that same relationship issued forth now the transformation of the entire drama toward a new world.

This angle of vision of the Bible was unprecedented in the ancient world. The Greek view of the world was cosmological; the ancient Orient understood the world in terms of mythology related to nature; the view of the Hellenistic world was that of demonic forces. In the Old Testament alone the course of history and—later in apocalypticism—the cosmic drama were also connected to the relationship between God and man. On the basis of this angle of vision the cyclical thought-structure of the ancient world oriented upon the seasonal rhythm of nature was overcome by a historical thought-structure. It was in the book of Daniel that for the first time the entire drama in time was conceived of as a teleological progression, i.e., as that which we call history. This angle of vision came about because God was encountered here not as the mute power of nature, but as the word addressing man, making promises to him that were to be honored in history. Thus, according to the Old Testament, history emerged out of the verbal encounter between God and man, and man shared responsibility for the future of the world.

The critical question for the book of Revelation of course was: Would man measure up to this his destiny? The doxology of the vision of the One upon the throne was uttered in the heavenly throne room, not upon the earth. For the situation upon the earth it was stated further in the prophecy that people would refuse to recognize their Creator in spite of all afflictions (9:20; 16:9, 11, 21).

3. THE EXALTATION OF CHRIST AS THE TURNING POINT OF HISTORY

a) The dominion of the Lamb. At the beginning of the seven-seal vision (5:1-7), Christ appeared as the One who alone was able to turn around the hopeless situation of the world. Since no one was able to open the book with the seven seals, i.e., to reveal and to realize the meaning of history, the seer saw "between the throne . . . a Lamb standing, as though it had been slain . . . , and he went and took the scroll from the right hand of him who was seated on the throne" (5:6f.). This image of the lamb appeared twenty-eight times in Revelation as its special symbol for the exalted Christ.

> This symbol came into being from early Christian symbolic language; in various New Testament writings the lamb was used as a symbol for Christ. The oldest reference was the quotation coming from the Passover homily in I Cor. 5:7: ". . . Christ, our paschal lamb, has been sacrificed" (cf. also Acts 8:32; I Pet. 1:19; Jn. 1:29, 36). In Revelation a visionary symbol of apocalyptic imagery developed out of this metaphor, though it used the Greek term *arnion* and not that of *amnos* as the other New Testament passages mentioned here. Perhaps the change of term was influenced by the fact that in the other passages the focus was on the crucified One, while here it was on the One exalted from the cross.

What this visionary symbol intended to express was made clear through two groups of epithets.

1) The lamb "has been sacrificed." It had the sacrificial mark upon the throat. That is to say, the exalted One stood before God as the One who died for all. That is important since the lamb was not at all the *Pantokratōr* or even the *Cosmokratōr* and Judge of the world, as was later painted on the apsides of old Christian basilicas. Here as in the rest of the New Testament Christ stood before God primarily as the One who on the basis of his dying made intercession for those who belonged to him (cf. Rom. 8:31-35; Heb. 8–10).

2) The lamb was, of course, at the same time the powerful One through whom the eschatological reign of God was established even in relationship to his adversaries. Revelation emphasized this side to a greater extent than the rest of the New Testament. Thus the seven horns[6] indicated that the lamb was given all authority and the seven eyes symbolized the full measure of the Spirit conveyed to him.

The lamb before the throne was both the One who died for all and the powerful ruler. Both these sides made repeated appearances throughout the entire book whenever the work of the lamb was in view. The lamb showed itself on the one hand to be the center of those set free through Christ's dying (7:9, 17; 14:1, 4; 19:7, 9; 21:9, 22f.). What counted was that one stood "in the book of life," i.e., "in the Lamb's book of life" (21:27). Corresponding to this the lamb's work of salvation, on the other hand, was that work which meant judgment. By opening the seal of the book (6:1, 3, 5) it unleashed the judgments that brought to a close history crafted by man (6:16; 14:10; 17:14).

It thus becomes clear what the point was for the event that in Revelation meant the decisive turning point in world history. The lamb received from God's hand the book with the seven seals (5:7); the carrying out of God's plan for history, also in relationship to the adversaries of God, was turned over to the One who had died for all. He was established as the end-time ruler who would bring history to its goal and precisely with respect to the adversaries. As can be seen at the opening of the seal, he will let the history that rejected the gospel die of its opposition.

b) The carrying out of God's plan for history. As portrayed in 5:8-10, the exalted One was "worthy," i.e., qualified before God, to carry out the plan for history even in relationship to the adversary because proleptically he had already realized that which was of decisive and positive importance. "Worthy art thou to take the scroll and to open its seals, for thou wast slain and by thy blood didst ransom men for God from every tribe and tongue and people and nation, and hast made them a kingdom and priests to our God, and they shall reign on earth." This was certainly the most central statement of Revelation; it stated that the exalted One by his dying had won for God people out of every group of society and had transferred them into his *basileia*. In it God's gracious will took place because evil had been overcome (Mt. 6:10, 13 par.). All members of the *basileia* became "priests"; they had direct access to God, and their whole life was a service of worship.

Rev. 5:8ff. did not go into detail about the missionary emergence of the community of faith out of all nations and about its outward appearance. It characterized the community rather by use of a kerygmatic indicative in accord with its essence; it was solely the work of Christ; he had "bought" it, he had "made" it. What it had become through his previous ministry, through his dying and his exaltation, was of course to be differentiated from what it would become

---

[6]The horn was already a symbol of power in Daniel (8:3); cf. I Enoch 90:9, 37; Syr. Bar. 66:2. The number seven symbolized fullness.

in the future through his *parousia*. This was stated at the end of the sentence: "and they shall reign on earth." This promise was repeated in the visions about the consummation brought by the *parousia* (20:6; 22:5; cf. Mt. 5:5). The "shall reign" would come when the new life became visible and all darkness had passed away (22:5; cf. I Cor. 4:8).

4. THE GOSPEL AND THE NATIONS OF THE WORLD

If one looks only at the surface of what was said about Christ in Rev. 6, the impression could arise that was articulated by H. J. Holtzmann: the Christ of Revelation was "the warrior, yes, the murdering Messiah who celebrated his triumphs in glaring contradiction to the peaceful Messiah-concept of Jesus. All this was taken over from Judaism. . . ."[7] In part this statement recognized an element of truth, even if it also drew an erroneous conclusion. What was said about the exalted Christ from ch. 6 on in the three groups of seven visions of seals, bowls, and trumpets was in fact regarded as an unrelenting chain of judgments! How is this image in overview to be understood?

It is critical that the presupposition developed from Rev. 5:10f., as we saw above, not be forgotten. These judgments were for Revelation strictly the negative reverse-side of the *basileia*, of the gracious dominion of the lamb. But it was characteristic of Revelation that this negative reverse-side was emphasized with greater breadth and intensity than anywhere else in the New Testament; this also resulted in its assuming a different character.

The latter becomes clear when a comparison is made between it and the closest corresponding statement in Paul, I Cor. 15:23-28. There it was also said, "For he must reign until he has put all his enemies under his feet. The last enemy to be destroyed is death" (I Cor. 15:25f.). Precisely in this last remark one can see that Paul had different enemies in mind than Revelation; he thought about death and other suprahuman forces hostile to God. Revelation, however, had in mind the nations of the world that were aligned with the Antichrist. The difference became especially clear at the conclusion of history. According to Rev. 19:19-21, the seer saw the beast and the kings of the earth and their armies gathered before the *parousia*, "to make war against him who sits upon the horse and against his army," i.e., against the Christ who had appeared for the *parousia*. This battle of the nations ended with the destruction of the aggressors.

Paul saw the end of history quite differently. "A hardening has come upon Israel, until the full number of the Gentiles come in [= into the reign of God], and so all Israel will be saved" (Rom. 11:25). At the end stood not the restoration of each individual, but yet the conversion of both the nations as a whole and Israel (§38,3). The Lukan historical composition could no longer expect this in a generation as the gospel's apocalyptic triumphal procession throughout the then-known world, like Paul in Rom. 15; rather, it looked for a long-lasting yet

---

[7]*Theologie* I, 541.

positive advancement of mission among the nations of the world (Acts 28:28; cf. §48,4).

If these other perspectives are placed alongside those of Revelation, then the special character of the latter becomes clear. Revelation maintained a different image of the encounter of the gospel with the nations of the world than Paul, Luke, and all the remaining documents of the New Testament, except for the Gospel of John. The *basileia* was, to be sure, gathered together out of all nations (Rev. 5:8ff.), but the mass of the nations of the world and particularly their political representatives rejected the *basileia*. This was therefore the scope of Revelation, that the exalted One would direct history to its goal, even though the nations and their political representatives would place themselves in large numbers against the gospel. In contrast to Paul (Rom. 9), this rejection of the gospel nevertheless was seen not merely as temporary, but as final.

Here we do not have simply an analysis of the new experiences of the community, e.g., those of persecution.[8] Rather, the seer saw the whole world centrally from the perspective of the cross;[9] he also seized upon a tendency making its mark in his environment to interpret that world prophetically. He observed a politico-religious view of the world to which the whole society of his time did homage, and which Christians, however, so far as they were Christians, must resist. This starting point was developed in depth in Rev. 13, the heart of the book.

5. POLITICAL ANTI-CHRISTIANITY AND THE TRUE DISCIPLES (REV. 13)

Rev. 13 depicted a situation that Christians throughout the centuries have recognized repeatedly as their own. In the vision of the seer two beast-figures emerged.

a) The first beast. The first beast (vv. 1-10) was characterized in appearance (vv. 1-4) in a threefold manner. (1) It combined in itself elements of the four beast-figures of Dan. 7. It thus represented the world-ruler *per se* whose might was embodied for people in biblical times in such figures as Nebuchadnezzar, Alexander, or even Caesar Augustus. (2) In addition, the beast was a reproduction of the dragon described in 12:3, of Satan. Like the latter, this world-ruler was the one who led people astray and was the adversary of Christ. (3) More importantly, the third characteristic was that one of his heads "seemed to have a mortal wound," and his mortal wound had been healed (13:3). He was one, therefore, who as it were had come back from the dead. This miracle prompted people to attribute divine honor to the beast (13:3b, 4); this was an element taken from the ancient Near Eastern myth of the god-king who returned from

---

[8]According to the letters to the seven churches the communities of Asia did not live in a distinct situation of persecution; only in 2:13 was the martyrdom of an individual community member mentioned.

[9]Thus the "great city" (11:8) was an image of the world "where their Lord was crucified."

the dead, and signified here the eschatological world-ruler as the counter-image to the lamb (5:6). As the lamb bore the mark of death and appeared as One raised from the dead, so too this one. The eschatological world-ruler came on the scene, therefore, not as a sinister tyrant but as the glistening counter-image of the Savior of the world; he would be honored and worshipped as the savior of the world! For this reason he was the political antichrist.

What was expressed by Revelation in its linguistic imagery found terminological expression elsewhere in the New Testament, characteristically enough, only in the Johannine writings. I Jn. 2:18, 22; 4:3; II Jn. 7 also spoke about the *antichristos*. This Antichrist of the Johannine epistles, however, was not a political but a theological figure. It referred to false teachers in the community of faith. Without using the designation, II Thess. 2:1-12 also depicted the Antichrist.[10]

The conduct of the Antichrist was marked by his blaspheming God (13:5f.) as he attributed the divine title to himself and thereby laid claim to being not "axe" and "rod" in the hand of God (Isa. 10:12ff.; 14:13f.), but himself the last word. His conduct was also marked by his persecuting the community of faith that refused to grant him the worship he demanded (13:7f.). To warn people against the worship of the Antichrist was the scope of Rev. 13. This calls to mind the ancient Near Eastern cult of the ruler that was applied to the Roman emperor in increasing measure through Roman imperial ideology. Domitian was one of the first emperors who insisted on divine adoration during his lifetime. This cult of the person was by no means merely an ideological game but an expression of genuine religious conviction. Since Augustus, the emperor was for many people actually the Deity who guaranteed sustenance and made a meaningful existence possible.[11] For this reason people gave him adoration. Christians were the only ones among the inhabitants of the earth (13:8) who did not ask for their daily bread from the world-ruler but from God. As such they appeared to their environment that was conditioned by ideology to be an arrogant crowd that disrupted the solidarity of autonomous humanity. Thus it came to the complete standoff between church and political ideology that in Rev. 13:7a ended with the defeat of the church (cf. 11:7f.). What emerged as a consequence for the community of faith, however, was not resistance (cf. Mt. 5:39) but "the endurance and faith of the saints" (13:9f.; cf. 12:11).

b) *The second beast.* The second beast (13:11-18) was like the lamb (v. 11) and spoke like the dragon; it was the false prophet. He would be empowered by the first beast to see to it that the inhabitants of the earth worshipped the first beast (vv. 12-17). It brought about worship through pseudo-miracles (vv. 13ff.) and through indirect force (vv. 16f.). Through this image of the false prophet the communities of John were reminded of the representatives of the empire's ideology, people like philosophers, poets, artists, and priests who each in their

---

[10]Regarding the prior history of this concept, cf. M. Dibelius, *Der Zweite Thessalonicherbrief* (HNT), at II Thess. 2:10 (excursus).

[11]From this perspective v. 8 becomes understandable; the only ones who do not ask their daily bread from the ruler of the world but from God are precisely those who stood in the book of life.

own way represented this ideology and propagated it publicly. Those who had been called to life through Jesus were not to succumb to either deceptive appearance or coercion. Their vision was to penetrate the fog of ideology when the offer of *pax et securitas* was made (I Thess. 5:3); they were not "to worship."

> The question that has been posed again and again since around the middle of our century for pressing concrete reasons whether our state is a state in the sense of Rom. 13 or of Rev. 13 is based, of course, on a false alternative when looked at from the New Testament. Political entities are ambivalent throughout. There is always the tendency to turn politics into something final, to deify it. The task of Christians is to expose this tendency with the help of Rev. 13 and to resist it, and precisely when the tendency is trimmed with theology.

c) The salvation-historical presuppositions of the conflict. The prophetic view of the conflict in Rev. 13 cannot be isolated from Rev. 12 where the salvation-historical presuppositions for it were brought to mind. This chapter noted two things.

1) The great decisions had already been made at the time the Savior of the world appeared (12:1-6) and was translated to God (12:7-12); the accuser of people has been toppled from power through Jesus' dying (12:13-18). Even the church as such has been sheltered. Thus, in these struggles the issue was no longer the existence or nonexistence of Christ and of the church, but of the loyalty of the individual disciple.

2) The attack of political ideology upon the church was not the product of a pre-Christian paganism but of the post-Christian world-situation. It was the reaction of the world—represented by Satan (12:9; 20:2, 7)—that denied God at the appearance of Christ and the establishment of the end-time community of salvation.

6. THE ESSENTIAL CHARACTERISTICS OF HISTORY'S CLIMAX (Rev. 6–11 and 15–19)

a) The community of faith within world history. In the sequence of images about the course of world history the community of faith only appeared in a single vision, the one about the fifth seal (6:9-11). The seer took down here the question of those who had become martyrs "for the word of God and for the witness they had borne": "how long before thou wilt judge and avenge our blood on those who dwell upon the earth?" This question of faith struggling with doubts—it was not, as often has been claimed, an un-Christian cry for revenge, but the question about God coming from the psalms of lament—was corrected through the reply (6:11): Christians were not to raise questions about God's conduct in relationship to the world, but about that which was their concern! They were to be patient yet for a brief time until the number of Christians was full who were yet to suffer martyrdom according to the plan of salvation. In the judgment of the seer, the church stood in history as the martyr-church although a current situation involving martyrdom was not yet its lot. The seer thus composed an image of essentials that corresponded to Jn. 15:19f.: "because . . . I chose you out of the world, therefore the world hates you. . . . If they persecuted me, they will persecute you." For this reason the church was not to concern itself with the question of the psalms of lament. In light of the cross of the righteous One, Revelation put to silence the question of the psalms about the suffering of the righteous ones among the Christians.

b) *Post-Christian world history under judgment.* The inhabitants of the earth afflicted the community because they rejected its witness. The reverse side of this rejection of the gospel was judgment. This was suggested in Rev. 8:3-5 and expressed in 19:2. From that vantage point the essential characteristics of the earthly drama that were portrayed in the threefold series of seven cycles become clear. World history was characterized by historical and cosmic catastrophes that finally brought the earthly drama to termination.

Here the affairs of this world no longer stood under the steadfast forbearance of God (*anochē*) as before Christ (according to Rom. 3:25); it had now fallen under the judgment of God's wrath. According to Rev. 15:7, the seven bowls, out of which were finally poured out terrors over the earth, were full of the wrath of God (cf. 15:1 and 16:1). All these shock waves poured out into the great day of the wrath of God (Rev. 6:16f.; 11:18; 14:10; 16:19; 19:15). Wrath poured forth because people did not repent of their "evil works," especially of their "idolatrous denial of their Creator" (9:20f.; 16:9ff.). Revelation painted in apocalyptic imagery for the course of history what Jn. 3:18 said for the individual: "he who does not believe is condemned already." This event of judgment in the threefold series of seven visions was focused concretely in the last cycle about the fall of "Babylon" (17:1–19:10), the decline of Rome, the decline of the flourishing capital of the world (ch. 19). Here it becomes clear once again that the seer did not live in a world shocked by wars and catastrophes. He did not analyze in images a situation that he could observe but developed an in-depth prophetic picture out of his insight into the backgrounds.

c) *Existence within the community of faith.* Chapters 7, 10, and 11 concerned themselves with existence within the community of faith. The community was seen here in two forms that were customarily distinguished with the terms *ecclesia militans* and *ecclesia triumphans*. The former appeared in 7:1-8; 14:1-5 as well as in chs. 10 and 11; the latter appeared in 7:9-17. From these images three things deserve special note.

1) Revelation knew nothing of a transfigured community presently existing in heaven that would be distinguishable from the community of the consummation that came forth after the *parousia* (Rev. 21:3f., 6). The seer saw rather in 7:9-17 as an eternity above time in heaven that which would first come true for those living in time at the end.

2) For the community in time everything depended on the *hypomonē*, the endurance of obedient faith (1:9; 2:2f.; 3:10; 12:19; 13:10; 14:12). This *hypomonē* corresponded to the affliction through tribulation. The community suffered

in two ways; it suffered along with the world under the judgments of God;[12] but mostly it suffered for the sake of its witness in the world (1:9; 2:9f.; 7:14). In the verification of the *hypomonē* was to be seen who really belonged to the community. Whoever stood in the book of the lamb, whoever was elected, that one did not worship the Antichrist.

3) This community beset by doubts bore the witness in relationship to the world (11:3-13). To this community was promised that it would be kept from profanation until the end as God's measured, holy domain (11:1f.) and would be able to convey its witness to the last (11:10). At the end, of course, would stand not the triumph of the mission to the world, but the witness having met defeat; the witnesses would lie "dead . . . in the street of the great city which is spiritually called Sodom and Egypt, where their Lord was crucified" (11:8). The voice of witness and the church would suffer defeat in the end by Anti Christianity (11:7; 13:7).

As already has become clear, all this was a different dimension of world history as well as church history than the one communicated by the other books of the New Testament. This dimension cannot be fixed absolutely, as has always happened during difficult times in the church's history, but it cannot be brushed aside either, as has been thought in times when Christianity enjoyed a privileged status.

7. THE CONSUMMATION

a) The consummation of the community of faith (20:1-10). The picture that Revelation depicted of the course of history as a whole concluded with the announcement of a transcendent future. This future was not conceptualized speculatively as a projection of human needs; rather, it was the consummation of that which encountered people in Jesus.

That is also and precisely true for the much misunderstood image of the millennial kingdom (20:1-10). After Satan, who according to 12:7-12 had already fallen from power in heaven through the exaltation of Jesus, was also eliminated on earth and thereby temptation and the struggle with doubt were at an end (20:1-3), there dawned the millennial kingdom of Christ (20:4-6). Christians were raised before all others who had died in order to reign with Christ for a thousand years.

What does this image say? Its scope lay in the statement about the participation of Christians in the first resurrection (vv. 5b, 6). It was the special resurrection of Christians that preceded the general resurrection of the dead.

This first resurrection was a peculiar expectation of the primitive Christian community; it was foreign to Jewish apocalypticism. It could be found as early as I Thess. 4:16ff. and I Cor. 15:23. The "first" here did not designate a temporal but rather a qualitative precedence. The resurrection of Christians had a different

---

[12]The only exception is Rev. 9:4.

meaning—this should be noted—than the resuscitation of all. Christians were not waiting to be resuscitated physically, a paradisiac life, but to be raised to the union with their Lord that meant life.

This center of the Christian end-time expectation was described, e.g., in I Pet. 1:8f.: ". . . you love him; though you do not now see him you believe in him and rejoice with unutterable and exalted joy. As the outcome of your faith you obtain . . . salvation. . . ." Corresponding to this was what the Gospel of John did with different categories and without the image of "first" (Jn. 5:29) by promising resurrection to life (cf. II Cor. 5:8; I Jn. 3:2).

Thus, this image of the "first resurrection" expressed the key moment of Christian end-time expectation. The union with the Lord in which even now one believed would not be something preliminary but the new life that cannot be surpassed. "Blessed and holy is he who shares in the first resurrection! Over such the second death [= damnation] has no power" (Rev. 20:6). This perfected fellowship with the Lord was then described in the second half of the image as ruling together with Christ.

> The chiliastic interpretation of Rev. 20 understood the statements here to mean a triumph of Christian mission and the realization of the messianic dominion on earth. Yet, not even half the image talked here about all this. In fact, the context made it impossible that the resurrected community should even come into contact with other people. The "ruling together with Christ" actually had more the meaning of total participation in his *basileia*. As Christians until now had been taken into the reign of salvation from God's perspective, so now they could truly serve God and each other without limitation.
>
> Chiliasm cannot base its claims, therefore, upon Rev. 20. As can be shown historically, chiliasm developed independent of Rev. 20 in the 2nd century out of Jewish traditions and then subsequently interpreted Rev. 20 in its interests. Rev. 20, however, only appropriated certain elements of the Jewish-apocalyptic concept of a messianic interim kingdom as the material of an image.

b) The universal judgment of the world (20:11-15).

We read in 20:12: "And I saw the dead, great and small, standing before the throne, and books were opened." All, including Christians, were judged according to their works, but according to the "books" of works no one could pass the test. Saved were only those who stood in the book of life, those who in Christ were elect and called (13:8).

The image of the books according to which people were judged was of great antiquity. We find that it was used as early as the ancient Egyptian representations of the judgment of the dead. But in this configuration it was quite unique. It expressed the specifically New Testament concept of the Last Judgment. According to Paul, everyone, including those justified by faith, would come into the judgment according to works (II Cor. 5:10) and their conduct would be weighed in dead earnest; there would be praise and reproach (I Cor. 3:12-15). Being acquitted in the judgment, however, was not to be expected from works and also not from the new obedience of Christians, but exclusively and solely from the ultimate intercession of Christ (Rom. 5:9). This expectation rested upon the saying of Jesus about the Son of man appearing for judgment; this One would confess those who had confessed Jesus here (Luke 12:8). The Judge of the world would be its Savior. Revelation portrayed this specifically Christian expectation through its version of the image of the books; it was accomplished by this peculiar setting off of the many books of works, on the one hand, over against deliverance through the book of life alone, on the other.

c) The new creation (21:1-8). There was also no attempt to describe pictorially in the concluding vision of the new creation (21:1-8); rather, what could be expected in the consummation was proclaimed. What was announced in vv. 1-5 as humanity's restored future was not the return of the golden age; the latter was construed idyllically in Virgil's Fourth Eclogue as the solution to the problems of human existence. Rather, it was the visual dawning of the kingdom of God that Jesus had promised in the Beatitudes and in his ministry had allowed to become present in secret. Each verse named an essential element of the consummation. A new world was created (v. 1), and into it descended from heaven the new Jerusalem (v. 2). This new Jerusalem was not the dwelling place of those who were perfected, but a symbol of the community of God. It was in fact the "bride," the symbol of the community of God (19:7). The new world had been created for the new community. This community, however, was identical to the new humanity. The community was what it was because God had made his dwelling among it (v. 3). Because God was with them, all evil would have disappeared (v. 4). As v. 5 announced in summary, "everything" would be "new" (and that was the first word of Revelation that directly was referred to as the word of God!). In the new creation that becoming-new begun in Jesus' resurrection would reach its goal.

8. STARTING POINT AND PROBLEMATIC OF END-TIME ESCHATOLOGY[13]

a) The expectation of a concrete prefection of man, of history, and of the world by no means grew naturally out of the world view of the environment for New Testament Christianity. Such was more than foreign to the thought of the Hellenistic world, just as it was also to that of Hellenistic Judaism. As early as I Cor. 15, Paul debated for this reason with a movement in Corinth that contested a concrete resurrection of those who believed. Palestinian apocalypticism with its absurd shaping of such concrete-historical expectations was more the occasion for misunderstanding than it was a positive point of departure. No differently than Jesus himself (§7,2), Paul opposed the expectation of Pharisaic apocalypticism according to which man would come again in the way he had departed

---

[13]Regarding the question of the so-called end-time eschatology, cf. F. Holmström, *Das eschatologische Denken der Gegenwart* (1936); W. Kreck, *Die Zukunft des Gekommenen* (1961); J. Moltmann, *Theology of Hope* (1967).

(Mk. 12:18-27 par.). Thus the Christian end-time expectation was an original formation within the surrounding world of thought.

b) Where was the starting point then of the New Testament expectation to be found? Just like Jesus, Paul understood that man in his in-person totality was claimed by God because the Creator intended to bring his creation as a whole to its goal. Hence for Paul coming to salvation stood or fell with the reality that those who believed would be raised just like Jesus himself in their in-person totality to an abiding existence before God. For him, the justification of those who believed had to come to its goal in the redemption of the body and of all creatures (Rom. 8:18-30). A new existence as person, however, also meant a new communication with others, a new fellowship and thereby a new situation for life—a "new world." The whole New Testament, including the Gospel of John, advocated this view. Even today, bound together with faith is the hope that the I-Thou relationship with God endures and will be consummated beyond death, and that the new human being that Jesus had claimed and mediated in secret will step forth in the way patterned by the Easter event.

c) The question of how has become for us, of course, incomparably more difficult than it already was for Hellenistic-Jewish man. In reply to his question, "How are the dead raised? With what kind of body do they come?" Paul answered, "You foolish man! . . . God gives it a body as he has chosen" (I Cor. 15:36, 38). For us this question of how has been wrenched from every mode of conceptualization much more than for Paul because of the uniformity and immenseness of the natural scientific view of the world. The end-time expectation lives today more than ever on the "nevertheless" of fellowship with God, as pronounced in Ps. 73. And it lives thereby on the just-as-incomprehensible reality of God itself.

d) Revelation remained fundamentally within this line demonstrated by the witness to Christ and by faith. Even in the final cycle, it did not conjure up objective descriptions, a time plan, or a succession of events in the spirit of Jewish apocalypticism. Here, too, it proclaimed in visionary images the essential characteristics of the event of the end time; these essential characteristics were made certain in faith coming from God's saving activity in Christ.

9. REVELATION AND I PETER—TWO DIMENSIONS

In conclusion, when we look back over the whole, we note the following. Revelation directed Christians into history under other dimensions than did I Peter. I Peter summoned to socio-political responsibility in a pre-Christian world that was viewed in its potential for Christ. Revelation, on the other hand, obligated in the direction of maintaining one's confession as well as one's witness in a post-Christian world that had fallen under anti-Christian ideology. Both dimensions provided directional guidelines for Christian existence in society. They did not provide such descriptively but kerygmatically, and therefore were by no means mutually exclusive; they complemented each other in a polarity.

These statements about Christian existence in society staked out the terrain for the life-situation of the community of faith in post-Pauline times. Corresponding to the word about enduring within the structures of society was a much more detailed and differentiating word about enduring in life's other connections, in the individual relationship of the Christian to one's neighbor, to the community of faith, and above all to oneself and to God. Here lie the intrinsic roots of being a Christian. Only when Christians remain Christians in these connections do they have a task in society (Rev. 3:16; Mt. 5:13).

The concerted effort of the post-Pauline writings on behalf of this internal situation of being a Christian produced differences that depended on the local situation within the individual ecclesiastical regions. For this reason, therefore, we intend in the following to represent the positions taken on this issue according to a breakdown of ecclesiastical regions.

Chapter II

THE PROCLAMATION OF THE EPISTLE OF JAMES AND OF MATTHEW IN THE CHURCH OF SYRIA

§45. The Epistle of James—A Parenetic Theology of Empiricism

A. Meyer, *Das Rätsel des Jakobusbriefes* (1930); G. Kittel, "Die Stellung des Jakobus zu Judentum und Heidenchristentum," *ZNW* 30 (1931), 145-156; H. Schammberger, *Die Einheitlichkeit des Jakobusbriefes im antignostischen Kampf* (1936); G. Kittel "Der geschichtliche Ort des Jakobusbriefes," *ZNW* 41 (1942), 71-105; K. Aland, *ThLZ* 69 (1944), 97-104; W. Rieder, "Christliche Existenz nach dem Zeugnis des Jakobusbriefes," *ThZ* 5 (1949), 93-113; K. Aland, "Der Jakobusbrief und die Apostolischen Väter," *ZNW* 43 (1950/51), 54-112; G. Eichholz, *Jakobus und Paulus. Ein Beitrag zum Problem des Kanons* (*ThEx* NF 39 [1953]); H. Thyen, *Der Stil der Jüdisch-Hellenistischen Homilie* (1956); G. Braumann, "Der theologische Hintergrund des Jakobusbriefes," *ThZ* 18 (1962), 401-410; E. Trocmé, "Les Églises pauliniennes vues du dehors: Jacques 2,1 á 3,13," *StEv* 2 (= *Texte und Untersuchungen* 87 [1964]), 660-69; G. Eichholz, *Glaube und Werke bei Paulus und Jakobus* (1961); U. Luck, "Der Jakobusbrief und die Theologie des Paulus," *Theologie und Glaube* 61 (1971), 161ff.; E. Lohse, "Glaube und Werke— Zur Theologie des Jakobusbriefes," in Lohse, *Die Einheit des Neuen Testaments* (1973), pp. 285-306. **Important Commentaries:** M. Dibelius (1921), KEK; A. Schlatter (1932); F. Mussner (1964), HTK (Eng. in prep.).

1. PRELIMINARY CONSIDERATION: COMPOSITIONAL CIRCUMSTANCES AND INTERPRETIVE PROBLEMATIC

Hardly any other document of the New Testament is more difficult to classify historically and theologically than the Epistle of James. Judgments about its historical and theological place have been extremely diverse, for this reason, in the ancient church, in the period of the Reformation, and in the exegesis of the modern era.

a) Compositional circumstances. The data given in the letter about its compositional circumstances are extremely sparse. It wanted to be understood as having been written by James the brother of the Lord, who directed and shaped the primitive community in Jerusalem since the Apostolic Council. Named as recipients were quite generally the twelve tribes in the Diaspora (1:1). This meant, however, not the Jewish Diaspora nor Jewish-Christianity, but the church as the new people of the twelve tribes. Hence the introduction was very ecumenical in nature; James the brother of the Lord was writing to the entirely new people of the twelve tribes. But in point of fact the letter was certainly not an ecumenical circular letter. Where then should one look for the first readers? Probably in that place where the name of the Lord's brother was held in regard, in the Palestinian-Syrian realm. In this direction one finds other indications, e.g., the comment about the early and late rains in 5:7. Concrete statements regarding the situation of the recipients, however, are not to be found anywhere in the letter; for that matter it really was not a letter at all, but a parenetic document of instruction with a letter-like introduction.

Chronologically speaking, its content presupposed the situation of post-Pauline times. It offered polemic in 2:14-26 against the Pauline slogan: faith alone! As we shall see, however, it did not mean Paul himself, but a flagging Christianity for which this Pauline formula had become simply a quietistic pillow. The debate in which Paul had formulated his slogan "justification by faith without the works of the Law" was for our letter a thing of the past. The question of a Gentile-Christianity free of the Law vs. a nomistic Jewish-Christianity was for the letter the question of a former period. The Epistle of James took its place not in the discussion among Paul's contemporaries, but in the post-Pauline period. For this and other reasons it could hardly have been written directly by James the brother of the Lord, who had already suffered martyrdom around A.D. 63 (Eus. *EH* 3.23.10-24). Within what historical and theological context is the letter then to be classified?

b) Historical and theological classification.[1] 1) The theological classification of the letter has been made repeatedly since the Reformation under the influence of Luther's judgment expressed in his introductory remarks to the (September) Bible of 1522. Luther measured it in comparison to Paul and therefore made the following judgment: "Therefore the Epistle of Saint James is purely an epistle of straw . . . , for it has no gospel in it."[2] It was "straightway contrary to Saint Paul and all other scriptures" because it "gives justification to works and says that Abraham was justified by his works . . . and does not once remember in such a long teaching as this Christ's suffering, resurrection, and Spirit. . . ."[3] For this reason, Luther altered its place in the canon by moving it to the end of the New Testament between Hebrews and Jude and before Revelation.

---

[1]W. G. Kümmel, *Introduction*, pp. 411-16.
[2]*WA, DB*, VI, 10.
[3]Ibid., VII, 384f.

2) This judgment of Luther appeared to have been confirmed literary-critically in relatively recent exegesis. In 1896, F. Spitta[4] posed quite one-sidedly the hypothesis that the letter was a thoroughly Jewish document that had undergone a minor Christian reworking. It did in fact contain the name of Jesus only twice (1:1 and 2:1). This hypothesis was then augmented so convincingly by A. Meyer[5] that H. Windisch also made it the basis of his commentary.[6] Today, of course, the hypothesis has been abandoned completely.[7] The substantively appropriate line of questioning for the evaluation of the Epistle of James has been found, and that through form-critical analysis!

3) In 1921, M. Dibelius furnished the letter with a new analysis that until now has not become obsolete.[8] He applied the form-critical line of questioning that he had developed in pioneering fashion for the synoptics to James and determined that it belonged to a special genre that he called parenesis.

Parenesis assembled traditional ethical admonitions without supplying a rational context. As was customary in oral tradition, the connection between the admonitions was often nothing more than key words. Thus it can be explained in terms of the genre of parenesis that in James one cannot find either in the whole or in larger subsections a progressive thought development. The letter offered throughout only groups of sayings and loosely arranged, brief hortatory sections.

4) This insight into the genre of the letter contained consequences for the substantively appropriate theological classification. We cannot consider it a compendium of Christian teaching and gauge it by how its content related to Paul; we must take it for what it was intended to be: a parenetic composition. In order to evaluate it in accord with its own intention we must ask: What sort of parenesis was this? Did it belong together with Jewish parenesis, as we find, e.g., in Jesus ben Sirach and in the Testaments of the Twelve Patriarchs, or with that of the early catholic period, as in the Didache and the Shepherd of Hermas, or with the parenesis of the Jesus tradition?

A. Schlatter pursued this latter line of questioning. He made a special point of the contact between the letter and the parenesis of Jesus;[9] in doing so he emphasized that the Beatitudes of Jesus (according to Matthew) could be detected shining through repeatedly as the supportive foundation of the admonitions.[10] This perspective was advanced with consistency in the recent commentary by F. Mussner whose introduction closed with the statements: "For James there were no thousand ifs and buts, but only the clear and simple requirement to help, to forgive, to be patient, to point one's entire life 'in an eschatological

[4] "Der Brief des Jakobus," in F. Spitta, Zur Geschichte und Literatur des Urchristentums II (1896), 1-155.
[5] Das Rätsel des Jakobusbriefes (1930).
[6] Der Jakobusbrief (1930).
[7] Cf. W. G. Kümmel, Introduction, p. 410.
[8] James (Hermeneia, 1976).
[9] Der Brief des Jakobus (1932), pp. 9-19.
[10] Jas. 1:9; 2:5 = Mt. 5:3; Jas. 2:13 = Mt. 5:7; Jas. 3:18 = Mt. 5:9; Jas. 5:16 = Mt. 5:6.

direction.' Hence it corresponded to the teaching of Jesus as it has been passed on to us above all in the Sermon on the Mount."[11]

An important qualification regarding one side was made in a posthumous article from G. Kittel;[12] in it was demonstrated through a collection of comprehensive material that the parenesis of James differentiated itself clearly through its rigorous posture from the tempered Christian ethos that the Apostolic Fathers represented. This is an important index point that the letter belonged, chronologically speaking, to a considerably earlier time frame, i.e., to the second generation.[13]

5) Taking note of this difference can also explain the riddle of its canonization. The parenetic tradition represented in the letter had already been appropriated in I Clement and the Shepherd of Hermas; on the other hand, however, the letter was first mentioned expressly by Origen at the beginning of the 3rd century. Its canonicity was first decided after long discussion in A.D. 367. This—to all appearances—contradictory development can be explained on the basis of the type of parenesis. It was so one-sided and rigorous that it could not generally be repeated any longer as worship-service lection since the beginning of the 2nd century. Documents, however, that were no longer read with regularity did not attain to canonical status. Why James was not read can be seen, e.g., if Jas. 5:1-6 is compared with the corresponding statements about rich and poor in the Shepherd of Hermas that sound like a commentary on the former. In Jas. 5:1f. it said: "Come now, you rich. weep and howl for the miseries that are coming upon you. Your riches have rotted and your garments are moth-eaten." In contrast, Herm. *Vis*. 3.9.2-6 threatened only the rich who did not support the hungry, and *Sim*. 2 recommended the coexistence of rich and poor in the community of faith—the rich were to support the poor, and the poor should pray for the rich! Wherever such an ethic of compromise reigned one could no longer prescribe the rigorous parenesis of the Epistle of James!

The decisive theological question directed at the letter thus runs: Was the parenesis of the Epistle of James eschatologically compatible with the demands of Jesus? Did it burst the bounds of society's immanent possibilities like the demands of Jesus did, and did it presuppose man's total change?

2. THE "PERFECT LAW OF LIBERTY"

While the whole New Testament emphasized that the *nomos* had been overcome for Christians, James referred to it eight times as the valid norm for the life of Christians. Christians should live by the Law since they would be judged by it (2:12).

Did the letter show itself to belong to early catholicism through this major

---

[11]*Der Jakobusbrief*, pp. 52f. (Eng. in prep.).

[12]"Der Jakobusbrief und die Apostolischen Väter," *ZNW* 43 (1950/51), 54-112.

[13]To be sure, it in no way belonged to the Pauline period, as Kittel would have it (op. cit.) (n. 12).

concept? Among the Apostolic Fathers Christian parenesis was designated in fact and expressed literally as "the new law of our Lord Jesus Christ" (Barn. 2:6 = LCL, *Apostolic Fathers*, I, 345). By this move, Christian existence was deeschatologized. Christians took their place alongside Jews and Greeks as the "third gender"; the former also lived each according to their *nomos*. Hence this catchword *nomos* threw open a far-reaching perspective. We must keep it in mind when we try to ascertain in what sense James introduced this key term.

   a) **The Law and the word (Jas. 1:25).** In the first passage in which the key term *nomos* (Law) appeared (1:25), James distinguished the *nomos* to which he would bind Christians from the *nomoi* of the environment through a demanding predicate. Christians were to take their orientation from the "perfect law of liberty."[14] This demanding expression must be explained in terms of its context. It was introduced in order to comment further about the word, i.e., about proclamation in the community

   1) In 1:22-25, a group of sayings about the hearing of the word led to the Law: "But be doers of the word, and not hearers only, deceiving yourselves. For if any one is a hearer of the word and not a doer, he is like a man who observes his natural face in a mirror; for he observes himself and goes away and at once forgets what he was like. But he who looks into the perfect law, the law of liberty, and perseveres, being no hearer that forgets but a doer that acts, he shall be blessed in his doing." In this group, the reference to the "law" in v. 25 replaced the previous commenting about the "word." The "word" according to general primitive-Christian usage was the good news that was proclaimed in the community, even the gospel. Did James understand the gospel, the Christian good news, therefore as Law? It is to be seen, however, that by no means did he align the two as synonyms; the word did not have merely parenetic character! According to 1:18, the word accomplished rebirth; according to 1:21, it was "implanted" in the baptized person, i.e., it was, as Jer. 31:33 promised for the day of salvation, written into the heart so that it would be lived from people's hearts. Thus, when in 1:25 the "word" was replaced by the "law," it meant that the Law was the imperative side of the word that not only made demands but also accomplished its ends.[15]

   2) If that which James called Law was related in this way to gospel, then it differentiated itself clearly from early catholicism. For early catholicism the gospel split into two parts: the one was the demonstration of grace—mediated above all in the sacrament (so first in Barn. 2:6); the other was the parenesis following it that was characterized as "the new law of our Lord Jesus Christ." In the Shepherd of Hermas the relationship between these two parts found drastic expression; for it baptism removed previously existing sins and mediated the

---

[14]Cf. H. Windisch, *Der Jakobusbrief*, at Jas. 1:25 (excursus); W. Gutbrod, *TDNT* IV, 1080ff.

[15]A. Schlatter, *Der Jakobusbrief*, p. 150, certainly reproduced the view of James correctly when he explained: "There was, therefore, no word of God that would also not be Law and it was this precisely when it proclaimed and secured salvation."

Spirit, and from then on the baptized were supposed to live in its power according to the Law of Christ (M. 4.3.1f.; Vis. 3.5.1-4).[16]

James, in contrast to this, did not designate as "Law" a part but one side of the word that also accomplished rebirth. He maintained thereby to some degree the interrelatedness of indicative and imperative, while for early catholicism the indicative of the removal of guilt and the imperative fell completely in two.

b) Law and freedom. James designated his Law as the "law of liberty" (1:25; 2:12). Analogies to this statement cannot be found in the New Testament; Paul spoke about Law and freedom in an entirely different way. For the latter, one did not become free through the Law; one was free who was free from the Law (Rom. 7:1-4; Gal. 4:25f.). Much the same could be said about all the rest of the New Testament, with certain reservations for Matthew. In contrast, the formula of James called to mind Hellenistic and Jewish analogies.

1) In both the Hellenistic and the Jewish worlds the—for us strange-sounding—concept was represented that man became free through law. Stoicism taught that the wise become free when they give themselves to the law that corresponded to world-reason.[17] Philo transferred this concept to the Mosaic Law and explained that just as those citizens who do not live under a tyrant but according to law were free, so the people who lived according to the Law were free in contrast to those over whom anger, lust, etc. reigned[18] (cf. IV Macc. 14:2). Whoever obeyed the Law became free, i.e., free from emotions.

More along Jewish lines the rabbis coupled this fascinating Greek term "freedom" with their Law. In Mishnah Aboth 6:2 it was said in reference to Exod. 32:16: "Read not harut [bury] but [pointed differently in Hebrew] herut (freedom), for thou findest no freeman excepting him that occupies himself in the study of the Law" (= Danby, Mishnah, p. 459). Whoever devoted oneself to the Torah was free from all earthly lords and powers because God alone was his Lord. That was the pride of the Jew, that he had no lord over him besides the Torah and its Lord (Jn. 8:33).

2) Was the formula in James "the law of liberty" to be understood in accordance with these analogies?[19] The formula as well as the context suggested another explanation. The genitive ("of liberty") could certainly mean only that it had to do with a law that belonged together essentially with freedom. It is hardly a coincidence that there were no Jewish analogies to this formula.[20] It was probably a specifically Christian formation.

In what way Law and freedom stood together essentially becomes understand-

---

[16]Thus the content of the gospel was, as it were, apportioned; cf. L. Goppelt, Christentum und Judentum im ersten und zweiten Jahrhundert (1954), pp. 216, 242.

[17]M. Dibelius, James, at 1:25 (excursus, pp. 116-120).

[18]Quod Omnis Probus Liber Sit I:7 (= LCL, Philo, IX, 15).

[19]Mussner, op. cit. (n. 11), p. 108, surely moved James too far into the vicinity of Philo when he expressed the opinion that the freedom that the Law created consisted "of the liberation from all selfishness that realizes itself in the loving move toward one's neighbor."

[20]The correspondence that some think is to be found in 1QS 10:6 was the result of an erroneous translation; cf. H. Braun, Qumran I, 279f.

able when viewed in terms of the contextual statement of James. The Law brought freedom because it was the imperative side of the word that was "implanted" in man and that transformed him from within (Jas. 1:18, 21). To put it differently, it was the Law of liberty because it was the eschatological Law in the sense of Jer. 31:31ff. It claimed man in such a way that it also made him free for a new form of conduct through grace. True for this Law was what Jn. 13:34 said of the new commandment: "A new commandment I give to you, that you love one another; even as I have loved you." A certain correspondence can also be found in Paul when he designated himself as *ennomos Christou*, i.e., as bound within to the claim of Christ (I Cor. 9:21).

c) The content of the Law. 1) In 1:25, the "law of liberty" was characterized as "perfect." "Perfect" (*teleios*) was for James in the Hebrew sense that which was "complete," and not in the Greek sense, the highest level (cf. 1:4). The Law was not perfect because it was the ideal type of law but because it claimed man entirely for his Creator, grasped him entirely from within, and made him free!

This explanation is confirmed through 2:8-14. Here the inseparable unity of the Law was emphasized: "For whoever keeps the whole law but fails in one point has become guilty of all of it. For he who said, 'Do not commit adultery,' said also, 'Do not kill.' If you do not commit adultery but do kill, you have become a transgressor of the law" (2:10f.). That intended to say that whoever fell short with respect to a single directive of the Law, did not merely make a singular mistake but had fallen short of the whole, for he did not stand before a sum of ordinances, but before "the One who had spoken."[21]

This understanding of the Law corresponded to the way in which Jesus interpreted the Mosaic Law. He forbade looking at the Law as a sum of statistical ordinances and thereby setting oneself off from the claim of God. Rather, he made every commandment transparent for the living claim of God (§9,3). On this very basis Matthew then developed the demand for perfection (Mt. 5:48; 19:21; cf. §46,5b).

2) Hence the Law was an expression of the all-encompassing claim of God. But how was it related to the Old Testament commandments? The demand for perfection, just mentioned, was developed in 2:10ff. in relationship to two of the Ten Commandments, and 2:8 pointed to the Old Testament commandment of loving one's neighbor. The commandments of the Decalogue were quoted here in reality not as constitutive parts of the Law, but as examples of the indivisible claim of God. Even 2:8 did not make the "royal law" equal to the love command, but explained that the "royal law," in accord with which Christians conduct themselves, corresponded to the love command of scripture!

---

[21]Thus the totality claim of the Law was understood differently here than in 1QS 5:8f., where the novitiate was enjoined to obey with the whole heart and soul what was revealed to the priests by the Torah. If it was a matter here of the complete obedience toward the entire sum of the ordinances, for James it was a matter of the total claim of the God who expressed himself in the Law.

Thus James too followed here the basic line of thought that had its origin with Jesus; individual commandments were always but illustrative restatements of the consistently vital and total claim of God. That claim could never be circumscribed as a sum of ordinances. This was underscored here through the expression "royal law"; the Law was "royal" because it went forth from the King of the eschatological reign of God. Out of that Law spoke the claim of that eschatological reign.

Thus it may be concluded that the "royal law" was not the religious-moral commandment of the Old Testament, the Decalogue supplemented by the love command,[22] as it became later in early catholicism all the way up to Irenaeus, but the claim of God that stood behind the Old Testament commandments. This claim was summarized illustratively in the love command; it was developed illustratively in the Decalogue, but it was never identical to a sum of ordinances. James developed his own parenesis therefore, not as interpretation of these commandments, but as illustrative restatements of this claim in acute focus upon the contemporary situation. The parenesis of the letter was a restatement of the "perfect law of liberty" and showed itself to be eschatologically compatible with Jesus.

d) Human judging according to the Law. 1) The neighbor and the Law. In a somewhat perplexing manner 4:11f. issued a warning against passing critical judgment upon one's neighbor and based it on a reference to the Law. "Do not speak evil against one another, brethren. He that speaks evil against a brother or judges his brother, speaks evil against the law and judges the law. But if you judge the law, you are not a doer of the law but a judge." To judge here meant, as in Mt. 7:1ff., to pass judgment and to condemn the conduct of the other person. How was it possible for this passing of judgment upon the other person to become a passing of judgment upon the Law? This becomes clear by holding up for contrast the Pharisaic manner of judging according to the Law.

The Pharisee considered himself obligated to measure and to judge the other person and himself regularly by the standards of the Law. For as long as the Law was a sum of statistical ordinances, the conduct of man could and should be judged by these ordinances. According to James' understanding of the Law, however, precisely this was not possible. For James the Law was not an objectively prescribed norm, as it was for the Pharisee, but the will of God that was written in the heart of the other person. It guided the other person in a special way through his conscience; it commanded the other person in a special way in every situation.

If the Law was this will of God that commanded each individual in the present from within, then Rom. 14:4 would have viable application here. "Who are you to pass judgment on the servant of another? It is before his own master that he stands or falls." In the specific terminology of James it would state that whoever

---

[22]Contra H. Windisch, *Der Jakobusbrief*, at this location.

judged another judged the Law that directed him. Passing of judgment on another became, therefore, a passing of judgment on the Law itself.

2) The Last Judgment and the Law. No less instructive for the character and content of the Law was Jas. 2:12f.: "So speak and so act as those who are to be judged under the law of liberty. For judgment is without mercy to one who has shown no mercy; yet mercy triumphs over judgment." This statement appeared to stand in contradiction to the entire New Testament; there was complete agreement from Lk. 12:8 and Rom. 5:9f. to Rev. 20:12f. that in the Last Judgment salvation was to be expected not through the Law but alone through Christ. But James too directed his hearers' attention not to a judgment according to the Mosaic Law, but according to the Law of liberty.

Whoever expected judgment according to the Law of liberty expected mercy for the merciful. This understanding of the goal formulated characteristically in the indicative becomes clear as soon as one recognizes that the expectation of mercy and one's own showing of mercy belonged together. Precisely this connection was developed in Matthew's Gospel; there the merciful were pronounced blessed (Mt. 5:7) and from the unfaithful servant, who refused to show his neighbor mercy, grace was withdrawn (Mt. 18:33). Here a twofold connection was operative. Whoever was not merciful toward his neighbor could expect no mercy; but, on the other hand, whoever lived entirely on the expectation of mercy would show mercy to his neighbor.

Thus also, according to Jas. 2:12f., the Law was the "law of liberty" because that Law itself accomplished the obedience it required. It was the imperatival side of the word that contained the pronouncement of blessing upon the merciful! It was of course characteristic for our letter that it concealed this promise under the imperative.

e) Summary. The peculiar usage of the term "Law" in the Epistle of James gave an indication of its perspective as a whole. It belonged to the peculiarity of the letter that it brought out the demanding side of the gospel one-sidedly and referred to it with the term "Law." The parenesis of the letter was a restatement of this Law. It intended to develop the royal and perfect Law of liberty; that is, it did not wish to give casuistically applicable ordinances, but examples that were to be appropriated by the individual in concrete settings of personal activity. Such appropriation was to occur for each one on the basis of faith in terms of his own responsibility as measured by what the situation called for. The Law James had in mind was thus neither the Law in the Jewish sense, nor that in the early catholic sense. It was the imperative of the gospel that corresponded to the indicative.

What was the reason behind the letter's one-sided emphasis on this side of the gospel? For a reply to this question one can make reference to the tradition in which the letter stood. It belonged to a stream of early Christian tradition that stretched from Matthew's Gospel to the Didache and further to the regulations of the Syrian church. In this Syrian-Palestinian tradition one tried to restate what it meant to be a Christian through regulations for living and thus to portray it in empirical terms. This way of doing things stood in tension with the conventional parenesis in the Pauline realm. Apparently, James and similarly Matthew (§46,5) did not expect to receive any help for their community situation from the Pauline way of doing things. Indeed, that which circulated from Paul among the Syrian-Palestinian communities appeared to them, instead, to recommend a break with that tradition (cf. Jas. 2:14-26; Mt. 5:17-19).

3. FAITH AND WORKS—THE PROGRAM OF A THEOLOGY OF EMPIRICISM

In the well-known section about faith and works (Jas. 2:14-26) the letter reached its theological peak. The theme addressed here is relevant for us for various reasons. For one thing because here Paul and thereby the unity of the canon was in question; for another because the letter was attacked by Luther and the Reformation tradition on account of these statements; and most of all because this theme has stirred renewed interest in the current theological discussion.

a) The line of argumentation in Jas. 2:14-26. 1) The section represented the thesis that it advanced in the form of a question. "What does it profit, my brethren, if a man says he has faith but has not works? Can his faith save him?" (2:14). The thesis ran: Faith without works cannot save.

2) The thesis was then furnished with a foundation in vv. 15-20 through two negative arguments. Vv. 15-17 stated that faith without works was just as empty as love of neighbor that expressed itself in words void of commitment. Vv. 18f. stated that the summons to faith alone—and that meant for James to faith without works—was empty since it had nothing to show and came near to a demonic possibility (v. 19b).

3) Then followed in vv. 20-25 two positive arguments that could be traced back to an early Christian interpretive tradition of the Old Testament. The faith of Abraham was brought to its goal through his work, i.e., his preparedness to sacrifice Isaac (vv. 21-24); Rahab too was justified in terms of works (v. 25).[23] Thus scripture promised salvation only to faith coupled with works.

b) The object of opposition for James. 1) Did James oppose Paul? It appears at first glance that James was directing polemic against the central Pauline statements of Rom. 3:28, Gal. 2:16, and Rom. 9:32 when he drew the conclusion: "You see that a man is justified by works and not by faith alone" (Jas. 2:24). This impression receives added support when one notes that James developed his thesis in 2:21ff. polemically in terms of an exegesis of Gen. 15:6, the word about Abraham's faith, which Paul had claimed for support in Rom. 4 and Gal. 3.

But this impression is a deception. The principle expressed in Rom. 3:28 was worded differently than the slogan contested by James. Rom. 3:28 proclaimed justification through faith "without the works of the Law" (*pistei chōris ergōn*

---

[23]The "alone" (*monon*) is found, by the way, only in James; it is missing in Rom. 3:28; 9:32; Gal. 2:16 (cf. §38,1c).

nomou), but not through faith "without works!" The polemic of James, there-fore, was not directed at the thesis of Paul, but at a slogan derived from it.

2) James was not being confronted with a heretical theory but a practical posture, a Christianity for which God and justification by faith alone had become metaphysical theories. People were so convinced of these theories that they no longer had any impact on conduct. Such a Christianity of conviction can come about in a variety of contexts. It can be a lifeless orthodoxy that suffocates in intellectualism; it can also be a middle-class Christian liberalism that lives in conformity with the world and turns grace into cheap grace. Seen within the context of compositional circumstances for the Epistle of James, it was a typical problem of the second generation; moreover, for the rational tradition out of which James came it was foreign and surprising.

The polemic of James against this problem found its closest New Testament counterpart in Matthew, who extended redactionally such a saying as that found in Luke 6:46 to the statement: "Not every one who says to me, 'Lord, Lord,' shall enter the kingdom of heaven, but he who does the will of my Father" (Mt. 7:21); and Matthew supplemented the Parable of the Royal Wedding with the question about the wedding garment (Mt. 22:11ff.).

c) James and Paul. If one compares James to Paul one must first try to ascertain the real differences.

1) James turned his attention to a different addressee when he directed polemic at a flagging Christianity of habit. In contrast, Paul struggled in Rom. 3 with a Jewish and in Gal. 3 with a Judaizing path to righteousness by the Law. Paul spoke with a view toward people who clung to the pre-Christian path of the Law; James with a view toward the flagging of Christian faith.

2) James made use of different terminology. The terminological difference has been reduced on occasion to the formula that James spoke jewishly about faith and christianly about works, Paul the other way around. This formula is appropriate to a certain extent as regards works, but not faith. The difference is better put as follows: for Paul faith was the function of its content. Man had faith precisely to the degree that he allowed himself to be determined by God through Christ. Faith was *creatura verbi*, a creation of the word (II Cor. 4:4, 6). Because faith was the function of its content, it was at work in love by the power of its content (Gal. 5:6). It only existed as *hypakoē pisteōs* (the obedience of faith, Rom. 1:5). What James called "works" was called therefore in Paul "the fruits of righteousness" or "the fruit of the Spirit" (Phil. 1:11; Gal. 5:22; cf. also Rom. 6:22). On occasion, he could also refer to this fruit as work (Col. 1:10); yet in general he used the term *ergon* in a theologically precise manner for the act of obedience that the Mosaic Law demanded.

For James faith was not a work alongside other works, as in rabbinic theology, but the foundation of Christian existence. For James too Christians were the believing ones (Jas. 1:3; 2:1, 5). Faith was not a work but it demonstrated itself in the work (1:3f.; 2:1, 18). Thus for James faith was the foundation quite in keeping with the common primitive-Christian sense. In contrast to Paul, however, James did not understand faith in terms of its content, but purely phenomenologically-empirically as a physical posture, as the act of believing. Hence he also had to demand so laboriously that this physical posture be combined with a corresponding conduct, "works." And finally as far as the different usage of the term "work" is concerned, it may be said that for Paul a "work" was what the Law demanded, while James understood by the term "work" what Paul called fruit of the Spirit. James did not at all speak about "works" in the sense of the Mosaic Law.

3) The recognition of these terminological differences supplies the direction one should go in characterizing the substantive-theological relationship between James and Paul. The decisive question is whether Paul could say about the fruits of righteousness what James said about works. Paul would have agreed with James in negation. Most certainly would a faith that did not work itself out in a corresponding conduct not count toward righteousness (I Cor. 6:9; 10:5-13). Of course, Paul would not designate this breakdown of obedience as faith without works; rather he would ask if faith were present at all where obedience was absent (II Cor. 13:5). He would not have demanded that works be added to faith, but that faith be brought to life. That, however, is not just a terminological difference!

Would Paul have been able to agree substantively as well with what James said positively about justification in his surprising terminology? How would he have responded to statements like Jas. 1:25 ("But he who looks into the perfect law, the law of liberty, and perseveres . . . he shall be blessed in his doing"), 2:22 and 24 ("a man is justified by works")? These statements were not, as we saw above, an intellectual doctrine of justification that required the keeping of accounts on one's conduct, but were a parenetic promise that summoned one to a demonstration of faith. It was no doubt far from James' intent that one should wish to calculate the result of the Last Judgment on the basis of works. Hardly any other document of the New Testament taught with greater emphasis than the Epistle of James that Christians also sinned much daily, "for we all make many mistakes" (3:2). And Jas. 5:16 admonished: "Therefore confess your sins to one another!" Thus James expected in judgment not a settling of accounts but mercy (2:12f.). But even when one considers this overall intention it still must be said that Paul would not speak this way when expressing parenetic promise. True, he also promised recognition of good deeds (I Cor. 3:14f.; II Cor. 5:10), but he never made the decision in the Last Judgment dependent upon the conduct of faith but alone upon faith's content, namely, Christ (Rom. 5:9f.). The assertive parenesis of James would destroy the certainty of salvation for Paul.

4) The intrinsic difference between Paul and James, however, becomes clear when we ask what actually prompted James to demand Christian conduct in this way. We come upon a difference of ways of looking at and expressing things that requires serious attention.

Paul spoke about Christian existence as it was established creatively by God's saving activity. For Paul's manner of speech the great indicatives that expressed what had been established by God were characteristic. James, on the other hand, described Christian existence analytically as to what it should look like empirically in the psyche and in the conduct of man. A different way of speaking corresponded to this different way of looking at things. Paul spoke kerygmatically; James, however, spoke psychologically-objectively. He attempted to describe phenomenologically-psychologically what a Christian posture should look like empirically.

5) It is easy to see what this way of putting things accomplished positively. The address of the Epistle of James was forthrightly concrete. It exposed a Christianity of appearances that lived in empty words and quietistic concepts. It pressed hard with the help of bold examples for the demonstration of faith, for an appropriate Christian conduct. If one acknowledges this, then one must also take note of the limitations of this manner of expressing things. The parenesis of James became a preliminary stage of the early catholic attempt to achieve through a psychological pedagogy that which only the proclamation that creatively transformed man could bring into being. In the final analysis, being a Christian can never be described as a form of living; one must have trust in the word from Christ that produces Christian existence, to be sure, trust only in the evident and concrete word. James knew that basically too; this became clear finally in his astonishing word about the judging of the Law (4:11f.). Thus, in spite of the empirical focus of his parenesis, James belonged quite justifiably to the New Testament.

§46. The Interpretation of Jesus' Life and Ministry through Matthew

E. von Dobschütz, "Matthäus als Rabbi und Katechet," *ZNW* 27 (1928), 338-348; A. Schlatter, *Die Kirche des Matthäus* (1929); G. D. Kilpatrick, *The Origins of the Gospel according to St. Matthew* (1950); C. H. Dodd, "Matthew and Paul," *NTS* 1 (1953/54), 53-66; K. Stendahl, *The School of St. Matthew* (1954); P. Nepper-Christensen, *Das Matthäusevangelium—ein judenchristliches Evangelium* (1958); G. Bornkamm— G. Barth—H.-J. Held, *Tradition and Interpretation in Matthew* (1963); J. Gnilka, "Die Kirche des Matthäus und die Gemeinde von Qumran," *BZ* NF 7 (1963), 43-64; R. Hummel, *Die Auseinandersetzung zwischen Kirche und Judentum im Matthäus-Evangelium* (1963); W. Trilling, *Das wahre Israel. Studien zur Theologie des Matthäus-Evangeliums* (1964[3]); G. Strecker, *Der Weg der Gerechtigkeit. Untersuchungen zur Theologie des Matthäus* (1971[3]); G. Baumbach, "Die Mission im Matthäus-Evangelium," *ThLZ* 92 (1967), 889-893; R. Walker, *Die Heilsgeschichte im ersten Evangelium* (1967); N. Walter, "Die Bearbeitung der Seligpreisungen durch Matthäus," *StEv* 4 (1968), 246-258; J. D. Kingsbury, *The Parables of Jesus in Matthew 13* (1969); W. G. Thompson, *Matthew's Advice to a Divided Community. Mt. 17,22–18,35* (1970); M. J. Suggs, *Wisdom Christology and Law in Matthew's Gospel* (1970); B. J. Malina, "The Literary Structure and Form of Matt. XXVIII.16-20," *NTS* 17 (1970/71), 87-103; U. Luz, "Die Junger im Matthäusevangelium," *ZNW* 62 (1971), 141-171; A. Vögtle, "Das christologische und ekklesiologische Anliegen von Mt 28,18-20," in Vögtle, *Das Evangelium und die Evangelien* (1971), pp. 253-272; W. Trilling, "Matthäus, das kirchliche Evangelium—Überlieferungsgeschichte und Theologie," in *Gestalt und Anspruch* (ed. J. Schreiner [1969]), pp. 186-199; C. Burger, "Jesu Taten nach Matthäus 8 und 9," *ZThK* 70 (1973), 272-287;

H. Frankemölle, "Amtskritik im Matthäus-Evangelium?", *Biblica* 54 (1973), 247-262; Frankemölle, *Jahwebund und Kirche Christi. Studien zur Form- und Traditionsgeschichte des "Evangeliums" nach Mätthaus* (Neutestamentliche Abhandlungen 10 [1974]); J. Lange, *Das Erscheinen des Auferstandenen im Evangelium nach Matthäus. Eine traditions- und redaktionsgeschichtliche Untersuchung zu Mt 28,16-20* (1973); J. D. Kingsbury, "The Structure of Matthew's Gospel and its Concept of Salvation History," *Catholic Biblical Quarterly* 35 (1973), 451-474; Kingsbury, "The Composition and Christology of Matt 28:16-20," *JBL* 93 (1974), 573-584. **Important Commentaries**: P. Bonnard (1963), Commentaire du Nouveau Testament; F. V. Filson (1960), Black's NT Commentaries; W. Grundmann (1968), ThHK; E. Klostermann (1971⁴), HNT; E. Lohmeyer, *Das Evangelium des Matthäus*, ed. W. Schmauch (1956), KEK (special volume); A. Schlatter (1959⁵); J. Schmid, *Das Evangelium nach Matthäus* (1959), Regensburger NT; J. Schniewind (1962¹⁰), NTD; E. Schweizer, *The Good News According to Matthew* (1975). **On 4a**: R. H. Gundry, *The Use of the Old Testament in St. Matthew's Gospel with Special Reference to the Messianic Hope* (1967); W. Rothfuchs, *Die Erfüllungszitate des Matthäusevangeliums* (1969); R. S. McConnell, *Law and Prophecy in Matthew's Gospel. The Authority and Use of the Old Testament in the Gospel of St. Matthew* (1969); M. D. Goulder, *Midrash and Lection in Matthew* (1974). **On 5**: W. D. Davies, "Matthew V.18," in *Mélanges Bibliques rédigés en l'honneur de André Robert* (1957), pp. 428-456; Davies, *The Setting of the Sermon on the Mount* (1964); R. A. Guelich, *"Not to Annul the Law Rather to Fulfill the Law and the Prophets"; an Exegetical Study of Jesus and the Law in Matthew with Emphasis on 5:17-48* (Diss. Hamburg [1967; pub. in prep.]). **On 6**: W. Pesch, "Die sogenannte Gemeindeordnung Mt 18," *BZ* NF 7 (1963), 220-235; K. Tagawa, "People and Community in the Gospel of Matthew," *NTS* 16 (1969/70), 149-162; E. Schweizer, *Matthäus und seine Gemeinde* (1974).

In the following section we shall set forth and summarize the kerygmatic-theological substance of the redactional achievement of the Gospel of Matthew.

In each of our Gospels three layers of material were woven together: (1) The image of Jesus as it was seen by his disciples, (2) the shaping of this image through the witnesses who related it and through the further transmission of that report, and (3) the redactional reworking of the tradition by the evangelists for their community situation. We shall concern ourselves here exclusively with the third layer.

What belonged to redactional material can be ascertained only by exegetical investigation. We shall begin with the material that clearly shows itself to be the redactional achievement of Matthew; it shows itself to be such through comparison with the other Gospels and through its terminological and substantive particularity.

1. THE SITUATION

Here a necessary differentiation is in order. The redaction-historical line of questioning needs to ask about the context out of which the document emerged and the situation for which it was written. Between the two lines of questioning there exists a difference that has been observed too little in the past. Precisely for the Gospel of Matthew it is, in fact, the case that the context from which its tradition stemmed was not straightway identical to the situation for which it was written!

a) The origin of the Matthean tradition. 1) The Gospel of Matthew presented pieces of tradition in its special source material that could be passed on only in the early Palestinian church because they had meaning for it only and actually were understood by it only. Thus, clearly reflected in the sayings about persecution (Mt. 10:17-23) was the fate of Christianity in Palestine when they spoke about the disciples' being delivered over to "their councils" (*synedria*, intended were the courts of the synagogues) and about their flight from the "cities of Israel"; the same can be said for the directive concerning the temple tax (Mt. 17:24-27).

2) But this was no longer the situation for which Matthew wrote. Rather, this was a time that for Matthew had already passed. According to Mt. 22:7, the king burned down the "city of the murderers," indignant over the treatment of his servants. This gospel was therefore written after the destruction of Jerusalem, but the new situation between the church and the synagogue was still being delineated; this was the situation that arose through the measures taken by the Council of Jamnia after A.D. 80. The Palestinian situation clearly stood behind these Palestinian special sources and was reflected in them. The community of Matthew did not pay temple tax any longer since the temple did not exist anymore. It would be just as incorrect to conclude from the sayings about persecution that the community of Matthew was still associated with the synagogue. It becomes fundamentally clear that the evangelist passed on traditions that were not referring to his community situation.

How is this phenomenon to be explained? In the opinion of the evangelist these statements referring to Palestine, which we ascribe today through history-of-tradition analyses to the situation of the Palestinian church, belonged to the Palestinian circumstances of Jesus. He wrote, therefore, fully aware that there was a historical distance to be reckoned with. He intended primarily to portray the preceding history of Jesus and then in turn to make clear how it was related to his community situation.

b) The situational goal. 1) The situation toward which the evangelist wished to direct his audience becomes fundamentally clear in the concluding verses of his Gospel, in the directive of the resurrected and exalted One: "Go therefore and make disciples of all nations!" (28:19). This Gospel was written with the universal church made up of Jews and Gentiles in mind. The time was past for which the directive of Mt. 10:5f. was originally intended: "Go nowhere among the Gentiles, and enter no town of the Samaritans, but go rather to the lost sheep of the house of Israel."

2) The universal church to which Matthew turned his attention was to be found according to many indicators within the geographical setting of Syria. The linguistic presuppositions already point one in that direction. The evangelist assumed that his readers were familiar with the language and customs of Palestinian Judaism; outside of Palestine itself this could only be presupposed in

Syria. The first traces of the use of Matthean tradition were also to be found there in the Didache and in the writings of Ignatius; there the conditions were also right for the intensive debate that the evangelist conducted with Judaism. It can therefore also be assumed—as many scholars agree—that this Gospel was written for a community of faith in Syria. Whether or not it should be sought in Antioch or in one of the Phoenician coastal cities can of course no longer be ascertained.

2. THE KERYGMATIC GOAL IN THE JUDGMENT OF SCHOLARLY RESEARCH

An impressive preliminary stage of the contemporary redaction-critical investigation of the Gospel was already available in 1910. A. Schlatter characterized in a section of his *Theologie der Apostel* the way in which Matthew shaped the account of Jesus for his community;[1] he reconstructed the community situation in his monograph *Die Kirche des Matthäus* (1929); this work of Schlatter was then later carried on in very detailed fashion by G. D. Kilpatrick (Lit., §46). In polar correspondence to Schlatter's writings H. J. Holtzmann characterized the Gospel as "good catholic" (we would say today, "early catholic").[2] The evangelist combined—thought Holtzmann—conflicting traditions into the catholic synthesis; thus he emphasized on the one hand that no iota of the Law should pass away (5:18) in order that he might then present the antitheses of Jesus that removed the Old Testament verbal expression of the commandments (5:21ff.). In the first instance, thought Holtzmann, Matthew accommodated the conservative Jewish-Christian, and in the second the freedom-oriented one.

After a long intermission filled with the work of form-critical research, Holtzmann's approach was taken up again when the Bultmann school turned to the redaction-critical line of questioning after 1950. In a collection of articles published in 1960, G. Bornkamm, together with his students G. Barth and H. J. Held, committed Matthew to the nomistic Jewish-Christian line.[3] In this view, the evangelist did not harmonize Mt. 5:18 and the antitheses—to remain by the previous example—but considered the antitheses to be interpretations of the Law! Bornkamm arrived at this one-sided view because he remained entirely obligated to the conceptual approach of classical form criticism. He thought that the statements of the evangelist had to have reflected directly his community situation and thus posited the thesis that Matthew's community still lived in association with the synagogue and still paid temple tax.[4]

It signaled a turning point in the Bultmann school when G. Strecker distanced himself thoroughly from this approach and stated as the scope of his book *Der Weg der Gerechtigkeit* (1962) that Matthew was thinking historically and not

---

[1] A. Schlatter, *Theologie* II, 16-38.
[2] *Theologie* I, 457-515, esp. 514.
[3] Op. cit. (Lit. §46), esp. pp. 153-164.
[4] Ibid., p. 20.

directly existentially; he differentiated, moreover, between the time of Jesus and the time of the church as he historicized the Jesus tradition. Of course, for Strecker this did not mean that the time of Jesus was simply a bygone epoch reflected in its distance from the ecclesiastical present of Matthew. Rather, "eschatological significance"[5] adapted itself to this present of Matthew through Jesus' eschatological demand and its exemplary fulfillment through him. Both aspects qualified the time of Jesus as belonging to salvation history.

This historicizing way of looking at Matthew was continued in a one-sided overstatement by R. Walker. His programmatic thesis stated: "The entire portrayal of Jesus' debate with Israel stood within a salvation-historical dimension; it was (kerygmatic) historiography, not the mirror of current controversies of the church with Israel."[6]

Equally as important in terms of the history of research was the antithesis to G. Strecker constituted by the independent study of the Roman Catholic exegete from Leipzig, W. Trilling, *Das wahre Israel*. Where Strecker maintained that the church represented only the eschatological demand and accordingly the kingdom of God, Trilling thought that messianic salvation was present in the church and thereby the situation of the world was altered in a saving way. Trilling's interpretation was in many ways more accurate than that of Strecker, although it took Matthew somewhat too far into the proximity of early catholicism.

3. THE SALVATION-HISTORICAL DESIGN

a) For Matthew the time of Jesus was the time of his encounter with Israel. Jesus' encounter with Israel did not stand beneath the heading "first to the Jews and then to the Greeks" as it did for Luke (§48,2); rather, for Matthew it stood beneath the watchword: to Israel alone in order to fulfill the scriptures (Mt. 15:24)! In the exclusive encounter of Jesus with Israel, Israel's history came to an end and God's plan of salvation reached its goal. In contrast to Luke, Matthew did not represent Jesus' life and ministry as a progression of events in time and space and as an epoch of a history divided into periods, but as a time uniquely qualified through prophecy.

b) Just exactly how this unique course of Jesus' life was connected fundamentally to the time of the community was expressed by the conclusion of the Gospel (Mt. 28:18f.). It constituted the key to understanding the whole Gospel. This word of the resurrected One expressed two things:
1) "All authority . . . has been given to me. Go therefore and make disciples

---

[5]Op. cit. (Lit., §46), p. 185.
[6]*Die Heilsgeschichte im ersten Evangelium* (1967), p. 9. This is the same one-sidedness as in G. Bornkamm, only directed at the other side; Matthew described—so Walker—only the past controversy, but not the present one. In truth, the evangelist combined both together: the past debate of Jesus with Israel and the apologetic-missionary debate with the Jews in his present. In addition to this, the work of R. Walker is not as reliable, in terms of research, as that of G. Strecker; the same is even more so the case for the work of R. Hummel (op. cit. [Lit., §46]), which stands in the proximity of G. Bornkamm.

of all nations. . . ." That meant that Jesus would not become the Teacher of the nations when they accepted the teachings of the earthly One like those of a rabbi, but when they turned to the resurrected and exalted One in person. After Jesus' exit discipleship was just as much being connected to Jesus' person as it was during his earthly ministry; it was not merely the acceptance of his teachings. Jesus' earthly ministry continued only on the basis of his resurrection and exaltation.

2) The word stated: "Make disciples of all nations, baptizing them in the name of the Father and of the Son and of the Holy Spirit, teaching them to observe all that I have commanded you!" Jesus' commandment—above all in the Sermon on the Mount—was to become, therefore, baptismal parenesis. Baptism, however, assumed the place in point of fact that had been occupied by Jesus' gracious turning of himself to the individual. This turning had won over the individual in discipleship and faith, and it was the image of this turning that Matthew drew in 8:1–9:34. Jesus' ministry was portrayed in the Gospel in terms of the new mediation through baptism and baptismal parenesis.

c) This portrayal was the connection to the community situation in two ways.

1) Matthew shaped Jesus' encounter with Israel with an eye toward an apologetic-missionary debate with Judaism. In this way the Jesus tradition was both interpreted in terms of its original circumstances and therefore understood in its depth dimension as in no other Gospel.

2) In all that which was presented as apologetics from the perspective of this compositional decision, the intention was embedded, nevertheless, to go beyond this to a theological understanding of Jesus' life and ministry so that the community could be told who its Lord was. The interplay of these two lines of thought becomes clear in particular when we represent more exactly in what follows the three theological themes characteristic for Matthew. They were the Messiahship of Jesus, the fulfillment of the Law through the command of Jesus, and the replacement of Israel by the church.

4. THE MESSIAHSHIP OF JESUS

It is by no means saying too much when one states that Matthew has shown the church throughout the centuries how it could understand Jesus as the Messiah of the Old Testament. It was Matthew, not Paul, who provided it with the key for the interpretation of Jesus' Messiahship, especially by means of his scriptural evidences.

a) The scriptural evidence. 1) Survey. No Gospel and certainly no other writing of the New Testament pointed so stereotypically to the fulfillment of Old Testament prophecies through Jesus' life and ministry as did the Gospel of Matthew. Not only did Matthew appropriate all the references direct and indirect to the Old Testament that were available to him in his sources Mark and Q, but he also supplemented them through a considerable number of his own supporting references, especially through the eleven so-called proof-from-prophecy quotations (*Reflexionszitate*).

Although the proof-from-prophecy quotations can be regarded correctly as especially characteristic for Matthew, it is doubtful that he formulated them himself. While the evangelist followed the LXX generally in regard to the other quotations, both those introduced by him and those coming from Mark and Q, the proof-from-prophecy quotations belonged in the main to another text-type that had greater affinities with the Masoretic text.[7] How is this difference to be understood? It has been assumed frequently that Matthew took over these proof-from-prophecy quotations from a collection of testimonia put together in the Palestinian church for the missionary-apologetic debate with the Jews. K. Stendahl conjectured, moreover, that they were developed in a school of Christian scribal learning from which Matthew, who designated himself as a scribe taught in the dominion of heaven, had come.[8]

While the issue of how the evangelist is to be related to the content of the quotations remains uncertain, the formulas of introduction definitely stemmed from him. They contained expressions quite typical for Matthew. Frequently they run: "This took place to fulfill (*hina plērōthē*) what the Lord had spoken (*ho rhētheis* or *to rhēten*). . . ."[9] What was Matthew intending to make people aware of through these extensive and expressly reflected pointers to the fulfillment of scripture through Jesus? The fulfillment aspect as such was connected with the Jesus tradition from the very beginning; it already was a part of the primitive kerygma in I Cor. 15:3-5. What special contribution was the Matthean scriptural evidence supposed to make?

2) The apologetic purpose. To be sure, Matthew wished to prove that certain prominent data of Jesus' course of life were prophesied. An especially conspicuous example of his intention was the reworking of the account of Jesus' entering Jerusalem, Mt. 21:1-9. In 21:5, Matthew inserted in relationship to the parallel section in Mk. 11:1-11 the proof-from-prophecy quotation out of Zech. 9:9 and then enlarged his text accordingly to achieve verbatim agreement by means of a second animal of burden (21:2, 7): "they brought the ass and the colt . . . and he sat thereon."[10] Also in 4:15f. and 27:9 narrational material was adapted to fit the particular quotation.

What kind of data from Jesus' course of life were those that Matthew wished to prove additionally as prophesied in this virtually calculable way? We find proof-from-prophecy quotations for the virgin birth (1:23), the birthplace of

---

[7]Individual support in Strecker, op. cit. (n. 5), pp. 21-29.

[8]Op. cit. (Lit., §46), pp. 194ff.

[9]*plēroun* ("to fulfill") was a typical term for Matthew. It is found sixteen times in his Gospel, while in Mark only twice and in Luke nine times. Even the expression *to rhēthen* ("that which was spoken" or "as it was said") was typically Matthean (1:22; 2:15, 17; 4:14; 8:17; 12:17; 13:35; 21:4; 22:31; 27:9). Thus the introductory formula of the proof-from-prophecy quotations and thereby the emphasized interpretation of history through the reference to fulfillment came in any case from Matthew.

[10]Zech. 9:9 was held in synthetic parallelism and spoke only of one beast of burden in both halves of the verse.

Bethlehem (2:6), the flight into Egypt (2:15), the murder of the children in Bethlehem (2:18), the surname of "Nazarene" (i.e., man from Nazareth) given him by the Jews (2:23), and the assuming of public ministry in remote Galilee (4:15f.). Then they were also used for Jesus' healings (8:17), as well as for his warning not to tell anyone else about them (12:18-21), for supporting references for his concealing speech in parables (13:35), as well as finally for the humble entry into Jerusalem (21:5) and the payment to Judas (27:9f.). The occurrences mentioned here have their common ground, no doubt, in that they were controversial matters in the conversation between the church and Judaism! Because of these matters the Jews rejected the Messiahship of Jesus and defamed him. According to Jewish polemic Jesus was an illegitimate child and had learned magic while in Egypt; his coming from Nazareth made every messianic claim impossible. The same was true for the concentration of his ministry in the area of Galilee, the humbleness of this ministry, and his concluding betrayal by his own disciple.[11]

Hence the proof-from-prophecy quotations were prompted by apologetic vis-à-vis Judaism. The degree to which Matthew was influenced by the apologetic battlefront against Judaism showed itself conspicuously in his narrative about the grave guards (27:62-66; 28:4, 11-15); it was not intended to demonstrate the facticity of the resurrection, but to negate the Jewish explanation for the empty tomb by a manipulative act of the disciples. Matthew's scriptural evidences were also, as long as they were apologetic, of a decidedly more defensive nature than they were of a demonstrative one. It was not Matthew's intent to produce by means of rationally calculable evidence from scripture, as it were, the historical or historical-philosophical demonstration of truth for Christianity; that would be attempted later by the apologist Justin Martyr.[12]

3) Salvation-historical understanding. If the proof-from-prophecy quotations were to have had a positive value beyond defensive apologetics, then it was that of opening up for the community a salvation-historical understanding. If one listens to them within their substantive context it can be seen that they pointed not only toward individual historical data but also toward the essential characteristics of the ministry of Jesus as Matthew saw them prophesied for the Messiah in the Old Testament. And in this sense the evangelist heard them and wished to bring them into the hearing of his community. He wanted—to anticipate it as thesis—to say to this community: Jesus was the promised One because he was the humbled and the compassionate One who came for the humbled and compassionate ones!

That the evangelist sought for himself and his community such a salvation-historical understanding of the substance of Jesus' life through references to

---

[11]Cf J. Klausner, *Jesus of Nazareth* (1929), pp. 17-127; H. L. Strack, *Jesus, die Häretiker und die Christen nach den ältesten jüdischen Angaben* (1910).

[12]Justin Martyr wanted to prove the truth of Christianity, as it were, in a historical-philosophical way through rationally calculable evidence from scripture. He explained in dialogue with Trypho the Jew (*Dial*. 28:2): "Since I bring forth from the Scriptures and the facts themselves both the proofs and the inculcation of them, do not delay or hesitate to put faith in me . . ." (= ANF, *Justin Martyr*, I, 208); cf. on this, L. Goppelt, *Christentum und Judentum*, pp. 286-301 (esp. pp. 286f., 296).

scripture becomes clear when one considers the two passages where he himself made pointed use of Hos. 6:6 (Mt. 9:13; 12:7). At two key junctures in Jesus' ministry, Matthew placed on his lips the prophetic word from God, "I desire mercy, and not sacrifice!" Matthew wanted to mark the fundamental principle that guided Jesus' action when he granted those following him in discipleship the freedom to break the sabbath in his service in order to quiet their hunger (12:1-8); the same was the case when he granted his fellowship to sinners that they might recover their health (9:9-13). Thus, in both cases the transgression of the Law as demand and order of salvation was justified as a demonstration of the compassion that God was seeking in the first place.

Accordingly, the proof-from-prophecy quotation in the narrative of Jesus' entry into Jerusalem (21:5) also sought not merely to point out the two animals of burden, but to designate Jesus in this decisive moment as the *praus*, the humbled One, who was precisely as such the promised One. What was demonstrated at the entry to Jerusalem in accord with scripture was not a calculable external event, but a basic element of Jesus' ministry! According to this in-depth salvation-historical interpretation Jesus was precisely not the promised One because he fulfilled individual predictions, but because he brought to reality the intrinsic intention of God for man. He was the promised One because he was the humbled and compassionate One who took into his care those who were humbled and compassionate.

This can also be seen in terms of Matthew's linguistic usage. The adjective *praus* (Heb. *'anaw*, lowly, humble), which is found only in Matthew among the synoptic Gospels, characterized Jesus in the famous "Come unto me" saying (11:28f.) and in the proof-from-prophecy quotation about the entry into Jerusalem (21:5); it was used in reference to the people to whom he brought salvation in the Beatitude fashioned by Matthew himself in Mt. 5:5. To the humbled belonged also "the small ones" (*hoi mikroi*). Their accentuation Matthew took up in 18:6 from Mk. 9:42 in order then to intensify it in 18:10, 14; 10:42 (all Sp. Mt.). Corresponding to this emphasized reference to the oppressed humbled ones, who were in need of comfort, was the reference to the compassion that reached out to help. In the Gospel of Matthew there was a prominent use of words coming from the root *eleein* (mercy, compassion) in order to express that, on the one hand, Jesus himself acted as the compassionate One and that, on the other, he sought compassion in others. Hence the cry, "Have mercy on us, Son of David!" in Mt. 20:30 was appropriated from Mk. 10:49, and in 9:27 it was repeated together with the entire story of the healing of the blind man in order to fill out the image of Jesus' ministry of salvation in chs. 8 and 9. Twice (Mt. 9:13 and 12:7), as we saw, Hos. 6:6 was quoted: "I desire mercy, and not sacrifice!" As Jesus himself acted mercifully, so he sought those who were merciful. For them the word to the unfaithful servant in 18:32f. had meaning: ". . . should not you have had mercy on your fellow servant, as I had mercy on you?"

This image of Jesus as the humbled and compassionate One who accepted the humbled and the compassionate was furnished with scriptural support. The same intentions that the evangelist developed here were at work in his redaction of the messianic titles of honor.

b) Messianic predicates. 1) Jesus the Son of David for Israel. Matthew altered considerably the christological predicates that he found available to him in Mark and Q. Most conspicuous was his preference for the designation "Son of David." No other New Testament writing even came close to placing it in such prominent light as did Matthew.

The results of a word-statistical analysis produce the following picture: In Mark, and taken over from him in Luke, the title "Son of David" appeared only twice (Mk. 10:47f. par. Lk. 18:38f.; [Mt. 20:29-34]; Mk. 12:35ff. par. Lk. 20:41-44; [Mt. 22:41-46]). In contrast to this, the title appeared in seven passages in Matthew (1:1; 9:27; 12:23; 15:22; 20:29ff.; 21:9ff.; 22:41ff.) and not at all in the rest of the New Testament. Of the seven passages in Matthew, the two parallels to Mark excepted (20:29ff. par. Mk. 10:47f.; 22:41ff. par. Mk. 12:35ff.), all five were redactional. One might think initially that this preferred redactional expression, the title "Son of David," was suggested to Matthew through his Palestinian special source. All indications do in fact make probable that the title was used for Jesus in the Palestinian church. Hence the book of Revelation, appropriating Palestinian tradition, used the title in an apocalyptic image (Rev. 5:5; 22:16); the christological formula of Rom. 1:3 that also came out of Palestine (II Tim. 2:8 was an extension of this formula) made mention of the Davidic origin of Jesus too (§26,4).

This Palestinian tradition that continued to influence the liturgy of the Syrian church (Did. 10:6) may have prompted Matthew to make use of the title redactionally. Matthew did not intend, to be sure, by doing this to transport a designation for Christ from his community back into the circumstances of Jesus. We can see evidence for this claim in the fact that the predicate was not to be found in a single confessional formula of the Syrian church, but only in liturgical traditions. He made use of the designation in a historicizing way, i.e., in order to make a statement about the course of Jesus' earthly life.[13] Apparently, a certain apologetic interest was thereby also at work vis-à-vis Judaism. In rabbinic Judaism "Son of David" (*ben-dawid*) was actually the dominant designation for the Messiah. Matthew did not, however, simply transfer this Jewish expectation to Jesus. What he said about the Son of David was not what Judaism was expecting in regard to *ben-dawid*. When he combined the title on four occasions with miraculous healings (9:27; 12:23; 15:22; 20:30f.) he was expressing that the Son of David brought salvation's dawning as the compassionate One who helped the needy; he brought salvation's dawning for Israel. The Canaanite woman, who expressly acknowledged the sending of Jesus to Israel, called out to him, "O Lord, Son of David" (15:22). In the same way Jesus was greeted by

---

[13]Strecker, op. cit. (n. 5), pp. 118ff.

tne people of Jerusalem with the words: "Hosanna to the Son of David!" (21:9, 15).

Thus, apologetically the use of the designation expressed that Jesus was the promised Son of David, and that he was this in a different manner than Judaism expected and still expects. No one expected of *ben-dawid* that he would heal beggars. But Jesus came as the compassionately helping One, as the humbled One who was received by the humbled ones (21:9, 15). In this we observe again the positive salvation-historical statement that went beyond the apologetic motif. Inspired by Palestinian tradition, Matthew filled out the title from Old Testament prophecy seen from the perspective of Jesus' life and ministry. Understood like this, the title expressed Jesus' unique sending to Israel.

2) The invoking as *kyrios* by the disciples. In Matthew's Gospel the use of *kyrios* as address and as designation was broadened considerably in comparison to Mark and Q. The intention behind this broadening makes itself clear in the type of usage. Jesus was addressed as "Lord" by those seeking his help and especially by his disciples; this address was ascribed with such consistency to the disciples that other forms of address required by the tradition were replaced by it. In 20:33, e.g., we find *kyrie* instead of the *rabbouni* of Mk. 10:51.[14] Especially characteristic were the following passages. At the betrayal, Judas addressed Jesus as *rabbi* (26:25) while the disciples used *kyrie* (26:22). In the sayings about discipleship, 8:18-22, the scribe said *didaskale* (teacher), but the disciples said once again *kyrie* (8:19, 21).

Attempts have been made to explain this redactional activity of Matthew as the projection back into the earthly ministry of the address to the exalted One as *kyrios* practiced in the later community.[15] If one pays attention to the context and the tradition, however, a more differentiated process of development shows itself to have been the case. Matthew shaped the address *kyrie*, which in the tradition was used in relationship to the earthly Jesus (§34,2), into the language of the community; he did this in order that, in turn, he might fill with pointed content the invoking of the exalted One practiced in the community. Whoever invoked Jesus as Lord could expect the help in type if not in form from him that was patterned by his earthly ministry!

In a series of passages Matthew combined the address "Lord" with the invocation *eleēson* ("have mercy!" 9:27; 15:22; 17:15; 20:30f.) or *sōson* ("save!" 8:25; 14:30). Connected with the invocation was often a *proskynein*—a worshipful and not merely a respectful obeisance (8:2; 9:18; 15:25; 20:20); in 14:33 it followed the granting of the request. According to 4:9f., this *proskynein* belonged to the invoking of God. Hence Jesus was correctly understood in the invocation as *kyrie* when in him was seen the One who offered help in God's stead. Matthew also wanted thereby to bring his community to the place where it would associate with the worship-service invocation of the exalted One as Lord an image that was concretely shaped in terms of the earthly One.

---

[14]Further passages in ibid., pp. 123f.

[15]Thus ibid., p. 124: Hahn, *Titles*, pp. 81f.

3) Son of God as confession of the disciples. The designation "Son of God" was already used frequently with reference to Jesus in the Gospel of Mark. It was heard with the voice from heaven at Jesus' baptism and at his transfiguration (Mk. 1:11; 9:7) and with the defensive exclamation of the demons (Mk. 3:11; 5:7). Among human beings, however, only the centurion at the cross confessed Jesus as the Son of God (Mk. 15:39; cf. Mt. 27:54). Matthew took Mark's lead here and turned the title that had various interpretive possibilities in Mark into a pregnant confession of the disciples: "You are the Christ, the Son of the living God" (Mt. 16:16). The designation summarized what Jesus was on the basis of his work of salvation coming from God. The content of the designation was demonstrated, moreover, through the linguistic imagery of God as "Father" and Jesus as "Son."

4) Jesus the Son—God the Father. The title "Son of God" developed, as we saw, independently of this linguistic imagery, but it was nevertheless filled with content indirectly from it. Thus the central word of Mt. 11:27, which was appropriated from Q, stated: "All things have been delivered to me by my Father; and no one knows the Son except the Father, and no one knows the Father except the Son and anyone to whom the Son chooses to reveal him." Hence Jesus was the exclusive Revealer of God because he himself stood in a unique relationship to God. Through him God was not unveiled as the Father, but mediated, i.e., Jesus opened for the disciples access to God as the Father. Because he was Jesus' Father, he was their Father.

Matthew greatly intensified and multiplied the designation of God as Father in comparison to both Mark and Q. In Mark God was introduced as Father only three times; he was addressed as 'abba' (Father), a unique address of prayer (Mk. 14:36), then absolutely in the image "the Father—the Son" (Mk. 13:32), and finally in the expression "your heavenly Father" (Mk. 11:25 [26]). In Q, Jesus spoke, moreover, exclusively of God as "my Father" (Lk. 10:22 par. Mt. 11:27). While Luke added only three more references (Lk. 2:49; 22:29; 24:49), Matthew added thirty references of his own! In twelve of them Jesus spoke about God as the One who was exclusively his Father and therefore confirmed his ministry eschatologically as Judge (e.g., Mt. 7:21; 10:32f.; 18:10, 19, 35). In the remaining passages, of which the majority are found in the Sermon on the Mount, God was the Father of the disciples; he claimed their conduct and then rewarded it when it was directed completely toward him without self-righteousness (e.g., Mt. 5:48; 6:1, 4, 6).

5) The interpretation of the Son of man title. While Matthew gave prominence to the two christological designations "Lord" and "Son" because they apparently played a role in his community, he suppressed or limited interpretively the older title "Son of man" (§18,2).

Matthew interpreted the Son of man title in two ways. (1) He inserted it redactionally into the question that introduced the confession of Peter: "Who do men say that the Son of man is?" (16:13). The reply thereto ran: "You are the Christ, the Son of the living God" (16:16). Matthew still recognized, therefore, that Son of man was an honorific title. Only a short time later the Syrian bishop Ignatius stated that Jesus was the Son of man and the Son of God (Ign. Eph. 20:2) in order to represent the mistaken interpretation that endured into the 19th century that "Son of man" referred to Jesus' belonging to the genus man; it was thought then that standing antithetically over against this was his belonging to God expressed in the Son of God predicate. (2) Since for Matthew the Son of man was the "Christ, the Son of the living God," he could frequently replace the veiled Son of man predicate of the tradition with a statement of Jesus about himself; such statements characterized him openly as "the Christ." A typical example is the change in the first announcement of coming suffering. In Mk. 8:31 it ran: "And he began to teach them that the Son of man must suffer many things. . . ." Matthew, however, formulated this in 16:21: "From that time Jesus Christ began to show his disciples that he must go to Jerusalem and suffer many things. . . ."[16] Matthew understood correctly, therefore, that the announcement of coming suffering did not predict the fate of the prophet from Nazareth, but taught God's saving will regarding Jesus as the promised One, the *Christos* (§18,6). Accordingly, he clarified the veiled announcement in Mark accurately. In the same way, he replaced the title "Son of man" with the personal pronoun in 5:11 (par. Lk. 6:22 [Q]) and in 10:32 (par. Lk. 12:8 [Q]).[17]

It should be noted in addition that corresponding to this interpretive reshaping of the Son of man sayings was a general emphasis in Matthew on *egō*-sayings. In the Sermon on the Mount he formulated Jesus' saying against divorce (Lk. 16:18 [Q]) and the command to love one's enemy (Lk. 6:27-30 [Q]) as antitheses and introduced thereby with emphasis *egō*-sayings (Mt. 5:31f., 38f., 43f.): "You have heard that it was said . . . but I say to you." This I was the I of the One who spoke in God's stead, the I of the revealing One. Other *egō* or *kagō*-expressions typical for Matthew also had this same meaning: "And I tell you . . ." (16:18; 21:24; cf. also 10:32f.; 11:28); further, *plēn legō hymin* ("but I tell you"; 11:22, 24; 26:64); more remote, *palin de legō hymin* ("again I say to you"; 18:19; 19:24). In this way, the *amēn*-formula that went back originally to Jesus' own formulation was clarified; characteristically, Matthew also multiplied them redactionally (Mt. 5:18, 26; 8:10; 10:15; 11:11; 18:13 and passim vis-à-vis Q, and 19:23; 24:2 vis-à-vis Mark).

c) The overall image of the Messiahship of Jesus. The way in which Matthew designated Jesus as the promised One permits recognition of certain constant structural indices that can be assembled without difficulty into an overall image.

1) Nowhere were Jewish Messiah predicates and the messianic concepts associated with them simply transferred to Jesus. Jesus was not God's Son in the sense that was intended by the high priest at Jesus' interrogation (26:63), but in keeping with his witness to himself (11:27) and his actions (14:33). He fit no

---

[16]Goppelt followed here the 25th ed. of the Nestle Greek New Testament (Alsup).
[17]It is therefore incorrect when J. Jeremias, *Theology*, pp. 262-64, assumed that the personal pronoun was original.

better the "Son of David" image of the rabbis. Rather, the predicates were developed from the perspective of Jesus' life and ministry in a debate with the Jewish predicates; they were filled out, moreover, in terms of the Old Testament understood in a Christian way. Jesus was the promised One of the Old Testament who fulfilled Jewish expectations only antithetically.

2) On this common basis the individual predicates designated him in various ways.[18] As the Son of David he brought Israel's history to its goal. As the Son of God he was the ultimate revealer. As the Lord he was the helping protector of people. Just as deliberately as these predicates were given prominence, the older predicates of the Gospel tradition—Son of man and Christ—were suppressed.

3) The affirmation of the proof-from-prophecy quotations corresponded to the use of predicates. They characterized Jesus as the One who in lowliness was the messianic King from the line of David (2:6 and 21:5; cf. also 1:1-17). They introduced him as the Son of God who like Israel once before was called out of Egypt (2:15), but especially as the helping One (8:17; 12:18-21) of whom it was true: "Emmanuel, . . . God with us" (1:23).

4) Thus, a view of Messiahship was developed here through a Christian interpretation of the Old Testament; this view shaped the image of Jesus, the Messiah, throughout the centuries in the church. Matthew spoke for a new Christian scribal scholarship that developed a messianic understanding of the earthly ministry of Jesus.

5) In this way, Matthew advanced the Markan image of Jesus' Messiahship a decisive step further. In Mark, Jesus spoke and acted as the hidden Messiah whose ministry stood beneath the heading of the messianic secret. In Matthew, he spoke and acted as the Messiah made known to the reader, the One who was this precisely as the humbled and compassionate One. With this portrayal, however, Matthew did not transpose his Christ-image back into the earthly ministry; rather he interpreted the circumstances of Jesus with substantive consistency. He did not identify those circumstances with the situation of the community, but he did make possible and initiated their application to the community situation.

5. THE FULFILLMENT OF THE LAW

a) The problematic. In the saying found only in Matthew and probably even formulated by him[19] (Mt. 5:17), Jesus stated: "Think not that I have come to abolish the law and the prophets; I have come not to abolish but to fulfill them." In this sentence as well an apologetic defense was being voiced once again vis-à-vis Judaism and a Christianity that thought in its terms; yet here too the positive intent was there to represent Jesus as the One who accomplished fulfillment.

---

[18]One cannot conclude from that which was said, as Walker, op. cit. (n. 6), pp. 129ff. did, that all these predicates had the same content for Matthew. Naturally it was common to all of them that they characterized Jesus as the promised One, but each of them did so in a different respect!

[19]Strecker, op. cit. (n. 5), p. 144.

With this word began the preamble of the subsequent antitheses of the Sermon on the Mount (5:21-48).

Here is to be found as well, of course, the center of the discussion persisting to the present hour over the soteriological scope of Matthew's Gospel; we touched on this discussion earlier (§46,2). G. Strecker summarized his position about this in the sentence: "The actual mission of Jesus in history was, therefore, in Matthean understanding the proclamation of the ethical demand in which the yet future reign of God has become a present dimension, a demand that also was represented by the exemplary conduct of Jesus during his life on earth; therefore, the entire life of Jesus through word and action represented the ethical demand and the 'path of righteousness.' "[20] S. Schulz then focused this statement into the thesis: "The properly understood and practiced Law was the gospel."[21] H. Conzelmann opposed this perspective according to which for Matthew the imperative would precede the indicative—indeed, the indicative would be absorbed by the imperative; he contended that with respect to the teaching about the Law by Matthew one could not "simply measure Matthew's teaching on the law against Paul and argue that Matthew represents the law."[22]

With this two questions are raised: (1) How did the Law relate to the directive of Jesus for Matthew? (2) How were imperative and indicative, the demands and the accomplishment of salvation, related to each other?

b) The Law and the directives of Jesus. 1) The term "law" (*nomos*) did not appear in Mark. In Luke it appeared—with the exception of its use as a circumscription for "scripture" (e.g., Lk. 2:23f.; 10:26; 24:44)—only in five passages (Lk. 2:22, 27, 39 [Sp. Lk.]; 16:16 par. Mt. 11:13; 16:17 par. Mt. 5:18 [Q]); in Matthew hardly more often (Mt. 5:18 par. Lk. 16:17; 11.13 par. Lk. 16:16 [Q]; 7:12; 15:6; 22:36, 40 [redac.]). But this external result should not keep one from recognizing that the term had a much different significance for Matthew. The way he emphasized *nomos* reminds one of the Epistle of James. But in contrast to the referent there (§45,2), here the *nomos* always referred to the Mosaic Law. Its content was represented for Matthew by the Decalogue (15:3, 6; 19:17) and was summarized in the twofold command to love (22:36-40). According to Matthew, Jesus did not claim this Law directly as his own. It was therefore emphasized in 5:17 that Jesus did not want to abolish but to fulfill; precisely in the redaction of Matthew, Jesus placed his own directives over against the Law. For these directives Matthew did not develop his own designation. He spoke simply about the "teaching activity" (*didaskein*) of Jesus (5:2) and referred to Jesus correspondingly as the teacher (*didaskalos*; *kathēgētēs*) par excellence (23:8-10; cf. NEB). Let us now examine this antithetical relationship more exactly!

2) As was already mentioned, one-half of the six antitheses (5:21-48) were constructed by Matthew (§9,2d). In point of fact, Matthew understood them as

---

[20] "Das Geschichtsverständnis des Matthäus," *EvTheol* 26 (1966), 57-74 (71).
[21] *Die Stunde der Botschaft* (1967), p. 185.
[22] *Theology*, p. 148.

antitheses against the Mosaic Law and not some notion like the Jewish interpretation of the Law. Thus, in 5:31f. he presented Jesus' word against divorce
as an antithesis against the Mosaic law of divorce.[23]

Why then, however, did the protases of the antitheses not reproduce the
Mosaic Law verbatim but instead with enlargements and compilations? When
Matthew formulated in the sixth antithesis (5:43ff.): "You have heard that it was
said, 'you shall love your neighbor and hate your enemy,' " he circumscribed
in this protasis how he saw the Old Testament commandment to love one's
neighbor from the perspective of Jesus' demand to love one's enemy. Here too,
Matthew spoke as a scribe of the reign of God and thus he interpreted in a
substantively accurate way both the Old Testament commandment and Jesus'
directive quite as Jesus had intended.

3) The most difficult problem, of course, is posed by the statement of the
preamble (5:17-20) that Jesus had not "come to abolish the law and the prophets
. . . but to fulfill them." G. Strecker reached back once again to the Neo-Prot-
estant explanation; "to fulfill" was intended to express that Jesus had brought
through his teaching, i.e., through his interpretation of the Law, the realization
of the Law that continued to be valid without limit.[24] This view not only contradicts the context—the antitheses and their understanding of the Law just
characterized above—but more importantly also the use of *plēroun* (to fulfill)
found elsewhere in Matthew. The term appears throughout Matthew in the proof-
from-prophecy quotations as a technical term for the eschatological realization
of prophecy. According to 5:17, Jesus brought the prophesied realization of the
Law for the time of salvation. In order to make this even clearer Matthew inserted
the expression "heaven and earth will pass away" stemming from the eschatological discourse of Jesus (Mk. 13:31 par. Mt. 24:35) into the following Q-
saying of 5:18; the Law was valid without the slightest diminution *heōs panta
genētai*, i.e., until it should be replaced by the eschatological event of fulfillment.

The eschatological fulfillment brought forth perfect obedience from the whole
heart. Precisely this perfect obedience was demanded by Jesus in the antitheses
according to Matthew. Giving interpretive direction to the whole, Matthew closed
them with the sentence: "You, therefore, must be perfect, as your heavenly
Father is perfect" (5:48). Only Matthew used here (and in 19:21) the term *teleios*
(complete) and meant by it the completeness of devotion to the will of God.
Whereas Matthew demanded "perfection" in this sense at the end of the antitheses, so also at their beginning righteousness, also a typical expression for
him: ". . . unless your righteousness exceeds that of the scribes and Pharisees
. . ." (5:20). Righteousness and perfection meant the same thing, each expressing
a different side. For both the eschatological fulfillment of man's relationship to

---

[23]It is to be derived from his formulation in Mt. 19:7 that he meant the Mosaic Law in the
protasis of the antithesis that spoke about the writ of divorce, and not a Jewish interpretation of the
Law. After all, the issuance of the writ of divorce was traced back there expressly to a commandment
of Moses, i.e., to the Law.

[24]Strecker, op. cit. (n. 5), pp. 144-47.

God was under consideration. Jesus' every directive in the antitheses demanded completeness, e.g., the total demonstration of love, also in relationship to one's enemy. This completeness was the righteousness that in point of fact was doing justice to one's relationship to God and neighbor.

c) Righteousness as imperative and indicative. 1) While the term "righteousness" (*dikaiosynē*) appeared for the remaining synoptic Gospels only in one passage of little consequence (Lk. 1:75), in Matthew it appeared seven times in key statements that show themselves throughout to be redactional in nature (3:15; 5:6, 10, 20; 6:1, 33; 21:32). Next to Matthew only one other author of the New Testament spoke with such emphasis about righteousness, namely, Paul. But Matthew used the term righteousness completely independent of Pauline tradition and in a different sense. H. Conzelmann stated the difference in terms of the rule of thumb: what for Paul was righteousness was the kingdom of God for Matthew.[25] There is a certain degree of truth in that, but it does not cover the decisive Matthean passage, 6:33, for there "righteousness" stood parallel to "kingdom of God."

2) In 5:20 and 6:1, righteousness as conduct was demanded. According to this context, righteousness was the right conduct in relationship to God and to one's neighbor that Jesus demanded. This right conduct, however, was not the sum of individual acts that corresponded to ordinances, but the total turning of one's attention to God and to neighbor that fulfilled completely the relationship to both. "Beware of practicing your piety before men in order to be seen by them; for then you will have no reward from your Father who is in heaven" (6:1). Precisely at this point Pharisees fell short of the mark; they wanted to obey God, but they also cast furtive glances at their own merit. "Righteousness," however, was only to be found where "your left hand [does not] know what your right hand is doing" (6:3). Also in Mt. 25:37, the righteous ones ask the Judge of the world: "Lord, when did we see thee hungry. . . ?" They acted therefore without calculating, out of the completeness of love. How was this complete turning to God or to the neighbor, the righteousness that Jesus demanded, possible?

Matthew inserted into the traditional Beatitude of those who were hungry the words: "Blessed are those who hunger and thirst for righteousness" (5:6). The experience of becoming satisfied was promised to them just as much as participation in the kingdom was in the first Beatitude. Correspondingly in 6:33, Matthew placed righteousness alongside the kingdom of God: "But seek first his kingdom and his [i.e., God's] righteousness!" In Strecker's view, even here the righteousness of God was not a gift but the action of man that corresponded to the will of God.[26] Now it is surely to be noted that Matthew did not speak in both passages like Paul about a righteousness that God offered, but about a righteousness after which man should hunger and thirst. Here too righteousness was that right conduct as a whole in relationship to God and to one's neighbor.

---

[25]*Theology*, p. 149.
[26]Op. cit. (n. 5), p. 155.

Yet even this conduct as a whole was to be given as a gift by God together with
the kingdom of God. That was the promise of the Beatitudes and that was what
the parallel placement of the terms in 6:33 meant.

3) Matthew arranged the demands of the Sermon on the Mount into a compositional context that indicated how God gave their fulfillment as gift along
with the coming of the kingdom. He connected the Sermon on the Mount (chs.
5–7) to Jesus' ministry of salvation in chs. 8 and 9 through the bracketing
summary statements in 4:23 and 9:35 in order to make clear that corresponding
to the *exousia*, the authority of Jesus to command in God's stead (7:29), was his
authority to heal and to forgive sins (8:9; 9:6, 8).[27] Through this authority faith
and discipleship were accomplished. Through both, however, the turning of
oneself to God was being accomplished that meant that completely new conduct.
The righteousness that 6:1-18 intended could only be practiced by faith, by the
faith that Jesus' ministry of salvation elicited from people.

Thus, for Matthew the imperative was by no means identical to the indicative.[28] Rather, in his representation of Jesus' earthly ministry the indicative of
the ministry of salvation that accomplished faith and discipleship, i.e., conversion, followed the imperative of the call to repentance in the demands of the
Sermon on the Mount.

4) In the situation of the community the indicative of baptism preceded the
imperative of parenesis. "Baptizing them . . . teaching them to observe all that
I have commanded you" (28:19f.). This should be noted all the more, since,
other than James, Matthew pressed more emphatically than anyone else in the
New Testament toward the verification of Christian existence through a new
conduct. He motivated the new conduct more emphatically than any other writer
through eschatological retribution. Matthew promised reward; reward, however,
for the one who did not count on reward but did that which was commanded by
God only for the sake of God's will (6:4, 6, 18). Nevertheless, the references
to reward were significantly increased in Matthew (e.g., 5:12, 46; 6:2, 5, 16)
from one in Mark (9:41) and two in Luke (6:23 [Q]; 6:35 [redac.]).

Still more emphatic than the promise of reward was the threat of condemnation. Each of the extended discourses culminated in an announcement of judgment. The condemnation thereby was phrased with great urgency; there would
be those "thrown into the outer darkness" (8:12; 22:13; 25:30); there would be
"wailing and gnashing of teeth." This imagery, which occurred only once in Q
(Lk. 13:28), appeared six times in Matthew (8:12; 13:42, 50; 22:13; 24:51;
25:30). The judgment applied to those who rejected from the outset Jesus' summons, but it also applied to the foolish disciple who after grace had summoned
him failed to acquire a "wedding garment" (Mt. 22:11-14).

---

[27]Strecker explained this composition with the remark: "The deeds of power of Jesus demonstrated his sending, the eschatological demand of *dikaiosynē* in relationship to Israel, just like the
resurrection was then the sign of Jonah that attested to him" (ibid., p. 177; cf. pp. 220f.). Yet this
contradicts the text. What was reported in chs. 8 and 9 as deeds of salvation can never, as it were,
authorize the demand.

[28]Contra Strecker, ibid., p. 175.

All of this did not represent by any means "righteousness by works," not even in the early catholic sense. Disciples were not left to succeed by their works after a single release from guilt (cf. in contrast Herm. *M*. 12.6.2ff.; 1.7). Judgment only came upon disciples who did not repent after a transgression and did not permit themselves to be forgiven. This, of course, first became quite concrete when represented against the backdrop of sociological relationships.

6. THE REPLACEMENT OF ISRAEL BY THE CHURCH

In view of his historical ministry one could ask if Jesus intended to establish the church at all (§19,1). He summoned Israel to repentance and proclaimed the coming kingdom of God. Matthew, however, related both to the church; he was the only synoptic evangelist who expressly mentioned the church (Mt. 16:18; 18:17). And it was the failure of Israel in relationship to Jesus' summons to repentance that led him to the emergence of the church. The kingdom in its eschatological coming took on form in the church. Thus Matthew related Jesus' summons to repentance and his proclamation of the kingdom directly to the church.

Both of these statements have greatly influenced the self-awareness—often understood more one-sidedly than they were intended by Matthew—of the church in relationship to Israel and to the kingdom-expectation of Jesus.

a) Israel's conclusive failure in relationship to Jesus. 1) Matthew shaped Jesus' encounter with Israel as a unique salvation-historical hour of decision. With respect to this its own scope Matthew's Gospel differentiated itself fundamentally both from Luke, for whom this encounter was a salvation-historical transit station for the word en route to the Gentiles (Lk. 4:24ff.; Acts 13:46), and from John, for whom the Jews in their posture toward Jesus represented the world that always categorically rejected its Creator and Redeemer.

For Matthew, Jesus' historical sending applied exclusively to Israel (15:24) and therefore it was true for the sending of his disciples during his earthly ministry (10:5). The sending of Jesus was extended to the Gentiles only after taking on the form that it received through the encounter with Israel.

2) Thus the course of this encounter was explained by Matthew in its particulars by use of apologetic and missionary-theological motifs. According to the genealogy that opened the Gospel, Jesus came as the son of Abraham and of David in order—as the etymological meaning of the name "Jesus" in 1:21 would have it—to "save his people from their sins." In the course of his ministry a peculiar split in the Jewish people took place; while the masses (*hoi ochloi*) repeatedly paid him the tribute of acclaim (8:27; 9:33; 15:31), the representatives of the Jewish people rejected him from the outset. Both were impressively exemplified in 9:33f. The portrayal of Jesus' ministry of salvation (chs. 8 and 9) concluded with this statement: "and the crowds marveled, saying, 'Never was anything like this seen in Israel.' But the Pharisees said, 'He casts out demons by the prince of demons!' "

Matthew designated the representatives of Israel in relationship to Jesus for the most part schematically as "the Pharisees." He frequently inserted this designation where the tradition gave no specific reference to Jesus' partners in conversation (3:7; 12:38; 22:34, 41). Above all, he coupled the Pharisees redactionally with the scribes into his own, nonhistorical formula *hoi grammateis kai hoi Pharisaioi* (the scribes and the Pharisees, 5:20; 12:38; 23:2). To them applied the seven pronouncements of woe (23:13-29) that in Luke—more accurate historically—were dispersed over the two disparate groups (Lk. 11:37-54).

3) There were two reasons motivating Matthew to emphasize the Pharisees so strongly. For one thing, rabbinic Pharisaism represented the contemporary Judaism with which the evangelist was confronted. But more importantly, Matthew understood that Pharisaism was the intrinsic counterpart during the course of Jesus' earthly life (§8,2). Hence he let Jesus' public preaching begin with the pronouncement of blessing on those who "hunger and thirst for righteousness" (5:6) and conclude with the woes over the satisfied who considered themselves righteous, i.e., the scribes and the Pharisees (23:12-29).

Thus, during the public ministry of Jesus the reactions of the Pharisees and "the masses," these two entities given schematic profile by Matthew, were opposing each other, but in the end the people adopted the judgment of the Pharisees. Matthew emphasized this in the account of the passion as he let the crowd of the Jewish people take upon itself the guilt for his blood, while the Roman judge refused to take responsibility for Jesus' death through the symbolic washing of the hands (27:24f.): "His blood be on us and our children!" Corresponding to this was the statement used to introduce the threat of judgment at the end of the pronouncements of woe upon the Pharisees: "Fill up, then, the measure of your fathers" (23:32) in order to conclude them with the words: ". . . that upon you may come all the righteous blood . . ." (23:35). Here the woe has become the word of judgment.

4) These moments received forceful interpretation through the Matthean redaction of the two parables about the evil tenants and the royal marriage (21:33-22:14). Matthew allegorized both parables in terms of Jesus' encounter with Israel and its outcome. The parable of the evil tenants (21:33-46) characterized the condemnation of Jesus as the concluding act of Israel's counter-covenantal conduct. In the past God's claim upon his covenant people Israel, which had been articulated by the prophets, was repeatedly rejected. But now the murder of the final messenger, the "son," had led to a severance of relationship. The lord of the vineyard "will put those wretches to a miserable death, and let out the vineyard to other tenants who will give him the fruits in their seasons" (v. 41). The redactional concluding statement (v. 43) expressed the replacement of the old through the new covenant people: "Therefore I tell you, the kingdom of God will be taken away from you and given to a nation producing the fruits of it."

According to the parable of the marriage feast (22:1-14), the king, who was angered over the rejection and mistreatment of the servants extending his invitation, sent his army and destroyed "those murderers and burned their city" (22:7). At the same time he invited others, but even of those whoever had not acquired a wedding garment was thrown out (22:11-14). Thus Matthew furnished both these parables with a barb, both in relationship to Israel and to the church. Israel's special place in the history of salvation has come to an end since its condemnation of Jesus (21:41; cf. 27:25). This was confirmed through the destruction of Jerusalem in A.D. 70 (22:7).

These severe statements of Matthew have often been appropriated in the church in the form of a self-serving theology of history. In doing so one has failed to hear that the one-sided words of judgment in relationship to Israel were combined with an equally one-sided and pointed threat of judgment in relationship to the church that did not bring forth fruit. Matthew was one-sided, moreover, in the fact that he brushed aside the secret of Israel that Paul pondered in Rom. 9–11. For Matthew, Israel had become one people among many through the crucifixion of Jesus.[29] Just how much Matthew had distanced himself from Israel—called since Mt. 28:15 "the Jews"—was evidenced in his references to "their" scribes and "their" synagogues, etc. (7:29; 9:35; 11:1; 12:9 and passim). All these statements about Israel enable one to recognize through analogy and antithesis how Matthew reflected about the church.

b) The church. Everything that was said in Matthew about Jesus' life and ministry first took on concrete shape when it had gone through its orientation toward the church. Several lines converged in the direction of the church. The course of Jesus' encounter with Israel that ended with his and thereby Israel's condemnation was one; another, however, was Jesus' promise of the kingdom of God that Matthew especially underscored; there was also the demand of perfection or righteousness. If we draw out these lines further to their point of intersection, we shall find there what Matthew considered the church to be.

1) The constituting of the church as following Jesus in discipleship. With the word addressed to Peter (Mt. 16:17-19) that came from the primitive church of Palestine, Matthew had Jesus announce the emergence of the church for the future: "you are Peter, and on this rock I will build my *ekkēsia*." The future tense of the verb meant the future after Jesus' end, i.e., after his condemnation by Israel. The church was not yet gathered together during the earthly ministry; it came about in keeping with the word of commission formulated by Matthew at the end of his Gospel (Mt. 28:19f.). Here the resurrected and exalted One sent out his own disciples to make disciples of all nations (cf. §25,2). *Mathēteusate panta ta ethnē* ("make disciples of all nations!"); so ran the decisive

---

[29]Nevertheless it must remain open whether or not this is all one can say in terms of the understanding of Matthew. It is at least exegetically uncertain that he may in fact have had in mind a saving encounter of Israel with the returning One at the *parousia* in 23:39 ("you will not see me again, until you say, 'Blessed is he who comes in the name of the Lord!' "). According to Strecker, ibid., pp. 113ff. and Trilling, op. cit. (Lit., §46), pp. 87f., one can only think of the recognition of the Judge here, of course in keeping with the overall perspective of Matthew; A. Schlatter, *Matthäus*, at this location, saw in contrast a statement about a saving return of Jesus for Israel. Regarding the discussion, cf. W. Grundmann, *Matthäus* (ThHK), at this location.

command. And this was to take place, as the two subordinate participial forms indicate, through baptism (*baptizontes*) and through the passing on of the teaching of Jesus (*didaskontes*).

By virtue of the use of the rabbinic term *mathētēs* (*talmid* = "disciple, student"), Matthew emphasized more than any other New Testament author that everyone should become Jesus' disciple, not the disciples of Christian apostles or of Christian teachers. Jesus' teachings could not be passed on, therefore, as those of a rabbi. In 23:8-10, the evangelist inserted into the Q tradition the directive: "But you are not to be called rabbi, for you have one teacher, and you are all brethren." The "one teacher" was here in the first instance God himself. In the church no teaching office comparable to the rabbinate was supposed to emerge; rather, in it that which had been prophesied for the eschatological community was to prevail: all would be instructed directly by God (Jer. 31:31ff.).

Hence the alternative between heteronomy and autonomy was obsolete. Man appropriated from within the teaching activity of God as his own; this teaching activity of God, however, was realized concretely through Christ. As Matthew added with emphasis, he was the "one Teacher" (23:10, NEB). The references were all the more noteworthy since the only community offices that were visible behind Matthew's Gospel were those of the prophets and teachers. Even the Didache presupposed in the Syrian realm an ecclesiastical situation in which there were only missionaries—they were called apostles—prophets, and teachers (Did. 11:1-12), while the remaining ecclesiastical offices of bishops and presbyters arose only gradually (Did. 15:1). In regard to the prophets, Matthew warned quite emphatically against false prophets (Mt. 7:15ff.); in contrast, he gave unlimited recognition to the teacher, the "scribe who has been trained for the kingdom of heaven" (13:52).

It corresponded to this understanding of the community as following Jesus in discipleship that the abiding new presence of Jesus was promised to the church in Matthew rather than as in Luke the coming of the Spirit (28:20: "I am with you always, to the close of the age"; 18:20: "where two or three are gathered in my name, there am I in the midst of them"). These frequently quoted words were in wording and concept entirely Matthew's own. 18:20 corresponded to a word—agreeing almost verbatim—of the rabbis about the *sh^ekinah*, the presence of God.[30] Hence Jesus' presence was not thought of as that of a transfigured human being, but in terms of the godhead. He was in and among them in such a way that he was at work in them like God.

The promise of the presence of Jesus corresponded substantively, therefore, to the promise of the Spirit! Matthew, like the Palestinian-Syrian tradition encountered in the Didache, appeared to have a certain reservation in relationship to the concept of the Spirit, since spirit can be interpreted variously. Spirit was claimed, after all, by enthusiasts in the community as well as by others in its environment. He who, in contrast, was the Jesus present in a divine way among

---

[30]Billerbeck I, 794f.

his disciples and at work in them was clarified by the evangelist through his account.

2) The church as the sphere of God's reign. The context for the above becomes immediately clear when we consider how Matthew designated the church in a singular way as the "kingdom" of "the Son of man" and its true members as "the sons of the kingdom" in his own interpretation of the parable of the wheat and the tares (13:36-43; cf. vv. 38 and 41). According to the statement of 21:43—also Matthew's own—the kingdom of God was given to the church, the kingdom that was taken from Israel. These peculiar expressions indicate that Matthew saw the kingdom of God, in accord with the kingdom parables in ch. 13, present in the church. The *parousia* parables in chs. 24f., in contrast, pointed only to the future *eschaton*.

These statements of Matthew, along with other reasons, prompted early catholic theologians to identify the kingdom of God with the true church. For Jesus, however, the kingdom of God was only present in his ministry and not in the existence of his disciples (§6,3). In reply to the question, in what sense for Matthew God's reign was present in the church, we would have to repeat everything that was said about his understanding of the demand and gift of Jesus (§46,5c). The kingdom of God was undoubtedly not present in the church merely in the form of the demand of Jesus.[31] Rather, to the church was given the kingdom because it was the "nation producing the fruits of it" (21:43). It was a matter of the "fruits of it," not only the demand! Put another way, to the church was given, with the kingdom righteousness, right conduct (6:33). Its members were made disciples through baptism, and the extended discourses of the Gospel circumscribed with urgency the teaching that the disciple was to keep on the basis of baptism: woe to the servant who hides the talent in the ground and does not invest it! (25:24-30).

3) The community rules in Matthew 18. The community rules in Mt. 18 confirmed finally the base line of the Gospel that we have noted. They did not at all proclaim a rigorous community discipline, the likes of which one would expect according to most of the portrayals of the theology of Matthew. Rather, they began in 18:1-14 with the rule: great in the kingdom of God and thereby in the community was the humbled one, the *'anaw*, who made the humbled ones his concern and took care not to offend them! In the same way, the concluding parable of the unfaithful servant (vv. 21-35) obligated one to encounter the brother with the same mercy that one had experienced from Jesus. Bracketed by both these directives stood the rule about how one ought to encounter the offending community members (vv. 15-20). Community members, and not just some of the officeholders, were to concern themselves with those going astray, to prompt them to repent, and to forgive them with authority. The most extreme measure was that the community assembly would exclude the one who in spite of attempts to persuade would not desist from his offense: "if he refuses to listen

---

[31]Contra Strecker, op. cit. (n. 5), p. 215.

even to the church, let him be to you as a Gentile and a tax collector," i.e., as one who did not belong to the community, but to whom the good news still applied (18:17). This exclusion nevertheless was not a pedagogically directed disciplinary measure as in the case of the synagogue ban. In 18:18, the office of the key, which according to 16:19 was given to Peter, was delivered to the community as a whole: "Truly, I say to you, whatever you bind on earth shall be bound in heaven, and whatever you loose on earth shall be loosed in heaven." The expressions "bind" and "loose" meant in the synagogue the power of instruction and discipline, i.e., the synagogue was authorized to decide on the basis of the interpretation of the Law what was just and unjust and to exercise community discipline. Disciples exercised here the binding and loosing, however, on the basis of the teaching of Jesus. As Jesus could condemn through his "woe," so they too. 9:8 also alluded to this motif: ". . . and they glorified God, who had given such authority to men."

In what sense the binding and loosing on the basis of Jesus' teaching was practiced becomes clear from the perspective of the goal this community discipline had. According to the concluding parable of the unfaithful servant (vv. 23-35) the disciple based his life on the mercy of his Lord. The exclusion from the community of disciples of the one who did not desire to desist from his visible offense was only supposed to indicate that forgiveness was not a license to sin, but not that the community could here and now already liberate itself of all impure members.

Therefore, one should not interpret this section as a disciplinary ordinance and not move the elements of church discipline one-sidedly to the fore.[32] The tendency to want to cull out through disciplinary measures the pure community, or the relatively pure community, was expressly rejected by Matthew in the interpretation of the parable about the tares among the wheat (13:36-43). Upon the field of the church tares and wheat would have to grow alongside each other until the end. It was a *corpus mixtum*. But it was not, therefore, simply like the world in which God let his sun shine upon good and evil (5:45). In the church the contrasts were no longer relative but absolute. In it, the claim of the reign of God established by Jesus and the claim of the reign of the adversary stood in opposition to each other. Precisely because this opposition had a truly eschatological character, it could not now be resolved through relative separations as both the Essenes and the Pharisees tried in view of the *eschaton* that for them was always just around the corner. Matthew prohibited the selecting out of the core-community although he insisted more rigorously than anyone else in the New Testament that fruit should grow. He knew that goodness could only be expected as fruit and that it finally could not be produced, as the Pharisees and Essenes wanted, through social and pedagogical pressure. He knew that the gracious turning of Jesus' person to people preceded all his demands.

4. The sending of the church. For Matthew, therefore, this convergence of

---

[32]Thus ibid., pp. 222ff.; Conzelmann, *Theology*, p. 146.

all lines upon the church precisely did not serve its self-preservation but its sending. Between the Beatitudes and the demands of the Sermon on the Mount Matthew placed the words about salt and about light; he interpreted them through the introductory statements that he inserted: "You are the salt of the earth . . . you are the light of the world" (5:13f.). Disciples would not become salt and light by turning themselves into reformers of the world, but by letting the light shine that was given to them, i.e., by bringing forth fruit.

It was neither coincidence nor at all unjust that the Gospel of Matthew became the chief Gospel of the church. It is therefore important to recognize the positive contribution it has made as well as its one-sided features that could give rise to erroneous developments. His scripture-gnosis could give occasion to various rationally based proofs from scripture; the understanding of the teaching of Jesus as the fulfillment of the Law could be misunderstood as a *nova lex*; his word about Israel and the church could set in motion an anti-Semitic theology of history, and the convergence of all statements in the direction of the church could prompt the self-presumption of the church as the representative of the kingdom of God. Thus, these one-sided statements of the first Gospel certainly offer an occasion for misunderstandings and erroneous developments. If, however, they are taken as they were actually meant, then this theological interpretation of the life and ministry of Jesus can induce important stimuli precisely in its rigorous one-sidedness.

The Gospel of Matthew and the similarly one-sided but much narrower and smaller Epistle of James were the contributions of the Syrian church to the New Testament canon. One becomes fully aware of the distinctiveness of these contributions to the ecclesiastical questions of the post Pauline period only after one compares to them the quite different kind of contributions that came from the church of the West: the Epistle to the Hebrews and the historical composition of Luke.

Chapter III

THE LONG PATH OF THE CHURCH IN HISTORY: THE THEOLOGY OF THE EPISTLE TO THE HEBREWS AND OF LUKE

§47. The Community on a Journey—Christ the Perfect High Priest (the Epistle to the Hebrews)

On the History of Research: E. Grässer, "Der Hebräerbrief 1938-1963," *ThR* NF 30 (1964), 138-236. **Important Commentaries:** H. Windisch (1931²), HNT; O. Michel (1966¹²), KEK; E. Riggenbach (1923²⁻³), ed. T. Zahn; C. Spicq, I/II (1952/53), Études Bibliques. **On 1:** L. Vaganay, "Le plan de l'Epitre aux Hébreux," in *Mémorial Lagrange* (1940), pp. 269-277; W. Nauck, "Zum Aufbau des Hebräerbriefes," in *Judentum—Urchristentum—Kirche, Festschrift für J. Jeremias*, ed. W. Eltester (1960), pp. 199-206; A. Vanhoye, *La structure littéraire de l'Épitre aux Hébreux* (1963). **On 2:** G. Harder, "Die Septuagintazitate des Hebräerbriefes. Ein Beitrag zum Problem der Auslegung des Alten Testaments," in *Theologia Viatorum* (1939), pp. 33-52; F. C. Synge, *Hebrews and the Scriptures* (1959); H. Koester, "Die Auslegung der Abraham-Verheissung in Hebräer 6," in *Studien zur Theologie der alttestamentlichen Überlieferungen. Festschrift für G. von Rad*, ed. R. Rendtorff and K. Koch (1961), pp. 95-109; F. Schröger, *Der Verfasser des Hebräerbriefes als Schriftausleger* (1968). **On 3:** O. Kuss, "Der theologische Grundgedanke des Hebräerbriefes," in Kuss, *Auslegung und Verkündigung* I (1963), 281-328; E. Fiorenza, "Der Anführer und Vollender unseres Glaubens—Zum theologischen Verständnis des Hebräerbriefes," in *Gestalt und Anspruch* (ed. J. Schreiner [1969]), pp. 262-281; U. Luck, "Himmlisches und irdisches Geschehen im Hebräerbrief," *NovTest* 6 (1963), 193-215; E. Käsemann, *Das wandernde Gottesvolk* (1961⁴); F. J. Schierse, *Verheissung und Heilsvollendung* (1955); M. Dibelius, "Der himmlische Kultus nach dem Hebräerbrief," in Dibelius, *Botschaft und Geschichte* II (1956), 169-176; G. Bornkamm, "Das Bekenntnis im Hebräerbrief," in *Aufsätze* II, pp. 188-203; W. Hillmann, "Einführung in die Grundgedanken des Hebräerbriefes," *Bibel und Leben* 1 (1960), 17-27, 87-99, 157-178, 237-252; G. Theissen, *Untersuchungen zum Hebräerbrief* (1969); O. Hofius, *Katapausis. Die Vorstellung vom endzeitlichen Ruheort im Hebräerbrief* (1970). **On 4:** G. Delling, *teleō/teleioō, TDNT* VIII, 57-61, 79-84; F. Büchsel, *Die Christologie des Hebräerbriefes* (1922); Schweizer, *Lordship*, pp. 88ff.; Cullmann,

Christology, pp. 89-107; E. Grässer, "Der historische Jesus im Hebräerbrief," *ZNW* 56 (1965), 63-91; M. Rissi, "Die Menschlichkeit Jesu nach Hebr 5,7-8," *ThZ* 11 (1955), 28-45; J. Gnilka, "Die Erwartung des messianischen Hohepriesters in den Schriften von Qumran und im Neuen Testament," *RQ* 2 (1959/60), 395-426; Hahn, *Titles*, pp. 229-239; G. Friedrich, "Das Lied vom Hohenpriester im Zusammenhang von Hebr 4,15–5,10," *ThZ* 18 (1962), 95-115; S. Nomoto, "Herkunft und Struktur der Hohepriestervorstellung im Hebräerbrief," *NovTest* 10 (1968), 10-25; E. Brandenburger, "Text und Vorlagen von Hebr V.7-10. Ein Beitrag zur Christologie des Hebräerbriefes," *NovTest* 11 (1969), 190-224; G. Schille, "Erwägungen zur Hohepriesterlehre des Hebräerbriefes," *ZNW* 46 (1955), 252-266; J. Roloff, "Der mitleidende Hohepriester. Zur Frage nach der Bedeutung des irdischen Jesus für die Christologie des Hebräerbriefes," in *Jesus Christus in Historie und Theologie, Festschrift für H. Conzelmann*, ed. G. Strecker (1975), pp. 143-166. **On 5:** K. Rahner, "Die Busslehre des Hirten des Hermas," *ZKTh* 77 (1955), 385-431; B. Poschmann, *Paenitentia secunda* (1940); O. Glombitza, "Erwägungen zum kunstvollen Ansatz der Paränese im Brief an die Hebräer X 19-25," *NovTest* 9 (1967), 132-150; C. K. Barrett, "The Eschatology of the Epistle to the Hebrews," in *The Background of the New Testament and its Eschatology, Festschrift for C. H. Dodd*, ed. W. D. Davies and D. Daube (1969), pp. 363-393; G. Bornkamm, "Sohnschaft und Leiden," in *Aufsätze* IV, 214-224; Goppelt, *Apostolic Times*, pp. 135-151; E. Grässer, *Der Glaube im Hebräerbrief* (1965).

1. PRELIMINARY CONSIDERATION: ORIGIN AND COMPOSITION

a) Time of composition. The Epistle to the Hebrews, like the epistles of Paul, was already being appropriated verbatim without express quotation in the First Epistle of Clement written in A.D. 96.[1] It must have been written, therefore, sometime before this date. On the other hand, the author, like his readers, belonged to the second Christian generation (Heb. 2:3). Based on that observation a time of composition after the year A.D. 70 would be thinkable. The statements about the priestly service in the Old Testament sanctuary, however, create the impression that the cult in the Jerusalem temple was still in operation; thus, e.g., in 9:9: "(which is symbolic for the present age). According to this arrangement, gifts and sacrifices are offered. . . ." But the letter spoke nowhere about the cult in the Jerusalem temple; it appropriated strictly and simply the statements of the Pentateuch about the cult in the tabernacle of Israel's wilderness wanderings. It illuminated the course of Christ's life and his ministry through comparison with the order of atonement from scripture, but not in terms of the cultic practice in Jerusalem. Thus it need not surprise anyone that the letter did not contain a reference to the destruction of the temple in Jerusalem, even though this is to be presupposed for the second generation; nothing stands in the way of accepting a time between A.D. 80 and 90—for which other indices also speak favorably—for its composition.

b) The addressees. When the New Testament writings were assembled in the 2nd century, the letter was given the title *pros Hebraious*, to the Hebrews; meant were people of Jewish, perhaps Palestinian, origin. This title was not based on tradition but was derived from the content. The letter's style of developing its statements from an extremely intensive and ingenious interpretation of the Old Testament seemed to presuppose Jewish readers. But neither does the letter itself

---

[1]In I Clem. 17:1, Heb. 11:37 was used; I Clem. 36:2-5 depended on Heb. 1:3-5; 7:13; especially in I Clem. 36:3, Ps. 104:4 was quoted in departure from the LXX in the same way as Heb. 1:7.

suggest this nor does it show itself to be substantively necessary. The extensive lines of argumentation from scripture in the Epistle to the Romans or in the First Epistle of Clement were intended for Gentile-Christians and were understandable to them. The Epistle to the Hebrews was therefore written to Christians as Christians without reflecting upon their Jewish or non-Jewish origin.

Where should we look for them? In 13:24, the addressees received greetings from Christians who came from Italy; this greeting probably applied to fellow-countrymen back home. Thus it suggests itself to look for the addressees in Italy, particularly in Rome. This becomes nearly certain when further indices are considered. The letter was first used, as noted above, in the First Epistle of Clement, which was written in Rome; this reference to Hebrews was not purely coincidental. In its terminology and in its problematic, Hebrews more than any other New Testament writing had points of contact with typical voices from the early community of Rome, with the First Epistle of Clement and the Shepherd of Hermas; it surely stood therefore, like them, directly in the community tradition of Rome.

The letter did not address itself to a local community as a whole. In 13:24, the addressees were requested to greet the community leaders and the remaining community members. Hence the addressees are to be sought in a house-community. From this perspective the lofty rational and spiritual standards that were deliberately directed at the readers in 5:12ff. also would be more easily understood.

c) The author. According to the traditional context mentioned above, the author too must have stood close to the community tradition of Rome. The letter itself did not mention any name and it began without mention of where it came from. Even in the ancient church people sought, therefore, to guess the name of the author. In the Eastern church since the 2nd century Paul was believed to have been the author. But the learned scholars of Alexandria, Clement and Origen, already recognized that the letter, if for no other reason than its diction, could not have come from Paul; so they developed secretarial hypotheses. Clement guessed that Paul wrote it to Hebrews in the Hebrew language, but that Luke translated it into Greek.[2] At least one thing was correct here: the Epistle to the Hebrews was written in such a polished Greek that only Luke can compare to it in the New Testament. Origen, however, wanted to leave the question of authorship open and stated: "But who wrote the epistle, in truth God knows."[3] To this day, that is about where the question rests.

From the style and content, however, it can be concluded that the author must have been a well-educated Christian who came out of Hellenistic Judaism. He quoted the Old Testament as a rule in the way that was customary in the Hellenistic Judaism of Alexandria. And yet, as shall become clear, he did not have direct points of contact with the theology of Philo.

d) Canonization. The discussion in the ancient church about the author had further effects upon the controversy regarding its canonization. In the Eastern

---

[2]Eus. *EH* 6.14.2ff. (= LCL, II, 47).
[3]Ibid. 6.25.11ff. (= LCL, II, 77-79; cf. quote, p. 79).

church since the 2nd century the letter was considered part of the Pauline epistles and therefore part of the canon. In contrast, the Western church first granted canonical recognition to it reluctantly under pressure from the East in the 4th century. The reason for this reluctance becomes clear in connection with a very instructive remark by Tertullian. In his Montanist period, Tertullian opposed the catholic doctrine of a second repentance and referred thereby to Heb. 6:4-8: "I wish, however, redundantly to superadd the testimony likewise of one particular comrade of the apostles. . . . For there is extant withal an Epistle to the Hebrews under the name of Barnabas. . . . And, of course, the Epistle of Barnabas is more generally received among the Churches than that apocryphal 'Pastor moechorum.' "[4] The Epistle to the Hebrews was therefore not canonized in the Western church where it was vigorously debated because it appeared to contradict the central ecclesiastical teaching and practice that represented the possibility of Christian repentance.

Finally, then, the Reformation stance of Luther took as its starting point the same central theme of the Western church, the doctrine of repentance. Luther too, however, took offense increasingly over the words of Hebrews against subsequent repentance and moved it together with the Epistle of James and Revelation to the end of the New Testament canon.[5] Thus, already in a discussion of authorship and canonization the substantive problems of this unusual document become apparent.

e) Literary structure and arrangement. 1) The Epistle to the Hebrews had a letter-type conclusion in 13:22-25, but had no letter-type introduction; moreover, in the body of the text the style was not that of a letter. It was, in fact, no letter but, as it stated in 13:22, a *logos paraklēseōs*, a word of exhortation, in the final analysis a sermon. O. Michel called it correctly the "first complete primitive-Christian sermon . . . that has been preserved for us."[6] Certainly the developments of thought were too long and too compact for oral presentation. But the character of the document is correctly designated with the term sermon.

2) Just as in form so too in arrangement the Epistle to the Hebrews differentiated itself fundamentally from the Pauline epistles. To begin with it is noticeable that didactic and parenetic sections were arranged together in a different manner than in Paul. In the theologically ordered Pauline epistles an "ethical" part followed the "dogmatic" one; e.g., following Gal. 1–4 came the parenesis of chs. 5 and 6. In Hebrews, however, didactic and parenetic sections follow each other alternately in the body of the text. The question is: How were these sections woven together into larger units? Was the principle of division based primarily on the didactic (i.e., christological) lines of thought or on the parenetic ones?

---

[4]Tert. *De pud.* 20 (= ANF, *Tertullian*, IV, 97). " 'Shepherd' of adulterers" was what he called the Shepherd of Hermas because this document advocated second repentance and at that time this was also connected to the deadly sin of adultery.

[5]In the Nestle Greek New Testament as in the Vulgate it has its place, in contrast, between the Pauline and the Catholic epistles.

[6]*Der Hebräerbrief*, p. 24.

W. Nauck and W. G. Kümmel considered the parenesis primary.[7] In this view, the goal of the parenesis in the three major portions was first to summon attention to the word (1:1–4:13), then to perseverance in confession (4:14–10:39), and finally to obedience of faith (11:1–13:17). But this arrangement fails to note the weight of the christological statements. For the readers the issue was apparently not religious zeal and morality; their problem was whether or not they had grasped eschatological salvation with the confession of Jesus as the Son of God when nothing had changed with regard to their circumstances in the world. Because it was a matter of this issue the christological sections demonstrated through comparison with the Old Testament revelation of salvation that Christ was precisely in his concealment and lowliness the eschatological revelation of salvation. The parenesis concluded from this that whoever joined himself to Christ and then abandoned him again lost his salvation irrevocably!

The parenetic sections each proceeded to express a negative and a positive side; the negative one warned against the loss of salvation, while the positive articulated the expectation that among the readers it would not come to this loss.

It appears to this writer an error to play off the christological and parenetic sections one against the other. I would therefore like to offer for discussion another breakdown of the material that, as I see it, would do justice more satisfactorily to the weight of the christological statements and thereby to the overall tenor of thought development.[8] Ch. 7:1–10:18 constituted the high point

---

[7]Nauck, op. cit. (Lit., §47); W. G. Kümmel, *Introduction*, pp. 388ff.

[8]A. (T [= Teaching] + P [= Parenesis]): Jesus the Preparer of the Way (guidance to understanding and holding fast to the confession): 1:1–6:20
  I. The Word mediated by Christ claimed incomparably more attention than the Law mediated by angels: 1:1–2:18.
    1. (T): 1:1-14 (Superiority of the Son over angels)
    2. (P): 2:1-4 (Contempt for preached salvation and its consequences)
    3. (T): 2:5-18 (Abasement of the Son as precondition for his high-priestly position)
  II. The promise mediated by Christ claimed a greater hearing than the one given to the people in the desert: 3:1–4:13.
    1. (T): 3:1-6 (Jesus' superiority over Moses)
    2. (P): 3:7–4:13 (The ominous consequences of callousness in relationship to Jesus' promise of salvation)
  III. Precisely through his lowliness Jesus became the eschatological high priest; to forfeit him means irreversible apostasy: 4:14–6:20.
    1. (T): 4:14–5:10 (Abasement of Jesus as presupposition for high-priestly service)
    2. (P): 5:11–6:20 (Preparation for the "perfect teaching" through warning against irreversible apostasy and challenge to hold fast to the promise)
  B. (T) Jesus the Eschatological High Priest (Interpretation of the Confession): 7:1–10:18
  I. The superior high-priestly position of Jesus: 7:1-28
  II. The high-priestly ministry of Jesus: 8:1–10:18
    1. 8:1-13 (The places of Jesus' priestly service)
    2. 9:1–10:18 (The high-priestly sacrifice of Jesus)
  C. (P) Parenetic Consequences of the Eschatological High Priest's Saving Work: 10:19–13:17
  I. Stay on the path to salvation opened up by Christ! 10:19-31
  II. The journey of faith of the ancients and that of the community: 11:1–12:29
    1. 11:1-40 (The witness to faith of scripture)
    2. 12:1-29 (Perseverance of the community along the way)
  III. Individual directives for the application of the fundamental parenesis to the situation of the community: 13:1-17
  Epistolary Conclusion: 13:18-25

of the letter. This section represented the theme "Jesus, the eschatological High Priest." Chs. 1–6 moved in the direction of this climax as they characterized Jesus as the *prodromos*, the "forerunner," who had now already entered into the heavenly sanctuary. The third major section, 10:19–12:29, constituted the anticlimax. Here the parenetic conclusions were drawn from that which went before. Ch. 13 manifested the character of a supplement that applied what had been developed to concrete issues in the community.

f) The community situation. It has frequently been assumed that the document wanted to counter a lapse of the readers into Judaism;[9] this was the reason—it is argued—for the repeated emphasis on the superiority of Jesus over the Old Testament mediation of salvation. This view fails to understand, however, the situation of the readers just as much as the intention of the "letter." The threat to the community was of a quite different sort than this. The community to which the author addressed himself was comparable to the people of Israel during the wilderness wanderings. Like Israel back then, so now the community too was in danger of succumbing to fatigue (3:12f.); it became disappointed that the path to the promised land had become so long and arduous. Without the imagery that meant: the community had become dismayed over the fact that the revelation of glory promised it had not come about visibly and instead it experienced one new affliction after another (3:7ff.; 6:12; 10:36ff.; 12:4-11). This sense of dismay produced a result typical for the second generation. Christians began to flag in their striving to lead a life by faith (2:13; 12:4) and conformed themselves once again to a life of worldly standards (13:13f.). Those who were called to be citizens of a new world were settling in once again in the old world. Hence, threatening them was the fate of Israel's desert generation that hardened itself in murmuring against the God who had caused their exodus and for this reason it had not been allowed to set foot in the promised land (3:7-19; 4:11). Thus the community had to be warned by confrontation with the example of Esau, who for a pitiful mess of pottage frivolously forfeited his birthright (12:16). In order to wrench the community from this ominous resignation the author held an image of Christ before their eyes. Christ was the perfect and ultimate revelation of the salvation of God precisely because he was the humbled One in this world. Whoever should forfeit him would no longer hope for salvation (4:1f.; 6:4-6; 10:26-31; 12:14-17)! Thus, for the author it was absolutely essential that he make the readers aware that Jesus really was God's perfect revelation of salvation.

In doing this the author traveled a different road than Matthew, who referred to Jesus as the One who was prophesied (§46,4a). The author of Hebrews compared the course of Jesus' life and his ministry with the way in which salvation was mediated according to the Old Testament. He did this to bring out the eschatological superiority of the mediation of salvation through Jesus and to demonstrate that Jesus himself was the eschatological revelation. The point of departure for the author was the presupposition that the provisions for salvation

---

⁹Thus, e.g., H. Strathmann, NTD (1949⁵), p. 65.

of the Old Testament did not represent the random cult of a Near Eastern people but the mediation of salvation of the covenant existing until that time—of course, restricted to Israel—between God and man. Hence the great comparison of the high priesthood of Christ to that of the Old Testament led to the challenge in which the parenesis of the "letter" reached its peak: "since we have a great priest . . . let us draw near [to God] with a true heart in full assurance of faith. . . . Let us hold fast the confession of our hope without wavering . . . all the more as you see the Day drawing near" (10:21-25).

Here become clear then the theological themes of Hebrews that we shall have to discuss below: the use of scripture; the concept of Christ's high priesthood as the replacement of the Old Covenant and its Law; the teaching concerning the singular nature of repentance; finally, the path tread by the community as the path of the faith that hopes.

2. THE USE AND UNDERSTANDING OF SCRIPTURE

a) The form of quotation. Very characteristic for the understanding of scripture in Hebrews was the way it made quotations.

1) It quoted the Old Testament throughout with a quotation formula that was not customary in the New Testament: "God [or Christ or the Holy Spirit] said."[10] On the other hand, the formulas that otherwise were dominant in the New Testament are not to be found at all: "it is written" (*gegraptai*) or "scripture [or the corresponding name of the human author, such as David] said" (*[hē graphē] legei*). A human author was mentioned only once (2:6), whereby this passage showed how inconsequential this was for the writer. It stated: "It has been testified somewhere" (cf. 4:7; 5:6). Otherwise almost throughout, Old Testament passages were introduced as the word of God, of Christ, or of the Spirit (exceptions: 10:37; 12:5; and 13:6). Even where in the Old Testament God was spoken of in the third person he was regarded as the One speaking (1:6, 9; 4:4, 7; 7:21; 10:30). Correspondingly, Old Testament passages were introduced directly as words of Christ as though they were sayings of Jesus (2:12ff.; 10:5-7).

2) Quotations were made throughout on the basis of the LXX text that for the most part was close to that of Codex Alexandrinus. The author also followed the LXX where it departed from our Masoretic text (1:6f.; 2:7; 10:38; 12:5f., 15, 20f.); sometimes he even based his interpretation on such departures from the Hebrew (10:5-10; 12:26).[11]

3) How is this way of making quotations to be explained on the whole? Formally speaking, it corresponded without doubt to the tradition of the Hellenistic synagogue as we find it represented above all by Philo.

---

[10]Also on occasion elsewhere in the New Testament (e.g., Rom. 9:15, 25) reference was made to a word of God in the Old Testament, but as quotation formula these expressions were peculiar to the Epistle to the Hebrews.

[11]This observation, of course, ought not to be overemphasized since we know neither to what extent our Masoretic text is original, nor whether the writer of Hebrews quoted freely from memory. In some passages he appears to have shaped quotations himself to fit his interpretation, such as the well-known quotation from Hab. 2:3f. in 10:37ff.

Many have therefore concluded the Epistle to the Hebrews represented the same theory of inspiration held by Philo. According to Philo the statements that Moses recorded in the Pentateuch only appear to come from him; in reality they were in all details utterances of God. This theory gave justification to his allegorical interpretations; it permitted him to derive secretive meaning from every word, indeed from each letter of the LXX text. The Old Testament text thus became an oracle that contained a system of Hellenistic philosophical mysticism.

The Epistle to the Hebrews, along with all of primitive Christianity, accepted formally from Judaism the concept of the inspiration of scripture (II Tim. 3:16). For Hebrews, however, the Old Testament was precisely not a collection of oracles all of which were valid in the same way. Rather it stated programmatically at the outset that God spoke in various ways "through the prophets" and at the conclusion of those days "has spoken to us in the Son" (1:1, NEB). In terms of this concluding address of God that which was said formerly was heard and even altered. Thus Hebrews could state that God had replaced what was said earlier by words that were spoken later (7:18; 8:13). The manner of quoting wanted to designate the Old Testament therefore, in spite of a formal similarity to Hellenistic Judaism, not as an inspired oracle but as the word of God that was "living" (4:12) and should be passed on "today" as a living word (4:7). From the perspective of the end-time address of God through Christ the author acquired a new understanding of scripture.

b) Exegetical method. 1) Here too the author followed initially the forms of thought of his environment. They emerged in rather peculiar fashion precisely where the author derived and founded his interpretations exegetically. Thus in 2:6-9, Ps. 8, and in 3:2ff., Num. 12:7, were interpreted; 3:7–4:11 was a midrash-like interpretation of Ps. 95:7-11. The interpretation of the Melchizedek-pericope (Gen. 14:17-20) in 7:1-10 created an especially strange impression. Here, e.g., as in Philo, an etymological secret meaning was elicited from the name "Melchizedek" (7:2); on the basis of the silence of scripture about the origin, birth, and end of Melchizedek it was concluded that he was eternal (7:3). The relationship between the word of scripture and the truth for the present in the adduced examples was secured at least formally through the exegetical methods practiced in the environment among Jews and Hellenists.

2) Again and again, however, this interpretive approach manifested a character of its own through its content. It was the case here that scripture was related with consistency to God's activity through Jesus! If, however, this activity of God through Jesus really was the goal of the Old Testament, then this interpretation, in spite of its ties to contemporary forms of thought, becomes substantively relevant. Let us turn our attention then to the direct relating of Old Testament words to Christ and his community!

Hebrews did not quote, as we saw above, Old Testament words as prophetic pronouncements and therefore also did not connect the Old Testament word and the Christ event according to the scheme of "prophecy–fulfillment." Rather, it allowed Christ or the community to be addressed by God directly in the Old

Testament words or to answer with these Old Testament words. For example, in 5:5-7, the key passage for the high priesthood, Ps. 110:4 was understood directly as God's word of appointment to Jesus: "So also Christ did not exalt himself to be made a high priest, but was appointed by him who said to him . . . 'Thou art a priest for ever, after the order of Melchizedek' " (bestowed upon him this honor). These connections were by no means drawn together arbitrarily. It can be shown that the author's procedure may be put into specific rules even, in fact especially, with the aid of criteria from a historical approach to things.

2.1 Old Testament words about the king of Israel were related to Christ: Ps. 2 in 1:5 and 5:5; Ps. 110 in 1:3, 13; 5:6; 7:15, 17, 21; 8:1; 10:13; 12:2; more distantly Ps. 45 in 1:8; and II Sam. 7:14 in 1:5.

2.2 The statements of the Psalms about the path of the righteous One were related to Jesus by way of the adoption of a primitive Christian interpretive tradition that went back to Jesus himself (§18,7c): Ps. 22 in 2:12; Ps. 8 in 2:6ff.; Ps. 40 in 10:5-15.

2.3 Old Testament words about prophets were perhaps applied to Jesus in 2:13 (= Isa. 8:17), in 3:2 (= Num. 12:7), and in 9:28 (= Isa. 53:12).

2.4 Old Testament words about the *kyrios* = Yahweh were related to Jesus in 1:6 (= Dt. 32:42) and in 1:10-12 (= Ps. 110).

2.5 Correspondingly, a word directed at Israel was understood to apply to the community in 3:7-11.

When we arrange and verify the pneumatic exegesis of Hebrews in this way we have already begun to make use of an optical lens that Hebrews itself developed elsewhere: the so-called typological interpretation of the Old Testament.

c) The typological interpretation of Old Testament history and provisions for salvation. The utilization of the history of Israel in the desert and of its cult described in the Old Testament occupied far more space in Hebrews than the interpretative application of Old Testament words to Christ. Both this history and this cult were related typologically by Hebrews throughout to the present. In chs. 1–6 and 11–13 the situation of the community was compared continuously with Israel's period in the desert. Correspondingly, in the central portion (chs. 7–10) the course of Jesus' life and his ministry were interpreted as the high-priestly act of atonement on the basis of the high-priestly atoning sacrifice of the Old Testament order of salvation (Lev. 16). The entire Epistle to the Hebrews, therefore, was furnished with a comprehensive salvation-historical optical lens according to which the history and order of salvation recounted in the Old Testament of Israel in the time of Moses were compared with Christ and his community. In 8:8ff., express reference was made to the announcement of the New Covenant in Jer. 31 in order to justify from its perspective this understanding of Old Testament provisions. This utilization of the Old Testament was therefore no allegorical game played with inspired jots and tittles, but the utilization of a relationship established by God between his activity in the Old Covenant and in the New. The typological salvation-historical lens showed itself by virtue of its scope and the consequences of its implementation to be representative for the theological position of the Epistle to the Hebrews.

3. THE THEOLOGICAL POSITION

a) H. J. Holtzmann made the problem apparent in his own provocative one-sidedness when he said: "So it was that the entire worldview of the Epistle to the Hebrews was at home within Alexandrianism's metaphysical contrasts of idea and appearance, eternal and finite, heavenly and cosmic, prototype and likeness."[12] Holtzmann was thinking here that according to Hebrews the high-priestly service of Christ took place in a heavenly sanctuary just as that of the levitical high priest was done in an earthly one (8:5; 9:1-11, 23). But was it really the case that Hebrews thought primarily, as it were, in this vertical cosmic-Hellenistic dualism, or did it think like Jesus and Paul in terms of the salvation-historical horizontal dimension? That would mean for Christology: Was Jesus for Hebrews the manifestation of an eternal idea or was he the One who brought history to its goal? And that would mean for soteriology: Was the salvation of man the translation of the soul into its home above or was it participation in the exodus of the new people of God?

The reply to this question about the fundamental optic through which Hebrews viewed things was signaled by its understanding and its utilization of scripture. The vertical dimension did in fact surface in its exegesis on two occasions. It spoke in 12:22 and 13:14 about the heavenly Jerusalem; above all, however, it explained in 8:5 and 9:1-11, 23 that Christ was the high priest in the heavenly sanctuary, while the levitical high priests performed their functions in the earthly sanctuary. That reminds one of Philo, who in the sense of a Platonic-gnosticizing dualism was regularly placing the ideal heavenly world over against the inferior earthly world. For Hebrews too the heavenly sanctuary was not merely an image borrowed from Ex. 25:40, but the symbol of a reality. It qualified this heavenly sanctuary and the heavenly priestly service with terms derived from dualistic vocabulary when it said: "For Christ has entered, not into a sanctuary made with hands, a copy of the true one, but into heaven itself, now to appear in the presence of God on our behalf" (9:24). The term *alēthinos* (true) referred here, as often in John, in a dualistic sense to that which was intrinsic over against that which was derivative. Yet in both Hebrews and John that which was intrinsic was not qualified cosmically, but through its immediacy to God. The Epistle to the Hebrews employed such dualistic conceptual elements from the Hellenistic as well as from the early Gnostic view of the world; they were for it, however, only auxiliary benchmarks helping to express the eschatological preeminence of Christ. The foundation of its theological thought processes was, in contrast, the

---

[12]*Theologie* II, 331f.

salvation-historical horizontal dimension that expressed itself in terms of the greatly predominating typological utilization of scripture.[13]

b) What intention was this utilization of scripture pursuing, standing as it did without peer in the whole New Testament when it came to intensity and formal cultivation? An apologetical or polemical intent has frequently been ascribed to it; in this view, the author desired to provide scriptural evidence for his Christology from the Old Testament since it was for his readers a recognized authority; by doing this, he could also claim the Old Testament polemically for Christians.[14] Polemical or apologetical barbs, however, are nowhere to be observed like we find in Matthew or in Paul's debate with Judaizers and Jews. The barbs that are to be observed in this document were directed exclusively in a parenetic sense at the readers. By means of a typological utilization of the Old Testament the contemporary situation of the community and the course of Jesus' life were to be interpreted in a binding way. As such, typology was by no means merely a secondarily employed form of thought that should serve the purpose of affixing to the Old Testament an image of Christ that was derived primarily from speculation. Rather, it was the specifically primitive Christian, productive method of utilizing scripture. Of course, Hebrews did not develop its image of Christ as the high priest in a purely spontaneous, exegetical manner from the Old Testament, but in the process availed itself of traditions. But its extended fashioning of this image was accomplished in large measure through independent acquaintance with scripture. This will become clear when we examine more closely this remarkable christological composition.

4. THE HIGH PRIEST CHRISTOLOGY

a) The designations for Christ. Two designations were emphasized in the Christology of the Epistle to the Hebrews: *ho huios* (the Son) and *ho archiereus* (the high priest).[15] Alongside these the remaining christological titles of the New Testament were used only occasionally. The Son of man predicate could be heard indirectly on only one occasion (2:6), something that is hardly surprising for a document that came out of the Hellenistic church. That makes it all the more noticeable when the designation that was dominant in the Pauline realm (§34), *ho kyrios* (the Lord), only appeared sporadically, mostly as a designation for the earthly One, i.e., in a pre-Pauline usage (2:3; 7:14). Finally, in 1:8 the Son was addressed as God (*ho theos*), something that occurred otherwise only in the Gospel of John. The customary christological name was *Iēsous*. The combination customary for Paul, *Iēsous Christos*, was used only sporadically (10:10; 13:8,

---

[13]With this accentuation of both lines our view of the rational structure of the Epistle to the Hebrews is exactly the reverse of H. J. Holtzmann (cf. n. 12) and E. Käsemann (Lit., §47); the latter considered the Gnostic world view as the foundation and regarded the typological interpretation of scripture as merely a secondary apologetic designed to meet the need of the readers.

[14]Cf. Schröger, op. cit. (Lit., §47), pp. 11-32.

[15]In place of *archiereus*, *hiereus megas* (10:21) was used on occasion with the same meaning or—according to Ps. 110:4—only *hiereus*.

21). Correspondingly, *Christos* was used alone and almost throughout with the definite article; it was not only a name but frequently also a messianic title (3:14; 5:5; 6:1; 9:14, 24, 28; without the article only in 3:16).

On the basis of this terminological overview we note the following: for Hebrews, Jesus was the Son of God just like he was for Paul and John. But whereas in Paul the Son was at work accomplishing salvation as the *kyrios*, in Hebrews the christological event of salvation was linked to the title *archiereus* (high priest).

b) The Son's path to perfection as the high priest. The first major section (chs. 1–6) took as its starting point christologically the concept of the Son and then moved to that of the high priest.

1) The starting point (Heb. 1:1-4). Just as the theology of the Epistle to the Romans took its starting point from the christological confession in 1:3f., so the Epistle to the Hebrews did so with the hymnic confession in 1:1-4. It gained access to the essence of Jesus much like the prologue of the Gospel of John (Jn. 1:1-18) by the equally central and specifically biblical concept that God communicated himself to people through human discourse. What Jn. 1:1 said more in Hellenistic terms ("In the beginning was the Word"), Hebrews formulated more in Old Testament terms:

1) In many and various ways God spoke of old to our
    fathers by the prophets;
2) but in these last days he has spoken
    to us by a Son,
    whom he appointed the heir of all things,
    through whom also he created the world.
3) He reflects the glory of God and bears the very stamp
    of his nature, upholding the universe by his word of power.
    When he had made purification for sins,
    he sat down at the right hand of the Majesty on high,
4) having become as much superior to the angels
    as the name he has obtained is more excellent than theirs.

The first two lines (vv. 1 and 2a) introduced the Son as God's end-time word of revelation. The next lines (vv. 2b and 3a) expressed his significance for the cosmos. Through the Son took place God's entire administration of the world; as the world was created through him, so too it would be perfected through him. A statement in line 5 was added to this cosmic affirmation that stated the Son's relationship to God: in the conceptual language of Hellenistic-Judaism he was the *apaugasma* (reflection) of the Deity of God and the *charaktēr* (stamp) of his essence; he was that which Paul called the *eikōn* (likeness) of God (II Cor. 4:4; Col. 1:15).

These statements about the relationship of the Son to the cosmos and to God were founded upon his soteriological function about which lines 7-10 (vv. 3b and 4) spoke. On the basis of his ministry of salvation Jesus inherited the name "Son." As support for this a quotation from Ps. 2:7: "Thou art my Son!" was

added in 1:5. In the same way 7:28 clarified that the Son became the perfected
Son in eternity and thereby heir of the universe through the path tread by the
Christ. Two things characteristic for Hebrews emerged in terms of this comprehensive christological confession. The one was that the subject behind the course
of Christ's life was not God—in contrast to the ancient Christology of exaltation
in Rom. 1:3—but the Son. He "sat down at the right hand" (line 8 = Ps. 110:1).
The other was that the course of the Son's life received special emphasis; it was
only through this course that the "Son" was perfected to the place of Son; i.e.,
the preexistent One became the messianic mediator of salvation (cf. Rom. 1:3f.).

2) The perfection of the Son and of the sons. The course of the Son's life
was christologically and soteriologically interpreted with the aid of the term
teleioun (to perfect). This verb, which was used nowhere else in the New Testament with such density as in Hebrews, meant in Greek "to perfect." Philo
used it frequently for moral perfection.[16] Hebrews used it, however, as it was
in the LXX, in a cultic sense; in 2:11 and 10:14 it was qualified (as in LXX Ex.
29:33) by means of *hagiazein* (to make holy). Used in this sense, *teleioun* meant
to make someone worthy to come before God, to bring someone to the goal
intended by God.[17] The term was used in this sense christologically; the Son
was "perfected" (7:28). How he was perfected was clarified by the example of
Gethsemane in the difficult statement of 5:7ff.: "In the days of his flesh [i.e.,
as human being], Jesus offered up prayers and supplications, with loud cries and
tears, to him who was able to save him from death, and he was heard for his
godly fear [or: because he was afraid]. Although he was a Son, he learned
obedience through what he suffered; and being made perfect he became the
source of eternal salvation to all who obey him."

In a way distinct from Paul, Hebrews seized upon individual events of the
course of Jesus' earthly life; here it was Gethsemane and elsewhere it was his
temptation (2:18; 4:15). Precisely through these events the Son had to prove his
sonship through struggles with doubt and suffering and was "perfected"; he
became the mediator of salvation who could come before God as the high priest.
The perfected Son was the high priest. In this sense the words of appointment
in 5:5f. were put in conjunction with both side by side: "So also Christ did not
exalt himself to be made a high priest, but was appointed by him who said to
him, 'Thou art my Son, today I have begotten thee'; as he says also in another
place, 'Thou art a priest for ever, after the order of Melchizedek.' " The appointment as Son in the sense of Ps. 2, Son as messianic mediator of salvation,
corresponded to that as high priest.

To both of these christological designations corresponded a soteriological
function that was different in each case. The soteriological function of the Son
can be summarized in advance thus: through his perfection the Son became the
preparer of the way who took care of his brothers, the remaining children of
God; he showed solidarity with them and opened to them the way out of death's

---

[16]Supporting references: G. Delling, *TDNT* VIII, 80.
[17]Similarly, ibid., 82.

grip to God. The function of the Son as preparer of the way was expressed in his designation as *archēgos tēs sōtērias* (pioneer of their salvation, 2:10; cf. 12:2). Less immediate, he was called the *prodromos* (forerunner) in 6:20 who broke the trail for those following him. And in 5:9 he was referred to as the *aitios* (source) of salvation.

The intent of this forerunner concept becomes clearer through consideration of its history-of-tradition background. Initially it calls to mind the synoptic concept of discipleship. But Hebrews did not use the term "to follow in discipleship." Besides this, the path of the forerunner was not a historical but a cosmic term; it led out of the realm under the angels (2:9) and under the fear of death (2:15), under temptation and suffering on "through the curtain, that is, through his flesh" (10:20)—i.e., through the boundary of finitude—and through heaven to God (2:8-10; 5:8f.; 9:26; 10:19f.). Thus the synoptic concept of discipleship has been transposed into the situation after Easter in such a way that the course of Jesus' life was featured as the breaking loose of the grip of death in which people live.

For this reason the statements about the preparer of the way also call to mind the concepts of Hellenistic Judaism and of gnosticism.[18] E. Käsemann also proposed, therefore, as history-of-religion background the Gnostic myth of the redeemer who led the souls related to him by essence through the spheres of the universe to their heavenly home.[19] The statement of Hebrews, however, distinguished itself characteristically from the Gnostic concept of the redeemer. The sons that the Son led to glory were not related to him by essence as they were in that context! To be sure, in 2:11 the "brotherhood" of him who "sanctifies" and of the "sanctified" was marked by the origin of each—of course in a different way—from God; yet this "brotherhood" was realized only by means of the pioneer having sanctified those who followed him.

The Son was the forerunner who prepared the way for those who belonged to him only as the One who at the same time was the high priest who purified them from sin. Hence the statements about the Son making common cause with the children of God always flowed into the notion of the high-priestly service on their behalf. This can be seen with telling clarity in 2:14-18 where the "with" and the "on behalf of" were directly interwoven. Thus 2:14f. stated: "Since therefore the children share in flesh and blood, he himself likewise partook of the same nature, that through death he might destroy him who has the power of death, that is, the devil, and deliver all those who through fear of death were subject to lifelong bondage." This statement about the breaking loose of the grip by the preparer of the way, as it were, from the bottom up was immediately supplemented through reference to his atoning intercession for those who be-

---

[18]The title *archēgos* ("pioneer"; "leader") probably played upon the designation of the patriarchs in Hellenistic Judaism. Supporting references are found in Schweizer, *Lordship*, p. 89 (the Ger. revision, pp. 138f., contains an extended footnote [n. 514] referred to here by Goppelt).

[19]Op. cit. (n. 13), p. 81.

longed to him: "Therefore he had to be made like his brethren in every respect, so that he might become a merciful and faithful high priest . . . to make expiation for the sins of the people. For because he himself has suffered and been tempted, he is able to help those who are tempted" (2:17f.). The functions of the preparer of the way and of the high priest who interceded for those who belonged to him were linked together in the same way in 4:14–5:10; 10:19-21; and 12:1f.

c) The origin of the high priest concept. 1) Nowhere else in the New Testament was Jesus referred to as the high priest. The title, however, and the concept belonging to it are found in the First Epistle of Clement and otherwise as well in the Apostolic Fathers as liturgical tradition.[20] Of special interest for us is I Clement. In the great prayer for the church that closed the letter (ch. 61) it was said: "We praise Thee through the high priest and guardian of our souls" (I Clem. 61:3; similarly also 64:1 = LCL, Apostolic Fathers, I, 121). In I Clem. 36:1 the exalted One was called "the high priest of our offerings" (= LCL, I, 71). Intended here was that he brought "offerings," namely prayers, before God.[21] With high probability, this liturgical-worship service concept of the high priest who interceded before God for those who belonged to him was not first developed in conversation with the Hebrews known to I Clement. Rather it was the other way around; the concept was the starting point from which Hebrews developed its high priest Christology. After all, in Heb. 2:17 the motif of the high priest who made intercession for his own was introduced quite spontaneously and was presupposed as familiar to the readers.[22]

2) In any case the tradition about the exalted One who interceded for those who belonged to him before God that developed into the high priest concept showed itself to be relatively ancient. It had been combined directly with the saying of the Psalm about sitting at the right hand (Ps. 110:1), as Rom. 8:34 shows. Just this Psalm, however, contained in v. 4 the leading statement from which Hebrews developed its high priest Christology: "Thou art a priest for ever, after the order of Melchizedek" (Heb. 5:6). Perhaps Ps. 110:4 had already very early provided the stimulus to designate the One who interceded on behalf of his own before God as the priest. Hebrews, however, also derived from Ps. 110:4 the decisive statement about the type of Christ's high priesthood. Christ was not a high priest like all other Jewish/Old Testament high priests of the house of Aaron or of Levi; he was the high priest after the order of Melchizedek (5:10; 6:20; 7:1-28)!

3) In the first two passages where Hebrews used this designation (3:1; 4:14) it pointed to the homologia, the confession of the community: "Since then we have a great high priest who has passed through the heavens, Jesus, the Son of

---

[20]I Clem. 36:1; Ign. Phld. 9:1; Pol. Phil. 12:2; Mart. Pol. 14:3; cf. W. Bauer et al., Die Apostolischen Väter (HNT Ergänzungsband, 1923), at Ign. Phld. 9:1= p. 261.

[21]Different, of course, are W. Bousset, Kyrios, p. 439 (cf. also pp. 361f.), and following him Theissen, op. cit. (Lit., §47), pp. 41f.

[22]Similarly, Hahn, Titles, pp. 229ff. (there overview representation of the discussion).

God, let us hold fast our confession" (4:14). And with a third reference to the confession it concluded in 10:19ff. the statements about the high priesthood. Thus the concept of the high priesthood was bound together with the confession of the community. The confession did not mean here the timely act of confessing but a formulated confession. This most certainly contained—among what other particulars of content one might imagine—the statement about "sitting at the right hand."[23] It not only appeared in the introductory hymnic confession of Christ (1:3), but was also appropriated in 8:1 and interpreted throughout that chapter in the sense of the One who interceded as high priest. Hence we see a further possible starting point for the statements about the high priest; through those statements the *homologia*, the confession, was supposed to be interpreted for the community. The confession provided the content of the high-priestly path: the high-priestly self-sacrifice as well as his passing through the heavens into the Holy of Holies before God.

4) The image of the high-priestly activity, however, was derived by the writer from the institution of the great day of atonement (Lev. 16). This was the central provision for atonement in the Old Covenant and was linked to the atoning death of Jesus in primitive Christianity before the composition of Hebrews (§35,4a). After this concept was addressed for the first time in 6:19, the course of Jesus' life and ministry were portrayed in 8:1–10:18 in correspondence to the service of the high priest on the day of atonement.

5) To what extent did the author employ Jewish interpretive tradition in the development of his image of the high-priestly activity of Jesus? The following possibilities have been considered in scholarly research.

5.1   The assumption emerging after the discovery of the Qumran texts, that Hebrews found suggestive impetus in the Essene expectation of the high priest-Messiah, has not found confirmation. The Essene high priest-Messiah came from the house of Aaron or of Levi, the one of Hebrews precisely did not (7:13). The Essene figure was a human being like the Davidic Messiah who stood next to him; the high priest of Hebrews, however, in 7:3 was like Melchizedek, having "neither beginning of days nor end of life, but resembling the Son of God." Also, the high-priestly service of the contexts under comparison have nothing in common.[24]

5.2   Attempts to derive the lofty developments of thought about Melchizedek, the priestly king of Salem in 7:1-10, from a Hellenistic-Jewish midrash on the Melchizedek pericope in Gen. 14 have also led to no satisfactory conclu-

---

[23]G. Bornkamm, *Aufsätze* II, 190ff., conjectured that Hebrews intended in 3:1; 4:14; and 10:39 a baptismal confession that like Acts 8:37 ran: "Jesus is the Son of God." In opposition then was to be seen in 13:15 a hymnic confession of the community or of the community's service of worship, something like what is found in the introductory confession of Christ (1:1-4). In my view, however, also and precisely in the first three passages was intended such a confession about the course of Jesus' life and not only an honorific statement.

[24]For this reason H. Braun, *Qumran* II, 181-84, also rejected this context.

sion.[25] Direct supports for such an interpretive tradition could not be produced. The baroque-style allegory of Philo on Gen. 14 was of another type.[26]

5.3 More probable would be the appropriation of a Hellenistic-Jewish source for the ascension and the heavenly service of the high priest according to Heb. 8 and 9. The concept of a heavenly sanctuary was not developed directly out of Ex. 25:40. The heavenly sanctuary was qualified to some extent in the sense of Hellenistic-Jewish dualism as the genuine, intrinsic one. For this reason alone the concept of a heavenly high priest could also have acquired impetus from Hellenistic-Jewish traditions.[27] Going beyond this conjecture, E. Käsemann[28] attempted a derivation of the statements of Hebrews as well as those of Philo about the heavenly high priest from Gnostic speculative thought regarding a primal man high priest in the context of Hellenistic-Judaism. This derivation, however, is without foundation when examined by the methodological principles for the study of gnosticism inaugurated by Bultmann.[29] One cannot postulate ostensibly pre-Christian concepts in this way on the basis of later sources!

Thus we may conclude regarding the history-of-religion background of the high priest concept that Hebrews or the preceding Christian community-tradition about Christ as the heavenly high priest may well have received stimuli from Hellenistic Judaism, but their significance should not be overestimated. In essence, the author of Hebrews started from a liturgical formula and composed this image with the aid of his interpretation of scripture as an interpretation of the confession of Christ in the community.

d) The typological interpretation of the course of Jesus' life and ministry seen from Lev. 16 in Heb. 8–10. With the aid of a typological utilization of Lev. 16, Jesus' life and ministry were interpreted in Heb. 8–10 as an integrated event of salvation in which each individual moment had its necessary and meaningful place. The same tradition that may have stood behind this utilization of Lev. 16 was also appropriated by Paul in Rom. 3:24ff. (cf. §35,4a). But let us now reconstruct how the Old Testament act of atonement looked in the view of Hebrews, the act that was depicted quite heterogeneously in a variously expanded text of Lev. 16!

Once a year on the day of atonement the high priest passed through the sanctuary and went behind the curtain into the Holy of Holies where God was present over the Ark of the Covenant (Heb. 9:7, 25; 10:1, 3 = Lev. 16:34; cf.

---

[25]Regarding the discussion, cf. O. Michel, *TDNT* IV, 569.

[26]The Christian-Gnostic sect of the Melchizedekians that arose in the 2nd century A.D. made use of the statements in Heb. 7 and not the reverse. The material germane to this question was provided by H. Windisch, *Der Hebräerbrief*, at Heb. 7:14 (excursus).

[27]Philo also characterized the heavenly logos as high priest; cf. G. Schrenk, *TDNT* III, 273. Conjecturing that the concept of the heavenly high priest in Hebrews was taken over directly from these speculative reflections were: Windisch, op. cit. (n. 26), at Heb. 1:4 (excursus) and C. Spicq, *L'Épitre aux Hébreux* 1 (1952), 39-91. As source for the high-priestly ascension, Windisch (op. cit., at Heb. 8:2) assumed the apocalyptic speculation about the ascension of Enoch (I Enoch 70:71; II Enoch 67:68) and especially about the ascension of Levi (Test. Levi 2–5).

[28]Op. cit. (n. 13), pp. 131-140.

[29]C. Colpe, *Die religionsgeschichtliche Schule* (1961); cf. above, §29,2.

16:15). Only with the blood of the atoning sacrifice was the high priest allowed to enter the Holy of Holies where it was graciously accepted by God (Heb. 9:7, 12f.; 10:4 = Lev. 16:2f.). With this blood he purified both himself and the people from sin (Heb. 5:3; 7:27 = Lev. 16:14f., 24, 30, 33).

That which the Aaronic high priest accomplished yearly in this way, Christ accomplished once for all time as true high priest. The stages of his destiny that were named by the confession became understandable in terms of typological correspondence.

Let us now consider this process of making typological correspondence from the perspective of its goal; in terms of the history of tradition that was also the perspective from which it was composed!

1) When the community, according to Heb. 1:3 and 8:1, confessed: "seated at the right hand," it was to see Jesus as the high priest who interceded for it in the heavenly Holy of Holies with his own blood (8:1f.; 9:24). This typological image expressed still more than the visionary symbol of the lamb in Revelation (§44,3a); it expressed the intrinsic meaning of the confession about sitting at the right hand. Sitting at the right hand meant not *imperium* but *dominium*, the eschatological dominion of salvation, because it meant primarily and simultaneously *intercessio*. It meant this because the typological image that interpreted this statement of the confession also provided the connection to the preceding course of Christ's life. According to Lev. 16, the presupposition for this *intercessio* was the atoning sacrifice and the entry into the Holy of Holies.

2) The entry into the Holy of Holies became for Christ his entry "into heaven itself" (9:24), a high-priestly ascension. This vivid concept replaced in Hebrews the traditional speech about arising or being-raised and being-exalted; these technical terms were not missing by accident! Having undergone interpretation the content represented by these terms was expressed by this typological image: resurrection and exaltation were Jesus' passing on into God's gracious turning of himself in salvation and thereby his perfecting as mediator of salvation.

3) This passing on to God, however, was only meaningful on the basis of his atoning sacrifice. No portion of the course of Jesus' life was so thoroughly clarified in Hebrews as Jesus' dying. The statement of 9:12 together with 10:19ff. was one of the two focal points of the document: "he entered once for all into the Holy Place, taking not the blood of goats and calves but his own blood. . . ." That meant that Jesus' dying was not an object-oriented sacrifice but a personal self-sacrifice. Jesus was he "who through the eternal Spirit offered himself without blemish to God" (9:14). Thus stood the typological supersession: "For if the sprinkling of defiled persons with the blood of goats and bulls . . . sanctifies for the purification of the flesh, how much more shall the blood of Christ . . . purify your conscience from dead works" (9:13f.).

This conclusion was only relevant when those Old Testament purifications, even if only as a shadow (10:1), made known God's order of salvation. It presupposed, therefore, that the atonement ritual of the day of atonement was God's gracious institution and that God wanted to save his bankrupt creature through atonement. That atonement was imperative, moreover, was the subject matter of the section 9:16-28; here the expressions *ananke* and *dei* (necessity; must be) that pointed back to God's plan of salvation came markedly to the fore (vv. 16, 23, 26). In its center (v. 22b) stood the concise statement: "without the shedding of blood [i.e., without atoning death] there is no forgiveness of sins."[30]

4) This self-sacrifice that became effective through the passing on to and interceding before God was the result of a life that stood the test during its days lived on earth. It was about that life that the preparatory chs. 1–6 spoke, especially in 5:7-10. Thus Jesus' life and ministry were interpreted as an integrated event of salvation that brought to realization God's order of salvation. By showing the mutual relationship to the Old Testament background the reader was to gain understanding about how it was necessary (*ananke*), how it had to be (*dei*), how it was compatible (*eprepen*) with God that salvation should have followed along this path.

5) Finally, we should touch on the much discussed question: When did Jesus become the high priest? He came into his office when he made his high-priestly self-sacrifice. The intrinsic exercise of the *munus sacerdotale*, however, was the *intercessio* before God.

e) The salvation-historical position and effect of Jesus as the mediator of the New Covenant. 1) The New Covenant. If Jesus offered the true sacrifice that eliminated the power of sin and thereby opened access to God, then the promised eschatological turning point in the relationship between the Creator and his creatures came about through him. It was in the final analysis this reality that stood behind the conclusion that was drawn in 8:6 in terms of the superiority of Jesus' high-priestly service: "But as it is, Christ has obtained a ministry which is as much more excellent than the old as the covenant he mediates is better, since it is enacted on better promises." Similarly it was said of Jesus in 7:22: "the surety of a better covenant."

The "better covenant" was the covenant promised in Jer. 31. This promise was quoted in detail at the beginning and at the end of the thought developments about the high-priestly service (8:8-12; 10:16); this promise had already guided the theological overview of Paul (II Cor. 3) and probably even already the self-understanding of Jesus (Mk. 14:24; §20,4b). If Jesus, however, was the mediator of the promised new relationship to God, then it could be concluded for the previous relationship, the Sinai Covenant: "In speaking of a new covenant he treats the first as obsolete. And what is becoming obsolete and growing old is ready to vanish away" (Heb. 8:13). This difficult statement intended to say that the Old Covenant was not simply replaced by the New in a chronological sense but that it, like the Law, was passing away along with the time frame of this world. Even Hebrews was familiar therefore with the presence of the *eschaton* in history.

2) The suspension of the Law. Along with the Sinai Covenant the manifes-

---

[30]This statement was in principle not Jewish but Christian, since according to the Pharisaic practice of repentance, atonement could also be accomplished through additional good works.

tation of Jesus suspended the Law, and that in keeping with the "promise" (8:6ff.) or the "word of the oath" (7:28) announced in the Old Testament. In a different way than Paul, Hebrews developed the suspension of the Law from the perspective of the priesthood. The high priesthood of Jesus after the order of Melchizedek that was set up through Ps. 110:4 suspended the priesthood of Aaron. 7:18f. stated programmatically: "On the one hand, a former command-ment [i.e., the Mosaic Law] is set aside because of its weakness and uselessness (for the law made nothing perfect); on the other hand, a better hope is introduced, through which we draw near to God." In spite of external terminological resem-blance, Law and Covenant were seen here in a way much different than in Paul.

3) The Law in Hebrews. For Jesus and Paul, the Law was the demanding will of God that insisted on obedience and promised life to the obedient one. In other words, the Law was the demand of obedience under the aegis of the order of retribution (Mt. 19:17-19; Rom. 10:5). In contrast, for Hebrews the regula-tions governing the service of the priests stood at the center of the Law (7:12; 8:4; 10:8). The center of the Law was therefore a provision for salvation through which sins were cancelled and access to God was made available. The order of the great day of atonement (Lev. 16) appeared as the center of the Law. Naturally, the demand of obedience represented the background of these provisions for salvation. The atoning sacrifices were necessary because "the message [of the Law] declared by angels was valid and every transgression or disobedience re-ceived a just retribution" (2:2; cf. 10:28).

If Hebrews gave prominence to the atonement order of the Covenant in such a way as this, it marked thereby a side of the Law that was passed over in silence in the writings of Paul, but has been emphasized today by Old Testament research as well as by the objections of Jewish theology. Hebrews clarified that for the Old Testament the demand of the Law was set within the framework of the Covenant of God, and that it was therefore already connected in the Old Covenant to atonement and forgiveness, indeed was based upon them.

This thesis of Hebrews, however, was wedded to the conclusion that the provisions for atonement in the Old Testament had not been effective. When one thinks about the sacrificial cult in Israel that spanned the centuries a judgment could hardly have been more radical than to state that it was impossible for sins to be removed through the blood of bulls and goats (10:4; cf. 9:9) and that therefore the priesthood (7:11) and the Law brought nothing to perfection (7:18), i.e., they put no one in fellowship with God.

The kerygmatic intention behind this radical thesis becomes clear from the viewpoint of 10:1: "the law has but a shadow of the good things to come instead of the true form of these realities." Paul put antitheses into writing against the righteousness of the Law propounded by Jews and Judaizers. Hebrews wrote with an eye toward an acquiescent community and wished to make clear to it in terms of the supersession of the Old Testament cult through Christ's self-sacrifice that a religious possibility had been opened up to it that could never be superseded.

No less impressive were then the parenetic conclusions of the document that were drawn from the christological developments of thought we have brought together in this section. If Jesus as high priest was the mediator and guarantor of the New Covenant, then the person who was committed to him in the way it was expressed in the transmitted confession stood already within the New Covenant in spite of all appearances to the contrary and thereby already upon the abiding foundation of the new world. "Therefore let us be grateful for receiving a kingdom that cannot be shaken" (12:28). For the one who had gained footing upon this abiding world there was no turning back. This one belonged to God's people of the Exodus, the people that was on a journey (3:12–4:11); this one belonged to the company of believers that had no abiding city here but looked for the future one (11:13f.).

5. THE PARENESIS

The theology of the Epistle to the Hebrews was like an elliptical lens with two focal points. The one was the high priest Christology, the other the parenesis that concentrated on the warning against irreversible apostasy. We shall represent as follows this parenesis from the perspective of the warning and the statement connected to it about the impossibility of a second repentance.

a) The soteriological terminology. The proper understanding of the warnings against irreversible apostasy (3:18f.; 6:14ff.; 10:26ff.; 12:16f.) depends on a substantively accurate explanation of the soteriological terminology used by them.

While Paul and John developed a new soteriological terminology of their own, Hebrews followed the soteriological terminology of the synoptic tradition and the missionary sermons of Acts. Paul spoke, e.g., about justification, reconciliation, or dying-with in order to live-with (§35,5; §39), and John spoke about new birth and about passing from death to life (§49,2). Hebrews, however, stayed with traditional expressions and spoke about *metanoia* (repentance, 6:1, 6 [NEB]; 12:17) and about *aphesis hamartiōn* (forgiveness of sins, 9:22; 10:18; cf. 10:26).

The same soteriological terminology continued then to play a dominant role in the early writings from the Roman community, in I Clement and in the Shepherd of Hermas, and was also passed on from them to the Western church. Concerning the history of terminology a curious circular movement took place here; as early as in the Shepherd of Hermas the content of these terms came close once again to the use in the synagogue from which Jesus had distanced himself. For the synagogue repentance was the active contrition to be repeated regularly for transgressions of the commandments and forgiveness was the cancellation of the debt accomplished by such active repentance. Jesus, however, demanded a once-for-all total repentance, man's complete turning of himself over to God that corresponded to God's turning of himself toward man, i.e., that corresponded to forgiveness (Lk. 15:11-32; cf. §12,5). Both repentance and forgiveness took place when Jesus summoned a person into discipleship.

In view of the history of this terminological spectrum we must ask: Did Hebrews with its doctrine of repentance stand with Jesus or with the synagogue to which the Shepherd of Hermas again came close? It certainly stood with Jesus by virtue of the fact that it emphasized the singularity of repentance and the singularity of the forgiveness corresponding to it. But did it understand them in the way that Jesus did?

b) **The impossibility of a second repentance.** 1) The impossibility of a second repentance was expressed in Heb. 6:4-6: "For it is impossible to restore again to repentance those who have once been enlightened, who have tasted the heavenly gift, and have become partakers of the Holy Spirit, and have tasted the goodness of the word of God and the powers of the age to come, if they then commit apostasy, since they crucify the Son of God on their own account and hold him up to contempt."

What did the impossibility consist of? Conversion and apostasy were looked at here as complete eschatological moments. The one who was converted had crossed over the threshold between the old and the new world; this was made clear by the four expressions that circumscribed in 6:4f. acceptance into the state of salvation. One cannot be led back across this threshold a second time. Whoever became apostate did not simply give up a world view; rather, this one knowingly repeated for himself, as 6:6b put it, what the Jews had done unknowingly to Jesus in his crucifixion.

2) That this "impossible" was not formulated with categories of psychological and pastoral empiricism in mind becomes clear in 10:26f. Here it was not a second repentance that was ruled out but its correspondence, the forgiveness of sins: "For if we sin deliberately after receiving the knowledge of the truth, there no longer remains a sacrifice for sins, but a fearful prospect of judgment, and a fury of fire which will consume the adversaries."

This thesis appeared on the surface to appropriate the Old Testament/Jewish differentiation between known sins and sins that were committed without deliberation. But Hebrews used the Old Testament/Jewish terminology of "sin deliberately" in order to say something new. It meant thereby not a single grave transgression of a commandment, but the renunciation of the knowledge of the truth, i.e., as in 6:6, apostasy. In this sense, 10:29 circumscribed the intended offense with three drastic expressions that had their correspondence in 6:6b: "the man who has spurned the Son of God, and profaned the blood of the covenant by which he was sanctified, and outraged the Spirit of grace"; he has committed the sin against the Spirit. A renewed recourse to the event of salvation was no longer possible here because the eschatological singularity of Christ's sacrifice, the *eph' hapax* marked with such emphasis by Hebrews (9:12, 28; 10:10, 12, 14), conditioned the eschatological singularity of repentance (6:4). The angle of vision of Paul ("where sin increased, grace abounded all the more" [Rom. 5:20]) was apparently not appropriated in this question.

3) In Heb. 12:16f. the situation was illustrated once again under the catchword "to repent" by way of the forfeiture of birthright by Esau: "that no one be immoral or irreligious like Esau, who sold his birthright for a single meal. For you know that afterward, when he desired to inherit the blessing, he was rejected, for he found no chance to repent, though he sought it with tears."

The offense here too was not the grave transgression of a commandment, but the forfeiture of the grace represented by Christ; this forfeiture was realized, of course, not in the theoretical realm but in concrete practice as the exchange of grace for life bound to this world. The expression "he found no chance to repent" characterized the impossibility of repentance both as a subjective and as an objective dimension; Esau was as subjectively contrite as Judas, but this contrition was not yet repentance; but also objectively there was "no chance" anymore because the blessing had been given away.

But could the grace of Christ—we should ask critically—like the blessing of Jacob be used up in terms of time and amount? Did not the eschatological gift encompass all the vicissitudes of life in the frame of time?

4) The statements we have just interpreted should not be understood as parts of a didactic theory. Rather they constituted the negative extreme possibility of a parenesis that was followed in each case by a positive promise. Thus, following the first reference to the impossibility of repentance after apostasy (6:4-7) came immediately the positive statement: "Though we speak thus, yet in your case, beloved, we feel sure of better things that belong to salvation" (6:9). The author did not want to enjoin the readers to exercise judgment over their brother or even over themselves. The boundary between the offense that stood under the patience of God and the forfeiture of Christ that cost a person one's life, "God alone decided."[31]

These statements were the negative side of a kerygmatic summons to hold fast to faith. They were a parenetic warning to Christians for whom faith and hope were steadily losing significance; they were in danger of succumbing to the fascination of a purely inner-worldly existence; with eyes wide open they were about to step over a boundary line from which one could never return. The warning said to them: whoever retreated in faith was nearing an abyss with one's back. The very next step backward could be one step too many. Whoever played with grace, because he knew it was eternal, would lose it.

5) The foregoing should not, however, cause one to miss the seriousness of the reference to the boundary line. Therefore we must inquire into the theological basis for representing this boundary, the *adynaton* (the "impossible," 6:4).

E. Grässer saw in its establishment a violation by Hebrews of the apostolic concept of grace and faith.[32] Such would imply that the new existence was no longer grasped as the constant decision of faith, but as the consequence of faith understood in terms of habit. Grässer was correct that an altered use of the term faith in Hebrews brought a shift in accent along with it. And yet, that does not

---

[31]A. Schlatter, *Erläuterungen* III, at Heb. 6 (pp. 306-326).
[32]*Der Glaube im Hebräerbrief*, pp. 192ff.

solve the problem. Certainly for Paul, baptism comprehended the rest of one's life as the summons to live out that baptism in a constantly relevant way through faith (Rom. 6:11); but for Paul too the baptized person's struggle with sin was not exhausted with this permanent posture of faith's decisions. He too was acquainted with the extreme focus upon the total breach of relationship, as his demand of excommunication for the one practicing incest showed (I Cor. 5). For Hebrews, however, the situation had become far more acute in this respect. It stood before the critical problematic of apostasy because of the lengthening of time (Heb. 10:25). In view of that issue it spoke about the boundary line.

6) So it can be said by way of summarizing the perspectives seen thus far: the rigorous reference to the boundary came about because Hebrews understood the eschatological singularity of Christ's work and of repentance, and because in terms of the community situation it stood over against a tendency toward apostasy. In relationship to this tendency the boundary that Judas represented must be considered. Coming into its statement, however, was the undertone of a quantitative limitation of grace because Hebrews did not understand faith as the relevant living out of baptismal repentance but as its consequence, as a stance that was maintained or given up.

7) Finally, we need now to illustrate the position taken by Hebrews on the question of a second repentance from the perspective of its substantive context. We shall do so as we look for comparable statements in the rest of the New Testament.

Only I Jn. 5:16 went a step further: "There is sin which is mortal; I do not say that one is to pray for that." Here the author not only called to remembrance the boundary established by God, but the community was instructed to refrain from intercessory prayer for sinners when a particular degree of offense had been reached. This "mortal sin" was for I John the willful departure from the love of God and the brethren. This departure could take on anti-Christian form in relationship to which the prayer of the community for forgiveness became mute.

In contrast, the warnings against offenses encountered throughout the New Testament that excluded inheriting "the kingdom of God" (e.g., Gal. 5:21) fell short of the position taken by Hebrews. They summoned to repentance and did not warn against the impossibility of repentance (e.g., I Cor. 10:12). Comparable to Hebrews were: the warning about the sin against the Spirit (Mt. 12:31f.), the warning about the fate of the foolish virgins (Mt. 25:10ff.) for whom exactly this "too late" was true, and also the already mentioned exclusion from the community of the one practicing incest (I Cor. 5).

Thus the Epistle to the Hebrews stood thoroughly within the framework of a substantive New Testament context even in terms of this extreme focus.

c) Hebrews and the early catholic practice of repentance. 1) The early catholic practice of repentance most probably took its point of departure from Hebrews in an antithetical manner. We meet up with the questioning of the Western church about repentance and the wrestling over an appropriate practice of repentance for the first time in the Shepherd of Hermas, an apocalyptic prophecy written in Rome between A.D. 120 and 140. The considerations of Hermas started with the thesis that there was fundamentally but one repentance.

In *M*. 4.3.1f. Hermas inquired of the *angelus interpres*: " 'I have heard, sir . . . from some teachers that there is no second repentance beyond the one given when we went down into the water and received remission of our former sins.' He said to me, 'You have heard correctly, for this is so. For he who has received remission of sin ought never to sin again, but to live in purity' " (= LCL, *Apostolic Fathers*, II, 83). We are not familiar with any teacher in the time prior to Hermas who had expressed exactly the singularity of baptismal repentance and the singularity of forgiveness in this way other than the author of Hebrews. Since the author stood within the tradition of the community of Rome he may have been the author from whom Hermas received the doctrine of the singularity of repentance. If that is correct, however, there was no other New Testament document that so directly shaped the origin and early history of Western Christianity than did Hebrews. Hermas then developed its message of second repentance in formal recognition of the thesis in Hebrews and yet in substantive contrast to it.

2) Hermas taught regarding the work of Jesus and the corresponding way to salvation: "When, therefore, he [Jesus] had cleansed the sins of the people, he showed them the ways of life, and gave them the Law . . ." (*Sim*. 5.6.3 = LCL, II, 167). Christ's work and the way to salvation corresponding to it were divided, therefore, into two parts. In baptism the sins committed before baptism were forgiven for the sake of Christ's sacrifice; baptism was the first repentance (*M*. 4.3.1ff.). The purity achieved in baptism had to be maintained through observance of the Law of Christ (*Sim*. 8.3.2) in order to be acquitted in the Last Judgment. After all, in the Last Judgment a tally would be made of forgiven guilt and accomplished obedience.

And then Hermas noted with deep consternation that neither he nor even less the community had maintained this purity after baptism. In the midst of this distress the possibility of a second repentance was revealed to the author through an apocalyptic vision: Prior to the new *parousia* the goodness of God once again granted acquittal to all baptized people if they demonstrated active contrition for their sins. That was the offer of a second repentance, the heart of the Shepherd of Hermas (*Vis*. 2.2.4f.).

When the imminent end expected by Hermas did not arrive, the ecclesiastical institution of repentance emerged necessarily from this prophetic message of a singular second repentance; controversial in the Western church of the 2nd and 3rd centuries was then only the matter of whether repentance was possible after baptism for *all* sins. Callixt even allowed adulterers to repent, though Tertullian objected, and Cyprian, opposed by Novatian, even allowed the apostate. Through Augustine and monasticism confessional penance for all Christians was developed out of the public ecclesiastical repentance for grave sins as the ancient church practiced it. Following Augustine then the church of the Middle Ages asked how human achievement and divine grace were related to each other in this confessional penance. But the presupposition for this entire development remained the notion about the way to salvation first appearing in Hermas; according to it, the issue was always the forgiveness of the sins committed after baptism with an eye toward a judgment that would add together acquittal and act of obedience.

Hermas knew on the basis of the apostolic tradition that repentance was a singular, saving possibility granted by God. What he no longer understood was that this singularity had an eschatological character. The eschatological act of baptism encompassed the whole life to its end and was lived out in relevance by faith in that same whole life. In Hermas this eschatological act of baptism became a temporally restricted acquittal that actually corresponded to the Old Testament day of atonement. Sin and forgiveness, sacrificial offering and Law thus took on once again Jewish/Old Testament meaning. The line that begins here could be followed throughout the history of the Western church.[33]

If one looks back from this line to Hebrews it becomes clear that Hebrews still represented the eschatological understanding of baptism that later was lost. As was expressed in the central parenesis of Heb. 10:22, baptism placed one beneath the heavenly high-priestly service of Christ, who opened up access to God. In this respect, the parenesis of Hebrews corresponded entirely to the baptismal parenesis of Rom. 6. The difference between the two can be seen precisely in the way each understood the concept of faith.

d) The concept of faith in Hebrews. 1) The function of faith. E. Grässer concluded in his monograph *Der Glaube im Hebräerbrief* (1965) that faith had been replaced here as a "soteriological category."[34] In Hebrews, in fact, the Christ event never appeared as the content of faith although that event was developed with such depth and thoroughness. In the same way faith did not appear as the permanent transformation of man into Christian existence. It is apparent, therefore, that faith did not have the soteriological interest as topic that it had for Paul and John. As we pursue the reasons for this below, the theological structure of the "letter" will become transparent again, this time from another side.

It is not appropriate to regard this difference in relationship to Paul as a "replacement." As we saw regarding the concept of repentance, Hebrews took a tradition with a different conceptual history as its starting point. This can be seen in terms of its statement concerning the goal of missionary preaching as "repentance from dead works and of faith toward God" (6:1f.). To refer to the starting point of Christian existence as "repentance and faith" alongside each

---

[33] At the Council of Trent the perspective developed by the Shepherd of Hermas basically became fixed; according to Sessio XIV there was no repetition of baptismal repentance because in baptism took place the singular forgiveness of sin alone for Christ's sake and without human assistance. After baptism human action and God's grace had to work together, though grace of course retained preeminence. In contrast to this, Luther discovered anew the eschatological character of baptism when he set forth in the Shorter Catechism that baptism was not the end but the beginning of an existence based on grace alone.

[34] Op. cit. (n. 32), pp. 215f.

other was characteristic for the conceptual language of the synoptic Gospels and the missionary sermons of Acts. Of course, fundamentally faith assumed a soteriological function precisely in the synoptic Gospels (e.g., Mk. 10:52 par.; Lk. 7:50; 17:19; 18:32; Acts 16:31; cf. §12,4f.). The faith that saved was the fundamental living-out of repentance. In contrast, for Hebrews faith did not appear as the soteriological living-out of repentance but rather as its consequence. And this consequence was seen as standing in harmony with that which always had been regarded as the appropriate posture of man in relationship to God. Hence in Heb. 11 it was shown that God's activity, especially his promise, could be appropriated by faith from the very beginning; this was true even if most of the Old Testament passages referred to did not speak expressly about faith.

In light of the above, Hebrews combined repentance and a concept of faith filled out exegetically from the Old Testament. This concept of faith expressed not the living-out but the consequence of repentance, namely, the orientation toward God and his promise.

2) Faith and Christology. This orientation corresponded to the structure of its Christology. For such, Christ was not the content, but "the pioneer and perfecter of our faith" (12:2). The final goal of faith for primitive Christianity—for Paul too—was always God. "To believe in Christ" meant to understand Christ as God's ultimate revelation of salvation. For Hebrews, however, in contrast to Paul Christ was not the revelation of God, but the preparer of the way to God (chs. 1–6) and the high priest who interceded for people before God (chs. 7–10). Seen from the perspective of both functions the relationship to Christ could, therefore, not be described in terms of "faith." Since the technical term "to follow in discipleship" was not appropriated, this relationship was expressed with a variety of terms. Thus Christians were seen as *metochoi Christou* (those who share in Christ, 3:14); they went "forth to him outside the camp" (13:13), or they "tread" upon the path opened up by him "toward God."[35] Thus the Christology of Hebrews prohibited the linking of faith directly to Christ precisely because in that Christology Christ was the subject.

3) The orientation of faith. On the other hand, the community situation required that faith be oriented upon the promise and the future and that it be stabilized as a posture. Paul oriented faith upon the Christ event from which the community arose; the post-Pauline documents—the Gospel of John excepted—oriented it throughout more upon that which was yet to come. For them the problem had now become how the long road to the finish line could be endured. Hence in the parenesis of Hebrews, faith was linked throughout with hope (6:11f.; 10:22f.; 10:36, 39; 11:1).

Of special importance for consideration in this context is the well-known statement in 11:1 that straightway defined faith as hoping. "Now faith is the

---

[35]Schweizer, *Lordship*, pp. 88ff.

assurance of things hoped for, the conviction of things not seen." The translation of both *hypostasis* and *elenchos* is a matter of considerable debate.

While the Vulgate translated *hypostasis* with *substantia* (substance, essence), Luther decided after considerable indecision to follow the advice of Melanchthon and to translate it with "firm assurance." Correspondingly, he rendered *elenchos* with "nondoubt" (certainty). Protestant and, to a great extent also, Roman Catholic exegetes over the last 400 years have followed this definition of faith as a subjective state of being convinced. According to the research of H. Dörrie, however, *hypostasis* elsewhere never had this subjective meaning.[36] The term was used only in Hebrews (1:3; 3:14; 11:1) with the exception of two passages in Paul (II Cor. 9:4; 11:17). It designated in Greek colloquial usage "that which was placed underneath," the substructure, the prop, and then assumed pregnant meaning in philosophy. For the latter *hypostasis* was the essence, the reality, the intrinsic substance in contrast to appearance.

Heb. 1:3 came close to this philosophical usage; there *hypostasis* was the essence or the reality of God, but still not actually the essence in the philosophical sense.

Hence it was a semantic short-circuit when H. Koester postulated from this perspective throughout Hebrews the exact philosophical meaning of the term and translated faith in Heb. 11:1 as "the reality of what is hoped for."[37]

It appears methodologically more reliable when E. Grässer[38] attempted to clarify the term on the basis of its general linguistic sense in context and in the way Hebrews otherwise spoke about faith. According to Grässer, *hypostasis* was "standing firm," "that which stood firm." This meaning was suggested by 3:14, the second passage that understood faith as *hypostasis*. There *hypostasis* was the opposite of *apostēnai* (to fall away, 3:12), as in 11:1 of *hypostolēs* (shrink back, 10:38f.). Thus 11:1 should be translated: "Faith, however, is a standing firm in that which is hoped for and a being convinced (*Überführtsein*) about things that one does not see." It was actually the second part of the statement that introduced an element from Greek thought that was otherwise foreign to the New Testament. It designated faith as a "being convinced" (*elenchos*)[39] about the unseen; this may also mean here: being convinced about intrinsic reality. This unseen reality, however, was in any case also the future eschatological one.

Thus, this statement did not express a theoretical definition, but articulated the hardships of the readers; salvation was for them unseen and future while the afflicting social situation, however, was present and visible. In order to counter this situation Hebrews designated faith as the basic posture in which precisely that which was essential and intrinsic in the earthly drama had been understood

---

[36] "*Hypostasis*. Wort und Bedeutungsgeschichte," *Nachrichten der Akademie der Wissenschaften in Göttingen*, Phil.-hist. Klasse (1955), pp. 35-92; H. Dörrie, "Zu Hebr 11,1," *ZNW* (1955), 196-202.
[37] *TDNT* VIII, 587.
[38] Op. cit. (n. 32), pp. 69ff.
[39] Ibid., pp. 126ff.

and held firm since time began. Hebrews designated faith thus in a long series of examples from the Old Testament (11:2-40).

All of this conditioned the function that the document ascribed to faith in its theology; faith was holding firm to the promised goal of God.

It remains for us to refer to several individual elements that underscored the static character of faith. It was repeatedly referred to as being patient, remaining firm, waiting for (6:12; 10:39; 11:9f.). In several passages faith appeared as a perception (*Einsicht*), regarded statically as well (6:4; 10:26; 11:3). And finally it was oriented less individually than collectively; to believe meant to hold fast to the confession of the community (3:1; 4:14; 10:19ff.) and not to abandon the fellowship of the people of God under the New Covenant.

e) The goal of hope—eschatology. It was the purpose of parenesis that hope would be maintained to the *telos*, to its goal (3:6; 6:11; 10:23). But what did the goal consist of for Hebrews?

Several passages conveyed the impression that this goal was nothing other than the impending *parousia*. Hence 9:28: "So Christ . . . will appear a second time . . . to save those who are eagerly waiting for him"; 10:25: "encouraging one another, and all the more as you see the Day drawing near"; 10:37: " 'For yet a little while, and the coming one shall come and shall not tarry!' "

But although the announcement of the imminent expectation was repeated in these statements, the near *parousia* was by no means the focal point toward which the "letter" pointed its readers. It directed their attention rather to the future that in fact already existed "in heaven," i.e., "above." What the frequently recurring expression *ta mellonta* (the things to come; e.g., 9:11; 10:1) meant was the future city (13:14) that was both the heavenly Jerusalem and everything else that was designated as "in heaven" in 12:22-24. In all of this, attention was focused on the consummation in God that Christ had attained as the forerunner and high priest. According to 6:18ff., hope was "a sure and steadfast anchor of the soul, . . . a hope that enters into the inner shrine behind the curtain, where Jesus has gone as a forerunner on our behalf, having become a high priest for ever after the order of Melchizedek."

Through this accentuation hope detached itself from the question about time and the passage of world history; it did so without being developed in any special way. The universal *parousia* eschatology became, as it were, permeable to the personal eschatology that thought of the perfection of the individual in the hour of death. The one who believed no longer asked: When and how? That one looked now only at the goal, the consummation, into which Christ had already entered. Thus the problem of time and world history with a view toward the *eschaton* was overcome by means of this concentration.

6. THE EPISTLE TO THE HEBREWS AND LUKE

In every respect Hebrews offered an interpretation of the gospel that is fully independent alongside of Paul and John. Its interpretation was written for the community on a long journey, the community that was growing tired under the pressure of faith in the context of society. In this orientation the document showed no greater affinity with any other New Testament writing than the composition of Luke. Yet this agreement went beyond such orientation to a whole series of particulars.

a) Conspicuous is the linguistic proximity of the two authors to each other.[40] This proximity rested not only on the fact that they both wrote a cultivated Greek. Belonging to common linguistic material were also characteristic technical terms of community parlance. Only these two writers referred to Christ, e.g., as the *archēgos* (Heb. 2:10; 12:2; Acts 3:15; 5:31) and to community leaders as the *hēgoumenoi* (Heb. 13:17, 24; Lk. 22:26; Acts 15:22). Both spoke about Jesus "having been perfected" (*teleiousthai*, Heb. 2:10; 5:9; 7:28; Lk. 13:32).

b) For both a comparable community situation was addressed in a similar direction; the situation was quite different from that of the Epistle of James or of John. The farewell address of Paul in Miletus (Acts 20:17-38) and also the farewell discourse of Jesus in Lk. 22:15-38 remind one in many ways of the concluding exhortation of Heb. 13:7ff.: "Remember your leaders, those who spoke to you the word of God; consider the outcome of their life and imitate their faith." The correspondence in the parenetic situation and especially in the concept of faith becomes clear when we read in comparison at Acts 14:22: "[Paul and Barnabas were] strengthening the souls of the disciples, exhorting them to continue in faith, and saying that through many tribulations we must enter the kingdom of God." If one asks how Luke understood this entering into the kingdom of God a further point of contact emerges.

c) Luke referred even less to the *parousia* than did Hebrews, and not at all to an imminent *parousia*, but he referred all the more to the exalted One. And this exalted One had already spoken to the thief on the cross in the words: "today you will be with me in Paradise" (Lk. 23:43). Even here there was obviously a degree of individual eschatology as we saw its way being paved in Hebrews.

Such points of contact in the line of questioning as in their conclusions suggest that the theology of Hebrews and that of Luke should be considered together. Both of these theologies were the most important documents of New Testament theology to come from the post-Pauline period out of the Western church.

§48. Luke—The Theologian of Salvation History

On the History of Research: E. Grässer, "Die Apostelgeschichte in der Forschung der Gegenwart," *ThR* NF 26 (1960), 93-167; A. J. and M. B. Mattill, *A Classified Bibliography of Literature on the Acts of the Apostles* (1966); E. Haenchen, *Acts of the Apostles* (1971), pp. 116-132; W. Gasque, *A History of the Criticism of the Acts of the Apostles* (1975). **Important Commentaries** (Gospel of Luke): E. Klostermann (1929[2]),

---

[40]Cf. C. P. Jones, "The Epistle to the Hebrews and the Lucan Writings," in *Studies in the Gospels, Essays in Memory of R. H. Lightfoot* (ed. D. E. Nineham [1957]), pp. 113-143.

HNT; W. Grundmann (1961), ThHK; E. E. Ellis (1966), New Century Bible; H. Schürmann (1969), HTK (Acts): O. Bauernfeind (1939), ThHK; E. Haenchen (1971), Westminster; G. Stählin (1962), NTD; H. Conzelmann (1963), HNT; cf. also §24, n. 2. **General:** G. Bouwman, *Das dritte Evangelium. Einübung in die formgeschichtliche Methode* (1968); F. Neyrinck, ed., *L'Évangile de Luc. Problèmes littéraires et théologiques. Mémorial Lucien Cerfaux* (1973). **On 1:** H. Conzelmann, *The Theology of St. Luke* (1960); W. C. Robinson, *Der Weg des Herrn. Studien zur Geschichte und Eschatologie im Lukasevangelium. Ein Gespräch mit H. Conzelmann* (1964); E. Lohse, "Lukas als Theologe der Heilsgeschichte," in Lohse, *Die Einheit des Neuen Testaments* (1973), pp. 145-164; G. Klein, "Lukas 1,1-4 als theologisches Programm," in Klein, *Rekonstruktion und Interpretation* (1969), pp. 237-261; P. Vielhauer, "Zum 'Paulinismus' der Apostelgeschichte," in Vielhauer, *Aufsätze zum Neuen Testament* (1965), pp. 9-27; H. Flender, *St. Luke: Theologian of Redemptive History* (1967; Ger. '68²); U. Wilckens, "Lukas und Paulus unter dem Aspekt dialektisch-theologisch beeinflusster Exegese," in Wilckens, *Rechtfertigung als Freiheit. Paulusstudien* (1974), pp. 171-202. **On 2:** H. von Baer, *Der Heilige Geist in den Lukasschriften* (Beiträge zur Wissenschaft vom Alten und Neuen Testament, 3. Folge H. 3 [1926]); O. Cullmann, *Salvation in History* (1967); W. Ott, *Gebet und Heil. Die Bedeutung der Gebetsparänese in der lukanischen Theologie* (1965); T. Holtz, *Untersuchungen über die alttestamentlichen Zitate bei Lukas* (= Texte und Untersuchungen 104 [1968]); K. Löning, "Lukas—Theologe der von Gott geführten Heilsgeschichte (Lk, Apg)," in *Gestalt und Anspruch* (ed. J. Schreiner [1969]), pp. 200-228; W. G. Kümmel, " 'Das Gesetz und die Propheten gehen bis Johannes'—Lukas 16,16 im Zusammenhang der heilsgeschichtlichen Theologie der Lukasschriften," in *Verborum Veritas, Festschrift für G. Stählin* (ed. O. Böcher und K. Haacker [1970]), pp. 89-102; G. Lohfink, *Die Sammlung Israels* (1975). **On 3:** G. W. H. Lampe, "The Lucan Portrait of Christ," *NTS* 2 (1955/56), 160-175; M. Rese, *Alttestamentliche Motive in der Christologie des Lukas* (1969). **On 4:** E. Grässer, *Das Problem der Parusieverzögerung in den Synoptischen Evangelien und in der Apostelgeschichte* (1957; 1960²); G. Klein, *Die zwölf Apostel. Ursprung und Gehalt einer Idee* (1961); U. Wilckens, *Die Missionsreden der Apostelgeschichte* (1961; 1974³); J. Dupont, "Les discours des Actes des Apôtres d'après un ouvrage récent," *RB* 69 (1962), 37-60; E. Haenchen, "Tradition und Komposition in der Apostelgeschichte," in Haenchen, *Gott und Mensch* (1965), pp. 206-226; E. E. Ellis, "Die Funktion der Eschatologie im Lukasevangelium," *ZThK* 66 (1969), 387-402; Ellis, *Eschatology in Luke* (1972).

1. INTRODUCTION: COMPOSITIONAL RELATIONSHIPS, LITERARY DISTINCTIVENESS, AND THEOLOGICAL PROBLEMATIC

a) The course of research.[1] 1) With a one-sidedly exaggerated judgment about Luke F. C. Baur established a decisive milestone for the "purely historical" position of biblical research. He thought that the image in the book of Acts concerning the emergence of the church was not historical, but the product of a theological tendency. This tendency was the intent to harmonize the apostles and the primitive church into the unity of the *Una Sancta*. The historical reality of Christianity at the beginning, as was reflected over against Acts in the epistles of Paul, was not unity, but was contrast, antithesis.[2] What the school of research inspired by Baur had to say at the end of the 19th century about the theology

---

[1] Overview of the course of scholarly research in W. G. Kümmel, *Introduction*, pp. 125-188.
[2] *Vorlesungen über neutestamentliche Theologie*, ed. F. F. Baur (1864 [repr. 1973]), pp. 328-338.

of Luke was recorded in the *Theology* of H. J. Holtzmann.[3] A contemporary of Holtzmann, A. Schlatter, wrote an opposing composition.[4]

2) After a lengthy interval this line of questioning was taken up once again after 1950. The line of Baur was extended by P. Vielhauer when he explained that Luke wrote a piece of history as salvation history and therefore also salvation history as a piece of history.[5] The ministry of Jesus—said Vielhauer—was deeschatologized in Luke and became a piece of church history; moreover, the Christology of Luke was pre-Pauline, while his natural theology, his understanding of the Law, and his eschatology were post-Pauline. For all of these reasons the theology of Luke no longer belonged to primitive Christianity, but to the emerging early catholic church.

Vielhauer's theses continued to resonate broadly in the school of Bultmann. They were appropriated particularly by his student G. Klein in several publications.[6] Alongside, E. Käsemann developed independently a point of view that tended in the same direction.[7] It emphasized the ecclesiological dimension: Luke described as his actual theme the hour of the church as the center of time.[8] Luke depicted—thought Käsemann—a church that demonstrated its legitimacy in relationship to heresy on the basis of continuity with the primitive apostolate and that had become a sanctified realm in the world. Luke was hereby the initial advocate of the early catholic theory of tradition and legitimation[9] and thus the first representative of an emerging early catholicism.[10]

A new phase of Lukan research was introduced by H. Conzelmann with his book *The Theology of St. Luke* (1960; Ger. 1964⁵). In a careful exegetical investigation he pushed beyond these cliché-ridden initial attempts, but he continued fundamentally in the same direction. This can be seen with respect to the following points. (1) The center of time was for Luke not the time of the church but the time of Jesus. (2) The theology of Luke must not be compared with that of Paul since it was faced with a problem that was not yet existent for Paul: "the delay of the Parousia and her existence in secular history."[11] (3) Characteristic for the historical composition through which Luke solved this problem was the compartmentalization of salvation-historical epochs; these fell into three sections: (a) the time of Israel (Lk. 16:16), (b) the time of the ministry of Jesus as the intrinsic time of salvation, the "center of time" (Lk. 4:16ff.; Acts 10:38), and (c) the time of the church as a time of struggle with doubt and of patience.[12] (4) Through this periodization Luke wanted to make clear to the church of his

---

[3]*Theologie* I, 515-539.

[4]*Theologie* II, 447-460

[5]Op. cit. (Lit., §48,1), esp. p. 115; cf. contra, L. Goppelt, *Christentum und Judentum*, pp. 227ff.

[6]Op. cit. (Lit., §48).

[7]*Essays on New Testament Themes*, pp. 88-94, and 18ff.

[8]Ibid., pp. 28f.

[9]Ibid., p. 91.

[10]Thus also S. Schulz, *Stunde* (1970²), p. 254.

[11]*The Theology of St. Luke* (1960), p. 14.

[12]Ibid., p. 17.

time that the forms of the church may change,[13] but the fundamental structure must be maintained.

Thus Conzelmann found the principle of Lukan theology as a whole in a salvation-historical continuity that was differentiated at the same time through epochs. Through this approach Luke made a positive existence possible for the church in the history that was expanding.[14]

We shall only make mention here of the publications of W. C. Robinson and H. Flender, which went beyond Conzelmann.[15] Though Flender's book mixed exegetical and systematic reflection much too freely, it criticized Conzelmann's unreflected use of the term salvation history and his too-schematic division of periods. Salvation history for Luke ran precisely not along one level, but along two levels, one over the other. Jesus belonged—continued Flender—in accord with his human mode of existence at the beginning of a new time; in accord with his heavenly mode of existence he stood, however, "sharing God's contemporaneity with all human time."[16] Hence for humankind Luke crossed horizontal eschatology with a vertical one; for the individual the hour of death became the *parousia* (Lk. 24:43).[17]

b) The compositional circumstances. 1) The third Gospel and the book of Acts came from the same author; the style and design of the two make this clear. They were conceived from the beginning as one compositional whole written in two separate books. This can be seen in the following example: In Lk. 24, the Gospel closed with an Easter account and an ascension narrative, both of which were composed as a conclusion to the Gospel; the book of Acts began in 1:1-11 with an Easter account and an ascension narrative that were fashioned into the introduction for the second book.

2) The composition was accomplished after A.D. 70 since in Lk. 21:20, 24 the author looked back to the destruction of Jerusalem. On the other hand, a stage of community development was presupposed that clearly preceded the one reflected in I Clement and Ignatius. Hence the composition was accomplished between A.D. 80 and 90.

3) As the place of composition Greece was named by the anti-Marcionite Prologue to the Gospels, the only information in this regard that has come down to us from the ancient church. Internal indices make clear in any case that the composition was accomplished in the region of the church toward which it

---

[13]Thus, e.g., the directives for the equipping of the apostles in the earthly days of Jesus (Lk. 9:1ff.; 10:1ff.) were removed for the period thereafter (22:35ff.), and the tie of the primitive community in Jerusalem to the temple and the Law was no longer in effect for the Gentile church according to Acts 15.

[14]This conception was taken over by G. Bornkamm, "Evangelien, synoptische," *RGG* II³, 763ff.; with it, however, O. Cullmann, "Unzeitgemässe Bemerkungen zum 'historischen Jesus' der Bultmannschule," in *Hist. Jesus*, pp. 266-280, also concurred in order, finally, to identify his own understanding of the entire theology of the New Testament to a large extent with H. Conzelmann's view of Lukan theology; O. Cullmann's programmatic book on this subject was his *Salvation in History* (1964; Eng. 1967). He contested, of course, that the Lukan conception of salvation history was a distortion of Pauline and Johannine thought.

[15]Op. cit. (Lit., §48,1).

[16]Flender, op. cit. (n. 15), p. 125.

[17]Ibid., pp. 13ff., 90-106, 159.

moved, in the West. Shared contacts with the Roman community tradition, which we have already encountered in comparison with the Epistle to the Hebrews, point to Rome.

4) As author the ancient church tradition—the Muratorian Canon and anti-Marcionite Prologue—named Luke and meant the associate of Paul mentioned in Col. 4:14 and Philem. 24. The historical evaluation of this tradition depends on the question of how the portrayal of the life and message of Paul in Acts compares to Paul's own statements in his letters. If there should be more than only a difference of accent and if the historical situation and the theological conception of Paul should be represented in a way contrary to Paul's personal witness, then it would be difficult for an associate of Paul to come into consideration here as author. We cannot pursue this question explicitly here but we shall try to make a contribution to it by way of our representation of Lukan theology.

c) *The literary intent.* 1) The literary character of the Lukan composition was signaled by the preface in Lk. 1:1-4. Luke was the only New Testament author who introduced his book in keeping with Hellenistic custom through a preface. "Inasmuch as many have undertaken to compile a narrative of the things which have been accomplished among us, just as they were delivered to us by those who from the beginning were eyewitnesses and ministers of the word, it seemed good to me also, having followed all things closely for some time past, to write an orderly account for you, most excellent Theophilus, that you may know the truth concerning the things of which you have been informed." This classically stylized, grammatically complicated sentence structure intended to express that the author of this book was aware of his historical distance from the origin of his faith, the public ministry of Jesus; moreover, he was trying thereby to bridge that gap in order to demonstrate the *asphaleia*, the truth/reliability of the witness that grounded faith.

But how did he intend to bridge that gap? Did he intend, as G. Klein concluded,[18] to ground the certainty of salvation with the help of historical certainty? Even the analysis of the prologue shows that Luke regarded the task he saw not as a matter of a simple theology of history; he looked upon the structure of the process of transmission as well as that of the transmitted object in a much clearer and deeper way than this.

2) According to Lk. 1:2, Luke was precisely not in search of purely historical tradition. Rather he inquired into what the eyewitnesses transmitted, those who had understood that which was perceived with the eyes of faith and therefore had proclaimed it as gospel; Luke inquired into apostolic tradition as understood in his own definition, Acts 1:21f.

3) The structure of this sought-out tradition corresponded to the object: what concerned Luke were "the things which have been accomplished among us" (*tōn peplērophorēmenōn en hēmin pragmatōn*, Lk. 1:1). The passive form

---

[18]*Rekonstruktion und Interpretation*, p. 260.

(*peplērophorēmenōn*) was certainly a divine passive; it intended to say that God had brought "these things," the history of Jesus, to fulfillment. Here a different dimension emerged than that in Matthew (§46,4); God had not brought prophecies to realization, but he had carried out his plan of salvation that was to be understood on the basis of scripture (Acts 3:18, 21, 24). What Luke wanted to portray were the events in history that corresponded to God's plan of salvation.

4) The portrayal that he made his goal because of this presupposition was characterized by two features and through them it distinguished itself from the Gospel writings already existing at this time (v. 3). This portrayal was based on a thorough examination of the tradition ("having followed all things closely for some time past"), and it attempted to depict events *kathexēs* (in succession, in order). When one compares Luke to Matthew and Mark it can in fact be observed that he went to great lengths to portray Jesus' ministry as a continuously progressing event. Continuity was an essential feature of history. Luke wanted, therefore, to portray the ministry of Jesus as a history that corresponded to the plan of salvation, as salvation history the way he understood it.

5) How could the reliability (*asphaleia*) of the witness to Jesus be determined by this procedure? It has become clear that for Luke both the Jesus event and its process of transmission were not purely historical, but were double layered. The reliability of the witness to Jesus, therefore, could not be demonstrated by the historical proof of historical factuality. Certainty could only be grounded by a portrayal that showed the correspondence existing between the progression of historical events and the plan of salvation, i.e., by a salvation-historical portrayal that for its part was a witness of faith.

Thus the preface contained the author's theological program draped in the language of an educated Hellenistic person.

d) **Language and style.** In its forward progress, the composition could speak a different language, apparently for the most part that of the appropriated tradition. If one wishes to develop the theology of the author by means of redaction-critical analysis, one must pay attention to the linguistic criteria that prompted this author himself to speak. Two observations in this respect are important and they stand in a certain tension to each other.

1) Synoptic comparison shows that Luke eliminated Semitic peculiarities of style when he appropriated material from Mark. Indices in the Gospel of his own style were plentiful, as one might expect, at the introductory and closing portions of pericopes, where he combined the various traditions he had received into a progressive portrayal. These peculiarities of his style became especially concentrated in the birth narrative (Lk. 1–2) and in the Easter chapter (Lk. 24); in Acts they are found mainly in the summary accounts about the life of the primitive community and in the speeches.

2) On the other hand, this typically Lukan style deviated considerably from the classical style of the preface (Lk. 1:1-4). The typical style was influenced heavily by the Septuagint. Apparently Luke deliberately employed the language of the Greek Bible as a stylistic measure. He wanted to portray the fulfillment

history that corresponded to the announced plan of salvation also in the style and in the language of its announcement in scripture; for him that was the Septuagint! Thus even the features of style lead one toward the substantive intention.[19]

2. THE LUKAN CONCEPTION OF SALVATION HISTORY

a) The dimension of history. 1) That Luke saw the world in which Jesus lived and ministered and in which the church arose in a fundamentally different way than Paul and Matthew becomes clear when we hold up the course of Christian mission as seen in Rom. 15 alongside that in the book of Acts.

Paul set forth in Rom. 15:19, 23 an apocalyptic view of history and the world. The gospel had been proclaimed in the Eastern hemisphere: "from Jerusalem and as far round as Illyricum I have fully preached the gospel of Christ" (15:19). Now the same was to take place in the Western half of the world (15:23); then would come the end. Jerusalem was the center from which everything went forth. The world and history were seen, as it were, from the perspective of an astronaut. In comparison to this the Lukan Acts could be compared to a travel diary; here the Pauline mission was the beginning of a long historical process that was not yet over. Luke understood the dimension of history as it is seen today by Western man.

2) This Lukan optic becomes even clearer when we compare by way of another example the historical framework of the birth of Jesus in Luke and in Matthew. Luke placed the birth of Jesus and the entry of the Baptist upon the scene into the framework of world history (Lk. 2:1f.); an edict of Caesar Augustus, who had founded the *Pax Romana* and who was considered the guardian of the empire, was responsible for Jesus' being born in Bethlehem, the city of David (Lk. 2:4, 11). Then an angel proclaimed the birth in terminology that was otherwise connected with Augustus: "Be not afraid; for behold, I bring you good news (*euangelizomai*) of a great joy which will come to all the people" (Lk. 2:10). The word of the angel meant *euangelizesthai*, the proclamation of good news for the "people"—intended in the first instance was Israel—but beyond that for all of humanity, especially for the poor. *Euangelia*, however, were the imperial edicts issued in accord with the ideology of the empire, and for the same reason that analogous application was made here to Jesus: he who was born was the *sōtēr* (Savior, Lk. 2:11), the One who brought *eirēnē* (peace, Lk. 2:14) on earth. It was customary to say such things about Augustus (§36,3). Thus Luke placed the birth in the framework of contemporary history.

Compared like this, the historical framework of the birth narrative of Matthew went in an entirely different direction; three magicians came from the East as representatives of the Gentiles (Mt. 2:1-12) and the king, Herod (Mt. 2:3-8, 13-19), stood as representative of Israel against the One "who has been born

---

[19]Cf. W. Grundmann, *Das Lukasevangelium*, pp. 23f.

king of the Jews" (Mt. 2:2), who like Israel of old would be saved out of Egypt (Mt. 2:15). Matthew spoke from the view of the world here of a Jewish rabbi; Luke, however, from that of Hellenistic man.

3) Yet Luke's view of the world was not simply that of Hellenistic man who was driven about by belief in fate, demonology, and ideology. His view rather was informed by the Old Testament. That was shown when, e.g., Luke inserted the appearance of John the Baptist into world history by utilizing the style of Old Testament accounts of the prophets: "In the fifteenth year of the reign of Tiberius Caesar, Pontius Pilate being governor of Judea, and Herod being tetrarch of Galilee . . . in the high-priesthood of Annas . . . the word of God came to John the son of Zechariah . . ." (Lk. 3:1f.). That was exactly the style in which the Old Testament prophetic books inserted the appearance of the prophets into history (cf., e.g., Jer. 1:2f.; 25:1; 32:1; Ezek. 1:1-3; Amos 1:1).

4) The history of Jesus was not merely written by Luke into history seen thus; rather Jesus' history grew out of this history. Just as his birth took place in Bethlehem because "everyone" had to be enrolled in his place of birth (Lk. 2:1ff.), so too it came to the baptism through John that began his ministry because "all the people were baptized" (Lk. 3:21).

b) The plan of salvation as God's plan of action. 1) The Lukan conception of the plan of salvation is found quite imposingly in the conclusion to the Gospel. A basic feature of the Easter account fashioned by Luke (Lk. 24) was that the resurrected One provided the disciples in the Easter appearances with the understanding that his final destiny as well as the further course of the disciples' lives and the emergence of the church were prescribed in a plan of salvation that was to be derived from scripture.

This reference to the plan of salvation was repeated three times: vv. 6f.; vv. 24-27; and vv. 44-49. At the end (vv. 45-49) it stated: "Then he opened their minds to understand the scriptures, and said to them, 'Thus it is written, that the Christ should suffer and on the third day rise from the dead, and that repentance and forgiveness of sins should be preached in his name to all nations, beginning from Jerusalem. You are witnesses of these things. And behold, I send the promise of my Father upon you; but stay in the city, until you are clothed with power from on high!' " These words stand at the place assumed by the so-called great commission in Matthew (Mt. 28:18-20; §46,6b). In contrast to Matthew, here only the last statement was a directive to the disciples; everything else was not a command but an announcement. The sending through the commission of the resurrected One was already presupposed in the ancient tradition of I Cor. 15:7f. Luke changed the sending to an announcement that appropriated and extended the announcements of coming suffering of the synoptic tradition (Mk. 8:31 par.; 9:31 par.; 10:33f. par.).

The affirmation that Christ had to suffer, die, and rise was lengthened to include: thus it must be that "repentance and forgiveness of sins should be preached in his name to all nations, beginning from Jerusalem." This "must be" (*dei*, v. 44) was understood by Luke—as already by the synoptic tradition before him (Mk. 8:31)—neither in the Greek sense as a development determined by an irrevocable fate nor in the apocalyptic sense as God's plan of history for the end time (cf. §18,6), but as God's intent for salvation that was marked out in scripture. But in Luke this intent for salvation was lengthened and connected to history; it became for him, as it were, a plan of salvation that was to be manifested in history.

To be sure, this plan of salvation was not a program that was set up for the disciples to carry out. It was to be carried out by God himself, as was evidenced outwardly even by the diminished use of the imperative mood in Lk. 24:45-49. The disciples were involved only as his tools (cf. Acts 9:15). The directive given them was restricted purely to the next step; they should remain in Jerusalem and wait for the "power from on high," the Holy Spirit. Everything thereafter would then be activated by God at the appointed time.

2) Corresponding to this conclusion to the Gospel was the introduction to the book of Acts (1:6-8). In reply to the disciples' question, "Will you at this time restore the kingdom to Israel?" it was answered, "It is not for you to know times or seasons which the Father has fixed by his own authority. But you shall receive power when the Holy Spirit has come upon you; and you shall be my witnesses in Jerusalem and in all Judea and Samaria and to the end of the earth." Here the negation is just as noteworthy as the positive promise. Luke prohibited apocalyptic calculating in terms of periods of time and dates as well as waiting for the establishment of the messianic reign in history. This meant for his church that he prohibited fixing one's eyes on the imminent *parousia*. The attentive look of the disciples should focus in an entirely different direction; they ought to attend to where and how the Spirit would establish them as witnesses. Through the direction and power of the Spirit a particular plan would be realized; the witness should be heard in Jerusalem, in Judea and Samaria, and to the very end of the earth (Acts 1:8).

Quite in keeping with this plan the course of Christian mission was portrayed in that which followed. This mission was not planned by the apostles and the community but alone by God, who made even those who resisted him his tools. This can be shown very effectively in terms of the portrayal of the circumstances surrounding the first baptism of an uncircumcised man (Acts 10:1–11:18). Through visions the resistant Peter was brought into the house of Cornelius (Acts 10:1-33) and there prompted by the prevenience of the Spirit to baptize him (10:44-48). Before the community in Jerusalem that was indignant over this step he excused his action with the statement characteristic for all of Acts: "If then God gave the same gift to them [i.e., the Gentiles] as he gave to us . . . who was I that I could withstand God?" (Acts 11:17).

In the same way, Paul finally reached the goal of the announcement in Acts 1:8 "to the end of the earth," namely, Rome. Paul did not come to Rome in the way that he planned and wished (Acts 19:21; Rom. 15:25), but by being transported there as a prisoner. Thus came to pass that which was expressed by the last words of the book of Acts: ". . . [he was] preaching the kingdom of God"—precisely in Rome—". . . quite openly and unhindered."

According to Luke, therefore, a plan of salvation marked out in scripture realized itself through the actions of the disciples. It was not planned and carried out by the disciples as a program, but realized "from above" through Christ and through the Spirit of God. The disciples always had to take but the next step that was opened up and shown to them. If, according to the portrayal of Luke, their action in fact produced a progressing context of activity—that which we call history—then that was provided from above. Luke did not, therefore, declare a segment of history delimited in a special way to be salvation history; rather he perceived disparate human action seen from a plan of salvation as having continuity and in this sense to be salvation history.

c) The continuity of salvation history. 1) But let us now examine more exactly this continuity pointed out by Luke in the book of Acts with regard to the emergence of Christianity.

It becomes clear that this continuity was not that of a historical development; this can be seen among other things by the way Luke portrayed the bridge from the church among Israel in Jerusalem to Gentile Christianity free of the Law in Antioch in Acts 8–11. 8:4 recounted the starting point; through the persecution of Stephen—once again not through the disciples' planning—it happened that disciples in missionary activity moved throughout the land. Acts 11:19 pointed to the preliminary conclusion of this occurrence; through some of those who were forced to flee the first Gentile-Christian community of faith arose in Antioch. Between 8:4 and 11:19, however, occurrences were related that from a substantive point of view led up to this result in a progressing line, but historically were not linked to each other in any way. Such was the role of the conversion of the Samaritans who did not belong to the Jewish cultic community (Acts 8:4-25), the baptism of the Ethiopian treasurer who though he was a God-fearer could not be circumcised as a eunuch (Acts 8:26-40), and finally the baptism of the first uncircumcised man through Peter (Acts 10:1–11:18). Through these occurrences the boundary line posed by circumcision was exceeded step by step and the community of Jerusalem was led to ecclesiastical fellowship with baptized members who were not circumcised. Accordingly, therefore, Luke portrayed a continuous development but its continuity was the substantive realization of the plan of salvation, not a historically connected development.

From this angle of vision the theological intention of Acts also becomes clear. The literary program proposed in 1:8 of recording the witness given by the disciples from Jerusalem to the ends of the earth was not discharged in the form of a portrayal of the mission's manifold paths. Instead Luke drew out but one line that led from the apostles in Jerusalem through Paul to Rome. But was "the end of the world" (1:8) reached in Rome? According to Acts 28:31, the last sentence of the book, the mission went on. Paul, however, its bearer until then, had reached the goal established for him in 13:47; he had become "a light for the Gentiles . . . to the uttermost parts of the earth." After all, along the road he had traveled from Jerusalem to Rome the church made up of all nations had taken shape fundamentally, the church that had already been portrayed in a programmatic way by the account of Pentecost (Acts 2:11).

The book of Acts did not intend to depict, therefore, the whole course of Christian mission but the salvation-historical base line upon which the church took shape. The intention behind the portrayal was to make plain that only that which stood within the extension of this line was worthy of the name church. Accordingly, the norm that continued to be valid for the church could only be sought in the extension of this line. The standard was by no means a primitive situation normative for all times; that is an understanding of decisive importance vis-à-vis many mistaken interpretations of Acts 1–6. The form of the primitive community was not for Luke the norm for the building of communities for all times.

This foundation line of Luke can be designated most appropriately with the term "continuity in progression." In Acts the most important "progression" was the apostolic decree (15:28f.). Through this decree the freedom of Gentile Christianity in relationship to the Law was decided once and for all. That which was finally achieved, according to the Pauline epistles, only in lengthy debate and in the battle against dangerous lapses was decided once and for all according to the undoubtedly much oversimplified and schematic portrayal of Luke, through the apostolic decree. It formed the conclusion to the salvation-historical development, characterized above, from Jerusalem to Antioch.[20]

2) In his Gospel as well, Luke was obviously concerned about showing continuity in what he portrayed. While Matthew arranged the tradition thematically, Luke worked at furnishing the pericopes with a framework to convey the impression of a connected progression for the ministry of Jesus. He raised the impression of a continuous course of Jesus' life from Galilee to the passion in Jerusalem (Lk. 23:5).

This course too ran in progressing phases or stages. The first phase was the peripatetic preaching in Galilee. In 4:14f., Luke reshaped the summary statement about the beginning of Jesus' public ministry in Galilee (Mk. 1:14) to an announcement that Jesus was teaching in the synagogues of Galilee as he traveled about. The first phase began as Jesus appeared publicly with a programmatic sermon in the synagogue at Nazareth (Lk. 4:16-30). The following account of his activity in Galilee (Lk. 4:31–9:50) came together out of originally loosely linked pericopes from the Markan tradition. Luke linked them together by means of skilled redactional bracket statements (e.g., 4:38, 40, 42) into a continuously progressing development of events.

In Lk. 9:51 this course of Jesus' life in Galilee closed with the words: "When

---

[20]According to H. Conzelmann, *St. Luke* (cf. n. 10), p. 224, Luke wanted to portray two salvation-historical levels in Acts that were separated from each other by Acts 15. But perhaps it corresponds better to the intention of Luke to speak rather about a constant progression of salvation history. Then Acts 15 would be the preliminary point in time of the development that started with the Gentile mission in Antioch (Acts 11:20f.), from which time then, moreover, further progression took place.

the days drew near for him to be received up, he set his face to go to Jerusalem." This comment provided the bridge to the second phase, to the so-called Lukan travel narrative that extended from 9:51 to 19:27. The controlling concept of a journey from Galilee to Jerusalem did not adhere originally to the pericopes gathered together here out of Q and out of the Lukan special source; it was introduced through redactional comments (13:22, 33; 17:11; 18:31, 35). The employed pericopes supported the impression of his being on a journey only by showing Jesus repeatedly as the One who was moving on or was the guest (9:56f.; 10:1, 38; 11:37; 14:1; 15:1f.; 19:5, 11). The travel narrative pursued the compositional goal of bringing Jesus in continuity from Galilee to Jerusalem. It especially wanted to show him as the One who was striding toward his *analēmpsis*, his being received up (9:51), through the process of suffering.

In the last phase, the period in Jerusalem (19:28–24:53), it was above all important for Luke that Jesus was greeted at his entry to Jerusalem as a king; he was greeted as such, however, not—as in Matthew (21:9)—by the people, but by his disciples (19:37). If from that day on "he was teaching daily in the temple" (19:47), then the goal of his earthly life had thereby been reached, the goal that was also the point of departure for the emergence of the church (Acts 2:46; 3:1; 5:42).

3) But another salvation-historical epoch already preceded the time of Jesus. To this epoch pointed the Lukan version of the so-called violent entry saying: "The law and the prophets were until John; since then the good news of the kingdom of God is preached, and every one enters it violently" (Lk. 16:16 par. Mt. 11:12f.). Accordingly, he allowed the public ministry of Jesus to begin with the programmatic proclamation: "Today this scripture [Isa. 61:1f.] has been fulfilled in your hearing" (Lk. 4:21); it was fulfilled in that the Holy Spirit now dwelt upon Jesus and the day of salvation had dawned (Lk. 4:17f.). And correspondingly, already as child in the temple Jesus was greeted by the elderly Simeon; "it had been revealed to him by the Holy Spirit that he should not see death before he had seen the Lord's Christ" (Lk. 2:26). Precisely the Simeon pericope makes clear that the manifestation of Jesus was linked directly to the preceding salvation history; moreover, it shows that the decisive feature of the true Israel, whose history also led up in continuity like this to the manifestation of Jesus, was the spirit of prophecy. This latter aspect was also emphasized in addition to Lk. 2:26 by the speech of Stephen (Acts 7); it compared the resistance of the Jews to the Christian mission with the resistance of the fathers to the prophets and came to the conclusion: "you always resist the Holy Spirit. As your fathers did, so do you!" (Acts 7:51).

d) Epochs of salvation history. Thus we can observe in Luke three epochs of salvation history that follow each other; they were three epochs of a progressing continuity according to God's plan of salvation. The chief feature of this continuity was the different work of the Spirit in each.

Following upon the work of the Spirit through the prophets that lasted until

John the Baptist—in the view of the rabbis it was already quenched with Ezra[21]—came a concentration of all work of the Spirit upon Jesus, and after that, moreover, the general working of the Pentecost-Spirit in the community.[22]

Luke demarcated these three epochs that followed each other in succession through distinct incisions so that the progression would be clear. In order to work out the salvation-historical succession—and that in contrast to historical continuity!—the imprisonment of John the Baptist was reported before his baptism of Jesus (Lk. 3:21f.); this imprisonment ended John's ministry (Lk. 3:18-20). In contrast to the portrayal of Paul and John, the Easter appearances of the resurrected One were also concluded after forty days (Acts 1:3) by the ascension, and after a ten-day interim the work of the Pentecost-Spirit began (Acts 2:1-13).

What kind of work of the Spirit was assigned variously to each of the epochs? In Israel it was always but individuals, the prophets, who were seized directly by the Spirit. At Pentecost, however, the realization of the general endowment of the Spirit (Joel 3:1-5) was fulfilled: "I will pour out my Spirit upon all flesh" (Acts 2:17). The giving of the Spirit to Jesus, however, distinguished itself from these forms of the giving of the Spirit before and afterward.

While Matthew and Mark had very little to say about Jesus and the Spirit, the Lukan Jesus emerged already in his earthly ministry as the Lord of the Spirit. According to Lk. 1:35 he was conceived by the Spirit; in terms of its roots his historical existence came from the Spirit. Since his baptism he was "full of the Holy Spirit" (Lk. 4:1); he was continuously filled with it, while of the prophets just as of the apostles it was only said that they were laid hold of by the Spirit (Lk. 1:67; cf. 1:15, 41; Acts 2:4; 4:8, 31; 9:17; 13:9). Jesus began his public ministry in Galilee "in the power of the Spirit" (Lk. 4:14) and therefore quoted Isa. 61:1 in his inaugural sermon: "The Spirit of the Lord is upon me, because he has anointed me" (Lk. 4:18). Thus he was the subject of the Spirit.[23] Through his exclusive possession of the Spirit he conquered Satan (Lk. 4:13), who withdrew from him until he returned again at the beginning of the passion (22:3).

Because Jesus was the Lord of the Spirit, after his resurrection he appropriately became the giver of the Spirit for the community (Lk. 24:49; Acts 2:33). This was already anticipated in his earthly ministry. While Jesus' healings were not traced to God (as in Mt. 12:28), but to the finger of God (Lk. 11:20), he promised those who prayed not good gifts (as in Mt. 7:11), but the Holy Spirit (Lk. 11:13). This indicated that the time of Jesus was not simply replaced chronologically by the time of the church, but that it went on instead in the ministry of salvation of the exalted One in the church.

  e) The problem of distance. Luke was the first to understand that which has

---

[21]Cf. R. Meyer, *TDNT* VI, 816f.

[22]This image was in essence already elaborated by H. von Baer in his dissertation from the year 1926 (Lit., §48).

[23]E. Schweizer, *TDNT* VI, 405.

been called since Lessing the "ugly, broad ditch."[24] To be sure, after Easter the disciples learned very early to differentiate between the circumstances of Jesus and the situation of the church (§24,2). Luke, however, understood this difference as historical distance. For him the quite elementary question was: What did the completed earthly ministry of Jesus mean to the community that while separated from him historically lived in the Spirit?

The link between the content of the gospel and the emergence of the church was produced for Luke by the announcement of the role of witness played by the disciples. While according to Mt. 28:20 the disciples were supposed to pass on the sayings of Jesus as teachers, according to Lk. 24:48f. they were supposed to give intelligible witness to the course of his life as the realization of the plan of salvation to be derived from scripture. This witness would have a convincing effect when the witness of the Spirit joined itself to it (Acts 5:32).

This giving witness to the course of Jesus' life was carried out kerygmatically in different ways. For one thing, in missionary sermons based on the course of Jesus' life the people of Jerusalem were summoned to repentance and the Gentiles to faith (Acts 5:30-32; 10:34-43). For another, however, in the situation of the community as well reference was made to the course of Jesus' life. The latter took place in the farewell discourse of Jesus put together by Luke (Lk. 22:21-38). It warned the disciples at the beginning against betrayal (Lk. 22:21ff.) and at the end against denial (22:34); between the two he summoned them to service (vv. 26f.) and to endurance in struggles with doubt (v. 32). The scope of this discourse can be summarized as follows: the disciples were to travel the path of Jesus. In this he was not for them an example, but the course of his life marked the trail they were to follow. Everything depended on their staying on this trail.

It corresponded to this emphasis on the course of Jesus' life when Luke used on occasion the principle of *synkrisis*, of comparison—one could also say, of historical analogy—frequently practiced in Hellenistic history writing; Luke used the principle to clarify the course of the disciples' lives in terms of the course of Jesus' life. Hence the martyrdom of Stephen was represented in analogy to the passion of Jesus (Acts 6:10-15; 7.54-60) and the trial of Paul in analogy to the trial of Jesus (Acts 22:30–23:9; 24:1-27). Apostles and missionaries appeared like their Lord as those who traveled about; through them God visited people. And this coming of the Lord and of his apostles and missionaries meant the "today" of the encounter with salvation (Lk. 4:21; 5:26; 19:5, 9; 23:43; Acts 10:25).

On the other hand, this dimension also shaped the portrayal of Jesus' ministry. His public appearance in the synagogue at Nazareth, e.g., was patterned after those of his disciples in the synagogues of Asia Minor (Acts 14:1-6; Lk. 4:16-30). His debate with the Pharisees was given typical character with respect to standard

---

[24]Reference to the "ugly, broad ditch which I cannot get across, however often and however earnestly I have tried to make the leap," in "On the Proof of the Spirit and of Power," *Lessing's Theological Writings* (ed. H. Chadwick [1957]), p. 55 (Alsup).

human response when the Pharisees were represented as types of self-righteous moral man (Lk. 20:20f.; cf. Acts 2:36). And the portrayal of the suffering of Jesus acquired in Luke elements of exemplary martyrdom (Lk. 22:43f.; 23:46).

It was in the same line when Jesus' praying was emphasized to a far greater degree than in the parallel tradition (Lk. 3:21; 9:28; etc.) and when the temptation narrative showed him as the One who triumphed in the struggle with the doubt (Lk. 4:13) that surrounded the course of the disciples' lives (Lk. 22:28).[25] What emerges from all this is that for Luke the course of Jesus' life was not the center of time, as H. Conzelmann thought, but rather the beginning and the foundation for the realization of God's plan of salvation.[26]

3. THE DISTINCTIVENESS OF LUKAN CHRISTOLOGY

a) The Savior (sōtēr) of the poor and of sinners. 1) For Luke, Jesus was the stranger who was passing through, the guest through whom God stopped in for communion with people. This stopping in meant salvation. As guest Jesus also— this would be unthinkable for Matthew—came into the homes of the Pharisees and concerned himself with them (Lk. 7:36; 11:37; 14:1). Above all, however, he went as guest to sinners (Lk. 15:1f.; 19:1-5). Wherever he was welcomed the word with which the Zacchaeus story concluded was true: "Today salvation has come to this house" (Lk. 19:9).

Jesus concerned himself, therefore, according to Luke not just with one group but with all; that would also correspond to the historical circumstances. He went into the homes of sinners and into those of the Pharisees.

2) For Luke, the starting point of Jesus' ministry was his position toward the poor and the rich; put more precisely, his stance toward the problem: poor and rich. With the exception of the Epistle of James, this problem was handled in the New Testament nowhere so thoroughly as in the Gospel of Luke. In the Magnificat Jesus was introduced with the announcement formulated from the Old Testament: "he has put down the mighty from their thrones, and exalted those of low degree; he has filled the hungry with good things, and the rich he has sent empty away" (Lk. 1:52f.). According to this, general social revolution could be expected of Jesus.

The first Beatitude (Lk. 6:20b) appeared to support this when it simply promised salvation to the "poor" without any additional qualification (cf. Mt. 5:3). That the poor in the literal sense of the word were really intended, was underscored by the "woe" over the rich added only in Luke (Lk. 6:24). How both the pronouncement of blessing upon the poor and the pronouncement of woe over

---

[25]Both the Jesus struggling with doubts and the Jesus in prayer as the preparer of the way for the community in Luke were studied in monograph publications in recent years. On the first, cf. F. Schütz, *Der leidende Christus* (1969); on the latter, cf. W. Ott, *Gebet und Heil* (1965).

[26]"The center of time" was the history of Israel including that of the church first for Irenaeus. For Luke, in contrast, the Old Testament was the announcing of the plan of salvation; the manifestation of Jesus, however, was its beginning realization. Regarding the comparison between Luke and Irenaeus, cf. L. Goppelt, *Christentum und Judentum*, pp. 304f.

the rich were intended, was commented upon by a series of parables about rich and poor; Luke derived them from his special source. They were the parables of the rich fool (Lk. 12:16-21) and of Lazarus and the rich man (Lk. 16:19-31). Of how much consequence these traditions were to Luke can be seen with regard to his reworking of the parable of the unjust steward. In contrast to its original meaning he applied this parable (Lk. 16:1-7) to the question of material possessions and their danger, as he added to it a series of sayings on this theme (Lk. 16:9-13).

In not one of these passages, however, did Luke advocate an Ebionitism; one might have expected he would after the Magnificat. Nowhere, not even in 16:19-31, did he introduce the concept that Jesus merely preached the overturning of the social situation. The rich person would not be lost simply because he was rich, and the poor person would not be blessed because he was poor. Instead the judgment stood throughout that was formulated in the introduction and conclusion of the parable of the rich fool (Lk. 12:15, 21): life was lost for the one who thought he could live on that which he had provided for himself! Luke marked this criterion for the relationship of man to God in antithesis to the usual viewpoint of the Hellenistic world. In the latter, whether the path to life was won or lost was decided by the position of man with respect to self-control and personal righteousness according to the Law. Since in the Gospel of Luke it was a matter of the path to life and thereby the relationship to God in the question "rich and poor," we hear nowhere that Jesus turned his attention directly to the poor as such, but rather that he took "sinners" under his care.[27]

3) For Luke, sinners were not characterized so much as they were for Matthew and Mark in terms of failure vis-à-vis the Law, but rather in terms of their failure vis-à-vis material possessions. Stereotypes of sinners were not only small-time tax-gatherers and prostitutes, but people who failed when it came to possessions; the chief tax-collector Zacchaeus had gained wealth by fraud (Lk. 19:8), the prodigal son had squandered his property (Lk. 15:13, 30), and both had lost their life and neighborly contact because of it; the decisive thing, however, was that both of them had run away from God in this way!

How Jesus cared for sinners was explained in Lk. 15 by means of the parable of the prodigal son; this chapter was the most characteristic for Luke. Through this composition of three parables Luke had Jesus address the situation that was portrayed redactionally in 15:1ff.; Jesus sat at table with sinners, people who had run away from God, and table-fellowship with him meant for them the joy of returning home to their Creator. In this way Jesus became for Luke the sōtēr, the Savior, of sinners; and only along this road did the poor become the poor pronounced blessed.

One element earned special attention thereby. According to redactional notations (15:2) the parables in Lk. 15 as well as those in Lk. 7:41-43 and 18:9-14 were not told to sinners, but to the righteous. The righteous ones were invited

---

[27]Lk. 5:1-11, 27-32; 7:36-50; 15:1-32; 18:9-14; 19:1-10; 23:39-43. All these pericopes were Lukan special material (5:27-32 excepted)!

through these parables, as was the elder brother of the prodigal son, to join in the fellowship of Jesus with the repentant "sinners" over whom they murmured (Lk. 7:39; 15:28).

Thus Luke showed Jesus to be the *sōtēr* who turned to sinners, people who had run away from God, and who invited the righteous too in order to make of them all the poor pronounced blessed.

4) In all this, the Gospel developed what was announced in Lk. 2:11: "for to you is born this day . . . a *sōtēr*." Jesus was characterized through the portrayal of his ministry as that which Augustus wanted to be and also was in an entirely different way. The accounts in Lk. 7:36-50 and 19:1-10 explained how the change of the situation in society promised in Lk. 1:62f. came about. The chief tax-collector Zacchaeus stated: "Behold, Lord, the half of my goods I give to the poor; and if I have defrauded any one of anything, I restore it fourfold" (Lk. 19:8). Hence Jesus brought change to social relationships as well when he changed the relationship of man to God and thereby to his entire environment.

The same perspective was documented through the Lukan summary account of the so-called community of goods in the primitive community of Jerusalem; this account is also worthy of note in this context (Acts 2:42-47; 4:32-35). Jesus ushered in not only a new perspective for the individual, but a new social situation. This new social situation, however, came about not through an alteration of the structures of society, but through the emergence of the freedom within the community of believers to place at the disposal of the other person also that which was economically necessary if the situation required it. This freedom was possible where the members of the community were turned toward each other in openness and saw themselves as new people. That this community in its various world situations also had a responsibility toward the structures of society was a necessary conclusion based on this principle, but it was not the starting point.

b) The interpretation of Jesus' dying. 1) While the Epistle to the Hebrews, akin to Luke in so many ways, focused the course of Jesus' life on the atoning high-priestly self-sacrifice, an atoning significance of Jesus' dying was mentioned by Luke only briefly in two formulaic expressions. The one is found in Acts 20:28 and appropriated the traditional redemption formula (I Pet. 1:18f.); the other is found in the word about the cup in the account of institution, Lk. 22:19f., and also contained traditional, liturgically shaped material.

Further observations correspond to this sparse finding. The chief Old Testament passage for the atoning death of Jesus, Isa. 53, was, of course, directly quoted in Lk. 22:37 and Acts 8:32f., but the statement about atonement was not appropriated. Even more conspicuous is the fact that the saying about the ransom (Mk. 10:45), the second Markan passage in addition to the word about the cup (Mk. 14:24) that spoke about Jesus' atoning death, was appropriated in Lk. 22:26f. without the expression about the ransom (*lytron*). Here the saying went: "But I am among you as one who serves." This secondary formulation came about, of course, not through a redactional reworking of Mk. 10:45, but through a special tradition.[28] But it is, nevertheless, to be assumed that Luke deliberately put this special tradition in the place of the saying about a ransom.

Thus Luke on the whole did not eliminate the interpretation of Jesus' dying as atonement, but he did, nevertheless, relegate it to a marginal position and did not make it relevant for his theological conception.

2) How then did Luke portray Jesus' dying? As we saw above, for him Jesus' ministry was a continuous path and therefore his dying was not an independent act, but only a transit station along this path that Luke saw on the whole in terms of the ancient Christology of exaltation; this Christology he appropriated in Acts 2:33ff.; 13:37f. As such a transit station Jesus' dying had for Luke a twofold significance.

For one thing, his dying made plain the guilt of the representatives of Judaism in Jerusalem. With the execution of Jesus they sealed their opposition to God in his gracious turning and claim (Acts 7:52). But they did it unwittingly (Lk. 23:34; Acts 3:17); this was once again an element peculiar to Luke. Hence they were summoned to repentance in the missionary sermons of the book of Acts (Acts 2:22f., 38; 3:19). This conduct of the Jews was not understood, of course, as representative for humanity; on this point Luke and John went their separate ways. For that matter, this conduct was not even representative for all Israel. The missionary sermons in the synagogues of the Diaspora recounted it merely as the transgression of those in Jerusalem: "For those who live in Jerusalem and their rulers, because they did not recognize him nor understand the utterances of the prophets which are read every sabbath, fulfilled these by condemning him" (Acts 13:27).

The other positive significance of Jesus' dying becomes evident here. It consisted of the fact that his dying belonged to God's plan of salvation. It was said to the disciples along the road to Emmaus who thought in their resignation, "But we had hoped that he was the one to redeem Israel" (Lk. 24:21), "Was it not necessary that the Christ should suffer these things and enter into his glory?" (Lk. 24:26). That meant in soteriological terms that the forgiveness that Jesus mediated in his earthly days through his turning in personal involvement was now offered to all from his resurrection: "through this man forgiveness of sins is proclaimed to you!" (Acts 13:38). It was still bound to the turning of Jesus' person, but it was not justified in any special way through an atoning death.

3) The reason for this theological gap is to be sought in the fact that for Luke the Sinai Covenant and its legal order did not play any role. Because of this he did not understand the new salvation as a breaking through the legal order of God that laid claim to atonement, but as the realization of the promised plan of salvation.

4) Thus for Luke, Jesus' dying was on the whole an integrated part of the course of Christ's life; through it the guilt of the Jews, but above all God's gracious turning to people, was declared. The atoning significance retreated for

---

[28]Cf. J. Roloff, "Anfänge der soteriologischen Deutung des Todes Jesu (Mk. X.45 und Lk. XXII.27)," *NTS* 19 (1972/73), 55ff.

Luke, on the one hand, because he spoke principally in a missionary style, and, on the other hand, most importantly because he did not link the course of Jesus' life to the legal order of the Sinai Covenant; in this latter respect he was to be differentiated from Paul and the other Jewish-Christian authors of the New Testament. This aspect becomes clear when we examine the Lukan version of the relationship of Jesus and the church to Israel.

4. JESUS—ISRAEL—THE CHURCH

a) Israel. The opinion has often been voiced in the scholarly discussion that for Luke Christianity was finally nothing other than true Judaism.[29] There is a considerable moment of truth in this perspective; yet only when "Judaism" is understood in the way Luke did.

1) For Luke, Israel was not, as it was for Paul, the people of promise that was held securely beneath the Sinai Covenant (Rom. 9:4). As we noted above, Luke never spoke of the Sinai Covenant. In the three passages that mentioned a covenant with Israel the promise given to the patriarchs, the Abrahamic Covenant, was intended (Lk. 1:72; Acts 3:25; 7:8).

2) To the question about the significance of this covenant for Israel, Luke answered that because the promises were given to their fathers the fulfillment of the promise, the dawning of salvation, was preached to the Jews first before all other nations initially by Jesus and then after Easter by his messengers. "You are the sons of the prophets and of the covenant which God gave to your fathers, saying to Abraham, 'And in your posterity shall all the families of the earth be blessed.' God, having raised up his servant, sent him to you first, to bless you" (Acts 3:25f.).

Accordingly, the Lukan historical composition, from the inaugural sermon of Jesus in Nazareth (Lk. 4:25ff.) to the proclamation of Paul before the Jews in Rome (Acts 28:25-31), was constantly based on the principle that the salvation brought by Jesus was offered first to the Jews and then to the other nations (Acts 13:46). This principle, advocated also by Paul (Rom. 1:16), was for Luke (differently than for Matthew) already in effect for Jesus' earthly ministry (Lk. 4:24), and basically, even though not expressed, also for the Old Testament and the patriarchal promise.

3) From this may be concluded: Israel was for Luke from start to finish a nation among nations that was simply the first to be encountered by God's revelation. Hence, in contrast to Matthew (§46,6), Luke did not speak about a suspension of the Covenant. The end of the parable of the evil tenants, e.g., in Lk. 20:16 was not emphasized in any special way at all. Israel's conduct in relationship to Jesus and the gospel was not representative, but seen as an example. Because Israel was always looked upon basically as the people first affected by God's gracious turning in salvation and not as the people held securely in God's Covenant from Sinai, the church was the continuation of pious Israel.

---

[29]Thus, e.g., H. J. Holtzmann, *Theologie* I, 538f.; E. Haenchen, *Acts*, at Acts 22:2-21.

b) *The church as the continuation of pious Israel.* Those Israelites who accepted the promise as well as its fulfillment distinguished themselves from the Israel that once rejected the prophets and now rejected Jesus and the apostles. They were few in number (Lk. 13:23). That Jesus and the church joined themselves to these few in continuity became apparent repeatedly in the entire conception of the Lukan historical composition.

In the name of these few, in the name of the true Israel, Jesus was welcomed already as a child by Simeon and Anna in the temple (Lk. 2:25-32, 37). There in his "Father's house" the parents found the twelve-year-old boy (Lk. 2:49). Correspondingly, in conclusion the entry of Jesus into Jerusalem and thereby his entire earthly ministry led to the temple (Lk. 19:47). The Gospel closed with the remark, "[They] were continually in the temple blessing God" (24:53). The assembly of the church took as its point of departure the teaching of the apostles in the temple (Acts 2:46; 3:1; 5:12). Even Paul declared his allegiance to this Christianity that came from the temple during his last residence in Jerusalem (Acts 21:20-24; 24:27f.). Luke therefore allowed the church to grow forth in historical continuity from the pious Israel that looked for the comfort of Israel in the temple.

In this way Luke also furnished the church with a historical self-understanding and provided it with an important apologetic argument in relationship to the Hellenistic world. Christianity was not "a new and mischievous superstition," as was claimed in that context (according to Suetonius *Nero* 16 = LCL, II, 111); rather it was the consummation of ancient Israelite religion. Before the Roman procurator Paul defended himself: "I worship the God of our fathers!" (Acts 24:14). And to the Jews in Rome he stated: "it is because of the hope of Israel that I am bound with these chains" (Acts 28:20).

c) *Jerusalem.* In no other Gospel was Jerusalem mentioned so often and with such emphasis as in Luke. Because he portrayed the coming of salvation in terms of a historical process, he also linked it to historical places. Jerusalem was seen thereby both positively and negatively.

1) The positive significance of Jerusalem was bound together to a large extent with the significance of the temple just discussed above. Jerusalem was the goal of the course of Jesus' earthly life and the starting point for the emergence of the church. Jesus had to die in Jerusalem (Lk. 13:33), and after his end the disciples had to remain in Jerusalem in order to receive the Spirit there (Lk. 24:49; Acts 1:4). For this reason, Luke also restricted the Easter appearances to the region in and around Jerusalem (Lk. 24:13, 18, 33, 52). Starting from Jerusalem the missionary outreach to the nations of the world had to be carried out (Lk. 24:47; Acts 1:8). The church grew outward from Jerusalem in a concentric way as the newly founded communities each established ecclesiastical fellowship with the primitive community in Jerusalem (Acts 8:14-25; 11:22; 12:25; 13:13). Christian Jerusalem did not assume for Luke the authoritarian position and the jurisdictional power that Jewish Jerusalem had for the Diaspora. The course of development led rather from Jerusalem to Rome. Perhaps Luke

wanted to suggest in this way that from now on Rome ought to constitute a central point as Jerusalem formerly did; moreover, that Rome was threatened with the same fate as Jerusalem. After all, Jerusalem was not only the city in which the decisive turning point—Jesus' exit and the beginning of the church—took place; it also bore responsibility in a special way through these events.

2) No other New Testament writer referred so emphatically to the destruction of Jerusalem as did Luke. Besides the words used in common with the other synoptics (Lk. 13:34f. par. Mt. and Lk. 21:20-24 par.) there are the following references from the Lukan special material: 13:1-5; 19:14, 27; Acts 6:14 and above all the brackets placed around the passion narrative consisting of the two words that predicted the impending judgment over the city: Lk. 19:41-44 (Jesus wept over Jerusalem) and Lk. 23:27-31 (the people, in contrast to the hierarchy of the priests, wept over Jesus' end).

Finally, at the heart of the temple discourse stood the announcement: "for these are days of vengeance to fulfill all that is written" (Lk. 21:22). Here in Lk. 21:20f., the historical event of the besieging of the city took the place of the eschatological "abomination" (par. Mk. 13:14; Mt. 24:15), the desolation of the temple. The destruction of Jerusalem became an exemplary historical event (Lk. 13:1-5; 23:29f.).

d) The Law. 1) The Law was viewed by Luke as a norm for living and not, as it was for Paul and—in a different way—for the Epistle to the Hebrews, as an order of salvation. This norm for living was observed by pious Judaism (Lk. 1:6; 2:22ff., 27, 39) as also by Jewish-Christianity (Acts 10:14; 21:20 and passim). Even Paul held to this norm, according to Luke, as a Jewish-Christian; according to Acts 16:3 he circumcised Timothy, who came from a religiously mixed marriage, before making him his co-worker. This appears to be a blatant contradiction to Paul's own statement, for according to Gal. 2:3 at the Apostolic Council he refused defiantly to allow his co-worker Titus to be circumcised. Yet both circumstances are historically thinkable, each according to a different situation. But it is characteristic that Luke emphasized the first and not the last. The conduct of Paul during his last residence in Jerusalem corresponded to this former compliance (Acts 21:21-26). Thus, according to Luke, the Jewish-Christians maintained the Law, although, according to Acts 15:10f., they hoped to be saved alone through the grace of the Lord Christ. Luke did not make of the Jewish-Christians Judaizers; but in terms of his leading notion of historical continuity he could not imagine it otherwise than that they continued to hold to the norm for living of the Law.

2) In contrast, the Gentile-Christians were free from the Law: "For it seemed good . . . to lay upon you [i.e., Gentile-Christians] no greater burden than these necessary things: that you abstain from what has been sacrificed to idols and from blood and from what is strangled and from unchastity" (Acts 15:28f.). In this summary of the conclusions of the Apostolic Council—and this is characteristic for Luke—certain regulations were taken from the Law that also should be in effect for the Gentile-Christians. Since, however, the Law was recognized

as an important norm for living for Christians too, a question became acute that until then had been discussed nowhere in the New Testament: How were the religious-moral directives of the Old Testament related to political and ritual laws? It is once again characteristic for Luke that he was the only one in the New Testament who separated the cultic and ceremonial laws from the Mosaic *nomos* and thereby introduced for the first time a necessary differentiation that did not exist for the Old Testament itself; this differentiation was then carried out by the early catholic fathers. Luke separated the "ordinances" (*ta ethē*) of Moses from the *nomos* of Moses (Lk. 10:26; 16:17; Acts 15:5; 21:20, 24) and understood by "ordinances" the ceremonial law. He characterized these cultic and ceremonial laws as "the ordinances" (*ta ethē*) Moses had passed on (Acts 15:1; 21:21; 26:3; 28:17; cf. Lk. 1:9; 2:42; Acts 16:21).

3) If one tries to classify this understanding of the Law it can be seen that a certain degree of contact existed with the understanding of early catholicism as it emerged in Justin Martyr and Irenaeus. Early catholicism also moved the accent from the order of salvation to the norm in its understanding of the Law so as to separate the norm from the ceremonial law as well. Nevertheless, even in this respect one cannot characterize Lukan theology as early catholic.[30] In contrast to Irenaeus and Justin Martyr, Luke taught neither synergism nor a new Law. That he sought to clarify the unclarified problem of the norm for the Gentile church of his time cannot be turned against him as accusation. He also wanted to equip the church thereby for a long journey through history.

e) Regarding eschatology. 1) Four times in the Lukan composition the question was raised about the "when" of the end or of the visible establishment of the kingdom and immediately rejected with emphasis. According to Lk. 17:20, Jesus answered the question with the pointer: "the kingdom of God is in the midst of you!" According to Lk. 4:18-21, Jesus' preaching was gospel, proclamation of the present coming (cf. Lk. 16:16).[31]

The second passage, Acts 1:6ff., referred the question of "when" to the present emergence of the church through the witness of the disciples. Similarly, the third passage (Lk. 19:11ff.) answered the question of the "when" with the reference to the talent entrusted to the disciples. Lk. 21:7-36 finally answered with the apocalyptic discourse and thereby through the reference to a long road through history.

2) These answers to the question of the "when" corresponded to the christological statements about the exaltation and the *parousia*. The traditional reference to the *parousia* remained; in fact, it was especially emphasized in Acts 1:11; the ascension showed symbolically that the disciples would no longer see Jesus until the *parousia*. But the accent lay clearly on the exaltation. Before the Sanhedrin Jesus answered the question of the high priest, according to Lk. 22:69,

---

[30]Cf. L. Goppelt, *Christentum und Judentum*, pp. 294ff., 304f.

[31]Luke for his part used this summation to replace the summaries found in Mk. 1:15 and Mt. 4:17 in which Jesus spoke about the drawing near of the kingdom. According to Luke, Jesus did not preach like this!

with the announcement of the exaltation and disregarded the announcement of the *parousia* that stood in the synoptic parallel tradition (Mk. 14:62; Mt. 26:64).

From this christological shift of accent to the exaltation H. Flender concluded for the issue of soteriology that Luke moved redemption to heaven, i.e., the hour of death became for the individual the *parousia* in which life would either be lost or won (Lk. 12:20; 23:43).[32] But one cannot make these statements of an individual eschatology that undeniably appear in Luke (Lk. 12:20; 23:43; cf. 16:19-31) into absolutes in this way. The universal concrete consummation at the *parousia* remained intact even for Luke as the ultimate goal (Lk. 14:14; 17:30-35). But attention was not directed primarily at the universal consummation, but at the exalted One and the assembling of the church through his Spirit. That meant: the expectation became permeable to an individual eschatology.

By bringing into connection exaltation, the gathering of the church through the Spirit, and individual eschatology Luke offered a polar correspondence to the book of Revelation. If the relationship to the world was focused in the resistance to the Antichrist in Revelation (Rev. 13), in Luke it found its most characteristic expression in the Areopagus address (Acts 17:16-34), the missionary debate with the world of the educated. If Revelation closed with the prayer: "Amen. Come, Lord Jesus!" (Rev. 22:20), the Lukan composition closed with the report of the unhindered proclamation of the message of salvation (Acts 28:31). If Revelation expected the first resurrection, the so-called millennial kingdom, Luke expected the fellowship with the exalted One that was not bound to the *parousia*: "You are those who have continued with me in my trials; as my Father appointed a kingdom for me, so do I appoint for you that you may eat and drink at my table in my kingdom" (Lk. 22:28-30).

---

[32]Flender, op. cit. (n. 16), pp. 91ff.

Chapter IV

THE PRESENCE OF THE *ESCHATON* IN THE SELF-REVELATION OF THE WORD BECOME FLESH (THE FIRST EPISTLE OF JOHN AND THE GOSPEL OF JOHN)

§49. The Structure of Johannine Theology

H. Windisch, *Johannes und die Synoptiker* (1926); W. von Loewenich, *Das Johannes-verständnis im zweiten Jahrhundert* (1932); C. Maurer, *Ignatius von Antiochien und das Johannesevangelium* (1949); E. Ruckstuhl, *Die literarische Einheit des Johannesevangeliums* (1951); Bultmann, *Theology* II, §§41-50; C. H. Dodd, *The Interpretation of the Fourth Gospel* (1953); Dodd, *Historical Tradition in the Fourth Gospel* (1963); B. Noack, *Zur johanneischen Tradition* (1954); Goppelt, *Apostolic Times*, pp. 128f., 157f.; E. Haenchen, "Johanneische Probleme," in Haenchen, *Gott und Mensch* (1965), pp. 78-113; E. Käsemann, *The Testament of Jesus. A study of the Gospel of John in the light of chapter seventeen* (1968); on this: G. Bornkamm, "Zur Interpretation des Johannesevangeliums," in *Aufsätze* III, 104-121; Conzelmann, *Theology*, pp. 321-358; C. K. Barrett, *The Gospel of John and Judaism* (1975); R. Fortna, *The Gospel of Signs* (1970); R. Schnackenburg, "Zur Herkunft des Johannes-Evangeliums," *BZ* NF 14 (1970), 1-23; S. S. Smalley, "Diversity and Development in John," *NTS* 17 (1970/71), 276-292; G. Klein, " 'Das wahre Licht scheint schon.' Beobachtungen zur Zeit und Geschichts-erfahrung einer urchristlichen Schule," *ZThK* 68 (1971), 261-326; Koester-Robinson, *Trajectories*, pp. 232-79; O. Cullmann, *The Johannine Circle* (1976). **On the History of Research:** E. Haenchen, "Aus der Literatur zum Johannesevangelium 1929-1956," *ThR* NF 23 (1955), 295-335; R. Schnackenburg, *The Gospel According to St. John* I (Herder, 1968), 11-217; E. Malatesta, *St. John's Gospel 1920-1965* (Analecta Biblica 32, 1967); Kümmel, *Introduction*, pp. 188-247; H. Thyen, "Aus der Literatur zum Johannesevangelium," *ThR* NF 42 (1974), 4ff. **Important Commentaries:** W. Bauer (1925), HNT; M. J. Lagrange, *L'Evangile selon Saint-Jean* (1936⁵); R. Bultmann, *The Gospel of John* (1971), Westminster; C. K. Barrett, *The Gospel according to St. John* (1954); R. Schnackenburg, *The Gospel According to St. John* I/II (Herder, 1968–); R. E. Brown, *The Gospel according to St. John* I/II (1966/70), Anchor Bible; S. Schulz (1972), NTD; B. Lindars, *The Gospel of John* (1972). **On 1:** J. Roloff, "Der johanneische 'Lieblingsjünger' und der Lehrer der Gerechtigkeit," *NTS* 15 (1968/69), 129-151; R. Schnackenburg, "Der Jünger, den Jesus liebte," in *Evangelisch-Katholischer Kommentar, Vorarbeiten* II (1970), 97-117. **On 2:** L. Schottroff, *Der Glaubende und die feindliche Welt. Beobachtungen zum gnostischen Dualismus und seiner Bedeutung für Paulus und das Johannesevangelium* (1970); O. Böcher, *Der johanneische Dualismus im Zusammenhang des nachbiblischen Judentums* (1965); H. Leroy, *Rätsel und Missverständnis* (1968). **On 3:** E. Schweizer, *Ego Eimi* (1939; 1965²); H. Becker, *Die Reden des Johannesevangeliums und der Stil der gnostischen Offenbarungsrede* (1956); S. Schulz, *Komposition und Herkunft der johanneischen Reden* (1960); H. Zimmermann, "Das absolute egō eimi als die neutestamentliche Offenbarungsformel," *BZ* NF 4 (1960), 54-69, 266-276; E. Haenchen, " 'Der Vater, der mich gesandt hat'," in Haenchen, *Gott und Mensch* (1965), pp. 68-77; Haenchen, "Probleme des johanneischen 'Prologs,' " ibid., pp. 114-143; J. Blank, *Krisis. Untersuchungen zur johanneischen Christologie und Eschatologie* (1964); J. Riedl, *Das Heilswerk Jesu nach Johannes* (1973). **On 4:** G. Kittel, *logos, TDNT* IV, 100-136; E. Käsemann, "The Structure and Purpose of the Prologue to John's Gospel," in Käsemann, *New Testament Questions*, pp. 139-167; W. Eltester, "Der Logos und sein Prophet," in *Apophoreta. Festschrift für E. Haenchen* (1964), pp. 109-134; J. Jeremias, "Zum Logos-Problem," *ZNW* 59 (1968), 82-85; H. Zimmermann, "Christushymnus und johanneischer Prolog," in *Neues Testament und Kirche. Festschrift für R. Schnackenburg* (1974), pp. 249-265.

1. ANONYMITY

a) Since the formation of the canon, three writings of the New Testament, besides the book of Revelation (§44,1), were ascribed to the Apostle John; he was referred to in Gal. 2:9 among the three "pillars" of the community of Jerusalem. The Gospel of John and two Epistles of John already belonged to the Muratorian Canon.[1]

The name John, however, appeared only in the book titles that arose subsequently and not in the writings themselves. The first two epistles of John named neither author nor recipient, and even the third, which was written in the conventional letter form, did not reveal the name of its author (III Jn. 1). This silence was neither coincidental nor—as in the case of Hebrews (§47,1)—conditioned by literary character. The author certainly did introduce himself in I John, as also in the Gospel of John; he did not designate himself with a name but with his function; he spoke as a witness of the Logos become flesh. He laid claim to being an eyewitness in order to let it be known also that he meant thereby more than being a historical witness. In I Jn. 1:1, 3 ("that which we have seen and heard we proclaim also to you") and in Jn. 1:14 ("we have beheld his glory") a "we" came to expression. Here spoke in fact an individual who had joined the company of a group.

b) This individual assumed a form in the so-called "beloved disciple" who was introduced by the Gospel of John for the first time in 13:23 (*ho mathētēs . . . hon ēgapa ho Iēsous*; cf. Jn. 19:26; 20:2; 21:7, 20). The supplementary chapter (ch. 21) identified this beloved disciple with a historical disciple of Jesus who also represented here the author of the Gospel (Jn. 21:24f.). The references

---

[1]Cf. W. G. Kümmel, *Introduction*, pp. 239, 492.

in the original Gospel, however, portrayed the beloved disciple not primarily as a historically identifiable disciple figure but as a model of the true disciple; this one on the one hand was directly familiar with the event of Jesus' earthly sojourn (Jn. 19:35f.), but on the other hand saw how it could be understood in retrospect (Jn. 20:8f.), the way the author of the Gospel understood it (Jn. 2:22).

c) Thus the manner in which the author introduced himself in the Gospel as in I John had theological meaning: he gained access to the manifestation of Jesus in a fundamentally different way than Luke who, in his foreword (Lk. 1:1-4), had made the gaining of such access into a program (§48,1). John too was concerned about eyewitness substantiation. But the kind of seeing he spoke about (I Jn. 1:1, 3) did not refer to the concrete, identifiable eyewitnesses (*autoptai*) of Lk. 1:3; Acts 1:21f.; it acquired rather a peculiar derived meaning; only the one who understood what he saw had really "seen" (Jn. 9:39; 19:35; 20:8). And whoever understood had seen and could bear witness, even if he no longer beheld Jesus with his own eyes (20:29).

In this way the author joined company in the "we" with all true witnesses of Jesus; he left open whether he himself was an eyewitness in the historical sense of the word or simply appropriated directly the eyewitness accounts of someone else.

Thus the historical question of whether these documents really came from the Apostle John was relativized in the Gospel and in I John. The anonymous but functional designation of witness indicated that for this as well as for the other Gospels and epistles the decisive question about apostolicity ran: Was the historical course of Jesus' life and ministry—and even here this was all-important—understood and interpreted on the basis of firsthand information in accord with its own intent?

2. THE NEW LANGUAGE

a) A distinguishing attribute of the Johannine interpretation of Jesus' life and ministry was its independent terminology that, of course, did not appear everywhere with the same pregnance and intensity. Hence the narrative portions of the Gospel were shaped less by this terminology than were the discourses, the prose portions of I John less than the statement-type antithetical couplets (e.g., I Jn. 2:12-17; 3:4-10, 13-24). With this varying intensity, however, it was applied with regularity in the Johannine writings.

This terminology was obviously not only a means of translation but also a vehicle of transportation into a particular conceptual world. The question of its origin and meaning is in any case a history-of-religion/philological as well as a theological problem.

Especially characteristic for the terminology and the theology of the Johannine writings were three forms of speech.

1) The dualistic antitheses: light and darkness (Jn. 1:4f.; 3:19; 8:12; 11:9f.;

12:35, 46), truth and falsehood (Jn. 8:44; I Jn. 1:6ff.; 2:21), life and death (Jn. 5:24; 11:25; I Jn. 3:14), above and below (Jn. 8:23), freedom and servitude (Jn. 8:33, 36).

2) The "I am" words: "I am the bread of life" (Jn. 6:35, 48); "I am the light of the world" (8:12); "I am the door of the sheep" (10:7); "I am the good shepherd" (10:11); "I am the resurrection and the life" (11:25); "I am the way, the truth, and the life" (14:6); "I am the true vine" (15:1).

3) The designation of Jesus as the Logos: within the New Testament only in Jn. 1:1; I Jn. 1:1; and Rev. 19:13.

b) In terms of the history of religion the origin of this terminology can be traced back to two roots.

1) The antithetical dualism is found in the analogous formulations of the Qumran texts. For example, the "sons of light" (Jn. 12:36; I Thess. 5:5; Eph. 5:8), not found otherwise prior to the New Testament, was used frequently in the Essene texts (e.g., 1QS 3:24f.), and in them, moreover, the "sons of light"— as in John—stood antithetically over against people who remained in darkness. Hence it frequently has been assumed today that the Johannine terminology had its origin in the Jewish baptismal movement of Palestine.[2] The contention is that Christians coming out of these circles developed this language and with it the Johannine tradition. Speaking against this single-track derivation, however, is the fact that the Essene documents do not provide analogies for the two other linguistic constructions characteristic for John.

2) In contrast, all three characteristics of the Johannine terminology had analogies in gnosticism; we find them expressed in the Odes of Solomon, among the opponents of Ignatius (e.g., Ign. Trall. 9:1–11:2; Sm. 4:1–7:2), and in the early Mandean traditions. These sources, however, were throughout chronologically later than the Johannine writings that had to have been composed between A.D. 90 and 100. Gnostic research in the meantime has shown, moreover, that John did not take over a developed Gnostic language system; he did not even rework, as R. Bultmann conjectured, Gnostic documents.[3]

The tradition of Johannine terminology that came out of Palestinian baptismal circles rather went on to develop independently in debate with Gnostic streams of thought. According to various indicators this debate took place in several geographical regions. It happened initially in Samaria (Jn. 4), then in Syria and in Asia Minor where it finally achieved literary fixation.[4] That John did in fact conduct a debate with Gnostic streams of thought is shown by I John, which continuously opposed a Docetic enthusiasm of a Gnostic cast (I Jn. 1:6, 8, 10; 2:4, 9 and passim). By way of defense it clearly incorporated expressions of its opponents into its own language.

---

[2]E.g., S. Schulz, *Komposition und Herkunft der johanneischen Reden* (1960), pp. 182-87; R. Schnackenburg, *The Gospel According to St. John* (HTK) I, 129ff.

[3]"Johannesevangelium," *RGG* III³, 842f.; H. Becker, *Die Reden des Johannesevangeliums und der Stil der gnostischen Offenbarungsrede*, ed. R. Bultmann (1956).

[4]Regarding further support, cf. Goppelt, *Apostolic Times*, pp. 157ff.

3. THE *EGO-EIMI* FORMULAS

The metaphysical character of the Johannine terminology and thereby the theological scope of the Johannine tradition can be demonstrated in a pragmatic way through the "I am" words.

a) The Gospel of John passed on the words of Jesus predominantly in another genre than the synoptics; it did not do so in sayings, parables, and controversy dialogues, but in connected or dialogical discourses. These discourses repeatedly reached their climax in the "I am" words. What this registered was that the Johannine words of Jesus, in contrast to those of the synoptics, did not address the colorful spectrum of concrete social exigencies, but concentrated upon that which alone was decisive, upon the self witness of Jesus for humanity. This self-witness was summarized in the "I am" words.

b) The Johannine "I am" words encompassed two constitutive parts; they were the *ego-eimi* formulas and a determinative word-picture. Such, e.g., were 6:35, 41, 48, 51: "I am the bread of life"; or 8:12: "I am the light of the world"; or 10:11, 14: "I am the good shepherd"; or 15:1, 5: "I am the true vine." A further development of the word-picture toward a direct statement was suggested in 14:6 ("I am the way, the truth, and the life") and was accomplished completely in 11:25 ("I am the resurrection and the life"). Both constitutive parts of the formulas were of direct theological significance for the reader of the Gospel.

c) The determinative word-picture designated in each case Jesus' gift—and that was finally Jesus himself—through a figure of something people depended on for life, such as water and bread. Jesus' gift was "living water" (7:38), as 4:14 explained, water that mediated life. In ch. 6 the expression "bread of life" (6:35) was used correspondingly along with the expression of the same meaning "living bread" (6:51). Decisive was that the gift of Jesus in these statements was not compared with the realities "bread" and "water" as known from the world of everyday experience. The word-pictures were neither similes nor metaphors, but intrinsic speech.[5] Hence the water that Jesus gave was not compared to but instead placed over against natural water when Jesus spoke with the Samaritan woman at the well; he explained that whoever drank from Jacob's well would constantly become thirsty again (4:13); he offered her in contrast to it a water that quenched thirst permanently. In the same way, he offered in 6:49f. a bread that would still all hunger forever. It was "bread from heaven," genuine, true bread (*ton arton . . . ton alēthinon*, 6:32).[6]

This manner of speaking distinguished itself fundamentally from corresponding Old Testament images. In the Old Testament we find a metaphor such as God "the fountain of living waters" (Jer. 2:13; cf. Ps. 36:10). It was appropriated in Revelation when it promised that the saved would be guided "to springs of living water" (Rev. 7:17; cf. 21:6, 22; 22:7). Here was promised quite under-

---

[5]Cf. E. Schweizer, *Ego Eimi* (1939; 1965²).

[6]The only analogy for this within the New Testament is found in Hebrews with its contrasting of the genuine heavenly and imperfect earthly sanctuary (8:2; 9:24).

standably a fountain of water from which one can drink again and again so that one should not suffer thirst again. In Jn. 4:14; 7:38, in contrast, water was promised that would quench thirst permanently. These statements corresponded to a dualistic-cosmic way of thinking that distinguished heavenly and earthly as intrinsic and derivative; what man sought vainly in the derivative, in the earthly realm—such as the quenching of the thirst for life—would be found when he grasped the intrinsic.

The roots of this dualistic way of thinking reached far back into the ancient Orient. The closest parallels to the Johannine statements, however, are found in early Syrian gnosticism. Thus one encounters in Od. Sol. 30:1 (cf. 11:6ff.), in Ign. Rom. 7:2, and in Mandean traditions the expression "water of life" as a standard designation for the salvation that came from above.

But John did not simply take over this manner of speaking from gnosticism; it needs to be observed that the same type of imagery was used in the book of Revelation in an Old Testament way. There—and only there within the New Testament—Jesus gave to eat of the "tree of life" (Rev. 2:7) and to drink of the "water of life" (Rev. 21:6) and was himself designated as the "light" (Rev. 22:5). In the Gospel of John, therefore, a complex of images that also existed in the book of Revelation as Old Testament tradition was transposed into a dualistic form of speech. The author himself developed this transposition in apologetic and polemical debate with a Hellenistic, in particular Gnostic, way of thinking. The similar statements in the Odes of Solomon and in the writings of Ignatius were probably analogous constructions.

With this dualistic form of speech John did not intend in any way to minimize the value of the natural side, e.g., earthly bread and water. Rather he intended on the negative side to make unmistakably clear that Jesus' gift was something radically different from that which man wished for himself, but was precisely the fulfillment of that for which man actually hungered. Jesus' gift was not the direct answer to the question of man and not the direct goal toward which the development of humanity (such as in the understanding of Hegel) led. All the more, however, John intended to say on the positive side that Jesus' gift was not only the salvation-historical fulfillment of the Old Testament promise; it also stilled the very hunger for life that comprehended the entire human race and came to abundant expression in its mythology.

In this way Jesus' gift was designated as that which it was in its essence: the present *eschaton*, the absolutely new thing that could not be reached along the road of historical development and yet must be reached if history was not to become meaningless. The dualistic form of speech designated Jesus' gift as the eschatologically new thing. This gift was present in the midst of history; it was identical to Jesus' person.

d) Such was claimed and clarified by the "I am" formulas placed at the head of the word-pictures. Among the synoptics an "I am he" (*egō eimi*) on the lips of Jesus is found in Mk. 14:62 as identification in response to the question of the high priest, "Are you the Christ?" The meaning of the Johannine formulas stood, nevertheless, in contrast to this usage. In them the "I am" did not identify

Jesus with something already known. It unveiled for man something otherwise unknown and inaccessible. According to the content of the statement the "I am" was a formula of revelation.

As such the "I am" was already current in the Old Testament. The absolute use of *'ani hu'* (I am He) is thus to be found above all in Second Isaiah. In Isa. 43:10 it was said at the end of a major theophanic discourse, ". . . that you may know and believe me and understand that I am He." This absolute "I am He" was appropriated in Jn. 8:24 in connection with Isa. 43:10, similarly as in Jn. 13:19 in connection with Isa. 42:9. The "I am" was disseminated as formula of revelation far beyond the Old Testament throughout the entire Near East, while it was unknown in the specifically Greek-speaking realm. Greek man did not wait for revelation; he even sought to grasp the divine by inquiry.

The connection of this "I am" to word-pictures of cosmic dualism cannot be demonstrated as existing prior to John; it can be found, however, in the post-Johannine Gnostic literature. John probably fashioned this connection himself in debate with Gnostic and generally with Hellenistic thought.

e) Now the overall meaning of the "I am" formulas also became evident among those used by John to summarize Jesus' words. In these formulas Jesus offered himself exclusively as that which man sought without knowing it: as the life! Man understood and yet finally did not understand what was meant; "water" (Jn. 4:14) was everything with which man satisfied his thirst for life, "bread" (Jn. 6:35, 41, 48, 50f., 58) everything that meant a living wage and standard of living, and "light" (Jn. 8:12; cf. 1:4f.; 3:19ff.; 9:5) everything that brought certainty and clarity into the threatening uncertainty of existence. The "shepherd" meant protection and guidance in every respect (Jn. 10:11-16), and the "vine" (Jn. 15:1, 5) was for ancient man the quintessence of the joy that reached beyond the routine of life. Jesus laid claim to being and to giving all this in an intrinsic and final sense.[7]

How could man appropriate this claim of revelation? This offer of that which was real turned the Gospel of John into that document of the New Testament in which philosophers, mystics, and Gnostics from time immemorial have found the way to Jesus that was congenial to them. For gnosticism that which was intrinsically real was the divine spark in man that was, as it were, awakened through revelation; thus, in the 2nd century the Gospel of John became the book of the Gnostics. Platonism and—in the 19th century—German Idealism sought that which was intrinsically real in the world of ideas; as early as in Clement of Alexandria the Gospel of John was understood, therefore, as the pneumatic Gospel that brought out the eternal spiritual truths. Fichte recommended it to the educated of the 19th century as the writing that most clearly represented the ideas of Christianity.[8] Finally, in the 1930s existential philosophy promoted "self-existence," the achievement of one's intrinsic existence, and R. Bultmann derived from this source important impulses for his commentary on John that had an enormous effect in the 1950s.

---

[7]Cf. Schweizer, op. cit. (n. 5).

[8]*Anweisung zum seeligen Leben* (1806).

But the Johannine "I am" formulas were intended to lead the reader neither into the world of ideas nor to his intrinsic existence, but to the eschatological renewal and perfection of his creatureliness. He should be "born anew" (Jn. 3:3). He was by nature the one born blind who should receive his sight (Jn. 9). As the prologue said, he should be led into fellowship with the Logos of whom he knew nothing and desired to know nothing, although he owed his existence to him (Jn. 1:4f., 12f.).

4. JESUS—THE *LOGOS* BECOME FLESH

When the prologue of the Gospel of John began: "In the beginning was the *logos* . . . all things were made through him" (Jn. 1:1a, 3a), and when it closed: "And the *logos* became flesh . . . we have beheld his glory" (Jn. 1:14), it addressed that which was the center of existence for Old Testament/primitive Christian as well as for Hellenistic peoples. The words of the prologue about the *logos* were connected to three comprehensive contexts of usage for this term.

a) The Old Testament background. The very first sentence of the prologue (1:1) calls to mind what the Old Testament said about the word of God that made heaven and earth. How the prologue here and elsewhere spoke about the *logos* would have been unthinkable without the language of the Old Testament about the word of God. In the entire ancient world only the Old Testament was familiar with a word that—as it said here in v. 3—allowed the world and history to come into being and also went out to people as human speech (v. 14). Only in the Old Testament do we find a word in the ancient world that went out through the prophets as human word and not only announced history but fashioned it (Isa. 55:10f.). On the basis of this activity of the word in history nature and the universe were also placed into relationship to it (Isa. 40:26). The cultic tradition too, Ps. 33:9, confessed about creation: "For he spoke and it came to be."[9]

The Old Testament concept of the word of God was the first substantive foundation of the prologue. Yet it did not establish its connection directly to the Old Testament manner of speech. Three things distinguished its *logos* from the Old Testament. 1) The Old Testament spoke about the word of God while the prologue spoke about the "Word." 2) Corresponding to this was a substantive difference; the Johannine *logos* stood as an independent, in-person quantity next to God, it was hypostatized. The Old Testament word of God, in contrast, was the voice of God, even if it was occasionally personified (e.g., Ps. 147; Isa. 55:11). 3) The Old Testament word appeared primarily as the salvation-historical declarations of God; the Johannine *logos*, however, was introduced as a cosmic quantity even if it was understood in terms of the Word become flesh.[10]

Thus we may conclude: on a substantive level the statements of the prologue

---

[9]What these references could suggest was developed by G. von Rad, *Theology* II, 80-98.

[10]How a statement about Jesus as the Word would appear linking up directly with the Old Testament can be seen in Heb. 1:1f.

about the *logos* presupposed the Old Testament declarations about the Word of God and were intended fundamentally in this sense, but in terms of form and content they were not placed in direct connection with the Old Testament concept.

b) The primitive Christian prior history. As regards the term's history, the space between the Old Testament and the prologue was occupied by its usage in primitive Christianity. The apostles and teachers of the primitive Christian communities presupposed that God had already spoken through Moses and the prophets (Heb. 1:1). But when Paul wrote that he preached "the word of God" or in the absolute sense "the word," he meant the message of Jesus Christ, the gospel. "Word of God" or "the word" was here and in general primitive Christian linguistic usage a technical term for the message of Christ (e.g., I Cor. 14:36; II Cor. 2:12; 4:2; Col. 1:25ff.).

In the New Testament, there are only two passages from Johannine writings that go beyond this linguistic usage. According to I Jn. 1:1 the historical Jesus was the "word of life," and in Rev. 19:13 the One appearing for the *parousia* received the symbolic name "the word of God."

But even between these two passages and the prologue a considerable distance can be seen, since only in the latter was the term used in an absolute sense and applied to the preexistent One. More than this, a prehistorical being was introduced in the prologue under this term. The *logos* of the prologue became Jesus; Jesus was the *logos* become flesh, but not the *logos* as such. Thus, once again a gap in the history of the term emerges between the rest of the New Testament writings, including I Jn. 1:1 and Rev. 19:13, and the prologue; this compels one to ask: Where was the *logos* spoken of as a cosmic quantity prior to John? Prior to John, the preexistence and mediator role of the Son in creation (§33,4) were known in the Hellenistic church. But how did it happen that the preexistent One was referred to as the *logos*?

c) The logoi of the environment. The designation was apparently prompted in part by an apologetic and missionary debate with the environment.

1) The Greeks had made the *logos* notion into a symbol of their understanding of the world and existence throughout a history of intellectual development over the centuries.[11] In New Testament times the Stoa placed it at the center of its system of thought; for the Stoics the *logos* was the law of reason according to which the events of the cosmos took place, as well as the power that maintained the cosmos as an organic whole; it was world-reason. Hence it was the destiny of man to live *kata logon*, not to follow a claim from without but the law residing in oneself and thereby God. Man came to himself and became free.

To be sure, the Hellenistic reader of the Gospel of John would also be reminded about these concepts. He would nevertheless notice very quickly that the *logos* of the prologue was not derived from them. It was not the world-principle dwelling within the cosmos, but the counterpart in relationship to the cosmos;

[11]H. Kleinknecht, *TDNT* IV, 77.

the world was brought into being by the *logos* (Jn. 1:3) and was to be redeemed by it (1:10, 14).

2) This relationship of the *logos* to the world calls to memory the realm of gnosticism in which R. Bultmann thought he had found the concept's place of origin.[12] But the supporting references put forth by him[13] nearly all came from sources that were later than the Gospel of John.[14] In view of the contemporary status of research into gnosticism it can be said at most that the author of the prologue received thought-provoking impetus through contact with Gnostic movements. The assumption, however, that a developed Gnostic myth was taken over here far exceeds that which can be ascertained historically.[15]

Apart from the question about origin, a comparison of the Johannine *logos* with later Gnostic *logos* concepts is very instructive because it shows that the Johannine *logos* stood in relationship to the world in a different way than did the Gnostic one. The latter was one of the emanations that were brought into existence between the supreme deity and the world at creation in order to distance this world from God. Hence it was later sent as the redeemer—not to redeem the world but to free the souls of light from entanglement in the dark, material world. From this is to be concluded, however, that the Gnostic, the Greek, and the Johannine *logos* concepts each expressed a distinctive understanding of the world. Through the Gnostic *logos* one was set apart from the world, through the Greek *logos* one was incorporated into it; the Johannine *logos*, however, redeemed the world that had been created by it.

3) The closest parallels to the Johannine way of talking about the *logos* were found in the theology of Hellenistic Judaism, especially in the speculative thought about wisdom. Even in the latest portion of Proverbs (3rd century B.C.) a cosmological function was ascribed to wisdom. It was the firstborn of God's works and participated in the work of creation (Prov. 8:22-36). Wisdom also had a soteriological function; whoever listened to its exhortations and continued in its path "finds life," and whoever hated it, however, "love[s] death" (Prov. 8:35f.; cf. Syr. Bar. 3:9-4:4).

Because Judaism from ancient times more or less placed wisdom and the Law on an equal plain (cf. Sir. 24:23), speculative thought about wisdom found continuation in the corresponding speculative thought of the rabbis about the Torah.[16] The Torah too was considered to have been created by God before the world, to have participated in the creation of heaven and earth, and to be life

---

[12] "The *Johannine Prologue*, or its source, speaks in the language of Gnostic mythology, and its *Logos* is the intermediary, the figure that is of both cosmological and soteriological significance" (*The Gospel of John* [1971], p. 28).

[13] Ibid., pp. 24ff.

[14] The chronologically closest source would be the Letters of Ignatius that were composed some twenty years later; they spoke of the *logos* in gnostically colored expressions. Thus Jesus was called *autou logos apo sigēs proelthōn* ("his Word proceeding from silence") in Ign. Magn. 8:2 (= LCL, *Apostolic Fathers*, I, 205).

[15] Cf. Goppelt, *Apostolic Times*, pp. 101f.

[16] Billerbeck II, 353-57; G. Kittel, *TDNT* IV, 135f.

and light for the world. Of course, there is little to support the thesis of G. Kittel that the Johannine *logos* statements were formulated in antithesis to rabbinic speculations about the Law.[17] It is more likely that the reverse was true.

The fact that late Jewish statements about wisdom in many respects distinguished themselves considerably from the *logos* statements of the prologue does not hinder them from having been of service here as elsewhere (e.g., Col. 1:15-20; Phil. 2:5-11; Heb. 1:1-4) to the Christology of preexistence as stimulus and vehicle of expression. It is still noteworthy, however, that although those Jewish statements had in mind the "word," the Law, they did not use the term *logos*.

4) A way of speaking about the *logos* comparable to the prologue is found sporadically in Wis. Sol. (7)9 and then extensively in Philo. What Philo said about the *logos* was as elusive and complex as his philosophy of religion on the whole. *Logos* was for him, on the one hand—and this was inherited from Platonic thought—the quintessence of the ideal world, the prototype of the visible world, and on the other—and this was inherited from Stoic thought— the power of the good and the true at work in the world, and finally—and this was inherited from Jewish thought—the representative of those angelic beings that were agents of world-creation and of revelation. The *logos* of Philo did not stand in an observable genetic connection to that of John, but it was an instructive analogous phenomenon. Philo too wished to bring the biblical word into confrontation with the *logoi* of the Hellenistic environment. But how different the results of this effort in both places!

The difference was even reflected in the type of language; Philo's *logos* was an elusive term that was supposed to captivate the environment. The Johannine term *logos* was, in contrast, sharply profiled on all sides. It did not wish to allure but to address. It was fashioned out of the traditions and stimuli mentioned above without substantive compromise in order to articulate the intended content. In terms of content as well, Philo's *logos* was an imprecise compromise with the world views of the environment that wanted to accommodate all needs of society and had nothing to say to any one of them. The Johannine *logos*, in contrast, articulated that the redeeming and creating word of God was present in person in Jesus. Distinct from all analogies it was precisely not an agent figure between God and the world, but God himself in his gracious turning to the world, and yet a Thou in relationship to God, exactly Jesus' real background.

Thus John clarified in relationship to all contemporary ways of talking about the *logos* that Jesus was the *logos* in person! He was it in the flesh, as mortal human being. He was it for those who could see in the speaking and acting as well as in the course of this human being's life the *doxa*, the very being of their

---

[17]Kittel, op. cit. (n. 16), pp. 134ff. But the statements of the rabbis about the Torah that G. Kittel put forward come in large part from the 2nd through the 4th centuries after Christ and—like many statements of later gnosticism about the *logos*—were likely composed in their time also in opposition to the *logos* Christology of the church.

Creator; they could so see because they were like those born blind who through the encounter with him had been made to see (Jn. 9:39).[18]

The distinctiveness of the Johannine interpretation of Jesus becomes apparent here in terms of the two examples we have examined concerning the *logos* theology and the "I am" formulas. In all the New Testament this interpretation made the most extensive inroads from the Old Testament/Jewish terminological and conceptual world into that of Hellenistic man. These inroads, however, did not lead to the Hellenization of Christianity that would have meant the depletion of its essence; rather they led to the result that the decisive matter of Jesus' manifestation, the presence of eschatological salvation in history, was grasped more profoundly and more clearly.

5. THE LORD'S SUPPER

a) In contrast to the synoptics, the Gospel of John did not present an account of institution. It was not silent for reasons of a community oath of secrecy, as has frequently been assumed,[19] since Justin (*Ap.* 1:67) was still speaking openly to outsiders about the eucharistic worship service. John wanted rather here as well to give greater interpretive depth to that which in the synoptic tradition known to the communities had been encountered through Christ.

In place of the account of institution we find in John the farewell discourses (Jn. 13–17). On the basis of independent tradition they developed what was said in the discipleship sayings of the synoptics about Jesus' exit and the time of the church and thereby especially about the promise of the Last Supper. In Jn. 14:18-24 (cf. 16:16-24) the disciples received a promise that also applied the terminology of the event of Pentecost[20] and of the *parousia*[21] to the coming of Jesus in the Easter appearances. In this way it was to become clear that the coming of the resurrected One in the Easter appearances was an eschatological event and that fundamentally the community would continue to be encountered as well; yet this would happen in a different form, namely, through the Spirit. Thus the overall promise of the account of institution was developed in the farewell discourses.

b) But John portrayed the special content of the Lord's Supper along with that of baptism by extending the speaking and acting of Jesus into the situation of the community. Thus the summons of Jesus to repentance with respect to the kingdom of God (Jn. 3:3) was extended in the conversation with Nicodemus into

---

[18]How this becoming sighted, this believing and knowing, was possible was something John reflected about with just as much thoroughness as the essence of the manifestation of Jesus itself. It was, e.g., in 6:44f. a being-drawn and a letting-oneself-be-drawn. It came about in the Johannine dialogues, e.g., in 4:7-30, in the conversation at the well with the Samaritan woman, or in 9:35-39, the conversation with the blind man.

[19]Thus, e.g., by J. Jeremias, *The Eucharistic Words of Jesus* (1966), p. 136 (there in n. 5 one finds further representatives of this view).

[20]E.g., "make our home with him" (v. 23); "I [am] in you" (v. 20).

[21]E.g., "in that day" (v. 20; cf. 16:23).

the post-Easter situation and was repeated as the challenge to be baptized (Jn. 3:5). This challenge was the form to which Jesus' summons to repentance focused itself after Pentecost (Acts 2:38). Correspondingly in Jn. 6, the action of Jesus at the meal was adapted in the bread-of-life discourse to the post-Easter situation; the community was not to anticipate from him a continuation of the miraculous provision of bread, but to accept him as the bread of life (6:26f., 35). In 6:51c-58, finally, the "flesh" that Jesus gave was offered to it instead of the bread of life. John 6:51c stated: "and the bread which I shall give for the life of the world is my flesh [given over to death]."

These expressions call to mind the account of institution. There it was said about the bread as it was given to the disciples: "this is my body." In John that meant: "the bread . . . is my flesh." There Jesus was handed over "for the many," i.e., for all, while for John it was "for the life of the world," i.e., for humanity. This accommodation to the terminology of the Eucharist—a phenomenon that was intensified in 6:53 (to eat his flesh and to drink his blood)—helped each hearer to understand what was imperative; the promise that Jesus gave here was not fully appropriated at the hearing of the word, but only by the eating and drinking of the eucharistic meal. John did not introduce the Lord's Supper along with baptism as an institution established in an incidental way, but allowed it to grow out of the self-offering of Jesus through his word.

c) What the entire section, Jn. 6:51c-58, stated about the Lord's Supper in this way was summarized in v. 53: "Truly, truly, I say to you, unless you eat the flesh of the Son of man and drink his blood, you have no life in you." Hence the gift of the meal was the flesh and blood of the Son of man. The "Son of man" was the end-time mediator between God and man (Jn. 1:51) who on the basis of his dying brought life to all who believed (Jn. 3:14f.). His "flesh" was his human existence that was handed over to death for all.[22] Correspondingly, the established image of "his blood" was also Jesus' dying in its saving significance. Thus the gift of the Lord's Supper was the exalted Son of man in the saving power of his dying. This interpretation is confirmed through 6:57, since there "flesh and blood" were replaced by the personal pronoun "me"; to take to oneself the flesh and blood of the Son of man meant, accordingly, the same as to take him to oneself.

How was the eating and drinking intended? Up to this point it was an image in the bread-of-life discourse of Jn. 6:35 for the acceptance of Jesus through a hearing in faith. Now it had to be intended actually as follows: the gift was received physically through sacramental eating and drinking. When some interpreters clarify that faith was no longer a matter of concern,[23] they fail to recognize that this section in accord with its context continued to be a revelation

---

[22]*Sarx* (flesh) was here and in v. 51, as in 1:14, man as mortal earthling; in 6:63 it was the sphere of mortality as it also was elsewhere in John.

[23]G. Bornkamm, *Aufsätze* II, 51-64; G. Richter, *Formgeschichte*, p. 39; cf. also regarding this problem, U. Wilckens, "Der eucharistische Abschnitt der johanneischen Rede vom Lebensbrot (Joh. 6,51c-58)," in *Neues Testament und Kirche. Für Rudolf Schnackenburg,* ed. J. Gnilka (1974), pp. 220-248.

discourse in which Jesus offered himself through his word. Even if they assumed here their intrinsic meaning, eating and drinking always remained, therefore, primarily an image for acceptance through hearing in faith; it was so because the moment of self-offering always remained here as well primarily an offer through the word.[24]

That meant that John combined here in an impressive way word and sacrament. From Jn. 6:51c on, the sacrament did not simply take its place alongside the word. Rather the word became, as it were, concentrated in the direction of the sacrament, and the sacrament received in this way verbal character. Only through the terminology of proclamation could it be made clear to the reader that Jesus' offering of himself was only then completely accepted when personal appropriation had taken place not only through hearing in faith but also through the eating and drinking of the sacrament in faith.[25]

That also makes understandable why this eating and drinking was characterized here as necessary for salvation: "unless you eat . . . you have no life in you." What was declared here as necessary for salvation was not an ecclesiastical institution, but the word that had become flesh. For the one who did not find access to the sacrament beyond hearing in faith, the vital essence of the word had not yet dawned, i.e., its becoming flesh.

d) The degree to which these Johannine statements set forth the apostolic understanding of the Lord's Supper at the conclusion of the apostolic period becomes clear when we compare them finally to the statements of Ignatius composed with the same terminology: "the Eucharist is the flesh of our Savior Jesus Christ who [scil. *tēn* = that] suffered for our sins, which [*hēn*] the Father raised up by his goodness" (Ign. Sm. 7:1 = LCL, *Apostolic Fathers*, I, 258f.). Here "flesh" was, in contrast to Jn. 6 and otherwise in New Testament anthropology as well, not the mortal human being or the sphere of mortality, but the human nature that was transfigured through the resurrection. Thus the gift of the Eucharist was here apparently understood as a heavenly substance (Ign. Eph. 20:2). Ignatius could not transfer this statement about the "flesh" to the "blood"; a resurrected, heavenly blood was unthinkable. Hence he characterized the gift of the blood and its effect in a way different from that of the flesh (Ign. Rom. 7:3; Phld. 4:1), while in the New Testament the two were spoken of in a strictly parallel sense.

Thus this brief comparison with Ignatius can illustrate why John should be seen together with Paul (§41,2) on a substantive level in spite of a different

---

[24]For this reason it was possible here to speak much more directly than in Paul (cf. §41,2) about an eating of the flesh and drinking of the blood without there being any association with a *manducatio capernaitica*.

[25]This exegetical understanding of the statement of Jn. 6:51c-58 as well as that of its connection to the bread-of-life discourse disproves the literary-critical hypothesis that ascribed the section to a redactor. Since the stylistic-critical arguments turned out to be indefensible, this hypothesis was based on the exegetical understanding, e.g., coming from the erroneous assumption that in 6:51c-58 the Eucharist was designated as *pharmakon athanasias*; regarding the discussion, cf. L. Goppelt, *TDNT* VI, 143f.; VIII, 236f.; U. Wilckens, op. cit. (n. 23).

terminology and form of address. In ch. 6 he made the bold attempt to introduce the gift of Jesus that finally was mediated in the Lord's Supper by using the language of Hellenistic dualism and of the mystery religions and to dispense with a direct connection to the Old Testament. And this attempt was successful because he interpreted the genuine Jesus tradition in the Spirit of truth.

6. THE DISTINCTIVENESS OF JOHANNINE ESCHATOLOGY

The problem of Johannine eschatology[26] can be shown paradigmatically in terms of Jn. 5:20b-30. Here we find statements that speak of the full realization of salvation in the present for believers (vv. 20-27) right alongside others that— in the sense of traditional primitive Christian eschatology—combine the realization of salvation with the *parousia* (vv. 28f.). On the one hand, we read: "Truly, truly, I say to you, he who hears my word and believes him who sent me, has eternal life; he does not come into judgment, but has passed from death to life!" (v. 24). On the other hand, it was stated: ". . . for the hour is coming when all who are in the tombs will hear his voice and come forth, those who have done good, to the resurrection of life, and those who have done evil, to the resurrection of judgment" (vv. 28f.). How is the obvious tension between these statements to be clarified?

a) It would appear at first glance that the literary solution proposed by R. Bultmann suggests itself most strongly.[27] According to it, a church redactor secondarily inserted into the Gospel the popular primitive Christian apocalyptic eschatology through the addition of vv. 28f.; this was the eschatology that the evangelist himself wanted to eliminate on the basis of his bold new conception. In this way the redactor made the Gospel acceptable for the church.

b) If one examines this hypothesis it becomes evident that it cannot be verified on the basis of formal criteria, i.e., through stylistic and terminological analysis. To be sure, R. Schnackenburg found it strange that our evangelist, with the exception of 5:28f., nowhere spoke in apocalyptic terminology about the future *eschaton*.[28] Nevertheless, in contrast, it can be objected that even the language about the presence of the *eschaton* with the aid of apocalyptic terminology as found in 5:24ff. is singular in the Gospel. The decision must be made here, therefore, on the basis of content as well.

c) Do vv. 28f. really introduce popular primitive Christian eschatology? Upon closer examination this question is to be answered in the negative. It can be seen rather that the expectation of the end here was expressed in a very particular

---

[26]The problem of the section was set forth poignantly by R. Bultmann's interpretation (*The Gospel of John*, at Jn. 5:19-30). The decisive contribution to the discussion is still the article by G. Stählin, "Zum Problem der johanneischen Eschatologie," ZNW 33 (1934), 225-259. Neither the monograph by J. Blank, *Krisis* (1964), nor the Basel dissertation by P. Ricca, "Die Eschatologie des vierten Evangelisten" (1966), went beyond it in any substantive way. Cf. most recently the excursus of R. Schnackenburg, *The Gospel According to St. John* (HTK) II, 114-17.

[27]*John* (cf. n. 26), at Jn. 5:28f.

[28]*St. John* (cf. n. 26), pp. 115f.

formulation; these verses did not speak about a general resurrection to judgment, but about a differentiated resurrection!

This concept had but modest preliminary stages in Old Testament/Jewish apocalypticism. Dan. 12:2, e.g., spoke about a resurrection of the righteous to salvation and about an arising of sinners to eternal torment. This differentiation was first developed then with emphasis in primitive Christian eschatology, although—and this is important—not in popular but in apostolic eschatology; Paul differentiated in I Thess. 4:16 and I Cor. 15:23 a first from a second resurrection. Precisely this differentiation was made graphic by Rev. 20:4-6 in the image of the millennial reign whose meaning was addressed in Rev. 20:5f.: "This is the first resurrection. Blessed and holy is he who shares in the first resurrection! Over such the second death has no power" (§44,7). The first resurrection was the resurrection of believers unto life.

This fundamental line of primitive Christian eschatology was apparently appropriated in Jn. 5:29 when the "resurrection of life" and the "resurrection of judgment" were differentiated here. This differentiation was in any case an expression of a particularly apostolic expectation about the end.

d) What was the differentiation based on? It presupposed that the decision had already been made prior to the resurrection and would not first come in the judgment of the world. At that point what now was already reality for faith would only become apparent.

That was the central content of primitive Christian believing and hoping. Paul too expected a general coming-back-to-life of all for a judgment according to works. He expected salvation in this judgment, however, as the verification of faith through Christ—as already now in the present (Rom. 5:9f.). Constitutive for the primitive Christian expectation of the end was the saving union with the Lord to whom the Christian now made confession in faith but then would see face to face (II Cor. 5:7; I Pet. 1:8). This form of hope was grounded in Jesus' own word: the Son of man would confess those at his coming who had confessed him here (Lk. 12:8).

Surprisingly enough, of course, Jn. 5:29 made the resurrection to life dependent not upon faith but upon doing good. John spoke here in apocalyptic terminology. The expression "to do good" is not found otherwise in his Gospel. What he wanted to say by using it here becomes clear from the perspective of 3:20f.; there those who do "what is true" (*poiein tēn alētheian*) were placed over against those who do "evil." "To do the truth" meant nothing other according to 6:29, however, than to believe in Jesus.

Thus 5:29 said: the kind of future, concrete resurrection for the individual depended on faith or disbelief in Jesus.

e) Can the statement of 5:28f. be combined substantively with that of 5:24-27? Vv. 24-27 emphasized the eschatological ultimacy of that which was encountered through Jesus; to faith was given not only the prospect of eternal life but eternal life itself. Did vv. 28f. still have a place next to that?

This must be affirmed as soon as one recognizes one thing; according to

vv. 28f. the decision had already been made so that from the very beginning the resurrection had a different character; through it would only be carried out what had previously been given. This act of carrying it out consisted of two aspects.

1) It consisted of the bodiliness of the resurrection; while v. 25 spoke of the spiritually dead, v. 28 focused on the dead in the grave.

2) According to v. 25 the eschatological hour was both present and coming; according to v. 28 the final hour was dawning also for the world. Thus vv. 28f. announced an hour in which Jesus' word would bring about concretely and ultimately that which it accomplished now for faith in secret, namely, life or judgment.

Did this hour have a place next to the hour of v. 25? V. 24 now made the entry upon life expressly dependent upon faith. Faith would also no longer be faith for John, if he were not expecting that which now for him was strictly a new relationship mediated by the word to become ultimate and concrete. Life was more than a definitive understanding of oneself; it was the new relationship of the believing "I" to the Thou of God. This relationship was designed to become concretely and ultimately visible.

V. 28 prevented a misunderstanding of present-oriented eschatology that was in circulation since the time of the First Epistle to the Corinthians. Already current among the enthusiast opponents of Paul in Corinth, this present-oriented eschatology was misunderstood perfectionistically; at the same time they denied a future concrete resurrection (I Cor. 4:8; 15:12-19). This misunderstanding also turned up in the contention quoted in II Tim. 2:18 that the resurrection had already taken place.

The Gospel of John emphasized more emphatically than any other document of the New Testament that in Jesus' ministry the *eschaton* was present; whoever believed had already passed from death to life! Whoever did not believe was already condemned! This apologetic antithesis did not aim at a perfectionistic decision, but at the faith that found in Jesus everything that was called the salvation of God: "I am the way, the truth, and the life" (14:6).

THE PUBLICATIONS OF LEONHARD GOPPELT

Books

1) *Typos. Die Typologische Deutung des Alten Testaments im Neuen* (*Beiträge zur För-derung christlicher Theologie* 2/43; Gütersloh, 1939).
   —(repr. Wissenschaftliche Buchgesellschaft; Darmstadt, 1973). Eng. trans. *Typos. The Typological Interpretation of the Old Testament in the New* (trans. Donald H. Madvig; Grand Rapids, 1982).

2) *Christentum und Judentum im ersten und zweiten Jahrhundert. Ein Aufriss der Ur-geschichte der Kirche* (*Beiträge zur Förderung christlicher Theologie* 2/55; Güter-sloh, 1954) Eng. trans. *Jesus, Paul und Judaism. An Introduction to New Testament Theology* (trans. and ed. E. Schroeder; 1964).

3) *Die apostolische und nachapostolische Zeit, Die Kirche in ihrer Geschichte* 1/A (ed. K. D. Schmidt, E. Wolf; Göttingen, 1962).
   —(2nd rev. ed., 1966). Eng. trans. *Apostolic and Post-Apostolic Times* (trans. R. A. Guelich; Grand Rapids, 1970; repr. 1977).

4) *Christologie und Ethik. Aufsätze zum Neuen Testament* (Göttingen, 1968).

5) *Theologie des Neuen Testaments*, Bd. 1: *Jesu Wirken in seiner theologischen Bedeu-tung* (ed. J. Roloff; Göttingen, 1975). Eng. trans. *Theology of the New Testament*, Vol. 1: *The Ministry of Jesus in Its Theological Significance* (trans. J. E. Alsup; Grand Rapids, 1981).

6) *Theologie des Neuen Testaments*, Bd. 2: *Vielfalt und Einheit des apostolischen Chris-tuszeugnisses* (ed. J. Roloff; Göttingen, 1976). Eng. trans. *Theology of the New Tes-tament*, Vol. 2: *The Variety and Unity of the Apostolic Witness to Christ* (trans. J. E. Alsup; Grand Rapids, 1982).
   —three further editions to date.

7) *Der erste Petrusbrief* (KEK XII/1, ed. F. Hahn; Göttingen, 1978). Introduction sup-plemented by J. Roloff.

Articles in Scholarly Journals and Essay Collections

1952
"Heilsoffenbarung und Geschichte nach der Offenbarung des Johannes," *ThLZ* 77 (1952), 513-522.

1954

"Die Autorität der Heiligen Schrift und die Bibelkritik," *Wort Gottes und Bekenntnis* (Sonderdruck zur Rüstzeit der 15. ordentlichen Landessynode in Loccum) (Pattensen, 1954).

1956

"Heinrich Schliers 'Weg zur Kirche,' " *ELKZ* 10 (1956), 443-46.

"Der Staat in der Sicht des Neuen Testaments," in *Macht und Recht* (ed. H. Dombois, E. Wilkens; (Berlin, 1956), pp. 9-21. Also in *Christologie*, pp. 190-207.

"Am dritten Tage auferstanden von den Toten," in *Das Wahrzeichen des Christenglaubens. Eine Besinnung auf das Apostolische Glaubensbekenntnis* (ed. H. Lamparter; Wuppertal-Barmen, 1956), pp. 131-142.

"Das hermeneutische Problem in der gegenwärtigen neutestamentlichen Wissenschaft," *Amtsblatt der Evangelisch-Lutherischen Kirche in Thüringen* 9 (1956), 90-94, 103-05.

1958

"Tradition nach Paulus," *KuD* 4 (1958), 213-233.

"Kirchengemeinschaft und Abendmahlsgemeinschaft nach dem Neuen Testament," in *Koinonia* (Arbeiten des Oekumenischen Ausschusses der VELKD; Berlin, 1958), pp. 24-33.

"Kirche und Häresie nach Paulus," in *Koinonia* (as above), pp. 42-56. An earlier version in the Gedenkschrift für W. Elert (1955), pp. 9-23.

1959

"Der Missionar des Gesetzes. Zu Röm. 2, 21 f.," in *Basileia* (Festschrift für W. Freytag, ed. J. Hermelink, H. J. Margull; Stuttgart, 1959), pp. 199-207. Also in *Christologie*, pp. 137-146.

1960

"Urkirche und Staat," in *Kirche und Staat* (ed. T. Heckel; München, 1960), pp. 7-21.

1961

"Die Freiheit zur Kaisersteuer. Zu Mk. 12, 17 und Röm 13, 1-7," in *Ecclesia und Res Publica* (Festschrift für K. D. Schmidt, ed. G. Kretschmar, B. Lohse; Göttingen, 1961), pp. 40-50. Also in *Christologie*, pp. 208-219. Eng. in *StEv* 2 (1964), 183-194.

"Der verborgene Messias. Zu der Frage nach dem geschichtlichen Jesus," in *Der historische Jesus und der kerygmatische Christus* (ed. H. Ristow, K. Matthiae; Berlin, 1961²), pp. 371-384 (1st ed. 1960). Also in *Christologie*, pp. 11-27.

1962

"The Existence of the Church in History According to Apostolic and Early Christian Thought," in *Current Issues in New Testament Interpretation* (Essays in Honor of O. A. Piper, ed. W. Klassen and G. F. Snyder; New York, 1962), pp. 193-209.

"Dare We Follow Bultmann?", *Christianity Today* (April 27, 1962), 14-17 (726-29).

1963

"Zum Problem des Menschensohns. Das Verhältnis von Leidens- und Parusieankündigung," in *Mensch und Menschensohn* (Festschrift für K. Witte, ed. H. Sierig, F. Wittig; Hamburg, 1963), pp. 21-32. Also in *Christologie*, pp. 66-78.

"Israel und Kirche, heute und bei Paulus," *Lutherische Rundschau* (hereafter *LuthRu*) 13 (1963), 429-452. Also in *Christologie*, pp. 165-189.

1964

"Apokalyptik und Typologie bei Paulus," *ThLZ* 89 (1964), 321-344; reprinted as appendix to *Typos* (Darmstadt, 1973; *Christologie*, pp. 234-267).

"Das Osterkerygma heute," *Lutherische Monatshefte* 3 (1964), 50-57; in revised form in *Christologie*, pp. 79-101. Eng. trans. "The Easter Kerygma in the New Testament," *The Easter Message Today*, essays by L. Goppelt, H. Thielicke, H.-R. Müller-Schwefe (1964), pp. 27-58. Also in *Diskussion um Kreuz und Auferstehung* (ed. B. Klappert; Wuppertal, 1967), pp. 207-221.

"Zehn Jahre Evangelisch-Theologische Fakultät Hamburg." in *Hamburger Kirchenkalender* (Hamburg, 1964), pp. 1-13 (rev. offset print).

"Das kirchliche Amt nach den lutherischen Bekenntnisschriften und nach dem Neuen Testament," *LuthRu* 14 (1964), 517-536. Also published in *Zur Aufer buuung des Leibes Christi* (Festschrift für P. Brunner; 1965), pp. 97-115.

1965

"Begründung des Glaubens durch Jesus" (Guest Lecture in Greifswald and Rostock. First published in *Christologie*, pp. 44-65).

"Wahrheit als Befreiung—Das neutestamentliche Zeugnis von der Wahrheit nach dem Johannesevangelium," in *Was ist Wahrheit?* (Hamburger Ringvorlesung, ed. H.-R. Müller-Schwefe; Göttingen, 1965), pp. 80-93.

"Kirchenleitung in der palästinischen Urkirche und bei Paulus," in *Reformatio et confessio* (Festschrift für W. Maurer, ed. F. W. Kantzenbach, W. Friedrich, and G. Müller; Berlin, 1965), pp. 1-8.

1966

"Paulus und die Heilsgeschichte: Schlussfolgerungen aus Röm. 4 und I Kor. 10, 1-13," *NTS* 13 (1966/67), 31-42. Eng. trans. "Paul and Heilsgeschichte: Conclusions from Romans 4 and I Cor. 10:1-13," *Int* 21 (July 1967), 315-326. Also in *Christologie*, pp. 220-233.

1967

"Das Problem der Bergpredigt. Jesu Gebot und die Wirklichkeit dieser Welt" (Address before the Theologischen Kommission des Luth. Weltbundes on June 24, 1967 in St. Peter/Minn.-USA; first published as *Die Bergpredigt und die Wirklichkeit dieser Welt* (Calwer Heft 96; Stuttgart, 1968). Republished in *Christologie*, pp. 28-43.

"Die Herrschaft Christi und die Welt," *LuthRu* 17 (1967), 22-50; revised and reprinted in *Christologie*, pp. 102-136. Eng. in *Lutheran World* 14 (1967), 263-69.

"Versöhnung durch Christus" (presented in formal discussion between theologians of the EKD and the Russ.-Orth. Kirche in Höchst on March 4, 1967; first published in *LuthMonh* 6 (1967), 263-69 and *Stimme der Orthodoxie* (1967), Heft 9, 42-46 and Heft 10, 38-43. Republished as "Versöhnung durch Christus nach dem Neuen Testament," in *Versöhnung* (ed. by Aussenamt der EKD, Studienheft 5; Witten, 1967), pp. 64-80; note also contributions to the discussion by Goppelt in the Diskussionsprotokoll. Also in *Christologie*, pp. 147-164.

1968

"Wege zum Verständnis des Kreuzes nach dem Neuen Testament," in *Das Kreuz Christi im Widerstreit der Meinungen* (Beiheft XI zum "Konvent Kirchlicher Mitarbeiter," ed. W. Baader; Kiel, 1968), pp. 19-33; here also "Zusammenfassende Thesen," pp. 75f.

"Kirchenleitung und Bischofsamt in den ersten drei Jahrhunderten," in *Kirchenpräsident oder Bischof?* (ed. J. Asheim, V. R. Gold; Göttingen, 1968), pp. 9-35. Eng. in *Episcopacy in the Lutheran Church?* (same eds.) (1970), pp. 1-29.

"Geschichtlich wirksames Sterben. Zur Sühnewirkung des Kreuzes," in *Leben Angesichts Des Todes* (Festschrift für H. Thielicke, ed. B. Lohse; Tübingen, 1968), pp. 61-68.

1969

"Verifizierung des Glaubens bei Paulus," in *Die Predigt zwischen Text und Empirie* (ed. H. Breit, L. Goppelt, J. Roloff. M. Seitz; Stuttgart, 1969), pp. 56-74.

"Mission ou revolution? La responsibilite du cretim dans la societe d'apres la Ie Ep de Pierre," *Positions luthériennes* 194 (1969), 202-216.

1970

"Kirchentrennung und Kirchengemeinschaft nach dem Neuen Testament (Paulus)" (Address presented to the Lutheran/Reformed discussions in Europe at Leuenberg bei Basel, April 8, 1969, and published in *Ökumenische Rundschau* 19 [1970], 1-11).

"Taufe und Neues Leben nach Joh 3 und Röm 6" (Address printed in *Taufe-Neues Leben-Dienst; Das Leningrader Gespräch über die Verantwortung der Christen für die Welt*, ed. Aussenamt der EKD, Studienheft Nr. 6; Witten, 1970), pp. 68-78. Also in *Stimme der Orthodoxie* (1970), Heft 4, 51-53 and Heft 5, 36-41.

"Die Auferstehung Jesu in der Kritik, ihr Sinn und ihre Glaubwürdigkeit," in *Grundlagen des Glaubens* (ed. P. Rieger and J. Strauss, Tutzinger Texte 8; München, 1970), pp. 55-74.

"Die Anfänge der Evangelisch-Theologischen Fakultät," *Ludwig-Maximilians-Universität Jahres-Chronik 1967/1968* (München, 1970), pp. 199-206.

1971

"Die Pluralität der Theologien im Neuen Testament und die Einheit des Evangeliums als ökumenisches Problem," in *Evangelium und Einheit* (ed. V. Vajta; Göttingen, 1971), pp. 103-125. Eng. trans. "The Plurality of New Testament Theologies and the Unity of the Gospel as an Ecumenical Problem," in V. Vajta, ed., *The Gospel and Unity* (1971), pp. 106-130.

1972

"Auf dem Weg zur Kirchengemeinschaft der reformatorischen Kirchen in Europa. Die Voraussetzungen der Konferenz in Leuenberg, 1971," *Nachrichten der ev. luth. Kirche in Bayern* (1972), pp. 185-87. Also published in *Die Zeichen der Zeit* (Berlin, 1972), pp. 305-08.

"Textpredigt und wissenschaftliche Exegese in der Krise," in *Die Predigt als Kommunikation* (ed. J. Roloff; Stuttgart, 1972), pp. 93-99.

"Prinzipien neutestamentlicher Sozialethik nach dem 1. Petrusbrief," in *Neues Testament und Geschichte* (Festschrift für O. Cullmann, ed. H. Baltensweiler; Zürich/Tübingen, 1972), pp. 285-296.

"Der Friede Jesu und der Friede des Augustus," *Wort und Wahrheit* 27 (1972), 243-251.

"Die Auferstehung Jesu: Ihre Wirklichkeit und ihre Wirkung nach 1. Kor 15," in *Der auferstandene Christus und das Heil der Welt* (ed. Aussenamt der EKD, Studienheft 7; Witten, 1972), pp. 98-111; note also contributions to the discussion by Goppelt in the Diskussionsprotokoll. Also in *J Mosh Patr* 6 (1974), 52-61.

Foreword to reprint of A. Schlatter, *Geschichte Israels von Alexander dem Grossen bis Hadrian* (Darmstadt, 1972).

1973

"Prinzipien neutestamentlicher und systematischer Sozialethik heute," in *Die Verantwortung der Kirche in der Gesellschaft* (ed. J. Baur; Stuttgart, 1973), pp. 7-30.

"Was kann die Gesellschaft vom Menschen erwarten?", in *Dem Wort Gehorsam* (Festschrift für H. Dietzfelbinger, ed. H. Maser; München, 1973), pp. 126-139.

"Jesus und die Haustafeltradition," in *Orientierung an Jesus* (Festschrift für J. Schmid, ed. P. Hoffmann; Freiburg, 1973), pp. 93-105.

"Die Religion und Gott (nach Paulus)," in *So sende ich euch!* (Festschrift für M. Pörksen, ed. O. Waack; Korntal bei Stuttgart, 1973), pp. 73-83.

"Der eucharistische Gottesdienst nach dem Neuen Testament," *Erbe und Auftrag, Benediktinische Monatsschrift* 49 (1973), 435-447. Also in *Die Eucharistie* (ed. Aussenamt der EKD, Studienheft 8; Bielefeld, 1974), pp. 28-41; note also contributions to the discussion by Goppelt in the Diskussionsprotokoll.

Articles in Theological Dictionaries

RGG³:
Art.: "Allegorie II," Vol. I, Cols. 239f. (Tübingen, 1957).
Art.: "Bund III," Vol. I, Cols. 1516-18 (Tübingen, 1957).
Art.: "Wiedergeburt II," Vol. VI, Cols. 1697-99 (Tübingen, 1962).

TDNT:
Art.: *peinaō*, Vol. VI, pp. 12-22 (Grand Rapids, 1968).
Art.: *pinō*, Vol. VI, pp. 135-160 (Grand Rapids, 1968).
Art.: *trapeza*, Vol. VIII, pp. 209-215 (Grand Rapids, 1972).
Art.: *trōgō*, Vol. VIII, pp. 236f. (Grand Rapids, 1972).
Art.: *typos*, Vol. VIII, pp. 246-259 (Grand Rapids, 1972).
Art.: *hydōr*, Vol. VIII, pp. 314-333 (Grand Rapids, 1972).

EKL:
Art.: "Johannes III, Apokalypse," Vol. II, Cols. 365-69 (Göttingen, 1958).
Art.: "Reich Gottes II," Vol. III, Cols. 555-59 (Göttingen, 1959).
Art.: "Sühne und Schuld III," Vol. III, Cols. 1220-22 (Göttingen, 1959).
Art.: "Urchristentum," Vol. III, Cols. 1581-86 (Göttingen, 1959).
Art.: "Urgemeinde," Vol. III, Cols. 1586-1591 (Göttingen, 1959).

The Encyclopedia of the Lutheran Church
Art.: "Theological Bible Study," Vol. I, pp. 239-246 (Minneapolis, 1965).

Baker's Dictionary of Christian Ethics
Art.: "Grace," pp. 273-75 (Grand Rapids, 1973).

Book Reviews

1950
"K. Buchheim, *Das messianische Reich*," *ThLZ* 75 (1950), 32-35.

"M. Doerne, *Grundriss des Theologiestudiums*," *Evangelisch-lutherische Kirchenzeitung* (hereafter *ELKZ*) (1950), 257f.

1951
"H.-J. Schoeps, *Theologie und Geschichte des Judenchristentums*," *ELKZ* (1951/52), 304f.

"H.-J. Schoeps, *Aus frühchristlicher Zeit*," *ELKZ* (1951/52), 305.

1953
"M. Dibelius, *Aufsätze zur Apostelgeschichte*," *ELKZ* (1953), 139f.

1955
"A. M. Hunter, *Die Einheit des Neuen Testaments*," *ELKZ* (1955), 290.

"J. Schneider, *Die Taufe im Neuen Testament*," *ELKZ* (1955), 360 and 363.

1956

"W. Mauer, *Kirche und Synagoge*," *ELKZ* (1956), 165.

"W. Bieder, *Die kolossısche Irrlehre und die Kirche von heute*," *ELKZ* (1956), 400.

1957

"M. Rissi, *Zeit und Geschichte in der Offenbarung des Johannes*," *ELKZ* (1957), 241.

"H.-J. Schoeps, *Urgemeinde, Judentum, Gnosis*," *ThLZ* 82 (1957), 429-431.

1958

"J.-L. Leuba, *Institution und Ereignis*," *ThLZ* 83 (1958), 110f.

1959

"M. Albertz, *Die Botschaft des Neuen Testaments*, Bd. 1 und Bd. 2," *ELKZ* (1959), 222f.

"L. H. Grollenberg, O.P., *Bildatlas zur Bibel*," *ELKZ* (1959), 253.

"G. van der Leeuw, *Phänomenologie der Religion*," *ELKZ* (1959), 305.

1961

"W. Nauck, *Die Tradition und der Charakter des ersten Johannesbriefes*," *ELKZ* (1961), 413.

1962

"K. Rudolph, *Die Mandäer*," *Lutherische Monatshefte* (hereafter *LuthMonh*) 1 (1962), 32 and 35.

1963

"E. Käsemann, *Exegetische Versuche und Besinnungen*, Bd. 1," *ThLZ* 88 (1963), 839-842.

"G. Bornkamm, *Die Vorgeschichte des sogenannten zweiten Korintherbriefes*," *ThLZ* 88 (1963), 895-97.

"E. Schweizer, *Erniedrigung und Erhöhung bei Jesus und seinen Nachfolgern*," *LuthMonh* 2 (1963), 11-12 (Literaturbeiheft!; hereafter Lit. bft.).

"R. Schnackenburg, *Die Johannesbriefe*, HTK III/3," *LuthMonh* 2 (1963), 13f. (Lit. bft.).

1964

"G. Eichholz, *Glaube und Werk bei Paulus und Jakobus*," *ThLZ* 89 (1964), 33f.

"Hilfsmittel für das Studium des NT: *Synopsis Quattuor Evangeliorum*, ed. K. Aland, E. Hennecke, W. Schneemelcher, *Neutestamentliche Apokryphen*; H. Kraft, *Clavis Patrum Apostolicorum; Die Texte aus Qumran*, E. Lohse (ed.)," *LuthMonh* 3 (1964), 18f. (Lit. bft.).

"Einleitungen in das NT: P. Feine, J. Behm, W. G. Kümmel, *Einleitung in das Neue Testament*; W. Marxsen, *Einleitung in das Neue Testament*," *LuthMonh* 3 (1964), 19f. (Lit. bft.).

"F. Hahn, *Christologische Hoheitstitel*," *LuthMonh* 3 (1964), 21 (Lit. bft.).

"Zur Apostelgeschichte: H. Conzelmann, *Die Apostelgeschichte*, HNT; G. Stählin, *Die Apostelgeschichte*, NTD 5; U. Wilckens, *Die Missionsreden der Apostelgeschichte*," *LuthMonh* 3 (1964), 21-23 (Lit. bft.).

"Zur Apostelamt: G. Klein, *Die Zwölf Apostel*; W. Schmithals, *Das kirchliche Apostelamt*," *LuthMonh* 3 (1964), 23f. (Lit. bft.).

"E. Schweizer, *Neotestamentica*," *LuthMonh* 3 (1964), 24 (Lit. bft.).

1965

"Forschungsgeschichtliche Einführungen: R. Schnackenburg, *Neutestamentliche Theologie*; B. Rigaux, *Paulus und seine Briefe*," *LuthMonh* 4 (1965), 11 (Lit. bft.).

"F. Mussner, *Der Jakobusbrief*, HTK XIII," *LuthMonh* 4 (1965), 14 (Lit. bft.).

"Religionsgeschichtliche Monographien: G. Jeremias, *Der Lehrer der Gerechtigkeit*; J. Becker, *Das Heil Gottes*," *LuthMonh* 4 (1965), 17f. (Lit. bft.).

"Chr. Burchard, *Bibliographie zu den Handschriften vom Toten Meer II, NR. 1557-4459*," *LuthMonh* 4 (1965), 18 (Lit. bft.).

"Aufsatzsammlungen: E. Haenchen, *Gott und Mensch*; W. G. Kümmel, *Heilsgeschehen und Geschichte*; E. Käsemann, *Exegetische Versuche und Besinnungen*, Bd. 2; E. Fuchs, *Glaube und Erfahrung; Zeit und Geschichte*, Festschrift für R. Bultmann, ed. E. Dinkler," *LuthMonh* 4 (1965), 18f. (Lit. bft.).

1966

"O. Cullmann, *Heil als Geschichte*," *ThZ* 22 (1966), 51-56.

"P. Stuhlmacher, *Gerechtigkeit Gottes bei Paulus*," *LuthMonh* 5 (1966), 392f.

"W. Schrage, *Das Verhältnis des Thomas-Evangeliums zur synoptischen Tradition und zu den koptischen Evangelienübersetzungen*," *LuthMonh* 5 (1966), 393f.

"K. Beyschlag, *Clemens Romanus und der Frühkatholizismus*," *LuthMonh* 5 (1966), 394.

1967

"E. Käsemann, *Exegetische Versuche und Besinnungen*, Bd. 2," *ThLZ* 92 (1967), 109-112.

"A. Safran, *Die Kabbala*," *LuthMonh* 6 (1967), 371.

"E. Gaugler, *Auslegung neutestamentlicher Schriften*," *LuthMonh* 6 (1967), 378.

"H. Braun, *Qumran und das Neue Testament*, Bd. 1/2," *LuthMonh* 6 (1967), 380.

"K. Rudolph, *Theologie, Kosmogonie und Anthropogonie in den mandäischen Schriften*," *LuthMonh* 6 (1967), 380f.

1968

"H. Conzelmann, *Grundriss der Theologie des Neuen Testaments*," *LuthMonh* 7 (1968), 371-73.

1969

"R. Schnackenburg, *Das Johannesevangelium 1. Teil HTK IV*," *LuthMonh* 8 (1969), 432f.

"W. Popkes, *Christus Traditus*," *LuthMonh* 8 (1969), 434f.

"E. Güttgemanns, *Der leidende Apostel und sein Herr*," *LuthMonh* 8 (1969), 435.

"Neue katholische Paulusinterpretation: P. Benoit, O.P., *Exegese und Theologie*; K. H. Schelkle, *Wort und Schrift;* H. Schürmann, *Traditionsgeschichtliche Untersuchungen zu den synoptischen Evangelien*; R. Schnackenburg, *Christliche Existenz nach dem Neuen Testament*," *LuthMonh* 8 (1969), 438f.

1970

"H. Braun, *Jesus*," *ThLZ* 95 (1970), 744-47.

"H. Braun, *Jesus*," *LuthMonh* 9 (1970), 437f.

"H. D. Betz, *Nachfolge und Nachahmung Jesu Christi im Neuen Testament*," *LuthMonh* 9 (1970), 438.

"P. Stuhlmacher, *Das paulinische Evangelium*," *LuthMonh* 9 (1970), 439.

"H. Conzelmann, *Geschichte des Urchristentums*," *LuthMonh* 9 (1970), 439f.

"H. Schürmann, *Das Lukasevangelium Teil 1*, HTK III/1," *LuthMonh* 9 (1970), 440.

1971

"Themen des NT: Taufe-Freiheit-Ostern: O. Böcher, *Dämonenfurcht und Dämonenabwehr*; W. Huber, *Passa und Ostern*; K. Niederwimmer, *Der Begriff der Freiheit im NT*," *LuthMonh* 10 (1971), 461f.

"Für Menschen unserer Zeit: D. Arenhoevel, A. Deissler, A. Vögtle, *Die Bibel*; U. Wilckens, *Das Neue Testament*," *LuthMonh* 10 (1971), 463.

1972

"Der Ertrag einer Epoche. Vier Darstellungen der Theologie des Neuen Testaments" (rev. of J. Jeremias, W. G. Kümmel, K. H. Schelkle, J. Schreiner [ed.]), *LuthMonh* 11 (1972), 96-98.

Sermon Meditations

Mt 11, 25-30, *Calwer Predigthilfen* (hereafter *CPH*) 7 (Stuttgart, 1968), pp. 85-91.
Mt 13, 10-17, *CPH* 7 (Stuttgart, 1968), pp. 91-95.

Röm 5, 12-21, *CPH* 8 (Stuttgart, 1969), pp. 55-62.
Röm 11, 25-32, *CPH* 8 (Stuttgart, 1969), pp. 62-67.
Eph 2, 17-22, *CPH* 8 (Stuttgart, 1969), pp. 67-74.

Mt 20, 20-28, *CPH* 9 (Stuttgart, 1970), pp. 187-194.
Joh 6, 47-57, *CPH* 9 (Stuttgart, 1970), pp. 180-86.

Offb 5, 1-14, *CPH* 10 (Stuttgart, 1971), pp. 160-68.
Offb 19, 11-16, *CPH* 10 (Stuttgart, 1971), pp. 168-175.
Offb 21, 1-7, *CPH* 10 (Stuttgart, 1971), pp. 175-180.
Offb 22, 12-21, *CPH* 10 (Stuttgart, 1971), pp. 180-85.
1. Petr. 1, 3-9, *CPH* 10 (Stuttgart, 1971), pp. 199-206.

Joh 2, 1-11, *CPH* 11 (Stuttgart, 1972), pp. 89-97.
Joh 6, 1-15, *CPH* 11 (Stuttgart, 1972), pp. 98-104.
Lk 24, 13-35, *CPH* 11 (Stuttgart, 1972), pp. 214-221.
Mt 25, 31-46, *CPH* 11 (Stuttgart, 1972), pp. 221-28.

Röm 6, 3-11, *CPH* 12 (Stuttgart, 1973), pp. 345-351.
1. Kor 10, 1-13, *CPH* 12 (Stuttgart, 1973), pp. 352-57.
1. Kor 11, 23-29, *CPH* 12 (Stuttgart, 1973), pp. 223-230.
1. Petr. 4, 7-11, *CPH* 12 (Stuttgart, 1973), pp. 315-321.
1. Petr. 5, 5-11, *CPH* 12 (Stuttgart, 1973), pp. 321-26.
1. Petr. 3, 8-15, *CPH* 12 (Stuttgart, 1973), pp. 326-332.

LITERATURE SUPPLEMENT:

A Selected Bibliography of Festschriften, Books, and Articles on the General Themes of *New Testament Theology, Biblical Theology, Methodology*, and *Hermeneutics*, 1973-1981.

NOTE: This bibliography spans the years from Leonhard Goppelt's death to the present. An exhaustive supplement to each section of the *Theology* proved to be far too extensive an undertaking, even with a focus on English-language publications: hence the concentration on four relevant, general themes. In the interest of promoting the international, multi-language discussion of New Testament theology to which Leonhard Goppelt was committed the following references are linguistically integrated and are listed alphabetically by author or editor for each year. In most cases, works or translations of works published after 1973 that are already included within the translation of Volumes I and II do not reappear in this supplement. The reader is encouraged to consult other bibliographical resources in further study of the individual sections of the *Theology*. Special note is made here, for example, of the excellent literary supplement by O. Merk to R. Bultmann, *Theologie des Neuen Testaments* (Uni-Taschenbücher 630) (Tübingen, 1980⁸), pp. 622-704, of *New Testament Abstracts* (Cambridge, Mass.), of the *Theologisches Wörterbuch zum Neuen Testament*, Vol. X, and of the *New Testament Exegetical Bibliographical Aids* (ed. G. Wagner) (Rüschlikon, Switzerland).

—John Alsup

1973

Aune, D. E., "The New Testament: Source of Modern Theological Diversity," *Direction* 2 (1973), 10-15.

Balz, H. and S. Schulz (eds.), *Das Wort und die Wörter*. Festschrift für Gerhard Friedrich zum 65. Geburtstag (Stuttgart, 1973).

Barr, J., "Reading the Bible as Literature," *Bulletin of the John Rylands University Library of Manchester* 56 (1973), 10-33.

———, *The Bible in the Modern World* (New York, 1973).

Betz, H. D. and L. Schottroff (eds.), *Neues Testament und christliche Existenz*. Festschrift für Herbert Braun zum 70. Geburtstag am 4. Mai 1973 (Tübingen, 1973).

Briggs, R. C., *Interpreting the New Testament Today. An Introduction to Methods and Issues in the Study of the New Testament* (Nashville, 1973).

Ebeling, G. et al. (eds.), *Festschrift für Ernst Fuchs* (Tübingen, 1973).

Geyer, H.-G. (ed.), *Freispruch und Freiheit: Theologische Aufsätze für Walter Kreck zum 65. Geburtstag* (München, 1973).

Hahn, F., "Der Beitrag der katholischen Exegese zur neutestamentlichen Forschung. Ein Überblick über die letzten 30 Jahre," *VF* 18 (1973), 83-98.

Harrington, W. J., *The Path of Biblical Theology* (Dublin, 1973).

Hengel, M., "Historische Methoden und theologische Auslegung des Neuen Testaments," *KuD* 19 (1973), 85-90.

Hübner, H., *Politische Theologie und existentiale Interpretation. Zur Auseinandersetzung Dorothee Sölles mit Rudolf Bultmann* (Glaube und Lehre 9) (Witten, 1973).

Käsemann, E., "The Problem of a New Testament Theology," *NTS* 19 (1973), 235-245.

Koch, K., "Reichen die formgeschichtlichen Methoden für die Gegenwartsaufgaben der Bibelwissenschaft zu?" *ThLZ* 98 (1973), 801-814.

Léon-Dufour, X. (ed.), *Dictionary of Biblical Theology* (New York, 1973).

Lindars, B. and S. S. Smalley (eds.), *Christ and Spirit in the New Testament*. Festschrift for C.F.D. Moule on his 65th Birthday (Cambridge, 1973).

Lindemann, W., *Karl Barth und die kritische Schriftauslegung* (Hamburg, 1973).

Livingstone, E. A. (ed.), *Studia Evangelica* VI (=Texte und Untersuchungen 112) (Berlin, 1973).

Lohse, E., *Die Einheit des Neuen Testaments. Exegetische Studien zur Theologie des Neuen Testaments* (Göttingen, 1973).

————, "Im Dienst des Evangeliums. Rudolf Bultmann als lutherischer Theologe," *Lutherische Monatshefte* 12 (1973), 422-24.

Morgan, R., *The Nature of New Testament Theology. The Contribution of William Wrede and Adolf Schlatter* (Studies in Biblical Theology 25) (London, 1973).

————, "Great Interpreters—V. Rudolf Bultmann (b. 1884)," *Scripture Bulletin* 4 (1973), 90f.

Moule, C.F.D., "The Distinctiveness of Christ," *Theology* 76 (1973), 562-572.

Riesenfeld, H., "Reflections on the Unity of the New Testament," *Religion* 3 (1973), 35-51.

Rogerson, J. W., "Biblical Studies and Theology: Present Possibilities and Future Hopes [review of Barr, *Modern World*]," *Churchman* 87 (1973), 198-206.

Schelkle, K. H., *Theology of the New Testament. III: Morality* (Collegeville, Minn., 1973) (I: 1971; II: *Salvation History-Revelation*, 1976; IV: *The Rule of God: Church-Eschatology*, 1978).

Schenk, W., "Die Aufgaben der Exegese und die Mittel der Linguistik," *ThLZ* 98 (1973), 881-894.

Schmid, H. H., "Schöpfung, Gerechtigkeit und Heil, 'Schöpfungstheologie' als Gesamthorizont biblischer Theologie," *ZThK* 70 (1973), 1-19.

Schnackenburg, R., "Biblische Sprachbarrieren," *Bibel und Leben* 14 (1973), 223-231.

1974

Banks, R. (ed.), *Reconciliation and Hope*. New Testament Essays on Atonement and Eschatology presented to L. L. Morris on his 60th Birthday (Grand Rapids, 1974).

Barr, J., "Trends and Prospects in Biblical Theology," *JThSt* 25 (1974), 265-282.

Barthes, R. et al., *Structural Analysis and Biblical Exegesis. Interpretational Essays* (Pittsburgh Theological Monograph Series 3) (Pittsburgh, 1974).

Black, M. and W. A. Smalley (eds.), *On Language, Culture, and Religion*: In Honor of Eugene A. Nida (The Hague, 1974).

Boutin, M., *Relationalität als Verstehensprinzip bei Rudolf Bultmann* (Beihefte zur Evangelischen Theologie 67) (München, 1974).

Conzelmann, H., *Theologie als Schriftauslegung. Aufsätze zum Neuen Testament* (Beihefte zur Evangelischen Theologie 65) (München, 1974).

Cox, C. E., "R. Bultmann: Theology of the New Testament," *Restoration Quarterly* 17 (1974), 144-161.

Dahl, N. A., *The Crucified Messiah and other essays* (Minneapolis, 1974).

Dantine, W., *Jesus von Nazareth in der gegenwärtigen Diskussion* (Gütersloh, 1974).

DeJonge, M., *Jesus: Inspiring and Disturbing Presence* (Nashville, 1974).

France, R. T. (ed.), *A Bibliographical Guide to New Testament Research* (Cambridge, 1974).

Frei, H. W., *The Eclipse of Biblical Narrative. A Study in Eighteenth and Nineteenth Century Hermeneutics* (New Haven, 1974).

Fuller, R. H., "The New Testament in Current Study," *Perspectives in Religious Studies* 1 (1974), 103-119.

Furnish, V. P., "The Historical Criticism of the New Testament: A Survey of Origins," *Bulletin of the John Rylands University Library of Manchester* 56 (1974), 336-370.

Gnilka, J. (ed.), *Neues Testament und Kirche*. Für Rudolf Schnackenburg (Freiburg, 1974).

Gross, H. and F. Mussner, "Die Einheit von Altem und Neuem Testament," *Internationale katholische Zeitschrift/Communio* 3 (1974), 544-555.

Ihde, D. (ed.), *P. Ricoeur—The Conflict of Interpretations*. Essays in Hermeneutics (Evanston, 1974).

Jackson, B. S. (ed.), *Studies in Jewish Legal History*. Essays in Honour of David Daube (London, 1974).

Jacobsen, R., "The Structuralists and the Bible," *Int* 28 (1974), 146-164.

Jansen, J. F., "The Biblical Theology of Geerhardus Vos," *Princeton Seminary Bulletin* 66 (1974), 23-34.

Johnson, R. A., *The Origins of Demythologizing. Philosophy and Historiography in the Theology of Rudolf Bultmann* (Studies in the History of Religions XXVIII; Supplement to Numen) (Leiden, 1974).

Kasper, W., *Jesus der Christus* (Mainz, 1974).

Ladd, G. E., *A Theology of the New Testament* (Grand Rapids, 1974).

Lehman, C. K., *Biblical Theology II. New Testament* (Scottsdale, Pa., 1974).

Lohff, W. and F. Hahn, *Wissenschaftliche Theologie in Überblick* (Göttingen, 1974).

Lohse, E., *Grundriss der neutestamentlichen Theologie* (Theologische Wissenschaft 5) (Stuttgart, 1974; 1979²).

Longenecker, R. N. and M. C. Tenney (eds.), *New Dimensions in New Testament Studies* (Grand Rapids, 1974).

Luz, U., "Theologia crucis als Mitte der Theologie im Neuen Testament," *EvTheol* 34 (1974), 116-141.

Merklein, H. and J. Lange (eds.), *Biblische Randbemerkungen*. Schülerschrift für Rudolf Schnackenburg zum 60. Geburtstag (Würzburg, 1974).

Morgan, R., "The New Testament in Religious Studies," *Religious Studies* 10 (1974), 385-406.

_____, "Great Interpreters—VI. W. G. Kümmel (b. 1905)," *Scripture Bulletin* 5 (1974), 28f.

Moule, C.F.D. and H. Willmer, "The Distinctiveness of Christ. A Correspondence," *Theology* 77 (1974), 404-412.

Murphy, R. E. (ed.), *Patrick W. Skehan Festschrift* (*Catholic Biblical Quarterly* 36/4) (Washington, 1974).

Nicol, I. G., "Event and Interpretation. Oscar Cullmann's conception of Salvation History," *Theology* 77 (1974), 14-21.

Perrin, N., "Eschatology and Hermeneutics: Reflections on Method in the Interpretation of the New Testament," *JBL* 93 (1974), 3-14.

Riesenfeld, H., "Criteria and Valuations in Biblical Studies," *Svensk Exegetisk Årsbok* 39 (1974), 74-89.

Sanders, J. A., "Reopening Old Questions About Scripture" [review of Barr, *Modern World*], *Int* 28 (1974), 321-330.

Schierse, F. J., "Probleme und Methoden heutiger Schriftauslegung," *Stimmen der Zeit* 99 (1974), 780-84.

Schubert, K. and N. Brox (eds.), *Festschrift für Endre Ivánka* (Salzburg, 1974) (=Kairos 15, 1973).

Seebass, H. *Biblische Hermeneutik* (Stuttgart, 1974).

Shires, H. M., *Finding the Old Testament in the New* (Philadelphia, 1974) (cf. review by J. A. Sanders, *Union Seminary Quarterly Review* 30 [1974], 241-46).

Spivey, R. A., "Structuralism and Biblical Studies: The Uninvited Guest," *Int* 28 (1974), 133-145.

Stramare, T., "Quod in novo patet in vetere latet," *Biblica et Orientalia* 16 (1974), 199-210.

Terry, M. S., *Biblical Hermeneutics. A Treatise on the Interpretation of the Old and New Testaments* (Grand Rapids, 1974²).

1975

Aune. D. E., "The Words of God Interpreting the Deeds of God" [review of G. E. Ladd, *A Theology*], *Int* 29 (1975), 424-27.

Barr, J., "Biblical Theology," *Interpreter's Dictionary of the Bible*, Supplementary Volume (Nashville, 1975), pp. 104-111.

Beardslee, W. A., "Narrative Form in the New Testament and Process Theology," *Encounter* 36 (1975), 301-315.

Brown, C. (ed.), *The New International Dictionary of New Testament Theology*, I: A-F (Grand Rapids, 1975); II: G-Pre (1977); III: Pri-Z (1978).

Brown, R. E., *Biblical Reflections on Crises Facing the Church* (New York, 1975).

Dornisch, L., "Symbolic Systems and the Interpretation of Scripture: An Introduction to the Work of Paul Ricoeur," *Semeia* 4 (1975), 1-21.

Drumwright, H. L. and C. Vaughan (eds.), *New Testament Studies*. Essays in Honor of Ray Summers in his Sixty-Fifth Year (Waco, 1975).

Ellis, E. E. and E. Grässer (eds.), *Jesus und Paulus*. Festschrift für Werner Georg Kümmel zum 70. Geburtstag (Göttingen, 1975).

Fiedler, P. and D. Zeller (eds.), *Gegenwart und kommendes Reich*. Schülergabe Anton Vögtle zum 65. Geburtstag (Stuttgart, 1975).

Flanagan, J. W. and A. Weisbrod Robinson (eds.), *No Famine in the Land*. Studies in Honor of John L. McKenzie (Missoula, Mont., 1975).

Frankemölle, H., "Exegese und Linguistik—Methodenprobleme neuerer exegetischen Veröffentlichungen," *Theologische Revue* 71 (1975), 1-12.

Frei, H. W., *The Identity of Jesus. The Hermeneutical Bases of Dogmatic Theology* (Philadelphia, 1975).

Giblet, J., "Unité et diversité dans les écrits du Nouveau Testament," *Istina* 20 (1975), 23-34.

Gisel, P., "E. Käsemann, oeuvre et projet théologique," *Bulletin du Centre Protestant d'Etudes* 27 (1975), 5-17.

Griffin, D. R., "Relativism, Divine Causation and Biblical Theology," *Encounter* 36 (1975), 342-360.

Hawthorne, G. F. (ed.), *Current Issues in Biblical and Patristic Interpretation*. Studies in Honor of Merrill C. Tenney Presented by His Former Students (Grand Rapids, 1975).

Hooker, M. and C. Hickling (eds.), *What About the New Testament?* Essays in Honour of Christopher Evans (London, 1975).

Kaye, B. N., "Recent German Roman Catholic New Testament Research," *Churchman* 89 (1975), 246-256.

Kistemaker, S. J., "Current Problems and Projects in New Testament Research," *Journal of the Evangelical Theological Society* 71 (1975), 17-28.

Kjeseth, P. [review of Goppelt, *Theologie I*], *Lutheran World* 3 (1975), 261f.

Klug, E. F., "The End of the Historical-Critical Method," *Springfielder* 38 (1975), 289-302.

Lewis, J. P., "The New Testament in the Twentieth Century," *Restoration Quarterly* 18 (1975), 193-215.

Lohse, E., "Die Einheit des Neuen Testaments als theologisches Problem. Überlegungen zur Aufgabe einer Theologie des Neuen Testaments," *EvTheol* 35 (1975), 139-154.

Longenecker, R. N., *Biblical Exegesis in the Apostolic Period* (Grand Rapids, 1975).

Menoud, P. H., *Jésus-Christ et la Foi. Recherches néotestamentaires* (Neuchatêl, 1975).

Mildenberger, F., "The Unity, Truth, and Validity of the Bible. Theological Problems in the Doctrine of Holy Scripture," *Int* 29 (1975), 391-405.

Neusner, J. (ed.), *Christianity, Judaism and Other Greco-Roman Cults.* Studies for Morton Smith at Sixty, Part 1: New Testament (Leiden, 1975).

Perrin, N., "The Interpretation of a Biblical Symbol," *Journal of Religion* 55 (1975), 348-370.

Pesch, R. and R. Schnackenburg (eds.), *Jesus und der Menschensohn.* Für Anton Vögtle (Freiburg, 1975).

Ricoeur, P., "Biblical Hermeneutics," *Semeia* 4 (1975), 27-148.

Schmidt, L., "Die Einheit zwischen Altem und Neuem Testament im Streit zwischen Friedrich Baumgärtel und Gerhard von Rad," *EvTheol* 35 (1975), 119-139.

Simon, U., *Story and Faith in the Biblical Narrative* (London, 1975).

Sobosan, J. G., "Man Before God," *New Blackfriars* 56 (1975), 22-31.

Strecker, G. (ed.), *Das Problem der Theologie des Neuen Testaments* (Wege der Forschung 367, Wissenschaftliche Buchgesellschaft) (Darmstadt, 1975).

———(ed.), *Jesus Christus in Historie und Theologie.* Neutestamentliche Festschrift für Hans Conzelmann zum 60. Geburtstag (Tübingen, 1975).

Stuhlmacher, P., *Schriftauslegung auf dem Wege zur biblischen Theologie* (Göttingen, 1975).

Talmaze, F. E. (ed.), *Disputation and Dialogue. Readings in the Jewish-Christian Encounter* (New York, 1975).

Via, Jr., D. O., *Kerygma and Comedy in the New Testament. A Structuralist Approach to Hermeneutic* (Philadelphia, 1975).

———, "A Quandary of Contemporary New Testament Scholarship: The Time between the 'Bultmanns,' " *Journal of Religion* 55 (1975), 456-461.

Vicentini, J. I., "Teologia del Nuovo Testamento," *Stromata* 31 (1975), 343-359.

Ward, W. (ed.), *Biblical Studies in Contemporary Thought.* The Tenth Anniversary Commemorative Volume of the Trinity College Biblical Institute 1966-1975 (Sommerville, MA, 1975).

1976

Aalin, S., "Bibel teologier til Det nye testamente" (Biblical Theologies of the New Testament), *Tidsskrift for Teologi og Kirke* 47 (1976), 21-46.

Baird, W., "The Significance of Biblical Theology for the Life of the Church," *Lexington Theological Quarterly* 11 (1976), 37-48.

Bauer, J. B. (ed.), *Encyclopedia of Biblical Theology* (New York, 1976).

Brown, R. E., "Difficulties in Using the New Testament in American Catholic Discussions," *Louvain Studies* 6 (1976), 144-158.

Cahill, P. J. [review of Goppelt, *Theologie I*], *Catholic Biblical Quarterly* 38 (1976), 105f.

Childs, B., *Biblical Theology in Crisis* (Philadelphia, 1976²) (cf. review by W. E. Ward, 1977).

Dahl, N. A., *Jesus in the Memory of the Early Church* (Minneapolis, 1976).

Elliott, J. K. (ed.), *Studies in New Testament Language and Text*. Essays in Honor of George D. Kilpatrick on the Occasion of his sixty-fifth Birthday (Novum Testamentum, Supplement 44) (Leiden, 1976).

Festorazzi, F., "Teologia biblica: problem e riflessioni," *Teologia* 1 (1976), 135-149.

Friedrich, J. et al. (eds.), *Rechtfertigung*. Festschrift für Ernst Käsemann zum 70. Geburtstag (Tübingen, 1976).

Fuchs, A. (ed.), *Jesus in der Verkündigung der Kirche* (Studien zum Neuen Testament und seiner Umwelt A, 1) (Linz, 1976).

Gaffin, R. B., "Systematic Theology and Biblical Theology," *Westminster Theological Journal* 38 (1976), 281-299.

Gisel, P., "Ernst Käsemann ou la solidarité conflictuelle de l'histoire et de la vérité," *Etudes théologiques et religieuses* 51 (1976), 21-37.

Güttgemanns, E., "Generative Poetics," *Semeia* 6 (1976), 1-220.

Hahn, F., "Das biblische Kerygma und die menschliche Existenz. Zum Werk und Wirkungsgeschichte Rudolf Bultmanns," *Herder-Korrespondenz* 30 (1976), 630-35.

Hamerton-Kelly, R. and R. Scroggs (eds.), *Greeks and Christians. Religious Cultures in Late Antiquity*. Essays in Honor of William David Daube (Studies in Judaism in Late Antiquity 21) (Leiden, 1976).

Johnson, Jr., A. M. (ed. and trans.), *The New Testament and Structuralism* (Pittsburgh Theological Monograph Series 11) (Pittsburgh, 1976).

Lindars, B. and P. Borgen, "The Place of the Old Testament in the Formation of New Testament Theology: Prolegomena and Response," *NTS* 23 (1976), 59-75.

Lindner, H., "Widerspruch oder Vermittlung? Zum Gespräch mit G. Maier und P. Stuhlmacher über eine biblische Hermeneutik," *Theologische Beiträge* 7 (1976), 185-197.

MacRae, G. W., "The Gospel and the Church," *Theology Digest* 24 (1976), 338-348.

Martin, G. M., *Vom Unglauben zum Glauben. Zur Theologie der Entscheidung bei Rudolf Bultmann* (Theologische Studien 118) (Zürich, 1976).

Martins Terra, J. E., "Teologia Biblica," *Revista de Cultura Biblica* 13 (1976), 99-143.

Marxsen, W., *Die Sache Jesu geht weiter* (Gütersloh, 1976).

McKay, J. R., and J. F. Miller (eds.), *Biblical Studies*. Essays in Honour of William Barclay (London, 1976).

Neill, S., *Jesus Through Many Eyes. Introduction to the Theology of the New Testament* (Philadelphia, 1976).

Obermüller, R., *Teología del Nuevo Testamento*, 3 vols. (4th in prep.) (Buenos Aires, 1976-78) (for a nonspecialist audience).

Patte, D. (ed.), *Semiology and Parables. Exploration of the Possibilities Offered by Structuralism for Exegesis* (Pittsburgh Theological Monograph Series 9) (Pittsburgh, 1976).

Roberts, R. C., *Rudolf Bultmann's Theology: A Critical Interpretation* (Grand Rapids, 1976).

Robinson, J. M., "The Future of New Testament Theology," *Religious Studies Review* 2 (1976), 17-23.

1977

Baird, W., *The Quest of the Christ of Faith. Reflections on the Bultmann Era* (Waco, 1977).

Baker, D. L., *Two Testaments, One Bible. A Study of some modern solutions to the theological problem of the relationship between the Old and New Testaments* (Downers Grove, Ill., 1977).

Berger, K., *Exegese des Neuen Testaments. Neue Wege vom Text zur Auslegung* (Uni-Taschenbücher 658) (Heidelberg, 1977) (cf. review by van Iersel, *Nederlands theologisch tijdschrift* 33 [1979], 69-77).

Bornkamm, G., "In Memoriam Rudolf Bultmann *20.8.1884 †30.7.1976," *NTS* 23 (1977), 235-242.

Bruce, F. F., *The Defense of the Gospel in the New Testament* (Grand Rapids, 1977; rev. ed.).

Cahill, P. J., "The Theological Significance of Rudolf Bultmann," *Theological Studies* 38 (1977), 231-274.

Crossan, J. D., "Perspectives and Methods in Contemporary Biblical Criticism," *Biblical Research* 22 (1977), 39-49.

Dieckmann, B., *"Welt" und "Entweltlichung" in der Theologie Rudolf Bultmanns. Zum Zusammenhang von Welt- und Heilsverständnis* (Beiträge zur ökumenischen Theologie 17 (München, 1977).

Dunn, J.D.G., *Unity and Diversity in the New Testament. An Inquiry Into the Character of Earliest Christianity* (Philadelphia, 1977).

Evans, C. F., *Explorations in Theology* 2 (London, 1977).

Frye, R. M., "A New Criticism" [review of Via, *Comedy*, 1975], *Int* 31 (1977), 299-302.

Fuchs, A. (ed.), *Theologie aus dem Norden* (Studien zum Neuen Testament und seiner Umwelt A,2) (Linz, 1977).

Gese, H., *Zur biblischen Theologie. Alttestamentliche Vorträge* (München, 1977).

Haacker, K. et al., *Biblische Theologie heute—Beispiele—Kontroversen* (Biblisch-Theologische Studien 1) (Neukirchen, 1977).

————, "Biblische Theologie und historische Kritik" [review of O. Merk, *Biblische Theologie des Neuen Testaments*], *Theologische Beiträge* 8 (1977), 223-26.

Hahn, F., "Exegese, Theologie und Kirche," *ZThK* (1977), 25-37.

Jervell, J. and W. A. Meeks, *God's Christ and His People. Essays in Honour of Nils Alstrup Dahl* (Oslo, 1977).

Kaiser, O. (ed.), *Gedenken an Rudolf Bultmann* (Tübingen, 1977).

Kieffer, R., *Nytestamentlig teologi* (Lund, 1977).

Köberle, A., "Evangelium und Natur. Zur Theologie von Adolf Schlatter," *EvK* 10 (1977), 539-541.

Kwiran, M., *Index to Literature on Barth, Bonhoeffer and Bultmann* [2048 references on the latter] (Basel, 1977).

Maier, G., *The End of the Historical-Critical Method* (St. Louis, 1977).

————, "Einer biblischen Hermeneutik entgegen? Zum Gespräch mit P. Stuhlmacher und H. Lindner," *Theologische Beiträge* 8 (1977), 148-160.

Marshall, I. H. (ed.), *New Testament Interpretation. Essays on Principles and Methods* (Grand Rapids, 1977).

Morgan, R., "A Straussian Question to 'New Testament Theology,'" *NTS* 23 (1977), 243-265.

————, "F. C. Baur's Lectures on New Testament Theology," *Expository Times* 88 (1977), 202-06.

Nineham, D. E., *Explorations in Theology 1* (London, 1977).

Purkiser, W. T., R. S. Taylor, and W. H. Taylor, *God, Man, and Salvation. A Biblical Theology* (Kansas City, Mo., 1977).

Regner, F., *"Paulus und Jesus" im neunzehnten Jahrhundert. Beiträge zur Geschichte des Themas "Paulus und Jesus" in der neutestamentlichen Theologie* (Studien zur Theologie und Geistesgeschichte Neunzehnten Jahrhunderts 30) (Göttingen, 1977).

Riesenfeld, H., "Zur Frage nach der Einheit des Neuen Testaments," *Erbe und Auftrag* 53 (1977), 32-45 (cf. Riesenfeld, 1973).

Roloff, J., *Neues Testament* (Neukirchen, 1977; 1979²).

Schnackenburg, R. et al. (eds.), *Die Kirche des Anfangs*. Festschrift für Heinz Schürmann zum 65. Geburtstag (Leipzig, 1977).

Seebass, H., "Zur Ermöglichung biblischer Theologie. Fragen an G. Klein zur 'zentralen urchristlichen Konstruktion des Glaubens,' " *EvTheol* 37 (1977), 591-600.

Stuhlmacher, P., *Historical Criticism and Theological Interpretation of Scripture. Toward a Hermeneutics of Consent* (Philadelphia, 1977) (cf. Stuhlmacher, *Schriftauslegung*, 1975).

————, "Biblische Theologie und kritische Exegese," *Theologische Beiträge* 8 (1977), 88-90.

Ward, W. E., "Towards a Biblical Theology" [review among others of B. Childs, *Crisis*, 1976], *Review and Expositor* 7 (1977), 371-387.

1978

Baarda, T. et al. (eds.), *Miscellanea Neotestamentica* (2 vols.; Novum Testamentum, Supplement 47/48) (Leiden, 1978).

Bammel, E. et al. (eds.), *Donum Gentilicum*. New Testament Essays in Honour of David Daube (Oxford, 1978).

Barr, J., *Does Biblical Study Still Belong to Theology?* (Oxford, 1978).

Beck, H. W., "Der ur- und endgeschichtliche Universalismus der Schrift als hermeneutischer Schlüssel für eine gesamtbiblische Theologie," *Theologische Beiträge* 9 (1978), 182-194.

Broer, I., "Die Gleichnisexegese und die neuere Lituraturwissenschaft," in H. Kreuzer and K. W. Bonfig (eds.), *Entwicklungen der siebziger Jahre* (Gerabonn, 1978), pp. 125-135.

Bruce, F. F., *The Time is Fulfilled. Five Aspects of the Fulfillment of the Old Testament in the New* (Exeter, 1978).

Cook, J. I. (ed.), *Saved by Hope*. Essays in Honor of Richard C. Oudersluys (Grand Rapids, 1978).

Crossan, J. D., "Waking the Bible, Biblical Hermeneutics and Literary Imagination," *Int* 32 (1978), 269-285.

Ellis, E. E., *Prophecy and Hermeneutic in Early Christianity. New Testament Essays* (Grand Rapids, 1978).

Forde, G. O., "Bultmann: Where Did He Take Us?" *Dialog* 17 (1978), 27-30.

Friedrich, J. H. (ed.), *Auf das Wort kommt es an*. Gesammelte Aufsätze [of G. Friedrich] zum 70. Geburtstag (Göttingen, 1978).

Fuchs, A. (ed.), *Probleme der Forschung* (Studien zum Neuen Testament und seiner Umwelt A,3) (Wien, 1978).

Gasque, W. W. and W. S. LaSor (eds.), *Scripture, Tradition, and Interpretation*. Essays Presented to Everett F. Harrison by His Students and Colleagues in Honor of His Seventy-Fifth Birthday (Grand Rapids, 1978).

Grässer, E. and O. Merk (eds.), *W. G. Kümmel, Heilsgeschehen und Geschichte II, Gesammelte Aufsätze 1965-1977* (Marburger theologische Studien 16) (Marburg, 1978).
Guelich, R. A. (ed.), *Unity and Diversity in New Testament Theology*. Essays in Honor of George E. Ladd (Grand Rapids, 1978).
Güttgemanns, E., "Sensus historisticus und sensus plenior oder Über 'historische' und 'linguistische' Methode. Thesen und Reflexionen zur erkenntnis-theologischen Funktion von Linguistik und Semiotik in der Theologie," *Linguistica Biblica* 43 (1978), 75-112.
Harrisville, R. A., "Somewhere between Burying and Praising Caesar," *Dialog* 17 (1978), 9-14.
Hasel, G. F., *New Testament Theology. Basic Issues in the Current Debate* [a companion to his *Old Testament Theology*, 1975²] (Grand Rapids, 1978).
Kindt, I., *Der Gedanke der Einheit. Adolf Schlatters Theologie und ihre historischen Voraussetzungen* (Stuttgart, 1978).
Klein, C., *Anti-Judaism in Christian Theology* (Philadelphia, 1978) (cf. review by G.W.E. Nickelsburg, *Religious Studies Review* 4 [1978], 161-68).
Maier, G., *Wie legen wir die Bibel aus?* (Giessen, 1978).
Megivern, J. J. (ed.), *Bible Interpretation, Official Catholic Teachings* (Wilmington, NC, 1978).
Müller, G. (ed.), *Israel hat dennoch Gott zum Trost*. Festschrift für Shalom Ben-Chorin (Trier, 1978).
Patte, D. and A. Patte, *Structural Exegesis: From Theory to Practice*. Exegesis of Mark 15 and 16. Hermeneutical Implications (Philadelphia, 1978).
Robbins, V. K., "Structuralism in Biblical Interpretation and Theology," *Thomist* 42 (1978), 349-372.
Scharlemann, R. P., "The Systematic Structure of Bultmann's Theology," *Dialog* 17 (1978), 31-35.
Schlatter, A., *Jesus—der Christus. Acht Aufsätze* (Giessen, 1978).
Schnackenburg, R., *Masstab des Glaubens. Fragen heutiger Christen im Licht des Neuen Testaments* (Freiburg, 1978).
Stegemann, W., *Der Denkweg Rudolf Bultmanns. Darstellung der Entwicklung und der Grundlagen seiner Theologie* (Stuttgart, 1978).
Stuhlmacher, P., "Adolf Schlatter's Interpretation of Scripture," *NTS* 24 (1978), 433-446 (short English version of his "Adolf Schlatter als Bibelausleger," *ZThK* [1978], 81-111).
————, "Hauptprobleme und Chancen kirchlicher Schriftauslegung," *Theologische Beiträge* 9 (1978), 53-69.
Terrien, S., *The Elusive Presence. Toward a New Biblical Theology* (Religious Perspectives 26) (New York, 1978) (cf. Frizzel, 1980).
Theissen, G., *Sociology of Early Palestinian Christianity* (Philadelphia, 1978) (cf. also his *The Social Setting of Pauline Christianity: Essays on Corinth* [Philadelphia, 1982]; cf. review by Luz, 1980).
Thiselton, A. C., "Keeping up with Recent Studies II. Structuralism and Biblical Studies: Method or Ideology?" *Expository Times* 89 (1978), 329-335.
Tuttle, G. A. (ed.), *Biblical and Near Eastern Studies*. Essays in Honor of William Sanford LaSor (Grand Rapids, 1978).
Wagner, S., " 'Biblische Theologien' und 'Biblische Theologie,' " *ThLZ* 103 (1978), 785-798.

1979

Andersen, C. and G. Klein (eds.), *Theologia crucis—Signum crucis*. Festschrift für Erich Dinkler zum 70. Geburtstag (Tübingen, 1979).

Best, E. and R. McL. Wilson (eds.), Text and Interpretation. Studies in the New Testament Presented to Matthew Black (New York, 1979).

Blank, J., "Exegese als theologische Basiswissenschaft," Theologische Quartalschrift 159 (1979), 2-23.

Boers, H., What Is New Testament Theology? The Rise of Criticism and the Problem of a Theology of the New Testament (Guides to Biblical Scholarship: NT Series) (Philadelphia, 1979).

Durken, D. (ed.), Sin, Salvation, and the Spirit. Commemorating the Fiftieth Year of the Liturgical Press (Collegeville, Minn., 1979).

Gasque, W. W., "The Promise of Adolf Schlatter," Crux 15 (1979), 5-9.

Goldingay, J., "The 'Salvation History' Perspective and the 'Wisdom' Perspective within the Context of Biblical Theology," Evangelical Quarterly 51 (1979), 194-207.

Grech, P. and G. Segalla, Metodologia per uno studio della teologia del Nuovo Testamento (Turin, 1979).

Grötzinger, E. (ed.), E. Fuchs. Wagnis des Glaubens. Aufsätze und Vorträge (Neukirchen, 1979).

Hadidian, D. Y. (ed.), From Faith to Faith. Essays in Honor of Donald G. Miller on his Seventieth Birthday (Pittsburgh Theological Monograph Series 31) (Pittsburgh, 1979).

Hengel, M., "Kein Steinbruch für Ideologien. Zentrale Aufgaben neutestamentlicher Exegese," Lutherische Monatshefte 18 (1979), 23-27.

Henry, P., New Directions in New Testament Study (Philadelphia, 1979).

Hermesmann, H.-G., Zeit und Heil. Oscar Cullmanns Theologie der Heilsgeschichte (Konfessionskundliche Schriftenreihe 43) (Paderborn, 1979).

Jobling, D., "Structuralism, Hermeneutics, and Exegesis: Three Recent Contributions to the Debate" [McKnight, Detweiler, Patte(s)], Union Seminary Quarterly Review 34 (1979), 135-147.

Johnson, A. M. (ed.), Structuralism and Biblical Hermeneutics. A Collection of Essays (Pittsburgh Theological Monograph Series 22) (Pittsburgh, 1979).

Klein, G. (ed.), P. Vielhauer. Oikodome. Aufsätze zum Neuen Testament II (Theologische Bücherei 65) (München, 1979).

Koenig, J., Jews and Christians in Dialogue: New Testament Foundations (Philadelphia, 1979).

Martin, B. L., "Some Reflections on the Unity of the New Testament," Studies in Religion/Sciences religieuses 8 (1979), 143-152.

Perrin, N., The Promise of Bultmann (Philadelphia, 1979).

Pfitzner, V. C., "Pointers to New Testament Studies Today," Lutheran Theological Journal 13 (1979), 7-14.

Piper, J., "A Reply to Gerhard Maier: A Review Article," Journal of the Evangelical Theological Society 22 (1979), 79-85.

Reumann, J. (ed.), Studies in Lutheran Hermeneutics (Philadelphia, 1979).

Ruh, U. and R. Schnackenburg, "Exegese: ihre Rolle in Theologie und Kirche. Ein Gespräch mit Prof. Rudolf Schnackenburg," Herder-Korrespondenz 33 (1979), 549-554.

Ryan, T. J. (ed.), Critical History and Biblical Faith. New Testament Perspectives (Villanova, Pa., 1979).

Segalla, G., "Quindici anni di Teologia del Nuovo Testamento. Una rassegna (1962-1977)," Rivista Bíblica 27 (1979), 359-395.

Schillebeeckx, E., Jesus. An Experiment in Christology (New York, 1979) (cf. Christ, 1980).

Smart, J. D., The Past, Present, and Future of Biblical Theology (Philadelphia, 1979).

Strecker, G., Eschaton und Historie. Aufsätze (Göttingen, 1979).

Stuhlmacher, P. and H. Class, Das Evangelium von der Versöhnung in Christus (Stuttgart, 1979).

Stuhlmacher, P., "The Gospel of Reconciliation in Christ—Basic Features and Issues of a Biblical Theology of the New Testament," *Horizons in Biblical Theology* 1 (1979), 161-190.

―――, *Vom Verstehen des Neuen Testaments*. *Eine Hermeneutik* (Grundrisse zum NT, NTD Ergänzungsreihe 6) (Göttingen, 1979).

Winter, A. et al. (eds.), *Kirche und Bibel*. Festgabe für Bischof L. Luard Schick (Paderborn, 1979).

1980

Achtemeier, P. and G. M. Tucker, "Biblical Studies: The State of the Discipline," *Bulletin of the Council on the Study of Religion* 11 (1980), 72-76.

Bartsch, C., *'Frühkatholizismus' als Kategorie historisch-kritischer Theologie. Eine methodologische und theologie-geschichtliche Untersuchung* (Studien zu jüdischem Volk und christlicher Gemeinde 3) (Berlin, 1980).

Bonnard, P., *Anamnesis. Recherches sur le Nouveau Testament* (Lausanne. 1980).

Brecht, M. (ed.), *Text—Wort—Glaube. Studien zur Überlieferung, Interpretation und Autorisierung biblischer Texte*. Dedicated to Kurt Aland (Arbeiten zur Kirchengeschichte 50) (Berlin, 1980).

Brown, R. E., "The Meaning of the Bible," *Theology Digest* 28 (1980), 305-320.

Bruce, F. F., "Charting New Directions for New Testament Studies," *Christianity Today* 24 (1980), 1117-1120.

Carmody, J., *Theology for the 1980s* (Philadelphia, 1980).

Dahl, N. A., "New Testament Theology in a Pluralistic Setting," *Reflection* 77 (1980), 16-18.

Farmer, W. R., "Critical Reflections on Werner Georg Kümmel's History of New Testament Research," *Perkins Journal* 34 (1980), 41-48.

Frizzel, L. E. (ed.), *God and His Temple. Reflections on Professor Samuel Terrien's The Elusive Presence: Toward a Biblical Theology* (South Orange, NJ, 1980).

Fuller, R. H., "What is Happening in New Testament Studies?" *Saint Luke's Journal of Theology* 23 (1980), 90-100.

Gaffin, R. B. (ed.), *Redemptive History and Biblical Interpretation. The Shorter Writings of Geerhardus Vos* (Phillipsburg, NJ, 1980).

Grässer, E., "Offene Fragen im Umkreis einer Biblischen Theologie," *ZThK* 77 (1980), 200-221 (cf. response below by Stuhlmacher, *ZThK*, 1980).

Grundmann, W., *Wandlungen im Verständnis des Heils. Drei nachgelassene Aufsätze zur Theologie des Neuen Testaments* (Arbeiten zur Theologie 65) (Stuttgart, 1980).

Hahn, F., "Auf dem Wege zu einer biblischen Theologie?" *Nachrichten der evangelisch-lutherischen Kirche in Bayern* 35 (1980), 281-87.

Hanson, P. D., "The Responsibility of Biblical Theology to Communities of Faith," *Theology Today* 37 (1980), 39-50.

Haubeck, W. and N. Bachmann (eds.), *Wort in der Zeit*. Neutestamentliche Studien (for K. H. Rengstorf on his 75th Birthday) (Leiden, 1980).

Holtz, T. [review of Goppelt, *Theologie II*], *ThLZ* 105 (1980), 599-602.

Jansen, J. F., *The Resurrection of Jesus Christ in New Testament Theology* (Philadelphia, 1980).

Kee, H. C., *Christian Origins in Sociological Perspective. Methods and Resources* (Philadelphia, 1980).

Kelsey, D. H., "The Bible and Christian Theology," *Journal of the American Academy of Religion* 48 (1980), 385-402.

Koester, H., *Einführung in das Neue Testament im Rahmen der Religionsgeschichte und Kulturgeschichte der hellenistischen und römischen Zeit* (Berlin, 1980).

Kubina, V. and K. Lehmann (eds.), *H. Schlier. Der Geist und die Kirche. Exegetische Aufsätze und Vorträge IV* (Freiburg, 1980).

Küng, H., Moltmann, J., and M. Lefébvre (eds.), *Conflicting Ways of Interpreting the Bible* (Concilium 138) (New York, 1980).

Lührmann, D. and G. Strecker (eds.), *Kirche*. Festschrift für Günther Bornkamm zum 75. Geburtstag (Tübingen, 1980).

Luz, U., "Soziologische Aspekte in der Exegese," *Kirchenblatt für die reformierte Schweiz* 136 (1980), 221.

March, W. E. (ed.), *Texts and Testaments*. Critical Essays on the Bible and Early Church Fathers (in Honor of S. D. Currie) (San Antonio, 1980).

Martin, R. P., "New Testament Theology: Impasse and Exit. The Issues," *Expository Times* 91 (1980), 264-69.

Merk, O., "Biblische Theologie II. Neues Testament," *Theologische Realenzyklopädie* VI (1980), 455-477 (Lit.).

Metzger, B. M., *New Testament Studies. Philological, Versional, and Patristic* (New Testament Tools and Studies 10) (Leiden, 1980).

Mudge, L. S. (ed.), *P. Ricoeur. Essays on Biblical Interpretation* (Philadelphia, 1980).

Piper, J., "Historical Criticism in the Dock: Recent Developments in Germany," *Journal of the Evangelical Theological Society* 23 (1980), 325-334 (review of Stuhlmacher, *Vom Verstehen* [1979] et al.).

Pokorný, P., "Das Wesen der exegetischen Arbeit," *Communio Viatorum* 23 (1980), 167-178.

Sabourin, L., *The Bible and Christ. The Unity of the Two Testaments* (Staten Island, NY, 1980).

Sandys-Wunsch, J., "G. T. Zachariae's Contribution to Biblical Theology," *ZAW* 92 (1980), 1-23.

————and L. Eldredge, "J. B. Gabler and the Distinction between Biblical and Dogmatic Theology: Translation, Commentary, and Discussion of His Originality," *Scottish Journal of Theology* 33 (1980), 133-158.

Schillebeeckx, E., *Christ. The Experience of Jesus as Lord* (New York, 1980) (cf. *Interim Report*, 1981).

Scroggs, R., "The Sociological Interpretation of the New Testament: The Present State of Research," *NTS* 26 (1980), 164-179.

Stancil, B., "Structuralism and New Testament Studies," *Southwestern Journal of Theology* 22 (1980), 41-59.

Strecker, G., "Historische Kritik und 'neue Exegese,' " *Communio Viatorum* 23 (1980), 159-166.

Stuhlmacher, P., "Zum Thema 'Hermeneutik,' " *Communio Viatorum* 23 (1980), 179-184.

————, ". . . in verrosteten Angeln," *ZThK* 77 (1980), 222-238.

Thiselton, A. C., *The Two Horizons. New Testament Hermeneutics and Philosophical Description with Special Reference to Heidegger, Bultmann, Gadamer, and Wittgenstein* (Grand Rapids, 1980).

Wells, P. R., *James Barr and the Bible. Critique of a New Liberalism* (Phillipsburg, NJ, 1980).

Zmijewski, J. and E. Nellessen (eds.), *Begegnung mit dem Wort*. Festschrift für Heinrich Zimmermann (Bonner biblische Beiträge 53) (Bonn, 1980).

1981

Bouttier, M., "Bulletin de Nouveau Testament: Théologies," *Études théologiques et religieuses* 56 (1981), 307-331.

Brown, R. E., " 'And the Lord Said'? Biblical Reflections on Scripture as the Word of God," *Theological Studies* 42 (1981), 3-19.

Fitzmyer, J. A., *To Advance the Gospel. New Testament Studies* (New York, 1981).

Hubbard, B. J. [review of four recent contributions to the discussion of resurrection and the New Testament: Alsup, Perrin, Wilckens, Lapide], *Religious Studies Review* 7 (1981), 34-38.

Hübner, H., "Biblische Theologie und Theologie des Neuen Testaments. Eine programmatische Skizze," *KuD* 27 (1981), 2-19.

Jeremias, J., *The Central Message of the New Testament* (Philadelphia, 1981).

Pokorný, P., "Probleme biblischer Theologie," *ThLZ 106 (1981), 1-8.*

Schillebeeckx, E., *Interim Report on the Books Jesus and Christ* (New York, 1981).

Stroup III, G. W., *The Promise of Narrative Theology* (Atlanta, 1981).

Thüsing, W., *Die neutestamentlichen Theologien und Jesus Christus*, I: *Kriterien aufgrund der Rückfrage nach Jesus und des Glaubens an seine Auferweckung* (Düsseldorf, 1981).

Index of Passages to Volume II

(Page references in boldface indicate more extensive interpretation.)

1. Old Testament

Subject Index to Volumes I and II

(Page references in boldface indicate more extensive discussion.)